DENISE LEVERTOV

COLLECTED POEMS

BOOKS BY DENISE LEVERTOV

POETRY

The Double Image
Here and Now
Overland to the Islands
With Eyes at the Back of Our Heads
The Jacob's Ladder
O Taste and See
The Sorrow Dance
Relearning the Alphabet
To Stay Alive
Footprints
The Freeing of the Dust
Life in the Forest
Collected Earlier Poems 1940–1960
Candles in Babylon
Poems 1960–1967
Oblique Prayers
Poems 1968–1972
Breathing the Water
A Door in the Hive
Evening Train
Sands of the Well
The Life Around Us
The Stream and the Sapphire
This Great Unknowing: Last Poems
Poems 1972–82
Making Peace
Selected Poems

PROSE

Poet in the World
Light Up the Cave
New & Selected Essays
Tesserae: Memories & Suppositions
The Letters of Denise Levertov & William Carlos Williams

TRANSLATIONS

Guillevic/Selected Poems
Joubert/Black Iris
In Praise of Krishna (with Edward C. Dimock)

DENISE LEVERTOV

COLLECTED POEMS

EDITED AND ANNOTATED BY
PAUL A. LACEY AND ANNE DEWEY

WITH AN INTRODUCTION BY
EAVAN BOLAND

A NEW DIRECTIONS BOOK

ACKNOWLEDGMENTS: Special thanks for help with the creation of this volume are due to William McPheron, Margaret Kimball, Bill O'Hanlin, and all the staff of Stanford University's Special Collections Library; to Robert Caspar at the Library of Congress; to Valerie Trueblood; to Helen Graves; and especially to the book's designer, Sylvia Frezzolini Severance.

PUBLISHER'S NOTE: Audio files of Levertov reading from her work are available for download or listening on the New Directions website:
http://ndbooks.com/LevertovReading

Book design by Sylvia Frezzolini Severance
Manufactured in the United States of America
New Directions Books are printed on acid-free paper
First published clothbound by New Directions in 2013
ISBN 978-0-8112-2173-3

Library of Congress Cataloging-in-Publication Data

Levertov, Denise, 1923–1997.
[Poems. Selections]
The Collected Poems of Denise Levertov / Introduction by Eavan Boland ;
Edited by Paul A. Lacey and Anne Dewey.
pages cm
"A New Directions Book."
"New Directions Books are printed on acid-free paper"—T.p. verso.
Includes index.
I. Boland, Eavan. II. Lacey, Paul A. III. Dewey, Anne Day. IV. Title.
PS3562.E8876A6 2013
811'.54—dc23
2013022660

New Directions Books are published for James Laughlin
by New Directions Publishing Corporation
80 Eighth Avenue, New York 10011

FOR NIKOLAI

CONTENTS

INTRODUCTION

BY EAVAN BOLAND

In 1960, when she was in her late thirties, Denise Levertov published a poem in *Poetry* magazine. In the free and bold tone which had become her signature, the first lines weighed origin and loss.

> Something forgotten for twenty years: though my fathers
> and mothers came from Cordova and Vitepsk and Caernarvon,
> and though I am a citizen of the United States and less a
> stranger here than anywhere else, perhaps,
> I am Essex-born:

The poem is brilliant and mysterious. In this it resembles its maker. When I met Denise Levertov, thirty years ago in Dublin, I found a smiling, debonair woman; a conversationalist of great charm, but with an elusive air. What was it? When I thought about it I was nearly certain I was looking at a drama of displacement. With her English birth, her American citizenship, her Russian inheritance, she seemed like one of those European exiles at a cafe table on a summer evening— able to understand every place because she had long ago lost the ability to belong to only one.

I came to think I was wrong; or at least only partially right. Some of the reasons are made plain in this splendid and inviting book. To see Denise Levertov's work in a *Collected* version assembled by New Directions—meticulously edited and annotated by Paul A. Lacey and Anne Dewey—is to be offered a new vantage point on one of modern poetry's greatest achievements.

The effect is transformative. All too often, working poets, in their lifetimes, are seen in fractions. Single volumes, *Selected Poems*, limited editions. All are welcome; none provide the information we need. But a *Collected Poems* is different; it offers a panoramic view. It shows the poet not merely moving through time, but inhabiting the questions that come jangling along with it. Through this wider lens, it is now possible to see Levertov in a broader, more complex way.

The complexity is rewarding. On page after page here, we can see Levertov's gifts engaging some of the major contests in twentieth-century poetry: between conscience and imagination, between individual and collective obligation. The poet who Robert Creeley describes as "dogged, determined, flooded with purpose" is more and more on view as the book goes on. Finally, she emerges from these pages as the maker of a fluid, mercurial lyric that is often breathtaking. She also emerges as a hero of the ethical imagination. And there are few.

Denise Levertov, a defining American poet, was born in England. She came into the world, in October 1923, as Priscilla Denise Levertoff. Her inheritance was a rich re-working of Russian and Jewish and Welsh. Her father, Paul Levertoff, was descended from Shneour Zalman, a Russian founding father of the Habad branch of Hasidism. He converted to the Church of England and became an Anglican priest. Her Welsh mother, Beatrice Spooner-Jones, encouraged her in both literature and spirituality. Their daughter described them as "exotic birds in the plain English coppice of Ilford, Essex."

Her Englishness, ardent and regional as the poem suggests, would always remain part of her. In the first volume here, *The Double Image*, published in 1946, it's possible to find phrases, lines, even whole stanzas to remind us she was a young poet in England at a moment of rhetoric and incantation. These after all were the years of Dylan Thomas and George Barker. Forever afterward, that first acoustic chamber would leave a watermark of musical noise under the conversational ease of her poems.

By her early thirties she was settled in America. She had married an American, Mitchell Goodman. It was a momentous transition. Even at this distance, it's possible to pause on one page or another here, and wonder at this young woman, who crossed from England to America four hundred years after Anne Bradstreet and, like Bradstreet, must have "found a new world and new manners."

In fact Levertov's real rite of passage may have come through another poet—William Carlos Williams: that obstinate, generous titan of demotic verse. His work guided her. In 1951 she wrote her first letter to him from Italy. "If a man is a force in one's life," she wrote, "he certainly ought to know it. So thank you."

For all that, the first five volumes here—*The Double Image* (1946), *Here and Now* (1957), *Overland to the Islands* (1958), *With Eyes at the Back of our Heads* (1960), and *The Jacob's Ladder* (1961)—make it clear no single influence can account for her. Kenneth Rexroth writes of her work: "It would be easy to say it came under the influence of

William Carlos Williams. It would be more true to say it moved into the mainstream of twentieth-century poetry."

So what does a Levertov poem look like as it moves into that mainstream? What energies, what formal properties show up in these poems that go from postwar England to America in the Kennedy years?

First and foremost is a stance, a receptivity. James Wright said of this: "her imagination is always religiously open and it always responds to what touches it awake." The openness is everywhere. Whether in "O Taste and See," the title poem of her 1964 volume, where a crude phrase from a subway Bible poster becomes a rush of syllables, guessing at the hiding places of the sacred—a theme that will last long into her life:

> grief, mercy language,
> tangerine, weather, to
> breathe them, bite,
> savor, chew, swallow, transform

or the assonantal magic at the end of "The Ache of Marriage":

> two by two in the ark of
> the ache of it.

In whatever manifestation, this is indeed an imagination that can be touched awake—whether by symbols or sonic values. In fact, one way of reading this early work may be to regard it as a sound studio. Levertov was trying her notes. Making a register for her voice both higher and lower than was usual in a mid-twentieth-century American poet. But the sounds are only part of it. At the edge of the poems in *O Taste and See* and *The Jacob's Ladder* are hints of an expanded role for the poet. "Pure poetry, diatribe, and passionate exhortation meet in the prophets," she would write in a later essay. These early poems may not be prophets. But they are meeting places for the crosscurrents of Levertov's energy and ambition.

In 1961, at the end of this cycle of early publication, Levertov was thirty-nine. She was plainly weighing her future as a poet. She dates a poem from the autumn of that year, "September 1961," which is later published in *O Taste and See*. In it, she writes of herself and others inheriting their responsibilities from an older poetic generation. The poem is somber, thoughtful. It is also different. This is no longer a private voice. Almost the opposite: this is an imagination reaching for the spoiled strengths of an older art—didacticism, revelation, witness. The lines from "September 1961" celebrate and warn. They also point forward to a difficult, exemplary future.

> for us the road
> unfurls itself, we count the
> words in our pockets, we wonder
>
> how it will be without them, we don't
> stop walking
> there is far to go

II

The 1960s and 1970s were years of change and upheaval. The Vietnam War was a polarizing event: a visible hurt, fracturing a public consensus. But something less visible was happening as well; and in many ways the poems Levertov wrote in these years defined it. That less visible entity was a radical shift in ideas of poetic responsibility. "The critical context in which politics and poetry were discussed in the late 1940s," wrote Robert Von Hallberg, "emphasized a poet's obligation to the private experiences out of which poetry can come."

But the volumes here from 1968 to 1982—from *The Sorrow Dance* to *Candles in Babylon*—show a woman in mid-life and a poet in mid-career, and both growing restless with that obligation. These are bold, intense collections. There are seven in all: *The Sorrow Dance* (1967), *Relearning the Alphabet* (1970), *To Stay Alive* (1971) *Footprints* (1972), *The Freeing of the Dust* (1975), *Life in the Forest* (1978), and *Candles in Babylon* (1982). They track a life becoming complicated and enriched by ideas and sorrows: the death of a sister, the pressures of both marriage and parenthood, the growth of political activism. Above all, they show a poet less and less convinced that poetic responsibility can be discharged through private vision

In letters to her friend, poet Robert Duncan, at the height of the Vietnam War—letters which eventually strained their friendship—Levertov begins to express her doubts about a private aesthetic. She writes of "trying to grasp with the imagination what does happen in war." In her 1967 essay, "The Poet in the World," she writes:

> People are always asking me how I can reconcile poetry and political action, poetry and the talk of revolution. Don't you feel, they say to me, that you and other poets are betraying

your work as poets when you spend time participating in sit-ins, marching in the streets, helping to write leaflets, etc. My answer is no; precisely because I am a poet, I know, and those other poets who do likewise know, that we must fulfill the poet's total involvement in life in this aspect also.

A volume like *To Stay Alive*, published in 1971, shows a deepening attachment to "total involvement." There is no doubt that, with such commitments, Levertov took risks with her subject matter which translated into risks with her audience. She was unswerving and even unapologetic in her purpose: "My didactic poetry," she wrote, "should be judged by the same criteria as my lyric poetry; in my opinion, it won't be found wanting." And yet, inevitably, some of these books, some of these poems remain a controversial part of her achievement.

Many of them, of course, found admirers. Who wouldn't read "Tenebrae" today, as a text that has survived any and all contexts? With its gusto, its front-loaded reproach to moral passivity, it remains a model of dark lyric purpose. Its eerie placing of human vanity next to public suffering draws us in: we look on, summoned and enchanted, as the poem lifts a time of war into the timelessness of moral outcry:

> Gowns of gold sequins are fitted,
> sharp-glinting. What harsh rustlings
> of silver moiré there are,
> to remind me of shrapnel splinters.

But for some readers—especially as they tracked the anti-war activist—there was a keen disappointment at the loss of their earlier lyric witness: that glowing poet who had written down their visionary dawns, their attitudes to marriage, their twilight winters in Central Park. Who now seemed focused on a different kind of experience; just no longer theirs.

But was that lyric witness really lost? Here again we can draw on the immense value of *The Collected Poems*. It shows us a near and distant view of her work; a foreground and a background. Certainly, poems like "Tenebrae" and "Life at War"—from *To Stay Alive* and *The Sorrow Dance* respectively—are anti-war poems. They breathe a tonic grief and anger.

But now thanks to Paul A. Lacey and Anne Dewey's editing, we can look into that distance. And what we see is continuance rather than rupture: a poetry of witness that is entirely coexistent with the old lyric life. Nothing has been lost; none of the music, brio, poise has been abandoned. We turn a page; we turn another. (This is the luxury of a *Collected Poems.*) And we can prove that continuance.

To start with, the poems of this time are made in Levertov's signature way—that is, from headlong syntax and conversational wildfire. Even the reader who disagrees with the politics can be excited by this throwaway, heraldic stylist, writing as freely of "the gray filth" or "the gas-fog" of an antiwar march as of taking down clothes from the line in "On the Roof": "gathering the washing as if it were flowers." Little has changed; much has been added. The beautiful, thrifty lines from "A Cloak" in *Relearning the Alphabet* still hold true:

> breathing in
> my life
> breathing out
> poems.

What's more, the additions are not to be found just in style or syntax. They are in the braiding of different imaginative components. Finally, it is this diligent weaving—of language, ethical responsibility, lyric craft—that makes Levertov's relation to her age so compelling, and the poems that emerge from it so essential.

III

In the last decade and a half of her life Levertov published six volumes of poetry, one posthumously: *Oblique Prayers* (1984*)*, *Breathing the Water* (1987), *A Door in the Hive* (1989), *Evening Train* (1992), *Sands of the Well* (1996), and *This Great Unknowing* (2000).

These later volumes show the same unswerving eloquence as earlier ones. But there is a focus that complicates their relation to the earlier work. It is not a matter of disrupting that past, so much as internalizing what had been external. In these books a political commitment has grown into something else: it is now a fully realized moral vision, absorbing both the private troubadour and the public poet.

Many of these poems are connected to Levertov's Christian conversion in 1984; and yet not confined to it. "Levertov's Christian faith," writes Albert Gelpi, "is the source of both her inspiration and her politics, her poetry of celebration as well as her poetry of opposition."

In the beautiful poem "Annunciation," for instance, from *A Door in the Hive*, we can see Levertov incorporate the ghosts of a past—

gender, faith and loss—into the body of a new poetic faith. The Virgin Mary is shown on the threshold of revelation. Even the theme is poignant. Women's lives had been central to Levertov at all stages of her work; women's issues much less so. In her 1982 essay "Genre and Gender v. Serving an Art" she wrote, "I don't believe I have ever made an aesthetic decision based on my gender."

And yet in this poem faith itself is gendered. A young woman is considered as an instrument of will. She faces her destiny, as a believer might; or even a young poet. *Aren't there annunciations / of one sort or another / in most lives?* the speaker asks. The poem widens out from there, almost as if the confluence of faith and femininity had brought both into a sharper relief.

> She was free
> to accept or refuse, choice
> integral to humanness.

In her final years Denise Levertov found new friends and further acclaim. At Stanford University, where she taught at this time, colleagues such as Albert Gelpi, Ken Fields and John Felstiner treasured her company. And still the poems moved forward, seeking and striving. In one of the finest, "Uncertain Oneiromancy," from *Sands of the Well*, a speaker guides a blind man through a museum at night. She is so concerned for his safety that she becomes beauty-blind. So busy is she guiding him, warning him, taking his arm, that she sees nothing else.

This may be Levertov's most subtle statement on imagination. As the poem progresses, the old convention of the blind poet is wonderfully reversed. It is not now the poet who is blind. The poet, the speaker, can see. It is the man she is guiding who is blind. But as the poem comes towards its powerful conclusion, the poet and the speaker, the blind man and his guide begin to shimmer and dissolve and—as can so easily happen in the best Levertov poems—a whole, mighty argument about vision and faith cracks open in a few lines.

> . . . I stood looking after him,
> watching as the street enfolded him, wondering
> if he would make it, and after I woke, wondering still
> what in me he was, and who
> the I was who took that long short-cut with him
> through room after room of beauty his blindness
> hid from me as if it had never been.

When Denise Levertov died in the late winter of 1997 I was at Stanford. We planned a small memorial service. Immediately we asked Adrienne Rich, who also had been at Stanford, to speak; immediately she agreed.

When she spoke she singled out one memory. Denise and herself, she said, had been young women and young mothers in Cambridge, Massachusetts. And, of course, young poets. Rich remembered their long talks at the kitchen table. Always, she said, Denise would press new discoveries on her: new poets, different voices, poems from another coast. Those conversations, Adrienne Rich said, opened a new, exciting poetic horizon. She felt indebted to them all her life.

A great poet generates a great conversation. Denise Levertov's ardent, eloquent body of work accomplishes this: craft, ethics, lyric reach are all part of it. This superb collection provides a vast new resource to continue it. But somehow it seems especially important to remember that the finished conversation was once a living one. And so I like to think of those winter twilights in Cambridge, and Denise Levertov bringing with her the news of poetry. As she does here. As she will always.

Eavan Boland
Stanford / Dublin

EARLY AND
UNCOLLECTED POEMS

Listening to Distant Guns

The roses tremble; oh, the sunflower's eye
Is opened wide in sad expectancy.
Westward and back the circling swallows fly,
The rooks' battalions dwindle near the hill.

That low pulsation in the east is war:
No bell now breaks the evening's silent dream.
The bloodless clarity of evening's sky
Betrays no whisper of the battle-scream.

1940

Sarnen

Under the harvest sun the heart
ripens on its wall;
under the heat of noon the mind
like a leaf is cool.
The angelus and the goatbell
sway across the grass;
butterflies in blue mid-air
touch and spin apart.
Any attempted dream must fall
to ruin in this light, must pass
before the mocking glance
of idle animals.
There is no need to escape
from the motionless mountain
there is no need to escape
when here the indifferent lake
accepts a nervous image,
demands no affirmation
of innocence or faith.

Switzerland, 1946

Interim

For K.S.

A black page of night
flutters: dream on or waken,
words will spring from darkness now,
gold-bright, to fill the hollow mind
laid still to hear them, as an iron cup
laid on the window-ledge, would fill with rain.
Not more alone
waking than sleeping, in darkness than in light,
yet it is now we can assume
an attitude more listening than longing,
extend invisible antennae towards
some intimation, echo, emanation
falling slowly like a destined feather
that lights at last before the feet
of hesitating fear. Not less alone
in city than in solitude, at least
this time—an hour or minute?—left between
dreaming and action, where the only glitter
is the soft gleam of words, affording
intimacy with each submerged regret,
awakes a new lucidity in pain,
so that with day we meet
familiar angels that were lately tears
and smile to know them only fears transformed.

London, 1946

A Dream of Cornwall

Footprint of fury quiet, now, on the salt sand
hills couched like hares in blue grass of the air
water lifting its glass to star and candle
time curled at rest in a ready hand.

No claw of wind plucking the strings of the sea
never a bough bent, no sad fruit falling;
never a rage of autumn's angry angel
but sails in to the haven of a tree.

O fear dissolves here and now I cease
to hear the hammer the axe the bone the bell,
shade of a shade grown still, grief of a grief
lulled in green hollows of a well of peace.

1946

The Anteroom

Out of this anteroom whose light is broken
by slatted blinds and rustling portières,
a tentative room too near the street,
pierced with street voices and the sound of horns,
uneasy halting place of travelling ghosts:

out of this season of uprooted hours,
where time, that should grow round as hanging fruit,
rushes like showers of dry and shrivelled leaves,
and no hour quickens into truth; where love,
confused, can never touch or penetrate
a growing dream, but hovers at its side:

that love, that dream, must travel
into wide landscapes where the heart has rest,
and quietly (as stones, pure on the still earth,
await a strange completion into dream,
by the slow rain, or by a man's desire)
await their transformation into life.

Florence, 1948

Folding a Shirt
For S.P.

Folding a shirt, a woman stands
still for a moment, to recall
warmth of flesh; her careful hands

heavy on a sleeve, recall
a gesture, or the touch of love;
she leans against the kitchen wall,

listening for a word of love,
but only finds a sound like fear
running through the rooms above.

With folded clothes she folds her fear,
but cannot put desire away,
and cannot make the silence hear.

Unwillingly she puts away
the bread, the wine, the knife,
smooths the bed where lovers lay,

while time's unhesitating knife
cuts away the living hours,
the common rituals of life.

London, 1946

Poem

Some are too much at home in the role of wanderer,
watcher, listener; who, by lamplit doors
that open only to another's knock,
commune with shadows and are happier
with ghosts than living guests in a warm house.
They drift about the darkening city squares,
coats blown in evening winds and fingers feeling
familiar holes in pockets, thinking: Life
has always been a counterfeit, a dream
where dreaming figures danced behind the glass.
Yet as they work, or absently stand at a window
letting a tap run and the plates lie wet,
while the bright rain softly shines upon slates,
they feel the whole of life is theirs, the music,
"colour, and warmth, and light"; hands held
safe in the hands of love; and trees beside them
dark and gentle, growing as they grow,

a part of the world with fire and house and child.
The undertone of all their solitude
is the unceasing question, "Who am I?
A shadow's image on the rainy pavement,
walking in wonder past the vivid windows,
a half-contented guest among my ghosts?
Or one who, imagining light, air, sun,
can now take root in life, inherit love?"

London, 1946

Fear of the Blind

The blind tap their way from stone to stone
feel from shadow to shadow, suncaressed
between the plane-trees.
I listen with closed eyes to the dry
autumnal sound of their searching.
Whom the tree grows in, whom clouds compel,
green enters, red, blue of a bell
of a ringing sky; whom wings delight
or waving weed on frayed sleeves of the sea,
I fear the blind: they cannot share my world
but stop its spinning with their heavy shadows.

Paris, 1947

'So You, too . . . '

So you, too, are a part of me. My solitude
always beginning, as grass grows, is a tide
running at daybreak out of the grayrose east
to slide over the sand, encircle
the drowned beauty, the dead bird, the old boot;
my life explores the caves, pours into pools,
hunts with the starry hunters. I stretch out
fingers of grass, fingers of flame, and touch
my own name engraved on air, own flesh
walking towards me down a dream. I wheel

as a wave pounces, unmask the stranger:
you too a part of me, I enter the gate of your eyes,
my beggar, my brother, answer of the sea.

Holland, 1947

Solace

For N.P.

Memories at best are old wives' ghosts,
    transparent and incredible, their chains
    clanking grotesquely. Only an unforeseen
    access of longing in the blood can bear
    the risen burden of true ghosts, that are
    powerful and near as, on a moor,
    the immanent spirit of a rock may seem; are warm
    to touch, and, fading, undermine
    the elaborate bulwarks of indifference.

Better to drift, happy, among stone faces
    which, looking back, are alive, but exact nothing,
    neither a past nor a future; to commune
    with Apollo's impersonal smile, which surrounds
    your listening silence like a phrase of music.

The head of Euripides or a tense
    Egyptian cat (so still, you feel
    it turns and stretches when you look away)
    are not more distant than a lover
    in a far country (*does it rain there,*
    the small rain in the streets of home?
    Do you sleep sound or hear the dripping eaves?)

Not less real, the melancholy, eager,
    black-olive eyes of lost Byzantium
    than recollected glances met
    last year or yesterday, and now forgotten
    even while longing strives to raise a ghost.

Paris, 1947

Too Easy: to Write of Miracles

Too easy: to write of miracles, dreams where the famous give
mysterious utterance to silent truth;
to confuse snow with the stars,
simulate a star's fantastic wisdom.

Easy like the willow to lament,
rant in trampled roads where pools
are red with sorrowful fires, and sullen rain
drips from the willows' ornamental leaves;
or die in words and angrily turn
to pace like ghosts about the walls of war.

But difficult when, innocent and cold,
day, a bird over a hill, flies in
—resolving anguish to a strange perspective,
a scene within a marble; returning
the brilliant shower of coloured dreams to dust,
a smell of fireworks lingering by canals
on autumn evenings—difficult to write
of the real image, real hand, the heart
of day or autumn beating steadily:
to speak of human gestures, clarify
all the context of a simple phrase
—the hour, the shadow, the fire,
the loaf on a bare table.

Hard, under the honest sun, to weigh
a word until it balances with love—
burden of happiness on fearful shoulders;
in the ease of daylight to discover
what measure has its music, and achieve
the unhaunted country of the final poem.

Sicily, 1948

Who He Was

One is already here whose life
bearing like seed its distant death, shall grow

through human pain, human joy, shall know
music and weeping, only because
the strange flower of your thighs
bloomed in my body. From our joy
begins a stranger's history. Who
is this rider in the dark? We lie
in candlelight; the child's quick unseen movements
jerk my belly under your hand. Who,
conceived in joy, in joy,
lies nine months alone in a walled silence?

Who is this rider in the dark,
nine months the body's tyrant,
nine months alone in a walled silence
our minds cannot fathom?
Who is it will come out of the dark,
whose cries demand our mercy, tyrant
no longer, but alone still, in a solitude
memory cannot reach?
Whose lips will suckle at these breasts,
thirsting, unafraid, for life?
Whose eyes will look out of that solitude?

The wise face of the unborn
ancient and innocent
must change to infant ignorance
before we see it, irrevocable third
looking into our lives; the child
must hunger, sleep, cry, gaze, long weeks
before it learns of laughter. Love can never
wish a life no darkness; but may love
be constant in the life our love has made.

New York, 1949

Kresch's Studio

Easels: a high & bare room:
some with charcoal, one with a brush,
some with loud pens in the silence,
at work. The woman
in taut repose, intent:

10

under violent light that pulls
the weight of breasts to answer the long
shadow of thighs,
confronts angles with receding
planes, makes play with elements.

That they work, that she will not move too soon,
opposes (as Bartok's plucked strings oppose)
the grinding, grinding, grinding of lives,
pounding constant traffic.

On paper, on canvas, stroke, stroke: a counterpoint:
an energy opposing
the squandered energy.

New York, early '50s

A Woman
For L.B.

Exciting not by excitement only; subtler:
'beautiful & unhappy' 's not enough:
a woman engrossed
in delight or anguish or simply in passing
from point to point: stretched proudly
ready to twang or sing at pluck or stroke.
Northward: now her green eyes
are looking, looking for a door
to open in a wall where
there's no door, none unless she make it:
an ice-wall to be broken by hand. Northward
in fact and in fact:
now her green eyes
spend their sea-depth & glitter
remotely; she's gone, who stays so strangely.
And we—we look at each other:
'Where should this music be?'

New York, early '50s

An Innocent (II)
(1st version)

At 9 on Hudson St., by 10
   through rotten mounds of foodscraps
in Chelsea, and on, north, with
perhaps some glove (or what?) to show for his pains.

Pink face, curved nose, white mustache,
white hair curling
over his collar; an army greatcoat. A blue sack
         or sometimes a white sack stencilled
         with faded dollar-signs.

It's not his thoroughness and speed
distinguish him so much as the invention
he wears, intimate as a hearing aid: an aid
      to delicate poking:
      a hook
      attached to his arm, projecting
      beyond the hand.

One, hearing of
this prince of scavengers, cried out
         in horror at that bad dream of a hook
         (methodical defilement coyly reduced)
and I too recoiled then; but later

thought my disgust false:
for I'd seen on the old man's face
only the calm intense look of a craftsman:
innocent!

He accepts what we reject, endlessly stuffing
his floursack, silent
      (no one speaks to him)
      from can to can—an endless
city of refuse. And makes
some kind of life from it. His face
                                    rebukes us.

New York, mid '50s

12

An Innocent (II)
(2nd version)

Pink faced, white haired, aquiline old man
endlessly stuffing your floursack—with what?
—Scraps from an endless
city of refuse—
                    Silent, all day from can to can
picking garbage with an ingenious hook—

It's the hook we most recoil from—
in false disgust—
                    Calm, intense—
          the face of a craftsman—innocent!

New York, mid '50s

The Whisper

Among the leaves & bell-flowers
he who carved them contrived to
entwine the letters of his name. Other
letters complete the
span of the small round table,
                    but these

don't seem to spell even
in Hungarian. They are probably
          not a code, not
          initials of a phrase, only
          part of a pattern.
                    Yet: it is

a message—some continuing whisper,
          the act of choice of Anders
Szoltesz, alive or dead, drawn to
just these from all the alphabet, to enhance
the table I love for its
solid stance and
involved, angular, delicate ornament.

New York, mid '50s

Today's Saint

O.K., so he's crazy,
        dowser, cloudbuster. But it's his goodness
makes him attempt so variously,
assuming rapports.
            He's looking
not at the fragments but for
the interplay. It's your pain,
      my grimace, torments him:
                      why, why
          the jagged lives.
He wanted, even in his first mistakes
      (the cold girl taken too often
        hating him at last, escaping)
that all should flower, everyone
joyful. If his imagination
proliferates, it is for you. If not,
he gave us the sudden rain last Sunday,
        the darkening. Maybe raindrops?
               It's a
'means of grace' he's trying to
secure for us.
          'The cloud
compact of energy.' That we may
live.

New York, late '50's

15th Street

Almost dark, and the wind off the river.
It's November. But quite a few
(kids mostly) out on the stoops. A bunch of young girls
posed on the steps of this one,
ladies of the court. Oh, one's the queen,
red hair, & that turn
of the head, a long neck.
A woman in black's going up between them now
slowly, bringing home groceries. 'Where's Johnnie tonight?'
     'Oh, I'm mad at him.'—Deirdre, tossing her head.

'Hah,'—the woman, over her shoulder, in fond contempt,
going on in.

       The sky has cleared itself of clouds
as always at this hour, preparing
for the stars it's hard to see.
Hockey players on roller skates are
shouting, hard, they glide subtly
to dodge a cab, not looking at it.
Here, a few doors down, two youths reveal & exchange
scraps of their work-world, still new.
'He pushes himself right to the front, this guy,
swearin' and hollerin'. So we said to him, "Listen, mister
there's other people waitin' besides you."'
We. It's here, here, here, 'it frees, it
creates relief.' Poetry, element, in which we move
as fish in water.

       The river-hooting, illusion of north-lights
shaking in fever over 14th, & away uptown, 42nd.
It's getting late, the kids drift off
indoors. Better get supper. Deirdre will forgive
Johnny, later, in this unlit doorway (launderette)
saying 'Goodnight. So long. Goodnight.
               I'll see you around.'

New York, late '50s

Down Here and up There

Swing of the scythe
illuminated, displaced
into my book of hours, the falling
grass, goldleafed
on the uneven
left upper windowpane—

But way up on the hill
the drift of field-air around you,
the scythe singing,
and what birds you may hear.

Maine, early '60s

THE DOUBLE IMAGE

Childhood's End

The world alive with love, where leaves tremble,
systole and diastole marking miraculous hours,
is burning round the children where they lie
deep in caressing grasses all the day,
and feverish words of once upon a time
assail their hearts with languor and with swans.
The pebble's shadow quivers in the sun;
the light grows low, and they become
tuned to the love and death of day, the instruments
of life and dream, as Syrinx flying
in fear from unimaginable sound, became
music's green channel; then they rise and go
up the inevitable stony slope
to search untravelled valleys for the land
of wonder and of loss; but on that hill
they find it, wound about them like a cloud.

'They, Looking Back, All Th' Eastern Side Beheld'

From darkness rose the vibrant grass, the first
step in a world of flowers, bees, bright birds:
the afternoons
were dazed with sun
as the world grew,
a garden flowing behind a rooted house.

Trees in the park were wearing coats of mail:
the nightly fairytale lived there by day—
flying Mary Anna,
little crying loaves,
the eight wonderful stones.
To bed by daylight meant a secret journey.

But time grew hostile, and the colours dull,
in silence and alone I saw the ramparts crumble;
the forest and the fool
darkened and were shades
crying 'Alas!
My love, my love, this is disaster's ghost'.

Now I travel on another road
climbing the long hill to a weary town,
but still sometimes
when fragile laughter breaks
I know the gold, the gold,
of Shelley's orange weighty as the world.

To the Inviolable Shade

Intimate trivial glow of cigarettes
shows me the soft and desultory smoke
gently rising; and murder overhead
knocks at our hearts like an impatient ghost
that batters window panes on stormy nights.

Incredible threats grown near as a raised hand
startle familiar dreams to dreaming life,
love on your lips a miracle, and words
magical flowers that bend bright heads to earth.

'Where is tomorrow?' says the pulse of darkness,
'but in the chance fall of a tossed coin?
Time is not master of felicity'.

The pain of the world is in the air we breathe:
tender satirical lover of the lost,
no pain but your loss can darken all my world.

The Ice Betrays

Sordid mornings or the dead end of dark
by tears made heavier; the lost élan
sought unavailingly with clumsy words
morose and nervous in mistaken streets—
all these are bearable; the living cells
will bridge those lacerations of deceit,
willowherb quickly clothe
the naked ruin. An organic love
makes green unyielding time, like moss upon a stone.

But there's an unimagined numb indifference,
a mockery, the beat of a dead heart,
that sets a black seal on the open rose.
For this incredible but certain thought,
cold with the grandeur of the evil grave
there is no help. There is no cure for death.

Durgan
For J.M.

At Durgan waves are black as cypresses,
clear as the water of a wishing well,
caressing the stones with smooth palms, looking
into the pools as enigmatic eyes
peer into mirrors, or music echoes
out of a wood the waking dream of day,
blind eyelids lifting to a coloured world.

Now with averted head your living ghost
walks in my mind, your shadow leans
over the half-door of dream; your footprint lies
where gulls alight; shade of a shade, you laugh.
But separate, apart, you are alive:
you have not died, therefore I am alone.

Like birds, cottages white and grey
alert on rocks are gathered, or low
under branches, dark but not desolate;
shells move over sand, or seaweed gleams
with their clear yellow, as tides recede.
Serene in storm or eloquent in sunlight
sombre Durgan where no strangers come
awaits us always, but is always lost:
we are separate, sharing no secrets, each alone;
you will listen no more, now, to the sounding sea.

The Barricades

If now you cannot hear me, it is because
your thoughts are held by sounds of destiny
or turn perhaps to darkness, magnetized,
as a doomed ship upon the Manacles
is drawn to end its wandering and down
into the stillness under rock and wave
to lower its bright figurehead; or else
you never heard me, only listening
to that implicit question in the shade,
duplicity that gnaws the roots of love.

If now I cannot see you, or be sure
you ever stirred beyond the walls of dream,
rising, unbroken battlements, to a sky
heavy with constellations of desire,
it is because those barricades are grown
too tall to scale, too dense to penetrate,
hiding the landscape of your distant life
in which you move, as birds in evening air
far beyond sight trouble the darkening sea
with the low piping of their discontent.

The Dreamers

The sleeping sensual head
    lies nearer than her hand,
but secret and remote,
    an impenetrable land.

Each, in the hardening crystal
    a prisoner of pride,
abstractedly caresses
    the stranger at his side,

duality's abyss
    unspanned by desire,
reason's cold salamander
    scatheless in the fire.

She hears the sound of midnight
    that breaks like a sea,
and leans above the sleeper
    as secretive as he.

Casselden Road, N.W. 10
    For Marya

The wind would fan the life-green fires that smouldered
under the lamps, and from the glistening road
draw out deep shades of rain, and we would hear
the beat of rain on darkened panes, the sound
of night and no one stirring but ourselves,
leaning still from the window. No one else
will remember this. No one else will remember.

Shadows of leaves like riders hurried by
upon the wall within. The street would fill
with phantasy, the night become
a river or an ocean where the tree
and silent lamp were sailing; the wind would fail
and sway towards the light. And no one else
will remember this. No one else will remember.

Five Aspects of Fear

I. Only Fear

Familiar images of mellow ruin—
of summer peering from under wistful arches,
the fall of leaves on leaden lakes—

fade into shadows, as the rainy larches
fade into a mist beneath the hill,
their pensive grace inadequate.

Happy to feel, at last, the hand fulfil
its promise of reality; to penetrate
the woollen forest and discover

an earthy path and unembroidered gate,
a credible living world of danger and joy,
regret grows obsolete, remote.

And only fear has power to destroy
the new immediacy of pain or pride
and steal your sleeping love;

words must be flesh and blood, not ghosts, to ride
over unbearable deserts of fear, and reach
the tangible city and desired embrace.

II. Fear the Fool

Fear in haste, like horses over heath
galloping black and shiny in the night,
spreads wing across the waste of calendars,
rags fluttering, fingers trembling, grabs at the hours
but finds them gone and laughing further on;
or hears, beguiled, the weeping of desire,
and with a candle discovers the face of love.

But love is too serious to be long a slave:
Fear wakes to find the sparkling wave a brackish
and sombre shade in his glass. 'O return',
he cries, 'caprice fairer than constancy!
What sail, what feather charmed you?
Summer shade, what sun do you follow,
and where is the westward sinking of my heart?'

Then Fear upbraids his dreams, 'These nymphs
were never mine, you lied!' And while the long
sonata hastens toward silence, he spins
round corners of blanched and secret streets, his whip
beating the dead air of night, and quickens
the beat of his drum, seeking the music of life.

III. Ominous Morning

Of ominous morning and the flight of stars
hunter and hawker and crimson fox

burning doors with intractable locks,
fear (like a weapon in darkness) mutters.

Stepping on comets I flew to the sea,
daylight revealed the wreck, the weed,
and no one to vanquish or impede
ominous morning and the flight of stars.

IV. Dreams

Comfort me: I wake from dreams of death,
I have seen the light of leaves grow red, the star
open its heart and mock me with decay,
my love a harlot in the halls of death.

Comfort me: I come with no desire;
the shadowed fire of rain in hollow streets,
the idle laughter and the glittering glass,
are images of fear and not desire.

Waken me: I fear to find you lost;
my dreams of music ended silently,
the sullen opening of heavy doors
revealed the ravaged landscape of the lost.

V. The Past Can Wait

In fear of floods long quenched, waves fallen,
shattered mirrors darken with old cries;
where no shot sounds the frightened birds go flying
over heights of autumn soft as honey:
each country left is full of our own ghosts
in fear of floods quenched, waves fallen.
Rags of childhood flutter in the woods
and each deserted post has sentinels;
bright eyes in wells watch for the sun's assassin:
the regions bereft of our desires are haunted,
rags of childhood flutter in the woods.
Now when the night is blind with stars
now when candles dazzle the day
now

turn from phantoms: they are preoccupied
with a solved conundrum and an old pursuit.
O, be deaf to what they say—
rumours of distant winters and a broken bough—
now when your love is a candle to dazzle the day.

To Death

Enter with riches. Let your image wear
brocade of fantasy, and bear your part
with all the actor's art and arrogance.
Your eager bride, the flickering moth that burns
upon your mouth, brings to your dark reserve
a glittering dowry of desire and dreams.

These leaves of lightness and these weighty boughs
that move alive to every living wind,
dews, flowers, fruit, and bitter rind of life,
the savour of the sea, all sentient gifts
you will receive, deserve due ritual;
eloquent, just, and mighty one, adorn
your look at last with sorrow and with fire.
Enter with riches, enviable prince.

The Conquerors

Love lies bleeding
alone, alone
lost beyond the air
whose palaces are sombre, far from sun,
far from the bitter brilliance of the sun;
or deep below the earth, as sunken streams
shed ever-darkening wine
in throbbing veins of stone,
dumb as a swan on reddening evening pools.
The conquerors in their cities
on hills no longer blue
fear each other and look away

fear the summer and look down
are lost in folds of fear and ask 'What hand
of sinister intent is laid upon my sleeve
arresting turns of thought away from those
surrendered proud façades, these empty streets?'
Night's hypnotic answer,
a gesture in the dark,
is not enough: the invaders lie awake
tormented by the treason in their hearts;
but love alone and deaf to their despair
lies like a rock,
an island in the sorrow of the air.

Christmas 1944

Bright cards above the fire bring no friends near,
fire cannot keep the cold from seeping in.
Spindrift sparkle and candles on the tree
make brave pretence of light; but look out of doors:
Evening already surrounds the curtained house,
draws near, watches;
gardens are blue with frost, and every carol
bears a burden of exile, a song of slaves.
Come in, then, poverty, and come in, death:
this year too many lie cold, or die in cold
for any small room's warmth to keep you out.
You sit in empty chairs, gleam in unseeing eyes;
having no home now, you cast your shadow
over the atlas, and rest in the restlessness
of our long nights as we lie, dreaming of Europe.

A painted bird or boat above the fire,
a fire in the hearth, a candle in the dark,
a dark excited tree, fresh from the forest,
are all that stand between us and the wind.
The wind has tales to tell of sea and city,
a plague on many houses, fear knocking on the doors;
how venom trickles from the open mouth of death,
and trees are white with rage of alien battles.
Who can be happy while the wind recounts
its long sagas of sorrow? Though we are safe

in a flickering circle of winter festival
we dare not laugh; or if we laugh, we lie,
hearing hatred crackle in the coal,
the voice of treason, the voice of love.

'One There Was'

One there was who a long while resisted
the soft descending cloud of feathered sleep
upright against a rough encrusted rock,
who pondered long and fiercely what cruel or crude
necessity of anguish brought them here
as dark grew colder and Athene's owl
saddened the hillside with a wise lament.

Sighing, at last he slept; and dreamed the sun
broke into flames. He could not warn the world,
and saw the earth burn, and the phoenix charred
and still unrisen from the ashen rose.

He heard the quick unbearable tattoo
of bleeding hands on bars he could not break,
finding it easier to turn away:
but on the plains of childhood where the deer
grazed undisturbed on amber afternoons
lay already the shadow of starving snow,
the first signs of fear.

'O waken me! Release me! Let me run
to lead the gentle doe across the moor,
to free the innocent grown corrupt with longing,
and raise my phoenix from the settling dust!'

Yet when a hand aroused him, and he saw
an early radiance show the mountain green
while cocks conversed from farm to far-off farm
and lingering stars shivered above the olives:
perceiving then no flames, no slaves, no menace,
what was the burden that oppressed his heart?
Why was he silent, and his step so heavy?

Extravagant Time

Extravagant Time still sprinkles days and hours
idly as evening wind blows sand inshore
to empty streets of moth-enticing lamps;
still flings away, in frenzy or despair
as terraces of stars obscure the sky
in white confusion clouding darkness over,
the unreturning dream, eternity.

What stone, what piled magnificence of stones
that raises up its towers in pride, is ever
unchanged one moment in the eye of Time?
Large in the lull of noon, at night the house
dwindles to ruin under invisible hills.
What word of love approaches ever again
lost words of yesterday, or holds the sound
of life one instant from the listener,
old sharp-eared Time, who eavesdrops on our dreams?
The poles of silence tear this hour apart
from all the other hours in history.

Two Voices

What can I give you? I am the unseizable
indigo and wandering sea. I give
no love but music, cold and terrible airs
to darken on your heart as albatross
obscures the gleaming water with a wing.

*Be silent. You are beautiful; I hear
only the summer whisper on the shore.*

What can I give you? I am that great tree,
the green penumbra of forgotten dreams.
I send a leaf to greet you, but no more;
my branches rustle in the wind of death.

*Be still; I hear no menace in the wind;
the tree is mine, and grows about my heart.*

I am the wind. *I hold you.* I am gone,
shade of no substance. What is it you hold?
Shadow, I love you.
Free me. I am death.

Meditation and Voices

The mortal failure is the perfect mask,
the adamant and long desired defence.
Assiduously, like soft approaching nightmare,
we amplify the sinister pretence,

ignore the fable which we dare not fear,
turn a deaf ear to death, cover our tracks.
But you and I lack skill in prison building;
anger and love still enter by the cracks.

    'Hard crust and bitter sky
    I pit against your words;
    clatter of clogs on stone,
    the frozen falling birds.'

    'And I will never confess
    my hunger and my guilt:
    A smile about my lips,
    my hand on the sword's hilt.'

The mortal failure is to turn away,
to lock the gates and throw away the key,
poison the well with droppings of deceit
and fossilize in false solemnity.

    'The blue-veined mountains, the sterile sun,
    hang above me as I run;
    but the hand that could point out the way
    plucks at the sheet, shrivels away.

    I cross the dry contemptuous sands
    and hear all night the shouting sea;
    if I should cross to other lands
    contemptuous waves will follow me.'

'The idle rain, and darkness at the door . . .
"There's room for questions here, Propinquio."
Do you hear the sullen wind along the floor?
Or feel the heavy foliage bending closer?'

'I hear the wind, and hear the unborn child's
heart like a drum; I feel the sullen hour;
yes, and I know the questions you will ask
and I would answer, but I lack the power.'

There's some paralysis of heart and hand
that checks the little word, the easy gesture;
and only they could make you understand
the incalculable, still, unhappy silence.

A mask's protection—ah, and there's the treason—
can make the hidden face its own dark image;
whip off that covering, no doubt you'll find
only the bright indifferent gaze of reason.

I found the shells of peace, the starry shore,
and heard the curlews crying as they flew,
mooring at sundown in a western haven:
but not with you, my love, nor yet with you.

These are my valid symbols, but to you
I know they are the distance and a veil.
How to transpose them to your native key,
or make them nearer than a fairy tale?

Green waves of passionate seas assail the caves
not more importunately than I dream; I take
a thousand dreams like stars in eager arms,
and, light as dust, they vanish when I wake;

and still the secrets dwell in other glances,
lost as a quiet well in summer woods,
when the brown hill is arid in its pride
and all day long the glittering heat advances.

'But where are we getting to?' my shadow said,
'The mortal failure is your vanity;

you watch in mirrors for your own dark head.
It flatters you to dream in discontent
of how the world is alien and unreal,
or what the phantoms of your childhood meant.

The cruel almond hastens to be new
each frivolous and unemotional spring.
Why must you hoard your sorrows, count your sins,
and hope to rub a genie from your ring?

Leave your dark autumn groves, the roads oppressed
by dropping alder and repining cloud—
lack-lustre follies, harvests of reproach.
Follow your sunrise shadow to the west!

Each voice that comes to trouble you is your own:
the hard, the hungry, lost or questioning.
To find what land your lover travels, turn
out to the waiting sea. You are alone.'

Ballad

Bravely in a land of dust
we set out, as pilgrims must,
you, who fear the dark, and I
fearing winter in the sky.

Dark and cold the winter cloud
hung above the hill of lies
and my phoenix cried aloud,
took flight toward the eastern skies.

Do you think I shall forget
the tried intent, the diamond set
solitary and forlorn
in a coronet of thorn?

Beyond the high and frozen hill
beyond the forest black and still
I shall find you, where the fire
burns the wings of my desire.

The Shadow

'Can we bring heaven nearer than a star,
Or lift the shadow from a world at war?'
—*Nicholas Moore*

I need a green and undulating line
the hill's long contours in my words, to tell
how by unwarranted grace I found this place.

I need the green astonishment of spring,
stillness of music in the mind, to give
the lie to darkness and release the lark.

The green of day assumes in dreams the shade
of eloquence I need, to tell how love
can lay the ghosts of childhood with a smile.

But the ancient lines of mountains break in craters,
destructive skies crack like decaying plaster;
the individual grace is out of place,

and history denies the structure of delight,
contemptuous of its tender vanity;
music refuses to ignore the black confusion of war.

For love must keep silence, remembering poverty's silence;
recalling the ghosts still living and enslaved,
must hide eternity away, and learn
that time engraves upon the prison wall
'spring' as the symbol of a bitter hope.

Return

I have been long in a land where birds
of plumage bright as flowers and soft to touch
cut the unchanging sky like knives in flight
or brood and scream on boughs, but never sing;
and where they nest the trees begin to droop,
green turns to brown beneath the weight of wings.

The men and women in that country wear
a glittering mail no coloured clothes can hide,
fearing the armoured music of a mood;
never alone, they walk in chains of laughter,
their dreams are desolate, and their eyes,
like diamonds out of darkness, or like waves'
dazzle at noon, enchant the traveller
but never give him back his look of love.

Out in the sunburnt street the hawkers cry,
the world goes by as though it were alive:
but sometimes watching, silent and unseen,
the people pass intent on their pursuits,
I thought their gaiety a play of ghosts,
the dress rehearsal of forgotten death's
amatory and embattled dance.

And yet in the elusive avenue
skirting the town, I heard the sound of tears
break on the night as rain into a lake,
and then it seemed the captives whom I sought
might be disguised in these impassive masks
as pulses stir in cold unmoving flesh,
bound by an evil spell to give no sign.

April (i)

Show me with lanterns how the days go down,
the gentle evening falling like a star;
show me the green and growing fire's decline,
and how we are the clowns of death
tumbling in a breath of wind and hushed
back into silence as the air grows still:
you will not give me news I have not heard
nor tell me what the summer has not told.

> The labyrinthine shell is deaf
> and on its shelf is wreathed in sleeping dust,
> the peacock's eyes are blind
> as statues' sockets staring out of stone;

you may call and call in the dark,
the dream's abyss may deepen, but your fall
will not be broken by the breaking sea,
no bird will warn you in the voice of day.

The sombre and enticing woods we see
from attic windows after rain, arose
to tell me this when I was wandering
over the open countries of the night.
Now add no more to what the leaves foretell:
mortality is lovely in your look.

April (ii)

Trees are green clouds that sail in light and wind
or sink in the drowning sound of shaken leaves;
they shine now, or grieve as the sombre sun
hides in the April wilderness of skies.

    So you, my shadow and fire, masked
    as love or lie, peering as ghosts do
    over my shoulder in the dusty glass
    now smile, now weep, now fade and now return,
    and empty sunlit streets of afternoon
    echo with other footsteps than my own.

Caught in the seasons as a moth is caught
in dancing lantern light that swings away,
the days like snakes cast off their brittle scales,
the hours like ashes fall without a sound.

    You are the lamp that grows into a star,
    you are the glitter of the serpent's skin
    in the green fire of the sea, the ship of leaves
    guiding elusive April through dark dreams;
    and in your changing aspect lies the seed
    of a living landscape, out of ash a flame.

Days

This day has no centre; it flows, blows,
like scents of a drowsy summer heath
or hesitant snows that glide,
silent as owl's wing, down to a silent field.

Yesterday was cut in stone, was bone
firm under flesh, inevitable line
of limb and purpose, hard
as a star's radiance, cold as a cold desire.

Days, like the emanations of a dream,
gather me up into their secret folds;
centred in sorrow, they fall
to the green pool of the evening, or burn
with solitude or love, a wandering flame of love.

Midnight Quatrains

I love to see, in golden matchlight,
intimate contours of a face
like discovered innocence
in dusty annals of disgrace.

Caught in a minute's spell of love,
a microcosm of sudden flame,
I learn this new geography—
wilderness I could never tame.

Listening to rain around the corner
we sense a dream's reality,
and know, before the match goes out,
ephemeral eternity.

For B. M.

I know an exiled shell,
that hears the sea, and can tell

of serpents and a distant shore;
a fruit whose inmost core
whispers 'near me is truth'; a voice that asks
no foolish questions of the durable masks
worn by the heart; a glove,
encasing the reasons for pain, for love;
I know a questioner who is aware
that the answerer is sleeping somewhere.

The Quest

High, hollowed in green
above the rocks of reason
lies the crater lake
whose ice the dreamer breaks
to find a summer season.

'He will plunge like a plummet down
far into hungry tides'
they cry, but as the sea
climbs to a lunar magnet
so the dreamer pursues
the lake where love resides.

Fable

There still are forests we must penetrate,
dark as silence and stricken suddenly
with scream of bright birds caught by flesh-eating flowers
and where the river green as tarnished gold
flows in slow thunder to unruffled lakes;
there still are mountains high as a proud heart
where the strong eagle dies, the lichens wither,
biting night air moans with the voice of rocks,
and every rock cries out to be released;
and there's the lustful sea, that longs to wrest
you to the south, me to the wasting north,
and woo you down from storm to lifeless sand
ravished for ever. These we must not fear

but walk like children stolen by a swan
and following in escape the innocent swallow
westward through danger to the shore of peace,
who saw no darkness though they passed this way,
but only love, and heard the wings of wisdom.

The Air of Life

The air of life is music; oh, be still
one moment while I listen! But the dark
consumes the sounding minutes constantly;
I cannot rest at any single word,
each is borne down by excess of desire,

is whirled away on rivers like a rose
thrown from a silent stony bridge by one
who cannot follow; or is swept too soon
into the greedy waiting hands of time
and death, the hooded beggars by the door.

I walk through rooms that flower in fronds of smoke
bluer than moonlight; colour and darkness sway
like lovers in the mind, insatiable,
beating their mortal wings upon the hours.
The air of life is music, and I live.

Listen!

Sitting up late, sometimes, do you hear,
drowning the whisper of thoughts, the wild
stamping of night, dancing alone in the road?
Or trees pulling away from earth, desiring
to possess the fluent body of the wind,
gesticulating in the starry air?

The wind escapes, and seeks the drunken sea
that leaps and splashes, shouting to the stones
that jostle in the tide along the shore,
forcing green music from symbolic shells.

As you sit musing of last year or the next,
the years of love, hate, lies, and the drab years
when days filed mutely by like prisoners,
do you feel night's arrogant hands caress you,
draw you out and away from the four
obstinate walls and the warm ashes?

One night you will follow. I can see
how you must lay aside the foxed pages,
lost faces ranged like an alphabet,
and go to meet the night, the dream, the sea,
already running in your blood like wine.

'The Sea's Wash in the Hollow of the Heart . . . '
(C.W.G.)

Turn from that road's beguiling ease; return
to your hunger's turret. Enter, climb the stair
chill with disuse, where the croaking toad of time
regards from shimmering eyes your slow ascent
and the drip, drip, of darkness glimmers on stone
to show you how your longing waits alone.
What alchemy shines from under that shut door,
spinning out gold from the hollow of the heart?

Enter the turret of your love, and lie
close in the arms of the sea; let in new suns
that beat and echo in the mind like sounds
risen from sunken cities lost to fear;
let in the light that answers your desire
awakening at midnight with the fire,
until its magic burns the wavering sea
and flames caress the windows of your tower.

Autumn Journey

Out of autumn like a blade
mysteriously engraved, flashes the frost;

stars and leaves are blown to the brown earth
and burning distantly
encircle evening in a web of smoke.

Now once again the wanderer deserts
the comfortable myth and drowsy mansion
where all these months he lay entranced, and heard
the soft forgetful murmur of his flowers
lovingly bent over their mirrored doubles.

As he looks back, a window lit—
fantastic lemon fruit in northern woods,
lost in a high façade—suggests
a latent music, and he knows the sound
is both 'Farewell' and promises of treasure
over the hill, among the burning worlds.

Regent Street, W. 1

The long street is silent under stars;
red, gold, green, the formal fugue of light
continues northward. Stones of curved façades
take on a lustre and a secret look,
awaiting miracles or poised for love.
Chill the wind round All Souls', the air
bitter as wine; but life is in each breath,
the stillness is not death's, but as it were
a hush in music or a dancer's pause.
Though once the trouble on a sleeping face
darkened my mood, and fear
lay like a leopard in the shade of joy,
to-night I know that pain is only a part
of fierce and beautiful life; that silent stone
anticipates the solitudes of Spring
I had no heart for; and I know the hour
grows like a branch, the promise of bright leaves.

HERE AND NOW

The Gypsy's Window

It seems a stage
backed by imaginations of velvet,
cotton, satin, loops and stripes—

A lovely unconcern
scattered the trivial plates, the rosaries
and centered
a narrownecked dark vase,
unopened yellow and pink
paper roses, a luxury of open red
paper roses—

Watching the trucks go by, from stiff chairs
behind the window show, an old
bandanna'd brutal dignified
woman, a young beautiful woman
her mouth a huge contemptuous rose—

The courage
of natural rhetoric tosses to dusty
Hudson St. the chance of poetry, a chance
poetry gives passion to the roses,
the roses in the gypsy's window in a blue
vase, look real, as unreal
as real roses.

Beyond the End

In 'nature' there's no choice—
                                   flowers
swing their heads in the wind, sun & moon
    are as they are. But we seem
almost to have it (not just
    available death)

It's energy; a spider's thread: not to
'go on living' but to quicken, to activate: extend:
    Some have it, they force it—

with work or laughter or even
    the act of buying, if that's
all they can lay hands on—

        the girls crowding the stores, where light,
            colour, solid dreams are—what gay
        desire! It's their festival,
            ring game, wassail, mystery.

It has no grace like that of
the grass, the humble rhythms, the
falling & rising of leaf and star;
it's barely
a constant. Like salt:
take it or leave it

The 'hewers of wood' & so on; every damn
craftsman has it while he's working
        but it's not
a question of work: some
shine with it, in repose. Maybe it is
response, the will to respond— ('reason
can give nothing at all / like
the response to desire') maybe
a gritting of the teeth, to go
just that much further, beyond the end
beyond whatever ends: to begin, to be, to defy.

The Innocent

The cat has his sport
and the mouse suffers
but the cat
        is innocent
    having no image of pain in him

    an angel
    dancing with his prey

carries it, frees it, leaps again
ith joy upon his darling plaything

a dance, a prayer!
How cruel the cat is to our guilty eyes

The Earthwoman and the Waterwoman

The earthwoman by her oven
        tends her cakes of good grain.
The waterwoman's children
are spindle thin.
            The earthwoman
        has oaktree arms. Her children
full of blood and milk
        stamp through the woods shouting.
            The waterwoman
sings gay songs in a sad voice
            with her moonshine children.
When the earthwoman
has had her fill of the good day
        she curls to sleep in her warm hut
        a dark fruitcake sleep
but the waterwoman
            goes dancing in the misty lit-up town
        in dragonfly dresses and blue shoes.

The Rights

I want to give you
something I've made

some words on a page—as if
to say 'Here are some blue beads'

or, 'Here's a bright red leaf I found on
the sidewalk' (because

to find is to choose, and choice
is made).   But it's difficult:

so far I've found
nothing but the wish to give. Or

copies of old words? Cheap
and cruel; also senseless:
                              Take

this instead, perhaps—a half-
promise: If

I ever write
a poem of a certain temper

        (willful, tender, evasive,
        sad & rakish)

I'll give it to you.

People at Night
(derived from Rilke)

A night that cuts between you and you
and you   and you   and you
and me : jostles us apart, a man elbowing
through a crowd.   We won't
                look for each other, either—
wander off, each alone, not looking
in the slow crowd. Among sideshows
        under movie signs,
            pictures made of a million lights,
            giants that move and again move
            again, above a cloud of thick smells,
            franks, roasted nutmeats—

Or going up to some apartment, yours
                    or yours, finding
someone sitting in the dark:
who is it, really? So you switch the
light on to see: you know the name but
who is it?
        But you won't see.

The fluorescent light flickers sullenly, a
pause. But you command. It grabs
each face and holds it up
by the hair for you, mask after mask.
      You   and you   and you and I repeat
        gestures that make do when speech
        has failed   and talk
        and talk, laughing, saying
        'I', and 'I',
meaning 'Anybody.'
               No one.

The Flight

     'The will is given us that
        we may know the
delights of surrender.' Blake with
tense mouth, crouched small (great forehead,
somber eye) amid a crowd's tallness in a narrow room.
                The same night
a bird caught in my room, battered
from wall to wall, missing the window over & over
                    (till it gave up and
                huddled half-dead on a shelf, and I
                put up the sash against the cold)

and waking at dawn I again
pushed the window violently down, open
        and the bird gathered itself and flew
        straight out
        quick and calm (over the radiant chimneys—

Love Poem

Maybe I'm a 'sick part of a
sick thing'
        maybe something
      has caught up with me

certainly there is a
mist between us
                    I can barely
see you
        but your hands
are two animals that push the
mist aside and touch me.

A Silence

Among its petals the rose
still holds
                    a few tears of the morning rain that
broke it from its stem.
                        In each
shines a speck of
                        red light, darker even
than the rose. Phoenix-tailed
slateblue martins pursue
        one   another, spaced out
in hopeless hope, circling
            the porous clay vase, dark from
the water in it. Silence
surrounds the facts. A language
still unspoken.

Something to Wear

To sit and sit like the cat
and think my thoughts through—
that might be a deep pleasure:

to learn what news
persistence might discover,
and like a woman knitting

make something from the
skein unwinding, unwinding,
something I could wear

or something you could wear
when at length I rose to meet you
outside the quiet sitting-room

(the room of thinking and knitting
the room of cats and women)
among the clamor of

cars and people,
the stars drumming and poems
leaping from shattered windows.

Le Bateleur

> *'Why should a legerdemainist be placed at the head of this mar-*
> *velous game? Was it to indicate that despite every effort to read*
> *order into the world one remains the victim of illusion?'*
>
> The Mirror of Magic

The bank teller has
a constant chance to play such
lovely games, flickering
so much money in such
brilliant fingers, the
clean nails glinting and
the bills forming myriad
patterns like a
magician's Japanese fan, then
coming to rest in little
neat blocks, secured by
rubber-bands, with which
one might build
makebelieve houses; and
always there is
more and more money for his
virtuoso hands to
exercise their trivial powers on,

as water
in the great fountains never
gives out, even
in times of drought, because
they don't waste it—the
same water goes
down and through the
pipes after
its supreme moment of
release—always back again, with
civic prudence.

The Hands

       Don't forget the crablike
hands, slithering
        among the keys.
                  Eyes shut, the downstream
      play of sound lifts away from
the present, drifts you
              off your feet : too easily let off.

      So look: that almost painful
        movement restores the pull, incites
           the head with the heart : a tension, as of
             actors at rehearsal, who move
this way, that way, on a bare stage, testing
        their diagonals, in common clothes.

Jackson Square

Bravo! the brave sunshine.
A triangle of green green contains
the sleek and various pigeons
the starving inventors and all
who sit on benches in the morning,
to sun tenacious hopes—indeed
a gay morning for hope to feed on

greedy as the green
        and gray
        and purple-preening birds
feeding in a flock, now here, now there,
parading for the pleasure of old heroes
and witches, all, all the forlorn.

Ink Drawings

black black on white white
not vague darkness
black defined, black concentrate
crystal-pointed white

rigging, a line of land
nails, wires
lines alive, acts of language
constellations of black

counter to 'unlived life' (passing
repassing, drooping,
senselessly reviving)

energy, gay, terrible, rare,
a hope, man-made.

Xmas Trees on the Bank's Façade

In wind & cold sun the small lights
wink rapidly, pale
            (excited) among
agitated green, the needle fringes of two
high trees. Wiring looped from branch to branch.
Babies, pushed by, look up, are reluctant
to pass, stretch back their arms.
    The tellers survey from their cages
    the silent swinging of gold-edged doors.
    Money come, money go.

Don't go in. Look: whether the wind,
or lights in daylight, or the
cut trees' lifelike movement, there's
something wild and
                    (beyond clerks & clients.)
joyful here. Answerable to no one; least to us.
                                        An idiot joy, to recall
the phoenix joys that mock dead fires
   and whisk
            the ashes with their wings.

Zest

DISPOSE YOUR ENERGIES
PRACTISE ECONOMIES
GO INDOORS, REFUSING
TO ATTEND THE EVENING LANGUORS OF SPRING

WORK BY A STRONG LIGHT
SCOUR THE POTS
DESTROY OLD LETTERS

FINALLY BEFORE SLEEP
WALK ON THE ROOF WHERE
THE SMELL OF SOOT RECALLS A
SNOWFALL.
                    UP
OVER THE RED DARKNESS DOLPHINS
ROLL, ROLL, AND TUMBLE, FLASHING THE
SPRAY OF A GREEN SKY.

Central Park, Winter, after Sunset

Below the
   darkening fading
rose
      (to which, straining
      upward, black

                branches address them-
            selves, clowns of alas)
the lights

in multitudinous
windows
                are
        bells in Java

A sense
of festival
    but
somewhere far-off;
            sounds from
over water

the frosty field un-
dulates from
Holland to Mexico:
                space, or
space as dreams
dissolve it

Homage

To lay garlands at your feet
because you stand
dark in the light, or lucent
in the dark air of the mind's world
solitary in your empire of magic,
undiminished

and doors are slammed in your face
and stony faces pass you wideawake
and you sing
dreaming wideawake with stone eyes
undiminished

wreaths of hummingbird color
at your feet

and white, and dark leaves, shadows
of moonlight where you sit in sunlight
near the bright sea, listening

to the crash and sighing, crash
and sighing dance of the words.

Mrs. Cobweb

Her dress was too tight, she had
fits & starts of violent memory that threw
daily memories down the airshaft, she looked
into the cupboard and found
a bone
   that changed into a shadow
         that stole
some treasure from its hiding place behind
the clock, she could not follow, her dress
clutched her,
    but there were days
when shreds of light, fringes of sun
caught her up & whizzed away with her
along serene trolley lines, she reached
for anything & could keep
whatever she could touch, she made:
   a collage of torn leaves she had touched,
   a glass moon-reflector,
often she almost spoke, sharp stars
got tangled in her hair, dazzled by the quietly
shining tracks she wondered if they had passed
the place of arrival?

Everything that Acts Is Actual

From the tawny light
from the rainy nights
from the imagination finding
itself and more than itself

alone and more than alone
at the bottom of the well where the moon lives,
can you pull me

into December? a lowland
of space, perception of space
towering of shadows of clouds blown upon
clouds over
         new ground, new made
under heavy December footsteps? *the only*
way to live?

The flawed moon
acts on the truth, and makes
an autumn of tentative
silences.
You lived, but somewhere else,
your presence touched others, ring upon ring,
and changed. Did you think
I would not change?

         The black moon
turns away, its work done. A tenderness,
unspoken autumn.
We are faithful
only to the imagination. *What the*
imagination
      seizes
as beauty must be truth. What holds you
to what you see of me is
that grasp alone.

The Lovers

She: Since you have made me beautiful
    I am afraid
         not to be beautiful.
    The silvery dark mirror
    looks past me: I
    cannot accept its silence

the silence of your
absence. I want
my love for you to
shine from my eyes and hair
        till all the world wonders
at the light your love has made.

He: At night, waking alone,
    I see you as if in a clear light
    a flower held in the
    teeth of the dark.
    The mirror caught in its solitude
    cannot believe you as I believe.

The Bird

That crazy bird
always laughing—
he sits on the wall they are building,
the wall
which will hide the horizon,
and laughs like mad every time
we open our mouths to say
I love you I hate you etc.
He came only since
the green rain came and
softened everything, making
mud of the cracked
selfrespecting earth and rotting
the red flowers from their stems. Yes,
the rain, the trucks full
of pink bricks, that crazy
eavesdropping bird, came
together and finished
the days of burning, and silence, and distance.

The Third Dimension

Who'd believe me if
I said, 'They took and

split me open from
scalp to crotch, and

still I'm alive, and
walk around pleased with

the sun and all
the world's bounty.' Honesty

isn't so simple:
a simple honesty is

nothing but a lie.
Don't the trees

hide the wind between
their leaves and

speak in whispers?
The third dimension

hides itself.
If the roadmen

crack stones, the
stones are stones:

but love
cracked me open

and I'm
alive to

tell the tale—but not
honestly:

the words
change it. Let it be—

here in the sweet sun
—a fiction, while I

breathe and
change pace.

The Marriage

You have my
attention: which is
a tenderness, beyond
what I may say. And I have
your constancy to
            something beyond myself.
The force
of your commitment charges us—we live
in the sweep of it, taking courage
one from the other.

The Marriage (II)

I want to speak to you.
To whom else should I speak?
It is you who make
a world to speak of.
In your warmth the
fruits ripen—all the
apples and pears that grow
on the south wall of my
head. If you listen
it rains for them, then
they drink. If you
speak in response
the seeds
jump into the ground.
Speak or be silent: your silence
will speak to me.

Laying the Dust

What a sweet smell rises
    when you lay the dust—
bucket after bucket of water thrown
on the yellow grass.
                The water
flashes
each time you
make it leap—
      arching its glittering back.
The sound of
          more water
pouring into the pail
almost quenches my thirst.
Surely when flowers
grow here, they'll not
smell sweeter than this
        wet ground, suddenly black.

Courage

That ancient rockface, rosecolor,
image of steadfastness,
              gathers the light
through the day and after sundown
and makes of it
something one cannot
     call light nor color : an artifact,
as if a smile
broke some ravaged face
           and remained
in the glowing eyes, innocent.

Tomatlán (Variations)

i

The sea quiet, shadow-colored and
without shadows.
From which shall rise
the sea wind, moving
swiftly towards the
steep jungles. The sea wind
the awakener.

ii

The sea wind is
a panther moving
swiftly towards the
mountain jungles.
Its silky fur
brushes me.

iii

The green palmettos of the
blue jungle
shake their
green breasts, their stiff
green hair—
the wind, the sea wind is come
and touches them
lightly, and strokes them, and
screws them, until they
are blue flames,
green smoke, and
screws them again.

iv

At the touch
of the sea wind
          the palms
shake their green breasts, their

                    rustling fingers—
flames of desire and pleasure.
The sea wind that

           moves like a panther
blows the spray inland.
              Voluptuous

and simple—the world is
larger than one had thought.
It is a

new peace
shades the mind here
with jungle shadows
              frayed by the
sea wind.

Poem from Manhattan

Green-spined
river-bounded
desired of summer storms

                     (city, act of joy

Spring evenings in sea-light
façades relax
steel & stone float among clouds

                     (city, act of power

And always nightfall flicks
fantasy on black air
           chips of light
flashing   scattered

                     (city, act of energy

Over littered avenues
& yawn of brakes at the lights
   hesitation of dawn
   dazed behind smoke feathers

      (city, act of hope

But down, past many windows
  each holding less,
less light—
    down—
each weak pane tossing, feebly handing, letting drop
  pale suns to lower panes—
    fall
  many fathoms down

      (city, desolation

   fall
to cracks between cages
where men are walking
jostled, in dirty light
(reflected light)
are running

      (city, gesture of greed

the derelict & diamond-sharp
in shadow of inordinate monuments

It is to them
who speaks must speak
Precise
as rain's first
spitting words on the pavement
   pick out
     the core
   lost impulse

     (give it back

OVERLAND TO THE ISLANDS

Overland to the Islands

Let's go—much as that dog goes,
intently haphazard. The
Mexican light on a day that
'smells like autumn in Connecticut'
makes iris ripples on his
black gleaming fur—and that too
is as one would desire—a radiance
consorting with the dance.
                    Under his feet
rocks and mud, his imagination, sniffing,
engaged in its perceptions—dancing
edgeways, there's nothing
the dog disdains on his way,
nevertheless he
keeps moving, changing
pace and approach but
not direction—'every step an arrival.'

The Palm Tree

The bright moon stranded like a whale
the east yellow
and the mistral furious
out of the back hills seawards in black flames.

How the mule-eared palm, half paralyzed
has quickened overnight! Scraping
leaves beating!
            (strained flags . . .)
The palm tree in frenzy!
At once the mind, agape,
                        scavenging:

What's human here? what hope is here?
thumbing the dry leaves
eager, eager, for the fabulous
poem there may be
in this delight or battle

day coming and the moon not gone.

And all morning the palm tree
thick trunk immobile
                    abandons
its awkward leaves
                    (all its life awake
                    in struggling leaves . . .)
And only after the wind
is quenched
the tree dull
a quietness come
does the scraping mind perceive
                              what is possible:
there are no miracles but facts.
To see! (there might be work
        a challenge, a poem)

The squat palm!

The Way Through

Let the rain plunge radiant
through sulky thunder
rage on rooftops

let it scissor and bounce its denials
on concrete slabs and black
roadways. Flood the streets. It's much

but not enough, not yet: persist,
rain, real rain, sensuous,
swift, released from

        vague skies, the tedium
up there.

        Under scared bucking trees
the beach road washed out—

trying to get by on the verge
is no good, earth crumbles into the
brown waterfall, but he backs up
the old car again and CHARGES.

The water flies in the halfwit's eyes
        who didn't move fast enough
'Who do you think I am, a horse?'
        but we made it—

        Drown us, lose us,
rain, let us loose, so,
to lose ourselves, to career
up the plunge of the hill

A Story, a Play

Not to take
that which is given, to overlook
the grace of it (these fragments
        of lives, broken off for you, or
        you might say drops of quicksilver
        alive, rolling for your eyes' pleasure)

not to take—that's
the morality:
only desire for money is proof
money's deserved:
only expected echoes
merit attention

        not generosities: that the one ('pointless')
        lights itself, its whole span,
        minute to minute, 'perception
        to perception,'—no crises
        dearly bought, forced up by leverage—
        but all of certain
        minutes of a certain life,

        while the other ('unplayable')
        lets you in—in!—to the presence of

two, alone, who speak
for a long time, a long
time hardly moving,
as people speak when alone, late, at last,
at last speaking.

God knows there's enough
deprivation without
self-deprivation—because they tell you
the rules are broken! They gull you!
    Let your senses work, let
    your head have its head. The end
    is pleasure, and the heart
    of pleasure: enlightenment,
                mystery:
rhythm
      of their alternations, or best
      rarest and best,
              their marriage—
a grace, fire, bread, what
keeps you moving, keeps your eyes
wide with seeing,
having something to see.

The Dogwood

The sink is full of dishes. Oh well.
Ten o'clock, there's no
hot water.
The kitchen floor is unswept, the broom
has been shedding straws. Oh well.

The cat is sleeping. Nikolai is sleeping,
Mitch is sleeping, early to bed,
aspirin for a cold. Oh well.

No school tomorrow, someone for lunch,
4 dollars left from the 10—how did that go?
Mostly on food. Oh well.

I could decide
to hear some chamber music
and today I saw—what?
Well, some huge soft deep
blackly gazing purple
and red (and pale)
anemones. Does that
take my mind off the dishes?
And dogwood besides.
Oh well. Early to bed, and I'll get up
early and put
a shine on everything and write
a letter to Duncan later that will shine too
with moonshine. Can I make it? Oh well.

Merritt Parkway

        As if it were
forever that they move, that we
        keep moving—

                Under a wan sky where
                as the lights went on a star
                        pierced the haze & now
                follows steadily
                                a constant
                above our six lanes
                the dreamlike continuum . . .

And the people—ourselves!
    the humans from inside the
    cars, apparent
    only at gasoline stops
                        unsure,
        eyeing each other
                        drink coffee hastily at the
            slot machines & hurry
        back to the cars

vanish
into them forever, to
keep moving—

Houses now & then beyond the
sealed road, the trees / trees, bushes
passing by, passing
      the cars that
          keep moving ahead of
      us, past us, pressing behind us
                    and
            over left, those that come
        toward us shining too brightly
moving relentlessly

    in six lanes, gliding
    north & south, speeding with
    a slurred sound—

Something

'Something to
nullify the tall women on Madison
sniffing, peering at windows, sharp-eyed,
the ones with
little hope beyond the next hat?'
'Unequal forces.'

            'But unmeasured.
That the whirlpool remains
    (tossing aside the 'Around Manhattan' boat)
that the rocks remain
snarling among dusty lawns—
that's something.
        It was you who leapt—'

'from Spuyten Duyvil into
the desert!'

'Into another whirlpool,
the pit of it, where money
rattles against the rocks as it's sucked down.
If it's a battle I'll take sides.'

                              'But
not with nature—she won't fight—not
this battle. There's no
sequence, beyond that they both exist as
elements of a city: your whirlpool, and my
boars stuffed with dollar bills, "alive"
only with maggots.'

                              'What then?'

'Whatever's animated: *that* fights back. Not
the neurotic thrust at subway doors
but, well, like the kids from Junior High
yelling when they let 'em out, chattering in
quick Spanish. Their faces change
from moment to moment
both the beautiful ones and those
deformed by want.
They yell and stamp
and cuff and wallop and shriek
as the bus sways off with them
and some before the enraged monitor
risk death each day
                    to cling to the backs of trucks, waving, and some
are grave, demure, but have earrings that shine & tremble.'

'You're almost lyrical!' 'Oh listen! It's
as if in their violent joy they were almost
about to be silent—all at once—
and weep in concourse.'

'And the minotaur will devour them.
It's life against death, and
                              death wins—
and will uproot the rocks, too, for pastime.'

'Deformed life, rather:
the maskfaced buyers of bric-a-brac
are the detritus only—of a
ferocious energy—'

                              'A monster.
Greed, is it? Alive, yes—'

'Whose victims
multiply quicker than it eats
and stubbornly
                    flourish in the shadow of it.'

Turning

The shifting, the shaded
          change of pleasure
Soft warm ashes in place of fire
          out, irremediably

and a door blown open:

planes tilt, interact, objects
          fuse, disperse,
          this chair further from that table . . . hold it!
Focus on that: this table
closer to that shadow. It's what appalls the
heart's red rust. Turn, turn!
Loyalty betrays.

          It's the fall of it, the drift,
             pleasure
          source and sequence
             lift
          of golden cold sea.

The Bereaved

. . . Could not speak
    could not speak
        no meeting was possible.

  We spoke without euphemism of their deaths
cheerfully of their lives.
At night a touch on the shoulder, wishes for sleep:
  no more. The children were dead.

Of one: he had grown thoughtful of late,
    read much, listened at night,
    was happy alone, but a sought companion.

                          The other:
    certain words delighted her to laughter
    her ways were quick and light.

  No more.
        Could not speak . . .

We could not speak:
a recoil from the abyss?
Did she see the mountain?
did she see the terraced olive-field, sunmist in hollows?
was the water cold and clear on her tongue?
the bucket risen
        heavy
            out of the black well-hole—
did she tremble before it?

The abyss was there.
          (Standing there
she sees them darken and fall.)
We did not touch her
        (she may not have seen us)
by fear or wisdom
did not touch her . . .

She left early
  before violets opened
under the crumbled wall.

The Instant

'We'll go out before breakfast, and get
some mushrooms,' says my mother.
Early, early: the sun
risen, but hidden in mist

the square house left behind
sleeping, filled with sleepers;

up the dewy hill, quietly, with baskets.

Mushrooms firm, cold;
    tussocks of dark grass, gleam of webs,
turf soft and cropped. Quiet and early. And no valley,

no hills: clouds about our knees, tendrils
of cloud in our hair. Wet scrags
of wool caught in barbed wire, gorse
looming, without scent.
                  Then ah! suddenly
the lifting of it, the mist rolls
    quickly away, and far, far—

'Look!' she grips me, 'It is
        Eryri!
             It's Snowdon, fifty
    miles away!'—the voice
a wave rising to Eryri,
falling.
        Snowdon, home
of eagles, resting place of
Merlin, core of Wales.

        Light
graces the mountainhead
for a lifetime's look, before the mist
    draws in again.

In Obedience

'The dread word has been spoken.
I expect, like myself, you have known it
all along. He does not guess it, I think,
and yet . . .' And yet he knows it. *'We live*
from day to day, not
dipping too far
below the surface, and therefore
quite happily.
                    You, too,
be happy, dear children' . . . So be it:
bow the head for once. Shall it be
in the red
almost-invisible spiders circling
a hot stone I shall take pleasure today?
The veery
            hidden, his song
      rippling downward, inward, over and over,
almost-visible spiral?

                    More:
let there be more joy!—if that
is what you would have. I dance
now that work's over and the house quiet:
alone among fireflies on the
dark lawn, humming and leaping.
'After all, life
is a journey to this goal
from the outset.' And Mr. Despondency's daughter
Muchafraid, went through the water singing?
                    I dance
for joy, only for joy
while you lie dying, into whose eyes
I looked seldom enough, all the years,
seldom with candid love. Let my dance
be mourning then,
now that I love you too late.

Continuing

From desire to desire
                plucking
white petals away from their
green centres.   *It was thus and thus*
repeats the head, the fantasist.
                      No matter:
that wind sweeps forward
again—life itself.
       Gather them, flawed, curled
       veined like a child's temple
       heaped one on another
                   irregular
displaced at a breath: secrets . . .
              So
one smiled, another turned pages:
steady, heartbeats apart; many
continuing variously—
And the stripped green? Alert, hard
on a thick stalk. So.

Spring in the Lowlands

Shout into leaping wind
alone by spring lakes
On muddy paths, yellow grass
stamp, laugh; no one
to hear.

The water, water, dazzles;
                    dark winds
pluck its feathers
       splash the hissing reeds.
Birches lean on the air.

Lean into solitude
you whose joy is a kite
now dragged in dirt, now
breaking the ritual of sky.

Nice House

How charming, the colored cushions
curtains of brocade, the fine baskets
filled with fruit, candy, logs for the fire!

It was well-praised and well-shared, Nice House.
And so, many years passed. Hyacinths
in the garden, whiskey
never wanting, music of course.

And many years passed.

One day, came from the terrace and saw
the faded rags, curls of
dust blowing softly
across and across the room. Yes, correct,
brown flowers, smoking fire, the garbage
tipping out of its bag in the kitchen.
            The smell was probably mice.

It seemed the place was empty
at first—then we made out
the police, their black clothes in the shadows
waiting. The chief sat feet apart
beefsteak hands on his knees.
Nobody said a word—only
the lonely icebox set up its sobbing and shaking
which gave us cover, anyway.

A Supermarket in Guadalajara, Mexico

In the supermercado the music
        sweet as the hot afternoon
wanders among the watermelons,
        the melons, the sumptuous tomatoes,
and lingers among the tequila bottles,
        rum bacardi, rompope. It
hovers like flies round the butchers
        handsome and gay, as they dreamily

sharpen their knives; and the beautiful
    girl cashiers, relaxed
in the lap of the hot afternoon,
    breathe in time to the music
whether they know it or not—
    at the glossy supermercado,
the super supermercado.

A Song

Red flowers on a leafless tree.

All day the light is clear
the baker boy with his basket
comes and goes in the sun
his bicycle shines in the sun.

Red flowers on a leafless tree.

The dust of the fields is blowing
the cattle are eating dust and grass
all day the light is clear
the flowers shine in the sun.

Red flowers, shine for me.
The dust is gray and comforts me
a woolen blanket of soft dust.
I want your red to anger me.

The Recognition

Since the storm two nights ago
the air
is water-clear, the mountains
tranquil and clear.
          Have you seen
an intelligent invalid—that look
about the eyes and temples?—one who
knows damn well

death is coming—in the guise let's say
of a carpenter, coming
to fix him for good
with his big hammer and
sharp nails.
                    The air and the horizon.
Clouds make
          gestures of flight but
remain suspended. The builders
continue to build the
house next door.
                    Nothing
will happen. A transparence
of the flesh, revealing
not bones but the shape of bones.

Scenes from the Life of the Peppertrees

i

The peppertrees, the peppertrees!

Cats are stretching in the doorways,
sure of everything. It is morning.
     But the peppertrees
stand aside in diffidence, with berries
of modest red.
                    Branch above branch, an air
of lightness; of shadows
scattered lightly.
                    A cat
closes upon its shadow.
Up and up goes the sun,
sure of everything.
     The peppertrees
               shiver a little.
Robust
and soot-black, the cat
leaps to a low branch. Leaves
close about him.

ii

The yellow moon dreamily
tipping buttons of light
down among the leaves. Marimba,
marimba—from beyond the
black street.
            Somebody dancing,
somebody
         getting the hell
outta here. Shadows of cats
weave round the tree trunks,
the exposed knotty roots.

iii

The man on the bed sleeping
defenseless. Look—
his bare long feet together
sideways, keeping each other
warm. And the foreshortened shoulders,
the head
barely visible.   He is good.
let him sleep.
        But the third peppertree
    is restless, twitching
thin leaves in the light
of afternoon.   After a while
it walks over and taps
on the upstairs window with a bunch
of red berries.   Will he wake?

The Sharks

Well then, the last day the sharks appeared.
Dark fins appear, innocent
as if in fair warning. The sea becomes
sinister, are they everywhere?
I tell you, they break six feet of water.
Isn't it the same sea, and won't we
play in it any more?

I liked it clear and not
too calm, enough waves
to fly in on. For the first time
I dared to swim out of my depth.
It was sundown when they came, the time
when a sheen of copper stills the sea,
not dark enough for moonlight, clear enough
to see them easily. Dark
the sharp lift of the fins.

Action

I can lay down that history
I can lay down my glasses
I can lay down the imaginary lists
of what to forget and what must be
done. I can shake the sun
out of my eyes and lay everything down
on the hot sand, and cross
the whispering threshold and walk
right into the clear sea, and float there,
my long hair floating, and fishes
vanishing all around me. Deep water.
Little by little one comes to know
the limits and depths of power.

Lonely Man

An open world
        within its mountain rim:
trees on the plain lifting
        their heads, fine strokes
        of grass stretching themselves to breathe
the last of the light.
                    Where a man
riding horseback raises dust
        under the eucalyptus trees, a long way off, the dust
is gray-gold, a cloud
        of pollen. A field

of cosmea turns
all its many faces
of wide-open flowers west, to the light.

It is your loneliness
your energy
           baffled in the stillness
        gives an edge to the shadows—
the great sweep of mountain shadow,
shadows of ants and leaves,
        the stones of the road each with its shadow
and you with your long shadow
closing your book and standing up
to stretch, your long shadow-arms
        stretching back of you, baffled.

One A.M.

The kitchen patio in snowy
moonlight.   That
snowsilence, that
abandon to stillness.
The sawhorse, the concrete
washtub, snowblue. The washline
bowed under its snowfur!
Moon has silenced
the crickets, the summer frogs
hold their breath.
Summer night, summer night, standing
one-legged, a crane
in the snowmarsh, staring
at snowmoon!

Pure Products

To the sea they came—
2000 miles in an old bus
fitted with brittle shelves and makeshift beds

and cluttered with U.S. canned goods
                    —to the Sea!
on which they paddle
innertubes   —and the lowhovering Sun!
from which the old woman hides her head
under what looks like
a straw wastebasket.
                    'Yep, they cured me all right,
but see, it made my breasts grow like a woman's.'
And she: 'Something hurts him in his chest,
I think
        maybe it's his heart,'—and hers
I can see beating at the withered throat.

To the Sea some force has driven them—
                    away from a lifetime.
And in this windless heat the purpose
to walk the 3 miles of shadeless beach to the store
to ask in Spanish (of which they know
only yes and no) for wholewheat flour
(which is unknown in the region) that she
may bake their bread!
                    They are dying
in their gentleness, adorned
with wrinkled apple smiles—nothing
remains for them
but to live a little, invoking
the old powers.

Illustrious Ancestors

The Rav
of Northern White Russia declined,
in his youth, to learn the
language of birds, because
the extraneous did not interest him; nevertheless
when he grew old it was found
he understood them anyway, having
listened well, and as it is said, 'prayed
            with the bench and the floor.' He used

what was at hand—as did
Angel Jones of Mold, whose meditations
were sewn into coats and britches.
             Well, I would like to make,
thinking some line still taut between me and them,
poems direct as what the birds said,
hard as a floor, sound as a bench,
mysterious as the silence when the tailor
would pause with his needle in the air.

Broken Glass

Two bean-fed boys set bottles on the wall
yesterday, and shied at them for a half-hour
with desperate energy, taking their stand
back a way in the rubbled lot.
Now the green fragments glitter.
Is that a lizard stirred among them?
The black goat that goes ahead of the cows
picks by in a hurry, her udders rocking.
She hears
             something I don't hear.
The young ivy leaves
are shining. Is it spring?

Sunday Afternoon

After the First Communion
and the banquet of mangoes and
bridal cake, the young daughters
of the coffee merchant lay down
for a long siesta, and their white dresses
lay beside them in quietness
and the white veils floated
in their dreams as the flies buzzed.
But as the afternoon
burned to a close they rose
and ran about the neighborhood

among the halfbuilt villas
alive, alive, kicking a basketball, wearing
other new dresses, of bloodred velvet.

The Lesson

Martha, 5, scrawling a drawing, murmurs
'These are two angels. These are two bombs. They
are in the sunshine. Magic
is dropping from the angels' wings.'
Nik, at 4, called
        over the stubble field, 'Look,
the flowers are dancing underneath the
tree, and the tree
        is looking down with all its apple-eyes.'
Without hesitation or debate, words
used and at once forgotten.

The Whirlwind

The doors keep rattling—I
stick poems between their teeth to
stop them. The brown dust
twirls up outside the window, off
the dead jicama field, scares the curtains,
spirals away to the dirty hollow
where the cesspools are, and the most ants,
and beyond—to the unfenced pasture land, where nothing
will get in its way for miles and it
can curtsey itself at last into
some arroyo.   The doors
keep rattling—I'm
shivering, desperate for a poem
to stuff into their maws that will
silence them. I know what they want:
they want
in all their wooden strength
to fly off on the whirlwind into
the great nothingness.

A Stir in the Air

A stir in the air, the proper space
holding existences in grave distinction—
If as you read I walk
      around you in a
            half circle
your response to the poem will
waver, maybe, like the lights just now
in the thunderstorm—the balance
is that fine—the dance
of hiving bees it is, that design
in air, joyfully
      reducing possibilities to
                    one, the next act.

The Absence

Here I lie asleep
or maybe I'm awake yet—

not alone—and yet
it seems by moonlight

I'm alone, hardly hearing
a breath beside me. And those shadows

on the wall indeed are
not shadows but the
featherweight dancing echoes
of headlights sliding by.

Here I lie and wonder
what it is has left me, what element.
I can't remember my dreams
by morning.
          Maybe, as Frazer tells,

my soul flew out in that moment
of almost-sleep.   If it should go

back to the scenes and times
of its wars and losses

how would I ever lure it
back? It would

be looking for something, it would be
too concentrated to hear me.

O moon, watching everything,
delay it in the garden among the white flowers

until the cold air before sunrise
makes it glad to come back to me through the screens.

The Springtime

The red eyes of rabbits
aren't sad. No one passes
the sad golden village in a barge
any more. The sunset
will leave it alone. If the
curtains hang askew
it is no one's fault.
Around and around and around
everywhere the same sound
of wheels going, and things
growing older, growing
silent. If the dogs
bark to each other
all night, and their eyes
flash red, that's
nobody's business. They have
a great space of dark to
bark across. The rabbits
will bare their teeth at
the spring moon.

WITH EYES AT

THE BACK OF OUR HEADS

The Artist

*(From the Spanish translation of Toltec Códice de la
Real Academia,* fol. 315, v. *With the help of
Elvira Abascal who understood the original Toltec.)*

The artist: disciple, abundant, multiple, restless.
The true artist: capable, practicing, skillful;
maintains dialogue with his heart, meets things with his mind.

The true artist: draws out all from his heart,
works with delight, makes things with calm, with sagacity,
works like a true Toltec, composes his objects, works dexterously, invents;
arranges materials, adorns them, makes them adjust.

The carrion artist: works at random, sneers at the people,
makes things opaque, brushes across the surface of the face of things,
works without care, defrauds people, is a thief.

El Artista

El artista: discípulo, abundante, múltiple, inquieto.
El verdadero artista: capaz, se adiestra, es hábil;
dialoga con su corazón, encuentra las cosas con su mente.

El verdadero artista todo la saca de su corazón,
obra con deleite, hace las cosas con calma, con tiento,
obra como un tolteca, compone cosas, obra hábilmente, crea;
arregla las cosas, las hace atildadas, hace que se ajusten.

El torpe artista: obra al azar, se burla de la gente,
opaca las cosas, pasa por encima del rostro de las cosas,
obra sin cuidado, defrauda a las personas, es un ladrón.

Toltecatl

In toltecatl; tlamachtilli, tolih, centozon, aman.
In qualli toltecatl: mozcaliani, mozcaliz, mihmati;
moyolnonotzani, tlalnamiquini.

In qualli toltecatl tlayollocopaviani,
tlapaccachivani, tlaiviyanchivani, tlamavhcachiva,
toltecati, tlatalia, tlahimati, tlayocoya;—
tlavipana, tlapopotia, tlananamictia.

In xolopihtli toltecatl; tlailivizviani, teca mocayavani,
tlaixpachoani, iixco quihquiza,
tlailivizvia, teca mocayava, ichtequi.

With Eyes at the Back of Our Heads

With eyes at the back of our heads
we see a mountain
not obstructed with woods but laced
here and there with feathery groves.

The doors before us in a façade
that perhaps has no house in back of it
are too narrow, and one is set high
with no doorsill. The architect sees

the imperfect proposition and
turns eagerly to the knitter.
Set it to rights!
The knitter begins to knit.

For we want
to enter the house, if there is a house,
to pass through the doors at least
into whatever lies beyond them,

we want to enter the arms
of the knitted garment. As one
is re-formed, so the other,
in proportion.

When the doors widen
when the sleeves admit us
the way to the mountain will clear,
the mountain we see with

eyes at the back of our heads, mountain
green, mountain
cut of limestone, echoing
with hidden rivers, mountain
of short grass and subtle shadows.

The Charge

Returning

       to all the unsaid
all the lost living untranslated
in any sense,
and the dead
unrecognized, celebrated
only in dreams that die by morning

is a mourning or ghostwalking only.
             You must make, said music

    in its voices of metal and wood
in its dancing diagrams, moving
apart and together, along
       and over and under a line
and speaking in one voice,

                make
my image.   Let be
what is gone.

The Departure

Have you got the moon safe?
Please, tie those strings a little tighter.
This loaf, push it down further
the light is crushing it—such a baguette
golden brown and so white inside

you don't see every day
nowadays. And for God's sake
don't let's leave in the end
without the ocean! Put it
in there among the shoes, and
tie the moon on behind. It's time!

The Five-Day Rain

The washing hanging from the lemon tree
in the rain
and the grass long and coarse.

Sequence broken, tension
of sunlight broken.
                    So light a rain

fine shreds
pending above the rigid leaves.

Wear scarlet! Tear the green lemons
off the tree!   I don't want
to forget who I am, what has burned in me
and hang limp and clean, an empty dress—

The Dead Butterfly

i

Now I see its whiteness
is not white but green, traced with green,
and resembles the stones
of which the city is built,
quarried high in the mountains.

ii

Everywhere among the marigolds
the rainblown roses and the hedges

of tamarisk are white
butterflies this morning, in constant
tremulous movement, only those
that lie dead revealing
their rockgreen color and the bold
cut of the wings.

The Lost Black-and-White Cat

Cockcrowing at midnight.   Broken
silence. Crickets skillfully re-
forming it in
                    minims and
quavers.   The child turns, bangs
        the headboard, struggles
with dreams. Last night in dreams
he found the cat in the bathroom.

                    Come back, cat.
Thrash the silence with your autonomous
feather tail. Imagination made fur,
come back, spring poems out of the whole
cloth of silence.

The Lagoon

This lagoon with its glass shadows
and naked golden shallows
the mangrove island, home of white herons,

recalls the Loire at La Charité
that ran swiftly in quiet ripples
brimful of clouds from the evening sky.

In both, the presence of a rippling quiet
        limpid over the sandbars, suspended,
        and drawing over the depths
long lines of beveled darkness,

draws the mind
down to its own depths

where the imagination swims,
shining dark-scaled fish,
swims and waits, flashes, waits and
wavers, shining of its own light.

Pleasures

I like to find
what's not found
at once, but lies

within something of another nature,
in repose, distinct.
Gull feathers of glass, hidden

in white pulp: the bones of squid
which I pull out and lay
blade by blade on the draining board—

    tapered as if for swiftness, to pierce
    the heart, but fragile, substance
    belying design.   Or a fruit, *mamey*,

cased in rough brown peel, the flesh
rose-amber, and the seed:
the seed a stone of wood, carved and

polished, walnut-colored, formed
like a brazilnut, but large,
large enough to fill
the hungry palm of a hand.

I like the juicy stem of grass that grows
within the coarser leaf folded round,
and the butteryellow glow
in the narrow flute from which the morning-glory
opens blue and cool on a hot morning.

The Offender

The eye luminous
in its box of ebony
saw the point of departure, a room
pleasant, bare, sunlit,
and space beyond it, time
extending to mountains, ending,
beginning new space beyond.

The eye, luminous, grayblue,
a moonstone,
brimmed over with mercury tears
that rolled and were lost in sunny dust.
The world in the lustre of a
black pupil moved its clouds
and their shadows. Time
had gathered itself and gone. The eye
luminous, prince of solitude.

Seems Like We Must Be Somewhere Else

Sweet procession, rose-blue,
and all them bells.

Bandstand red, the eyes
at treetop level seeing it. 'Are we
what we think we are or are we
what befalls us?'

The people from an open window
the eyes
seeing it!   Daytime!   Or twilight!

Sweet procession, rose-blue.
If we're here let's be here now.

And the train whistle? who
invented that? Lonesome man, wanted the trains
to speak for him.

Obsessions

Maybe it is true we have to return
to the black air of ashcan city
because it is there the most life was burned,

as ghosts or criminals return?
But no, the city has no monopoly
of intense life. The dust burned

golden or violet in the wide land
to which we ran away, images
of passion sprang out of the land

as whirlwinds or red flowers, your hands
opened in anguish or clenched in violence
under that sun, and clasped my hands

in that place to which we will not return
where so much happened that no one else noticed,
where the city's ashes that we brought with us
flew into the intense sky still burning.

Triple Feature

Innocent decision: to enjoy.
And the pathos
of hopefulness, of his solicitude:

—he in mended serape,
she having plaited carefully
magenta ribbons into her hair,
the baby a round half-hidden shape
slung in her rebozo, and the young son steadfastly
gripping a fold of her skirt,
pale and severe under a
handed-down sombrero—

                    all regarding
the stills with full attention, preparing

to pay and go in—
to worlds of shadow-violence, half-
familiar, warm with popcorn, icy
with strange motives, barbarous splendors!

A Letter

I know you will come, bringing me
an opal. Good! I will come
to meet you. And walk back with you
to meet whatever it is raves to us
for release.   New courage
has stirred in me while you were gone.
They are stripping the bark from the trees
to make soup
and sitting down I crush fifty
blackeyed susans, each no bigger than a
one-cent piece.   I'm tired
of all that is not mine. Lighting
two cigarettes by mistake, lying back
one in each hand, surprised,
Buddha of the anthill. A great day!
The first to waken as a bear
from cosy smelly comfort ("a rock
dressed in brown moss, little eyes
glinting") and walk out
to the hunt.

Another Journey

From a world composed, closed to us,
back to nowhere, the north.
                    We need
a cold primrose sting
of east wind; we need
a harsh design of magic lights at night over
drab streets, tears
salting our mouths, whether the east wind

brought them or the jabbing
of memories and perceptions, who knows.
                    Not history, but our own histories,
a brutal dream drenched with our lives,
intemperate, open, illusory,

        to which we wake, sweating to make
substance of it, grip it, turn
its face to us, unwilling, and see the
snowflakes glitter there, and melt.

The Take Off

The mountains through the shadowy
flickering of the propellers, steady,
melancholy, relaxed, indifferent, a world
lost to our farewells.
                    The rising of the smoke
from valleys, the pearly waters, the
tight-lipped brown fields, all is relaxed,
melancholy, steady, radiant with dawn stillness,
the world indivisible, from which we fly—
sparks, motes, flickers
of energy, willful, afraid, uttering
harsh interior cries, silent, waving and smiling to the
invisible guardians of our losses.

Girlhood of Jane Harrison

At a window—
so much is easy to see:

an outleaning from indoor darkness
to garden darkness.

But marzipan! Could so much sweetness
not seem banal?

No: it was a calling of
roses by other names.

Now from, as it may be,
the cedar tree

out went the points of the star.
The dance was a stamping in

of autumn. A dance in the garden
to welcome the fall. The diagram

was a diamond, like the pan
for star-cake.   Multiplied,

the dancer moved outward to all the
promontories of shadow, the

forest bays, the moon islands. With
roses of marzipan
the garden dissolved its boundaries.

A Happening

Two birds, flying East, hit the night
at three in the afternoon; stars came out
over the badlands and the billowy
snowlands; they floundered on
resolving not to turn back in search
of lost afternoon; continuing
through cotton wildernesses
through the stretched night
and caught up with dawn in a rainstorm
in the city, where they fell
in semblance of torn paper sacks
to the sidewalk on 42nd St., and resumed
their human shape, and separated:
one turned uptown, to follow
the Broadway river to its possible source,
the other downtown, to see

the fair and goodly harbor; but each,
accosted by shadows that muttered to him
pleading mysteriously, half-hostile, was drawn
into crosstown streets, into
revolving doorways, into nameless
small spaces back of buildings,
airless airshafts, till no more
was known of man, bird, nor paper.

The Vigil

When the mice awaken
and come out to their work of searching
for life, crumbs of life,
I sit quiet in my back room
trying to quiet my mind of its chattering,
rumors and events, and find
life, crumbs of life, to nourish it
until in stillness, replenished,
the animal god within the
cluttered shrine   speaks.   Alas!
poor mice—I have left
nothing for them, no bread,
no fat, not an unwashed plate.
Go through the walls to other kitchens;
let it be silent here.
I'll sit in vigil
awaiting the Cat
who with human tongue
speaks inhuman oracles
or delicately, with its claws, opens
Chinese boxes, each containing
the World and its shadow.

The Room

With a mirror
I could see the sky.

With two mirrors or three
justly placed, I could see
the sun bowing to the evening chimneys.

Moonrise—the moon itself might appear
in a fourth mirror placed high
and close to the open window.

          With enough mirrors within
and even without the room, a cantilever
supporting them, mountains
and oceans might be manifest.

I understand perfectly
that I could encounter my own eyes
too often—I take account
of the danger—
                    If the mirrors
are large enough, and arranged
with bravura, I can look
beyond my own glance.

With one mirror
how many stars could I see?

I don't want to escape, only to see
the enactment of rites.

The Sage

The cat is eating the roses:
that's the way he is.
Don't stop him, don't stop
the world going round,
that's the way things are.
The third of May
was misty; fourth of May
who knows. Sweep
the rose-meat up, throw the bits
out in the rain.

He never eats
every crumb, says
the hearts are bitter.
That's the way he is, he knows
the world and the weather.

The Communion

A pondering frog looks
out from my eyes:

dark-red, veiled blue, plums
roll to the center of a bowl

and at close horizon water-towers
hump and perch.

               Leap
frog, to a lake: leaves
support the lilies, water holds

erect the long, strong stems,
reflects gleaming

rosy petals, pollen-yellow lily-buds,
clouds lilac-tinted and dissolving.
Back to the plums—

eggs in a blue nest—the squat
peaked assembly of towers.

What is it?
         An accord.

Break out, frog,
sing, you who don't know

anything about anything.
'To dance without moving' shall be your burden.

February Evening in New York

As the stores close, a winter light
   opens air to iris blue,
    glint of frost through the smoke,
    grains of mica, salt of the sidewalk.
As the buildings close, released autonomous
   feet pattern the streets
    in hurry and stroll; balloon heads
    drift and dive above them; the bodies
    aren't really there.
As the lights brighten, as the sky darkens,
   a woman with crooked heels says to another woman
   while they step along at a fair pace,
   'You know, I'm telling you, what I love best
   is life. I love life! Even if I ever get
   to be old and wheezy—or limp! You know?
   Limping along?—I'd still . . . ' Out of hearing.
To the multiple disordered tones
   of gears changing, a dance
    to the compass points, out, four-way river.
   Prospect of sky
    wedged into avenues, left at the ends of streets,
    west sky, east sky: more life tonight! A range
    of open time at winter's outskirts.

A Straw Swan under the Christmas Tree

Its form speaks of gliding
   though one had never seen a swan

   and strands of silver, caught
   in the branches near it, speak

of rain suspended in a beam of light,

   one speech conjuring the other.

   All trivial parts of
   world-about-us speak in their forms
   of themselves and their counterparts!

Rain glides aslant,
   swan pauses in mid-stroke,
      stamped on the mind's light, but aloof—

and the eye that sees them refuses
to see further, glances off the
surfaces that
           speak and conjure,
rests

   on the frail
   strawness of straw, metal sheen of tinsel.

   How far might one go
   treading the cleft the swan cut?

The Dead

Earnestly I looked
into their abandoned faces
at the moment of death and while
I bandaged their slack jaws and
straightened waxy unresistant limbs and plugged
the orifices with cotton
but like everyone else I learned
each time nothing new, only that
as it were, a music, however harsh, that held us
however loosely, had stopped, and left
a heavy thick silence in its place.

Notes of a Scale

i

A noon with twilight overtones
from open windows looking down.
Hell! it goes by. The trees
practice green in faithful measure.
It could be what I'm waiting for is

not here at all. Yet
the trees have it, don't they?
Absorbed in their own magic,
abundant, hermetic, wide open.

ii

The painting within itself,
a boy that has learned to whistle,
a fisherman. The painting
living its magic, admitting
nothing, being, the boy
pushing his hands further into his
pockets, the fisherman
beginning the day, in dew and half-dark,
by a river whose darkness
will be defined as brown in a
half-hour. The painting
suspended in itself, an angler
in the suspense of daybreak,
whistling to itself.

iii

Where the noon passes
in camouflage of twilight

doesn't cease to look
into it from his oblique
angle, leafwise,
'. . . maintains dialog with his heart,'

doesn't spill the beans
balances like a papaya tree on a single
young elephant-leg.

iv

A glass brimming, not spilling,
the green trees
practising their art.
                    'A wonder

from the true world,'
he who accomplished it
        'overwhelmed with the wonder
which rises out of his doing.'

Terror

Face-down; odor
of dusty carpet. The grip
of anguished stillness.

Then your naked voice, your
head knocking the wall, sideways,
the beating of trapped thoughts against iron.

If I remember, how is it
my face shows
barely a line? Am I
a monster, to sing
in the wind on this sunny hill

and not taste the dust always,
and not hear
that rending, that retching?
How did morning come, and the days
that followed, and quiet nights?

A Ring of Changes

i

Shells, husks, the wandering
of autumn seeds, the loitering
of curled indoor leaves holding
by a cobweb to the bark
many days before falling.

Cracking husk, afraid
it may reveal a dirty emptiness
afraid its hazelnut may be green,
bitter, of no account.

.   .   .   .

Seed, cling
to the hard earth, some footstep
will grind you in,

new leaf, open your green hand,
old leaf, fall and rot
enriching your rich brotherhood,

hazelnut, know when ripeness
has hardened you and sweetened you.

ii

To shed this fake face
as a snakeskin, paper
dragon the winds will tear—
to dig shame up, a buried bone
and tie it to my breast—

(would it change, in time,
to an ornament? Could it serve
to be carved with new designs?)

iii

I look among your papers
for something that will give you to me
until you come back;
and find: 'Where are my dreams?'

Your dreams! Have they not nourished my life?
Didn't I poach among them, as now on your desk?
My cheeks grown red and my hair curly
as I roasted your pheasants by my night fire!

My dreams are gone off to hunt yours,
I won't take them back unless they find yours,
they must return torn by your forests.

Unremembered
                          our dreams move together
in our dark heads, wander
in landscapes unlit by our candle eyes
eyes of self love and self disgust
eyes of your love for me kindling my cold heart
eyes of my love for you flickering at the edge of you.

iv

Among the tall elders of the hereafter
my father had become
                          a blissful foolish rose
his face beaming from among petals
(of sunset pink) 'open as a daisy'—
a rose walking, tagging at the heels
of the wise, having found
a true form.

v

The tree of life is growing
in a corner of the living-room
held to its beam by nails
that encircle, not pierce, its stem.
From its first shoots, many leaves,
then a long, curved, and back-curving bare stretch,
and above, many leaves, many new shoots,
spreading left along the wall, and right,
towards your worktables.

Casals' cello (a live broadcast: the resistances
                          of the live bow, the passion manifest
                          in living hands, not smoothed out on wax)
speaks from across the room
and the tree of life answers
with its green silence and apparent stillness.

The cello is hollow and the stems are hollow.
The space of the cello is shaped; no other form would resound
with the same tones; the stems at their branchings-off
widen, and narrow to a new growth.
As bow touches strings, a voice is heard;
at the articulations of green, a path
moves toward a leaf. There is space in us

but the lines and planes of its form
are what we reach for and fall,
touching nothing (outside ourselves and yet
               standing somewhere within our own space,
               in its darkness).
Buds are knots in our flesh, nodules of pain.

What holds us upright, once we have faced
immeasurable darkness, the black point
at our eyes' center? Were we suspended,
museum butterflies, by a filament, from a hidden nail?
Has it broken when we begin to
fall, slowly, without desire?
(But we don't fall. The floor is flat, the round earth
is flat, and we stand on it, and though we lie down
and fill our lungs with choking dust
and spread our arms to make a cross
after a while we rise and creep away,
walk from one room to another
'on our feet again.')

Your worktable
is close to the tree—not a tree perhaps,
a vine.
In time the leaves
will reach the space above it, between the windows.

Cello and vine commune
in the space of a room.

What will speak to you?
What notes of abundance
strike across the living room
to your bowed head and down-curved back?

Watch the beloved vine. We can't
see it move.

Listen, listen . . .
We are in this room
together. You are alone
forming darkness into words
dark on white paper,
I am alone with the sense of your anguish.
The tree of life is growing in the room,
the living-room, the work-room.

vi

Between the white louvers, nectarine
light, and on the carpets earthbrown, amber,
entered, filled unpeopled space with presence.
From the doorway we saw
harmonies and heard
measured colors of light, not quite awake and so awake
to correspondences. A room in a house in the city
became for a space of fine, finely-drawn,
November morning, a Holy Apple Field.

And from the table to the crimson
blanket, from the other, carved, table
to the ashes of last night's fire, slanted
louvered light, passing without haste.
We watched from the doorway between sleeping and waking.
Green to the white ceiling drew the vine.

The Goddess

She in whose lipservice
I passed my time,
whose name I knew, but not her face,
came upon me where I lay in Lie Castle!

Flung me across the room, and
room after room (hitting the walls, re-

bounding—to the last
sticky wall—wrenching away from it
pulled hair out!)
till I lay
outside the outer walls!

There in cold air
lying still where her hand had thrown me,
I tasted the mud that splattered my lips:
the seeds of a forest were in it,
asleep and growing! I tasted
her power!

The silence was answering my silence,
a forest was pushing itself
out of sleep between my submerged fingers.

I bit on a seed and it spoke on my tongue
of day that shone already among stars
in the water-mirror of low ground,
and a wind rising ruffled the lights:
she passed near me returning from the encounter,
she who plucked me from the close rooms,

without whom nothing
flowers, fruits, sleeps in season,
without whom nothing
speaks in its own tongue, but returns
lie for lie!

Under the Tree

Under an orange-tree—
not one especial singular
orange-tree, but one among

the dark multitude. Recline
there, with a stone winejar

and the sense
of another dream
concentration would capture—
but it doesn't matter—

and the sense
of dust on the grass, of infinitesimal
flowers, of
cracks in the earth

and urgent life
passing there, ants and transparent
winged beings in their intensity
traveling from blade to blade,

under a modest orange-tree
neither lower nor taller
neither darker-leaved nor aglow
more beneficently

than the dark multitude
glowing in numberless lanes
the orange-farmer counts, but
not you—recline

and drink wine—the stone
will keep it cold—with the sense
of life yet to be lived—rest, rest,
the grass is growing—

let the oranges
ripen, ripen above you,
you are living too, one
among the dark multitude—

Fritillary

A chequered lily,
fritillary, named
for a dicebox, shall be
our emblem

and the butterfly
so like it one would see
a loose petal blowing
if it flew over
                    where the flowers grew.

A field flower
but rare,
chequered dark and light,

and its winged semblance
lapsing from sky to earth,

fritillary, a chance word
speaking of glancing shadows, of
flying fluttering delights, to be

our talisman in sorrow.

The Wife

A frog under you,
knees drawn up
ready to leap out of time,

a dog beside you,
snuffing at you, seeking
scent of you, an idea unformulated,

I give up on
trying to answer my question,
Do I love you enough?

It's enough to be
so much here. And
certainly when I catch

your mind in the
act of plucking
truth from the dark surrounding nowhere

as a swallow skims a
gnat from the
deep sky,

I don't stop to ask myself
Do I love him? but
laugh for joy.

At the Edge

How much I should like to begin
a poem with And—presupposing
the hardest said—
the moss cleared off the stone,
the letters plain.
How the round moon
would shine into all the corners
of such a poem and show
the words! Moths and dazzled
awakened birds
would freeze in its light!
The lines would be
an outbreak of bells
and I swinging on the rope!

Yet, not desiring apocrypha
but true revelation,
what use to pretend the stone discovered,
anything visible?
That poem indeed
may not be carved there, may lie
—the quick of mystery—
in animal eyes gazing
from the thicket,
a creature of unknown size,
fierce, terrified, having teeth or
no defense, but whom
no And may approach suddenly.

An Ignorant Person

Way out there where words jump
in the haze
is the land of hot mamas.

Or say, in the potato patch
a million bugs glittering green and bronze
climb up and down the stems
exchanging perceptions.

                    I in my balloon
light where the wind
permits a landing,
in my own province.

The Great Dahlia

Great lion-flower, whose flames
are tipped with white,
so it seems each petal's fire
burns out in snowy ash,

a dawn bird will light
on the kitchen table
to sing at midday for you

and have you noticed?
a green spider came with you
from the garden where they cut you,
to be the priest of your temple.

Burn, burn the day. The wind
is trying to enter and praise you.
Silence seems something you have chosen,
withholding your bronze voice.
We bow before your pride.

Bread

As florid berries to the oak, should I pin
sequins to this Rockland County bouquet
of bare twigs?—as roses
to pineboughs?—While a primrose-yellow
apple, flushed with success, levitates quietly
in the top right-hand corner of a small canvas,
giving pleasure by its happiness?
But these are thin pleasures, to content
the contented. For hunger:
the bare stretching thorny branches that may never speak
though they conceal or half-reveal
sharp small syllables of bud; and the ragged laughter
—showing gaps between its teeth—
of the anonymous weeds, tousle-heads,
yellow-brown like the draggled undersides of
dromedary and llama basking
proud and complete in airy wedges
of April sun—something
of endurance, to endure
ripeness if it come, or suffer
a slow spring with lifted head—
good crust of brown bread for the hungry.

The Dog of Art

That dog with daisies for eyes
who flashes forth
flame of his very self at every bark
is the Dog of Art.
Worked in wool, his blind eyes
look inward to caverns and jewels
which they see perfectly,
and his voice
measures forth the treasure
in music sharp and loud,
sharp and bright,
bright flaming barks,
and growling smoky soft, the Dog

of Art turns to the world
the quietness of his eyes.

A Dream

A story was told me of the sea, of time suspended as calm seas balance and hover, of a breaking and hastening of time in sea tempest, of slow oil-heavy time turning its engines over in a sultry night at sea. The story belonged not to time but to the sea; its time and its men were of the sea, the sea held them, and the sea itself was bounded by darkness.

The man who told it was young when it began—a young ship's officer on that ship whose name he did not tell.

Among the crew—many of whom had sailed together many times before the young officer joined them—were two, Antonio and Sabrinus, who were regarded by the rest with a peculiar respectful affection.

These two were friends; and in the harmony of their responses, their communing quietness, seemed twin brothers, more than friends.

Their friendship, while it enclosed them in its ring, did not arouse jealousy or contempt; a gentle and serene light glowed out from it and was seen as something fair and inviolable.

The Captain himself (rarely seen on deck) allowed them a special privilege: In an idle time Antonio had built with matchless skill a small boat of his own, which when completed he and Sabrinus painted a glowing red, not scarlet but bright carmine. This—slight and elegant as a shelf model, but fully seaworthy—Antonio was permitted to keep in special davits; and when the ship anchored in roads or harbor, or lay becalmed in midvoyage, he and Sabrinus would go fishing in her— sailing if there were wind enough, or rowing at times of glassy lull.

Even this caused no resentment. That they seemed to share thoughts as well as words—not many of the men understood their language, which may have been Portuguese or Catalan, or some island dialect—and that the catboat or skiff held only two, was tacitly accepted. An unfailing gentleness and kindly composure compensated for their reserve.

As for daily work, the ship's life, Antonio and Sabrinus were quick, sagacious, and diligent.

Indeed the young man soon came to realize that a belief had grown among the men that Antonio and Sabrinus were luck-bringers and that no evil would come to them or to the ship as long as those two were there.

So that when one night (or it may have begun on a dark day) a storm came up that grew fiercer hour by hour, it appeared to them at first 'only' a storm. The wind became a thing, solid, heavily insistent, lacking only visibility—and yet remained only the wind; and the spiring waves it whipped up, though they rose higher than the ship itself, and seemed about to devour everything they could reach, were still only waves; and confident that ship and voyage were under the protection of a special providence, manifested in the incandescent companionship of the holy friends, the crew staggered and gripped and moved as they could about the lunging decks without true fear.

But there was an end to this time of brave activity; for as life slid violently aside and back, and the storm achieved its very orgasm, a chill silent fear struck the men, at seeing Antonio and Sabrinus in a new aspect—hatred marking their faces and bitter words breaking out between them. The cause of the quarrel was the crimson boat. Antonio, believing the ship about to sink, determined to loose and launch his artifact, and counted on his friend to take his chance of life in her with him, frail though she was in such a sea. But it seemed less the chance of life he desired than to give his boat her freedom, so that if she were destroyed it would be in open combat with the great ocean, not as a prisoner bound fast to the body of the ship. And Sabrinus refused.

Though the greater number of the listening men surrounding them on three sides (on the fourth was the sea itself) could not understand their language, and those who did could catch only a few words from the storm's clamor, all understood that Sabrinus was saying, No, they must always as before stand by the ship to which they were committed, and help their fellows save her if they could—must share the common fate as if they were common men. Neither would be swayed by the other, and in a moment the two men, set apart in hatred as in love, set upon one another, oblivious of all that encircled them, in a murderous fight. As the young officer saw it, this hatred was the long-secreted flower of their love, the unsuspected fearful harvest of long calm voyages, of benevolent quietness and exclusive understandings.

Not a man but clung to whatever rail or stanchion he could find on the steep decks to see this abominable flowering, cold at heart. But no one thought for a moment of stepping between them, it was the storm itself intervened: as Antonio and Sabrinus held one another in choking grip, the vessel was lifted in the sea's gleaming teeth. The deck shuddered and pitched them overboard into a great trough of the waters, as if to appease the great mouth.

Then the wind was no longer a thing, but an evil, multiple, personage; and the waves swept up upon them with intent of malice. The blessed cord that bound ship and men to happy fortune had broken. No one listened to what orders they could hear, the Captain vanished from the bridge, and in half an hour the ship had split and sunk. The survivors, reaching shore, dispersed, and of them the storyteller had no more to say.

But the story of Antonio and Sabrinus was not ended. This is what he told:

Many years later it happened that he found himself without a berth in an obscure, sleazy tropical port—perhaps in Central America, at all events in a hot, moist climate. Eager to get away from the sultry city, he shipped as first mate on the freighter *Jacobi* at very short notice, the officer he replaced having been taken seriously ill. The owners, only eager for the perishable cargo to reach its destination by a certain date, concealed from him the fact that there was fever aboard.

He joined the ship at dusk; by midnight they were well out to sea, and having soon become aware of the crew's depletion, he was musing angrily at the deception practiced on him, which the captain had shiftily admitted once they were out of port. A little after midnight he descended into the sick men's quarters.

The steaming darkness here was in sharp contrast to the bright moonlight he had just left. Dim lights swung here and there; crowded with hammocks and cramped bunks, the space in which these men were isolated seemed a hellish writhing mass of discolored and tormented forms.

He passed from one to another grimly inspecting the disorder, flashing a shielded light now on faces wild with delirium, now on swollen unmoving bodies, perhaps already dead. Nor was the horror all to the eyes; piercing cries and deep groans rose from this multitude into the sweating air in a unison to which the engines played ground-bass.

At length, in the furthest corner, he came to two men whose faces made him start; he bent to examine them more closely. The serenely joyful days of the long-ago voyage returned to his mind; Antonio and Sabrinus in all their luck-bringing radiance; and the fearful term of it, their flight, their plunge to death. But had they somehow swum to safety? Was it possible that they had after all been rescued? For here they lay—they or their doubles?

Long he looked—turned away—looked again. The features were the same; yet the faces looked darker. And the torn clothing on their thin bodies was of a kind traditional to one of the Malay Islands. Moreover the language in which, unconscious of him, they muttered in their fever, was not the Mediterranean tongue of Antonio and Sabrinus. But they lay, in their hammocks, so close to one another—a ring of difference invisibly separating them from the mass of men, as it had separated Antonio and Sabrinus. Could it be that, rescued unimaginably from the storm, they had landed together on some island and in amnesia, or from mysterious will to obliterate all that had been, made its language their own? What of their hatred? If they had lived, then, had it passed, had they resumed their calm affection?

Or were they without substance, were they images and shadows of himself?

He turned to see if others saw them, or if he had conjured them to his private sight. But there was no one to ask, for all were absorbed in their own agonies. Back to the darkened faces, changed and yet the same, he looked, and saw that they were dying. Each was speaking, long and low, neither seeming to hear the other. Whether they had objective life or were parts of himself, he knew the same spirit informed them that had lit and darkened the forms of Antonio and Sabrinus.

Next day they did indeed die and with others were buried at sea. But—he told me—not only then but now at the moment of recounting—he felt they would return to him, or he to them.

His inquiries clarified nothing—they were two among a crowd of Lascar hands. He left the ship at her port of destination and stayed ashore for over a year, drifting from one occupation to another; but at length returned to the sea. He has not yet seen them again, Antonio and Sabrinus.

A darkness enclosed the whole story
though in the beginning
a serene, even, sourceless light
veiled the darkness.

Did they know one another?
The hammocks were slung
one alongside the other
but the two sailors each addressed darkness.

Was it Antonio and Sabrinus or his double shadow?
Were they his shadow and themselves?
Had their intensity a substance
out of his sight?

Darkness enclosed his story. He would be waiting
to see them again.

Relative Figures Reappear

She, returned in the form of youth
black of hair and dress
curls deaf in a poem.

He, returned, sits as he would never sit
perched on a radiator, smoking,
balking sullenly at an obscure outrage.

Only she who still lives, not as then but in
the white hair of today, awkwardly
laughs, at a loss for right words.
Three familiar spirits present to me.

The lamb and the ram removed
from the packing case are neither
gentle nor potent, but gray dead
of having never lived, weightless
plaster forms. What comes

live (though a toy) out of the box
is a black fox. Is it a fox?

The dead girl rejoices (But wait—
only now I remember she too is living
changed by time and inward fires.)
She takes the black animal I give her
in her arms, its sharp nose
poked at the long poem she is sunk in.

He is gone to another room angry
because the boy-child has seen
a diagram of the womb. Why?
Implacably laughing

(now I laugh too) but unsure
of my justice, I turn to assuage
a quick fear my black sister is prying

into my world, but the garnered
poems, stirring letters, dreams,
are undisturbed on the open desk.
She reads on and is dear to me.

Xochipilli

Xochipilli, god of spring
                                    is sitting
on the earth floor, gazing
into a fire. In the fire
a serpent is preening, uncoiling.

'From thy dung
the red flowers,' says the god.

By the hearth
bodies of hares and mice,
food for the snake.

'From thy bones
white flowers,' says the god.

Rain dances many-footed
on the thatch. Raindrops
leap into the fire, the serpent hisses.

'From this music
seeds of the grass
that shall sing when the wind blows.'
                    The god stirs the fire.

The Quarry Pool

Between town and the
old house, an inn—
the Half-Way House.
So far one could ride, I remember,

the rest was an uphill walk,
a mountain lane with
steep banks and sweet
hedges, half walls of

gray rock. Looking
again at this looking-glass face
unaccountably changed in a week,
three weeks, a month,

I think without thinking of
Half-Way House. Is it
the thought that this far
I've driven at ease, as in a bus,

a country bus where one could talk to the driver?
Now on foot towards the village;
the dust clears, silence
draws in around one. I hear
the rustle and hum of the fields: alone.

It must be the sense
of essential solitude that chills me
looking into my eyes.
I should remember

the old house at the walk's ending,
a square place with a courtyard,
granaries, netted strawberry-beds,
a garden that was many

gardens, each one
a world hidden from the
next by leaves, enlaced trees,
fern-hairy walls, gilly-flowers.

I should see, making
a strange face at myself,
nothing to fear in the thought of
Half-Way House—

the place one got down
to walk—. What is
this shudder, this
dry mouth?

Think, please, of the quarry pool,
the garden's furthest
garden, of your childhood's
joy in its solitude.

The Park

A garden of illusions!
Hidden by country trees, elm, oak,
wise thorn, and the tall green hedges of a maze,
the carpenters are preparing marvels!

But across the street the family
only glance toward the park gates,
stand clustered,
hesitant in their porch.

Already a ghost of fire
glides on the lake! In a mist
the flames of its body
pass shuddering over the dark ripples.

But they turn their heads
away, the tall people,
they talk and delay.

Waiting, I leap over
beds of glowing heart's-ease,
leaf-gold, fox-red, violet, deep
fur-brown, sailing high and slow

above them, descending
light and soft at their far borders.

But across the ice-crackling roadway
the house stands in midwinter daylight
and my friends neither in nor out of the house
still ignore the preparations of magic

the darkening of the garden
the flashes that may be summer lightning or
trials of illusion, the balconies
carved in a branchless towering oak.

Only the boy, my son, at last
ready, comes, and discovers joyfully
a man playing the horn
that is the true voice of the fire-ghost,

and believes in all wonders to come
in the park over-the-way,
country of open secrets where the elm
shelters the construction of gods
and true magic exceeds all design.

Art
  (after Gautier)

The best work is made
from hard, strong materials,
  obstinately precise—
the line of the poem, onyx, steel.

It's not a question of
false constraints—but
  to move well and get somewhere
wear shoes that fit.

To hell with easy rhythms—
sloppy mules that anyone can
  kick off or
step into.

Sculptor, don't bother with modeling
pliant clay; don't let
        a touch of your thumb
set your vision while it's still vague.

Pit yourself against granite,
hew basalt, carve hard ebony—
        intractable
guardians of contour.

Renew the power men had in Azerbaijan
to cast ethereal intensity in bronze
        and give it
force to endure any number of thousand years.

Painter, let be the 'nervous scratches' the
trick spontaneity; learn to see again,
        construct, break through
to 'the thrill of continuance with the appearance of all its changes,'

towards that point where 'art becomes
a realization with which the urge to live
        collaborates as a mason.' Use
'the mind's tongue, that works and tastes into the very rock heart.'

Our lives flower and pass. Only robust
works of the imagination live in eternity,
        Tlaloc, Apollo,
dug out alive from dead cities.

And the austere coin
a tractor turns up in a
        building site
reveals an emperor.

The gods die every day
but sovereign poems go on breathing
        in a counter-rhythm that mocks
the frenzy of weapons, their impudent power.

Incise, invent, file to poignance;
make your elusive dream
        seal itself
in the resistant mass of crude substance.

To the Snake

Green Snake, when I hung you round my neck
and stroked your cold, pulsing throat
        as you hissed to me, glinting
arrowy gold scales, and I felt
        the weight of you on my shoulders,
and the whispering silver of your dryness
        sounded close at my ears—

Green Snake—I swore to my companions that certainly
        you were harmless! But truly
I had no certainty, and no hope, only desiring
        to hold you, for that joy,
                    which left

a long wake of pleasure, as the leaves moved
and you faded into the pattern
of grass and shadows, and I returned
smiling and haunted, to a dark morning.

THE JACOB'S LADDER

To the Reader

As you read, a white bear leisurely
pees, dyeing the snow
saffron,

and as you read, many gods
lie among lianas: eyes of obsidian
are watching the generations of leaves,

and as you read
the sea is turning its dark pages,
turning
its dark pages.

The Ladder

> *Rabbi Moshe (of Kobryn) taught: It is written: "And he
> dreamed, and behold a ladder set up on the earth." That "he" is
> every man. Every man must know: I am clay, I am one of count-
> less shards of clay, but "the top of it reached to heaven"—my soul
> reaches to heaven; "and behold the angels of God ascending and
> descending on it"—even the ascent and descent of the angels
> depend on my deeds.*
>
> Tales of the Hasidim: Later Masters *by Martin Buber.*

A Common Ground

i

To stand on common ground
here and there gritty with pebbles
yet elsewhere 'fine and mellow—
uncommon fine for ploughing'

there to labor
planting the vegetable words
diversely in their order
that they come to virtue!

To reach those shining pebbles,
that soil where uncommon men
have labored in their virtue
and left a store

of seeds for planting!
To crunch on words
grown in grit or fine
crumbling earth, sweet

to eat and sweet
to be given, to be eaten
in common, by laborer
and hungry wanderer . . .

ii

In time of blossoming,
of red
buds, of red
margins upon
white petals among the
new green, of coppery
leaf-buds still weakly
folded, fuzzed
with silver hairs—

when on the grass verges
or elephant-hide rocks, the lunch hour
expands, the girls
laugh at the sun, men
in business suits awkwardly
recline, the petals
float and fall into
crumpled wax-paper, cartons
of hot coffee—

to speak as the sun's
deep tone of May gold speaks
or the spring chill in the rock's shadow,
a piercing minor scale running across the flesh
aslant—or petals
that dream their way
(speaking by being white
by being
curved, green-centered, falling
already while their tree
is half-red with buds) into

human lives! Poems stirred
into paper coffee-cups, eaten
with petals on rye in the
sun—the cold shadows in back,
and the traffic grinding the
borders of spring—entering
human lives forever,
unobserved, a spring element . . .

iii

> . . . *everything in the world must*
> *excel itself to be itself.*
> > *Pasternak*

Not 'common speech'
a dead level
but the uncommon speech of paradise,
tongue in which oracles
speak to beggars and pilgrims:

not illusion but what Whitman called
'the path
between reality and the soul,'
a language
excelling itself to be itself,

speech akin to the light
with which at day's end and day's
renewal, mountains
sing to each other across the cold valleys.

The World Outside

i

On the kitchen wall a flash
of shadow:
        swift pilgrimage
of pigeons, a spiral
celebration of air, of sky-deserts.
And on tenement windows
a blaze
        of lustered watermelon:
stain of the sun
westering somewhere back of Hoboken.

ii

The goatherd upstairs! Music
from his sweet flute
roves from summer to summer
in the dusty air of airshafts
and among the flakes
of soot that float
in a daze from chimney
to chimney—notes
remote, cool, speaking of slender
shadows under olive-leaves.   A silence.

iii

Groans, sighs, in profusion,
with coughing, muttering, orchestrate
solitary grief; the crash of glass, a low voice
repeating over and over, 'No.
No. I want my key. No you did not.
No.'—a commonplace.
And in counterpoint, from other windows
the effort to be merry—ay, maracas!
—sibilant, intricate—the voices wailing pleasure,
        arriving perhaps at joy, late, after sets
have been switched off, and silences
are dark windows?

The Part

*In some special way every person completes the universe.
If he does not play his part, he injures the pattern of
all existence. . . .*

Rabbi Judah Loew

Homer da Vinci
with freckles on your nose
don't hang there

by the heels.
Sad everyman. I mean
let go, or jerk
upright.

They say gooseflesh
is the body's shudder when someone
walks over its grave-to-be,

but my hair rises
to see your living life
tamped down.

Blue mysteries
of the veronica florets
entertain
your modest attention:

there, where you live,
live:
start over,
everyman, with
the algae of your dreams.

Man gets his daily bread
in sweat, but no one said
in daily death. Don't eat

those nice green dollars your wife
gives you for breakfast.

A Sequence

i

A changing skyline.
A slice of window filled in
by a middle-distance oblong
topped by little
moving figures.
You are speaking
flatly, 'as one drinks a glass of

milk' (for calcium).
        Suddenly the milk
spills, a torrent of black milk hurtles
through the room, bubbling and
seething into the corners.

ii

'But then I was another person!'
The building veiled
in scaffolding. When the builders leave,
tenants will move in, pervading
cubic space with breath and dreams.
Odor of newmade memories
will loiter in the hallways,
noticed by helpless dogs and young children.
That will be other, another
building.

iii

I had meant to say
only, 'The skyline's changing,
the window's allowance of sky is
smaller
        but more
intensely designed, sprinkled
with human gestures.'

That's not enough.
Ah, if you've not seen it
it's not enough.
Alright.
It's true.
Nothing

is ever enough. Images
split the truth
in fractions. And milk
of speech is black lava. The sky
is sliced into worthless
glass diamonds.

iv

Again: middle of a night.
Silences lifting
bright eyes that brim with
smiles and painful
stone tears.
                    Will you believe it,
in this very room
cloud-cuckoos unfledged themselves,
shedding feathers and down,
showed themselves small,
monstrous,
paltry in death?
In the dark
when the past lays its hand on your heart,
can't you recall that hour of
death and new daylight?

v

But how irrelevantly
the absurd angel of happiness walks in,
a box of matches in one hand,
in the other a book of dream-jokes.
I wake up laughing, tell you:
'I was writing an
ad for gold—gold cups,

gold porridge-bowls—**Gold,
beautiful, durable**—While I mused
for a third adjective, you were
preparing to leave for
three weeks—**Here's the check. And
perhaps in a week or so
I'll be able to send you a
pound of tomatoes.'** Then
you laugh too, and we clasp
in naked laughter, trembling
with tenderness and relief.
Meanwhile the angel,
dressed for laughs as a plasterer,
puts a match to whatever's
lying in the grate: broken scaffolds,
empty cocoons, the paraphernalia
of unseen change.
Our eyes smart from the smoke but
we laugh and
warm ourselves.

The Rainwalkers

An old man whose black face
shines golden-brown as wet pebbles
under the streetlamp, is walking
two mongrel dogs of dis-
proportionate size, in the rain,
in the relaxed early-evening avenue.

The small sleek one wants to stop,
docile to the imploring soul of the trashbasket,
but the young tall curly one
wants to walk on; the glistening sidewalk
entices him to arcane happenings.

Increasing rain. The old bareheaded man
smiles and grumbles to himself.
The lights change: the avenue's
endless nave echoes notes of
liturgical red. He drifts

between his dogs' desires.
The three of them are enveloped—
turning now to go crosstown—in their
sense of each other, of pleasure,
of weather, of corners,
of leisurely tensions between them
and private silence.

Partial Resemblance

A doll's hair concealing
an eggshell skull delicately
throbbing, within which
maggots in voluptuous unrest
jostle and shrug. Oh, Eileen, my
big doll, your gold hair was
not more sunny than this
human fur, but
your head was
radiant in its emptiness,
a small clean room.

Her warm and rosy mouth
is telling lies—she would
believe them if she could believe:
her pretty eyes
search out corruption. Oh, Eileen,
how kindly your silence was, and
what virtue
shone in the opening and shutting of your
ingenious blindness.

Night on Hatchet Cove

The screendoor whines, clacks
shut.   My thoughts crackle
with seaweed-seething diminishing
flickers of phosphorus.   Gulp

of a frog, plash
of herring leaping;
                    interval;
squawk of a gull disturbed, a splashing;
pause
while silence poises for the breaking
bark of a seal: but silence.
                                        Then
only your breathing. I'll
be quiet too. Out
stove, out lamp, let
night cut the question with profound
unanswer, sustained
echo of our unknowing.

The Tide

While we sleep
mudflats will gleam
in moonwane, and mirror
            earliest wan daybreak
            in pockets and musselshell hillocks, before
a stuttering, through dreams, of
lobsterboats going out, a half-
awakening, a re-

living of ebbing dreams as morning ocean
returns to us, a turning
from light towards more dreams, intelligence of
what pulls at our depths for

design.
I hear

the tide turning. Last
eager wave over-
taken and pulled back
by first wave of the ebb. The pull back
by moon-ache. The great knots
of moon-awake energy
far out.

The Depths

When the white fog burns off,
the abyss of everlasting light
is revealed. The last cobwebs
of fog in the
black firtrees are flakes
of white ash in the world's hearth.

Cold of the sea is counterpart
to this great fire. Plunging
out of the burning cold of ocean
we enter an ocean of intense
noon. Sacred salt
sparkles on our bodies.

After mist has wrapped us again
in fine wool, may the taste of salt
recall to us the great depths about us.

Six Variations

i

We have been shown
how Basket drank—
and old man Volpe the cobbler
made up what words he didn't know
so that his own son, even
laughed at him: but with respect.

ii

Two flutes! How close
to each other they move
in mazing figures,
never touching, never
breaking the measure,
as gnats dance in
summer haze all afternoon, over

shallow water sprinkled
with mottled blades of willow—
two flutes!

iii

Shlup, shlup, the dog
as it laps up
water
makes intelligent
music, resting
now and then to
take breath in irregular
measure.

iv

When I can't
strike one spark from you,
when you don't
look me in the eye,
when your answers
come
      slowly, dragging
their feet, and furrows
change your face,
when the sky is a cellar
with dirty windows,
when furniture
obstructs the body, and bodies
are heavy furniture coated
with dust—time
for a lagging leaden pace,
a short sullen line,
measure
of heavy heart and
cold eye.

v

The quick of the sun that gilds
broken pebbles in sidewalk cement

and the iridescent
spit, that defiles and adorns!
Gold light in blind love does not distinguish
one surface from another, the savor
is the same to its tongue, the fluted
cylinder of a new ashcan a dazzling silver,
the smooth flesh of screaming children a quietness, it is all
a jubilance, the light catches up
the disordered street in its apron,
broken fruitrinds shine in the gutter.

vi

Lap up the vowels
of sorrow,
              transparent, cold
water-darkness welling
up from the white sand.
Hone the blade
of a scythe to cut swathes
of light sound in the mind.
Through the hollow globe, a ring
of frayed rusty scrapiron,
is it the sea that shines?
Is it a road at the world's edge?

A Map of the Western Part of the County of Essex in England

Something forgotten for twenty years: though my fathers
and mothers came from Cordova and Vitepsk and Caernarvon,
and though I am a citizen of the United States and less a
stranger here than anywhere else, perhaps,
I am Essex-born:
Cranbrook Wash called me into its dark tunnel,
the little streams of Valentines heard my resolves,
Roding held my head above water when I thought it was
drowning me; in Hainault only a haze of thin trees
stood between the red doubledecker buses and the boar-hunt,
the spirit of merciful Phillipa glimmered there.

Pergo Park knew me, and Clavering, and Havering-atte-Bower,
Stanford Rivers lost me in osier beds, Stapleford Abbots
sent me safe home on the dark road after Simeon-quiet evensong,
Wanstead drew me over and over into its basic poetry,
in its serpentine lake I saw bass-viols among the golden dead leaves,
through its trees the ghost of a great house. In
Ilford High Road I saw the multitudes passing pale under the
light of flaring sundown, seven kings
in somber starry robes gathered at Seven Kings
the place of law
where my birth and marriage are recorded
and the death of my father. Woodford Wells
where an old house was called The Naked Beauty (a white
statue forlorn in its garden)
saw the meeting and parting of two sisters,
(forgotten? and further away
the hill before Thaxted? where peace befell us? not once
but many times?).
All the Ivans dreaming of their villages
all the Marias dreaming of their walled cities,
picking up fragments of New World slowly,
not knowing how to put them together nor how to join
image with image, now I know how it was with you, an old map
made long before I was born shows ancient
rights of way where I walked when I was ten burning with desire
for the world's great splendors, a child who traced voyages
indelibly all over the atlas, who now in a far country
remembers the first river, the first
field, bricks and lumber dumped in it ready for building,
that new smell, and remembers
the walls of the garden, the first light.

Come into Animal Presence

Come into animal presence.
No man is so guileless as
the serpent. The lonely white
rabbit on the roof is a star
twitching its ears at the rain.
The llama intricately

folding its hind legs to be seated
not disdains but mildly
disregards human approval.
What joy when the insouciant
armadillo glances at us and doesn't
quicken his trotting
across the track into the palm brush.

What is this joy? That no animal
falters, but knows what it must do?
That the snake has no blemish,
that the rabbit inspects his strange surroundings
in white star-silence? The llama
rests in dignity, the armadillo
has some intention to pursue in the palm-forest.
Those who were sacred have remained so,
holiness does not dissolve, it is a presence
of bronze, only the sight that saw it
faltered and turned from it.
An old joy returns in holy presence.

Air of November

In the autumn brilliance
feathers tingle at fingertips.

This tingling brilliance
burns under cover of gray air and

brown lazily
unfalling leaves,

it eats into stillness zestfully
with sound of plucked strings,

steel and brass strings of the zither,
copper and silver wire

played with a gold ring,
a plucking of crinkled afternoons and

evenings of energy, thorns under the pot.
In the autumn brilliance

a drawing apart of curtains
a fall of veils

a flying open of doors, convergence
of magic objects into
feathered hands and crested heads, a prospect
of winter verve, a buildup to abundance.

Song for a Dark Voice

My black sun, my
Odessa sunflower,
spurs of Tartar gold
ring at your ankles,
you stand taller before me than the ten
towers of Jerusalem.

Your tongue has found
my tongue, peonies
turn their profusion towards
the lamp, it is you that burn there,
the Black Sea sings you awake.

Wake the violoncellos of Lebanon,
rub the bows with cedar resin,
wake the Tundra horsemen
to hunt tigers.
           Your skin
tastes of the salt of Marmora,
the hair of your body casts
its net over me.
           To my closed eyes
appears a curved
horizon where darkness
dazzles in your light. Your arms
hold me from falling.

A Window

Among a hundred windows shining
    dully in the vast side
of greater-than-palace number such-and-such
    one burns
these several years, each night
    as if the room within were aflame.
Some fault in the glass
    combines with the precise distance and
my faulty eyes to produce
    this illusion; I know it—
yet still I'm ready to believe perhaps
    some lives
tremble and flare up there, four blocks away
    across the sooty roofs and
the dusk,
    with more intensity than what's lived
behind the other windows,
    and the glowing of those brands of life
shows as seraphic or demonic flames
    visible only to weak and distant eyes.

' . . . Else a great Prince in prison lies'

All that blesses the step of the antelope
all the grace a giraffe lifts to the highest leaves
all steadfastness and pleasant gazing, alien to ennui,
dwell secretly behind man's misery.

Animal face, when the lines
of human fear, knots of a net, become transparent
and your brilliant eyes and velvet muzzle
are revealed, who shall say you are not the face of a man?

In the dense light of wakened flesh
animal man is a prince. As from alabaster
a lucency animates him from heel to forehead.
Then his shadows are deep and not gray.

FIVE POEMS FROM MEXICO

i The Weave

The cowdung-colored mud
baked and raised up in random
walls, bears the silken
lips and lashes of erotic
flowers towards a sky of
noble clouds. Accepted
sacramental excrement
supports the ecstatic half-sleep
of butterflies, the slow
opening and closing of brilliant
dusty wings. Bite down
on the bitter stem of your nectared
rose, you know
the dreamy stench of death and fling
magenta shawls delicately
about your brown shoulders laughing.

ii Corazón

When in bushy hollows between
moonround and moonround of hill, white clouds
loiter arm-in-arm, out of curl,
and sheep in the ravines
vaguely congregate, the heart
of Mexico sits in the rain
not caring to seek shelter,
a blanket of geranium pink drawn up
over his silent mouth.

iii The Rose
   (for B.L.)

In the green Alameda, near the fountains,
an old man, hands

clasped behind his shabby back
shuffles from rose to rose, stopping
to ponder and inhale, and I
follow him at a distance, discovering
the golden rose, color of bees' fur, odor of honey,
red rose, contralto, roses
of dawn-cloud-color, of snow-in-moonlight,
of colors only roses know,
but no rose
like the rose I saw in your garden.

iv   Canticle

Flies, acolytes
of the death-in-life temple
buzz their prayers

and from the altar
of excrement arises
an incense

of orange and purple
petals.   Drink,
campesino,

stain with ferment
the blinding white that clothes
your dark body.

v   Sierra

Golden the high ridge of thy back, bull-mountain,
and coffee-black thy full sides.
The sky decks thy horns with violet,
with cascades of cloud. The brown hills
are thy cows.   Shadows
of zopilotes cross and slowly
cross again
thy flanks, lord of herds.

Three Meditations

i

Breathe deep of the
freshly gray morning air, mild
spring of the day.
Let the night's dream-planting
bear leaves
and light up the death-mirrors with
shining petals.
Stand fast in thy place:
remember, Caedmon
turning from song was met
in his cow-barn by One who set him
to sing the beginning.
Live
in thy fingertips and in thy
hair's rising; hunger
be thine, food
be thine and what wine
will not shrivel thee.
Breathe deep of
evening, be with the
rivers of tumult, sharpen
thy wits to know power and be
humble.

ii

Barbarians
throng the straight roads of
my empire, converging
on black Rome.
There is darkness in me.
Silver sunrays
sternly, in tenuous joy
cut through its folds:
mountains
arise from cloud.
Who was it yelled, cracking
the glass of delight?
Who sent the child
sobbing to bed, and woke it
later to comfort it?
I, I, I, I.
I multitude, I tyrant,
I angel, I you, you
world, battlefield, stirring
with unheard litanies, sounds of piercing
green half-smothered by
strewn bones.

iii

> *And virtue? Virtue lies in the heroic response to the creative*
> *wonder, the utmost response.*
> > *D. H. Lawrence*

Death in the grassblade
a dull
substance, heading blindly
for the bone

and bread preserved without
virtue,
sweet grapes sour to the children's children.

We breathe an ill wind,
nevertheless our kind
in mushroom multitudes
jostles for elbow-room
moonwards

an equalization of
hazards
bringing the poet
back to song
as before

to sing of death
as before
and life, while he
has it, energy

being in him a singing,
a beating of gongs, efficacious
to drive away devils,
response to

the wonder that
as before
shows a double face,

to be
what he is
being his virtue

filling his whole space
so no devil
may enter.

In Memory of Boris Pasternak

i

The day before he died, a burnet moth
come to town perhaps on a load of greens,
took me a half-hour out of my way, or what
I'd thought was my way.   It lay bemused
on the third step down of the subway entrance.
I took it up—it scarcely fluttered. Where
should I take it for safety,
away from hasty feet and rough hands?

We went through the hot streets together,
it lay trustingly in my hand,
awkwardly I shielded it from the dusty
wind, a glitter of brine
hovered about the cement vistas.
At last I found
a scrap of green garden
to hide the stranger, and silently took leave.

Not his soul—
I knew that dwelled always on Russian earth
—yet it was spoken in me
that the dark, narrow-winged, richly
crimson-signed being, an
apparition at the steps to the underworld,
whose need took me upwards again and further than
I had thought to walk, was a word,
an emanation from him, fulfilling
what he had written—'I feel
that we shall be friends.'

ii

Seen through what seem
his eyes (his gift) the gray barn
and the road into the forest,
the snipe's dead young I am burying among
wild-strawberry leaves, all
lifts itself, poises itself to speak:

and the deaf soul
struggles, strains forward, to lip-read what it needs:
and something is said, quickly,
in words of cloud-shadows moving and
the unmoving turn of the road, something
not quite caught, but filtered
through some outpost of dreaming sense
the gist, the drift. I remember
a dream two nights ago: the voice,
'the artist must
create himself or be born again.'

'Ce bruit de la mer . . . '

(after Jules Supervielle)

That sound, everywhere about us, of the sea—
the tree among its tresses has always heard it,
and the horse dips his black body in the sound
stretching his neck as if towards drinking water,
as if he were longing to leave the dunes and become
a mythic horse in the remotest distance,
joining the flock of foam-sheep—
fleeces made for vision alone—
to be indeed the son of these salt waters
and browse on algae in the deep fields.
But he must learn to wait, wait on the shore,
promising himself **someday** to the waves of the open sea,
putting his hope in certain death, lowering
his head again to the grass.

Stems

(after Jules Supervielle)

A poplar tree under the stars,
what can it do.
And the bird in the poplar tree
dreaming, his head
tucked into
far-and-near exile under his wing—
what can either of them
in their confused alliance of
leaves and feathers
do to avert destiny?

Silence and the
ring of forgetting
protect them until the moment when
the sun rises
and memory with it.
Then the bird
breaks with his beak the thread
of dream within him,

and the tree unrolls
the shadow that will guard it
throughout the day.

Resting Figure

The head Byzantine or from
Fayyum, the shoulders naked,
a little of the
dark-haired breast visible
above the sheet,

from deep in the dark head
his smile glowing
outward into the
room's severe twilight,

he lies, a dark-shadowed
mellow gold against
the flattened white pillow,
a gentle man—

strength and despair
quiet there in the bed,
the line of his limbs
half-shown, as under stone
or bronze folds.

The Jacob's Ladder

The stairway is not
a thing of gleaming strands
a radiant evanescence
for angels' feet that only glance in their tread, and need not
touch the stone.

It is of stone.
A rosy stone that takes

a glowing tone of softness
only because behind it the sky is a doubtful, a doubting
night gray.

A stairway of sharp
angles, solidly built.
One sees that the angels must spring
down from one step to the next, giving a little
lift of the wings:

and a man climbing
must scrape his knees, and bring
the grip of his hands into play. The cut stone
consoles his groping feet. Wings brush past him.
The poem ascends.

The Well

The Muse
   in her dark habit,
trim-waisted,
     wades into deep water.

The spring where she
   will fill her pitcher to the brim
wells out
     below the lake's surface, among
papyrus, where a stream
     enters the lake and is crossed
by the bridge on which I stand.

She stoops
   to gently dip and deep enough.
Her face resembles
     the face of the young actress who played
Miss Annie Sullivan, she who
   spelled the word 'water' into the palm
of Helen Keller, opening
     the doors of the world.

In the baroque park,
   transformed as I neared the water
   to Valentines, a place of origin,
I stand on a bridge of one span
and see this calm act, this gathering up
   of life, of spring water

and the Muse gliding then
   in her barge without sails, without
oars or motor, across
   the dark lake, and I know
no interpretation of these mysteries
   although I know she is the Muse
and that the humble
   tributary of Roding is
one with Alpheus, the god who as a river
   flowed through the salt sea to his love's well

so that my heart leaps
   in wonder.
Cold, fresh, deep, I feel the word 'water'
   spelled in my left palm.

The Illustration

Months after the Muse
had come and gone across the lake of vision,
arose out of childhood the long-familiar
briefly forgotten presaging of her image—

'The Light of Truth'—frontispiece
to 'Parables from Nature,' 1894—a picture
intending another meaning than that which it gave
(for I never read the story until now)

intending to represent Folly
sinking into a black bog, but for me having meant
a mystery, of darkness, of beauty, of serious
dreaming pause and intensity

where not a will-o'-the-wisp but
a star come to earth burned before the
closed all-seeing eyes
of that figure later seen as the Muse.

By which I learn to affirm
Truth's light at strange turns of the mind's road,
wrong turns that lead
over the border into wonder,

mistaken directions, forgotten signs
all bringing the soul's travels to a place
of origin, a well
under the lake where the Muse moves.

Deaths

i
Osip Mandelstam

With a glass of
boiled water
not yet cold
by a small stove
not giving out
much heat
he was sitting
and saying over
those green words
Laura and laurel
written in Avignon

when out of the somber
winter day entered
Death in green clothing
having traveled
by train and on foot
ten thousand kilometers to
this end,
and moving aside to give him

a place at the fire, the poet
made him welcome, asking
for news of home.

ii
César Vallejo

Darling Death
shouted in his ear,
his ear made to record
the least, the most finespun
of worm-cries and
dragonfly-jubilations,
and with that courtesy he accorded
all clumsy living things
that stumble in broken boots
he bowed and
not flinching from her black breath
gave her his arm and
walked back with her the
way she had come and
turned the corner.

A Music

Melody
        moving
                downstream
a string of barges
                just
lit
against blue evening, the fog
giving each light
a halo

moving with
the river but not
adrift, a little
                faster perhaps
        or is it

slower?—a
singing
sung if it is sung
quietly

within the scored
crashing and the
almost inaudible hum impinging
upon the river's
                seawardness

A Letter to William Kinter of Muhlenberg

Zaddik, you showed me
the Stations of the Cross

and I saw
not what the almost abstract

tiles held—world upon world—
but at least

a shadow of what
might be seen there if mind and heart

gave themselves to meditation,
deeper

and deeper into Imagination's
holy forest, as travelers

followed the Zohar's dusty
shimmering roads, talking

with prophets and
hidden angels.

From the bus, Zaddik,
going home to New York,

I saw a new world
for a while—it was

the gold light on a rocky slope,
the road-constructors talking to each other,

bear-brown of winter woods, and later
lights of New Jersey factories and the vast

December moon. I saw
without words within me, saw

as if my eyes
had grown bigger and knew

how to look without
being told what it was they saw.

Clouds

The clouds as I see them, rising
urgently, roseate in the
mounting of somber power

surging in evening haste over
roofs and hermetic
grim walls—

       Last night
as if death had lit a pale light
in your flesh, your flesh
was cold to my touch, or not cold
but cool, cooling, as if the last traces
of warmth were still fading in you.
My thigh burned in cold fear where
yours touched it.

But I forced to mind my vision of a sky
close and enclosed, unlike the space in which these clouds move—
a sky of gray mist it appeared—

and how looking intently at it we saw
its gray was not gray but a milky white
in which radiant traces of opal greens,
fiery blues, gleamed, faded, gleamed again,
and how only then, seeing the color in the gray,
a field sprang into sight, extending
between where we stood and the horizon,

a field of freshest deep spiring grass
starred with dandelions,
green and gold
gold and green alternating in closewoven
chords, madrigal field.

Is death's chill that visited our bed
other than what it seemed, is it
a gray to be watched keenly?

Wiping my glasses and leaning westward,
clearing my mind of the day's mist and leaning
into myself to see
the colors of truth

I watch the clouds as I see them
in pomp advancing, pursuing
the fallen sun.

The Thread

Something is very gently,
invisibly, silently,
pulling at me—a thread
or net of threads
finer than cobweb and as
elastic. I haven't tried
the strength of it. No barbed hook
pierced and tore me. Was it
not long ago this thread
began to draw me? Or
way back? Was I

born with its knot about my
neck, a bridle? Not fear
but a stirring
of wonder makes me
catch my breath when I feel
the tug of it when I thought
it had loosened itself and gone.

From the Roof

This wild night, gathering the washing as if it were flowers
        animal vines twisting over the line and
        slapping my face lightly, soundless merriment
        in the gesticulations of shirtsleeves,
I recall out of my joy a night of misery

walking in the dark and the wind over broken earth,
        halfmade foundations and unfinished
        drainage trenches and the spaced-out
                        circles of glaring light
        marking streets that were to be,
walking with you but so far from you,

and now alone in October's
first decision towards winter, so close to you—
        my arms full of playful rebellious linen, a freighter
        going down-river two blocks away, outward bound,
        the green wolf-eyes of the Harborside Terminal
                glittering on the Jersey shore,
and a train somewhere under ground bringing you towards me
to our new living-place from which we can see

a river and its traffic (the Hudson and the
hidden river, who can say which it is we see, we see
something of both. Or who can say
the crippled broom-vendor yesterday, who passed
just as we needed a new broom, was not
one of the Hidden Ones?)

Crates of fruit are unloading
across the street on the cobbles,
and a brazier flaring
to warm the men and burn trash. He wished us
luck when we bought the broom. But not luck
brought us here. By design

clear air and cold wind polish
the river lights, by design
we are to live now in a new place.

The Presence

To the house on the grassy hill
where rams rub their horns against the porch

and your bare feet on the floors of silence
speak in rhymed stanzas to the furniture,

solemn chests of drawers and heavy chairs
blinking in the sun you have let in!

Before I enter the rooms of your solitude
in my living form, trailing my shadow,

I shall have come unseen. Upstairs and down with you
and out across road and rocks to the river

to drink the cold spray. You will believe
a bird flew by the window, a wandering bee

buzzed in the hallway, a wind
rippled the bronze grasses. Or will you

know who it is?

Luxury

To go by the asters
and breathe
the sweetness that hovers

in August about the tall milkweeds,
without a direct look, seeing
only obliquely what we know

is there—that
sets the heart beating fast!
And through

the field of goldenrod,
the lazily-humming waves of
standing hay, not to look up

at the sea-green bloom on the mountain—
the lips part, a sense
of languor and strength begins

to mount in us. The path leads
to the river pool, cold and
flashing with young trout. The sun

on my whiteness and your
tawny gold. Without looking
I see through my lashes the iridescence

on black curls of sexual hair.

The Tulips

Red tulips
living into their death
flushed with a wild blue

tulips
becoming wings

ears of the wind
jackrabbits rolling their eyes

west wind
shaking the loose pane

some petals fall
with that sound one
listens for

The Grace-Note

In Sabbath quiet, a street
of closed warehouses and wholesale silence,
Adam Misery, while the cop frisks him

lifts with both hands his lip and
drooping mustache to reveal
horse-teeth for inspection.

        Nothing
is new to him and he is not afraid.
This is a world. As the artist

extends his world with
one gratuitous flourish—a stroke of white or
a run on the clarinet above the

bass tones of the orchestra—so he
ornaments his with
fresh contempt.

The Fountain

Don't say, don't say there is no water
to solace the dryness at our hearts.
I have seen

the fountain springing out of the rock wall
and you drinking there. And I too
before your eyes

found footholds and climbed
to drink the cool water.

The woman of that place, shading her eyes,
frowned as she watched—but not because
she grudged the water,

only because she was waiting
to see we drank our fill and were
refreshed.

Don't say, don't say there is no water.
That fountain is there among its scalloped
green and gray stones,

it is still there and always there
with its quiet song and strange power
to spring in us,
up and out through the rock.

The Necessity

From love one takes
petal to **rock** and **blessèd**
away towards
descend,

one took thought
for frail tint and spectral
glisten, trusted
from way back that stillness

one knew
that heart of fire, rose
at the core of gold glow,
could go down undiminished,

for love and
or if in fear knowing
the risk, knowing
what one is touching, one does it,

each part
of speech a spark
awaiting redemption, each
a virtue, a power

in abeyance unless we
give it care
our need designs in us. Then
all we have led away returns to us.

Matins

i

The authentic! Shadows of it
sweep past in dreams, one could say imprecisely,
evoking the almost-silent
ripping apart of giant
sheets of cellophane. No.
It thrusts up close. Exactly in dreams
it has you off-guard, you
recognize it before you have time.
For a second before waking
the alarm bell is a red conical hat, it
takes form.

ii

The authentic! I said
rising from the toilet seat.
The radiator in rhythmic knockings
spoke of the rising steam.
The authentic, I said
breaking the handle of my hairbrush as I
brushed my hair in

rhythmic strokes: That's it,
that's joy, it's always
a recognition, the known
appearing fully itself, and
more itself than one knew.

iii

The new day rises
as heat rises,
knocking in the pipes
with rhythms it seizes for its own
to speak of its invention—
the real, the new-laid
egg whose speckled shell
the poet fondles and must break
if he will be nourished.

iv

A shadow painted where
yes, a shadow must fall.
The cow's breath
not forgotten in the mist, in the
words. Yes,
verisimilitude draws up
heat in us, zest
to follow through,
follow through,
follow
transformations of day
in its turning, in its becoming.

v

Stir the holy grains, set
the bowls on the table and
call the child to eat.

While we eat we think,
as we think an undercurrent
of dream runs through us

faster than thought
towards recognition.

Call the child to eat,
send him off, his mouth
tasting of toothpaste, to go down
into the ground, into a roaring train
and to school.

His cheeks are pink
his black eyes hold his dreams, he has left
forgetting his glasses.

Follow down the stairs at a clatter
to give them to him and save
his clear sight.

Cold air
comes in at the street door.

vi

The authentic! It rolls
just out of reach, beyond
running feet and
stretching fingers, down
the green slope and into
the black waves of the sea.
Speak to me, little horse, beloved,
tell me
how to follow the iron ball,
how to follow through to the country
beneath the waves
to the place where I must kill you and you step out
of your bones and flystrewn meat
tall, smiling, renewed,
formed in your own likeness.

vii

Marvelous Truth, confront us
at every turn,

in every guise, iron ball,
egg, dark horse, shadow,
cloud
of breath on the air,

dwell
in our crowded hearts
our steaming bathrooms, kitchens full of
things to be done, the
ordinary streets.

Thrust close your smile
that we know you, terrible joy.

DURING THE EICHMANN TRIAL

i When We Look Up

> *When we look up*
> *each from his being*
>   *Robert Duncan*

He had not looked,
pitiful man whom none

pity, whom all
must pity if they look

into their own face (given
only by glass, steel, water

barely known) all
who look up

to see—how many
faces?   How many

seen in a lifetime? (Not those
that flash by, but those

into which the gaze wanders
and is lost

and returns to tell
Here is a mystery,

**a person, an
other, an I?**

Count them.
Who are five million?)

'I was used from the nursery
to obedience

all my life . . .
Corpselike

obedience.' Yellow
calmed him later—

'a charming picture'
yellow of autumn leaves in

Wienerwald, a little
railroad station
nineteen-o-eight, Lemburg,

yellow sun
on the stepmother's teatable

Franz Joseph's beard
blessing his little ones.

It was the yellow
of the stars too,

stars that marked
those in whose faces

you had not
looked. 'They were cast out

as if they were
some animals, some beasts.'

'And what would disobedience
have brought me? And

whom would it have served?'
'I did not let my thoughts

dwell on this—I had
seen it and that was

enough.' (The words
'slur into a harsh babble')

'A spring of blood
gushed from the earth.'
Miracle

unsung. I see
a spring of blood gush from the earth—

Earth cannot swallow
so much at once

a fountain
rushes towards the sky

unrecognized
a sign—.

Pity this man who saw it
whose obedience continued—

he, you, I, which shall I say?
He stands

isolate in a bulletproof
witness-stand of glass,

a cage, where we may view
ourselves, an apparition

telling us something he
does not know: we are members

one of another.

ii The Peachtree

The Danube orchards
are full of fruit
but in the city one tree
haunts a boy's dreams

a tree in a villa garden
the Devil's garden
a peach tree

and of its fruit one peach
calls to him

he sees it yellow and ripe
the vivid blood
bright in its round cheek

Next day he knows
he cannot withstand desire
it is no common fruit

it holds some secret
it speaks to the yellow star within him

he scales the wall
enters the garden of death
takes the peach
and death pounces

mister death who rushes out
from his villa
mister death who loves yellow

who wanted that yellow peach
for himself
mister death who signs papers
then eats

telegraphs simply: **Shoot them**
then eats
mister death who orders
more transports
then eats

he would have enjoyed
the sweetest of all the peaches on his tree
with sour-cream
with brandy

Son of David
's blood, vivid red
and trampled juice
yellow and sweet
flow together beneath the tree

there is more blood than
sweet juice
always more blood—mister
death goes indoors
exhausted

iii Crystal Night

From blacked-out streets
    (wide avenues swept by curfew,
    alleyways, veins
    of dark within dark)

from houses whose walls
    had for a long time known
the tense stretch of skin over bone
as their brick or stone listened—

The scream!
The awaited scream rises,
the shattering
of glass and the cracking
of bone

a polar tumult as when
black ice booms, knives
of ice and glass
splitting and splintering the silence into
innumerable screaming needles of
yes, now it is upon us, the jackboots
are running in spurts of
sudden blood-light through the
broken temples

the veils
are rent in twain
terror has a white sound
every scream
of fear is a white needle freezing the eyes
the floodlights of their trucks throw
jets of white, their shouts
cleave the wholeness of darkness into
sectors of transparent white-clouded pantomime
where all that was awaited
is happening, it is Crystal Night

it is Crystal Night
these spikes which are not
pitched in the range of common hearing
whistle through time

smashing the windows of sleep and dream
smashing the windows of history
a whiteness scattering
in hailstones
each a mirror
for man's eyes.

A Solitude

A blind man. I can stare at him
ashamed, shameless. Or does he know it?
No, he is in a great solitude.

O, strange joy,
to gaze my fill at a stranger's face.
No, my thirst is greater than before.

In his world he is speaking
almost aloud. His lips move.
Anxiety plays about them. And now joy

of some sort trembles into a smile.
A breeze I can't feel
crosses that face as if it crossed water.

The train moves uptown, pulls in and
pulls out of the local stops. Within its loud
jarring movement a quiet,

the quiet of people not speaking,
some of them eyeing the blind man,
only a moment though, not thirsty like me,

and within that quiet his
different quiet, not quiet at all, a tumult
of images, but what are his images,

he is blind? He doesn't care
that he looks strange, showing
his thoughts on his face like designs of light

flickering on water, for he doesn't know
what **look** is.
I see he has never seen.

And now he rises, he stands at the door ready,
knowing his station is next. Was he counting?
No, that was not his need.

When he gets out I get out.
'Can I help you towards the exit?'
'Oh, alright.' An indifference.

But instantly, even as he speaks,
even as I hear indifference, his hand
goes out, waiting for me to take it,

and now we hold hands like children.
His hand is warm and not sweaty,
the grip firm, it feels good.

And when we have passed through the turnstile,
he going first, his hand at once
waits for mine again.

'Here are the steps. And here we turn
to the right. More stairs now.' We go
up into sunlight. He feels that,

the soft air. 'A nice day,
isn't it?' says the blind man. Solitude
walks with me, walks

beside me, he is not with me, he continues
his thoughts alone. But his hand and mine
know one another,

it's as if my hand were gone forth
on its own journey. I see him
across the street, the blind man,

and now he says he can find his way. He knows
where he is going, it is nowhere, it is filled
with presences. He says, **I am.**

O TASTE AND SEE

Song for Ishtar

The moon is a sow
and grunts in my throat
Her great shining shines through me
so the mud of my hollow gleams
and breaks in silver bubbles

She is a sow
and I a pig and a poet

When she opens her white
lips to devour me I bite back
and laughter rocks the moon

In the black of desire
we rock and grunt, grunt and
shine

The Elves

Elves are no smaller
than men, and walk
as men do, in this world,
but with more grace than most,
and are not immortal.

Their beauty sets them aside
from other men and from women
unless a woman has that cold fire in her
called poet: with that

she may see them and by its light
they know her and are not afraid
and silver tongues of love
flicker between them.

The Ache of Marriage

The ache of marriage:

thigh and tongue, beloved,
are heavy with it,
it throbs in the teeth

We look for communion
and are turned away, beloved,
each and each

It is leviathan and we
in its belly
looking for joy, some joy
not to be known outside it

two by two in the ark of
the ache of it.

Love Song

Your beauty, which I lost sight of once
for a long time, is long,
not symmetrical, and wears
the earth colors that make me see it.

A long beauty, what is that?
A song
that can be sung over and over,
long notes or long bones.

Love is a landscape the long mountains
define but don't
shut off from the
unseeable distance.

In fall, in fall,
your trees stretch
their long arms in sleeves
of earth-red and

sky-yellow. I take
long walks among them. The grapes
that need frost to ripen them

are amber and grow deep in the
hedge, half-concealed,
the way your beauty grows in long tendrils
half in darkness.

The Message

Cross-country, out of sea fog
comes a letter in dream: a Bard
claims from me 'on whose land they grow,'
seeds of the forget-me-not.

'I ask you
to gather them for me,' says
the Spirit of Poetry.
                            The varied blue
in small compass. In multitude
a cloud of blue, a river
beside the brown river.

Not flowers but
their seeds, I am to send him.
And he bids me
remember my nature, speaking of it
as of a power.
And gather
the flowers, and the flowers
of 'labor' (pink in the dream,
a bright centaury with more petals.
Or the form changes to a sea-pink.)

Ripple of blue in which are
distinct blues. Bold
centaur-seahorse-salt-carnation
flower of work and transition.
Out of sea fog, from a hermitage,
at break of day.

Shall I find them, then—
here on my own land, recalled
to my nature?
                    O, great Spirit!

The Breathing

An absolute
patience.
Trees stand
up to their knees in
fog. The fog
slowly flows
uphill.
            White
cobwebs, the grass
leaning where deer
have looked for apples.
The woods
from brook to where
the top of the hill looks
over the fog, send up
not one bird.
So absolute, it is
no other than
happiness itself, a breathing
too quiet to hear.

September 1961

This is the year the old ones,
the old great ones
leave us alone on the road.

The road leads to the sea.
We have the words in our pockets,
obscure directions. The old ones

have taken away the light of their presence,
we see it moving away over a hill
off to one side.

They are not dying,
they are withdrawn
into a painful privacy

learning to live without words.
E. P. "It looks like dying"—Williams: "I can't
describe to you what has been

happening to me"—
H. D. "unable to speak."
The darkness

twists itself in the wind, the stars
are small, the horizon
ringed with confused urban light-haze.

They have told us
the road leads to the sea,
and given

the language into our hands.
We hear
our footsteps each time a truck

has dazzled past us and gone
leaving us new silence.
One can't reach

the sea on this endless
road to the sea unless
one turns aside at the end, it seems,

follows
the owl that silently glides above it
aslant, back and forth,

and away into deep woods.

But for us the road
unfurls itself, we count the
words in our pockets, we wonder

how it will be without them, we don't
stop walking, we know
there is far to go, sometimes

we think the night wind carries
a smell of the sea. . .

Kingdoms of Heaven

Paradise, an
endless movie. You
walk in, sit down in the dark, it
draws you into itself.

Slowly
an old man crosses
the field of vision, his passions
gathering to the brim of his soul.
And grasses
bow and straighten,

the pulse of wind irregular,
gleam of twilight.

Anything, the attention
never wavers. A woman, say,
who is sleeping or laughing or making
coffee.
A marriage.

Stir of time, the sequence
returning upon itself, branching
a new way. To suffer, pains, hope.
The attention
lives in it as a poem lives or a song
going under the skin of memory.

Or, to believe it's there
within you
though the key's missing

makes it enough? As if
golden pollen were falling

onto your hair from dark trees.

The Ripple

On white linen the silk
of gray shadows
threefold, over-
lapping, a
tau cross.
Glass jug and
tumblers rise from
that which they
cast.

And luminous
in each
overcast of
cylindrical shade,
image
of water, a brightness
not gold, not silver,
rippling
as if with laughter.

Sparks

In today's mail a poem
quotes from Ecclesiastes:
**Whatsoever thy hand
findeth to do, do it with thy might:
for there is no work,**

nor device,
nor knowledge,
nor wisdom,
in the grave, whither thou goest.
A letter with it
discloses, in its words and between them,
a life opening, fearful, fearless,
thousand-eyed, a field
of sparks that move swiftly
in darkness, to and from
a center. He is beginning
to live.
The threat
of world's end is the old threat.
'Prepare
for the world to come as thou shouldst
die tomorrow' says
the Book of Delight,
and:
'Prepare for this world as thou
shouldst live forever.'

Another Spring

In the gold mouth of a flower
the black smell of spring earth.
No more skulls on our desks

but the pervasive
testing of death—as if we had need
of new ways of dying? No,

we have no need
of new ways of dying.
Death in us goes on

testing the wild
chance of living
as Adam chanced it.

Golden-mouth, the tilted smile
of the moon westering
is at the black window,

Calavera of Spring.
Do you mistake me?
I am speaking of living,

of moving from one moment into
the next, and into the
one after, breathing

death in the spring air, knowing
air also means
music to sing to.

The Film

Turtle Goddess
she of the hard shell
soft underneath
awaits enormously
in a dark grotto
the young Heroes—

Then the corridor
of booths—in each
Life enshrined in
veils of light, scenes
of bliss or
dark action.
Honey and fog, the nose
confused.

And at the corridor's end
two steps
down into Nothing—

The film is over
we're out in the street—

The film-maker's wife grieves and tells him
good-by for ever, you were wrong,
wrong to have shown the Turtle Mother.
The darkness
should not be revealed.
Farewell.

Maker of visions
he walks with me
to the gate of Home and leaves me.
I enter.

Mother is gone,
only Things remain.

So be it.

A Cure of Souls

The pastor
of grief and dreams

guides his flock towards
the next field

with all his care.
He has heard

the bell tolling
but the sheep

are hungry and need
the grass, today and

every day. Beautiful
his patience, his long

shadow, the rippling
sound of the flock moving

along the valley.

The Secret

Two girls discover
the secret of life
in a sudden line of
poetry.

I who don't know the
secret wrote
the line. They
told me

(through a third person)
they had found it
but not what it was
not even

what line it was. No doubt
by now, more than a week
later, they have forgotten
the secret,

the line, the name of
the poem. I love them
for finding what
I can't find,

and for loving me
for the line I wrote,
and for forgetting it
so that

a thousand times, till death
finds them, they may
discover it again, in other
lines

in other
happenings. And for
wanting to know it,
for

assuming there is
such a secret, yes,
for that
most of all.

Above the Cave

The cave downstairs,
jet, obsidian, ember
of bloodstone, glisten
of mineral green.
And what
hangs out there
asleep.

If a serpent were singing,
what silence.
Sleeping, sleeping,
it is the
thunder of the serpent
drumroll of
the mounting smell of

gas.
Unable to wake, to
blurt out the unworded
warning . . .

Augh!

Transformed.
A silence
of waking at night into speech.

Leaving Forever

He says the waves in the ship's wake
are like stones rolling away.

I don't see it that way.
But I see the mountain turning,
turning away its face as the ship
takes us away.

To the Muse

I have heard it said,
and by a wise man,
that you are not one who comes and goes

but having chosen
you remain in your human house,
and walk

in its garden for air and the delights
of weather and seasons.

Who builds
a good fire in his hearth
shall find you at it
with shining eyes and a ready tongue.

Who shares
even water and dry bread with you
will not eat without joy

and wife or husband
who does not lock the door of the marriage
against you, finds you

not as unwelcome third in the room, but as
the light of the moon on flesh and hair.

He told me, that wise man,
that when it seemed the house was
empty of you,

the fire crackling for no one,
the bread hard to swallow in solitude,
the gardens a tedious maze,

you were not gone away
but hiding yourself in secret rooms.
The house is no cottage, it seems,

it has stairways, corridors, cellars,
a tower perhaps,
unknown to the host.

The host, the housekeeper, it is
who fails you. He had forgotten
to make room for you at the hearth
or set a place for you at the table
or leave the doors unlocked for you.

Noticing you are not there
(when did he last see you?)
he cries out you are faithless,

have failed him,
writes you stormy letters demanding you return
it is intolerable

to maintain this great barracks without your presence,
it is too big, it is too small, the walls
menace him, the fire smokes

and gives off no heat. But to what address
can he mail the letters?
                              And all the while

you are indwelling,
a gold ring lost in the house.
A gold ring lost in the house.
You are in the house!

Then what to do to find the room where you are?
Deep cave of obsidian glowing with red, with green,
with black light,
high room in the lost tower where you sit spinning,

crack in the floor where the gold ring
waits to be found?

                    No more rage but a calm face,
trim the fire, lay the table, find some
flowers for it: is that the way?
Be ready with quick sight to catch
a gleam between the floorboards,

there, where he had looked
a thousand times and seen nothing?
                              Light of the house,

the wise man spoke
words of comfort. You are near,
perhaps you are sleeping and don't hear.

Not even a wise man
can say, do thus and thus, that presence
will be restored.
                    Perhaps

a becoming aware a door is swinging, as if
someone had passed through the room a moment ago—perhaps
looking down, the sight
of the ring back on its finger?

The Crack

While snow fell carelessly
floating indifferent in eddies of
rooftop air, circling the black
chimney cowls,

a spring night entered
my mind through the tight-closed window,
wearing

a loose Russian shirt of
light silk.
            For this, then,
that slanting
line was left, that crack, the pane
never replaced.

A Figure of Time

Old Day the gardener seemed
Death himself, or Time, scythe in hand

by the sundial and freshly-dug
grave in my book of parables.

The mignonette, the dusty miller and silvery
rocks in the garden next door

thrived in his care (the rocks
not hidden by weeds but clear-

cut between tufts
of fern and saxifrage). Now

by our peartree with pruning-hook,
now digging the Burnes's neat, weedless

rosebeds, or as he peered
at a bird in Mrs. Peach's laburnum,

his tall stooped person appeared, and gray
curls. He worked

slow and in silence, and knew perhaps
every garden around the block, gardens

we never saw, each one,
bounded by walls of old brick,

a square plot that was
world to itself.

When I was grown
and gone from home he remembered me

in the time of my growing, and sent,
year by year, salutations,

until there was no one there, in
changed times, to send them by. Old Day,

old Death, dusty
gardener, are you

alive yet, do I live on
yet, in your gray

considering eye?

The Victors

In June the bush we call
alder was heavy, listless,
its leaves studded with galls,

growing wherever we didn't
want it. We cut it
savagely, hunted it from the pasture, chopped it

away from the edge of the wood.
In July, still everywhere, it appeared
wearing green berries.

Anyway it must go. It takes
the light and air and the good of the earth
from flowers and young trees.

But now in August
its berries are red. Do the birds
eat them?   Swinging

clusters of red, the hedges are full of them,
red-currant red, a graceful
ornament or a merry smile.

A Turn of the Head

Quick! there's that
low brief **whirr** to tell

Rubythroat is at the
tigerlilies—

only a passionate baby
sucking breastmilk's so

intent. **Look
sharply after your thoughts** said
Emerson, a good
dreamer.

**Worlds may lie
between you
and the bird's return.** Hummingbird

stays for a fractional sharp
sweetness, and's gone, can't take

more than that.
The remaining
tigerblossoms have rolled their petals
all the way back,

the stamens protrude entire,
there are no more buds.

The Resolve

To come to the river
the brook
hurtles through rainy
woods, over-
topping rocks that
before the rain were
islands.

Its clearness
is gone, and
the song.
It is a rich brown, a load

of churned earth
goes with it.

The sound now
is a direct, intense
sound of
direction.

Overheard

A deep wooden note
when the wind blows,
the west wind.
The rock maple is it,
close to the house?
Or a beam, voice
of the house itself?
A groan, but not
gloomy, rather
an escaped note of
almost unbearable
satisfaction, a great
bough or beam
unaware it had
spoken.

Claritas

i

The All-Day Bird, the artist,
whitethroated sparrow,
striving
in hope and
good faith to make his notes
ever more precise, closer
to what he knows.

ii

There is the proposition
and the development.
The way
one grows from the other.
The All-Day Bird
ponders.

iii

May the first note
be round enough
and those that follow
fine, fine as
sweetgrass,
              prays
the All-Day Bird.

iv

Fine
as the tail of a lizard,
as a leaf of
chives—
the *shadow of a difference*
falling between
note and note,
a *hair's breadth*
defining them.

v

The dew is on the vineleaves.
My tree
is lit with the
break of day.

vi

Sun
light.
     Light
light light light.

202

Shalom

A man growing old is going
down the dark stairs.
He has been speaking of the Soul
tattooed with the Law.
Of dreams
burnt in the bone.

He looks up
to the friends who lean
out of light and wine
over the well of stairs.
They ask his pardon
for the dark they can't help.

Starladen Babylon
buzzes in his blood, an ancient
pulse. The rivers
run out of Eden.
Before Adam
Adam blazes.

'It's alright,' answers
the man going down,
'it's alright—there are many
avenues, many corridors of the soul
that are dark also.
Shalom.'

The Coming Fall

The eastern sky at sunset taking
the glow of the west:
       the west a clear stillness.

The east flinging
nets of cloud
to hold the rose light a moment longer:
       the western hill dark to blackness.

The ants
on their acropolis
prepare for the night.

. . . .

The vine among the rocks
heavy with grapes

the shadows of September
among the gold glint of the grass

among shining
willow leaves the small birds moving

silent in the presence of a new season.

. . . .

In the last sunlight
human figures dark on the hill
outlined—

a fur of gold
about their shoulders and heads,
a blur defining them.

. . . .

Down by the fallen fruit in the old orchard
the air grows cold. The hill
hides the sun.

A sense of the present
rises out of earth and grass,
enters the feet, ascends

into the genitals, constricting
the breast, lightening
the head—a wisdom,

a shiver, a delight
that what is passing

is here, as if
a snake went by, green in the
gray leaves.

The Ground-Mist

In hollows of the land
in faults and valleys
        the white fog
bruised
    by blue shadows
a mirage of lakes

and in the human
faults and depths
        silences
floating
    between night and daybreak
illusion and substance.

But is illusion
so repeated, known
        each dawn,
silence
    suspended in the
mind's shadow

always, not substance
of a sort?
     the white
bruised
    ground-mist the mirage
a true lake.

Say the Word

A woman had been picking flowers in the half-wild garden of an old
farmhouse. Before going indoors to put the flowers in water and begin
making supper, she walked around to the back of the house and up the

pasture a little way to look across the valley at the hills. The pasture sloped steeply up to a line of trees and a stone wall half-concealed with vines and bushes, then beyond that up again to where the woods began.

The woman waded through the uncut grass and the milkweeds—not yet in flower—to a corner near the stone wall. Beyond this point—the highest point near the house from which to look to the eastern horizon—the ground dropped toward the curving road in a tangle of bracken, alder, young birches. Away across the valley, the unseen meadows of the intervale, she could see the nearest dark green hills, strong presences; and here and there, where these dipped, or sometimes higher than their highest ridges, another rank, green too but lightly dusted with distance. The woman was glad to be able to see them. She felt herself nourished by the sense of distance, by the stillness and mass of the hills. They were called mountains, locally; and they were almost mountains. They had the dignity of mountains. She couldn't quite bring herself to call them mountains, herself, having known higher ones—towering, unforested, sharp-peaked and snowy. But these old hills, rounded, softened by their woods, gave her joy in any case. A few white clouds followed each other across the sky, and their shadows moved darkly over the hills revealing contours the full sun did not show. The afternoon hummed with insects. The stems of the irises she had picked near the driveway felt cool in her hand. Not far away she could hear the voices of her son and her husband. They were cutting brush in the upper part of the pasture.

A view of the hills and a feeling of openness around the house were as important to her husband as to herself. This was their first whole summer here—they had bought the old farm, its fields mostly gone back to woodland, two years ago—and he had spent most of his free time, in these first weeks of it, cutting back the alder bushes that threatened to take over the pasture. The boy liked to help him. Each day, too, they pulled up innumerable milkweeds and dug out dock and burdock from around the edges of the dooryard.

It was still hot in the fields though the shadows were lengthening. Soon they would be coming in, sweaty and hungry. She turned to go, sighing deeply with pleasure. But her last look at the horizon as she turned revealed a flaw she had not realized before: in a great dip of the ridge, to the northeast, some still more distant, and higher, hills—mountains—would have been visible from this lookout, had not a tall and full poplar tree blocked the view. She could glimpse the pale blue of them on either side of its rippling leaves.

At supper the man was speaking of the alders he had cut and meant to cut. The alders were not beautiful and grew with a weedlike insistence. If one did not keep after them they would smother everything. She agreed. There was a coarseness to the leaf, a formlessness about the whole plant, one could not love. The boy—who when this clearing of brush began a week or so before had opposed it, almost with tears, frightened of changing what was already good—was full of pride and enthusiasm for the work done that day. So far they had worked only with machetes and a pair of bush-cutters or with their bare hands, but soon they would get a man with a power-saw to come and fell some of the trees that were crowding each other out. And there were others they could fell with an axe—not wholesale but with judgment—to reveal the form of the land and give back some of the space years of neglect had stolen, the man added.

"I know one tree that needs cutting," the woman said, speaking suddenly as if she had been holding it back and the words had now pushed their way out of her by themselves.

"Where's that?" her husband asked, looking up from his plate, his fork poised.

"Well—it's up there beyond that corner . . . I'll show you. There are some far-away mountains one could see from there, but it gets in the way."

The meal continued, they talked of other things, the woman went back and forth between the kitchen and the dining table with dirty plates and dessert and coffee. She was smoking a cigarette and sitting idle while the boy cleared the table when her husband said to her, "Come out a moment and show me which tree you mean."

She looked up at him as if she had not heard what he said.

"Let's go out and look at that tree," he said.

Only a few days before they had gone to picnic near an abandoned hill farm that had seemed, the summer before, very beautiful in its dreaming solitude, as if at rest after a life of achievement; but they found a year's growth of the eager woods had begun to close it in, block the horizon. She had been melancholy there; the blackflies were biting, the grass around the old house had been long and rank, brambles had almost hidden the wellhead and the rhubarb patch. They had eaten quickly, feeling bad tempered, and left almost at once. It had made him very eager to preserve the feeling of lightness and calm there was about their own place.

The woman looked at him and stood up, brushing away a slight unease she felt.

"Come on out with us," the man said to the boy, who was scraping the plates over a box of garbage before stacking them. "We can still do a bit more before the light goes."

The man put an arm around the woman's shoulder as they came out of the kitchen door and began stepping unevenly up the diagonal slope toward the stone wall and the line of trees. In his free hand he carried an axe. The boy followed them whistling. He had the two machetes with him. When they came to the lookout corner she stopped.

"Which tree did you mean?" the man asked.

"It's that popple—look—that tall one."

"Oh, yes—you're right. Yes, that would make a big difference. Funny we didn't notice it before."

The tree was one of the common field poplars people called popples, which grew almost as thick as alders in the neglected lands of a once-prosperous farming country. But where the alders were dull leaved and somehow shapeless, the little poplars were always graceful, and she loved their tremulous ways, the gray green of bark and leaves. In the upper pasture they advanced from the woods into the open in little lines as if hand in hand. They must not be allowed to take over, but a few should remain, to catch the light and the breezes. This one, however, grew not in the open grass but out of what was already a thicket of smaller popple, alder and bramble. The white blossom of the blackberry bushes glimmered in the fading light. The tree that was to be felled grew on the downslope but was tall enough to far overtop the line of the northeast horizon, and full enough to block off almost all of that swooping valley among the nearer hills beyond which lay the far-away mountains she longed to see.

The man and the boy after a moment's pause had gone on down the slope and were hidden now behind the bushes. The woman stood looking at the tree. The sun was just gone down, in back of her, but the eastern sky, which had clouded over while they were indoors, was not yet dark. Dove grays were flushed with wild-flower hues of mauve and pink, the white edges of high cumulus were veiled in transparent gold. The tree's gray green was still more green than gray. It stood at just such a distance from her that she could hear the voices of her husband and son, who were struggling now with the tangle of brush that surrounded it, but could not distinguish their words unless they shouted. As she looked, a rift in the clouds gave to the poplar's topmost branches a last gleam of sunlight which began almost immediately to fade. A thrill of wind ran through the tree, and its leaves even in the dulled light flickered like sequins. No other tree picked up the wind until after the poplar had rippled with it, but as the poplar grew almost still again all the lower trees began to stir. The rustling passed from tree to tree until if she closed her eyes she could think herself on a pebble beach. It slowly hushed, a wave powerfully sucking small pebbles and shells with it in its retreat, and no wave succeeded it.

Now the man and the boy had evidently come right up to the trunk of the tree. By the sound of their voices she knew they were arguing about what angle to begin chopping from. A wood thrush was singing somewhere beyond them. The woman began to feel cold, and pulled down the rolled sleeves of her sweater, nervously. She was ill at ease. There was every reason for the tree to come down; she knew those mountains were more truly mountains than the nearer ones that could already be seen; they were more truly mountains not only because of their height and their defined forms but because of their distance. She knew that on days when a sense of triviality or of nagging anxiety beset her, the sight of them, so far removed from her, would give her courage. But the tree stood out from among the blur of many trees, differentiated, poised in air, a presence, and her word had condemned it. She had spoken so quickly; it had been as if she had heard herself speaking words she had not first spoken in herself. And at once these actions began. Could she not have retracted, not shown the tree—or put off showing it for tonight at least? Or even now she could go down the slope and beg off—he would disagree but he would respect her feeling; and the boy would laugh at her or be indignant at her caprice, but within himself he would understand!

The disputing voices were silent but something was delaying the use of the axe. Swishing and hacking sounds, the rustle of pushed-aside leaves, told her they were still cutting away the bushes near the trunk. "So the axe can swing free," she thought. She stood as if unable to move, crossing her arms tightly as the evening grew colder. Her husband was full of a new liveliness these days. He moved from his desk to the fields and back again with a new lightness, as if such transitions were easy or as if there were no question of transition, as if the use of the mind and the use of the body were all one rhythm. She knew that was good, that was the way life should be lived. Could she—with her persistent sense of the precariousness of happiness, the knife-edge balance of his confidence, of all sureness—could she run to him now with a plea to stop what she had begun? To stop, when it was as much in his concern for her needs as for any need of his own to see those particular mountains, that he was felling this tree?

And while she stood came the first blow of the axe. Thwock. The leaves of a poplar are never completely still; but as yet there was no increase in their rippling. Thwock. The tree seemed to her to grow taller, to stretch itself, to smile in the sequin freedom of its flickering leaves. Thwock. With the third blow the whole tree moved—the trunk with a convulsive jerk and the leaves and branches shuddering deeply.

There was a pause. A murmur of voices, the tree seeming to hold its breath. The woman brushed away insects that were biting her bare legs and buzzing around her ears. Another phrase came from the thrush, from further away. The colors were gone from the sky now; the light that remained was toneless. All the varied greens of the woods had become a single dull green. Should she go down close to the tree and see the axe breaking into it? She had never been close to it, never touched its trunk. Should she go back to the house, heat the water and wash the dishes? The tree was as good as felled now, it was too late to stop it. How fearful when possibility becomes irremediable fact! But she remained where she stood, sullenly enduring the biting of the flies and mosquitoes that had gathered around her, not even trying again to wave them away with a piece of bracken.

The blows of the axe resumed. At each blow the tree shook a little, but after that first great jerk and shudder it was as if it only patiently awaited its fall. But how long it took! How could it take so long to hack through quite a slender stem? She heard her husband give a short roar through clenched teeth. Then it seemed the boy was taking a turn at the axe. The blows came hastily one after another, but not so loud. And now the man had the axe again—slowly, heavily, thwock. Thwock.

"Now!" came the boy's voice high and loud, a yell. Very slowly at first the tree began to lean away backwards, then with gathering momentum it was falling, had fallen. The crash was no louder than the sound a man or a large animal might make, shouldering roughly through the thicket. The man let out a low shout of triumph.

The woman began to run clumsily downhill toward them but caught her foot in something, stumbled, and stopped, her heart beating fast and a feeling of loneliness and confusion overwhelming her.

"Did you see it fall?" the boy cried, coming up to her, breathlessly.

"It was a lot tougher than I expected," her husband said, drawing near, smiling warmly and pushing the sweat off his forehead. He turned to see what had been revealed.

"Wow! That was worth doing. Just look at that!"

They gazed through and beyond the space the poplar had occupied. There to the northeast, in the scooped-out hollow of the pass, was an area of unclouded sky still pale with the last of daylight, and

against it the far mountains were ranged, a wistful blue, remote and
austere.

The Old Adam

A photo of someone else's childhood,
a garden in another country—world
he had no part in and has no power to imagine:

yet the old man who has failed his memory
keens over the picture—'Them happy days—
gone—gone for ever!'—glad for a moment to suppose

a focus for unspent grieving, his floating
sense of loss.
He wanders

asking the day of the week, the time,
over and over the wrong questions.
Missing his way in the streets

he acts out
the bent of his life,
the lost way

never looked for, life
unlived, of which he is dying
very slowly.

'A man,'
says his son, 'who never
made a right move in all his life.' A man

who thought **the dollar was sweet** and
couldn't make a buck, riding the subway
year after year to untasted sweetness,

loving his sons obscurely, incurious
who they were, these men, his sons—
a shadow of love, for love longs

to know the beloved, and a light goes with it
into the dark mineshafts of feeling . . . A man
who now, without knowing,

in endless concern for the smallest certainties,
looking again and again at a paid bill,
inquiring again and again, 'When was I here last?'

asks what it's too late to ask:
'Where is my life? Where is my life?
What have I done with my life?'

Who Is at My Window

Who is at my window, who, who?
Go from my window, go, go!
Who calleth there so like a stranger?
Go from my window, go!
                                    J. Wedderburn, 1542

Who is at my window, who, who?
It's the blind cuckoo, mulling
the old song over.

The old song is about fear, about
tomorrow and next year.

Timor mortis conturbat me, he sings
What's the use?   He brings me

the image of **when,** a boat
hull down, smudged on the darkening ocean.

I want to move deeper into today;
he keeps me from that work.
Today and eternity are nothing to him.
His wings spread at the window make it dark.

Go from my window, go, go!

Puñal

As if that hand
squeezing crow's blood
        against a white sky
        beside an idiot's laughing face
were real.

Having set out
in shoes that hurt
by the bog road
        and missed the way.

A cold day
dragging to a
        cold end.

The blood congealing
black
        between the pleased fingers.

Grey Sparrow Addresses the Mind's Ear

In the Japanese
tongue of the
mind's eye one
two syllable word
tells of
the fringe of rain
clinging to the eaves
and of the grey-green
fronds of
wild parsley.

O Taste and See

The world is
not with us enough.
O taste and see

the subway Bible poster said,
meaning **The Lord**, meaning
if anything all that lives
to the imagination's tongue,

grief, mercy, language,
tangerine, weather, to
breathe them, bite,
savor, chew, swallow, transform

into our flesh our
deaths, crossing the street, plum, quince,
living in the orchard and being

hungry, and plucking
the fruit.

In Abeyance

   No skilled hands
   caress a stranger's flesh with lucid oil before
a word is spoken
          no feasting
before a tale is told, before
the stranger tells his name.

The ships come and go
along the river and
in and out of the Narrows
and few among us know it

we are so many

   and many within themselves
travel to far islands but no one
asks for their story

nor is there an exchange of gifts, stranger
   to stranger

nor libation
nor sacrifice to the gods

and no house has its herm.

Eros at Temple Stream

The river in its abundance
many-voiced
all about us as we stood
on a warm rock to wash

slowly
smoothing in long
                    sliding strokes
our soapy hands along each other's
slippery cool bodies

quiet and slow in the midst of
the quick of the
sounding river

our hands were
flames
stealing upon quickened flesh until

no part of us but was
sleek and
on fire

The Novices

They enter the bare wood, drawn
by a clear-obscure summons they fear
and have no choice but to heed.

A rustling underfoot, a
long trail to go, the thornbushes grow
across the dwindling paths.

Until the small clearing, where they
anticipate violence, knowing some rite
to be performed, and compelled to it.

The man moves forward, the boy
sees what he means to do: from an oaktree
a chain runs at an angle into earth

and they pit themselves to uproot it,
dogged and frightened, to pull the iron
out of the earth's heart.

But from the further depths of the wood
as they strain and weigh on the great chain
appears the spirit,

the wood-demon who summoned them.
And he is not bestial, not fierce
but an old woodsman,

gnarled, shabby, smelling of smoke and sweat,
of a bear's height and shambling like a bear.
Yet his presence is a spirit's presence

and awe takes their breath.
Gentle and rough, laughing a little,
he makes his will known:

not for an act of force he called them,
for no rite of obscure violence
but that they might look about them

and see intricate branch and bark,
stars of moss and the old scars
left by dead men's saws,

and not ask what that chain was.
To leave the open fields
and enter the forest,

that was the rite.
Knowing there was mystery, they could go.
Go back now! And he receded

among the multitude of forms,
the twists and shadows they saw now, listening
to the hum of the world's wood.

The Stonecarver's Poem

Hand of man
hewed from
the mottled rock

almost touching
as Adam the hand of God

smallest inviolate
stone violet

Gone Away

When my body leaves me
I'm lonesome for it.
I've got

eyes, ears,
nose and mouth
and that's all.

Eyes
keep on seeing the
feather blue of the

cold sky,
mouth takes in
hot soup,
nose

smells the frost,

ears hear everything, all
the noises and absences,
but body

goes away to I don't know where
and it's lonesome to drift
above the space it
fills when it's here.

The Garden Wall

Bricks of the wall,
so much older than the house—
taken I think from a farm pulled down
       when the street was built—
narrow bricks of another century.

Modestly, though laid with panels and parapets,
a wall behind the flowers—
roses and hollyhocks, the silver
pods of lupine, sweet-tasting
phlox, gray
lavender—
         unnoticed—
              but I discovered
the colors in the wall that woke
when spray from the hose
played on its pocks and warts—

a hazy red, a
grain gold, a mauve
of small shadows, sprung
from the quiet dry brown—

          archetype
of the world always a step
beyond the world, that can't
be looked for, only
as the eye wanders,
found.

The Disclosure

From the shrivelling gray
silk of its cocoon
a creature slowly
      is pushing out
to stand clear—
              not a butterfly,
                  petal that floats at will across
                  the summer breeze

              not a furred
              moth of the night
                  crusted with indecipherable
                  gold—

some primal-shaped, plain-winged, day-flying thing.

Melody Grundy

Take me or leave me, cries
Melody Grundy. I
like my face.
I am gaily alone.

On my cast-iron horse I was swiftly
everywhere, and no one
saw it for what it was.
That was romance. I leaned

on the mighty tree-stump to watch
an other life at play.
That was joy, I wept, I
leapt into my ship

to sail over grass. Melody
Plenty-of-Friends-Elsewhere
doesn't care,
will sing for all to hear.

Into the Interior

Mountain, mountain, mountain,
marking time. Each
nameless, wall beyond wall, wavering
redefinition of
horizon.

And through the months. The arrivals
at dusk in towns one must leave at daybreak

—were they
taken to heart, to be seen
always again,
or let go, those faces,

a door half-open, moss
by matchlight on an inscribed stone?

And by day
through the hours that
rustle about one dryly,
tall grass of the savannah

up to the eyes.
No alternative to the
one-man path.

The Novel

A wind is blowing. The book being written
shifts, halts, pages
yellow and white drawing apart
and inching together in
new tries. A single white half sheet
skims out under the door.

And cramped in their not yet
halfwritten lives, a man and a woman
grimace in pain. Their cat

yawning its animal secret,
stirs in the monstrous limbo of erasure.
They live (when they live) in fear

of blinding, of burning, of choking under a
mushroom cloud in the year of the roach.
And they want (like us) the eternity
of today, they want this fear to be
struck out at once by a thick black
magic marker, everywhere, every page,

the whole sheets of it crushed, crackling,
and tossed in the fire
       and when they were fine ashes
       the stove would cool and be cleaned
       and a jar of flowers would be put to stand
       on top of the stove in the spring light.

Meanwhile from page to page they
buy things, acquiring the look of a
full life; they argue, make silence bitter,
plan journeys, move house, implant
despair in each other
and then in the nick of time

they save one another with tears,
remorse, tenderness—
hooked on those wonder-drugs.
Yet they do have—
don't they—like us—
their days of grace, they

halt, stretch, a vision
breaks in on the cramped grimace,
inscape of transformation.
Something sundered begins to knit.
By scene, by sentence, something is rendered
back into life, back to the gods.

Threshold

A form upon the quilted
overcast, gleam, Sacré
Coeur, saltlick
to the mind's
desire—

how shall the pulse
beat out
that measure,
under devious
moon
wander swerving

to wonder—

hands turn
what stone to uncover
feather of broken
oracle—

Looking-glass

I slide my face along to the mirror
sideways, to see
that side-smile,
a pale look, tired
and sly. Hey,

who is glancing there?
Shadow-me, not with
malice but mercurially
shot with foreknowledge of
dread and sweat.

About Marriage

Don't lock me in wedlock, I want
marriage, an
encounter—

I told you about the
green light of
May

        (a veil of quiet befallen
        the downtown park,
        late

        Saturday after
        noon, long
        shadows and cool

        air, scent of
        new grass,
        fresh leaves,

        blossom on the threshold of
        abundance—

        and the birds I met there,
        birds of passage breaking their journey,
        three birds each of a different species:

        the azalea-breasted with round poll, dark,
        the brindled, merry, mousegliding one,
        and the smallest, golden as gorse and wearing
        a black Venetian mask

        and with them the three douce hen-birds
        feathered in tender, lively brown—

                I stood
                a half-hour under the enchantment,
                no-one passed near,
                the birds saw me and

                    let me be
                    near them.)

          It's not
          irrelevant:
          I would be
          met

          and meet you
          so,
          in a green

          airy space, not
          locked in.

Hypocrite Women

Hypocrite women, how seldom we speak
of our own doubts, while dubiously
we mother man in his doubt!

And if at Mill Valley perched in the trees
the sweet rain drifting through western air
a white sweating bull of a poet told us

our cunts are ugly—why didn't we
admit we have thought so too? (And
what shame? They are not for the eye!)

No, they are dark and wrinkled and hairy,
caves of the Moon . . .   And when a
dark humming fills us, a

coldness towards life,
we are too much women to
own to such unwomanliness.

Whorishly with the psychopomp
we play and plead—and say
nothing of this later.   And our dreams,

with what frivolity we have pared them
like toenails, clipped them like ends of
split hair.

In Mind

There's in my mind a woman
of innocence, unadorned but

fair-featured, and smelling of
apples or grass. She wears

a utopian smock or shift, her hair
is light brown and smooth, and she

is kind and very clean without
ostentation—
                      but she has
no imagination.
                      And there's a
turbulent moon-ridden girl

or old woman, or both,
dressed in opals and rags, feathers

and torn taffeta,
who knows strange songs—

but she is not kind.

Our Bodies

Our bodies, still young under
the engraved anxiety of our
faces, and innocently

more expressive than faces:
nipples, navel, and pubic hair
make anyway a

sort of face: or taking
the rounded shadows at
breast, buttock, balls,

the plump of my belly, the
hollow of your
groin, as a constellation,

how it leans from earth to
dawn in a gesture of
play and

wise compassion—
nothing like this
comes to pass
in eyes or wistful
mouths.
        I have

a line or groove I love
runs down
my body from breastbone
to waist. It speaks of
eagerness, of
distance.

        Your long back,
the sand color and
how the bones show, say

what sky after sunset
almost white
over a deep woods to which

rooks are homing, says.

Losing Track

Long after you have swung back
away from me
I think you are still with me:

you come in close to the shore
on the tide
and nudge me awake the way

a boat adrift nudges the pier:
am I a pier
half-in half-out of the water?

and in the pleasure of that communion
I lose track,
the moon I watch goes down, the

tide swings you away before
I know I'm
alone again long since,

mud sucking at gray and black
timbers of me,
a light growth of green dreams drying.

The Prayer

At Delphi I prayed
to Apollo
that he maintain in me
the flame of the poem

and I drank of the brackish
spring there, dazed by the
gong beat of the sun,
mistaking it,

as I shrank from the eagle's
black shadow crossing
that sky of cruel blue,
for the Pierian Spring—

and soon after
vomited my moussaka
and then my guts writhed
for some hours with diarrhea

until at dusk
among the stones of the goatpaths
breathing dust
I questioned my faith, or

within it wondered
if the god mocked me.
But since then, though it flickers or
shrinks to a

blue bead on the wick,
there's that in me that
burns and chills, blackening
my heart with its soot,

flaring in laughter, stinging
my feet into a dance, so that
I think sometimes not Apollo heard me
but a different god.

October

Certain branches cut
certain leaves fallen
the grapes
         cooked and put up
for winter

mountains without one
shrug of cloud
no feint of blurred
wind-willow leaf-light

their chins up
in blue of the eastern sky
their red cloaks
wrapped tight to the bone

A Walk through the Notebooks

Let me walk through the fields of paper
touching with my wand
dry stems and stunted
butterflies—

let Sluggard Acre send up
sunflowers among its weeds,
ten foot high—let its thistles
display their Scottish magnificence,
mauve tam-o'-shanters and barbed plaids—

yes, set fire to frostbitten crops,
drag out forgotten fruit
to dance the flame-tango,
the smoke-gavotte,
to live after all—

let the note **elephant** become a song,
the white beast wiser than man
raise a dust in the north woods,
loping on corduroy roads to the arena.

A March

> '. . . *in those wine- and urine-stained hallways,*
> *something in me wondered,* What will happen
> to all that black beauty?'
>
> *James Baldwin*

Out of those hallways
crossing the street to blue
astonished eyes

as though by first light
made visible, dark
presences slowly
focus

revelation of
tulip blacks, delicate
browns, proportion
of heavy lip to bevelled
temple bone

  The mind
of a fair man at the intersection
jars
at the entering of this
beauty, filing

endlessly through his blue
blinking eyes into
the world within him

Earth Psalm

I could replace
God for awhile, that old ring of candles,
that owl's wing brushing the dew
off my grass hair.
If bended knee calls up
a god, if the imagination of idol
calls up a god, if melting
of heart or what was written as
bowels but has to do
      not with shit but with salutation of
      somber beauty in what is mortal,
calls up a god by recognition and power of
longing, then in my forest
God is replaced awhile,
awhile I can turn from that slow embrace
to worship *mortal*, the summoned
god who has speech, who has wit
to wreathe all words, who laughs
wrapped in sad pelt and without hope of heaven,
who makes a music turns the heads
of all beasts
as mine turns, dream-hill grass
standing on end at echo even.

Seedtime

There are weeds that flower forth in fall
in a gray cloud of seed that seems
from a not so great distance
plumblossom, pearblossom,
or first snow,

as if in a fog of feather-light
goosedown-silvery seed-thoughts
a rusty mind in its autumn
reviewed, renewed
its winged power.

A Psalm Praising the Hair of Man's Body

My great brother
> *Lord of the Song*
wears the ruff of
> *forest bear.*

Husband, thy fleece of silk is black,
> a black adornment;
lies so close to the turns of the flesh,
burns my palm-stroke.

My great brother
> *Lord of the Song*
wears the ruff of
> *forest bear.*

Strong legs of our son are dusted
> dark with hair.
Told of long roads,
we know his stride.

My great brother
> *Lord of the Song*
wears the ruff of
> *forest bear.*

Hair of man, man-hair, hair of
breast and groin, marking contour as
     silverpoint marks in cross-
     hatching, as river-
     grass on the woven current
     indicates ripple,
praise.

The Runes

> *(These words were given me in a dream. In the dream
> I was a Finnish child of 8 or 9 who had been given by her
> teacher the task of writing out these 3 ancient runes of
> her people. This is how they went:)*

(1) Know the pinetrees. Know the orange dryness of sickness and death in needle and cone. Know them too in green health, those among whom your life is laid.

(2) Know the ship you sail on. Know its timbers. Deep the fjord waters where you sail, steep the cliffs, deep into the unknown coast goes the winding fjord. But what would you have? Would you be tied up to a sandwhite quay in perpetual sunshine, yards and masts sprouting little violet mandolins?

(3) In city, in suburb, in forest, no way to stretch out the arms—so if you would grow, go straight up or deep down.

THE SORROW DANCE

I ABEL'S BRIDE

The Wings

Something hangs in back of me,
I can't see it, can't move it.

I know it's black,
a hump on my back.

It's heavy. You
can't see it.

What's in it? Don't tell me
you don't know. It's

what you told me about—
black

inimical power, cold
whirling out of it and

around me and
sweeping you flat.

But what if,
like a camel, it's

pure energy I store,
and carry humped and heavy?

Not black, not
that terror, stupidity

of cold rage; or black
only for being pent there?

What if released in air
it became a white

source of light, a fountain
of light? Could all that weight

be the power of flight?
Look inward: see me

with embryo wings, one
feathered in soot, the other

blazing ciliations of ember, pale
flare-pinions. Well—

could I go
on one wing,

the white one?

Abel's Bride

Woman fears for man, he goes
out alone to his labors. No mirror
nests in his pocket. His face
opens and shuts with his hopes.
His sex hangs unhidden
or rises before him
blind and questing.

She thinks herself
lucky. But sad. When she goes out
she looks in the glass, she remembers
herself. Stones, coal,
the hiss of water upon the kindled
branches—her being
is a cave, there are bones at the hearth.

Face to Face

A nervous smile as gaze meets
gaze across

deep
river.
What place
for a smile here;
            it edges away

leaves us each at ravine's edge
alone with our bodies.

We plunge—
O dark river!
towards each other—
into that element—

a deep fall,
the eyes closing as if forever,
the air ripping, the waters
cleaving and closing upon us.

Heavy we are, our flesh
of stone and velvet goes down,
goes down.

Stepping Westward

What is green in me
darkens, muscadine.

If woman is inconstant,
good, I am faithful to

ebb and flow, I fall
in season and now

is a time of ripening.
If her part

is to be true,
a north star,

good, I hold steady
in the black sky

and vanish by day,
yet burn there

in blue or above
quilts of cloud.

There is no savor
more sweet, more salt

than to be glad to be
what, woman,

and who, myself,
I am, a shadow

that grows longer as the sun
moves, drawn out

on a thread of wonder.
If I bear burdens

they begin to be remembered
as gifts, goods, a basket

of bread that hurts
my shoulders but closes me

in fragrance. I can
eat as I go.

Bedtime

We are a meadow where the bees hum,
mind and body are almost one

as the fire snaps in the stove
and our eyes close,

and mouth to mouth, the covers
pulled over our shoulders,

we drowse as horses drowse afield,
in accord; though the fall cold

surrounds our warm bed, and though
by day we are singular and often lonely.

The Son

i   The Disclosure

He-who-came-forth was
it turned out
a man—

Moves among us from room to room of our life
in boots, in jeans, in a cloak of flame
pulled out of his pocket along with
old candywrappers, where it had lain
transferred from pants to pants,
folded small as a curl of dust,
from the beginning—

unfurled now.

The fine flame
almost unseen in common light.

ii   The Woodblock

He cuts into a slab of wood,
engrossed, violently precise.
Thus, yesterday, the day before yesterday,
engines of fantasy were evolved
in poster paints. Tonight
a face forms under the knife,

slashed with stern
crisscrosses of longing, downstrokes
of silence endured—
                            his visioned
own face!—
down which from one eye

rolls a tear.
                    His own face
drawn from the wood,

deep in the manhood his childhood
so swiftly led to, a small brook rock-leaping
into the rapt, imperious, seagoing river.

A Man

'Living a life'—
the beauty of deep lines
dug in your cheeks.

The years gather by sevens
to fashion you. They are blind,
but you are not blind.

Their blows resound,
they are deaf, those laboring
daughters of the Fates,

but you are not deaf,
you pick out
your own song from the uproar

line by line,
and at last throw back
your head and sing it.

Hymn to Eros

O Eros, silently smiling one, hear me.
Let the shadow of thy wings
brush me.
Let thy presence
enfold me, as if darkness
were swandown.
Let me see that darkness
lamp in hand,
this country become
the other country
sacred to desire.

Drowsy god,
slow the wheels of my thought
so that I listen only
to the snowfall hush of
thy circling.
Close my beloved with me
in the smoke ring of thy power,
that we may be, each to the other,
figures of flame,
figures of smoke,
figures of flesh
newly seen in the dusk.

II   THE EARTH WORM

Thirst Song

Making it, making it,
in their chosen field
the roses fall
victim to a weakness of the heart.

Scoring
        so high
no one counts the cost.
The blue moon
light on their profusion darkens.

The Earth Worm

The worm artist
out of soil, by passage
of himself
constructing.
Castles of metaphor!
Delicate
        dungeon turrets!
He throws off
artifacts as he
contracts and expands the
muscle of his being,
ringed in himself,
tilling. He
is homage to
earth, aerates
the ground of his living.

The Unknown

for Muriel Rukeyser

The kettle changes its note,
the steam sublimed.

Supererogatory divinations one is
lured on by!
              The routine
is decent. As if the white page
were a clean tablecloth,
as if the vacuumed floor were
a primed canvas, as if
new earrings made from old shells
of tasty abalone were nose rings for the two most beautiful
girls of a meticulous island, whose bodies are oiled as one oils
a table of teak . . . Hypocrisies
of seemly hope, performed to make a place
for miracles to occur; and if the day
is no day for miracles, then the preparations
are an order one may rest in.

                        But one doesn't want
rest, one wants miracles. Each time that note
changes (which is whenever you let it)—the kettle
(already boiling) passing into enlightenment without
a moment's pause, out of fury into
quiet praise—desire
wakes again. *Begin over.*

                It is to hunt a white deer
                in snowy woods. Beaten
                you fall asleep in the afternoon
on a sofa.
           And wake to witness,
softly backing away from you, mollified,
all that the room had insisted on—
                    eager furniture, differentiated planes . . .
Twilight has come, the windows
are big and solemn, brimful of the afterglow;
and sleep has swept through the mind, loosening
brown leaves from their twigs to drift

<pre>   out of sight
</pre>
beyond the horizon's black rooftops.
A winter's dirt
makes Indian silk squares of the windowpanes,
semi transparent, a designed
middle distance.
<pre>   The awakening is
</pre>
to transformation,
word after word.

For Floss

Brown and silver, the tufted
rushes hold sway
by the Hackensack

and small sunflowers
freckled with soot
clamber out of the fill

in gray haze of
Indian summer
among the paraphernalia

of oil refineries, the crude
industrial débris,
leftover shacks

rusting under dark
wings of Skyway—

tenacious dreamers
sifting the wind
day and night, their roots

in seeping waters—

and fierce in each disk
of coarse yellow the archaic

smile, almost
agony, almost

a boy's grin.

Eros

The flowerlike
animal perfume
in the god's curly
hair—

don't assume
that like a flower's
his attributes
are there to tempt

you or
direct the moth's
hunger—
simply he is
the temple of himself,

hair and hide
a sacrifice of blood and flowers
on his altar

if any worshipper
kneel or not.

III   THE CRUST

Joy

i

Joy, the, 'well . . . *joyfulness* of
joy'—'many years
I had not known it,' the woman of eighty
said, 'only remembered, till now.'

Traherne
in dark fields.
              On Tremont Street,
on the Common, a raw dusk, Emerson
'glad to the brink of fear.'
              It is objective,

stands founded, a roofed gateway;
we cloud-wander

away from it, stumble
again towards it not seeing it,

enter cast-down, discover ourselves
'in joy' as 'in love.'

ii

              'They knocked an
old scar off—the pent blood
rivered out and out—
                    When I

white and weak, understood what befell me

speech quickened in me, I
came to myself,'
                    —a poet
fifty years old, her look a pool
whose sands have down-spiralled, each grain

dream-clear now, the water
freely itself, visible transparence.

iii

Seeing the locus of joy, as the gate
of a city, or as a lych-gate,

I looked up lych-gate: it means
body-gate—here the bearers

rested the bier till the priest came
(to ferry it into a new world).
                            'You bring me

life!' Rilke cried to his
deathbed visitor; then, 'Help me
towards my death,' then, 'Never forget,
dear one, life is
magnificent!'
                I looked up 'Joy'
in *Origins*, and came to

'Jubilation' that goes back
to 'a cry of joy or woe' or to 'echoic
iu of wonder.'

iv

Again the old lady
sure for the first time there is a term
to her earth-life

enters the gate—'Joy is
so special a thing, vivid—'

her love for the earth
returns, her heart lightens,
she savors the crust.

The Willows of Massachusetts

Animal willows of November
in pelt of gold enduring when all else
has let go all ornament
and stands naked in the cold.
Cold shine of sun on swamp water,
cold caress of slant beam on bough,
gray light on brown bark.
Willows—last to relinquish a leaf,
curious, patient, lion-headed, tense
with energy, watching
the serene cold through a curtain
of tarnished strands.

Message

Arbor vitae, whose grooved bole
reveals so many broken
intentions, branches
lopped or
wizened off,

in the grass near you
your scions are uprising,
fernlike, trustful.

Living While It May

The young elm that must be cut
because its roots push at the house wall

taps and scrapes my window
urgently—but when I look round at it

remains still. Or if I turn by chance,
it seems its leaves are eyes, or the whole spray
of leaves and twigs a face flattening
its nose against the glass, breathing a cloud,

longing to see clearly my life whose term
is not yet known.

Annuals

('Plants that flower the first season
the seed is sown, and then die')

All I planted came up,
balsam and nasturtium and
cosmos and the Marvel of Peru

first the cotyledon
then thickly the differentiated
true leaves of the seedlings,

and I transplanted them,
carefully shaking out each one's
hairfine rootlets from the earth,

and they have thriven,
well-watered in the new-turned earth;
and grow apace now—

but not one shows signs of a flower,
not one.
              If August passes
flowerless,
and the frosts come,

will I have learned to rejoice enough
in the sober wonder of
green healthy leaves?

The Cat as Cat

The cat on my bosom
sleeping and purring
—fur-petalled chrysanthemum,
squirrel-killer—

is a metaphor only if I
force him to be one,
looking too long in his pale, fond,
dilating, contracting eyes

that reject mirrors, refuse
to observe what bides
stockstill.
          Likewise

flex and reflex of claws
gently pricking through sweater to skin
gently sustains their own tune,
not mine. I-Thou, cat, I-Thou.

Revivals

When to my melancholy
All is folly
         then the whirr
of the hummingbird
at intervals throughout the day

is all that's sure
to stir me, makes me
jump up, scattering

papers, books, pens—
            To the bay window,
and certainly

there he is below it
true-aimed at the minute cups of
Coral Bells, swerving

perfectly,
the fierce, brilliant faith
that pierces the heart all summer

and sips bitter insects steeped in nectar,
prima materia
of gleam-and-speed-away.

A passion so intense
It driveth sorrow hence . . .

IV   THE SORROW DANCE

A Day Begins

A headless squirrel, some blood
oozing from the unevenly
chewed-off neck

lies in rainsweet grass
near the woodshed door.
Down the driveway

the first irises
have opened since dawn,
ethereal, their mauve

almost a transparent gray,
their dark veins
bruise-blue.

The Mutes

Those groans men use
passing a woman on the street
or on the steps of the subway

to tell her she is a female
and their flesh knows it,

are they a sort of tune,
an ugly enough song, sung
by a bird with a slit tongue

but meant for music?

Or are they the muffled roaring
of deafmutes trapped in a building that is
slowly filling with smoke?

Perhaps both.

Such men most often
look as if groan were all they could do,
yet a woman, in spite of herself,

knows it's a tribute:
if she were lacking all grace
they'd pass her in silence:

so it's not only to say she's
a warm hole. It's a word

in grief-language, nothing to do with
primitive, not an ur-language;
language stricken, sickened, cast down

in decrepitude. She wants to
throw the tribute away, dis-
gusted, and can't,

it goes on buzzing in her ear,
it changes the pace of her walk,
the torn posters in echoing corridors

spell it out, it
quakes and gnashes as the train comes in.
Her pulse sullenly

had picked up speed,
but the cars slow down and
jar to a stop while her understanding

keeps on translating:
'Life after life after life goes by

without poetry,
without seemliness,
without love.'

The Whisper

In world, world
of terror,
filling up fast with
unintelligible
signs:

imploring pinkpalmed hand
twitching, autonomous,
hung from an ordinary
black arm

        (the lights change,
          it's gone)

wind
skirting the
clots of spittle,
smears of
dogshit, pushing

shadows of unknown
objects across and
away and
half across the
sidewalks, arrhythmic.

Travels

The impasto of what is past,
the purple!
        Avalanches
of swarthy yellow!
                But the unremembered
makes itself into a granite-hued
nylon scarf, tight at the throat—
flies out
        backwards, a drifting
banner, tangles
the wheel.

In a landscape of boxed interiors,
among clefts, revealed strata, roofed-over
shafts, the road roves.
                    A shadow

not of a bird, not of a cloud,
draws a dark stroke over
the hills, the mind.
And another, another.
Our fears keep pace with us.
We are driven.
We drive

on, shift gears, grind
up into the present in first, stop,
look out, look down.
In dust
          the lace designs incised

by feet of beetles:
paths crossing, searching—
here a broad swathe
where manna was found, and dragged
away to be savored.
                    At the horizon

flowers
vaster than cathedrals
are crowding. The motor idles.
Over the immense upland
the pulse of their blossoming
thunders through us.

As It Happens

Like dogs in Mexico,
furless, sore, misshapen,

arrives from laborious nowhere
Agony. And proves

to have eyes of kindness,
a pitiful tail; wants

love. Give it some, in form of
dry tortilla, it

grabs and runs off
three-leggéd, scared,

but tarries nearby and will
return. A friend.

A Lamentation

Grief, have I denied thee?
Grief, I have denied thee.

That robe or tunic, black gauze
over black and silver my sister wore
to dance *Sorrow*, hung so long
in my closet. I never tried it on.
        And my dance
was *Summer*—they rouged my cheeks
and twisted roses with wire stems into my hair.
I was compliant, Juno de sept ans,
betraying my autumn birthright pour faire plaisir.
Always denial. Grief in the morning, washed away
in coffee, crumbled to a dozen errands between
busy fingers.

        Or across cloistral shadow, insistent
intrusion of pink sunstripes from open
archways, falling recurrent.

Corrosion denied, the figures the acid designs
filled in. Grief dismissed,
and Eros along with grief.
Phantasmagoria swept across the sky
by shaky winds endlessly,
the spaces of blue timidly steady—

blue curtains at trailer windows framing
the cinder walks.
There are hidden corners of sky
choked with the swept shreds, with pain and ashes.

Grief,

have I denied thee? Denied thee.
The emblems torn from the walls,
and the black plumes.

Skew Lines

Ugly look, close to tears, on a man's face—
      hath compassion
      no name for it?
Look not unlike a fearful animal's
snarl as the hunter backs him up,
      but here
      no bite showing,
      the lips drawn down not back.

Drawn down, sweet lips
      of a man
as if Laurel were about
to cry—compassion
      turns in on itself
biting its tongue, unable to cry out
      or give it a name.

The Closed World

      'If the Perceptive Organs close, their
      Objects seem to close also.'
Blake: Jerusalem

The house-snake dwells here still
under the threshold
but for months I have not seen it
nor its young, the inheritors.

Light and the wind enact
passion and resurrection
day in, day out
but the blinds are down over my windows,
my doors are shut.

When after the long drought at last
silver and darkness swept over the hills
the dry indifferent glare in my mind's eye
wavered but burned on.

To Speak

To speak of sorrow
works upon it
         moves it from its
crouched place barring
the way to and from the soul's hall—

out in the light it
shows clear, whether
shrunken or known as
a giant wrath—
           discrete
at least, where before

its great shadow joined
the walls and roof and seemed
to uphold the hall like a beam.

Psalm Concerning the Castle

Let me be at the place of the castle.
Let the castle be within me.
Let it rise foursquare from the moat's ring.
Let the moat's waters reflect green plumage of ducks, let the shells of
    swimming turtles break the surface or be seen through the rip-
    pling depths.
Let horsemen be stationed at the rim of it, and a dog, always alert on
    the brink of sleep.
Let the space under the first storey be dark, let the water lap the stone
    posts, and vivid green slime glimmer upon them; let a boat be kept
    there.
Let the caryatids of the second storey be bears upheld on beams that
    are dragons.
On the parapet of the central room, let there be four archers, looking
    off to the four horizons. Within, let the prince be at home, let
    him sit in deep thought, at peace, all the windows open to the log-
    gias.
Let the young queen sit above, in the cool air, her child in her arms;
    let her look with joy at the great circle, the pilgrim shadows, the
    work of the sun and the play of the wind. Let her walk to and fro.
    Let the columns uphold the roof, let the storeys uphold the
    columns, let there be dark space below the lowest floor, let the
    castle rise foursquare out of the moat, let the moat be a ring and
    the water deep, let the guardians guard it, let there be wide lands
    around it, let that country where it stands be within me, let me be
    where it is.

Perspectives

The dawn alps,
the stilled snake of
river asleep in its
wide bed,

'to exemplify something we desire in our
own nature.'

Or six miles down
below our hawkstill swiftness

                              the sea
                              wakening.

And when we
come to earth the roofs
are made of tiles,
pigeons
are walking on them,

little bushes
become shade trees.

The Postcards: A Triptych

The Minoan Snake Goddess is flanked by a Chardin still-life, somber
and tranquil, and by Mohammedan angels
brilliantly clothed and with multicolored wings,
who throng round a fleshcolored horse with a man's face
on whose back rides a white-turbanned being without a face,
merely a white, oval disk, and whose hands too are unformed, or
                                                          hidden
in blue sleeves.
                    Are the angels bringing attributes
           to this unconscious one?
Is he about to be made human?
                              One bends to the floor of heaven in
                                                          prayer;
one brings a bowl (of water?) another a tray (of food?); two
point the way, one watches from on high, two and two more
indicate measure, that is, they present
limits that confine the way to a single path;
two debate the outcome, the last
prays not bowed down but looking
level towards the pilgrim.

Stars and the winding
ceintures of the angels surround
the gold cloud or flame before which he rides; heaven itself
is a dark blue.
                    Meanwhile the still-life offers, makes possible,
a glass of water, a wine-bottle made of glass so dark it is
almost black yet not opaque, half full of
perhaps water; and beside these, two courgettes
with rough, yellow-green, almost reptilian skins,
        and a shallow basket
of plums, each almost cleft
with ripeness, the bloom upon them, their skin
darker purple or almost crimson where a hand
touched them, placing them here. Surely
this table, these fruits, these vessels, this water
stand in a cool room, stonefloored, quiet.
And the Goddess?
                    She stands
between the worlds.
                    She is ivory,
her breast bare, her bare arms
braceleted with gold snakes. Their heads
uprear towards her in homage.
Gold borders the tiers of her skirt, a gold hoop
is locked round her waist. She is a few inches high.
And she muses, her lips are pursed,
beneath her crown that must once have been studded with gold
she frowns, she gazes
at and beyond her snakes as if
not goddess but priestess, waiting
an augury.
                    Without thought I have placed these images
over my desk. Under these signs
I am living.

Remembering

How I woke to the color-tone
as of peach-juice
dulcet bells were
tolling.

And how my pleasure
was in the strength of my back,
in my noble shoulders, the cool
smooth flesh cylinders of my arms.
How I seemed a woman tall and
full-rounded, ready
to step into daylight sound as a bell

but continued to awake
further, and found myself
myself, smaller,
not thin but thinner, nervous,
who hurries without animal calm.
And how the sweet
blur of the bells

lapsed, and ceased,
and it was not morning.

City Psalm

The killings continue, each second
pain and misfortune extend themselves
in the genetic chain, injustice is done knowingly, and the air
bears the dust of decayed hopes,
yet breathing those fumes, walking the thronged
pavements among crippled lives, jackhammers
raging, a parking lot painfully agleam
in the May sun, I have seen
not behind but within, within the
dull grief, blown grit, hideous
concrete façades, another grief, a gleam
as of dew, an abode of mercy,
have heard not behind but within noise
a humming that drifted into a quiet smile.
Nothing was changed, all was revealed otherwise;
not that horror was not, not that the killings did not continue,
not that I thought there was to be no more despair,
but that as if transparent all disclosed
an otherness that was blesséd, that was bliss.
I saw Paradise in the dust of the street.

A Vision

*'The intellectual love of a thing is the understanding
of its perfections.'*
Spinoza, quoted by Ezra Pound

Two angels among the throng of angels
paused in the upward abyss,
facing angel to angel.

Blue and green glowed the wingfeathers
of one angel, from red to gold the sheen
of the other's. These two,

as far as angels may dispute, were poised
on the brink of dispute, brink of
fall from angelic stature,

for these tall ones, angels
whose wingspan encompasses entire
earthly villages, whose heads if their feet touched earth

would top pines or redwoods, live by their vision's harmony
which sees at one glance
the dark and light of the moon.

These two hovered dazed before one another,
for one saw the seafeathered, peacock breakered
crests of the other angel's magnificence,
different from his own,

and the other's eyes flickered with vision of
flame petallings, cream-gold grainfeather glitterings,
the wings of his fellow,

and both in immortal danger of dwindling, of dropping
into the remote forms of a lesser being.

But as these angels, the only halted ones
among the many who passed and repassed,
trod air as swimmers tread water, each gazing

on the angelic wings of the other,

the intelligence proper to great angels flew into their wings,
the intelligence called *intellectual love*, which,
understanding the perfections of scarlet,

leapt up among blues and greens strongshafted,
and among amber down illumined the sapphire bloom,

so that each angel was iridescent with the strange newly-seen
hues he watched; and their discovering pause
and the speech their silent interchange of perfection was

never became a shrinking to opposites,

and they remained free in the heavenly chasm,
remained angels, but dreaming angels,
each imbued with the mysteries of the other.

VI   LIFE AT WAR

The Pulse

Sealed inside the anemone
in the dark, I knock my head
on steel petals
curving inward around me.

Somewhere the edict is given:
petals, relax.
Delicately they arch over backward.
All is opened to me—

the air they call *water*,
saline, dawngreen over its sands,
resplendent with fishes.
All day it is morning,

all night the glitter
of all that shines out of itself
crisps the vast swathes of the current.
But my feet are weighted:

only my seafern arms
my human hands
my fingers tipped with fire
sway out into the world.

Fair is the world.
I sing. The ache
up from heel to knee
of the weights

gives to the song its
ground bass.
And before the song
attains even a first refrain

the petals creak and
begin to rise.
They rise and recurl
to a bud's form

and clamp shut.
I wait in the dark.

Didactic Poem

The blood we give the dead to drink
is deeds we do at the will of the dead spirits in us,
not our own live will.
The dead who thirst to speak
had no good of words or deeds when they lived,
or not enough, and were left in longing.
Their longing to speak, their thirst
for the blood of their deeds done by us,
would leave no time, place, force,
for our own deeds, our own
imagination of speech.
Refuse them!
If we too miss out, don't create our lives,
                          invent our deeds, do them, dance
                          a tune with our own feet,
we shall thirst in Hades,
in the blood of our children.

Second Didactic Poem

The honey of man is
the task we're set to: to be
'more ourselves'
in the making:
                  'bees of the invisible' working
in cells of flesh and psyche,
filling
        'la grande ruche d'or.'

Nectar,
　　　the makings of the
incorruptible,
　　　　　is carried upon the
corrupt tongues of
mortal insects,
fanned with their wisps of wing
　　　　　'to evaporate
excess water,'
　　　　　enclosed and capped
with wax, the excretion
of bees' abdominal glands.
Beespittle, droppings, hairs
of beefur: all become honey.
Virulent micro-organisms cannot
survive in honey.
　　　　　The taste,
the odor of honey:
each has no analogue but itself.
In our gathering, in our containing, in our
working, active within ourselves,
slowly the pale
dew-beads of light
lapped up from flowers
can thicken,
darken to gold:

honey of the human.

Two Variations

i Enquiry

You who go out on schedule
to kill, do you know
there are eyes that watch you,
eyes whose lids you burned off,
that see you eat your steak
and buy your girlflesh
and sell your PX goods

and sleep?
She is not old,
she whose eyes
know you.
She will outlast you.
She saw
her five young children
writhe and die;
in that hour
she began to watch you,
she whose eyes are open forever.

ii The Seeing

Hands over my eyes I see
blood and the little bones;
or when a blanket covers
the sockets I see the
weave; at night the glare softens
but I have power now
to see there is only gray
on gray, the sleepers, the
altar. I see the living
and the dead; the dead are
as if alive, the mouth of
my youngest son pulls my
breast, but there is no milk, he
is a ghost; through his flesh
I see the dying of those
said to be alive, they
eat rice and speak to me but
I see dull death in them
and while they speak I see
myself on my mat, body
and eyes, eyes that see a
hand in the unclouded sky,
a human hand, release
wet fire, the rain that gave
my eyes their vigilance.

The Altars in the Street

On June 17th, 1966, The New York Times *reported that, as part of the Buddhist campaign of non-violent resistance, Viet-Namese children were building altars in the streets of Saigon and Hue, effectively jamming traffic.*

Children begin at green dawn nimbly to build
topheavy altars, overweighted with prayers,
thronged each instant more densely

with almost-visible ancestors.
Where tanks have cracked the roadway
the frail altars shake; here a boy

with red stumps for hands steadies a corner,
here one adjusts with his crutch the holy base.
The vast silence of Buddha overtakes

and overrules the oncoming roar
of tragic life that fills alleys and avenues;
it blocks the way of pedicabs, police, convoys.

The hale and maimed together
hurry to construct for the Buddha
a dwelling at each intersection. Each altar

made from whatever stones, sticks, dreams, are at hand,
is a facet of one altar; by noon
the whole city in all its corruption,

all its shed blood the monsoon cannot wash away,
has become a temple,
fragile, insolent, absolute.

Living

The fire in leaf and grass
so green it seems
each summer the last summer.

The wind blowing, the leaves
shivering in the sun,
each day the last day.

A red salamander
so cold and so
easy to catch, dreamily

moves his delicate feet
and long tail. I hold
my hand open for him to go.

Each minute the last minute.

VII   A POEM BY OLGA LEVERTOFF

The Ballad of My Father

'Yáchchiderálum, pútzele mútzele:
    why is your fóotzele burnt to the bone?'
'Hail, dear Rabboni! We would not leave you lonely!
    We come from the limepit where millions were
        thrown!'

My father danced a Hassidic dance the day before he died.
His daughters they were far away, his wife was by his side.

'Yes, from concentration camps, and yes, from gas chambers:
    from thousand years' ghettos, from graves old and new—
Our unremembered bones come to caper in your
        drawingroom,
    and join in the death-dance of one holy Jew!'

He danced for Jesus his Messiah who rose up from the dead
And left the tomb for the upper room and was known
        in the breaking of bread.

'Those who were faithful, and those who betrayed them,
    those who did nothing, and those who defied—
Here they come crowding—the grave has but delayed them:
    your people surround you, in shame and in pride.'

Except you become as a little child my kingdom
        you shall not see.
So he danced in his joy as he did when a boy
        and as often he danced for me.

'Yáchchiderálum, pútzele mútzele:
    faster and faster the measure we tread!
Your hand in my hand, your foot to my footzele—
    partners for ever, the living and the dead!'

He danced for those he left long ago and for those
      he never knew,
For an end of strife for eternal life for behold
      I make all things new.

'Come, tread the winepress! The blood of the ages
      squeezed from our flesh shall be our loving cup:
Red river of life, drawn from martyrs and sages,
      shall bear you on its tide till your Lord
         shall raise you up!'

My father danced a Hassidic dance and sang
      with his latest breath
The dance of peace it will never cease till life
      has conquered death.

'Yáchchiderálum, pútzele mútzele—
      who will remember and who will forget?'
Twirling down time's corridors I see your shadow dancing—
      your song echoes clear down the years whose
         sun has set.

My father danced and then he died and his name
      is a long time gone.
His voice was stilled and his task fulfilled for a people
      that shall be born.

'Yáchchiderálum, pútzele mútzele—
      now if I couldzele I'd speak to you true:
But your dance it is ended and all the tears expended—
      so sleep on and take your rest, my father, my Jew.

Olga Levertoff
November, 1963

272

RELEARNING THE ALPHABET

ELEGIES

The Broken Sandal

Dreamed the thong of my sandal broke.
Nothing to hold it to my foot
How shall I walk?
               Barefoot?
The sharp stones, the dirt. I would
hobble.
And—
Where was I going?
Where was I going I can't
go to now, unless hurting?
Where am I standing, if I'm
to stand still now?

The Cold Spring

i

Twenty years, forty years, it's nothing.
Not a mirage; the blink
of an eyelid.

Life is nibbling us with little
lips, circling our knees, our
shoulders.
         What's the difference,
a kiss or a fin-caress. Only sometimes
the water reddens,
we ebb.

Birth, marriage, death, we've had them,
checked them off on our list,
and still stand here

tiptoe on the mud,
half-afloat,
water up to the neck.

It's a big pond.

ii

What do I know?
            Swing of the
            birch catkins,
            drift of
            watergrass,
            tufts of
            green on the
            trees,
            (flowers, not leaves,
            bearing intricately
            little winged seeds
            to fly in fall)
            and whoever
            I meet now,
            on the path.
It's not enough.

iii

Biology and the computer—
the speaker implies
we're obsolescent,

we who grew up
towards utopias.

In this
amnesia of the heart
I'm wondering,

I almost believe him.
What do I know?
A poem, turn of the head,

some certainty
of mordant delight—
five notes, the return
of the All Day Bird—:

truces, for the new moon
or the spring solstice,
and at midnight the firing resumes,

far away.
It's not real.
We wanted
more of our life to live in us.
To imagine each other.

iv

Twenty years, forty years,
'to live in the present' was a utopia
moved towards

in tears, stumbling, falling,
getting up, going on—
and now the arrival,

the place of pilgrimage curiously
open, not, it turns out,
a circle of holy stones,

no altar, no
high peak,
no deep valley, the world's navel,

but a plain,
only green tree-flowers
thinly screening the dayglare

and without silence—
we hear the traffic, the highway's
only a stonesthrow away.

Is this the place?

v

This is not the place.
The spirit's left it.
Back to that mud my feet felt
when as a child I fell off a bridge
and almost drowned, but rising

found myself dreamily upright,
water sustaining me,
my hair watergrass.

vi

Fishes bare their teeth to our flesh.
The sky's drifting toward our mouths.
Forty years redden the spreading circles.
Blink of an eyelid,
nothing,
obsolete future—

vii

If I should find my poem is deathsongs.
If I find it has ended, when
I looked for the next step.

Not Spring is unreal to me,
I have the tree-flowers by heart.
Love, twenty years, forty years, my life,
          is unreal to me.
I love only the stranger
coming to meet me now
up the path that's pinpricked with
yellow fallen crumbs of pollen.

I who am not about to die,
I who carry my life about with me openly,
health excellent, step light, cheerful, hungry,
my starwheel rolls. Stops
on the point of sight.

Reduced to an eye
I forget what
            I
was.

Asking the cold spring
what if my poem is deathsongs.

At David's Grave

for B. and H. F.

Yes, he is here in this
open field, in sunlight, among
the few young trees set out
to modify the bare facts—

he's here, but only
because we are here.
When we go, he goes with us

to be your hands that never
do violence, your eyes
that wonder, your lives

that daily praise life
by living it, by laughter.

He is never alone here,
never cold in the field of graves.

Despair

While we were visiting David's grave
I saw at a little distance

a woman hurrying towards another grave
hands outstretched, stumbling

in her haste; who then
fell at the stone she made for

and lay sprawled upon it, sobbing,
sobbing and crying out to it.

She was neatly dressed in a pale coat
and seemed neither old nor young.

I couldn't see her face, and my friends
seemed not to know she was there.

Not to distress them, I said nothing.
But she was not an apparition.

And when we walked
back to the car in silence

I looked stealthily back and saw she rose
and quieted herself and began slowly

to back away from the grave.
Unlike David, who lives

in our lives, it seemed
whoever she mourned dwelt

there, in the field, under stone.
It seemed the woman

believed whom she loved heard her,
heard her wailing, observed

the nakedness of her anguish,
and would not speak.

The Gulf

(During the Detroit Riots, 1967)

Far from our garden at the edge of a gulf,
where we calm our nerves in the rain,

(scrabbling a little in earth to pull weeds
and make room for transplants—

dirt under the nails, it
hurts, almost, and yet feels good)

far from our world the heat's on.
Among the looters a boy of eleven

grabs from a florist's showcase (the *Times* says)
armfuls of gladioli, all he can carry,

and runs with them. What happens?
I see him

dart into a dark entry where there's no one
(the shots, the shouting, the glass smashing

heard dully as traffic is heard).
Breathless he halts to examine

the flesh of dream: he squeezes
the strong cold juicy stems, long as his legs,

tries the mild leafblades—they don't cut.
He presses his sweating face

into flower faces, scarlet and pink and purple,
white and blood red, smooth, cool—his heart is pounding.

But all at once an absence
makes itself known to him—it's like

a hole in the lungs,
life running out. They are without

perfume!
        Cheated, he drops them.
White men's flowers.

They rustle in falling,
lonely he stands there, the sheaves

cover his sneakered feet ...
                         There's no place to go
with or without his prize.

Far away, in our garden he cannot imagine,
I'm watching to see if he picks up the flowers

at last or goes,
leaving them lie.

But nothing happens.
He stands there.

He goes on standing there,
useless knowledge in my mind's eye.

Nothing will move him.
We'll live out our lives

in our garden on the edge of a gulf,
and he in the hundred years' war ten heartbeats long

unchanging among the dead flowers,
no place to go.

Biafra

i

Biafra.   Biafra.   Biafra.
Small stock of compassion
grown in us by the imagination
(when we would let it) and by
photos of napalmed children and by
the voice of Thich Nhat Hanh
has expended itself, saying
Vietnam, Vietnam: trying
to end that war.
                    Now we look sluggishly
at photos of children dying in Biafra: dully

accumulate overdue statistics: Massacre
of the Ibos: Do nothing: The poisoning
called 'getting used to'
has taken place: we are
the deads: no room
for love in us: what's left over
changes to bile, brims over: stain on the cushion:
And the news from Biafra (doesn't make the headlines,
not in today's paper at all)
doesn't even get in past our eyes.

ii

Biafra, Biafra, Biafra.
Hammering the word against my breast:
trying to make room for more knowledge
in my bonemarrow:
And all I see
is coarse faces grinning, painted by Bosch
on TV screen as Humphrey
gets nominated: then, flash,
patient sadness,
eyes in a skull: photo
of Biafran boy (age 5?)
          sitting down to die:
And know
no hope: Don't know
what to do: Do nothing:

The Heart

At any moment the heart
breaks for nothing—

poor folk got up in their best,
rich ones trying, trying to please—

each touch and a new fissure appears,
such a network, I think of an old
china pie-plate
left too long in the oven.

If on the bloody muscle its namesake
patiently pumping in the thoracic cavity

each flick of fate incised itself,
who'd live long?—but this beats on

in the habit of minute response,
with no gift for the absolute.

Disasters
of history weigh on it, anguish

of mortality presses
in on its sides

but neither crush it to dust nor
split it apart. What

is under the cracked glaze?

For Paul and Sally Goodman

Between waking and sleeping I saw my life
in the form of an egg made of colored stones,
half-made, yet the dome of it implied
by the built-up set and curve of the mosaic.
Star stones, lozenges, triangles, irregular pebbles,
brilliants and amber, granite and veined chips of
dark rock, glints of silver and fool's gold and gold;
and each was the sign of someone I had known, from whose life
of presence or word my soul's form,
egg of my being,
had taken its nourishment and grown.

Life yet unlived was space defined
by that base of uncountable, varied fragments,
each unique but all fitting close,
shining or somber, curve meeting curve, or angle
laid next to angle with unpredictable precision
—except in one place: and there a gap was,

a little hole, an emptiness
among the chips and flakes of spirit-stone.
It was a life missing that might have touched mine,
a person, Mathew Ready,
now never to be known, my soul-egg
always to be incomplete for lack of one
spark of sapphire gone from the world.

What Wild Dawns There Were

What wild dawns there were
        in our first years here
when we would run outdoors naked
to pee in the long grass behind the house
            and see over the hills such streamers,
            such banners of fire and blue (the blue
            that is Lilith to full day's honest Eve)—
What feathers of gold under the morning star
        we saw from dazed eyes before
stumbling back to bed chilled with dew
to sleep till the sun was high!

Now if we wake early
        we don't go outdoors—or I don't—
        and you if you do go
        rarely call me to see the day break.
I watch the dawn through glass: this year
            only cloudless flushes of light, paleness
            slowly turning to rose,
            and fading subdued.
We have not spoken of these tired
risings of the sun.

FOUR EMBROIDERIES

An Embroidery　　(I)

Rose Red's hair is brown as fur
and shines in firelight as she prepares
supper of honey and apples, curds and whey,
for the bear, and leaves it ready
on the hearth-stone.

Rose White's grey eyes
look into the dark forest.

Rose Red's cheeks are burning,
sign of her ardent, joyful
compassionate heart.
Rose White is pale,
turning away when she hears
the bear's paw on the latch.

When he enters, there is
frost on his fur,
he draws near to the fire
giving off sparks.

Rose White catches the scent of the forest,
of mushrooms, of rosin.

Together Rose Red and Rose White
sing to the bear;
it is a cradle song, a loom song,
a song about marriage, about
a pilgrimage to the mountains
long ago.
　　　　Raised on an elbow,
the bear stretched on the hearth
nods and hums; soon he sighs
and puts down his head.

He sleeps; the Roses
bank the fire.
Sunk in the clouds of their feather bed
they prepare to dream.

Rose Red in a cave that smells of honey
dreams she is combing the fur of her cubs
with a golden comb.
Rose White is lying awake.

Rose White shall marry the bear's brother.
Shall he too
when the time is ripe,
step from the bear's hide?
Is that other, her bridegroom,
here in the room?

An Embroidery   (II)

(from Andrew Lang and H. J. Ford)

It was the name's music drew me first:
Catherine and her Destiny.
And some glow of red gold, of bronze,
I knew there—glint from the fire
               in a great hearth   awakening
the auburn light in her hair
               and in the heaped-up treasure
weighed in the balance.
                         The events
were blent in this light,
out of sequence.

But always
there seemed a flaw in the tale as told.
If, as it said, she chose sorrow in youth,
what power would she have to welcome joy
               when it came at last to her worn hands,
               her body broken on Destiny's strange little wheel?
How could she take pleasure, when grief was a habit,
in the caprice of a cruel King's making her Queen?

And my Catherine, who would have chosen joy at once,
now while her hair sparked as she brushed it
    and her face was already sad with beauty's sadness
    and had no need for the marks of care—
            (yes, surely she did choose so:
                the tale as told breaks down, grows vague)
—how she laughed when she found her Destiny
            tucked under seven quilts of down,
laughed at the ball of silk
held out impatiently by those fingers of bone,
all that power half asleep on the cloudy mountain!
Catherine threw down her cloak on Destiny's bed
for an eighth coverlid,
and merrily took the thread,
stepped out of her youth's brocade slippers
        and set out barefoot, strong from her years of pleasure,
        to wander the roads of the second half of her life.

An Embroidery   (III) Red Snow

(after one of the Parables from Nature *by Mrs Gatty)*

Crippled with desire, he questioned it.
Evening upon the heights, juice of the pomegranate:
who could connect it with sunlight?

He took snow into his
red from cold hands.
It would not acknowledge the blood inside,
stayed white, melted only.

And all summer, beyond how many plunging valleys,
                remote, verdant lesser peaks,
still there were fields
        by day silver,
        hidden often in thunderheads,
but faithful before night, crimson.
He knew it was red snow.

He grows tall, and sets out.
The story, inexorably, is of arrival long after, by dark.

Tells he stood waiting
   bewildered
     in stinging silver towards dawn,
    and looked over abysses, back:

  the height of his home, snowy, red,
  taunted him. Fable snuffs out.
           What did he do?

     He grew old.
      With bloodbright hands he wrought
     icy monuments.
    Beard and long hair flying he rode the whirlwind,
keening the praises of red snow.

An Embroidery   (IV) Swiss Cheese
(after a lost poem, 1947)

Lost wooden poem,
cows and people wending
downmountain slowly
to wooden homesteads

cows first, the families
following calmly their swaying,
their pausing, their moving ahead in dreamy
constancy.
Children asleep in arms of old men,
healthy pallor of smooth cheeks facing
back to high pastures left for the day,
are borne down as the light
waits to leave.

Upper air glows with motes color of hay,
deep valley darkens.
Lost poem, I know
the cows were fragrant
and sounds were of hooves and feet on earth,
of clumps of good grass torn off, to chew
slowly; and not much talk.

They were returning
to wooden buckets, to lantern-beams
crisp as new straw.

Swiss cheese with black bread,
meadow, wood walls, what

did I do with you, I'm looking
through holes, in cheese, or
pine knotholes, and

who were those peaceful folk, the poem
was twenty years ago, I need it now.

WANTING THE MOON

Wings of a God

The beating of the wings.
Unheard.
        The beat rising from dust
        of gray streets
        as now off pale fields.

'A huge crowd of
friends and well-wishers . . . '
                        Someone
figureskates brilliantly
across the lacquer lid of a box
where dreams are stored.
Something
          has to give.

The wings unheard
                felt as a rush of air,
        of air withdrawn, the breath
taken—
        The blow falls,
        feather and bone
                    stone-heavy.
I am felled,
        rise up
        with changed vision,
      a singing in my ears.

Wanting the Moon   (I)

Not the moon. A flower
on the other side of the water.

The water sweeps past in flood,
dragging a whole tree by the hair,

a barn, a bridge. The flower
sings on the far bank.

Not a flower, a bird calling,
hidden among the darkest trees, music

over the water, making a silence
out of the brown folds of the river's cloak.

The moon. No, a young man walking
under the trees.   There are lanterns

among the leaves.
Tender, wise, merry,

his face is awake with its own light,
I see it across the water as if close up.

A jester.   The music rings from his bells,
gravely, a tune of sorrow,

I dance to it on my riverbank.

Not to Have . . .

Not to have but to be.
The black heart of the poppy,
O to lie there as seed.

To become the belovéd.
As the world ends, to enter
the last note of its music.

Wanting the Moon   (II)

Not the moon. To be a bronze head
inhabited by a god.
          A torso of granite

left out in the weather ten thousand years,
adored by passing clouds.
Their shadows painting it, brushstrokes of dust blue.
Giving themselves to it in infinite rain.

      To be a cloud. Sated with wandering, seize
the gaiety of change from within, of dissolution,
of raining.
          To lie down in the dreams
of a young man whose hair
is the color of mahogany.

A Cloak

      'For there's more enterprise
      In walking naked.'
              W. B. Yeats

And I walked naked
from the beginning

breathing in
my life,
breathing out
poems,

arrogant in innocence.

But of the song-clouds my breath made
in cold air

a cloak has grown,
white and,
        where here a word
        there another
froze, glittering,
stone-heavy.

A mask I had not meant
to wear, as if of frost,
covers my face.
        Eyes looking out,
a longing silent at song's core.

A Defeat

        Wanted
to give away pride,
like donating one oil well when you know
you own a whole delta.

Gave away nothing: no takers.
The derricks are idle.

Punt through the shallows,
pushing fat lilies aside,
my shadow,
                in your dark boat.

Craving

Wring the swan's neck, seeking
a little language of drops of blood.

How can we speak of blood, the sky
is drenched with it.

A little language
of dew, then.

It dries.

A language
of leaves underfoot.
Leaves on the tree, trembling
in speech. Poplars
                tremble and speak
if you draw near them.

Swan That Sings and

Swan that sings and
                does not die.

Aimless, the long neck stretched out,
the note held, death
withheld.　　　Wings
creaking in strong flight,
not,
　　　not giving way,
weary of strength

　　　　　　　　the music
ending without conclusion

Earth Dust

So slowly I am dying
you wouldn't know it.
They say birth begins it.
　　　　　　　　　But for three decades, four,
　　　　　　　　the sky's valves lie open,
　　　　　　　　or close to open over again,
a green pearl revealed.

Slowly, slowly,
I spin towards the sun.

Waiting

I am waiting.
On benches, at the corners
of earth's waitingrooms,
by trees whose sap rises, rises
to escape in gray leaves and lose
itself in the last air.
Waiting
for who comes at last,
late, lost, the forever
longed-for, walking
not my road but crossing
the corner where I wait.

Dream

Someone imagined
who was real too

and did not want me to
imagine him,
to violate

his dream of himself.

. . . .

The touch of dream
upon the fine white

skin of someone caught
in someone else's imagined life.

Nails of imagination
tenderly scratching the back of

someone who isn't there,
who's there heavy-hearted,

and won't look up.

. . . .

Who won't look up to enter
the dream that violates
his imagined order.

Gently, insistently,
re-entering
the order of himself,

inviolate dream,
unimagined.

Mad Song

My madness is dear to me.
I who was almost always the sanest among my friends,
one to whom others came for comfort,
now at my breasts (that look timid and ignorant,
        that don't look as if milk had flowed from them,
        years gone by)
cherish a viper.
           Hail, little serpent of useless longing
that may destroy me,
that bites me with such idle
needle teeth.

I who am loved by those who love me
for honesty,
to whom life was an honest breath
          taken in good faith,
I've forgotten how to tell joy from bitterness.

Dear to me, dear to me,
blue poison, green pain in the mind's veins.
How am I to be cured against my will?

The Gulf   (II)
   (Late December, 1968)

'My soul's a black boy with a long way to go.
a long way to know if black is beautiful.'
'But doesn't your soul fly, don't you know who you are?'

'Flies, has flown, yes, poems and praise
known to it—but like a worn kite, old silk
mended with paper,
          bucks the wind, falters, leans
sideways, is falling.'
          'And you spoke of it
as a boy?'
        'That boy with long, cold
stems of stolen gladioli aching his arms:
No place to go.'

A Hunger

Black beans, white sunlight.
These have sufficed.

Approval of mothers, of brothers,
of strangers—a plunge of the hands
in sifted flour, over the wrists.
It gives pleasure.

And being needed. Being loved for that.
Being forgiven.

What mountains there are
to border solitude and provide
limits, blue or
dark as raisins.

But hunger: a hunger there is
refuses. Refuses the earth.

Not Yet

A stealth in air that means:

the swallows have flown
south while I flew
north again.

Still, in the quiet there are
chickadees,
to make me grudgingly smile,
and crickets curious about
my laundry put out to bleach
on brown grass.

So I do smile.
What else to do?
Melancholy is boring.

And if the well goes dry—
and it has;
and if the body-count goes up—
and it does;
and if the summer spent
itself before I took it
into my life—?

Nothing to do but take
crumbs that fall from the chickadee's table
—or starve.
But the time for starving is not yet.

Riders at Dusk

Up the long street of castles, over cobbles
we rode at twilight, alone.

Harlech, Duino, Azay-le-Rideau,
and many more,

neighboring one another.
Of all the windows

none were lit. The sky shone
in some, pale.

Through silence moved
the creak of saddles, jingle of gear.
Uphill,

though not very steep,
the road lay, and was white.

High stepped the horses' feet.

But as I woke I saw I could not see
who that belovéd was that rode with me.

Why Me?

No reason: hyacinthine, ordinary,
extraordinary, creature:

on your two legs, running,
the grey brain above
transmitting its poetry—

just that you are, man, someone,
wings at your heels, the gods sent

to tell me.

Adam's Complaint

Some people,
no matter what you give them,
still want the moon.

The bread,
the salt,
white meat and dark,
still hungry.

The marriage bed
and the cradle,
still empty arms.

You give them land,
their own earth under their feet,
still they take to the roads.

And water: dig them the deepest well,
still it's not deep enough
to drink the moon from.

The Rain

Trying to remember old dreams. A voice. Who came in.
And meanwhile the rain, all day, all evening,
quiet steady sound. Before it grew too dark
I watched the blue iris leaning under the rain,
the flame of the poppies guttered and went out.
A voice. Almost recalled. There have been times
the gods entered. Entered a room, a cave?
A long enclosure where I was, the fourth wall of it
too distant or too dark to see. The birds are silent,
no moths at the lit windows. Only a swaying rosebush
pierces the table's reflection, raindrops gazing from it.
There have been hands laid on my shoulders.
               What has been said to me,
     how has my life replied?
The rain, the rain . . .

Souvenir d'amitié

Two fading red spots mark on my thighs
where a flea from the fur of a black, curly, yearning dog
bit me, casually, and returned into the fur.

Melanie was the dog's name. That afternoon
she had torn the screen from a door and littered fragments
of screen everywhere, and of chewed-up paper,

stars, whole constellations of paper, glimmered
in shadowy floor corners. She had been punished, adequately;
this was not a first offense. And forgiven,

but sadly: her master knew she would soon discover
other ways to show forth her discontent, her black humor.
Meanwhile, standing on hind legs like a human child,

she came to lean her body, her arms and head,
in my lap. I was a friendly stranger. She gave me
a share of her loneliness, her warmth, her flea.

THE SINGER

Keeping Track

Between chores—
                    hulling strawberries,
                    answering letters—
or between poems,

returning to the mirror
to see if I'm there.

Dance Memories

Plié, the knees bend,
a frog flexing to spring;
grand battement, the taut leg
flails as if to beat
chaff from the wheat;
attitude, Hermes brings
ambiguous messages
and moves dream-smoothly
yet with hidden strain
that breaks in sweat,
into *arabesque* that traces
swan-lines on vision's stone
that the dancer not seeing
herself, feels in the bone.
Coupé, the air is cut
out from under the foot,
grand jeté, glissade, grand jeté, glissade,
the joy of leaping, of moving by
leaps and bounds, of gliding
to leap, and gliding
to leap becomes, while it lasts,
heart pounding, breath hurting,
the deepest, the only joy.

Liebestod

Where there is violet in the green of the sea
the eye rests, knowing
a depth there.
In the depth where the violet changes, the sea
surrenders to the eye
a knowledge.
Where the blue of shadow rests upon green the sea
knows desire, sorrow
becomes joy
where there is violet in the eye of the sea.
In the changing
depth of desire
the I knows it is open, the distant sea
withholds nothing, surrenders
nothing,
save to the eye. Rests in the sea
desire of joy,
heart's
sorrow. Where there is violet in the green of the sea.

Wind Song

Whó am I? Whó am I?
It is the old cry wandering in the wind
and with it interwoven
words of reply: I am fiery ember, dispersed
in innumerable fragments
flying in the wind, gray cinders
and black, and all still burning, all bearing
a point of flame
hidden in ashes. Flying upon the nameless
winds and upon those that men
know and name: sirocco,
bise, northeaster, tramontana. I die and again
life is breathed
into me. Whó am I? Whó am I?
My dust burns
in the past and flies before me

into the whirling future,
the Old World, the New World, my soul is scattered
across the continents
in the named places and the named and unnamed
shadowy faces, my years
a hearth from which the sparks wander
and to its stones
blow back at random upon the winds
to kindle the brand again that fades and flares.

Initiation

Black,
    shining with a yellowish
    dew,
erect,
    revealed by the laughing
    glance of Krishna's eyes:
the terrible lotus.

July 1968

Topmost leaves of young oak,
    young maple,
        are red—a delicate red
almost maroon.

I am not young,
    and not yet old. Young enough not to be able
        to imagine my own old age. Something in me

puts out new leaves that are red also,
    delicate, fantastic, in June,
        early summer, late spring in the north.

A dark time we live in. One would think
    there would be no summer. No red leaves.
        One would think there would be

no drawings-up of the blind at morning
    to a field awake with flowers.
        Yet with my tuft of new leaves

it is that field I wake to,
    a woman foolish with desire.

The Curve

Along the tracks
counting
always the right foot awarded
        the tie to step on
the left stumbling all the time in cinders

towards where
    an old caboose
samples of paint were once tried out on
is weathering in a saltmarsh
        to tints Giotto dreamed.

'Shall we
ever reach it?'   'Look—
the tracks take a curve.
We may
       come round to it
if we keep going.'

He-Who-Came-Forth

Somehow nineteen years ago
    clumsily passionate
I drew into me the seed
of a man—
      and bore it, cast it out—

man-seed that grew
       and became a person
       whose subtle mind and quick heart

though I beat him, hurt him,
while I fed him, loved him,

now stand beyond me, out in the world
                                        beyond my skin
beautiful and strange as if
        I had given birth to a tree.

A Marigold from North Vietnam
for Barbara Deming

Marigold   resurrection flower
that the dead   love and come forth
by candlelight to inhale
scent of   sharp   a smoke-of-watchfires
odor.   The living
taste it as if   on the tongue
acrid.   In summer it tells   of fall
in fall   of winter   in winter
of spring.   The leaves
very fine   delicate.   The flowers
petal-crowded   long-lasting.
Drooping in dryness   the whole plant
in minutes   lifts itself   resilient
given water.   The earth in the pot was dug
in quick kindness   by moonlight   for gift
in Maine   but to the root-threads cling still
some crumbs of Vietnam.   When I water
the marigold these too   are moistened
and give forth   nourishment.

Equilibrium

How easy it is to return
into the great nowhere!

Two weeks incommunicado
on the border of somebody else's life
equals two months at sea.

Whom did I anciently
pine for? What were my passions?

The plains of the sea
modulate quiet songs that light
hums to itself.
                The decks
are holystoned. Smoothly
the ship makes way, no shoreline
to mark her passage.

The wake fading.
Translated.

If even so I tremble sometimes,
if I scan the horizon for land-shadow;

it is because I am so unused
to the sufficiency of
random essentials:

moon, box, marigold, *Two Hundred and One
French Verbs*.

I practise breathing, my spirit acquires
color and texture of unbleached linen.

I am unused to
the single ocean,
the one moon.

Secret Festival; September Moon

Pandemonium of owls
plying from east to west and
west to east, over the full-moon sea of
mown grass.
                The low-voiced
and the wailing high-voiced
hooting together, neither in dialogue
                nor in unison,

                                an overlapping
antiphonal a fox
                        barks to,
as if to excel, whose obbligato
the owls ignore.
They raise
the roof of the dark; ferocious
            their joy in the extreme silver
                        the moon has floated out from itself,
luminous air in which their eyes
don't hurt or close,
                        the night of the year
            their incantations have raised—
            and if
foxes believe it's theirs, there's enough to slip
over and round them, earthlings, of owlish fire.

Moon Tiger

The moon tiger.
In the room, here.
It came in, it is
prowling sleekly
under and over
the twin beds.
See its small head,
silver smooth,
hear the pad of its
large feet. Look,
its white stripes
in the light that slid
through the jalousies.
It is sniffing our
clothes, its cold nose
nudges our bodies.
The beds are narrow,
but I'm coming in with you.

The Singer

Crackle and flash almost in the kitchen sink—the
thunderclap follows even as I
jump back frightened,
afraid to touch metal—

        The roof gutters pouring down
          whole rivers, making holes in the earth—
    The electric bulbs fade and go out,
      another thin crackling lights the window
    and in the instant before the next onslaught of kettle-drums,

a small bird, I don't know its name,
among the seagreen tossed leaves
                begins its song.

Somebody Trying

'That creep Tolstoy,' she sobbed.
'He. . . He. . . couldn't even. . .'
Something about his brother dying.

The serfs' punishments
have not ceased to suppurate on their backs.
Woodlots. People. Someone crying

under the yellow
autumn birchgrove drove him
wild: A new set of resolves:

When gambling, that almost obsolete fever,
or three days with the gypsies
sparked him into pure ego, he could,

just the same, write home, 'Sell them.'
It's true. 'Still,' (someone who loved her said,
cold and firm while she dissolved,

hypocrite, in self disgust, *lectrice*)
'Still, he kept on. He wrote
all that he wrote; and seems to have understood

better than most of us:
to be human isn't easy. It's not
easy to be a serf or a master and learn

that art. It takes nerve. Bastard. Fink.
Yet the grief
trudging behind his funeral, he earned.'

The Open Secret

My sign!
       —yours, too—
anyone's—
         aloft in the coppery
afterglow, gulls or pigeons,
         too high to tell,
way above downtown highrise
wheeling serene,
           whether to feed or
for flight's sake
         makes no difference
sliding the air's
         mountains,
unhastening

the bows of their winged bodies drawn
sostenuto over the hover of
        smoke, grey gauze tinged with rust:
over the traffic of our lives—a sign
if I look up—
        or you—
anyone.

Bullfrogs to Fireflies to Moths

i

At the dump bullfrogs
converse as usual.
It's their swamp
    below the garbage tip,
where they were masters
long before towns had
dumps.   Rapid
the crossfire of their
utterance.
Their eyes
        are at water level.
Rats prowl
among the soiled bulrushes.
The frogs sound angry.
    But they have not
    hopped away in the time of rains.
    They inhabit their heritage,
    pluck the twilight
              pleasurably.
Are they irascible?
Yes, but not bored.
    It is summer,
    their spirits are high.
Urgently,
      anxiously,
above their glistening heads,
           fireflies
    switch
    on and
          off.

ii

The fireflies desperately
entreat their unknown bridegrooms,
their somewhere brides,
    to discover them.
      Now while there is time.

But what of the moths?
Their lives also are brief,
but hour after hour—
                    their days and years—
they choose to cling upon windows
ingazing to lighted rooms.
Silk of their bodies unruffled,
dust on spread wings unsmirched.

          Their eyes' lamps
          when mens' lights are put out
          glow steadily—they try
          still to look in towards departed splendor
that may return?

          What secret, worth
          this impassioned stillness
is it they dream of?

A Dark Summer Day

I want some funny jazz band
        to wake me,
tell me life's been dreaming me.
I want something like love, but made
        all of string or pebbles,
          oboe of torn air
to tear me to my senses.
          Emily's black birds
don't bate their banjos nor the throbbing
        of their quick hearts.
The leaves part to reveal
        more leaves, and darkness,
        darkness and the intense
        poised sequence of leaves.
I want to take the last of all leaves
          between my lips and taste
            its weight of stone.

Snail

Burden, grace,
artifice coiled
brittle on my back, integral,

I thought to crawl
out of you,

yearned for the worm's
lowly freedom that can go

under earth and whose
slow arrow pierces
the thick of dark

but in my shell
my life was,

and when I knew it
I remembered

my eyes adept to witness
air and harsh light

and look all ways.

A Tree Telling of Orpheus

White dawn. Stillness.   When the rippling began
    I took it for sea-wind, coming to our valley with rumors
    of salt, of treeless horizons. But the white fog
didn't stir; the leaves of my brothers remained outstretched,
unmoving.
          Yet the rippling drew nearer—and then
my own outermost branches began to tingle, almost as if
fire had been lit below them, too close, and their twig-tips
were dying and curling.
            Yet I was not afraid, only
          deeply alert.

I was the first to see him, for I grew
        out on the pasture slope, beyond the forest.
He was a man, it seemed: the two
moving stems, the short trunk, the two
arm-branches, flexible, each with five leafless
                twigs at their ends,
and the head that's crowned by brown or gold grass,
bearing a face not like the beaked face of a bird,
      more like a flower's.
              He carried a burden made of
some cut branch bent while it was green,
strands of a vine tight-stretched across it. From this,
when he touched it, and from his voice
which unlike the wind's voice had no need of our
leaves and branches to complete its sound,
                came the ripple.
But it was now no longer a ripple (he had come near and
stopped in my first shadow) it was a wave that bathed me
      as if rain
         rose from below and around me
       instead of falling.
And what I felt was no longer a dry tingling:
      I seemed to be singing as he sang, I seemed to know
      what the lark knows; all my sap
        was mounting towards the sun that by now

had risen, the mist was rising, the grass
was drying, yet my roots felt music moisten them
deep under earth.

He came still closer, leaned on my trunk:
    the bark thrilled like a leaf still-folded.
Music! There was no twig of me not
                        trembling with joy and fear.

Then as he sang
it was no longer sounds only that made the music:
he spoke, and as no tree listens I listened, and language
                came into my roots
                            out of the earth,
                into my bark
                        out of the air,
                into the pores of my greenest shoots
                        gently as dew
and there was no word he sang but I knew its meaning.
He told of journeys,
            of where sun and moon go while we stand in dark,
    of an earth-journey he dreamed he would take some day
deeper than roots . . .
He told of the dreams of man, wars, passions, griefs,
            and I, a tree, understood words—ah, it seemed
my thick bark would split like a sapling's that
                        grew too fast in the spring
when a late frost wounds it.

                    Fire he sang,
that trees fear, and I, a tree, rejoiced in its flames.
New buds broke forth from me though it was full summer.
        As though his lyre (now I knew its name)
        were both frost and fire, its chords flamed
up to the crown of me.
                I was seed again.
                    I was fern in the swamp.
                    I was coal.

And at the heart of my wood
(so close I was to becoming man or a god)
        there was a kind of silence, a kind of sickness,
            something akin to what men call boredom, something
(the poem descended a scale, a stream over stones)

that gives to a candle a coldness
in the midst of its burning, he said.

It was then,
when in the blaze of his power that
reached me and changed me
I thought I should fall my length,
that the singer began
to leave me.   Slowly
moved from my noon shadow
to open light,
words leaping and dancing over his shoulders
back to me
rivery sweep of lyre-tones becoming
slowly again
ripple.

And I
in terror
but not in doubt of
what I must do
in anguish, in haste,
wrenched from the earth root after root,
the soil heaving and cracking, the moss tearing asunder—
and behind me the others: my brothers
forgotten since dawn. In the forest
they too had heard,
and were pulling their roots in pain
out of a thousand years' layers of dead leaves,
rolling the rocks away,
breaking themselves
out of
their depths
You would have thought we would lose the sound of the lyre,
of the singing
so dreadful the storm-sounds were, where there was no storm,
no wind but the rush of our
branches moving, our trunks breasting the air.
But the music!
The music reached us.

Clumsily,
stumbling over our own roots,

                                 rustling our leaves in answer,
we moved, we followed.

All day we followed, up hill and down.
                                  We learned to dance,
for he would stop, where the ground was flat,
                                 and words he said
taught us to leap and to wind in and out
around one another in figures the lyre's measure designed.
The singer
          laughed till he wept to see us, he was so glad.
                                   At sunset
we came to this place I stand in, this knoll
with its ancient grove that was bare grass then.
       In the last light of that day his song became
farewell.
       He stilled our longing.
       He sang our sun-dried roots back into earth,
watered them: all-night rain of music so quiet
                                we could almost
          not hear it in the
                 moonless dark.
By dawn he was gone.
             We have stood here since,
in our new life.
        We have waited.
                He does not return.
It is said he made his earth-journey, and lost
what he sought.
         It is said they felled him
and cut up his limbs for firewood.
               And it is said
his head still sang and was swept out to sea singing.
Perhaps he will not return.
               But what we have lived
comes back to us.
         We see more.
                We feel, as our rings increase,
something that lifts our branches, that stretches our furthest leaf-tips
further.
       The wind, the birds,
                   do not sound poorer but clearer,
recalling our agony, and the way we danced.
The music!

RELEARNING THE ALPHABET

Gifts

I want to give away the warm coat
I bought but found
cold and ungainly.
      A man's wife will wear it,
    and in exchange the man will tear
an ugly porch off an old empty house,

leave it the way it was,
bare and sightly.

Dialogue

'I am an object to you,' he said.
'My charm, what you call
my charm—
     alien to me.'
'No! No!' she is crying.
'Indissoluble—' The tears hurt her throat,
'—idiosyncratic—you—not an object—'

       (That smiling glance from under
       fair-lashed long lids—complicit—
       :he cannot help it.)

    'Fire of the mind—
your vision—unique—
aware the lynx is there in smoky light,
a god disdained, unrecognized, dragged in darkness
out to sea—'

Fire, light, again,
beginning to dry tears: awaken, illumine.
Pain tears at her with lynx claws

but her throat relaxes.
Still he suspects. (—Not I but your idea
                    of who I am.)
                              (Why should he care,
                    not wanting the love I keep holding out
                    stupidly, like a warm coat on a hot day?)

She reflects out loud, 'Aren't all, whom we love,
not *objects*, but—symbols—impersonal—
molten glass in our desire, their dailiness
translucent—?
                    The gods in us,
you said: what violence more brutish
than not to see them:
                              I am not doing you
                              that violence:
                                        I see
what is strange in you, and surpasses
with its presence your history . . .'

But she knows the wall is there she can't pass.
The god, the light, the fire,
live in his body she may not touch.
It does not want to touch hers.
Tropism, one of those words she always
had to look up, before its meaning
took root in her, says itself back of her tongue.
She is dark,
            a blackness sinks on her.—*He has*
no tropism towards me, that knowledge.
And yet, and yet, he wants to be known to her,
hungers for love—even from *her* dark source—
      not to pass godlike from form to form, but dig in its claws:
even now, love that he does not want.

And he—(he does not say it now, there's nothing
            said now but re-sayings, but it was written already,
            she has the letter)
'You know
better than I
the desolation is gestation. Absence
                    an absolute

            presence
            calling forth
            the person   (the poet)
    into desperate continuance, toward
    fragments of light.'

Relearning the Alphabet
   (June, 1968–April, 1969)

   For G. who could not help it, I. who saw me,
   R. who read me, and M. for everything.

   "The treasure . . . lies buried. There is no need to seek it in a
   distant country . . . It is behind the stove, the center of the life
   and warmth that rule our existence, if only we knew how to un-
   earth it. And yet—there is this strange and persistent fact, that
   it is only after . . . a journey in a distant region, in a new land,
   that . . . the inner voice . . . can make itself understood by us.
   And to this strange and persistent fact is added another: that he
   who reveals to us the meaning of our . . . inward pilgrimage
   must be himself a stranger. . . . "
                                            —Heinrich Zimmer

A

Joy—a beginning.   Anguish, ardor.
To relearn the ah! of knowing in unthinking
joy: the belovéd stranger lives.
Sweep up anguish as with a wing-tip,
brushing the ashes back to the fire's core.

B

To be. To love an other only for being.

C

Clear, cool? Not those evasions. The seeing
that burns through, comes through to
the fire's core.

D

In the beginning was delight. A depth
stirred as one stirs fire unthinking.
Dark   dark   dark   . And the blaze illumines
dream.

E

Endless
returning, endless
revolution of dream to ember, ember to anguish,
anguish to flame, flame to delight,
delight to dark and dream, dream to ember

F

that the mind's fire may not fail.
The *vowels of affliction*, of unhealed
not to feel it, uttered,
transformed in utterance
to song.
            Not farewell, not farewell, but faring

G

forth into the grace of transformed
continuance, the green meadows
of Grief-Dale where joy grew, flowering
close to the ground, old tales recount,

H

and may be had yet for the harvesting.

                    •

I, J

Into the world of continuance, to find
I-who-I-am again, who wanted
to enter a life not mine,
            to leap a wide, deep, swift river.

At the edge, I stand yet. No, I am moving away,
walking away from the unbridged rush of waters towards
'Imagination's holy forest,' meaning to thread its ways,
                        that are dark,
and come to my own clearing, where 'dreamy, gloomy,
friendly trees' grow, one by one—but
            I'm not looking where I'm going,
            my head's turned back, to see
                    whom I called 'jester': someone dreamed
            on the far bank: not dreamed, seen
in epiphany, as Picasso's bronze *Head of a Jester*
was seen.
        I go stumbling
                    (head turned)
                            back to my origins:
(if that's where I'm going)
                    to joy, my Jerusalem.
Weeping, gesturing,
I'm a small figure in mind's eye,
diminishing in the sweep of rain or gray tears
that cloud the far shore as jealous rage
clouds love and changes it, changes vision.

                    •

K

Caritas is what I must travel to.
Through to the fire's core,
an alchemy:
            caritas, claritas,
But find my face clenched
when I wake at night
                    in limbo.

L

Back there forgetting, among the
letters   folded and put away.
Not uttered.
            'The feel of
not to feel it
was never said . . . ' Keats said.

'Desolation . . . Absence an absolute
presence
              calling forth . . . ' the jester said
from the far shore ('gravely, ringing his bells,
a tune of sorrow.' I dance to it?)
'You are offhand. The trouble
is concealed?' Isak said,
calling me forth.

                    •

I am called forth
from time to time.

I was in the time
of desolation.
What light is it
waking me?
              Absence has not become
a presence.
              Lost in the alphabet
              I was looking for
              the word I can't now say
(love)
        and am called forth
        unto the twelfth letter
        by the love in a question.

                    •

M

Honest man, I wanted
              the moon and went
              out to sea to touch
              the moon and

              down a lane of bright
              broken vanishing
              curled pyramids of
              moonwater
              moving
              towards the moon
          and touched
          the luminous dissolving

half moon
cold
I am
come back,
humbled, to warm myself,
honest man,

our bed is
        upon the earth
your soul is
        in your body
your mouth
        has found
my mouth once more
—I'm home.

N

Something in me that wants to cling
to *never*,
        wants to have been
        wounded deeper
        burned by the cold moon to cinder,

shrinks as the disk
dwindles to vision
        numb not to continuance
        but to that source
        of mind's fire

        waning now,
        no doubt to wax again—

        yet I perhaps not be there
        in its light.

O

Hostile.   Ordinary.   Home.
Order.   Alone.   Other.
Hostile longing.   Ordinary rose, omnivorous.
        Home, solitude.

Somnolence grotto.
Caught. Lost. Orient almost,
volition.
Own.   Only.

Pain recedes, rising from heart to head
and out.

                    Apple thunder, rolling over the
attic floor.

                         Yet I would swear
                         there had been savage light
                         moments before.

P, Q

In childhood dream-play I was always
the knight or squire, not
the lady:
quester, petitioner, win or lose, not
she who was sought.
The initial of quest or question
branded itself long since on the flank
of my Pegasus.
Yet he flies always
home to the present.

R

Released through bars of sorrow
as if not a gate had opened but I
grown intangible had passed through, shadowy,
from dark of yearning into
a soft day, western March;
a thrust of birdsong
parts the gold flowers thickbranching
that roof the path over.

Arms enfold me
tenderly. I am trusted, I trust
the real that transforms me.

And relinquish
in grief
the seeing that burns through, comes through
to fire's core: transformation, continuance,
            as acts of magic I would perform, are no longer
            articles of faith.

                    •

S

Or no: it
slowly becomes known to me:
articles of faith are indeed
rules of the will—graceless,
                faithless.
The door I flung my weight against
was constructed to open   out
                        towards me.

In-seeing
to candleflame's
blue ice-cavern, measureless,

may not be forced by sharp
desire.
        The Prince
        turns in the wood: 'Retrace
                        thy steps, seek out
        the hut you passed, impatient,
        the day you lost your quarry.
        There dwells
        a secret. Restore to it
        its life.
        You will not recognize
        your desire until
        thou hast it fast, it goeth
        aside, it hath
        the cunning of quicksilver.'

                    •

I turn in the forest.
About me the tree-multitudes
twist their roots in earth
to rip it, draw

hidden rivers up into
branch-towers.
Their crowns in the light sway
green beyond vision.
                    All utterance
takes me step by hesitant step towards

T

—yes, to continuance: into
                            that life beyond the dead-end where
(in a desert time of
dry strange heat, of dust
that tinged mountain clouds with copper,
turn of the year impending unnoticed,
the cactus shadows brittle thornstars,
time of
desolation)   I was lost.

                            •

The forest is holy.
The sacred paths are of stone.
A clearing.
The altars are shifting deposits of pineneedles,
                    hidden waters,
                    streets of choirwood,
not what the will
thinks to construct for its testimonies.

U

Relearn the alphabet,
relearn the world, the world
understood anew only in doing, under-
stood only as
looked-up-into out of earth,
the heart an eye looking,
the heart a root
planted in earth.
Transmutation is not
under the will's rule.

V

Vision sets out
journeying somewhere,
walking the dreamwaters:
arrives
not on the far shore but upriver,
a place not evoked, discovered.

.

W

Heart breaks but mends
like good bone.
It's the vain will
wants to have been wounded deeper,
burned by the cold moon to cinder.

Wisdom's a stone
dwells in forgotten pockets—
lost, refound, exiled—
revealed again
in the palm of
mind's hand, moonstone
of wax and wane, stone pulse.

Y

Vision will not be used.
Yearning will not be used.
Wisdom will not be used.
Only the vain will
strives to use and be used,
comes not to fire's core
but cinder.

Z

Sweep up
anguish as with a wing-tip:

the blaze addresses
a different darkness:
absence has not become
the transformed presence the will
looked for,
but other: the present,

that which was poised already in the ah! of praise.

Invocation

Silent, about-to-be-parted-from house.
Wood creaking, trying to sigh, impatient.
Clicking of squirrel-teeth in the attic.
Denuded beds, couches stripped of serapes.

Deep snow shall block all entrances
and oppress the roof and darken
the windows.   O Lares,
don't leave.
The house yawns like a bear.
Guard its profound dreams for us,
that it return to us when we return.

TO STAY ALIVE

PRELUDES

Olga Poems
(Olga Levertoff, 1914–1964)

i

By the gas-fire, kneeling
to undress,
scorching luxuriously, raking
her nails over olive sides, the red
waistband ring—

(And the little sister
beady-eyed in the bed—
or drowsy, was I? My head
a camera—)

Sixteen. Her breasts
round, round, and
dark-nippled—

who now these two months long
is bones and tatters of flesh in earth.

ii

The high pitch of
nagging insistence, lines
creased into raised brows—

Ridden, ridden—
the skin around the nails
nibbled sore—

You wanted
to shout the world to its senses,
did you?—to browbeat

the poor into joy's
socialist republic—
What rage

and human shame swept you
when you were nine and saw
the Ley Street houses,

grasping their meaning as *slum*.
Where I, reaching that age,
teased you, admiring

architectural probity, circa
eighteen-fifty, and noted
pride in the whitened doorsteps.

Black one, black one,
there was a white
candle in your heart.

iii

        i

Everything flows
        she muttered into my childhood,
pacing the trampled grass where human puppets
rehearsed fates that summer,
stung into alien semblances by the lash of her will—

everything flows—
I looked up from my Littlest Bear's cane armchair
and knew the words came from a book
and felt them alien to me

but linked to words we loved
        from the hymnbook—*Time
like an ever-rolling stream / bears all its sons away*—

        ii

Now as if smoke or sweetness were blown my way
I inhale a sense of her livingness in that instant,
feeling, dreaming, hoping, knowing boredom and zest like anyone
        else—
a young girl in the garden, the same alchemical square
I grew in, we thought sometimes

too small for our grand destinies—
                              But dread
was in her, a bloodbeat, it was against the rolling dark
oncoming river she raised bulwarks, setting herself
to sift cinders after early Mass all of one winter,

labelling her desk's normal disorder, basing
her verses on Keble's *Christian Year*, picking
those endless arguments, pressing on

to manipulate lives to disaster . . . To change,
to change the course of the river! What rage for order
disordered her pilgrimage—so that for years at a time

she would hide among strangers, waiting
to rearrange all mysteries in a new light.

                    iii

Black one, incubus—
          she appeared
riding anguish as Tartars ride mares

over the stubble of bad years.

In one of the years
     when I didn't know if she were dead or alive
I saw her in dream

haggard and rouged
          lit by the flare
from an eel- or cockle-stand on a slum street—

was it a dream? I had lost

all sense, almost, of
     who she was, what—inside of her skin,
under her black hair
                    dyed blonde—

it might feel like to be, in the wax and wane of the moon,
in the life I feel as unfolding, not flowing, the pilgrim years—

iv

On your hospital bed you lay
in love, the hatreds
that had followed you, a
comet's tail, burned out

as your disasters bred of love
burned out,
while pain and drugs
quarreled like sisters in you—

lay afloat on a sea
of love and pain—how you always
loved that cadence, 'Underneath
are the everlasting arms'—

all history
burned out, down
to the sick bone, save for

that kind candle.

v

i

In a garden grene whenas I lay—

you set the words to a tune so plaintive
it plucks its way through my life as through a wood.

As through a wood, shadow and light between birches,
gliding a moment in open glades, hidden by thickets of holly

your life winds in me.   In Valentines
a root protrudes from the greensward several yards from its tree

we might raise like a trapdoor's handle, you said,
and descend long steps to another country

where we would live without father or mother
and without longing for the upper world. *The birds
sang sweet, O song, in the midst of the daye,*

and we entered silent mid-Essex churches on hot afternoons
and communed with the effigies of knights and their ladies

and their slender dogs asleep at their feet,
the stone so cold—   *In youth*

is pleasure, in youth is pleasure.

                    ii

Under autumn clouds, under white
wideness of winter skies you went walking
the year you were most alone

returning to the old roads, seeing again
the signposts pointing to Theydon Garnon
or Stapleford Abbots or Greensted,

crossing the ploughlands (whose color I named *murple*,
a shade between brown and mauve that we loved
when I was a child and you

not much more than a child) finding new lanes
near White Roding or Abbess Roding; or lost in Romford's
new streets where there were footpaths then—

frowning as you ground out your thoughts, breathing deep
of the damp still air, taking
the frost into your mind unflinching.

How cold it was in your thin coat, your down-at-heel shoes—
tearless Niobe, your children were lost to you
and the stage lights had gone out, even the empty theater

was locked to you, cavern of transformation where all
had almost been possible.
                    How many books
you read in your silent lodgings that winter,
how the plovers transpierced your solitude out of doors with their
                                        strange cries
I had flung open my arms to in longing, once, by your side
stumbling over the furrows—

Oh, in your torn stockings, with unwaved hair,
you were trudging after your anguish
over the bare fields, soberly, soberly.

vi

Your eyes were the brown gold of pebbles under water.
I never crossed the bridge over the Roding, dividing
the open field of the present from the mysteries,
the wraiths and shifts of time-sense Wanstead Park held suspended,
without remembering your eyes. Even when we were estranged
and my own eyes smarted in pain and anger at the thought of you.
And by other streams in other countries; anywhere where the light
reaches down through shallows to gold gravel. Olga's
brown eyes. One rainy summer, down in the New Forest,
when we could hardly breathe for ennui and the low sky,
you turned savagely to the piano and sightread
straight through all the Beethoven sonatas, day after day—
weeks, it seemed to me. I would turn the pages some of the time,
go out to ride my bike, return—you were enduring in the
falls and rapids of the music, the arpeggios rang out, the rectory
trembled, our parents seemed effaced.
I think of your eyes in that photo, six years before I was born,
the fear in them. What did you do with your fear,
later? Through the years of humiliation,
of paranoia and blackmail and near-starvation, losing
the love of those you loved, one after another,
parents, lovers, children, idolized friends, what kept
compassion's candle alight in you, that lit you
clear into another chapter (but the same book) 'a clearing
in the selva oscura,
a house whose door
swings open, a hand beckons
in welcome'?
                    I cross
so many brooks in the world, there is so much light
dancing on so many stones, so many questions my eyes
smart to ask of your eyes, gold brown eyes,
the lashes short but the lids
arched as if carved out of olivewood, eyes with some vision

of festive goodness in back of their hard, or veiled, or shining,
unknowable gaze . . .

May–August, 1964

A Note to Olga (1966)

i

Of lead and emerald
the reliquary
that knocks my breastbone,

slung round my neck
on a rough invisible rope
that rubs the knob of my spine.

Though I forget you
a red coal from your fire
burns in that box.

ii

On the Times Square sidewalk
we shuffle along, cardboard signs
—Stop the War—
slung round our necks.

The cops
hurry about,
shoulder to shoulder,
comic.

Your high soprano
sings out from just
in back of me—

We shall—I turn,
you're, I very well know,
not there,

and your voice, they say,
grew hoarse
from shouting at crowds . . .

yet *overcome*
sounds then hoarsely
from somewhere in front,

the paddywagon
gapes. —It seems
you that is lifted

limp and ardent
off the dark snow
and shoved in, and driven away.

Life at War

The disasters numb within us
caught in the chest, rolling
in the brain like pebbles. The feeling
resembles lumps of raw dough

weighing down a child's stomach on baking day.
Or Rilke said it, 'My heart . . .
Could I say of it, it overflows
with bitterness . . . but no, as though

its contents were simply balled into
formless lumps, thus
do I carry it about.'
The same war

continues.
We have breathed the grits of it in, all our lives,
our lungs are pocked with it,
the mucous membrane of our dreams
coated with it, the imagination
filmed over with the gray filth of it:

the knowledge that humankind,

delicate Man, whose flesh
responds to a caress, whose eyes
are flowers that perceive the stars,

whose music excels the music of birds,
whose laughter matches the laughter of dogs,
whose understanding manifests designs
fairer than the spider's most intricate web,

still turns without surprise, with mere regret
to the scheduled breaking open of breasts whose milk
runs out over the entrails of still-alive babies,
transformation of witnessing eyes to pulp-fragments,
implosion of skinned penises into carcass-gulleys.

We are the humans, men who can make;
whose language imagines *mercy*,
lovingkindness we have believed one another
mirrored forms of a God we felt as good—

who do these acts, who convince ourselves
it is necessary; these acts are done
to our own flesh; burned human flesh
is smelling in Vietnam as I write.

Yes, this is the knowledge that jostles for space
in our bodies along with all we
go on knowing of joy, of love;

our nerve filaments twitch with its presence
day and night,
nothing we say has not the husky phlegm of it in the saying,
nothing we do has the quickness, the sureness,
the deep intelligence living at peace would have.

What Were They Like?

1) Did the people of Vietnam
   use lanterns of stone?
2) Did they hold ceremonies
   to reverence the opening of buds?

3) Were they inclined to quiet laughter?
4) Did they use bone and ivory,
   jade and silver, for ornament?
5) Had they an epic poem?
6) Did they distinguish between speech and singing?

1) Sir, their light hearts turned to stone.
   It is not remembered whether in gardens
   stone lanterns illumined pleasant ways.
2) Perhaps they gathered once to delight in blossom,
   but after the children were killed
   there were no more buds.
3) Sir, laughter is bitter to the burned mouth.
4) A dream ago, perhaps. Ornament is for joy.
   All the bones were charred.
5) It is not remembered. Remember,
   most were peasants; their life
   was in rice and bamboo.
   When peaceful clouds were reflected in the paddies
   and the water buffalo stepped surely along terraces,
   maybe fathers told their sons old tales.
   When bombs smashed those mirrors
   there was time only to scream.
6) There is an echo yet
   of their speech which was like a song.
   It was reported their singing resembled
   the flight of moths in moonlight.
   Who can say? It is silent now.

Advent 1966

Because in Vietnam the vision of a Burning Babe
is multiplied, multiplied,
                              the flesh on fire
not Christ's, as Southwell saw it, prefiguring
the Passion upon the Eve of Christmas,

but wholly human and repeated, repeated,
infant after infant, their names forgotten,
their sex unknown in the ashes,

set alight, flaming but not vanishing,
not vanishing as his vision but lingering,

cinders upon the earth or living on
moaning and stinking in hospitals three abed;

because of this my strong sight,
my clear caressive sight, my poet's sight I was given
that it might stir me to song,
is blurred.
                There is a cataract filming over
my inner eyes. Or else a monstrous insect
has entered my head, and looks out
from my sockets with multiple vision,

seeing not the unique Holy Infant
burning sublimely, an imagination of redemption,
furnace in which souls are wrought into new life,
but, as off a beltline, more, more senseless figures aflame.

And this insect (who is not there—
it is my own eyes do my seeing, the insect
is not there, what I see is there)
will not permit me to look elsewhere,

or if I look, to see except dulled and unfocused
the delicate, firm, whole flesh of the still unburned.

Tenebrae
(Fall of 1967)

Heavy, heavy, heavy, hand and heart.
We are at war,
bitterly, bitterly at war.

And the buying and selling
buzzes at our heads, a swarm
of busy flies, a kind of innocence.

Gowns of gold sequins are fitted,
sharp-glinting. What harsh rustlings

of silver moiré there are,
to remind me of shrapnel splinters.

And weddings are held in full solemnity
not of desire but of etiquette,
the nuptial pomp of starched lace;
a grim innocence.

And picnic parties return from the beaches
burning with stored sun in the dusk;
children promised a TV show when they get home
fall asleep in the backs of a million station wagons,
sand in their hair, the sound of waves
quietly persistent at their ears.
They are not listening.

Their parents at night
dream and forget their dreams.
They wake in the dark
and make plans. Their sequin plans
glitter into tomorrow.
They buy, they sell.

They fill freezers with food.
Neon signs flash their intentions
into the years ahead.

And at their ears the sound
of the war. They are
not listening, not listening.

STAYING ALIVE

Prologue: An Interim

i

While the war drags on, always worse,
the soul dwindles sometimes to an ant
rapid upon a cracked surface;

lightly, grimly, incessantly
it skims the unfathomed clefts where despair
seethes hot and black.

ii

Children in the laundromat
waiting while their mothers fold sheets.
A five-year-old boy addresses
a four-year-old girl. 'When I say,
Do you want some gum? say *yes.*'
'Yes . . . ' 'Wait!—Now:
Do you want some gum?'
'Yes!'   'Well yes means no,
so you can't have any.'
He chews. He pops a big, delicate bubble at her.

O language, virtue
of man, touchstone
worn down by what
gross friction . . .

        And,
' "It became necessary
to destroy the town to save it,"
a United States major said today.
He was talking about the decision
by allied commanders to bomb and shell the town
regardless of civilian casualties,
to rout the Vietcong.'

O language, mother of thought,
are you rejecting us as we reject you?

Language, coral island
accrued from human comprehensions,
human dreams,

you are eroded as war erodes us.

iii

To repossess our souls we fly
to the sea. To be reminded
of its immensity, and the immense sky
in which clouds move at leisure,
transforming their lives ceaselessly,
sternly, playfully.

Today is the 65th day since de Courcy Squire, war-resister,
began her fast in jail. She is 18.

And the sun
is warm bread, good to us, honest.
And the sand gives itself to our feet
or to our outstretched bodies,
hospitable, accommodating, its shells
unendingly at hand for our wonder.

. . . arrested with 86 others Dec. 7. Her crime:
sitting down in front of a police wagon
momentarily preventing her friends from being
hauled to prison. Municipal Judge Heitzler
handed out 30-day suspended sentences to several others
accused of the same offense, but condemned
Miss Squire to 8 months in jail and fined her
$650. She had said in court 'I don't think there should be
roles like judge and defendant.'

iv

Peace as grandeur. Energy
serene and noble. The waves
break on the packed sand,

butterflies take the cream o' the foam,
from time to time a palmtree lets fall
another dry branch, calmly.
                              The restlessness
of the sound of waves
transforms itself in its persistence
to that deep rest.
                    At fourteen
after measles my mother took me
to stay by the sea. In the austere presence

of Beachy Head we sat long hours
close to the tideline. She read aloud
from George Eliot, while I half-dozed
and played with pebbles. Or I read
to myself Richard Jefferies'
The Story of My Heart, which begins

in such majesty.
                          I was mean and grouchy
much of the time, but she forgave me,

and years later remembered
only the peace of that time.

The quiet there is
in listening.
              Peace could be

that grandeur, that dwelling
in majestic presence, attuned
to the great pulse.

v

                    The cocks crow all night
                    far and near. Hoarse with expectation.
                    And by day stumble red-eyed in the dust
                    where the heat flickers its lizard tongue.

In my dream the city
was half Berlin, half Chicago—
midwest German, Cincinnati perhaps,

where de Courcy Squire is.
There were many of us
jailed there, in moated fortresses—
five of them, with monosyllabic
guttural names. But by day
they led us through the streets,
dressed in our prisoners' robes—
smocks of brown holland—
and the people watched us pass
and waved to us, and gave us
serious smiles of hope.

          Between us and the beach
          a hundred yards of trees, bushes, buildings,
          cut the breeze. But at the *verge*
          of the salt flood, always
          a steady wind, prevailing.

While we await your trial,
(and this is no dream) we are

free to come and go. To rise
from sleep and love and dreams about
ambiguous circumstance, and from
waking in darkness to cockcrow, and moving
deliberately (by keeping still) back into
morning sleep; to rise and float
into the blue day, the elaborate rustlings
of the palmtrees way overhead; to hover
with black butterflies at the lemon-blossom.
The sea awaits us; there are sweet oranges
on our plates; the city grayness has been
washed off our skins, we take pleasure
in each other's warmth of rosy brown.

vi

'Puerto Rico, Feb. 23, 1968.

          . . . Some people, friends sincerely con-
cerned for us but who don't seem to understand what it's really all
about, apparently feel sorry for us because Mitch has been indicted.

One letter this morning said, shyly and abruptly, after talking about quite unrelated matters, "My heart aches for you." Those people don't understand that however boring the trial will be in some ways, and however much of a distraction, as it certainly is, from the things one's nature would sooner be engaged with, yet it's quite largely a kind of pleasure too, a relief, a satisfaction of the need to confront the war-makers and, in the process, do something to wake up the by-standers.

. . . Mitch and the others have a great deal of support, people who think of them as spokesmen; they have good lawyers, and have had and will have a lot of publicity of the kind one hopes will be use-ful—I don't mean useful for their case, saving them from going to jail, I mean useful towards clarifying the issues, stopping the draft, helping to end the war.'

> But something like a cramp
> of fury begins to form
> (in the blue day, in the sweetness
> of life we float in, allowed
> this interim before the trial)
> a cramp of fury at the mild,
> saddened people whose hearts ache
> not for the crimes of war,
> the unspeakable—of which, then,
> I won't speak—
> and not for de Courcy Squire's
> solitary passion
>   but for us.

Denied visitors, even her parents;
confined to a locked cell without running water
or a toilet.
*   On January 29th, the 53rd day of her fast,*
Miss Squire was removed to a hospital.
All the doctors would do was inform her that
the fast may cause her permanent brain injury.

> 'The sympathy of mild good folk,
> a kind of latex from their leaves;
> our inconvenience draws it out.

The white of egg without the yolk,
it soothes their conscience and relieves
the irritations of their doubt.'

' . . . You see how it is—I am angry that they feel no outrage. Their
feeling flows in the wrong directions and at the wrong intensity. And
all I can bring forth out of my anger is a few flippant rhymes. What I
want to tell you—no, not you, you understand it; what I want them
to grasp is that though I understand that Mitch may have to go to jail
and that it will be a hard time for him and for me, yet, because it's for
doing what we know we must do, that hardship is imaginable, encom-
passable, and a small thing in the face of the slaughter in Vietnam and
the other slaughter that will come. And there is no certainty he will
go to jail.'

And the great savage saints of outrage—
who have no lawyers,
who have no interim
in which to come and go,
for whom there is no world left—
their bodies rush upon the air in flames,
sparks fly, fragments of charred rag
spin in the whirlwind, a vacuum
where there used to be this monk or that,
Norman Morrison, Alice Hertz.

Maybe they are crazy. I know I could never
bring myself to injure my own flesh, deliberately.
And there are other models of behavior
to aspire to—A. J. Muste did not burn himself
but worked through a long life to make from outrage
islands of compassion others could build on.
Dennis Riordon, Bob Gilliam, how many others,
are alive and free in the jails. Their word is good,
language draws breath again in their *yes* and *no*,
true testimony of love and resistance.

But we need
the few who could bear no more,
who would try anything,
who would take the chance
that their deaths among the uncountable
masses of dead might be real to those who

don't dare imagine death.
Might burn through the veil that blinds
those who do not imagine the burned bodies
of other people's children.
We need them.
Brands that flare to show us
the dark we are in,
to keep us moving in it.

vii

To expand again, to plunge
our dryness into the unwearying source—

but not to forget.
Not to forget but to remember better.

We float in the blue day
darkly. We rest behind half-closed louvers,
the hot afternoon clouds up,
the palms hold still.

'I have a medical problem that can be cured'—
Miss Squire said last week when she was removed
from the city workhouse to Cincinnati General Hospital,
'I have a medical problem that can be cured
only by freedom.'

Puerto Rico, February–March, 1968

Part I
    (October '68–May '69)

i

Revolution or death. Revolution or death.
Wheels would sing it
                but railroads are obsolete,
we are among the clouds, gliding, the roar
a toneless constant.

Which side are you on?
Revolution, of course. Death is Mayor Daley.
This revolution has no blueprints, and
          ('What makes this night different
          from all other nights?')
is the first that laughter and pleasure aren't shot down in.

Life that
      wants to live.
                    (Unlived life
              of which one can die.)
        I want the world to go on
    unfolding. The brain
not gray except in death, the photo I saw
of prismatic radiance pulsing from live tissue.
      I see Dennis Riordon and de Courcy Squire,
      gentle David Worstell, intransigent Chuck Matthei
      blowing angel horns at the imagined corners.
      Jennie Orvino singing
      beatitudes in the cold wind
            outside a Milwaukee courthouse.
I want their world—in which they already live,
they're not waiting for demolition and reconstruction. 'Begin here.'
Of course I choose
revolution.

ii

And yet, yes, there's the death
that's not the obscene sellout, the coprophiliac spasm
that smears the White House walls with its desensitized thumbs.

      Death lovely,
      whispering,
      a drowsy numbness . . .
                'tis not
      from envy of thy happy lot
                lightwingéd dryad . . .
Even the longest river . . .

Revolution or death. Love
aches me.   *. . . river*
winds somewhere to the sea.

iii

Shining of Lorie's hair, swinging
  alive, color of new copper—

who has died and risen.
'What am I doing here? I had died—'
(The nurses are frightened. The doctor
refuses to tell what happened those four hours.)
whose body at twenty-three is at war
within itself
trying to die again,

whose 'psychic energy' pulls her ten ways:
sculpture poetry painting
psychology photography teaching
cookery love Chinese philosophy
physics

   If she can live I can live.

iv

Trying one corner after another
to flag down a cab
    at last unthinking as one at last
    seems to see me,
       I run into the traffic—
screech of brakes,
human scream, mine,
anger of drivers and shocked pedestrians
yelling at me!
    Is that how death is,
     that poor, that trivial? I'm
not even frightened, only ashamed,
the driver almost refusing me,
scolding me half the way to the airport, I
strenuous to convince him I'm not
a habitual public danger.
So close to death and thinking only
of being forgiven by strangers.

v

Gliding among clouds.   The will to live
pulses.   Radiant emanations
of living tissue, visible only
to some photo-eye we know
sees true because mind's dream-eye,
inward gage, confirms it.
                    Confirmation,
a sacrament.

                    Around the Fish
(it's reproduced here in the magazine the air-hostess gives me)
                    rearranges itself as *Around the—*
                    Nature of Death, is it? *How*
                    to Live, What to Do?

                                        Back in my room
after yet another return home,
first thing I see is a picture postcard
that stood on the windowledge all summer,
somehow not seen. An Assyrian relief. The wings
(as I look at the words I've written, 'gliding among clouds')
draw me to pick it up and examine it:
a sturdy muscular being it shows,
thick-bearded, heavy-sandalled;
wings made for crossing from world to world.
His hair is bound with a wreath;
in his left hand he grips
a thickstemmed plant bearing five blossoms.
                                        Who sent him?
I turn the card over—ah! at once
I know the hand—Bill Rose's. This was his message to me,
six months ago, unanswered. Is now the newly dead—
less than three weeks—trying to speak to me
one last time?
            How to live and the will to live,
            what was recalled to me of those
            rainbow pulsations some Russian scientist
            discovered,
            the choosing
            always before me now that sings itself

quietly, *revolution or death*
       cluster about some center
       unknown, shifting but retaining—
       snowflake forms in a kaleidoscope—
       a character that throughout all transformations
       reveals them connatural.
                     And to that cluster
this winged genie from Nimrud
now adds himself,
last sign from a friend whose life
failed him in some way long before death:
       a man my age
       a man deeply dissatisfied
       as he told me once.

            'It came on very suddenly; he found out
at the end of the summer that nothing could be done for him, so to
make the waiting easier, he decided to go on teaching. But within a
few weeks of that decision, he was dead.'
       And someone else writes: 'Mr Rose was such a lone
figure; he lived alone; you mostly saw him alone; and that's what's so
hard to take: he died alone. I never knew him except by sight.'

       Is there anything
       I write any more that is not
       elegy?
         Goldengrove
is unleaving all around me; I live
in goldengrove; all day
yesterday and today the air has been filled
with that hesitant downwardness;
the marigolds, the pumpkin, must be sought out
to be seen, the grass
is covered with that cloth, the roads'
margins illuminated.

vi

Learned—not for the first time—my 'roots in the
19th century' put me
           out of touch.

Born in the '20s, but a late child, my parents' memories pivoting on
their first meeting, Constantinople, 1910, and returning into the '90s.
Reading, I went straight from Grimm and Andersen to the 19th-
century novel. Until the war—1939—there was a muffin-man who
came by in foggy winter dusks, tea-time, ringing his bell, his wares
balanced on his head according to the mysteries of his trade as if Dick-
ens were still alive—
The 'Ode to a Nightingale' was the first and only poem I ever learned
by heart. Thus, when I wrote, translating, *'purged* of legend,' the
reader's thought was of Stalin, while my intention was something more
graphic than the literal 'cured'—

and again when I said the sun approached
'to study the flower,' the reader—
                                    to whom I would give
                                    all that arms can hold, eyes
                                    encompass—
alas, thought of a tedious process,
grade-points, term-papers—while I had meant 'study—e.g,
                    I study your face intently
                            but its secret eludes me,'
                or, 'he took her hand and studied
                the strong fingers, the veins,
                the curious ring.'

Without a terrain in which, to which, I belong,
language itself is my one home, my Jerusalem,

yet time and the straddled ocean
undo me, maroon me,
(roadblocks, the lines down)—
                        I choose
                                revolution but my words
often already don't reach forward
                        into it—
                                (perhaps)

            Whom I would touch
            I may not,
            whom I may
            I would
            but often do not.

My diction marks me
untrue to my time;
change it, I'd be
untrue to myself.
                    I study
a face intently.
Learning.
Beginning to learn.
And while
        I study,
                O, in that act
of passionate attention
A drowsy numbness
pains my sense.
                Too happy in thy happiness.
Love of living.   *That wants to live.*   *Unlived life.*
whisper
of goldengrove . . .

Entr'acte

i

Last of October, light thinning
towards the cold. Deep shadow.

Yellow honey, the ridge, a grove 'thrown into relief,'
of tamaracks, lurid, glamorous
upon the breast of
moving darkness, clouds thick with
gunmetal blue.
It becomes
November without one's knowing it.
Broad rays from southwest-by-west
single out one by one
the fixed parts of earthscape.

And into the first snowstorm   (marooned)
the lines down
no phone

no lights
no heat
gastank for cooking about to give out
car stuck in the driveway.

        We find candles.
        We light up the woodstove which was all we
        used to have anyway, till a few weeks back.

ii

A fly I thought dead
on its back on the windowsill,
grayed, shrivelled,

slowly waves.
               Yes, what would be its right arm
dreamily moves—out—in—out again
twice, three times.
            It seems
flies dream in dying.

iii

Four p.m.—pleasure
in exercise
in air,
in sound of brook
under and out from
thin ice

pleasure
of chest and shoulders
pushing air that's
not cold enough to hurt.

Jumping
into snowbank—
no sound—

pleasure—

But to the eye
terror of a kind:

black-and-white photo world
not night yet
but at four p.m.
no light we know

hemlock and cedar a toneless black,
snowtufted trunks and boughs
black, sky white, birches
whiter, snow
infinitely whiter: all things
muted: deprived
of color, as if
color were utterance.
A terror
as of eclipse.
The whites graying.

iv

George told me, and then I read it in Beckett,
Proust had a bad memory,
                              the only kind worth having,
Beckett argues: there's no remembrance
                    and so no revelation,
    for those Admirable, terrifying, unimaginable Crichtons
    who don't disremember nothing, keep
    the whole works in mind.
No pain. No sharp stabs of recall. No revelation.

I stretch in luxury; knowledge of the superb badness
of my memory gives me a sense of having thick fur,
a tail, and buried somewhere
a sweet bone, rotten, enticing . . .

What pain! What sharp stabs of recall! What revelations!
The black taste of life, the music
angel tongues buzz when my paws nuzzle it
out into light!

v

Again to hold—'capture' they say—
moments and their processions in palm
of mind's hand.
                    Have you ever,
in stream or sea,
                    felt the silver of fish
pass through your hand-hold? not to stop it,
block it from going onward, but feel it
move in its wave-road?
                    To make
            of song a chalice,
                of Time,
            a communion wine.

Part II

Can't go further.
If there's to be a
second part, it's not
a going beyond, I'm
still here.

To dig down,
to re-examine.

                    . . . .

What is the revolution I'm driven
to name, to live in?—that now roars,
a toneless constant, now
sings itself?

                    It's in the air: no air
                            to breathe without
                scent of it,
                        pervasive:
                odor of snow,
                            freshwater,

360

                                        stink of dank
                              vegetation recomposing.

—Yet crisply
the moon's risen,
full, complete.
Secret uprising (last time I looked,
                    surely not long since,
                    dark was
                    as complete).
The snowfields have been
taken over
(glistening crust of ice upon snow
in driftwaves, curves of stilled
wind-caress, bare to the moon
in silence of adoration).

                    If it were so for us!
                    But that's the moon's world.

                    . . . .

Robert reminds me *revolution*
implies the circular: an exchange
of position, the high
brought low, the low
ascending, a revolving,
an endless rolling of the wheel. The wrong word.
We use the wrong word. A new life
isn't the old life in reverse, negative of the same photo.
But it's the only
word we have . . .

                    . . . .

Chuck Matthei
travels the country
                    a harbinger.
(He's 20. His golden beard was pulled and clipped
          by a Wyoming sheriff, but no doubt has grown again
          though he can't grow knocked-out teeth.
          He wears sneakers even in winter,
          to avoid animal-hide; etc.)

And on his journeyings bears
my poem 'A Man'
to prisoners in the jails.
               Of Mitch I wrote it,
               even before anyone heard
               the voice he
               brought to song.
               But Chuck has found in it
a message for all who resist war,
               disdain to kill,
               try to equate
               'human' with 'humane.'
(And if his intransigeance
brings us another despair
and we call it 'another form of aggression,'
don't we confess—
               wishing he had a sense of humor—
our own extremity?)

'Living a life' the poem begins.
'—the beauty of deep lines
dug in your cheeks'
               and ends,
'you pick out
your own song from the uproar,

line by line,
and at last throw back
your head and sing it.'
               Next on the mimeograph follows:
'THERE IS ONLY AS MUCH PEACE AS THERE ARE
PEACEFUL PEOPLE'
               (A. J. Muste)
               Then Chuck has written:
This is your only life—live it well!

No one man can bring about a social change—
    but each man's life is a whole and necessary part of his society,
    a necessary step in any change,
    and a powerful example of the possibility of life
    for others.

Let all of our words and our actions speak the possibility of peace and
cooperation between men.
Too long have we used the excuse:
  'I believe in peace, but that other man does not—when
  he lays down his arms, then I will follow.'

  Which of us deserves to wait to be the last good man
  on earth; how long will we wait if all of us wait?

Let each man begin a one-man revolution of peace and mutual aid—
  so that there is at least that much peace . . . a beginning . . .

A beginning.
Where shall we
begin?
Can't go
further.
            Time, says the old Canon,
in Denis Saurat's *Death and the Dreamer*,
            is not a sequence,
            as man's simplicity thinks, but radiates
out from a center
            every direction,
            all
                dimensions
                        (pulsations, as from living cells,
radiant—

                . . . .

May 14th, 1969—Berkeley
Went with some of my students to work in the People's Park. There
seemed to be plenty of digging and gardening help so we decided, as
Jeff had his truck available, to shovel up the garbage that had been
thrown into the west part of the lot and take it out to the city dump.

                O happiness
                in the sun! Is it
                that simple, then,
                to live?
                —crazy rhythm of
                scooping up barehanded

(all the shovels already in use)
careless of filth and broken glass
—scooping up garbage together
poets and dreamers studying
joy together, clearing
refuse off the neglected, newly recognized,
humbly waiting ground, place, locus, of what could be our
New World even now, our revolution, one and one and
one and one together, black children swinging, green
guitars, that energy, that music, no one
                    telling anyone what to do,
                    everyone doing,

        each leaf of
        the new grass near us
        a new testament . . .

Out to the dump:
acres of garbage glitter and stink in wild sunlight, gulls
float and scream in the brilliant sky,
polluted waters bob and dazzle, we laugh, our arms ache, we
                                work together
shoving and kicking and scraping to empty our truckload over
                                the bank
even though we know
the irony of adding to the Bay fill, the System has us there—
but we love each other and return to the Park.

Thursday, May 15th
At 6 a.m. the ominous zooming, war-sound, of helicopters
breaks into our sleep.
To the Park:
ringed with police.
Bulldozers have moved in.
Barely awake, the people—
those who had made for each other
a green place—
begin to gather at the corners.

Their tears fall on sidewalk cement.
The fence goes up, twice a man's height.
Everyone knows (yet no one yet
believes it) what all shall know
this day, and the days that follow:

now, the clubs, the gas,
bayonets, bullets. The War
comes home to us . . .

. . . .

WHAT PEOPLE CAN DO

1. Be in the streets-they're ours!
2. Report any action you have witnessed or been involved in that should be broadcast to keep the people informed. Especially call to report the location of any large groups of people, so those people who have been separated may regroup . . .
3. The Free Church and Oxford Hall medical aid stations need medical supplies, especially:
   –gauze pads
   –adhesive tape
   –plastic squeeze bottles.
4. PLEASE do not go to the Free Church unless you have need to.
5. Photographers and filmmakers: Contact Park Media Committee.
6. Bail money will be collected at tables outside the COOP grocery stores:
   –Telegraph Ave. store: Monday
   –University Ave. store: Tuesday
   –Shattuck Ave. store: Wed. & Thurs.
7. BRING YOUR KITE AND FLY IT. Use nylon strings. Fly it when you are with a crowd. A helicopter cannot fly too near flying kites.
8. Be your brothers' and sisters' keeper.
9. Take care.

'change is now
change is now
things that seem to be solid are not'

The words came through, transistor
turned up loud. The music, the beat,
lost now, but
the words hang on.

Revolution: a crown of tree
        raises itself out of the heavy
        flood.
            A branch lifts
            under null skies' weight
        pushes against
        walls of air, flashing
        clefts in it.

The floodwaters
stir, mud
swirls to the surface.

        A hand, arm,
        lifts in the crawl—
        hands, arms, intricate
            upflashing—
                    a sea full of swimmers!
            their faces' quick steady
            lift for air—

Maybe what seems
evanescent is solid.

Islands
step out of the waves on rock feet.

Entr'acte

i   **At the Justice Department**
           November 15, 1969

Brown gas-fog, white
beneath the street lamps.
Cut off on three sides, all space filled
with our bodies,
    Bodies that stumble
in brown airlessness, whitened
in light, a mildew glare,
    that stumble

hand in hand, blinded, retching.
Wanting it, wanting
to be here, the body believing it's
dying in its nausea, my head
clear in its despair, a kind of joy,
knowing this is by no means death,
is trivial, an incident, a
fragile instant.   Wanting it, wanting
        with all my hunger this anguish,
        this knowing in the body
the grim odds we're
up against, wanting it real.
Up that bank where gas
curled in the ivy, dragging each other
up, strangers, brothers
and sisters.   Nothing
will do but
to taste the bitter
taste. No life
other, apart from.

ii   **Gandhi's Gun (and Brecht's Vow)**

Vessels of several
shapes and sizes—

bowls, pots,
a tall vase

and the guitar's
waiting body:

forms drawn
by a hand's
energy.

            'Never

        run away from the stormcenter.

            Cultivate

cool courage, die without killing—'

Strong orange, deep
oil-pastel green

but at the center, strange
upstroke of black

stronger, deeper
than all.
    —'but if one has not

   that courage'—

(or singing, *'Keiner
oder Alle, Alles
oder Nichts!')*
    —'cultivate

 the art of killing and being killed

 rather than in a cowardly manner

   to flee from danger.'

Vessels, counterparts
of the human; primal
vessel of music

towards which like a rifle
that harsh stroke blackly
points upward

would fail, fall from their whirling
dance, without

the terror patiently
poised there,

ultimate focus.

iii   The Year One

Arn says it's
the Year one.

And I
know such violent

revolution has ached
my marrowbones, my

soul changing
its cells, my

cracked heart tolling
such songs of

unknown morning-star
ecstatic anguish, the clamor

of unquenched desire's
radiant decibels shattering

the patient wineglasses
set out by private history's ignorant

quiet hands,   —I keep
enduring such pangs of giving

birth or being
born,
        I dream

maybe he's right.

iv   **Looking for the Devil Poems**
      'Tell Denise to write about the devil.'

i

Tell Sam
it is (perhaps) the devil
made me so goddamned strong

that I have made myself
(almost)
numb,
almost unable
to feel in me
(for now)
the beautiful outreaching of desire.

And tell him
it is perhaps the devil
inserted these parenthetical
qualifications.

ii

It's the devil
swarms into 'emptiness'
not
    waiting
            until it slowly
            as a jar let stand
            at fountain's edge, fills,
            drop by drop,
but busily, as if not water
but flies buzzing were what
'emptiness' were to hold.

iii

Looking for the devil I walked
down Webster St. and across on

Cottage St. and down
Sumner to Maverick Square
and saw
3 dogs nosing the green plastic
    garbage bags on the sidewalk,
5 children screaming cheerfully together, sliding
                                upon a strip of gray ice,
1 simpleton (Webster St.'s own) who waved and called
                                    'Hi!' to me,
4 elderly Italian peasant women (separately)
                            lugging home groceries
    in big shopping bags, their faces solemn
                            as at some ritual,
2 twelve-year-old girls in cheap maxicoats,
10 more or less silent teen-aged boys
                            in groups of 3 or 4 standing
    on several corners, collars up, seeming
                            to wait for something which
    was not about to happen,
2 middle-aged bookies, one wearing
    a seedy chesterfield—the same guys I saw
    one day at the Buffalo Meat Market ordering
    some big steaks, but today
    down on their luck—

and no doubt some other persons, but these
were all I noticed:
and in none of these
could I discern the devil
(under the sullen January sky) nor was the devil,
surely, the east wind
blowing garbage out of the bags after
the dogs succeeded in ripping them,
nor was the devil the ugly
dogshit innocently smeared on the pavement.
Was he then
my eyes that searched for him?
Or was he the inexorable
smog of tedium that we breathed,
I and all these, even
the children at play, even, quite possibly, the dogs?

Or was he
the toneless ignorance all that I saw
had of itself?

v   Today

Just feeling human
the way a cloud's a cloud
tinged with blue or
walking slow across the sky or
hastening,
but not a Thursday cloud
formed for the anxious glance of Thursday people,
simply a cloud, whose particles
may fall Tuesday, just as well,
on anyone's springy hair, on any
taciturn winter buds it chooses
and no one say no. Human,
free for the day from roles assigned,
each with its emblem
cluttering the right hand,
scroll of words in the left.
Human, a kind of element, a fire,
an air, today.
Floating up to you I enter, or you
enter me. Or imagine
a house without doors,
open to sun or snowdrifts.

vi   Casa Felice (I)

Getting back into
ordinary gentle morning, tide
          wavelessly dreaming in,
          silent gulls at ease on wheatsheaf sandbars—

Off the limb of
desperation
          I drop
          plumb into peace for a day—

it's
    not easy.
        But easier—
             O blessèd
             blue!
        —than fear and reason
        supposed of late.

vii   Casa Felice (II)

Richard, if you were here
would you too be peaceful?

(I am angry
all of the time, not just sometimes,
you said. *We must*
smash the state.
Smash the state.)

If you were here
for these two days at Casa
Felice, if you were here and listened
to the almost soundless tide
incoming,
            what would it say to you?
Would you feel new
coldness towards me
because this April morning, gentle light
on the unglittering sea and pale sands,
I am not angry and not tense?

viii   Revolutionary

When he said
'Your struggle is my struggle'
a curtain was pushed away.

A curtain was pushed away revealing
an open window
and beyond that

an open country.
For the first time I knew it was actual.
I was indoors still

but the air from fields
beyond me touched my face.

It was a country
of hilly fields, of many
shadows and rivers.

The thick heavy dark
curtain had hidden
a world from me;

curtain of sorrow, world
where far-off I see
people moving—

struggling to move, as I
towards my window
struggle, burdened but not

each alone. They move
out in that air together
where I too

will be moving,
not alone.

ix   'I Thirst'

Beyond the scaffolding set up for
TV cameras, a long way
from where I sit among 100,000 reddening
white faces,
          is a big wooden cross:

and strapped upon it, turning
his head from side to side in pain
in the 90-degree shadeless Washington midafternoon

May 9th, 1970,
　　　　　　　a young black man.

'We must *not* be angry, we must
L-O-O-O-V-E!' Judy Collins
bleats loud and long into the P.A. system,

but hardly anyone claps, and no one
shouts *Right On.*
　　　　　　　That silence cheers me.
Judy, understand:
there comes a time when only anger
is love.

Part III
　　　　(Europe after 10 years; England after
　　　　20 years; summer of 1970)

i

Silver summer light of Trieste early evening

　　　　　(a silver almost gold
　　　　　almost grey).

Caffè,
little cup
black and sweet.

　　　　　　　The waiter
　　　　　　　tall and benevolent
　　　　　　　gives some change to a wanderer
　　　　　　　(not a beggar,
　　　　　　　he has a pack,
　　　　　　　is maybe 30 and
　　　　　　　no taller than a boy of 11).
　　　　　　　Almost weeping with weariness.
　　　　　　　Stands to gaze at a green plant.

Droops.
Sinks to the pavement.
The waiter
gently sends him across the street
to a marble bench set in the church wall.

'Where is he from, that man?'
A shrug—'É Italiano . . . '

Maybe from Sicily. Later I pause
to watch him
curled like a tired child on the stone.

                              •

Caffè, another
sweet and black
little cup.

Cop-out, am I,
or merely,
        as the day fades

        (and Amerika
        far away
        tosses in fever)

on holiday?

ii

            And David said
            in England

            What's a cop-out? Is it
            the same as
            opting out?

            And I said
            Yes, but

opting out sounds like
cool choice

and copping-out
means fear and weakness
but he said
No,
we mean that too.

iii

Strange, a rusty freight train's passing
between the cafés and the sea
(a long train of cars
veiled in old Europe's dust—maybe
they've shuttled up and down the Adriatic
since before the War, and inland,
anywhere)

cutting between the sidewalk tables
                and the view
to no one's surprise but mine

and when they've gone by
the dim sea
has vanished,

vague silver
tarnished to blue;

points of amber
show where the suburbs
drift over down-grey hills.

iv

Summer dusk,
Triestino,
deep blue now.

The port, its commerce:
a few gold bars
broken upon the water.

A ship from Genoa
riding at anchor,
Port light, starboard.

The sky   the water
    warm   blue   blurred.

v

On the broad Riva
among young couples
taking the air with their babies

men still prowl as they used to,
laughably. Buona sera. Buona sera, Signorina.
                (That spring of '48, the weeks
                alone in Florence, waiting for Mitch.
                And I used to talk to the Israeli terrorist,
                if that's what he was, in the Pensione,
                but the Signora told me to watch out for him,
                a young bride should watch out.)
                                        Buona sera.
No sexual revolution here, no Women's Lib.
That's the third car to slow down.
        (The difference is, more cars,
            new ones too, I see.)
Buona sera, signorina. Each driver
leans out, affable.
                Evidently
I must give up my
slow stroll.
                (And in me the difference
                is, I'm not scared,
                I find them only foolish, they're
                in my way.
                        But do they spend every evening
                        cruising?   No whores around,
                        too early maybe. Whom do they hope for?)

378

I turn briskly along a one-way street.
In the hotel lobby, *terza classe*,
a young man, thickly handsome,
looks at me over the *Corriere della Sera*
and jumps up to follow me
but I get upstairs to my door and in and
shut it, just as his mechanical shadow
precedes him into the corridor.

'*Honestly*! I *ask* you!'
some English voice laughs in my head.

                                        Buona notte.

vi

Back in Boston a month ago I wrote:

'At my unhappiest,
like the next guy, I want

oblivion

          but even when
a couple of sleeping pills or
total immersion in an almost-boring fiction

          at last succeed in
shutting my eyes and
whatever torment ails me shuts off
and I get what I wanted

oblivion,

          I don't want it for long.
                    I don't know
how to be mute, or deaf, or blind,
for long, but
wake and plunge into next day
talking, even if I say *yesterday* when I mean *tomorrow*,
listening, even if what I'm hearing
has the *approaching* sound of terror,

seeing, even if the morning light
and all it reveals appear
pathetic in ignorance,
             like unconscious heroes trapped on film,
raised shadows about to descend and smash their skulls.

And when I'm not
unhappy but am
alone, then specially some hunger for revelation
keeps me up half the night
wandering from book to music to painting to book, reluctant
to give any time at all to oblivion—

only the hope of memorable dreams
at last luring me
exhausted to bed.'

Now I can barely remember what it is
to want oblivion. 'The dreamy lamps
of stonyhearted Oxford Street'—
             de Quincy wandered
   in hopeless search beneath them,
             Olga rushed back and forth
   for years beneath them, working
   in her way for Revolution
and I too in my youth
knew them and was lonely, an ignorant girl.
             But I forget anguish
             as I forget joy

returning after 20 years
to 'merry London' as to a nest.

             (Say what one will,
             know what one must
             of Powell, of the farm hand's
             £ 13 a week—and they vote
             Tory—yet

             there is a gentleness
             lost in anxious Amerika—

it's in the way
three young workmen in the Tube
smiled to each other
admiring their day-off purchases,
new shirts—

it's in the play-talk
of children, without irony:
not *cool*, not
                    joshing each other,

and in the way
men and women of any age maintain
some expectation of love,

(not pickups, but love) and so
remain beautiful:
there
            'in merry London, my most kindly nurse,
that to me gave this life's first native source'

my friends whose lives
have been knit with mine a quarter century
are not impaled on the spears of the cult of youth).
Aie, violent Amerika, aie, dynamic
deathly-sick America, of whose energy,
in whose fever, in whose wild
cacophonous music I have lived
and will live,

            what gentleness, what kindness
of the *private life* I left, unknowing,

and gained instead the tragic, fearful
knowledge of *present history*,
of doom . . . 'Imagination of disaster. . .life
ferocious and sinister'. . .

                    •

                    But shall I forget
            euphoria on the bus from
        Trafalgar Square to Kings Cross?

                                        What a laugh,
            there's nothing so great about Kings Cross,

            but life is in me, a love for
            what happens, for
            the surfaces that are their own
            interior life, yes, the
            Zen buildings! the
            passing of the
            never-to-be-seen-again
            faces! I bless
            every stone I see, the
            'happy genius' not of my household perhaps

            but of my solitude . . .

vii

Two hours after reaching Rijeka
(that once was Fiume)
I'm drinking *vinjak* with five Sudanese.

(Four days ago I was in Dorset. We drank
cider and walked in the rain.)

Jugoslavia still unknown, mysterious,
slow train-ride, rocky fields in heat haze
                        and now
a roomful of subtle
black faces!
They refill my glass and give me
The Baghdad Observer: 'Al-Ali Reviews
Revolutionary Achievements.' I give them
the news about Bobby Seale.

I ask one for a towel,
he gives me his own.

I help clear the ash trays,
they say, No, that's *our* work.

They sing, and drum on whatever comes to hand,
(one makes a bell of knife and glass)
and two of them dance.
                    Outside,

oleanders astir in folds of
dense night.
To Abubakar I gave
my Panther button, the yellow one
with the great Black Cat emerging
in power from behind bars.

they read, and repeated it
to each other in Arabic.

And he gave me
a photo of turbanned dancers
and one of a bridge crossing the Blue Nile.

Abubakar, gat-toothed
like me.   'They say it's lucky,'
I told him, 'and means you will journey
very far.'

            In that room I knew the truth of what José Yglesias
writes, in his book on revolutionary Cuba that I'm reading here on
this Adriatic island 3 days later: he had been to a film, a good one but
these Cuban country people took it with 'none of the tension, the con-
centration there would have been in New York. . . . Their presence
made me see that for all its artistry . . . it was a false picture of life:
[they] knew that the easy-going goodness of people was missing from
it, that it allowed no avenue for joy, such as they knew exists as soon

as any bar to its enjoyment is let down. Nor does it take a revolution
to know this, just a bit of living.'

And I remembered the time, just a few months ago, a bitter
March night in Boston, I went to see *Rock Around the Clock* with
Richard and Boat and someone else from their collective, that was the
same, gave me the same joy as this roomful of friends, there was the
same sense of generosity and good humor, but more frantic, a sense
of stolen time, of pleasure only taken in recognition of desperate need
sometimes to let up, a respite from the chills of fevered Amerika—

and here a leisure,
a courtesy unhurried

as if the bare student pad
were full of flowers, jasmine,
roses . . .
Selah.
Abubakar—I gave him
my promise to find out in what country
he might enter medical school:
'If I have to, I'll go
to a capitalist country.'
And he (20, slender, beardless,
gentle, and warm to touch as a nectarine
ripe in the sun)

asked for and gave
a kind of love.

viii

After the American lava
has cooled and set in new forms,
will you Americans have
more peace and less hope?
wonders Sasha, socialist,
('but not a Party member')
(We have not been asked, adds his wife

primly, the smallest smile
whisking across her elegant, honest face).

Is that what *you* have—
peace without hope?
                    I counter;

(and it seems perhaps
that *is* what they have
—at least,
none of the fervor here
that blazes in Cuban cane fields).

I swim out
over sharp rocks, sea urchins,
thinking, When I go back,

when I go back into the writhing lava,
will I rejoice in
fierce hope, in
wanhope, in
'righteous' pleasurable hope?

        Could struggle be enough, even
        without hope?

                For that I'm not
                enough a puritan. Or not yet.
                (Richard might say: history intervenes
                to weld endurance, revolution
        builds character—
                        but he is young,
        a young dreamer, willful, stern).
                                And peace—
I think I have
        not *hope* for it,
only a longing . . .

ix

        But on a hill in Dorset
            while the bells of Netherbury
            pealed beyond the grove of

                    great beeches,
                              and Herefords,
            white starred on tawny ample brows,
            grazed, slow, below us,
                              only days ago,
        Bet said:
        There was a dream I dreamed always
        over and over,

            a tunnel
            and I in it, distraught

            and great dogs blocking
            each end of it

            and I thought I must
            always go on
            dreaming that dream,
            trapped there,

            but Mrs. Simon listened
            and said

            why don't you sit down
            in the middle of the tunnel
            quietly:

            imagine yourself
            quiet and intent sitting there,
            not running from blocked
            exit to blocked exit.

    Make a place for yourself
    in the darkness
    and wait there. *Be* there.

    The dogs
    will not go away.
    They must be transformed.

    Dream it that way.
    Imagine.

Your being, a fiery stillness,
is needed to TRANSFORM
the dogs.

And Bet said to me:
Get down into your well,

it's your well

go deep into it

into your own depth as into a poem.

Entr'acte

'Let Us Sing Unto the Lord a New Song'

There's a pulse in Richard
that day and night says
revolution   revolution   revolution

and another
not always heard:

poetry   poetry

rippling through his sleep,
a river pulse.

Heart's fire
breaks the chest almost,
flame-pulse,
revolution:

and if its beat
falter
life itself
shall cease.

Heart's river,
living water,
poetry:

and if that pulse
grow faint
fever shall parch the soul, breath
choke upon ashes.

But when their rhythms
mesh
then though the pain of living
never lets up

the singing begins.

Part IV

i   **Report**

I went back.
Daily life
is not lava.
            It is
a substance that expands and contracts, a rhythm
different from the rhythm of history,
though history is made of the same
minutes and hours.
                    Tony writes from Ohio:
            'An atomistic bleakness drags on students this fall
            after the fiery fusion of last spring.'

Airplane life: the fall for me
spent like a wildgoose that has lost
the migrating flock and lost
the sense of where the south is—
zigzagging—'gliding among clouds.'

England, back there in summer, and especially
the two Davids, turned out to be home: but my literal
home, these rooms, this desk, these small
objects of dailiness each with its history,
books, photos, and in the kitchen
the old breadknife from Ilford that says
Bread Knife on its blade—the least details—
are what pull me. No, it's not true that I'm
a defective migrant, I know as I fly
where I long to be. But the wind blows me
off course.

            (Bromige writes: 'I recall the muffin man too, and
the naphtha lamps, I think they were, in the open-air market, High
Rd. Kilburn, after early December dark. Now I sit up here on a Cal-
ifornia hillside. This difficulty of what resonance has the language, for
you, for me,—I need to take up but the push and shove of events (
that's a telling phrase of Merleau-Ponty's!) has me, and meanwhile I
go on writing poems sometimes like shouting down a deep well.')

    Those are the same lamps
    of my dream of Olga—the eel or cockle stand,
    she in the flare caught, a moment, her face
    painted, clownishly, whorishly. Suffering.

'It's your own well.
Go down
into its depth.'

ii   **Happiness**

Two nights dancing (Workingman's Dead)
with someone of such grace and goodness, happiness
made real in his true smile,
                that it has seemed
I know now forever:
             The reason for happiness is,
             happiness exists,
Good Day Sunshine. The moon's vast aureole
of topaz was complete;
             utterly still;
                  a covenant,
its terms unknown. / Waving arms! Swaying!
                  The whirling of the dance!

Soon after
more (but not deeper) depth of joy
was given me at the show of Zen paintings.
                              Camus wrote:
        'I discovered inside myself, even in the very midst of
            winter, an invincible summer.'
Again—
                as in the act of clearing garbage off the land
together with those I loved,
and later dodging with them
                                        the swinging clubs of the cops,
living
in that momentary community—
again happiness
astonished me, so easy, 'amazing grace.'
Easy as the undreamed
dreamlike reality
of Abubakar and his friends.

But before this
came the death of Judy. Yes,
Judy had killed herself a full two weeks
before my hours of dancing began,
I found out the night I read to raise money
for the Juche Revolutionary Bookstore,

iii   **Two from the Fall Death-News**

and still I've not begun the poem,
the one she asked for ('If you would write me a poem
I could live for ever'—postmarked
the night she died, October twenty-ninth.)
I've begun though
to gather up fragments of it,
fragments of her: the heavy tarnished
pendant I don't wear,
the trapped dandelion seed in its transparent cube,
three notched green stones for divination, kept in green velvet,
a set of the *Daily Californian* for all the days
of the struggle for the People's Park,
a thick folder of her letters,

and now (come with the Christmas mail, packed
in a pink cosmetic box grotesquely labelled,
          'The Hope Chest'),
four cassettes recording (or so they are marked,
I've not played them) her voice speaking to me . . .

Revolution or death. She chose
as her life had long foretold. I can't lose her,
for I don't love her. In all her carefully kept
but unreread letters, all I remember sharply is the green
cold of the water in the deep pool she evoked,
the rock pool said to be bottomless,
where as a young girl she swam naked, diving
over and over, seeking
to plumb its roaring silence.

                    .   .   .   .

                    But Grandin, he could have lived!
His death, a year ago, hits me now,
reading his poems, stitched into order before he too
stopped himself.
                    Rage and awe
shake me.
And the longing to have spoken
long hours with him, to have gone
long walks with him beside rivers—
all I don't feel
for Judy, who in some fashion loved me,
lived through (for an hour, for recurring instants)
towards Grandin, to whom when he was alive
I was peripheral, as he to me . . .
  'By the post house • windblown reed-fronds.
  In some city tavern you dance the *Wild Mulberry Branch*.'
Rollicking, eyes flashing.   I resent your death
as if it were accidental.
          'Now snowstorms will fill the lands west of the Huai.
      I remember last year • broken candlelight upon
                    travelling-clothes.'
Last I heard of you, you were 'feeling better,'
up in some ghost town out West . . .
                    I feel life in your words,
tortured, savage.

Further away than 17th-century China,
nearer than my hand, you smashed
the world in the image of yourself, smashed
the horror of a world lonely Judy,
        silently plunging forever
into her own eyes' icy green, never even saw;
you raged bursting with life into death.

iv   **Daily Life**

Dry mouth,
            dry nostrils.
Dry sobs, beginning
abruptly, continuing
briefly,
        ending.
            The heart
dragging back sand through steelblue veins,
scraping it back out into the arteries: and they take it.
Living in the gray desert and
getting used to it.   Years ago, Juan wrote:
'We can never forget ourselves, and our problems involve
others and deform them.'
            And Hopkins:
        'Sorrow's springs áre the same.'
Then rainbow day comes in flashing
off the snow-roofs. By afternoon, slogging
through falling snow,
yellow snowlight, traffic slowed to
carthorse pace,
            exhilaration, East Boston
doubling for London.
            I'm frivolous.
            I'm alone.
                I'm Miriam
(in *Pilgrimage*) fierce with joy
                in a furnished room near Euston.
I'm the Tailor of Gloucester's cat.
                I live in one day
a manic-depressive's year.
            I like
            my boots, I like

the warmth of my new long coat. Last winter
running through Cambridge with Boat and Richard, afraid of
                                                    the ice they
slid on fearlessly—I must have been cold all winter
without knowing it, in my short light coat.
Buffalo Meat Market offers me a drink, (Strega),
                                        I lug home
the ham for Christmas Eve, life
whirls its diamond sparklers before me.
Yes, I want
                revolution, not death: but I don't
care about survival, I refuse
to be provident, to learn automechanics,
                        karate,
                        soybean cookery,
                        or how to shoot.

            O gray desert,
            I inhabit your mirages,
            palace after palace . . .
                    pineforest . . .
                    palmgrove . . .

v   **Report**

Judy ignored the world outside herself,
Grandin was flooded by it.
There is no suicide in our time
unrelated to history, to whether
each before death had listened to the living, heard
the cry, 'Dare to struggle,
            dare to win.'
heard and not listened, listened and turned away.

And I? 'Will struggle without hope
        be enough?' I was asking
on a sunny island in summer.
                            Now in midwinter
not doing much to struggle, or striving mainly
to get down into my well in hope
that force may gather in me
                from being still in the grim
                middle of the tunnel . . .

(And meanwhile Richard and Neil in their collectives
get down to it: get into work: food co-ops, rent strikes;
and 'Jacob and Lily' create
an active freedom in 'open hiding';
and Mitch has finished his book, 'a tool
for the long revolution.')
                              (And meanwhile Robert
                    sees me as Kali! No,
          I am not Kali, I can't sustain for a day
that anger.
          'There comes
                    a time
                              when only anger
                                        is love'—
I wrote it, but know such love
only in flashes.
                    And the love that streams
towards me daily, letters and poems, husband and child,
sings . . .)
                    Mayakovsky wrote,
                    in the 3-stepped lines that Williams
                    must have seen and learned from,
'Life
     must be
                started quite anew,
when you've changed it,
                    then
                              the singing can start up'—
but he too
took his own life. Perhaps he was waiting,
not with that waiting that is itself a
                                        transforming energy—
               'Stone
               breaks stone to reveal
               STONE in stone!'—but waiting
to *set all things right*, (to 'rearrange all mysteries
                              in a new light')
before beginning to live? Not understanding
only conjunctions
               of song's
                    raging magic

394

                              with patient courage
                          will make   a new life:
we can't wait: time is
                    not on our side:
                                  world
in which those I respect
                                'already live, they're not waiting
for demolition and reconstruction.' No more
'learning as preparation for life.'
                              In my own days and nights
(crawling, it feels like, on hands and knees—leaping
up into the dance!—to fall again, sprawled, stupid—)
I'm trying to learn
the other kind of waiting: charge, or recharge, my batteries.
Get my head together. Mesh. Knit
idiom with idiom in the
'push and shove of events.'
                    What I hold fast to
                    is what I wrote last May, not Kali speaking:
              'When the pulse rhythms
              of revolution and poetry
              mesh,

              then the singing begins.'
                          But that *when* must be
                          now!
Timid, impatient, halfblinded by
the dazzling abyss, nauseous under
the roar of the avalanche,
'imagination of disaster' a poison
that lurches through me the way
a sickened killer might lurch
through streets of charred straw—
                                    —what I hold fast to, grip

in my fist for amulet, is my love
of those who dare, who do dare
to struggle, dare to reject
unlived life, disdain
to die of *that*.

'Let us become men' says Dan Berrigan.
'Maybe you see it all, whiteman, or maybe you blind,'
        says Etheridge Knight to Dan.
'We gotta work
at our own pace, slow if need be,
work together and learn from within,'
        Richard said to me just today, the day
news of invasion of Laos started to be 'official.'
O holy innocents! I have
no virtue but to praise
you who believe
life is possible . . .

FOOTPRINTS

to J. Laughlin

The Footprints

Someone crossed this field last night:
day reveals
a perspective of lavender caves
across the snow.   Someone
entered the dark woods.

Hut

Mud and wattles.   Round almost.
Moss. Threshold: a writing,
small stones inlaid, footworn.
'Enter, who
so desires.'

Floor, beaten earth.   Walls
shadows.   Ashpit at center.
By day, coming in from
molten green, dusk
profound.   By night, through smokehole,
the star.

A Defeat in the Green Mountains
(Memory of Summer, 1955)

On a dull day she goes
to find the river,
accompanied by two
unwilling children, shut in
among thorns, vines, the
long grass

stumbling, complaining, the
blackflies biting them,
but persists, drawn
by river-sound close beyond
the baffling scratchy thicket

and after a half-hour they emerge
upon the water
                    flowing by
both dark and clear.
          A space and
          a movement crossing
          their halted movement.
But the river is deep

the mud her foot stirs up
frightens her; the kids are
scared and angry. No way
to reach the open fields over there.
Back then:
swamp underfoot, through the

perverse thickets, finding
a path finally to the
main road—defeated,
to ponder the narrow
depth of the river,
its absorbed movement past her.

The Rebuff

Yes, I'm nettled.
I touched a leaf
because I like to touch leaves
(even though this one
as it happens, had nothing
of special grace, no shine)

and though it had no spikes,
or thorns attached to it,
nothing like that
to warn the hand,
here I am tingling, it
hurts. I must look

for the coarse, patient
dockleaves nearby,

faithfully awaiting
nettled hands
to soothe with their juice,
wasted otherwise.

Living with a Painting
for Albert Kresch

It ripens
while I sleep, afternoons, on the old sofa,

the forms ready themselves for dazed, refreshed,
wakening senses to bite on,
'taste with the mind's tongue.'

Yes, that confusion
comes of sleep, and all was ripe
before, and I green.
                    Yet it's true
'One who makes it, and one who needs it.'

The work ripens
within the temper of living round about it,
that brings as tribute, as rain,
many awakenings

until a once-cold
arbitrary violet reveals itself
as radiance, a defining halo

and discovered
geometries in interplay

show in their harvest-time
vase, lute, beaker.

1962

An Old Friend's Self-Portrait

i

Somber, the mouth pinched and twisted,
eyes half-fierce, half-sad,
the portrait of my old friend stares at me
or at the world; that face
I remember as it laughed
twenty years ago, not untroubled but
more certain, face of an artist who
now with a master's hand paints
the image of his own
in-sight.

ii

Strong, the brow
revealed in volume, the ears
listening,
the eyes
watching time purse the
gentle smiling lips I remember,
this face
writes itself on triple-S board,
signs itself in thick
ridges of paint,
breaks through the mirror.

1970

Novella

In love (unless loved) is not *love*.
You're right: x needs—

with azure sparks down dazedly
drifting through vast night
long after—

the embrace of y to even
begin to become z.
                        To x alone
something else happens. Example:

a woman painter returns,
younger than she should be, from travels
in monotone countries

and on arrival, bandages of fatigue
whipped off her eyes,
                        instantly
looks, looks at whose shadow
first falls on her primed (primal) canvas
(all the soul she has left
for the moment)—:

At once the light
(not the gray north of journeys)
colors him! Candle-gold,

yet not still, but shivering,
lit white flesh for her (who preferred brown)
and hair light oak or walnut
was mahogany on the dream-palette.

Setting to work, the painter
paints what she sees: the object
moves, her eyes change focus
faithfully, the nimbus
dances.

        All one year she paints:
the works are known later by titles—
'Fiery Clouds,' 'Alembic,' '*Du Bleu Noir*,' 'The Burning-Glass.'
Rectangles, ovals, all the landscapes are portraits,
x kneels at the feet of y, barbaric frankincense
enclouds her. But y, embarrassed,
and finally indifferent, turns
away. Talking (he is a poet)

talking, walking away, entering
a small boat, the middle distance,

sliding downstream away.
She has before her

a long scroll to paint on, but no room
to follow that river.   The light's going.

'*L'homme est un drôle de corps,*
qui n'a pas son centre de gravité en lui-même,'
she reads, pages falling from trees
at need around her.   She continues

to paint what she saw:

y is a brushstroke now
in furthest perspective, it hurts

the eyes in dusk to see it, no one,
indeed, will know that speck of fire

but x herself, who has not
(in this example) even begun to become

z, but remains
x, a painter; though not perhaps
unchanged. Older. We'll take

some other symbol to represent
that difference—a or o.

June, 1969

Intrusion

After I had cut off my hands
and grown new ones

something my former hands had longed for
came and asked to be rocked.

After my plucked out eyes
had withered, and new ones grown

something my former eyes had wept for
came asking to be pitied.

August, 1969

Overheard over S.E. Asia

'White phosphorus, white phosphorus,
mechanical snow,
where are you falling?'

'I am falling impartially on roads and roofs,
on bamboo thickets, on people.
My name recalls rich seas on rainy nights,
each drop that hits the surface eliciting
luminous response from a million algae.
My name is a whisper of sequins. Ha!
Each of them is a disk of fire,
I am the snow that burns.
                              I fall
wherever men send me to fall—
but I prefer flesh, so smooth, so dense:
I decorate it in black, and seek
the bone.'

Scenario

The theater of war. Offstage
a cast of thousands weeping.

Left center, well-lit, a mound
of unburied bodies,

or parts of bodies. Right,
near some dead bamboo that serves as wings,

a whole body, on which
a splash of napalm is working.

Enter the Bride.

She has one breast, one eye,
half of her scalp is bald.

She hobbles towards center front.
Enter the Bridegroom,

a young soldier, thin, but without
visible wounds. He sees her.

Slowly at first, then faster and faster,
he begins to shudder, to shudder,

to ripple with shudders.   Curtain.

Time to Breathe

(Adapted from a prose poem by Jean-Pierre Burgart)

Evenings enduring, blending
one with the next. Ocean calmly
rocking reflected docks and those
indecipherable roads that
inscribe themselves in sky
way above trajectories of the swifts.

That freshness, over
and over: summer
in folds of your dress, mysterious fabric.
And in the disturbing
gentle grace of your neck.
The same summer shadow
looking out of your eyes.

Night seems to stop short
at the horizon. Perhaps it never
will quite arrive. Perhaps,
renewed in the breath of these
first summer days,
we shall leave off dying.

Hope It's True

Wonder if this very day the Hunza
are leading their charmed lives.
Their limbs anointed with oil of apricot,
are they singing, walking the
high paths? Himalayan
blues you couldn't
cry to, it's
like almond milk, sesame, such goodness,
the blues of joy?

While Nevada whores wake anxious
at airconditioned noon,
figuring a blast some time
may shatter the casinos . . .
While Mississippi babies grunt and die,
tired of hunger
and 'small clashes' rip human guts per
daily usual, closer to Hunza-land than here . . .
While an absurd flag
clatters in dust of lunar winds . . .

is the royal apricot-taster
even now stepping sideways from tree to tree
to check on bitterness?—that no Hunza,
the length of the land, shall eat sorrow?

July, 1969

M.C. 5

for John Sinclair

Not to blow the mind but
focus it again, renew its
ferocious innocence, hot-pepper sting of
wonder, impatient love.

Enough energy
to save the world; could be.

'Come Together' winds down,
grimly slow-spiralling,
                              only to recoil
with a snap! We're off!
Some zephyr rising
from choppy seas
        charges itself, lifts to a steady
        sweep, it picks me up, it
picks us up, lift up your heads
O ye gates.

(World's heart
keeps skipping a beat,
sweat crawls on the moon's white
stony face.
                Life's
winding down.) Tighten the spring.
Something is breathing deep. Ozone, oxygen.
Even yet. Kick out the jams.

July 30, 1969

Love Poem
for Mitch

Swimming through dark, slow,
breaststroke—
                not to startle
                walls or chairs and
                wake you—
I almost sundered the
full to the brim with moonlight
mirror

September, 1969

A Place to Live

Honeydew seeds: on impulse
strewn in a pot of earth. Now,

(the green vines) wandering
down over the pot's edges:

certainly no room here to lay
the egg of a big, pale,
green-fleshed melon.
                                    Wondering

where the hell to go.

The News

East Boston too, like the fields
somewhere, from which the snow's
        melting to show forth black
        earth and timid
        tips of grass, is preparing
for spring. In the windows
of candy stores are displayed
jump-ropes: white cord and glossy
red-and-green handles.

Obstinate Faith

Branch-lingering oakleaves, dry
brown over gray snowglare,
make of a gust of wind
an instrument, to play
'spring rain.'

Fragment

Not free to love where their liking chooses,
lacking desire for what love proposes,
they wander indoors and out, calling
'Eros, Eros' to the winged one,
who will not listen, for he will bear no bondage . . .

Only Connect

Gary with deer and bear
in the Sierras, in poems.
Acting his dreams out:
kind man,
practical.
Knows
how to kill and skin deer
and how to eat them
and love their life,
love them to life.
Daily his year-old son
runs out to greet them, they browse
deep in his green,
he knows them.

And another Gary
(McDonald) in
New Britain, dreams me
         a letter to live from—
that day's bread:
'I am just
thinking, writing, breathing here,
phantom of air . . . the
face of the world is
a million eyes.'
Wakes me to know
'there is a way
to the journey. A love grows into itself.'

And a third

(Aspenberg) planning
a Chronicle of the
End of the World, meanwhile
reads my chart: 'Many
loves at first sight.
Visions are presented.
You must choose
the worthy ones to follow.
Your death
may come in a
public place . . . '

'Horoscopes,' he says, 'would make
perfect poems if I could get into them.
Everything relates to all.'

Under a Blue Star

Under a blue star, dragon   of skygate . . .
Such wakenings into twilight, foreboding intermingled
with joy, beyond
hope of knowledge. The days
a web of wires, of energies vibrating
in chords and single
long notes of song; but nights
afloat on dream, dreams
that float silent, or leave word
of blue sky-dragons, to seduce
the day's questions, drown them
in twilight before dawn . . . What gate
opens, dim there in the mind's
field, river-mists of the sky
veiling its guardian?

Exchange

Seagulls inland.
Come for a change of diet,

a breath of
earth-air.

I smell the
green, dank, amber, soft
undersides of an old pier in their cries.

3 a.m., September 1, 1969
for Kenneth Rexroth

Warm wind, the leaves
rustling without dryness,
hills dissolved into silver.

It could be any age,
four hundred years ago or a time
of post-revolutionary peace,
the rivers clean again, birth rate and crops
somehow in balance . . .

In heavy dew
under the moon the blond grasses
lean in swathes on the field slope. Fervently
the crickets practice their religion of ecstasy.

A New Year's Garland for My Students / MIT: 1969–70

i   Arthur

In winter, intricately wrapped, the buds
of trees and bushes
are firm and small and go unnoticed,
though their complexity is as beautiful
now as eventual
                silky leaves in spring.

ii   Barry

What task is it
hidden just beyond vision yet,
your frown tries
to touch, as if
there, almost within
reach of
your eyes' blue light, as if
frowning were weight that
would pin phantoms to the
ground of
knowledge—
         What Gorgon is it
that shall be given you
(revealed)
        to strike?

iii   Bill

There is a fence around the garden
but the gate stands open.

And the garden within
is pleasant—
neither drearily formal
nor sad with neglect:

oldfashioned, with shade-trees and places
to take the sun, with paths
planted with fragrant resilient herbs.

But looking
out of the thickest, darkest branches—
back of the stone pool,
behind the arbor—

eyes of some animal:

blue-green gray, are they?
Topaz?

They question
and propose

no answers yet; disquieting
in the still garden,
and disquieted.

iv   Don

If the body is a house,
the house a temple,

in that temple
is a labyrinth,

in that labyrinth's core
a vast room,

in the room's remote depths
an altar,

upon the altar
a battle raging, raging,

between two angels, one feathered
with spines, with sharp flames,

one luminous, the subtle
angel of understanding,

and from time to time a smile flickers
on the face of the mean angel

and slips, shadowy, over
to the gentle face.

v   Ernie

Hey Ernie, here you come suavely
round the corner in your
broken-windowed bus

and brake elegantly and swing
open the door so I can get in and ride on, sitting
on crumpled poems among guitars and
percussion sets.
What can I say, Ernie?—
Younger than my son, you are
nevertheless my old friend

whom I trust.

vi   **Judy**

You have the light step
of Ariel, the smile of Puck,
something of Rosalind's
courage, I think, though you are small
as I imagine Perdita to have been

(and why Shakespeare gets into all this at all
I don't know—but he does, insistently)

but when you set off alone, winter nights,
coat collar up, and in your pocket
that invisible flute,

it's myself I think of, 12 years old,
trudging home from the library lugging
too many books, and seeing

visions in Ilford High Road,

the passing faces oblivious
to all their own strange beauty under the street-lamps,

and I drunk on it.

vii   **Lucy**

Lucy taking
the family cat
along on her pilgrimage.

Lucy's nineteenth-century face
gazing steadfastly into the twenty first century.

Jewish Lucy
rooted in Emily's
New England fields.

Aquarian Lucy searching
for rhymes that dance,

for gestures that speak of
the rhyming seasons,

for the community
of poems and people.

viii   Margo

The one who can't say it
says it.

The one who can't figure how
pictures what.

The song no one can sing
sounds, quiet
air in air.

ix   Mark

Ripple of clear water
in the sun—inscape of moving, curling wavelets,
and the murmuring of them: an ideogram
for 'happiness'—

a buddha spring upwelling
in deep woods
where light must climb
down ladders of somber
needled branches.

x   Richard

i

The old poet, white-bearded
showing an antique motorcycle
to the children of the revolution.

The old poet overhearing
lovers telling one another poems,
and the poems are his.
His laugh rings out in sudden joy
as it did when he was twenty-one.
I hunger for a world
you can
live in forever.

ii

'The very essence
of destiny hung over this house'
(this time) *'and how was he,*
a membrane stretched between the
light and darkness of the world,
not to become conscious of it?'

I want
a world you can live in.

'The blood ran to his head
and his heart beat like a trip-hammer
when he thought of
encountering the man,
of finding himself in his presence.

It was not cowardice; it was only that he had become
shudderingly aware of the tremendous task he had undertaken
and when he had realized it completely,
to the very tips of his fingers and the depths of his soul,
he smiled,
feeling rather like a man standing on the roof of a burning house,
and marking

the spot on which he must without fail alight . . .
He must indeed be
a good jumper,
and something of a magician besides.'

I want
a world.

xi   Roger

'Mad prince'—OK—that's it—
a madness
of such simplicity
                   under the crown of
                   too much knowledge
                             (heavy on your head its
                             velvet and stupidly
                             glaring stones, as
                             on all our heads
                             that burden, all of us
                             weighed down with its despair)
that it lifts
out and through it

like your Jewish natural would escape
a rabbi's hat, and send it sailing
crazy into the sky
of pale funny blue like your eyes.

xii   Ted

The people in you:
some are silent.

Two I see clear:

a girl at the edge of the sea
who dances in solitude
for joy at the sea's dance;
and she is one who speaks.

And an old man nearby
in a dark hut, who sits looking
into a pit of terror: hears
horror creeping upon the sea.
And he is silent.

Her voice lifts, silvery,
a flying shower in the sunlight

but the sky darkens, sea-music
twists into hideous tumult.
Other shadowy figures

move on the shore of my dream of you:
their lips form words but no sound
comes forth. None can speak

until the old man raises
his grim head and shouts
his curse or warning.

xiii   Vic

The dog, Stalin, is free and foolish
as a holy hasid.
Wonder, arf, wonder wags his tail,
in him your soul
takes its rest and,
         twitching, sighing,
         lifting sensitive ears at odd noises,
grows.

To Kevin O'Leary, Wherever He Is

Dear elusive Prince of Ireland,
I have received
from Arizona
your letter, with no return address
                    but telling me

my name in Hebrew, and its meaning:
     entrance, exit,
     way through of
     giving and receiving,
     which are one.
Hallelujah! It's as if you'd sent me
in the U.S. mails
a well of water,
     a frog at its brim, and mosses;
sent me a cold and sweet freshness
dark to taste.
                    Love from the door,
                         Daleth.

The Day the Audience Walked Out on Me, and Why
(May 8th, 1970, Goucher College, Maryland)

Like this it happened:
after the antiphonal reading from the psalms
and the dance of lamentation before the altar,
and the two poems, 'Life at War' and
                              'What Were They Like?'
I began my rap,
and said:

Yes, it is well that we have gathered
in this chapel to remember
the students shot at Kent State,

but let us be sure we know
our gathering is a mockery unless
we remember also
the black students shot at Orangeburg two years ago,
and Fred Hampton murdered in his bed
by the police only months ago.

And while I spoke the people
—girls, older women, a few men—
began to rise and turn
their backs to the altar and leave.

And I went on and said,
Yes, it is well that we remember
all of these, but let us be sure
we know it is hypocrisy
to think of them unless
we make our actions their memorial,
actions of militant resistance.

By then the pews were almost empty
and I returned to my seat and a man stood up
in the back of the quiet chapel
(near the wide-open doors through which
the green of May showed, and the long shadows of late afternoon)
and said my words
desecrated a holy place.

And a few days later
when some more students (black) were shot
at Jackson, Mississippi,
no one desecrated the white folks' chapel,
because no memorial service was held.

Animal Rights

Pig and wasp are robbed of their names.
OK! Let brutal
Amerikan polizei
and tightassed DAR's be known forever
as pigs and wasps, but let's think up
new names for those we ripped off:

the roguish Black Berkshires, the intelligent
rangy ginger roamers of Mexican beaches,
Iowan acorn-eaters, fast on their small feet,
even the oppressed pink fatbacks in smelly
concentration-pens,
                    deserve a good name.

And the bees' ornery cousins—
oh, in the time of ripened pears,

of plum and fig burst open for very languor
of sweetness and juicy weight—
then you shall see the spiteful, buzzing, honeyless ones
graceful with ecstasy, clumsy with passion,
humble in pleasure no pale wasp
knows. What
shall their new name be?

Leather Jacket

She turns, eager—
hand going out to touch
his arm. But touches
a cold thick sleeve.

1970

The Needles

He told me about
a poem he was writing.
For me.

He told me it asked,
'When I mean only to brush her gently
with soft feathers,

do the feathers
turn into needles?'
His telling me

was a cloud of
soft feathers, I closed
my eyes and sank in it.

Many weeks
I waited. At last,
'Did you, were you able

to finish that poem
you told me about,
once?'

'No,' he said,
looking away.
Needles paused

for an instant on my skin
before they drew blood.

1970

The Poem Unwritten

For weeks the poem of your body,
of my hands upon your body
    stroking, sweeping, in the rite of
    worship, going
    their way of wonder down
    from neck-pulse to breast-hair to level
    belly to cock—
for weeks that poem, that prayer,
unwritten.
        The poem unwritten, the act
left in the mind, undone. The years
a forest of giant stones, of fossil stumps,
blocking the altar.

1970

The Good Dream

Rejoicing
because we had met again
we rolled laughing
over and over upon the big bed.

The joy was
not in a narrow sense
erotic—not
narrow in any sense.
It was

that all impediments,
every barrier, of history,
of learn'd anxiety,
wrong place and wrong time,

had gone down,
vanished.
It was the joy

of two rivers
meeting in depths of the sea.

1970

Goethe's Blues

      (Fantasia on the Trilogie der Leidenschaft*)*

i

The hills stirring under their woven
leaf-nets, sighing, shimmering. . .
High summer.
          And he with
April anguish tearing him,
heart a young animal, its fur
curly and legs too long.

But he is old. Sere.

        'O love, O love,
        not unkind,
        kind,

        my life goes out of me
        breath by breath

thinking of your austere
compassion.'

ii

Fame tastes 'sweet' to him,
too sweet, and then sour,
and then not at all.

It is not a substance
to taste, it is a box
in which he is kept.

He is a silver
dandelion seed entrapped
in a cube of plexiglass.

iii

'Stop the coach! I want to get out
and die!'
      His friends
wonder what he's scribbling,
'furiously,' as it is said,
all the way back.
They're doing 80, the freeway's
all theirs.
      'Nature smiles,
and smiles, and
says nothing. And I'm
driving away from the gates of
Paradise.'

1970

February Evening in Boston, 1971

The trees' black hair electric
brushed out,
      fierce haloes.

And westward
veils of geranium hold their own,
even yet. Transparent.

People are quickly, buoyantly
crossing the Common
into evening, into
a world of promises.

It was the custom of my tribe
to speak and sing;
not only to share the present, breath and sight,
but to the unborn.
Still, even now, we reach out
toward survivors. It is a covenant
of desire.

          Shall there be, by long chance,
one to hear me after the great, the gross,
                  the obscene silence,
to hear and wonder that in the last days
the seasons gave joy,
that dusk transmuted
          brilliant pink to lilac, lilac
          to smoke blue?

And lovers sat on a bench in the cold as night drew in,
laughing because the snow had melted.

The Sun Going Down upon Our Wrath

You who are so beautiful—
your deep and childish faces,
your tall bodies—

Shall I warn you?

Do you know
what it was to have
certitude of grasses waving

426

upon the earth though all
humankind were dust?
Of dust returning
to fruitful dust?

Do you already know
what hope is fading from us
and pay no heed,
see the detested grave-worm shrivel,
the once-despised,
and not need it?

Is there an odyssey
your feet pull you towards
away from now to walk
the waters, the fallen
orchard stars?
    It seems
your fears are only the old fears, antique
anxieties, how graceful;
they lay as cloaks on shoulders
of men long dead,
skirts of sorrow wrapped
over the thighs of legendary women.

Can you be warned?

If you are warned will your beauty
scale off, to leave
gaping meat livid with revulsion?

No, who can believe it.
Even I in whose heart
stones rattle, rise each day
to work and imagine.

Get wisdom, get understanding, saith
the ancient. But he believed
there is nothing new under the sun,
his future
rolled away in great coils forever
into the generations.

Among conies the grass
grew again
and among bones.
And the bones would rise.

If there is time to warn you,
if you believed there shall be
never again a green blade in the crevice,
luminous eyes in rockshadow:
if you were warned and believed
the warning,

would your beauty
break into spears of fire,

fire to turn fire, a wall
of refusal, could there be
a reversal I cannot

hoist myself high enough
to see,
plunge myself deep enough
to know?

Forest Altar, September

The gleam of thy drenched
floors of leaf-layers! Fragrance
of death and change!
                    If there is only
now to live, I'll live
the hour till doomstroke
crouched with the russet toad,
my huge human size
no more account than a bough fallen:

not upward,
searching for branch-hidden sky:
I'll look
down into paradise.

Thy moss gardens, the deep
constellations of green, the striate
rock furred with emerald,
inscribed with gold lichen,
with scarlet!
          Thy smooth
acorns in roughsurfaced
precise cups!
          Thy black
horns of plenty!

Joie de Vivre

All that once hurt
(healed) goes on hurting
in new ways. One same heart
—not a transplant—
cut down to the stump
throbs, new, old.
Bring paper and pencil
out of the dimlit into
the brightlit room, make sure
all you say is true.
'Antonio, Antonio,
the old wound's
bleeding.' 'Let it bleed.'
The pulse of life-pain
strong again, count it,
fast but
not fluttering.

The Wanderer

The chameleon who wistfully
thought it could not suffer
nostalgia

now on a vast sheet of clear glass
cowers, and prays for vision
of russet bark and trembling foliage.

Brass Tacks

i

The old wooden house a soft
almost-blue faded green
embowered in southern autumn's
nearly-yellow green leaves,
the air damp after a night of rain.

ii

The black girl sitting alone in the back row
smiled at me.

iii

Yes, in strange kitchens
I know where to find the forks,

and among another woman's perfume bottles
I can find the one that suits me,

and in the bedrooms
of children I have not met
I have galloped the island
of Chincoteague at 3 a.m., too tired to sleep—

but beyond that

at how many windows I have listened
to the cricket-quivering of borrowed moonlight.

iv

Brass tacks that glint
                    illumination of dailiness
          and hold down feet to earth
                         ears to the rush and whisper of
                              the ring and rattle of
                                   the Great Chain—
brass tacks that rivet
the eyes to Consolation,
               that *are* Consolation.

v

Weighed down by two shopping bags she trudges
uphill diagonally across the nameless (but grassy)
East Boston square—Fort Something,
it was once. Her arms ache, she wonders
if some items she is carrying deserve to be classed
as conspicuous consumption. It would be nice
if a gray pet donkey came by magic
to meet her now, panniers ready
for her burdens . . . She looks up,
and the weight
lifts: behind the outstretched eager
bare limbs and swaying twigs of two
still-living elms

in moonstone blue of dusk
the new moon itself is swinging
back and forth on a cloud-trapeze!

vi

The spring snow
is flying
          aslant
                over the crocus gold
                and into evening.

vii

Returning tired towards his temporary
lodging, wondering again
if his workday was useful at all

the human being saw the rose-colored leaves
of a small plant growing among
the stones of a low wall

unobtrusively, and found himself
standing quite still, gazing,
and found himself
smiling.

The Old King
for Jim Forest

The Soul's dark Cottage, batter'd and decay'd,
Lets in new Light through chinks that Time hath made.

And at night—
the whole night a cavern, the world
an abyss—

lit from within:

a red glow
throbbing at the chinks.

Far-off a wanderer
unhoused, unhouseled,
wonders to see
hearthblaze:
fears, and takes heart.

The Roamer

The world comes back to me
eager and hungry, and often
too tired to wag its tail,

a dog with wanderlust
back from South Boston or the Reservoir.

Keeps coming back,
brought by triumphant strangers
who don't understand he knows the way well.
Faint jingle of collartag breaking
my sleep, he arrives
and patiently scratches himself on the front steps.
I let in blue
daybreak,
in rushes the world,

visible dog concocted
of phantasmagoric atoms.
Nudges my hand with wet nose,
flumps down, deeply sighing,

smelling of muddy streams, of thrown-away treasures,
of some exotic news, not blood, not flowers,
and not his own fur—
                  unable
except by olifact
to tell me anything.
                  Where have I been
without the world? Why am I glad
he wolfs his food and gathers
strength for the next journey?

'Life Is Not a Walk across a Field'

crossing furrows from green hedge to hedge,
rather a crawling out of one's deep hole

in midfield, in the moist
gray that is dawn, and begins

to hurt the eyes;
                        to sit on one's haunches
gazing, listening, picking up
the voices of wheat, trail of other
animals telling the nose the night's news.

To be at the hollow center of a field
at dawn; the radius
radiant. Silver
to gold, shadows
violet dancers.

                        By noon the builders
scream in, the horizon
blocks afternoon, a jagged
restlessness. To be
an animal dodging
pursuers it smells but can't
see clear, through labyrinths

of new walls. To be mangled or
grow wise in escape.
To bite, and destroy the net.

                        To make it maybe
into the last of day, and witness
crimson wings
                        cutting down after
the sun gone down in wrath.

To stay perhaps,

        one throat far-off
        pulsing to venture
        one note from its feathers,
        one bell,

on into dewfall, into
peculiar silence.

The multitude gone, labyrinths
crumbling.
                    To go down
back into the known hole.

Alice Transfixed

When your huge face
whipped by the highest branches
finds itself peering into a nest,
pathos of scraggly twigs and tiny eggs:

and the appalled mother-bird is shrieking
'Serpent! Serpent!' at you,
her beak grazing your ear—

that's when you wonder
if the first wish, the first question,
were worth it.
Mournfully
the feet you have bade-farewell-to
trample in cloudhidden thickets,
crushing the slow beasts.

Memories of John Keats
for Mitch

Watchfulness and sensation as John Keats
said to me
for it was to me
he said it
                    (and to you)

Side by side we lay full-length
upon a spumy rock, envisioning
Ailsa Craig

                    The sea tumult

bore away
          a word
      and a word

And again *that which is creative*
must create itself   he said
We skirted
the murmurous green hollow
Vale of Health

strolling the spiral road, the
Vale of Soulmaking

He would stop to pluck
a leaf, finger
a stone

watchfulness was his word
sensation
            and watchfulness in itself
the Genius
of Poetry must work out
its own salvation in a man

I leapt   he said
headlong into the sea . . .

Earthwards

Blue of Ireland quickens in the sea,
green fish
            deep below the fathoms
of glass air.

My shadow
if I were floating free

would stroke the mountains' bristles
pensively, a finger of dark

smaller even than the plane's
tiny shadow, unnoticed,

nearing the edge of
                    the old world.

By Rail through the Earthly Paradise,
Perhaps Bedfordshire

The fishermen among the fireweed.

Towpath and humpbacked bridge. Cows
in one field, slabs of hay
ranged in another.

Common day
precious to me.
There's nothing else
to grasp.

The train
moves me past it too fast, not much,
just a little, I don't want
to stay for ever.
                    Horses,
three of them, flowing across a paddock
as wind flows over barley.

Oaks in parkland, distinct,
growing their shadows.
A man from Cairo across from me
reading *A Synopsis of Eye Physiology*.
The brickworks,
fantastical slender chimneys.

I'm not hungry,
not lonely. It seems
at times I want nothing,
no human giving and taking.
Nothing I see
fails to give pleasure,

no thirst for righteousness
dries my throat, I am silent
and happy, and troubled only
by my own happiness. Looking,

looking and naming. I wish the train now
would halt for me at a station in the fields,
(the name goes by
unread).
                In the deep aftermath
of its faded rhythm, I could become

a carved stone
set in the gates of the earthly paradise,

an angler's fly
lost in the sedge to watch the centuries.

The Cabbage Field

Both Taine and the inland English child
were mocked for their independent
comparison of the sea to a field of cabbages:

but does this field
of blue and green and purple curling
turmoil of ordered curves, reaching

out to the smoky twilight's immense
ambiguousness we call
horizon, resemble

anything but the sea?

In Silence

Clear from the terraced mountainside
through fretwork of laden vines, red apples, brown
heavy pears poised to fall, and not falling,

I saw a woman deep in the valley
wrapped in a blue cloak as if autumn
veiled in the ripe sun
were running its cutting-edge over her skin,
hurry from her house out to the garden swimming pool
and bend to greet a child there, and again hurry
round the pool to the far side,
and drop the cloak from her shoulders,
kick off her shoes in haste
and at last slowly, smoothly,
flowingly as if all her being
were blue water,
enter the blue water.

Brunnenburg, 1971

To Antonio Machado

Here in the mountain woods
a furious small fountain
is channelled through pipes of hollow sapling
into a great wooden vat bevelled with moss,
and thence brims over into a concrete cistern
and from the cistern quietly
in modest rills
into the meadow where cows graze
and fringed wild carnations, white and sweet,
grow by the path.
Machado,
       old man,
            dead man,
      I wish you were here alive
to drink of the cold, earthtasting, faithful spring,
to receive the many voices
of this one brook,
to see its dances
of fury and gentleness,
to write the austere poem
you would have known in it.

Brunnenburg, 1971

Sun, Moon, and Stones

> *'I longed to go away, to take to the desolate, denuded mountains opposite me and walk and walk, without seeing anything but sun, moon, and stones.'*
> —*Nikos Kazantzakis*

Sun
moon
stones

        but where shall we find
        water?

Sun

    hoists all things upward and outward
    thrusts
    a sword of thirst into the mouth.

Moon

    fills the womb with ice.

Stones: weapons that carry
        warmth into night
        dew into day, and break
        the flesh of stumbling feet

And we were born to that sole end:
    to thirst and grow
    to shudder
    to dream in lingering dew, lingering warmth
    to stumble searching.

But O the fountains,
    where shall we find them.

Man Alone

When the sun goes down, it writes
a secret name in its own blood for remembrance,
the excess of light
an ardor slow to cool:
and man has time to seek shelter.

But when the moon
gains the horizon, though it tarries
a moment, it vanishes
without trace of silver

and he is left with the stars only,
fierce and remote, and not revealing
the stones of the dark roads.

So it is with the gods,
and with the halfgods,
and with the heroes.

Road

The wayside bushes waiting, waiting.
There's no one,
no one to meet them.
Golden in my sunset dustcloud
I too pass by.

The Malice of Innocence

A glimpsed world, halfway through the film,
one slow shot of a ward at night

holds me when the rest is quickly
losing illusion. Strange hold,

as of romance, of glamor: not because
even when I lived in it I had

illusions about that world: simply because
I did live there and it was

a world. Greenshaded lamp glowing
on the charge desk, clipboards
stacked on the desk for the night,

sighs and waiting, waiting-for-morning stirrings
in the dim long room, warm, orderly,
and full of breathings as a cowbarn.

Death and pain dominate this world, for though
many are cured, they leave still weak,

still tremulous, still knowing mortality
has whispered to them; have seen in the folding
of white bedspreads according to rule

the starched pleats of a shroud.
                                        It's against that frozen
counterpane, and the knowledge too
how black an old mouth gaping at death can look

that the night routine has in itself—
without illusions—glamor, perhaps. It had

a rhythm, a choreographic decorum:
when all the evening chores had been done

and a multiple restless quiet listened
to the wall-clock's pulse, and turn by turn

the two of us made our rounds
on tiptoe, bed to bed,

counting by flashlight how many pairs
of open eyes were turned to us,

noting all we were trained to note,
we were gravely dancing—starched

in our caps, our trained replies,
our whispering aprons—the well-rehearsed

pavanne of power. Yes, wasn't it power,
and not compassion,
                                        gave our young hearts
their hard fervor? I hated

to scrub out lockers, to hand out trays of
unappetizing food, and by day, or the tail-end of night

(daybreak dull on gray faces—ours and theirs)
the anxious hurry, the scolding old-maid bosses.
But I loved the power
of our ordered nights,

       gleaming surfaces I'd helped to polish
making patterns in the shipshape
halfdark—
              loved
the knowing what to do, and doing it,
list of tasks getting shorter

hour by hour. And knowing
all the while that Emergency
might ring with a case to admit, anytime,

if a bed were empty. Poised,
ready for that.
                 The camera
never returned to the hospital ward,

the story moved on into the streets,
into the rooms where people lived.

But I got lost in the death rooms a while,
remembering being (crudely, cruelly,

just as a soldier or one of the guards
from Dachau might be) in love with order,

an angel like the *chercheuses de poux*, floating
noiseless from bed to bed,

smoothing pillows, tipping
water to parched lips, writing

details of agony carefully into the Night Report.

At the 'Mass Ave Poetry Hawkers' Reading in the Red Book Cellar

When even craning my neck
I couldn't see over and round
to where poems were sounding from

I found eyesight wasn't so utterly
my way of being
as I'd supposed: each voice

was known to me, I could name
each, and conjure seven
faces, seven heads of

mysteriously intense and living
hair, curly, wavy, straight, dark, light,
or going further, *not* conjure

any picture: solely hear
person in voice: further:
to listen deeper:

deep listening: into the earth
burrowing, into the water courses
hidden in rockbed.

And songs from these
beloved strangers, these close friends,
moved in my blind illumined head,
songs of terror, of hopes unknown to me,
terror, dread: songs of knowledge, songs
of their lives wandering

out into oceans.

1972

444

Small Satori

Richard's lover has the look,
robust and pure, of a nineteenth-century
Russian heroine. Surely her brows and chin,
smooth hair, free walk,
        and the way she can sit poised and quiet,
speak of depth.

        Across the room
his profile—all I can see
beyond the range of heads and shoulders,
in smoke, in candlelight—
looks off into inner distance,
poignant, a little
        older than last year,
still very young though.

I think she is watching him too.

Calmly, calmly, I am seeing them both.
Reassured.

1972

The Life around Us
for David Mitchell and David Haas

Poplar and oak awake
all night. And through
all weathers of the days of the year.
There is a consciousness
undefined.
Yesterday's twilight, August
almost over, lasted, slowly changing,
until daybreak. Human sounds
were shut behind curtains.
No human saw the night in this garden,
sliding blue into morning.

Only the sightless trees,
without braincells, lived it
and wholly knew it.

Knowing the Way

The wood-dove utters
slowly
          those words he has
to utter,
and softly.
                    But takes flight
boldly,
and flies fast.

THE FREEING OF
THE DUST

ONE

From a Plane

Green water of lagoons,
brown water of a great river
sunning its muscles along intelligent
rectangular swathes of
other brown, other green,
alluvial silvers.
                    Always air
looked down through, gives
a reclamation of order, re-
visioning solace: the great body
not torn apart, though raked and raked
by our claws—

Bus

The turnpike, without history, a function
of history, grossly
cut through the woods,

secondgrowth woods without memory,
crowded saplings, bushes entangled,
sparse weedcrop on burned-over sandy embankments.

Brutally realized intentions speed us
from city to city—a driver's world:
and what is a driver? Driven? Obsessed?
These thickarmed men
seem at rest, assured, their world
a world of will and function.

Journeyings

Majestic insects buzz through the sky
bearing us pompously from love to love,
grief to grief,
                        expensively,
motes in the gaze of that unblinking eye.

Our threads of life are sewn into dark cloth,
a sleeve that hangs down over
a sinister wrist. All of us.
It must be Time whose pale fingers
dangle beneath the hem . . .

Solemn filaments, our journeyings
wind through the overcast.

Knowing the Unknown

Our trouble
is only the trouble anyone,
all of us, thrust from the ancient
holding-patterns, down toward
runways newbuilt,
knows; the strain
of flying wing by wing, not knowing
ever if both of us will land: the planet
under the clouds—
does it want us? Shall we be welcome,
we of air, of metallic
bitter rainbows,
of aching wings? Can we dissolve
like coins of hail,
touching down,
                        down to the dense, preoccupied,
skeptical green world, that does not know us?

TWO

In Summer

Night lies down
in the field when the moon
leaves. Head in clover,
held still.

It is brief,
this time of darkness,
hands of night
loosefisted, long hair
outspread.

Sooner than one would dream,
the first bird
wakes with a sobbing cry. Whitely

dew begins to drift
cloudily.
Leafily naked, forms of the world
are revealed,
all asleep. Colors

come slowly
up from behind the hilltop,
looking for forms to fill for the day,
dwellings.
Night
must rise and
move on, stiff and
not yet awake.

An Ancient Tree

'Can't get that tune
out of my head,'

can't get that tree
out of

some place in me.
And don't want to:

the way it
lifts up its arms,
opens them, and—

patient the way an
elderly horse is patient—
crosses them, aloft,

to curve and recross:

the standing, the being
rooted, the look
as of longing.
At each divide,
the choice endured, branches
taking their roads in air.

Glance up
from the kitchen window;
that tree word,
still being said,
over the stone wall.

Fall mornings, its head of twigs
vaguely lifted,
a few apples
yellow in silver fog.

Romance

i

Dark, rainsoaked
oaklimbs

within thorny
auburn haze
of brush at wood's edge.

Secretly
I love you, whom
they think I have abjured.

ii

Secretly,
blueveiled
moody
autumn auburn,

you are the very wood I knew
always, that grew up
so tall, to hold at bay

the worldly princes,
baffled and torn
upon the thorns
of your redberried thickets,
may and rose.

April in Ohio

Each day
the cardinals call and call in the rain,
each cadence scarlet
among leafless buckeye,

and passionately
the redbuds, that can't wait
like other blossoms, to flower
from fingertip twigs,
break forth

as Eve from Adam's
cage of ribs,
straight from amazed treetrunks.

Lumps of snow
are melting in tulip-cups.

THREE

A Time Past

The old wooden steps to the front door
where I was sitting that fall morning
when you came downstairs, just awake,
and my joy at sight of you (emerging
into golden day—
                              the dew almost frost)
pulled me to my feet to tell you
how much I loved you:

those wooden steps
are gone now, decayed,
replaced with granite,
hard, gray, and handsome.
The old steps live
only in me:
my feet and thighs
remember them, and my hands
still feel their splinters.

Everything else about and around that house
brings memories of others—of marriage,
of my son. And the steps do too: I recall
sitting there with my friend and her little son who died,
or was it the second one who lives and thrives?
And sitting there 'in my life,' often, alone or with my husband.
Yet that one instant,
your cheerful, unafraid, youthful, 'I love you too,'
the quiet broken by no bird, no cricket, gold leaves
spinning in silence down without
any breeze to blow them,
                              is what twines itself
in my head and body across those slabs of wood

that were warm, ancient, and now
wait somewhere to be burnt.

Fragment

All one winter, in every crowded hall,
at every march and rally,
first thing I'd look for was your curly head.

One night last summer in a crowded room
across the ocean,
my heart missed a beat—it seemed I saw you
in the far corner.

You who were so many thousand miles away.

Face

When love, exaltation, the holy awe
of Poetry entering your doors and lifting you
on one finger as if you were a feather
fallen from its wings, grasp you, then your face
is luminous. I saw the angel
of Jacob once, alabaster, stone and not stone,
incandescent.
              That look, the same,
illumines you, then.
                    But when
hatred and a desire of vengeance
make you sullen, your eyes grow smaller,
your mouth turns sour, a heaviness
pulls the flesh of your poet's face
down, makes it a mask
of denial. I remember:
from the same block of stone Jacob was carved,
but he was thick, opaque. The sculptor showed
Jacob still unwounded, locked into combat, unblest,
the day
not yet dawning.

What She Could Not Tell Him

I wanted
to know all the bones of your spine, all
the pores of your skin,
tendrils of body hair.
To let
all of my skin, my hands,
ankles, shoulders, breasts,
even my shadow,
be forever imprinted
with whatever of you
is forever unknown to me.
To cradle your sleep.

Ways of Conquest

You invaded my country by accident,
not knowing you had crossed the border.
Vines that grew there touched you.
                              You ran past them,
shaking raindrops off the leaves—you or the wind.
It was toward the hills you ran,
inland—

I invaded your country with all my
'passionate intensity,'
pontoons and parachutes of my blindness.
But living now in the suburbs of the capital
incognito,
              my will to take the heart of the city
              has dwindled. I love
its unsuspecting life,
its adolescents who come to tell me their dreams in the dusty park
among the rocks and benches,
I the stranger who will listen.
I love
the wild herons who return each year to the marshy outskirts.
What I invaded has
invaded me.

FOUR

Photo Torn from The Times

A story one might read and not know
                                    (not have to know)
the power of the face—

> 'Ten-year-old Eric
> was killed during racial tension last summer'

> Testimony . . .
> 'tears . . .
> in her eyes . . .
> *"I am not afraid*
> *of anyone.*
> *Nothing else*
> *can happen to me*
> *now that my son*
> *is dead." '*

But the power is there to see, the face
of an extreme beauty, contours
of dark skin luminous
as if candles shone unflickering
on beveled oiled wood.

Her name, Alluvita,
compound of earth, river, life.

She is gazing
way beyond questioners.

Her tears
shine and don't fall.

News Items

i   America the Bountiful

After the welfare hotel
crumbled suddenly (after repeated warnings)
into the street,

Seventh Day Adventists brought supplies
of clothing to the survivors,
' "Look at this," exclaimed
Loretta Rollock, 48 years old,
as she held up a green dress
and lingerie. "I've never worn
such nice clothes. I feel like
when I was a kid and my mom
brought me something." Then
she began to cry.'

ii   In the Rubble

For some the hotel's collapse meant
life would have to be started
all over again.
Sixty-year-old Charles, on welfare
like so many of the others, who said,
'We are the rootless people,' and
'I have no home, no place that I can say I
really live in,' and,
'I had become used to it here,'
also said:
'I lost
all I ever had,
in the rubble.
I lost my clothes,
I lost the picture of my parents
and I lost my television.'

A Sound of Fear

There's a woman (you tell the gender by the noise of her heels)
lives in this 12-story building,
who won't use the elevator: hurries
down the emergency stairs from a floor higher than sixth
clop, clop, clop, every night
about the same time.
If I'm awake I hear her slowly
reascend
much later, pausing
to rest her legs
and breathe,
like someone climbing inside a monument
to see the view and say
I climbed it.
Every night.

Too Much to Hope

Twisted body and whitesocked
deformed legs (evidently
too hard to get stockings on).
And little, booted, braced, feet,
swinging along
beside the crutches and under
the huge winglike shoulders . . .

Always the tap and creak and
tap and creak of
crutch and brace,
in effort always, and whirr
of wings revving up and not
getting the human, female, botched body
off the ground.
The sound never
letting up, no hushed pinewoods walk,
no slipping unseen through lakes of shadow.
Has she
some blessèd deafness given

along with starved bones?
                    It seems
too much to hope.

The Distance

While we lie in the road to block traffic from the air-force base,
over there the dead are strewn in the roads.

While we are carried to the bus and off to jail to be 'processed,'
over there the torn-off legs and arms of the living
hang in burnt trees and on broken walls.

While we wait and sing in ugly but not uninhabitable cells,
men and women contorted, blinded, in tiger cages, are
                                        biting their tongues
to stifle, for each other's sake, their cries of agony.
And those cruel cages are built in America.

While we refuse the standard prison liverwurst sandwiches,
knowing we'll get decent food in a matter of hours,
over there free fighters, young and old, guns never laid aside,
eat a few grains of rice and remember
Uncle Ho, and the long years he ate no better, and smile.

And while we fear
for the end of earth-life, even though we sing
and rejoice in each other's beauty and comradeship,

over there they mourn
the dead and mutilated each has seen.

They have seen and seen and heard and heard
all that we will ourselves with such effort to imagine,
to summon into the understanding . . .

And they too sing.
They too rejoice
in each other's beauty and comradeship:

they sing and fight. I see their spirits
visible, crowns of fire-thorn
flicker over their heads.

Our steps toward struggle
are like the first tottering of infant feet.
Could we,
          if life lasts
                          find in ourselves
that steady courage, win
such flame-crowns?

Weeping Woman

She is weeping for her lost right arm.
She cannot write the alphabet any more
on the kindergarten blackboard.

She is weeping for her lost right arm.
She cannot hold her baby and caress it at the same time
ever again.

She is weeping for her lost right arm.
The stump aches, and her side.

She is weeping for her lost right arm.
The left alone cannot use a rifle
to help shoot down the attacking plane.

In the wide skies over the Delta
her right hand that is not there
writes indelibly,
                'Cruel America,
when you mutilate our land and bodies,
it is your own soul you destroy,
not ours.'

The Pilots

Because they were prisoners,
because they were polite and friendly and lonesome and homesick,
because they said Yes, they knew
                              the names of the bombs they dropped
        but didn't say whether they understood what these bombs are
                                   designed to do
                                   to human flesh, and because
        I didn't ask them, being unable to decide
        whether to ask would serve
        any purpose other than cruelty, and
because since then I met Mrs. Brown, the mother of one of their
                                              fellow prisoners,
and loved her, for she has the same lovingkindness in her
that I saw in Vietnamese women (and men too)
and because my hostility left the room and wasn't there when I
                                    thought I needed it
while I was drinking tea with the POW's,

because of all these reasons I hope
they were truly as ignorant,
            as unawakened,
                        as they seemed,
I hope their chances in life up to this point
have been poor,
I hope they can truly be considered
victims of the middle America they come from,
their American Legionnaire fathers, their macho high schools,
their dull skimped Freshman English courses,

for if they did understand precisely
what they were doing, and did it anyway, and would do it again,

then I must learn to distrust
my own preference for trusting people,

then I must learn to question
my own preference for liking people,

then I must learn to keep
my hostility chained to me
so it won't leave me when I need it.

And if it is proved to me
that these men understood their acts,

how shall I ever again
be able to meet the eyes of Mrs. Brown?

A Place of Kindness

Somewhere there is a dull room
where someone slow is moving,
stumbling from door to chair

to sit there patiently
doing nothing but be,
enjoying the quiet and warmth,

pleased with the gradual
slope of day's light
into his corner. Dull

illiterate saint, never imagining
the atrocious skills his kin
devise and use,

who are avidly, viciously active,
refining quality, increasing quantity—
million by million—
of standardized Agony-Inflicters.

Somewhere there is a dull room
no phosphorescence of guile illumines.
No scintillations
of cruelty.

Imagination could put forth
gentle feelers there.
Somewhere there must be

such a room, and someone dumb
in it, unknown to cruelty,
unknowing.

May Our Right Hands Lose Their Cunning

Smart bombs replace
dumb bombs. 'Now we can aim
straight into someone's kitchen.'

Hard rice
sprays out of the cooking pot
straight into the delicate jelly of eyes.

Invisible pellets,
pointed blobs of mist,
        bite through smooth pale-brown skin
        into perfect bodies,
chewing them into bloody mincemeat.
This is smart.

        There is
a dumb fellow, a mongoloid,
40 years old, who, being cherished,
learned recently to read and write,
and now has written a poem.
        'Summer in the West when
                everything is quiet
        And clear, with everything
                beautiful and green,
        With wild flowers of all colors,
                and a small water creek,
And a beautiful blue sky. And
        the trees,' he wrote,
forming the letters carefully, his tongue
protruding, 'are very still.
        And sometimes a small breeze.'

He has been cherished,
slowly learned
what many learn fast, and go on
to other knowledge. He
knows nothing of man's devices,
        may die without discovering that
he's dumb, and they
are smart, the killers.

And the uncherished idiots,
tied in cots, smelling
of shit—
        exquisite dumbness,
guaranteed not to know,
ever, how smart
a man can be,
        homo faber of laser beams, of
quaintly-named, flesh-directed, utterly ingenious
mutilating spit-balls,
        yes,
the smartest boys, obedient to all the rules, who never
aimed any flying objects across the classroom,
now are busy with finely calibrated equipment
fashioning spit-balls with needles in them,
that fly at the speed of light multiplied
around corners and into tunnels to arrive
directly at the dumb perfection of living targets,
icily into warm wholeness to fragment it.

We who
        know this
tremble
at our own comprehension.
Are we infected,
viciously, being smart enough
to write down these matters,
        scribes of the unspeakable?
We pray to retain
something round, blunt, soft, slow,
dull in us,
not to sharpen, not to be smart.

In Thai Binh (Peace) Province
for Muriel and Jane

I've used up all my film on bombed hospitals,
bombed village schools, the scattered
lemon-yellow cocoons at the bombed silk-factory,

and for the moment all my tears too
are used up, having seen today
yet another child with its feet blown off,
          a girl, this one, eleven years old,
patient and bewildered in her home, a fragile
small house of mud bricks among rice fields.

So I'll use my dry burning eyes
to photograph within me
dark sails of the river boats,
warm slant of afternoon light
apricot on the brown, swift, wide river,
village towers—church and pagoda—on the far shore,
and a boy and small bird both
perched, relaxed, on a quietly grazing
buffalo.   Peace within the
          long war.

It is that life, unhurried, sure, persistent,
I must bring home when I try to bring
the war home.
          Child, river, light.

Here the future, fabled bird
that has migrated away from America,
nests, and breeds, and sings,

common as any sparrow.

Fragrance of Life, Odor of Death

All the while among
the rubble even, and in
the hospitals, among the wounded,
                    not only beneath
                    lofty clouds

                              in temples
                    by the shores of lotus-dreaming
                    lakes

a fragrance:
flowers, incense, the earth-mist rising
of mild daybreak in the delta—good smell
of life.

It's in America
where no bombs ever
have screamed down smashing
the buildings, shredding the people's bodies,
tossing the fields of Kansas or Vermont or Maryland into the air
to land wrong way up, a gash of earth-guts . . .
it's in America, everywhere, a faint seepage,
I smell death.

Hanoi–Boston–Maine, November 1972

A Poem at Christmas, 1972, during the Terror-Bombing of North Vietnam

Now I have lain awake imagining murder.
At first my pockets were loaded with rocks, with knives,
wherever I ran windows smashed, but I was swift and unseen,
        I was saving the knives until I reached
certain men . . .
                Yes, Kissinger's smile faded,
he clutched his belly, he reeled . . .
But as the night
wore on, what I held
hidden—under a napkin perhaps,
        I as a waitress at the inaugural dinner—
was a container of napalm:
and as I threw it in Nixon's face
and his crowd leapt back from the flames with crude yells of horror,
and some came rushing to seize me:
        quick as thought I had ready
a round of those small bombs designed
to explode at the pressure of a small child's weight,
and these instantly
dealt with the feet of Nixon's friends and henchmen,
who fell in their own blood

while the foul smoke of his body-oils
blackened the hellish room . . .
It was of no interest
to imagine further. Instead,
the scene recommenced.
Each time around, fresh details,
variations of place and weapon.
All night imagining murder,
O, to kill
the killers!

It is
to this extremity

the infection of their evil

thrusts us . . .

Goodbye to Tolerance

Genial poets, pink-faced
earnest wits–
you have given the world
some choice morsels,
gobbets of language presented
as one presents T-bone steak
and Cherries Jubilee.
Goodbye, goodbye,
                    I don't care
if I never taste your fine food again,
neutral fellows, seers of every side.
Tolerance, what crimes
are committed in your name.

And you, good women, bakers of nicest bread,
blood donors. Your crumbs
choke me, I would not want
a drop of your blood in me, it is pumped
by weak hearts, perfect pulses that never
falter: irresponsive
to nightmare reality.

It is my brothers, my sisters,
whose blood spurts out and stops
forever
because you choose to believe it is not your business.

Goodbye, goodbye,
your poems
shut their little mouths,
your loaves grow moldy,
a gulf has split
                    the ground between us,
and you won't wave, you're looking
another way.
We shan't meet again—
unless you leap it, leaving
behind you the cherished
worms of your dispassion,
your pallid ironies,
your jovial, murderous,
wry-humored balanced judgment,
leap over, un-
balanced? . . . then
how our fanatic tears
would flow and mingle
for joy . . .

January 1973

Dragon of Revolutionary Love

i

All the grievous wounds the murderers
crudely disguised as surgeons, inflict on the innocent—
gouging their flesh and the earth and rivers of their flesh—
are only debridements, light scrapings
of the layer just below the skin.

Breathing their own stale breath inside their masks,
fingers itching in bloody gloves,

they fail to touch the spirit-dragon
alive in the bone and marrow of their prey.

ii

From the Red River's many mouths
uprises
        a spirit-song.
Glittering drops that fall free from the nets
as fishermen take their catch
are the bright scales of the spirit-dragon.

iii

To live
beyond survival.
When a whole child
hurries to school with a legless child
on his back,
both of them flushed with pride,

the spirit-dragon
flies alongside them.

Hanoi, 1972–Temple, Maine, 1973

FIVE

Craving

Wring the swan's neck, seeking
a little language of drops of blood.

How can we speak of blood, the sky
is drenched with it.

A little language
of dew, then.

It dries.

A language
of leaves underfoot.
Leaves on the tree, trembling
in speech. Poplars
          tremble and speak
if you draw near them.

Dream Inscape

Mycelium, the delicate white threads
mushrooms weave in their chosen earth
(or manure or leafmold) to grow from

and milkweed silk orioles knit
into hammock nests their eggs
lilt in

and silver timbers
of old barns near salt water—

all of these
dreamed of, woven, knit, mitered
into a vision named 'A Visit Home'
(as if there were a home I had,
beyond the houses I live in, or those
I've lived in and hold
dimly in mind)
                    that waking
shook apart, out of
coherence, unwove, unraveled, took
beam by beam away, splintered.

The Way It Is

More real than ever, as I move
in the world, and never out of it,
Solitude.

Typewriter, telephone, ugly names
of things we use, I use. Among them, though,
float milkweed silks.

Like a mollusk's, my hermitage
is built of my own cells.
Burned faces, stretched horribly,

eyes and mouths forever open,
weight the papers down on my desk.
No day for years I have not thought of them.

And more true than ever the familiar image
placing love on a border
where, solitary, it paces, exchanging
across the line a deep attentive gaze
with another solitude pacing there.

Yet almost no day, too, with no
happiness, no
exaltation of larks uprising from the heart's
peat-bog darkness.

The Balance

At the door, some *never*, some *let it be*,
those pestering halftruths of impatience . . .

Yet the daily bread gets baked,
a rush of initiative takes the stairs
three at a time.
                    Crippled by their feet,
the swans waddle to water,
the first of them already
slowly and silently has ripped the silk of evening.

Canción

When I am the sky
a glittering bird
slashes at me with the knives of song.

When I am the sea
fiery clouds plunge into my mirrors,
fracture my smooth breath with crimson sobbing.

When I am the earth
I feel my flesh of rock wearing down:
pebbles, grit, finest dust, nothing.

When I am a woman—O, when I am
a woman,
my wells of salt brim and brim,
poems force the lock of my throat.

SIX

The Woman

It is the one in homespun
you hunger for
when you are lonesome;

the one in crazy feathers
dragging opal chains in dust
wearies you

wearies herself perhaps
but has to drive on
clattering rattletrap into

fiery skies for trophies,
into the blue that is bluer
because of the lamps,

the silence keener because it is solitude
moving through multitude on the night streets.

But the one in homespun
whom you want is weary
too, wants to sit down

beside you neither silent
nor singing, in quietness. Alas,
they are not two but one,

pierce the flesh of one, the other
halfway across the world, will shriek,
her blood will run. Can you endure
life with two brides, bridegroom?

Crosspurposes

i

With dread she heard the letter
fall into the drop.

    Playing frisbee
  turns out to be a graceful merriment,
  almost like chasing butterflies.
Even she herself
could not have said for sure, as she played,
the letter was moving north already
to indict her history.

Decision, and fear, and then–
a picnic.
  'If I should come upon myself
suddenly,' she thinks, 'nothing would show I knew the letter was
             crawling

grayly north to pronounce sentence,
to send a lifetime out into exile.'

Magically the tangerine disc
glides and curves and chooses
to land in someone's outflung hand, sometimes
even in unpracticed hers; gracious caprice.
Or circles back to fingers that sent it forth.
The game is a dance.
                    Incandescent
the round charcoals, lambent
the white ash.
            Sun's fire
scatters between dark branches for those few
           passionate moments it takes each night to say
           farewell, and drop
                        over the world's edge.
Laughter around the picnic table
lightly skims the ungathered dusk.

ii

Two letters passed each other, carried
north and south.
In the first was written: 'Our journey has come to a dead end,
we mustn't cower by that wall,
skin our fingers trying to scale it,
batter shoulder and head pushing against it,
perish there.
I have come to believe
it towers to the sky
and is thick through with layers of stone to the horizon.
We can only admit defeat,
and the road being closed to us by which we came—
closed like an ocean-furrow—
now we must each take one of the narrow paths,
left and right, parallel
to the wall at first,
then bearing away from it,
                    wider and wider apart
from it and from
each other.'
          In the second letter was written
'We must return

to sunrise and morning freshness, to seeing
one
another
anew.
     When I'm clear,
I see you, when I see you
I love you. How much life
we have lived together. Life begins
to wake new in me.'
The first letter is still
on its way, the second
has been received.
          They are two songs
          each in a different key,
          two fables told
          in different countries,
          two pairs of eyes looking past each other
          to different distances.

Summer 1972

Living for Two

Lily Bloom, what ominous fallen crowfeathers of shadow
the nightlight scattered around your outspread hair
on feverish cumulus of pillows—
demonic darkness, hair, feathers, jabs of greenish
sickroom light.
          And your sallow face, long, lost, lonely,
O Lily Bloom, dying,
          looked into mine those nights,
searching, equine, for life to be lived—
but not believing. Believing yourself fit for the knacker's yard . . .

What I told you—promised you—
though I meant it, didn't make sense:
Friendship, Life of Art, Love of Nature.
You had no correlatives, I had
no holiness.

You saved me the exact shame of not coming across. But Lily—
whom I remember not in my head (or barely once a year)
but in my nerves—what brimming measure of living
your death exacts from me! And when the fire of me smokes
or gasps as flames will do when a contending element
chokes their utterance, and they burn livid instead of red,

then I know I am cheating you. Living this half-life in my fiftieth
                                                                    year
cheats you. If I can't give you water, give myself
water, then I must give you, give myself, some icy spirits,
diamonds on the tongue,
                              to sear cracked lips and
                              quicken the heart: a ceremony
of living.
Love, lovers, husband, child, land and ocean, struggle and solitude:
you've had these, and more, but you need more.
                              We have other years
to go, Lily. I thirst too.
                    We're not free
of our covenant, Enemy, Burden, Friend.

Living Alone (I)

In this silvery now of living alone,
doesn't it seem, I ponder,
anything can happen?
On the flat roof of a factory
at eye level from my window,
starling naiads dip in tremulous rainpools
where the sky floats, and is no smaller
than long ago.
Any strange staircase, as if I were twenty-one—
any hand drawing me up it,
could lead me to my life.
Some days.

And if I coast, down toward home, spring evenings, silently,
a kind of song rising in me to encompass
Davis Square and the all-night

cafeteria and the pool hall,
it is childhood's song, surely no note is changed,
sung in Valentines Park or on steep streets in the map of my mind
in the hush of suppertime, everyone gone indoors.
Solitude within multitude seduced me early.

Living Alone (II)

Some days, though,
living alone,
there's only knowledge of silence,
clutter of bells cobwebbed
in crumbling belfry,
words jaggéd,
in midutterance broken.

Starlings, as before,
whistle wondering at themselves,
crescendo, diminuendo.
My heart pounds away,
confident as a clock.
Yet there is silence.

New leafed, the neighbor trees
round out. There's one,
near my window,
seems to have no buds, though.

Living Alone (III)

I said, the summer garden I planted
bears only leaves—leaves in abundance—
but no flowers.
And then the flowers,
    many colors and forms,
    subtle, mysterious,
came forth.

I said, the tree has no buds.
And then the leaves,
       shyly, sparse, as if reluctant,
in less than two days appeared,
and the tree, now,
       is flying on green wings.

What magic denial
shall my life utter
to bring itself forth?

Cloud Poems
for Mitch

i.   The Cloud

We have entered sadness
as one enters a mountain cloud.

One stands in the midst of rain that is not raining.
Summits vanish, sheepdog's bark is dim.

Move and the cloud moves too,
and sighs with a million infinitesimal white breaths.

In single file, slowly,
clouds take to the sheep paths,

cloudy sadness, vague arms around us,
carries us like a bundle.

ii.   The Recollection

There was once a cloud—remember?
—with swift undulations drew away from our feet,
revealed that where we stood edged a precipice:

and deep below was a radiant valley,
rivers, fold and fields, gleaming villages,

iii.   The Cutting-beam

Imagine this blur of chill, white, gray, vague, sadness
burned off.

Imagine a landscape
of dry clear sunlight, precise shadows,
forms of pure color.

Imagine two neighboring hills, and
your house, my house, looking across, friendly:
imagine ourselves
meeting each other,
bringing gifts, bringing news.

Yes, we need the heat
of imagination's sun
to cut through our bonds of cloud.

And oh, can the great and golden light
warm our flesh that has grown so cold?

Don't You Hear That Whistle Blowin' . . .

The 4 a.m. freight comes pounding and shaking through the
                                        fall night
and I go to the Middle Door to watch,
                        through the plain glass
            that has stained glass around it,
pressing my forehead against the pane,

and Steve hurries along to look too—for he's out of Appalachia,
the lonesome romance of the rails West is in his bones;

and Richard comes close behind, gazing intently over my
                                        shoulder—
out of the Midwest and the rails West are in his blood,
and our friend Bo is at this very moment hopping freight in Oregon
                                        to pick pears;

and I seem to smell iron and rust, an animal smell, red and dusty,
even through the glass that's steaming up with our breaths.
So I start to open the door, to hear the last cars and the
                                        caboose louder
and the sound of going away, and to see the stars,

and I want you, Mitch, to step out with me into the dark garden,
for you're standing back of me too, taller than anyone;

but as the cold air comes in I turn toward you and you're not there.
Then I realize I'm waking up: the train really is going by
but the Middle Door's back in my childhood, not in America,

and there's no one in the house but you and me,
you asleep beside me in bed, and soon you'll have left
and this moment of dark boxcars just visible
under the paling stars, a train of looming forms from faraway states
lurching through the edge of Boston,

is just the beginning of a long train of times I'll turn
to share a vision with you and find I'm dreaming.

September 6–7, 1974

Divorcing

One garland
of flowers, leaves, thorns
was twined round our two necks.
Drawn tight, it could choke us,
yet we loved its scratchy grace,
our fragrant yoke.

We were Siamese twins.
Our blood's not sure
if it can circulate,
now we are cut apart.
Something in each of us is waiting
to see if we can survive,
severed.

Strange Song

A virtuoso dog at midnight—high wavering howl
resolved in three staccato low barks.
Three times the same utterance
repeated, insisted on.
It makes sure, like a bird practicing,
        through the day,
        its phrase.
I listen half asleep, aware
of pleasure in listening,
not afraid of my solitude.
Yet the fear nags me: is the wound
my life has suffered
        healing too fast,
shutting in bad blood?
Will the scar
pucker the skin of my soul?
'Shut up,' someone shouts at the dog
who again lifts his complaint
into the fall night in strange song.

Grief

When your voice breaks
I'm impaled on the jaggéd
edges of its fracture.

It is visible
to mind's eye, bone or grained
splintering wood.

Bone-voice, O wooden
sobbing. The flesh of my spirit
is sore. I'm powerless

to mend you. Marrow,
or sap rising in the fibers
that hold, must do it.

I suffer
less your pain than my
helplessness,

hoisted off the
earth of my energies like
a bug overturned,

feet waving
wild and feeble.

Libation

Raising our glasses, smilingly
we wish one another not luck
but happiness. After half a lifetime
with and without luck,
we know we need more than luck.
It makes no difference that we're drinking
tomato juice, not wine or whiskey—
we know what we mean,
and the red juice of those virtuous
vegetable-fruits is something we both enjoy.
I remember your wonder, as at a miracle,
finding them growing on sturdy vines
in my old aunt and uncle's sun-room
ripe to pluck at the breakfast table!
We were twenty-three, and unappeasably hungry . . .

We agree on tomatoes, then—and happiness?
yes, that too: we mean growth, branching,
leafing, yielding blossoms and fruit and the sharp odor of dreams.
We mean knowing someone as deeply,
no, deeper, than we've known each other,
we mean being known. We are wishing each other
the luck not to need luck. I mill
some pepper into my juice, though,
and salt in the ancient gesture; and what would be wrong
with tipping out half a glass
for the gods?

We smile.
After these months of pain we begin
to admit our new lives have begun.

February 1975

SEVEN

Seth Thomas: A Love Poem
for Fran and Tom

Rejoining Time after fifty years,
not slow, not fast.
Pendulum beaming gold in miniature cupboard.
Confident lame tock *tock*.
Melodious chime of three at one a.m.,
midnight at seven.

The Quality of Genius

i

Trees that lift themselves like clouds
above the woods,

crest of the woods and then
more, a breath

in winter air, a web
of fiber, from afar

so tenuous, near
a stiff hard complication

of live sticks.

ii

Eve's lavender
from a garden gone
        seven years now
under concrete—

fragrant.
       (The church wanted
        money: but Eve,
    moneyless, with a poet's
    humor, or lack of it,

    did not waste the pink
    Thank Offering envelope,
    'To Be Used Any Time God Has Blessed You,'

    ideal for mailing lavender,
    mint leaves, or winged seeds

    when the spirit
            moved her.)

iii

Encircling gold faded
to gray, stalks
tough still but leaves
frost bitten,

what large brown faces
—smiling,
seedy—
the sunflowers have.

iv

Which of them has it
it's too soon to tell—

David, John,
    Naomi, Carlene . . .

Confusion, growth, the analogies
perceived.   Seed of words
that didn't come up three
or five or seven
years back putting out
green shoots now, small
sturdy shrubs, vine tangles not resembling
remembered cotyledons.
                         Paul, Andrea, Aaron . . .
Letters
come in from
             far away
as if in bottles.
             (What was
the ancient children's game,
some token
concealed and passed
from hand to hand? Pincushion, button, ring—
some common
talisman . . .)

Flames upspring
feline
      to illumine
one face or another, moments
of profound chiaroscuro,
definition of feature—

but not yet
from inside out through their skulls
or through one skull
persistently

the fiery moonlight,
      the tattered rage
         of the sun . . .

Growth of a Poet

i

He picks up crystal buttons from the ocean floor.
Gills of the mind pulse in unfathomed water.

In the infinite dictionary he discovers
gold grains of sand. Each has its twin
on some shore the other side of the world.

Blind to what he does not yet need,
he feels his way over broken glass
to the one stone that fits his palm.

When he opens his eyes he gives to what he gazes at
the recognition no look ever before granted it.
It becomes a word. Shuddering, it takes wing.

ii

> *'What is to give light must endure burning.'*
> *Viktor Frankl,* The Doctor and the Soul

Blind until dreaming gray
sparks green, his eyes
set fire to an ashen street,
a dancer's
bitter flesh in daybreak,
the moon's
last noontime look
over its shoulder.
They fade; the flames
go on burning,
enduring.

iii

Deaf till he hears
what answers:

                    Grandfatherly
bell, tolling
and telling
of faithful Time, that flood
(ever-rolling), of faithful blood.
The answers pushing
boundaries over,
(those proud embankments),
the asking revealed.

The asking, stones
bared of earth,
hammers at the door, a pulse
in the temple:
the insistent dance
of Who and How and Where,
the arms-akimbo of When.

iv

One at a time
books, when their hour is come
step out of the shelves.
Heavily step (once more, dusty, fingermarked,
                but pristine!)
to give birth:

each poem's passion
ends in an Easter,
a new life.

            The books of the dead
shake their leaves,
word-seeds fly and
lodge in the black earth.

v

Coffee cups fall out of his hands,
doorknobs slip his grasp and
doors slam,

antique writing desks break under his
leaning elbows—Taurus
is bucking and thudding, head down across
the cramped field.
                    But scraps of wood
found on the street, one night when winds were
scraping the thick dark to a steely shine,
                        become in the poet's hands
a table,
        round and
set firm on its one leg.

vi

To make poems is to find
an old chair in the gutter
and bring it home
into the upstairs cave;
a stray horse from the pound,
a stray boat on the weedy shore,
phosphorescent.
Then in the broken rocking chair
Take off—to reality!
Realm of ambrosia and hard crusts
earnest trudging doesn't lead to.

Only when feet begin
to dance, when the chair
creaks and gallops,
do the gates open
and we
        discover ourselves
inside
the kingless kingdom.

vii

The wild moonbull
                    who is the poet
grazes alone
a field of infinite, dewdrenched,

drops of red clover,
sharp spears of grass
                which are words.

Over the barbed fence a troop
of boys and young men
                        who are the poet
throng,
        breathless, silent,
to the encounter.

They desire
to practice the dance.
Secretly to prepare.
He breathes
his green, fresh, breath at them,
still distant,
gazing innocent
through full-moon silver
toward them
and viciously
rushes them, they step
each aside,
old coats for capes,
they taunt him,
he tosses
his deadly flourish of horns,
they love him, they imagine
the hot sunlight of the sacred kill.

Implacable silver
fades. By moonset

they vanish, he hears
the wire fence
twang where they climbed it.

viii

Shadowdog
blocking the threshold.

Only a shadow. But
bites!
     Try
to get out, try
to get in:
        the obstacle
sinks its
teeth in
flesh, and

blood flows,
they are not
shadowteeth,
are sharp, and
dirty.

     •

The venom rises
from torn foot to
heart. Makes
a knot in the heart.

A screeching:
of brakes on the street,
of an unsuspected
voice outcrying
through the poet's
lips, denying
poetry,
      violent
palpitating beat of
the mind's wings caged.

Dust on the tongue.

Storm
of torn feathers.

Falling.
    Falling—

ix

Hasidic rocking
is always back and forth,
       back and forth,
in perfect measure with the words,
over and over,
every day of the year—

except one:

on the day the Temple is destroyed
      which is also
the day the Messiah is born,
on that day alone, the rocking
moves from side to side,
       side to side,
a swaying,
as trees sway in the wind.

x

On his one leg that aches
the poet
learns to stand firm
upholding
the round table of his
blank page.
When the wind blows
his wood
shall be tree again.
Shall stir,
shall sigh and sing.

xi

    'Whatever has black sounds, has duende.'
    Manuel Torres, quoted by Federico García Lorca

And now the sounds
are green, a snowdrop's quiet
defiant insignia:

and now the sounds
crackle with mica glitterings,
rasp with cinder,
call with the oboe calm of rose quartz:

and now the sounds
are bone flutes, echo
from deepest canyon, sounds
only the earliest, palest stars may hear:

and now the sounds
are black. Are black sounds.
Black. The deep song
delves.

Conversation in Moscow

Red wine
        from the
                Black Sea.
                        Glasses
filled and refilled,
Georgian shishkebab has been eaten,
                        plates pushed back, voices
of other diners surround us—

Sometimes the five of us speak at once, so much is lost, we are all
in our forties, it is perhaps ten at night—

the woman who is
                our interpreter
                knows, she knows
poignantly: now is the night she must speak for us—

People look round to see who's come in, all
members of the tribe of the word. Chairs are pushed back,
                          swing door
lets out moments of kitchen clatter—
                  She knows she must *be*
each of us turn by turn and
each at once.

I see their eyes:

The fat poet I barely know, but surely
love,
who pours the wine
quietly, his eyes
kind, small, and sorrowful.
Blue, blue eyes in a tanned face, the veriest *azure* eyes
I've looked to ever: the poet's trusted friend; historian,
fresh from the re-examined lives of the Nihilists.

(Will you have ice cream?—the waiters
returning and leaving again)—

                Pale eyes of the biologist, pale face,
white beard,
though not old. He's O.K.,
a good guy—
but the others
know things he doesn't know.
He has
an aura of limits . . .

And I, I'm looking
from one to the other, trying to read
language in gesture, grasping
what Russian words I know, turning
to her who so often
looks either acutely anxious or deeply amused—
my sister the medium-interpretress! Oracle!—to give me
what these brothers are saying (for there's a spirit
has touched us, pulled us
suddenly close).

             Frown-lines and laugh-lines leave her face,
she is looking
          upward through smoke to the high ceiling,
              and through it
                searching—

'Each cell,' the biologist says, 'has in it
the whole body's potential.'

(And I think of the module, of detail
giving to inscape its signature, the great
web of analogy)—
but it seems he implies
some kind of determinism (I've been saying
I don't see *enough* communism here, no struggling toward
a classless society). Communism to him
is only the best we can do
with the historic, the social, shell, in which
the creature lives
                    unregenerate.
                              The historian faults him,
but I lose that, people come by, greetings exchanged—

Red wine from the black sea.
She searches
and finds the eloquent, accurate words of translation: the poet now
out of his stillness is talking: 'Poems,' he says,
'poems are of two kinds: those with mystery,
                              those without mystery.'
'And are poems without mystery poems at all?' 'Well . . . yes;
one cannot say
a poem wellmade, effective, but unmysterious,
has no value. But for myself—
I prefer the mysterious . . .'
                    'And Dostoyevsky—
why is it he, who's so often
clearly reactionary, pessimistic, all for
personal redemption and against
common action—antirevolutionary!—why is it he's
the 19th-century writer I see is most read, most loved,
in the Soviet Union?—Whereas Turgeniev, for instance,
whose work surely—(I think of the *Sportsman's Sketches* especially)—'
'*Ah*! But Dostoyevsky!' (Historian and poet, both are speaking)
'Who reached as he did into the hot and strange—'
                              'the cold and shadowy—'
'the intricate depths of life? We read him—'
                              'We read him because:
in him—'
          '—in him we know
our own darknesses and illuminations,
tortures and ecstasies: our human reality.'

Tea in glasses. Thick black coffee. Vodka? Vodka.
'To *Serve the People*,' I venture, 'is often thought of
—wrongly, narrowly—merely as mutual encouragement.
But to serve the people in truth one must do, I think,
what Pasternak said one must do: *excel oneself
in order to be oneself*.'
                                'To serve the people,' (the poet again
holds us in his hands, we are listening shells to whom
a heartbeat speaks),
                                'to serve the people
one must write for the ideal reader. Only for the ideal reader.
And who or what is that ideal reader? God. One must imagine,
one must deeply *imagine*
                                that great Attention.
Only so,
in lonely dialogue, can one reach—
the people.'

After our musing silences
have traveled away, each on its own road,
and returned again to this night, this place
of meeting—island of our eternity in the bustle and clatter
of passing time—now the biologist
(pale, skeptical, yet a friend: I see he's at bottom innocent
as only the trained skeptic can be,
whose imagination
is weak as fine hair) is telling,
when I've asked if anyone reads Kropotkin, that,
'Lenin said, after he'd talked for hours with Kropotkin,
What a charming old man! and shook his head, and added,
But he understands nothing. Nothing. But later Lenin sent
a train, a special train back and forth to the place where he,
the old man, lay dying, only to ask each day after him . . .'

He smiles, he is pale and gentle.
                                'To me it seems,'
I say, going slowly, waiting for her: she's ready:
'To me it seems perhaps
Kropotkin understood half
                                of what we need to know,
and Lenin perhaps
knew half, and true revolution . . . true revolution
must put these two halves together?'

A flash
of sapphire!
I hear
the historian's words, and understand them,
and wonder:
my woman friend
repeats in English, 'How young! How pure!'

I'm abashed, though he is speaking
without mockery, almost tenderly.
'I young, pure? Why, I'm two years older
than our friend here, the poet . . . And what have I spoken of
but doubts, of perplexity?'
'Human doubts, human longing,' he utters the words
solemnly,—'human longing
for ineffable justice and mercy:
in these lies purity
and the worth of men's lives—
new as a birch bud in spring.'

His mind has touched, moved into and out of,
as if into seacarved hollows bristling with hidden spines,
venomous tentacles,
the life of Nechaev,
killer, shaman. He has known
the sacrament of the absolute.

And then he says,
'In the end
we must follow Christ.' 'Is he joking?'—
I turn to my woman friend again, confused.
'No. No,' the historian says, understanding my question,
'I am not joking. I'm speaking
of spirit. Not dogma but spirit. The Way.'

(Not the corrupt Church—
bejeweled priests with dirty beards
prostrating themselves before the atrocious Czars—
its indispensable beggars encrusting the entrances
of every shrine, kissing with pus
the infinite insensibility of relics.

Not this but
the frail trust we have
when our hearts flutter, and we look
each to each,
and our eyes hold.

                  The Way.)
And the poet—it's midnight, the room is half empty, soon
                  we must part—
the poet, his presence
ursine and kind, shifting his weight in a chair too small for him,
quietly says, and shyly: 'The Poet
          never must lose despair.'
Then our eyes indeed
meet and hold.
        All of us know, smiling
in common knowledge—
even the palest spirit among us, burdened
as he is with weight of abstractions—
        all of us know he means
we mustn't, any of us, lose touch with the source,
pretend it's not there, cover over
the mineshaft of passion
         despair somberly tolls its bell
             from the depths of,

and wildest joy
sings out of too,
      flashing
        the scales of its laughing improbable music,

grief and delight entwined in the dark down there.

'The Poem Rising By Its Own Weight'

The poet is at the disposal of his own night.
        Jean Cocteau

The singing robes fly onto your body and cling there silkily,
you step out on the rope and move unfalteringly across it,

and seize the fiery knives unscathed and
keep them spinning above you, a fountain

of rhythmic rising, falling, rising
flames,

and proudly let the chains
be wound about you, ready
to shed them, link by steel link,
padlock by padlock—

                    but when your graceful
confident shrug and twist drives the metal
into your flesh and the python grip of it tightens
and you see rust on the chains and blood in your pores
and you roll
over and down a steepness into a dark hole
and there is not even the sound of mockery in the distant air
somewhere above you where the sky was,
no sound but your own breath panting:
then it is that the miracle
walks in, on his swift feet,
down the precipice straight into the cave,
opens the locks,
knots of chain fall open,
twists of chain unwind themselves,
links fall asunder,
in seconds there is a heap of scrap-
metal at your ankles, you step free and at once
he turns to go—

but as you catch at him with a cry,
clasping his knees, sobbing your gratitude,
with what radiant joy he turns to you,
and raises you to your feet,
and strokes your disheveled hair,
and holds you,
               holds you,
                    holds you
close and tenderly before he vanishes.

499

EIGHT

Prayer for Revolutionary Love

That a woman not ask a man to leave meaningful work to follow her.
That a man not ask a woman to leave meaningful work to follow him.

That no one try to put Eros in bondage.
But that no one put a cudgel in the hands of Eros.

That our loyalty to one another and our loyalty to our work
not be set in false conflict.

That our love for each other give us love for each other's work.
That our love for each other's work give us love for one another.

That our love for each other's work give us love for one another.
That our love for each other give us love for each other's work.

That our love for each other, if need be,
give way to absence. And the unknown.

That we endure absence, if need be,
without losing our love for each other.
Without closing our doors to the unknown.

Modes of Being
for Nguyen Cong Hoan

January's fist
unclenches.
        Walls of brick
are bastions of coral, welltempered, basking,
and shadows yawn and
stretch to the east.
            Watching the afternoon,
from the window watching it slowly brim
and not spill, not yet, into evening,
soothes and gives pleasure.

Near Saigon,
in a tiger-cage, a man
tries to stretch out his hand
and cannot.

Indoors, reading, talking,
we reach and enter
               a new landscape of knowledge,
as if coming through a high mountain pass together,
that wonder of other flora, different
ways of constructing rooves and
terracing fields, the haymakers
dressed differently.
               What more
can love be than epiphany!

Near Saigon,
in a tiger-cage, a woman
tries to straighten her cramped spine
and cannot.

Unclenched fist,
cinnamon warmth of winter light,
revelation, communion . . .
Unable
          to know for long
what we know; neither intense love
nor intense pain. Nature itself
allows the delight of sparrows
ruffling an inchdeep lake of rain
in the jailhouse yard.
                    Joy
is real, torture
is real, we strain to hold
a bridge between them open,
and fail,
or all but fail.

Near Saigon, in cages
made in America, jailers
force fluid down the prisoners' throats,
stomp on their swollen bellies.
This has been happening

for a long time.
This is happening
now, while I write, January
nineteen seventy-four.

What wings, what mighty arch
of feathered hollow bones, beyond
span of albatross or eagle,
mind and heart must grow
                    to touch, trembling,
with outermost pinion tips,
not in alternation but both at once,
in one
violent eternal instant
that which is and
that which is . . .

A Letter to Marek about a Photograph
for Mark Pawlak

This carpentered, unpainted, aging house,
one of many alike in some white ghetto,
is filled to the uninsulated seams with a face:
the brooding face of anxiety.   —Or the house
(one cannot say which is
superimposed on the other) is so montaged,
waking and sleeping, into that mind, it is
the house fills the outgazing head,
extends its boundaries with wooden angles.
                    And the face
is the face of your father, Marek,
a Polish workman, or of his brother, or—
for, beardless and hair dragged back,
it could be the face of a woman—your mother,
your grandmother in the 1930s,
just staying off the breadline . . .
any young woman quickly grown old, forehead
deeply wrinkled, eyes unable to laugh. Whatever else
—store-boughten furnishings, tawdry treasures, stories—
is inside the house, at the door

that *look* looks out,
worry without hope.
                    But the house itself
though cheaply built, has its share of ornaments turned on the lathe
of humor and trust, a human, unique
identity fronting the weather. In houses like these
your family of millions, Polacks, Wops,
Scotch-Irish, people shut now into 'projects,'
used to live. You would have known its
familiar mystery, its faint, sour charm,
even by dark, even before you had seen
its fretted gable, Marek:
your in-feeling comprehension
would touch with probing finger
the concealed wounds of those who built,
those who dwelt, those who moved on
or died here. Your gift is to reveal
poetry in the cries caught in nameless throats,
in eyes gazing into the street of trouble,
and foolish tender joys suspended
in half-light of memory; to lift
griefs out of the blind pit of unknowing,
placing glass and mercury under the tongue of dreams—
magical quick-
silver that measures
the fever it is to be human.

Room

> *for D. Mitchell and D. Hass*

Shelf of worn, chipped, exquisite china oddments,
for daily use.
Baskets, for fruit, potatoes, shopping.
Stove with grill where David
makes such good brown toast.
Left of the sink, above the counter,
Mary Wollstonecraft, fair face, dark shadows, energy.
Slightly unsteady, the small table. Notes to each other,
and soon, when David and David come home,
strong cups of tea.

It's the kitchen, its window viewless,
and not the handsome calm of the living room,
I find myself in, at peace,
though the presence across the hall of
that room too is part of being here:
the threadbare gracious carpet,
surreal romances of the Victorian *découpage* screen,
poplars and oaks and sunsets the large windows look to.
Afternoon, an ample easy quiet.
                                        But it breaks

sharply: the Davids
have moved, all the objects
stand at new angles, a kitchen I've never seen,
light from another compass point.
This room, my refuge, is nowhere but in my mind,
more blurred for them than for me, their memories
too many to sift and focus. 'Bees of the invisible,'
take this nectar, transform it, internalize it! If I lose
the knowledge of this place,
my soul shall be diminished. There is a song in all
humankind, that rooms, houses, parks, streets, fields
and particular corners of fields, rivers and certain
eye-span reaches of rivers, are notes in, as people are.
Give me the power
to sound this note, the disappeared-
as-if-torn-down, but clear, cool, tranquil kitchen
on Downside Crescent present in me,
a place to *be* in, not pretending
no tears were shed in it, no hard words ever shouted,
no gray mornings caught in the small mirror over the sink—
but seeing despite that, precisely because of that,
(grief not being turned away, a place
made for grief to be) one could
be there, and breathe easy, uncrowded.
A note or chord of notes
sustained, hushing, recurrent
in the stream of song.

Voyage

for Barbara Fussiner and Richard Edelman

Fluttering strips of paper strung on cord
tied to the ship's rail.
Each inscribed.
Read them:

'How deep the waves' blue!'

'How bright the foam!'

'Wind and light
sparkle together!'

'How the sea's plumage
preens itself!'

These are prayers.
To celebrate,
not to beseech.
Among them, leaning
toward the water, we voyage,
are voyaged, seeing.
We share among us
the depth of day, are borne
through it
swiftly as arcs of spray.

Salt glitters
on our lips,
on ruffled paper. Soon
the words will fly on their torn strips
beyond vision.

        Silent, smiling, receiving
joyfully what we are given,
we utter
each to each
our absolute presence.

NINE

Waving to the Devil

Tasted (and spat out)
Satan's Boletus.
Delicious!

Consulting the Oracle

I asked a blind man the way east,
because I'd not seen him,
not looked before asking.
He smiled, and walked on,
sure of his felt way,
silent.

The Life of Others

Their high pitched baying
as if in prayer's unison

remote, undistracted, given over
utterly to belief,

the skein of geese
voyages south,
                hierarchic arrow of its convergence toward
                the point of grace
swinging and rippling, ribbon tail
of a kite, loftily

over lakes where they have not
elected to rest,

over men who suppose
earth is man's, over golden earth

preparing itself
for night and winter.
                        We humans
are smaller than they, and crawl
unnoticed,

about and about the smoky map.

Freedom

Perhaps we humans
have wanted God most as witness
to acts of choice
made in solitude. Acts of mercy,
of sacrifice. Wanted
that great single eye to see us,
steadfast as we flowed by.
Yet there are other acts
not even vanity,
or anxious hope to please, knows of—
bone doings, leaps of nerve, heart-
cries of communion: if there is bliss,
it has
been already
and will be; out-
reaching, utterly.
Blind
to itself, flooded
with otherness.

The Freeing of the Dust

Unwrap the dust from its mummycloths.
Let Ariel learn
a blessing for Caliban
and Caliban drink dew from the lotus
open upon the waters.
Bitter the slow

river water: dew
shall wet his lips with light.
Let the dust
float, the wrappings too
are dust.
         Drift upon the stir
of air, of dark
river: ashes of what had lived,
         or seeds
       of ancient sesame,
        or namelessly
pure dust that is all
in all.   Bless,
weightless Spirit. Drink,
Caliban, push your tongue
heavy into the calyx.

The Wealth of the Destitute

How gray and hard the brown feet of *the wretched of the earth*.
How confidently the crippled from birth
push themselves through the streets, deep in their lives.
How seamed with lines of fate the hands
of women who sit at streetcorners
offering seeds and flowers.
How lively their conversation together.
How much of death they know.
I am tired of 'the fine art of unhappiness.'

LIFE IN THE FOREST

"We work in the dark. We do what we can.
We give what we have. Our doubt is our passion.
Our passion is our task. The rest is the madness of art."

Henry James

HOMAGE TO PAVESE

Human Being

Human being—walking
in doubt from childhood on: walking

a ledge of slippery stone in the world's woods
deep-layered with wet leaves—rich or sad: on one
side of the path, ecstasy, on the other
dull grief.   Walking

the mind's imperial cities, roofed-over alleys,
                              thoroughfares, wide boulevards
that hold evening primrose of sky in steady calipers.

Always the mind
walking, working, stopping sometimes to kneel
in awe of beauty, sometimes leaping, filled with the energy
of delight, but never able to pass
the wall, the wall
of brick that crumbles and is replaced,
of twisted iron,
of rock,
the wall that speaks, saying monotonously:

       Children and animals
                  who cannot learn
       anything from suffering,
       suffer, are tortured, die
       in incomprehension.

This human being, each night nevertheless
summoning—with a breath blown at a flame,
                              or hand's touch
on the lamp-switch—darkness,
                              silently utters,
impelled as if by a need to cup the palms
and drink from a river,
                    the words, 'Thanks.

Thanks for this day, a day of my life.'

                              And wonders.

Pulls up the blankets, looking
into nowhere, always in doubt.
And takes strange pleasure
in having repeated once more the childish formula,
a pleasure in what is seemly.
And drifts to sleep, downstream
on murmuring currents of doubt and praise,
the wall shadowy, that tomorrow
will cast its own familiar, chill, clear-cut shadow
into the day's brilliance.

Writing to Aaron

. . . after three years—a 3-decker novel
in fifteen pages? Which beginning
to begin with? 'Since I saw you last,
the doctor has prescribed me artificial tears,
a renewable order . . . ' But that leaves out
the real ones. Shall I write about them?
What about comedy, laughter, good news?
'I live in a different house now,
but can give you news
of most of the same people . . .' That ignores
the significance of the house, its tone of voice,
and the sentence by sentence
unfolding of lives into chapters.
'Your last letter told about sand-dunes in winter,
and having the sea to yourself.
Beautiful; I read it to the strangers
in whose midst I was at the time.
And that's the way we lost touch for so long,
my response was the reading aloud
instead of a letter,
and we both moved house—
a shifting of sand underfoot . . .'

Well, I could echo
the sound of facts, their weather—

thunderclaps, rain hitting stone, rattle of windows.
And spaces would represent sunlight,
when the wind gave over and everyone rested
between the storms.
Or chronological narrative? 'In the spring
of '73,' . . . 'That summer,'
'By then it was fall . . .'
      All or nothing—
and that would be nothing,
dust, parchment dried up, invisible ink.
Maybe I'll leave the whole story
for you to imagine,
telling you only, 'A year ago,
I said farewell to that poplar you will remember,
that gave us its open secret,
pressed on us all we could grasp, and more,
of vibrating, silvergreen being,
a tree tripping over its phrases in haste,
eloquent aspen.'

I know you know
it took my farewell for granted:
what it had given, it would never take back.
I know you know
about partings, tears, eyedrops, revisions, dwellings, discoveries,
mine or yours; those are the glosses,
Talmudic tractates, a lifetime's study. The Word itself
is what we heard, and shall always hear, each leaf
imprinted, syllables in our lives.

The Cabdriver's Smile

Tough guy. Star of David
and something in Hebrew—a motto—
hang where Catholics used to dangle
St. Christopher (now discredited).
No smile. White hair. American-born,
I'd say, maybe the Bronx.
When another cab pulls alongside
at a light near the Midtown Tunnel, and its driver

rolls down his window and greets this guy
with a big happy face and a first-name greeting,
he bows like a king, a formal acknowledgement,
and to me remarks,
                              deadpan,
            'Seems to think he knows me.'

'You mean you don't know him?'— I lean forward laughing,
close to the money-window,
                                   'Never seen him before in my life.'
Something like spun steel floats invisible, until questions strike it,
all round him, the way light gleams webs among grass in fall.
And on we skim
in silence past the cemeteries, into
the airport, ahead of time. He's beat
the afternoon traffic. I tip him well.
A cool acceptance. Cool? It's
cold as ice.

            Yet I've seen,
squinting to read his license,
how he smiled—timidly?—anyway,
smiled, as if hoping to please,
at the camera. My heart
stabs me. Somewhere this elderly
close-mouthed skeptic hides
longing and hope. Wanted
—immortalized for the cops, for his fares, for the world—
to be looking his best.

Nightingale Road

How gold their hair was,
and how their harps
and sweet voices called out into the valley
summer nights!

The boys black-haired,
coming home black with coal dust, same as us all,
but milk-skinned when they'd had their wash.

One of the boys, Arthur,
went down the pit the first time
same day as me.

And the girls—that gold hair
twining like pea-vine tendrils,
and even the youngest could play her harp.

Up on the mountain their house was,
up Nightingale Street, and then as you leave the village
it's Nightingale Road.
Mother and father, the three boys
and the six girls; all of them singing,
you'd think the gates of Heaven were open.

And funny thing—
the T.B. didn't stop them
each one, till a few weeks only
before it took them.
One by one
the whole family went, though.

Oh, but the sound was fine!
I'd be a young boy, lying awake,
and I'd smell my Mam's
honeysuckle she'd got growing
up the house wall, and I'd hear them singing,
a regular choir they were,
and the harps rippling out

and somehow as I'd be falling asleep
I couldn't tell which was the music
and which was that golden hair they had,
and all with that milky skin. The voices
sweet and gold and shrill and the harps
flowing like milk.

S. Wales, circa *1890*

Chekhov on the West Heath

for Jim McConkey
who spurred me into writing it
and for Rebecca Garnett
who was and is 'Bet'

A young girl in a wheelchair,
another girl pushing the chair.
Up from Heath Mansions they go,
past the long brick wall of the Fenton House garden.
The invalid girl's hands move as she speaks, delicately,
describing the curve of a cloud.
The other, younger one comes into focus;
how could I know so well
the back of my own head? I could touch the hair
of the long plait . . . Ah,
that's it: the young girl painting
in Corot's *L'Atelier*, upright, absorbed,
whose face we don't see. *There I am,*
I thought, the first time I saw it,
startled.
Up through small streets they go,
the crest of the hill, a stonesthrow of unpaved lane,
and out to the terrace: a few
lopsided benches, tussocky grass,
and the great billowing prospect north.
This is Hampstead. This
is Judge's Walk. It is nineteen hundred
and forty-one.
The war? They take it for granted;
it was predicted while they were children,
and has come to pass. It means
no more ballet school, Betty is ill,
I am beginning to paint in oils.
The war is simply
how the world is, to which they were born.
They share
the epiphanies of their solitudes,
hardly knowing or speaking to anyone else
their own age. They have not discovered men
or sex at all. But daily
they live! Live

intensely. Mysterious fragrance
gentles the air
under the black poplars.
And Bet, looking off towards hawthorn and willow,
middle-distance of valley and steep small hills,
says she would like to bounce
from one round-topped tree to another,
in the spring haze.

Often and often, as they talk and gaze,
that year and the next,
                              Chekhov is with them.
With us.
          The small, dark-green volumes.
          The awkward, heroic versions.
We're not systematic,
we don't even *try* to read all of them, held secure
in conviction of endless largesse.

                              Bet's glinting hair
in tendrils around her face. Her hands
thin. A spirit
woven of silk, has grown in her, as if bodily strength,
dwindling, had been a cocoon,
                              and only by this strange weakness
could her intelligence be freed, that instructs
the poet in me.
Alone at home, in between visits, I write, paint,
read and read, practice *Für Elise* with feeling
                              (and too much pedal)
help with the housework or shirk it,
and wait.
What did he say to us, Chekhov? Who was this Chekhov
pacing the round of the Whitestone Pond,
his hand on the chair coming down Heath Street,
telling the tale of Kashtanka in the gloomy sickroom
back at Heath Mansions?
                              Ah, even though
the dark gaze of youth
swaddled us,
          while airraids and news of battle
were part of each ominous day, and in flashes of dread

we glimpsed invasion, England and Europe gone down
utterly into the nightmare;
                              even though Bet
was fading, month by month, and no one knew why—
we were open to life and hope: it was that he gave us,
generous, precise, lifting us
into the veins of a green leaf, translucent,
setting our hearts' tinder alight,
                              sun striking on glass to release
the latent flames.

When the Black Monk
swiftly drew near, a whirlwind column grown from a pinpoint
to giant size, then—shrinking to human measure,
and passing inaudibly—moved through the solid trees
to vanish like smoke,
                              we thrilled to the presence of a power,
unquestioning. We knew
everything and nothing, nothing and everything.
Glimpsing a verity we could not define,
we saw that the story is not about illusion,
it's about what is true: 'the great garden
    with its miraculous flowers,
    the pines with their shaggy roots,
    the ryefield, marvellous science, youth,
    daring, joy . . .' That was the Chekhov we knew.

And the betrothed girl, who listens and listens
to a different and useful life calling her, and *does*
wrench herself free and go to study—and more,
comes back and *again* frees herself, journeying forth
(because a man dying, who himself
could not be free, gave her
his vision) into the hard, proto-revolutionary future,
her step forward for all of us,
as his words were for her—she was the Chekhov
who slipped unrecognized into our dreaming days.
She was at Bet's side when Bet,
a woman with grown children, so changed
from the girl in the wheelchair, a woman alone
with years of struggle behind her, sturdy—
yet still afraid—began, in spite of her fear,
to learn to teach. And at *my* side

in Berkeley, Boston, Washington, when we held our line
before advancing troopers, or sang out, 'Walk,
don't run,' retreating from gas and billyclubs, trying to learn
to act in the world.
    She, The Betrothed,
whose marriage was not with her fiancé but with her life's
need to grow, to work for Chekhov's
        'Holy of holies—the human body, health, intelligence,
        inspiration, love,
        and the most absolute
        freedom from violence and lying'—she
was the Chekhov we knew.

                    What he would mean to us
we still can know only in part. (What has the Heath,
which Bet has lived close to always, and I,
through decades away, never quite lost sight of,
meant in our lives? A place of origin
gives and gives, as we return to it,
bringing our needs.) What he has meant
and goes on meaning, can't be trapped
into closed definition. But it has to do
not with failure, defeat, frustration,
Moscows never set out for,
but with love.
        The sharp steel
of his scorn for meanness and cruelty gleamed
over our sheltered heads only half-noticed,
and irony was beyond our grasp,
we couldn't laugh with him; nevertheless
some inkling of rectitude and compassion
came to us, breathed in
under the fragrant leaves in wartime London, to endure
somewhere throughout the tumult of years. How, in our crude,
vague, dreamy ignorance could we recognize
    'the subtle, elusive beauty of human grief'?
Yet from between the dark green bindings
it rose, wafting into us, ready
to bide its time. The man who imagined a ring
inscribed with the words, 'Nothing passes,'
that rich man's son whom the townsfolk called 'Small Gain,'
who suffered loss after loss, and was
                        'left with the past,'

he too—for beyond despair
he carried in him the seed of change, the vision,
seeing not only *what is* but *what might be*—
he too was the Chekhov we knew, unknowing.

                        As we looked out
into the haze from that open height
familiar to Keats and Constable in their day—
a place built not only of earth but of layers
of human response, little hill
in time, in history—
your smile, Chekhov, 'tender, delightful, ironic,'
looked over our shoulders; and still looks, now,
half of our lifetime gone by, or more,
till we turn to see
who you were, who you are, everpresent, vivid,
luminous dust.

A Woman Meets an Old Lover

'He with whom I ran hand in hand
kicking the leathery leaves down Oak Hill Path
thirty years ago,

appeared before me with anxious face, pale,
almost unrecognized, hesitant,
lame.

He whom I cannot remember hearing laugh out loud
but see in mind's eye smiling, self-approving,
wept on my shoulder.

He who seemed always
to take and not give, who took me
so long to forget,

remembered everything I had so long forgotten.'

520

A Woman Alone

When she cannot be sure
which of two lovers it was with whom she felt
this or that moment of pleasure, of something fiery
streaking from head to heels, the way the white
flame of a cascade streaks a mountainside
seen from a car across a valley, the car
changing gear, skirting a precipice,
climbing . . .
When she can sit or walk for hours after a movie
talking earnestly and with bursts of laughter
with friends, without worrying
that it's late, dinner at midnight, her time
spent without counting the change . . .
When half her bed is covered with books
and no one is kept awake by the reading light
and she disconnects the phone, to sleep till noon . . .
Then
selfpity dries up, a joy
untainted by guilt lifts her.
She has fears, but not about loneliness;
fears about how to deal with the aging
of her body—how to deal
with photographs and the mirror. She feels
so much younger and more beautiful
than she looks. At her happiest
—or even in the midst of
some less than joyful hour, sweating
patiently through a heatwave in the city
or hearing the sparrows at daybreak, dully gray,
toneless, the sound of fatigue—
a kind of sober euphoria makes her believe
in her future as an old woman, a wanderer,
seamed and brown,
little luxuries of the middle of life all gone,
watching cities and rivers, people and mountains,
without being watched; not grim nor sad,
an old winedrinking woman, who knows
the old roads, grass-grown, and laughs to herself . . .
She knows it can't be:
that's Mrs. Doasyouwouldbedoneby from
                                        The Water-Babies,

no one can walk the world any more,
a world of fumes and decibels.
But she thinks maybe
she could get to be tough and wise, some way,
anyway. Now at least
she is past the time of mourning,
now she can say without shame or deceit,
O blessèd Solitude.

A Young Man Travelling

He is scared of the frankness of women
which attracts and, when he draws near to listen,
may repulse or ignore him. This morning
in lazy sunlight's veil of clear and pale honey
poured from the sky's blue spoon,
they were laughing, talking over coffee about
misadventures, lovers, their own bodies,
and didn't stop when he came to join them, stepping
from indoor shade onto the charmed
and dappled stone ground of their terrace.

If any one of them had been
alone there, surely
his presence would have changed her,
he'd have seen that flicker, the putting aside
of her solitude to make room for him?
Together they seem almost blind to him.

Later, when they have gone to see bubbles of glass
blown into phantasmagoric precisions,
he takes a gondola, sliding past the palazzos,
and counts bridges. It's not (he thinks to himself
at some dark place in his mind, an intersection
of narrow seldom-navigated canals) that I want
their entire attention: that would demand—oh,
a response
nothing assures me I can give.
It's that when I see
their creature freedom, the way they can

fling themselves into the day!—as I,
being a strong swimmer, fling myself sometimes
into the ocean off a sailboat:
then I envy them.

If they had stopped (he wonders)
when I came out to their table,
interrupted themselves to acknowledge me alien,
would I have felt more excluded or less?
Their frankness, their uninterrupted friendship,
the sunlight lacing their hair, their
bright clothes, the three of them, their eyes
friendly but without mercy, without
the mercy of distance . . . When they
admit me, passing the creamjug,
to their laughter, laughter and even
   the confession of their own
troubles, about which they speak
so simply, so freely,
I am afraid.

The gondola shoots back out
as if with a sighing triumph into the breadth
and glitter of the Grand Canal,
the golden façades, vaporetti bustling,
pigeons wheeling up from the piazza.
He pays the silent gondolier, to whom
he has nothing to say, no way
to convince him he is a person,
and lands, to stroll
back to the hotel, back to wait
till the women return,
drawn by what he fears.

Fellow Passengers

A handsome fullgrown child, he seems,
in his well-chosen suit and wedding-ring,
hair not too long or short, taking
a business trip, surely one of his first—

listening enthralled to the not-much-older
bearded man in the window seat,
a returned mercenary, bragging of Africa:
bronzed, blondish, imperial pirate
half audible, thrillingly, under the jet's monotonous
subdued growling.

The baby businessman, naïf, laughs, excitement
springing from him in little splashes—his aura
fragmented—at a whiff of
soiled romance. It is something morbid
that flutters his dark thick lashes, gestures
with such well-cared-for hands,

hands his young wife
must want to bite, when they fumble,
innocent and impatient,
at her tense thighs.

May 1976

A Mystery (Oaxaca, Mexico)

A gust of night rain lightly
sweeps the dusty *Zócalo*, and the moon is down.
Mariachis are wrapping soft old cloths
around their instruments, and laying them reverently
in dingy cases, the way peasant grandsons
wrap ancient grandmothers,

                     laying them back in their cribs.
The last tourists, watched by waiters whose features
are carved by obsidian knives to regard
bloodsacrifice, are on the move
under the *portales*, pushing back chairs,
draining a last *cerveza Moctezuma*, leaving
here a forgotten *US News*, there
                   a half-full pack of Luckies
some beer spilled on;
            and the sound of their voices,
Texans, New Englanders, hippies from California,

all the same to him, nasal and familiar, dwindles
as they scatter to sleep or sex or cards
or whatever the *yanquis* do by night.
Decades he has passed
back and forth and around and back and forth
in this square; and always the weight
of many *serapes*, heavy, and in the sun, hot,
on his shoulder. Of course he makes sales,
he spreads out the topmost one so they can see
the whole design. Some ignore him, some
wave him away, some he knows and nods to sometimes, they come
year after year and no longer buy, but they once did or still might—
but always there are some new ones, eager, easily impressed—yes,
he sells, he is not poor—no, looking around him he can see that
                                        anyone
looking from him to the shoeshine men, even,
not to speak of the barefoot boys with trays of quivering
ruby and gold and emerald *gelatinas*,
or the women nursing their babies down in the dust, ignoring
the ceaseless buzzing of wasps that are drunk all day
on candied fruits that sell by the piece,
women who take home scarcely the price of supper—
anyone looking from them to him can see he's not poor,
as poor goes. He's in business,
that's how he likes to think of himself. But still
he keeps walking, leaning always a bit
to one side from the weight.
                        He can't remember
his boyhood well. When he was young there was
                        something he wanted badly,
some desire that flamed in his eyes once,
like a spiralling saint's-day star it was,
rising from the heart when someone, something,
put a match to it . . . What was it? He's calm, but there's something
he can't remember.

The *tejedoras*, weavers,
Trixe women from the mountains, who all day
sit at work in the *Alameda* under the trees,
have gone with their little looms, their children, the two or three men
who come down from their villages with them, gone for the night
to sleep wherever they sleep.

The dome of the bandstand gleams, rainsprinkled, lit
by the tall street-lamps whose light
is somehow more silent and steady than darkness.
Here and there, now, one can see a few grayish figures
that have not left for the night's rest
but have begun to take it, tucked
as best they can into the angle of wall and sidewalk
or, if they dare, in a doorway,
some drunk, some homeless, all, certainly
of a poverty he has no truck with. Still,
he keeps walking. The bells of two unsynchronized
clocks are ringing:—eleven—midnight. A dog's howling
down by the market somewhere. The chairs and tables
from the cafés on three sides of the *Zócalo*
have been taken in or stacked—the fourth side,
floodlit, elegant, menacing, guarded always, is The Police,
The Government—a palace.
                              There's no-one
to whom to open the topmost *serape*,
outshaking its firm folds, to display
a god, a bird, a geometry some say
has some intention. No one to speak to. '*Este jardín
es suyo. Cuídelo,*' say the signs among grass and flowers;
deterrent branches of thorns have been strewn on the neat parterres.
                                                        A stranger,
crossing the *Zócalo* at a distance, solitary, glances his way.
He doesn't know that the stranger thinks,
'Doesn't the old man ever long
simply to put down his weight of woven wool
and lie down? Lie down and rest?
Here, anywhere, now,
and be still? He's been carrying through the years
a nest of blankets, a bed—heavier
than I can imagine . . . If that temptation were mine,
what could keep me walking, walking,
always carrying my wares? I'd lie down
as if in the snow . . .'

The 90th Year

for Lore Segal

High in the jacaranda shines the gilded thread
of a small bird's curlicue of song—too high
for her to see or hear.
                              I've learned
not to say, these last years,
'O, look!—O, listen, Mother!'
as I used to.

                   (It was she
who taught me to look;
to name the flowers when I was still close to the ground,
my face level with theirs;
or to watch the sublime metamorphoses
unfold and unfold
over the walled back gardens of our street . . .

It had not been given her
to know the flesh as good in itself,
as the flesh of a fruit is good. To her
the human body has been a husk,
a shell in which souls were prisoned.
Yet, from within it, with how much gazing
her life has paid tribute to the world's body!
How tears of pleasure
would choke her, when a perfect voice,
deep or high, clove to its note unfaltering!)

She has swept the crackling seedpods,
the litter of mauve blossoms, off the cement path,
tipped them into the rubbish bucket.
She's made her bed, washed up the breakfast dishes,
wiped the hotplate. I've taken the butter and milkjug
back to the fridge next door—but it's not my place,
visiting here, to usurp the tasks
that weave the day's pattern.
Now she is leaning forward in her chair,
          by the lamp lit in the daylight,
rereading *War and Peace*.
                              When I look up

from her wellworn copy of *The Divine Milieu*,
which she wants me to read, I see her hand
loose on the black stem of the magnifying glass,
she is dozing.
'I am so tired,' she has written to me, 'of appreciating
the gift of life.'

A Daughter (I)

When she was in the strangers' house—
    good strangers, almost relatives, good house,
    so familiar, known for twenty years,
    its every sound at once, and without thought,
    interpreted:
                but alien, deeply alien—
when she was there last week, part of her wanted
only to leave. It said, *I must escape*—no,
crudely, in the vernacular: *I gotta get outta here*,
it said.

And part of her
ached for her mother's pain,
her dying here—at home, yet far away from home,
thousands of miles of earth and sea, and ninety years
from her roots. The daughter's one happiness
during the brief visit that might be her last
(no, last but one: of course there would always be
what had stood for years at the end of some highway of
factual knowledge, a terminal wall;
there would be words to deal with: funeral, burial, disposal
                  of effects;
the books to pack up)—her one happiness *this* time
was to water her mother's treasured, fenced-in garden,
a Welsh oasis where she remembers adobe rubble
two decades ago. Will her mother now
ever rise from bed, walk out of her room, see if her yellow rose
has bloomed again?
Rainbows, the dark earthfragrance, the whisper of
                  arched spray:
the pleasure goes back

to the London garden, forty, fifty years ago,
her mother younger than *she* is now.
And back in the north, watering the blue ajuga
                    (far from beginnings too, but it's a place
                    she's chosen as home)
the daughter knows
another, hidden part of her longed—or longs—
for her mother to be her mother again,
consoling, judging, forgiving,
whose arms were once
                    strong to hold her and rock her,
who used to chant
                    a ritual song that did magic
to take away hurt. Now mother is child, helpless; her mind
is clear, her spirit proud, she can even laugh—
but half-blind, half-deaf, and struck down
in body, she's a child in being at the mercy
of looming figures who have the power
to move her, feed her, wash her, leave or stay
at will. And the daughter feels, with horror,
metamorphosed: *she's* such a looming figure—huge—a tower
of iron and ice—love
shrunken in her to a cube of pain
locked in her throat. O, long and long ago
she grew up and went
away and away—and now's bereft
of tears and unable
to comfort the child her mother's become.
Instead, by the bedside, briskly, nervously,
carries out doctor's orders;
                    or travelling endlessly
in the air-conditioned sameness of jet-plane efficiency,
withdraws into lonely distance
(the patient left in the best of hands).

Watering the blue ajuga in her Boston yard
she imagines her mother may, after all,
be needing her—should she have left?
Imagines her mother at six years old in the riverfield,
twelve years old in her orphan's mourning,
twenty, forty, eighty—the storied screen unfolding,
told and told——and the days untold. A life!

A life—ninetythree years unique in the aeons.
She wants to go back to Mexico, sit by her mother,
have her be strong and say, *Go, child, and I bless you.*
She did say it! But weakly; it wasn't enough; she wants
to hear it again and again.

But she does not go back. Remembers
herself as a monstrous, tall, swift-moving nurse.
And remembers the way
she longed to leave, while she was there,
trapped in the house of strangers.
Something within her twists and turns,
she is tired and ashamed. She sobs, but her eyes
cannot make tears. She imagines herself
entering a dark cathedral to pray, and blessedly
falling asleep there, and not wakening
for a year, for seven years, for a century.

A Daughter (II)

Heading south, above
thick golden surf of cloud.
Along the western earthcurve,
eternal sunset, a gaunt red,
crouches, a wing outstretched,
immobile.
Southward, deathward, time inside the jet
pauses. A drone of deafness—'Would you care
to purchase a cocktail?' mouthed
ritually. She clings, drink in hand,
to her isolation.

A day later begins
the witnessing. A last week of the dying.
When she inserts
quivering spoonfuls of violently
green or red *gelatina*
into the poor obedient mouth,
she knows it's futile. Hour by hour
the body that bore her

shrinks and grows colder
and suffers. But days go by, and the long nights.

Each dawn the daughter, shivering,
opens the curtained door
and steps out on the balcony; and from time to time
leans there during the days. Mornings,
emphatic sunlight seizes the bougainvillea's
dry magenta blossoms. Among sharp stones, below,
of the hospital patio,
                      an ugly litter of cigarette stubs
thrown down by visitors leaning, anxious or bored,
from other balconies. No one sweeps up.
Sobs shake her—no tears. She hates
the uncaring light.

                    Afternoons
it's better, when impetuously
the rain hurls itself earthward for an hour.
Abruptly it stops, the steep streets
are full of the voice of rivers, adobe-brown,
sky still dark for a while.

Mostly, when there's no help to be given the nurse,
no feeding, moving, changing of sheets to be done,
and vital signs have been checked once more,
she sits with her back to the light
and listens—eyes on whatever book her mind
hungrily moves in, making its way
alone, holding on—listens
to hiss of oxygen and the breathing,
still steady,
she knows will
change rhythm, change
again,
and stop.

            Some force roaming the universe,
malicious and stupid, affixed, she feels,
this postscript to so vivid a life.
This tide that does not ebb, this persistence
stuck like a plane in mournful clouds,

what can it signify?
                          is any vision
—an entrance into a garden
of recognitions and revelations, Eden
of radiant comprehensions, taking
timeless place in the wounded head, behind
the closed, or glazed half-open, eyes?
Are words of deserved joy
singing behind the sunken lips that bent
stiffly into a formal smile when the daughter arrived again,
but now shape only *no* when pain
forces them back to speech?

There are flies in the room. The daughter
busies herself, placing wet gauze
over her mother's mouth and eyes.
                          What she wants
she knows she can't have: one minute
of communion, here in limbo.
                          All the years of it,
talk, laughter, letters. Yet something
went unsaid. And there's no place
to put whatever it was, now,
no more chance.

Death in Mexico

Even two weeks after her fall,
three weeks before she died, the garden
began to vanish. The rickety fence gave way
as it had threatened, and the children threw
broken plastic toys—vicious yellow,
unresonant red, onto the path, into the lemontree;
or trotted in through the gap, trampling small plants.
For two weeks no one watered it, except
I did, twice, but then I left. She was still conscious then
and thanked me. I begged the others to water it—
but the rains began; when I got back there were violent,
sudden, battering downpours each afternoon. Weeds flourished,
dry topsoil was washed away swiftly

into the drains. Oh, there was green, still,
but the garden was disappearing—each day
less sign of the ordered,
thought-out oasis, a squared circle her mind
constructed for rose and lily, begonia
and rosemary-for-remembrance.
Twenty years in the making—
less than a month to undo itself;
and those who had seen it grow,
living around it those decades,
did nothing to hold it. Oh, Alberto did,
one day, patch up the fence a bit,
when I told him a future tenant would value
having a garden. But no one believed
the garden-maker would live (I least of all),
so her pain if she were to see the ruin
remained abstract, an incomprehensible concept,
impelling no action. When they carried her past on a stretcher,
on her way to the *sanatorio*, failing sight
transformed itself into a mercy: certainly
she could have seen no more than a greenish blur.
But to me the weeds, the flowerless rosebushes, broken
stems of the canna lilies and amaryllis, all
a lusterless jungle green, presented—
even before her dying was over—
an obdurate, blind, all-seeing gaze:
I had seen it before, in the museums,
in stone masks of the gods and victims.
A gaze that admits no tenderness; if it smiles, it
only smiles with sublime bitterness—no,
not even bitter: it admits
no regret, nostalgia has no part in its cosmos,
bitterness is irrelevant.
If it holds a flower—and it does,
a delicate brilliant silky flower that blooms only
a single day—it holds it clenched
between sharp teeth.
Vines may crawl, and scorpions, over its face,
but though the centuries blunt
eyelid and flared nostril, the stone gaze
is utterly still, fixed, absolute,
smirk of denial facing eternity.

Gardens vanish. She was an alien here,
as I am. Her death
was not Mexico's business. The garden though
was a hostage. Old gods
took back their own.

CONTINUUM

A Visit

i

Milk to be boiled
egg to be poached
pot to be scoured.

Bandage to bind
firm around old bones
cracked in a fall:

White hair to be brushed
cold feet to be warmed
gnarled toenails to cut.

When there is work to be done
moonwavering images
of sentiment and desire
ride away into the forest

and sexual songs
shake their preened wings
and fly off, casting
a few loose feathers

scarlet and purple

soon invisible.

ii

Over the mountains
lean the clouds
as if their shadows were mirrors.

Lay down poison
in the track of the ants
who devour the roses.

When there is work to do
one laughs at oneself,
the intense life of the heart
stops talking.

How frail, how small,
the body that bore me.
She too
is laughing:

'Skin and bones' she says.
'The bandage is like
a knight's armour,' she says.
'What dragons
are to be vanquished?'

Death Psalm: O Lord of Mysteries

She grew old.
She made ready to die.
She gave counsel to women and men, to young girls and young boys.
She remembered her griefs.
She remembered her happinesses.
She watered the garden.
She accused herself.
She forgave herself.
She learned new fragments of wisdom.
She forgot old fragments of wisdom.
She abandoned certain angers.
She gave away gold and precious stones.

She counted-over her handkerchiefs of fine lawn.
She continued to laugh on some days, to cry on others,
                        unfolding the design of her identity.
She practiced the songs she knew, her voice
                              gone out of tune
                 but the breathing-pattern perfected.
She told her sons and daughters she was ready.
She maintained her readiness.
She grew very old.
She watched the generations increase.
She watched the passing of seasons and years.
She did not die.

She did not die but lies half-speechless, incontinent,
                 aching in body, wandering in mind
                 in a hospital room.
A plastic tube, taped to her nose,
    disappears into one nostril.
Plastic tubes are attached to veins in her arms.
Her urine runs through a tube into a bottle under the bed.
On her back and ankles are black sores.
The black sores are parts of her that have died.
The beat of her heart is steady.
She is not whole.

She made ready to die, she prayed, she made her peace,
    she read daily from the lectionary.
She tended the green garden she had made,
    she fought off the destroying ants,
    she watered the plants daily
    and took note of their blossoming.
She gave sustenance to the needy.
She prepared her life for the hour of death.
But the hour has passed and she has not died.

O Lord of mysteries, how beautiful is sudden death
    when the spirit vanishes
    boldly and without casting
    a single shadowy feather of hesitation
    onto the felled body.

O Lord of mysteries, how baffling, how clueless
    is laggard death, disregarding
    all that is set before it
        in the dignity of welcome—
    laggard death, that steals
        insignificant patches of flesh—
    laggard death, that shuffles
    past the open gate,
    past the open hand,
    past the open,
            ancient,
            courteously waiting life.

A Soul-Cake

Mother, when I open a book of yours
your study notes fall out into my lap.
'Apse, semicircular or polygonal recess
arched over domed roof,' says one. I remember
your ceiling, cracked by earthquake,
and left that way. Not that you chose to leave it;
nevertheless, 'There's nothing less real
than the present,' you underlined.

My throat clenches when I weep and
can't make tears,
the way my feet clenched when I ran
unsuspecting into icy ocean
for 'General swim,' visiting Nik at summercamp.
What hurts is not your absence only,
dull, unresonant, final,
it's the intimate knowledge of your aspirations,
the scholar in you, the artist reaching
out and out.
            To strangers your unremitting
struggle to learn appears
a triumph—to me, poignant. I know
how baffled you felt.
I know only I
knew how lonely you were.

The small orphan,
skinny, proud, reserved, observant,
irreverent still in the woman of ninety,
but humble.

"To force conscience," you marked in Panofsky,
'is worse,' says Castellio, 'than cruelly
to kill a man. For to deny one's convictions
destroys the soul.'"
                              And Bruno's lines,
"The age
Which I have lived, live, and shall live,
Sets me atremble, shakes, and braces me."

Five months before you died you recalled
counting-rhymes, dance-games for me;
gaily, under the moon, you sang and mimed,

> My shoes are very *dir*ty,
> My shoes are very *thin*,
> I haven't got a *pocket*
> To put a penny in.

> *A soul-cake, a soul-cake,*
> *Please, good missis, a soul-cake . . .*

But by then for two years
you had hardly been able to hear me,
could barely see to read.
                              We spoke together
                              less and less.

There's too much grief. Mother,
what shall I do with it?
Salt grinding and grinding from the magic box.

Talking to Grief

Ah, grief, I should not treat you
like a homeless dog

who comes to the back door
for a crust, for a meatless bone,
I should trust you.

I should coax you
into the house and give you
your own corner,
a worn mat to lie on,
your own water dish.

You think I don't know you've been living
under my porch.
You long for your real place to be readied
before winter comes. You need
your name,
your collar and tag. You need
the right to warn off intruders,
to consider
my house your own
and me your person
and yourself
my own dog.

Earliest Spring

Iron scallops border the path, barely
above the earth; a purplish starling lustre.

Earth a different dark, scumbled, bare
between clumps of wintered-over stems.

Slowly, from French windows opened
to first, mild, pale, after-winter morning,

we inch forward, looking: pausing, examining
each plant. It's boring. The dry stalks
are tall as I, up to her thigh. But then—
'Ah! Look! A snowdrop!' she cries,
satisfied, and I see

thin sharp green darning-needles
stitch through the sticky gleam of dirt,

belled with white!
                  'And another!
And here, look, and here.'
                         A white carillon.
Then she stoops to show me precise
bright green check-marks

vivid on inner petals,
each outer petal
filing down to a point.

              And more:
'Crocuses—yes, here they are . . .'

and these point upward closed
tight as eyelids waiting a surprise,

egg-yolk gold or mauve;
and she brings my gaze

to filigree veins of violet
traced upon white, that make

the mauve seem. This is the earliest
spring of my life. Last year

I was a baby, and what I saw then
is forgotten. Now I'm a child. Now I'm not bored

at moving step by step,
slow, down the path. Each pause

brings us to bells or flames.

Emblem (I)

Dreaming, I rush
thrust from the cave of the winds,
into the midst of a wood of tasks.
The boughs part, I sweep
poems and people with me a little way;
dry twigs, small patches of earth
are cleared and covered.
Then I find myself
out over open heath, a sigh that holds
a single note, heading
far and far to the horizon's bent firtree.

Emblem (II)

A silver quivering cocoon that shakes
from within, trying to break.
                              What psyche
is wrestling with its shroud?
Blunt diamonds
scrape at its casing,
urging it out.
But there is too much grief. The world
is made of days, and is itself
a shrouded day.
It stifles. It's our world, and we
its dreams, its creased
compacted wings.

Kindness

> *'Was it eyes of friendship the dog had?'*
> *Robert Duncan, 1964, writing about*
> *a poem, 'As It Happens.'*

Eyes of kindness that the dog had,
the 3-legged beggar dog,
were not eyes of friendship—no:

in its hunger, dog
gave over to the stricken
heart of a watcher—not a giver—
(bereaved, an alien
for a time among the living)
agony. Shared it. As that watcher
would share a used-up bone, a crust.
In a fog of dust and grief
in the sun
the dog's hurt life
was itself
a kindness. Timidly
the beast took
the afterthought of bread.
The traveller took
in exchange
its gift
for a while, and
wept in it, enabled.

Split Second

What a flimsy shred of the world
I hold by its tenuous, filmy edge!
All my multitudes,
the tribes of my years passing
        into murmurous caverns,
the glassblades, flinty paths,
words, baled reams of inscribed paper, cities,
cities recurring composite
in dream,
            skin, breath, lashes, hair,
closeups, perspectives—a hive of knowledge
no bigger than a bead of sweat.

Fish are uttering silence in the ocean's holes—
and all about me,
unconceived,
the foundries, steelmill flames aloft flaring, clangor,
the vast routine of power,

what it is to be threadbare,
breathe asbestos,
daily for fifty years to tread
certain adamantine steps,
                    kill, to have killed.

Unknown lurchings into calculus, landing
the plane I fly in. And each other dreamer
clutching (wideawake) a different frayed
scrap of fabric!
                Are there gods whose pleasure
is to make rag rugs, deftly
braiding? Quilts for eternity? Needled blood
from Chthonian fingers speckling
the ritual patterns?

Scornful Reprieve

Curtly the sky
plucks
at knots of cloud;
from the unfurled bundles
out roll pellets
of leaden rain,
singly, savagely,
dropping, to pock
the pale
          dust of the earth.
Something cannot believe
a gift has been given.
Shall grass indeed
grow here?

Alongside

Catbird cadenzas from the bushes
issue like edicts. See him! Fearless,
intent upon invention, slate blue
among the dewy leaves, his puffed throat

pumping. Alongside
the human day, his day,
fully engaged.
                    Miaow!
A bright glance registers
old Two-legs passing by. Not his concern,
pah! A billion leaves
demand utterance, he has the whole
hillside to sing, the veil of vapor.
Azaleas must be phrased! And dandelions—
a golden pizzicato!
Soon enough
it will be noon, and hot, and silent.

Run Aground

A brown oakleaf, left over from last year,
turns into a bird and flies off singing.

That should encourage you!   I know it—
but I'm not an oakleaf.

I'm not singing.

I'm not watching the brown wings
cleave the air.

The cold half-moon
sits obstinate in this warm, middle-of-the-day,
middle of the month.

I'm looking sullenly back at it,
human, thrown
back on my own resources.

Intimation

Some trick of light

in the reflection of sunny kitchen against
a dark wall in back of the yard

makes this morning's daffodils
that shout for joy, thronging their stone vase,
leaning outward in a ring,
golden, hilarious, ready for anything,
for spring—

makes them into a cluster
of yellow chrysanthemums,
no less beautiful,
                    but very still,
facing November,
facing frost.

Autumnal

Through the high leafy branches
rush of wind-flood.   Gleam
of the wind's teeth
at dead of night, *calavera*.
Dark of the moon.
Under the smiling skin
bloodstream furtively
slower.   The wind sweeping aside
the weir of leaves. Meshing
of counterrhythms. So,
is this how time
takes one? Bricks returned to clay
in Nineveh? Sheba's gazebo
silted over, under
the desert tides?

The Long Way Round
for Alice Walker and Carolyn Taylor

i

'The solution,' they said to my friend,
'lies in eventual total'—they said (or 'final'?),
'assimilation. Miscegeny. No more trouble—'
            Disappear, they said.

I in America,
        white, an
               indistinguishable mixture
of Kelt and Semite, grown under glass
in a British greenhouse, a happy
old-fashioned artist, sassy and free,

had to lean in yearning towards
the far-away daughters and sons of
Vietnamese struggle
before I could learn,
        begin to learn,
by Imagination's slow ferment,
what it is to awaken
each day Black in White America,
each day struggling
           to affirm
a who-I-am my white skin never
has to pay heed to.
          Who I am
slowly, slowly
            took lessons
from distant Asia; and only then
from near-as-my-hand persons, Black sisters.

ii

Pushing open my mind's
door on its grating hinges
to let in the smell of
pain, of destroyed
flesh, to know

for one instant's agony,
insisted on for the sake of knowing
anything, anything at all
in truth,
that that flesh belonged
to one's own most dear,
child, or lover, or mother—

pushing open my door I began
to know who I was and
who I was not.
And slowly—for though
it's in a flash we
know we know,
yet before that flash there's a long
slow, dull, movement of fire
along the well-hidden
line of the fuse—

I came to know,
                in the alembic
of grief and will and love,
just barely to know, by knowing
it never
        ever
                would be what I could
know in the flesh,

what it must be to wake each day
to the sense of one's own beautiful
human skin, hair, eyes, one's
whole warm sleep-caressed body
as something that others
hated,
        hunted,
                haunted by its otherness,
something they wanted to see disappear.

iii

Swimming, we are, all of us, swimming
in the rectangular indoor claustrophobic pool

—echoing, sharply smelling of chlorine,
stinging our eyes—
that is
our life,

      where,
    scared and put off our stroke
    but righting ourselves with a gasp
       sometimes we touch
an Other,
    another
breathing and gasping body,
'yellow,' but not yellow at all,
'black,' but most often
brown; shaped like ourselves, bodies we could
embrace in relief, finding
ourselves not alone in the water.

      And someone,
       some fool of a coach,
strutting the pool's edge, wading
the shallow end, waves his arms at us,
shouting,
      'If you're White
      you have
      the right of way!'
          While we
swim for dear life, all of us—'not,'
as it has been said, '*not* waving,
but drowning.'

On the 32nd Anniversary of the Bombing of Hiroshima and Nagasaki

A new bomb, big one, drops
a long way beyond the fence of our minds'
property. And they tell us, *'With this
the war is over.'*
      We are twenty years old, thereabouts—

now stale uniforms
can fall off our backs, replaced
by silk of youth! Relief,
not awe, gasps from our
mouths and widens
ignorant eyes. We've been used
to the daily recitation of death's
multiplication tables: we don't notice
the quantum leap: eighty-seven thousand
killed outright by a single bomb,
fifty-one thousand missing or injured.
We were nurses, refugees, sailors, soldiers,
familiar with many guises of death: war had ended our childhood.
We knew about craters, torpedoes, gas ovens.
This we ignored.
The rumor was distant traffic. Louder
were our heartbeats,
                summer was springtime:
'The war is over!'

And on the third day no-one
rose from the dead at Hiroshima,
and at Nagasaki
the exploit was repeated, as if
to insist we take notice:
seventy-three thousand
killed by one bomb,
seventy-four thousand injured or missing.
Familiar simple-arithmetic of
mortal flesh did not serve,
                yet I cannot remember,
and Sid, Ruth, Betty, Matthew, Virginia
cannot remember August sixth or
August ninth, nineteen-
forty-five. *The war was over* was all we knew
and a vague wonder, *what next? What will ordinary
life be like, now ordinary life as we know it
is gone?*

But the shadow,
the human shadowgraph sinking itself
indelibly upon stone at Hiroshima

as a man, woman or child was consumed
in unearthly fire—
                              that shadow
already had been for three days
imprinted upon our lives.
Three decades now we have lived
with its fingers outstretched in horror clinging
to our future, our children's future,
into history or the void.
The shadow's voice
cries out to us to cry out.
Its nails dig
                    into our souls
                              to wake them:
'*Something*,' it ceaselessly
repeats, its silence
a whisper, its whisper
a shriek,
                    while 'the radiant gist'
is lost, and the moral labyrinths of
humankind convulse as if made
of snakes clustered and intertwined and stirring
from long sleep—
'. . . *something can yet*
be salvaged upon the earth:
try, try to survive,
try to redeem
the human vision
from cesspits where human hands
have thrown it, as I was thrown
from life into shadow. . . .'

For Chile, 1977

It was a land where the wingéd mind
could alight.
Andean silver dazzling the Southern Cross;
the long shore of gold beaten by the Pacific
into translucency, vanishing
into Antarctica—

                    yes, these:
            but not for these
our minds flew there,

but because they knew
the poor were singing there
and the homeless
were building there
and the downtrodden
were dancing.

How brief it was, that time
when Chile showed us how to rejoice!
How soon the executioners
arrived, making victims
of those who were not born to be victims.

The throats of singers
were punched into silence,
hands of builders
crushed,
dancers herded
into the pens.

                How few
all over the earth,
from pole to pole, are the lands
where our minds can perch and be glad,
clapping their wings, a phoenix flock!

From Chile now
they fly affrighted, evil smoke
rises from forest and city,
hopes are scorched.

When will the cheerful hammers sound again?
When will the wretched begin to dance again?
When will guitars again
give forth at the resurrected touch
of broken fingers
a song of revolution reborn?

Greeting to the Vietnamese Delegates to the U.N.

Our large hands
Your small hands

Our country's power
Our powerlessness against it

Your country's poverty
The power of your convictions

Our corrupted democracy
The integrity of your revolution

Our technology and its barbarity
Your ingenuity and simple solutions

Our bombers
Your bicycles

Our unemployed veterans
Your re-educated prostitutes

Our heroin addicts rotting
Your wounded children healing

Our longing for new life
Your building of new life

Our large hands
Your small hands

Continuum

Some beetle trilling
its midnight utterance.

Voice of the scarabee,
dungroller,
working survivor . . .

I recall how each year
returning from voyages, flights
over sundown snowpeaks,
cities crouched over darkening lakes,
hamlets of wood and smoke,
I find
        the same blind face upturned to the light
        and singing
        the one song,

        the same weed managing
        its brood of minute stars
        in the cracked flagstone.

MODULATIONS FOR SOLO VOICE

These poems were written in the winter and spring of 1974–75,
and might be subtitled, from the cheerful distance of 1978,
Historia de un amor. *They are intended to be read as a sequence.*

There are the lover and the beloved, but these two come from
different countries.
                          Carson McCullers, The Ballad of the Sad Café

From Afar

The world is round.
Amber beads
I took from around my neck
before we lay down, before
you left to go onward and homeward,
remind me, and the saying:
'Each place on earth is
the middle of the world.'

A certain blue would be
your color, no? Dark
as your irises
that ringed black tarns

I looked into,
                that looked
back at me,
gaze holding.

        •

I could sail around the world looking
for your country
and never find it—what would it mean to me
unless you were in it,
it is you I want, to look
with love into me,
to come into me,
you who came out of the
bluest furthest distance.
Who left so soon, going
inexorably
north into snow,
            like a messenger gone into Lapland
            with runes for the watchful sages,
            with gentleness wrapped in linen to give
            their crystal princess
            under those stern auroras.

        •

I wanted to learn you by heart.
There was only time
for the opening measures—a minor key,
major chords, arpeggios of desire that ripple
            swifter than I can hum them—
and through all
a lucid, dreaming tune
that gleaners sing
alone in the fields.

I am wayfaring
in the middle of the world,
treading water, the blue
of your absence,
cold ocean; trudging

the dusty earth-curves
to unending distance,
round and round.
Listening for that music,
singing within me
the first notes over,
as if in the middle of the
round world you could hear me?

Silk

i

Halfawake, I think
silky hair, cornsilk, his voice
of one substance with
his words, with
his warm flesh.
I put my hand out
in the dark to touch
his letter, placed
in reach for the night's
shoals of waking.
What I know of him
is a flow unbroken
from word to touch,
from body to thought's
dance or stillness.
Therefore into my palm
off the paper
rises what soothes me,
indivisible;
I can return
into the sea of sleep.

ii

Today the telephone
brought me his voice itself:
the silk of it

is darker than I remembered,
and warmer.
I took the folds of it up
to wrap myself in,
to keep off the cold of
all the snowfields between us.

The Phonecall

Big bluejay black,
white sky in back; brittle;
twisting bare random
branches.   Morning
persists in rain, rain
that last night
dripped from the eaves
in pacing footsteps.
Awake and awake
I was ashamed:
only lonely private sorrows
took my sleep—
(*only lonely, only lonely* . . . as if a child
sat in a treehouse,
moping). Politics,
the word I use to mean
striving for justice and for
mercy, never
keeps me so long
open-eyed. The world's
crowded with crowded
prisons; if Debs
was truthful, humankind
can feel more than
I know or
for more than a moment
can sustain. What turns
the jay blue
again in gray
rainlight is not,
this morning, news

of any justice or freedom
but (o infinitesimal,
fragile, vast, only!)
the mercy of one voice
speaking from far away
lowpitched, loving,
one to one . . .

Psyche in Somerville

I am angry with X, with Y, with Z,
for not being you.
Enthusiasms jump at me,
wagging and barking. Go away.
Go home.

I am angry with my eyes for not seeing you,
they smart and ache and see the snow,
an insistent brilliance.

If I were Psyche how could I not
bring the lamp to our bedside?
I would have known in advance
all the travails my gazing
would bring, more than Psyche
ever imagined,
and even so, how could I not have raised
the amber flame to see
the human person I knew
was to be revealed.
She did not even know! She dreaded
a beast and discovered
a god. But I
know, and hunger
to witness again the form
of mortal love itself.

I am angry with everything that is filling
the space of your absence,
breathing your air.

                    Psyche,
how blessèd you were
in the dark, knowing him in your flesh:
I was wrong! 1f I were Psyche
I would live on in darkness, and endure
the foolish voices, barking of aeolian dogs, the desert glitter
of days full of boring treasures,
walking on precious stones till my feet hurt,

to hold you each night and be held
close in your warmth in a pitchblack cave of a room

and not have to wait
for Mercury, dressed in the sad gray coat of a mailman
and no wings on his feet,
to bring me your words.

A Woman Pacing Her Room, Rereading a Letter, Returning Again and Again to Her Mirror

i

Poised on the edge of ugliness,

a flower whose petals
are turning brown.
                    I never liked
to keep them—a word of farewell
discreetly whispered, and out they go,
the discolored water after them,
the vase to be scrubbed.
                    A few flowers
dry into straw-crisp comeliness
without fetor. But
for most
            beauty is balanced upon
the poignance of brevity.

I have almost fallen already,
an ordinary flower.
But my lover talks about two years from now . . .

In two years I may be richly
gone into compost—juice and fiber
absorbed in the dark of
time past, my fever
a flame remembered,
                    old candle,
                    old shadow.
Or in two years I may be straw.

                    Flowers of straw,
everlastings, are winter makeshifts
pleasant to see, but not to touch.
Their voice is a faint crackling under the hand.
By spring the settled
                dust is dull
                        upon brittleness,

                and someone brings in
posies of fragrance from the meadows,
violets, the forgotten, now-to-be-known-freshly
primrose;
                dew is on them,
                what could one ever
                desire but to sink with closed eyes
                into their cold, sweet, brief,
                silent music?

ii

**(The Woman Has Ceased to Pace, She Sits Down on the
    Edge of Her Bed, Still Holding the Letter)**

We can't save
our tears in precious vials,
or if we do, we don't know
what to do with them then,
iridescent amphorae
            coated with salt . . .
                                    We can't save
ourselves, I cannot hold

my fleeting, fading, ordinary hedgerow rays
                              of sun or star homage
from falling, from leaving
                    nothing but the small nub they flare from
—and that itself
swiftly or slowly must turn
from gold to mole-dark gray.

Dream: Château de Galais

In dream you ask me
to care for your child while its mother
rides in the tapestry forest.
The whole château

is thronged with fair and strange
folk, both Frantz de Galais and his friends, and
your friends, my friends, and many
personages without whom my story
would have been a blank.

I lie down beside the child
to lull her to sleep, and I lull myself
to sleep. A remote attic, daytime, a room
where perhaps the godmother sometimes sits at her spinning.

And when I awake, the belovéd
rosy and longlashed daughter, fragrant
with infant sweat, is curled
confidingly into my circling protective arm,
and you have entered the room

searching for me, for now at last
we can meet alone for an hour.
Smiling, your hand on the door, eager to leave.
It is a subtle and delicate task to rise
so softly she will not wake.
Tendrils of hair, silky like yours,
cling damp to my cheek
where her head nestles.
But you want me. You take my hands,

we steal from the safe room quickly.
This was a dream
of sadness, of sleep, of a place
known to our minds, of seeking each other,
of joy.

Like Loving Chekhov

Loving this man who is far away
is like loving Anton Chekhov.
It is true, I do love Anton Chekhov,
I have loved him longer than I have known this man.
I love all the faces of Chekhov in my collection
of photos that show him in different years of his life,
alone, or with brothers and sisters, with actors,
                                    with Gorki,
with Tolstoi, with his wife, with his undistinguished
endearing pet dogs; from beardless student to pince-nez'd
famous and ailing man.
                    I have no photo
of the man I love.

I love Chekhov for travelling alone
to the prison island without being asked.
For writing of the boiling, freezing, terrible seas
around the island and around the lives of its people
that they 'resembled the scared dreams
of a small boy who's been reading
                    Lost in the Ocean Wastes
before going to sleep, and whose blanket has fallen off,
so he huddles shivering
and can't wake up.'
For treasuring the ugly inkstand a penniless seamstress
gave him in thanks for his doctoring.
If there's an afterlife,
I hope to meet Anton Chekhov there.

        Loving the man I love
is like that, because he is far away,
and because he is scrupulous, and because surely
nothing he says or does can bore me.

But it's different too. Chekhov had died
long before I was born. This man is alive.
He is alive and not here.
This man has shared my bed, our bodies
have warmed each other and given each other
delight, our bodies
are getting angry with us for giving them to each other and then
allowing something they don't understand to pry them apart,
                                                    a metallic
cruel wedge that they hear us call
necessity.
            Often it seems unreal to love
a man who is far away, or only real to the mind,
the mind teasing the body. But it's real,
he's alive, and it's not in the afterlife
I'm looking to see him,
but in this here and now, before I'm a month older,
before one more gray hair has grown on my head.
If he makes me think about Chekhov it's not because
he resembles him in the least but because the ache
of distance between me and a living man I know and don't know
grips me with pain and fear, a pain and fear
familiar in the love of the unreachable dead.

Fantasiestück

'My delicate Ariel'—
can you imagine,
Caliban had a sister?
Not ugly, brutish, wracked with malice,
but nevertheless
earthbound half-sibling to him,
and, as you once were,
prisoned within a tree—
but that tree being
no cloven pine but the sturdy wood
her body seemed to her,
its inner rings revealing
slow growth,
its bark incised

with hearts and arrows,
all its leaves wanting to fly, and falling—
    and ever in spring again
    peering forth small as flint-sparks?

Spirit whose feet touch earth
only as spirit moves them,
imagine
      this rootbound woman,
Prospero's bastard daughter,
his untold secret, hidden from Miranda's
gentle wonder.
              Her intelligent eyes
watch you, her mind
can match your own, she loves
your grace of intellect.
But she knows
what weight of body is, knows her flesh
(her cells, her magic cell)
mutters its own dark songs.
              She loves
to see you pass by,
grieves that she cannot hold you,
knows it is so and *must* be;
offers the circle of her shade,
silvery Ariel,
for your brief rest.

Modulations

    'The laws of modulation are found in The Science of Harmony,
    which treats of the formation and progression of chords.'
        Simple & Complete Primer for the Pianoforte, *1885*

i

Easily we are happy, I was thinking, no need
for so much grieving,
ashen mind, heart flaming, flaming
from core of stone.

Easy days, nights when our bodies
were learning each other.

ii

But that perfection, nectarine of light—
you bruised it.
Impeccably conscientious,
gave it a testing pinch,

reminding me of my status
in the country of your affections:
secondclass citizen,

Don't you know I hate to be told
what I know already?
Remember the custodian telling us,
'This chair is beautiful,
this is a beautiful table'?
What I knew I'd taken already
on terms of my own:
not as defeat but with new freedom—
            from false pride,
            from measuring my value to you
            in a jeweller's finicky scale.

(And *the heart's affections* are *holy*,
we have known that, but have loved
to hear it again for the sake of
his life who said it. And *what the Imagination seizes
as beauty must be truth*—
yet there are hierarchies within that truth.)

iii

Nectarine of our pleasure,
enclosed in its own fragrance,
poised on its imaginary branch!
I imagine too quickly, giving to tenuous things
hasty solidity,
to irresolute shadows
a perfect equilibrium.

For you, then,
our days and nights had not been a river
flowing at leisure between grassy banks?

You thought I would try
to force the river
out of its course?

You didn't trust me . . .

iv

Or perhaps indeed
we did after all
share our pleasure,
halving the nectarine—

but even as we drifted
downstream at ease
and golden juices
stained your mind's tongue,

anxiety arrived from your hometown
wearing black,
waving her umbrella?

v

Since I must recover
my balance, I do. I falter
but don't fall; recalling
how every vase, cut sapphire, absolute
dark rose, is not indeed
of rarest, of most cherished
perfection unless flawed,
offcentered, pressed
with rough thumbprint, bladescratch, brown
birthmark that tells
of concealed struggle from bud to open ease
of petals, soon
to loosen, to drop and
be blown away.

                    The asymmetrical
tree of life, fractionally lopsided
at the trunk's live-center
tells where a glancing eye,
                    not a ruler,
drew, and drew strength
from its mistake.

The picture of perfection
must be revised.
Allow for our imperfections,
welcome them,
consume them into its substance.
Bring from necessity
its paradoxical virtue,
mortal life, that makes it
give off so strange a magnetic
shining, when one had thought
darkness had filled the night.

vi

These questions
that have walked beside all that I say,
waiting their turn for utterance:

        How do I free myself
        from pain self-imposed,

                pride-pain,
                will-pain,

                pain of wanting
                never to feel superfluous?

        How are you acted on
        by anxiety, by a coldness
        taught to you as a boy?

—these questions
are not mine only.
The vision

of river, of nectarine,

is not mine only.
All humankind,

women and men,

hungry,

hungry beyond the hunger
for food, for justice,

pick themselves up and stumble on
for this: to transcend barriers, longing

for absolution of each by each,
luxurious unlearning
of lies and fears,

for joy, that *throws down the reins*
on the neck of
                    the divine animal
who carries us through the world.

'Elle est Débrouillarde'

High on vitamins, I demonstrate to my friends
the *lezginka, mazurka, gavotte.* With a
one two three, hop, one two three, hop, teach
someone the polka.
                    Laughter's a joy
even next day at breakfast.
Do I really suffer
that his letters arrive so seldom—
unwritten or unmailed?
Is it love or pride that hurts?
Am I maybe
fully as jocund as I seem?

(Only twice I've cried
in weeks now—once

writing of my mother's
extreme old age, the slow
race between heart and sight;
once when I read about Li-li's
lost first love, when her parents
pulled her away to Taiwan,
away from her comrades.
Did they die in the struggle against Chiang Kai-shek?)

Is 'the fine art of unhappiness' truly
losing its allure?

From Afar (II)

The first poem
becomes the last.

The world
is round.
I am wayfaring.

I learned
the tense and slender
warmth of your body
almost by heart.

The bluest, furthest distance
is what you carry
within you—
the cold of it
inexorable.

I know
you can't hear me.

I'm gleaning
alone in a field
in the middle of the world,

you're listening
for a song that
I don't know,

that no one
yet has sung.

This is not
farewell.
I have
your word for it,
inviolate.
The last poem

enclosed in the lucid
amber of the world

becomes the first.

Epilogue

I thought I had found a swan
but it was a migrating snow-goose.

I thought I was linked invisibly to another's life
but I found myself more alone with him than without him.

I thought I had found a fire
but it was the play of light on bright stones.

I thought I was wounded to the core
but I was only bruised.

The Blue Rim of Memory

The way sorrow enters the bone
is with stabs and hoverings.
From a torn page
a cabriolet
approaches over the crest of a hill,
first the nodding, straining head of the horse
then the blind lamps, peering;

the ladies within the insect eagerly
look from side to side awaiting the vista—
and quick as a knife
are vanished. Who were they? Where is the hill?

Or from stoked fires of nevermore
a warmth constant as breathing hovers out
to surround you, a cloud of mist
becomes rain, becomes cloak, then skin.

The way sorrow enters the bone
is the way fish sink through dense lakes
raising smoke from the depth
and flashing sideways in bevelled
syncopations.
It's the way the snow
drains the light from day but then,
covering boundaries of road and sidewalk,
widens wondering streets
and stains the sky yellow
to glow at midnight.

For the Blind

Listen: the wind in new leaves
whispers, smoother than fingertips,
than floss silk smoothing through fingertips . . .

When the sighted
talk about *white* they may mean
silence of sullen cold, that winter—
no matter how warm your rooms
—waits with at the door.
(Though there's another whiteness,
more like the weightlessness of a flake of snow
of a petal, a pine-needle . . .)

When they say *black* they may mean the persistence
of cold wind hopelessly, angrily,
tearing and tearing through leafless boughs.
(Though there's another blackness,
round and full as the notes of cello and drum . . .)

But this:
this lively, delicate shiver
that whispers itself caressingly
over our flesh
when leaves are moist and small
and winds are gentle,
is green. Light green. Not weightless,
light.

The Emissary

Twice now this woman for whom my unreasonable dislike
has slowly turned to loathing
has come up to me and said, 'Ah, yes,
we shall have plenty of time soon to talk.'

Twice she has laid her cold hand heavily
on mine,
and thrust her pallid face, her puffy cheeks,

close to mine.
I went to wash in the hottest water, to oil myself
in fragrant oils.

I know who she is in the world; others know her;
many seem not to notice she brings
a chill into rooms.
She is who she is,
ordinary, venal, perhaps sad.
Perhaps she is not aware of her own task:
but death sends her about the world.

I have always been afraid of pain
but not of death.
I am not afraid of death, but I don't want
to have time
to sit and talk with this woman.

I have watched her condescend
to those who don't know her name,
and smirk at the ones who do.
I have seen her signature
hiding under pebbles,
scratched into chips of ice.

She can have nothing to tell me
I could be glad to hear.
Twice she has looked at me
with eyes that gleam dull, a pewter gray.
Twice she has looked at me with a look
that gives me nothing I shall ever want.

Death is for everyone. I shall never willingly
give her the right to bring me my share.
I shall refuse to take what is mine
from her gray hands.

A Look at the Night (Temple, Early '60s)

The plough
the only constellation we are
sure of

turning
the sky's earth, faithful
among its furrows of wind—

And the fierce moon
a barn-owl, over
boughs and
bright clouds—

No one

       will speak for us
       no one
       but ourselves knows
       what our lives
       are.
       We step outdoors at
       2 a.m., our minds
       dilated by deep
       early sleep,
to the quick of
           brilliant night
alone:
such words as
carry our testimony
          singular,
          incontrovertible,
          breath and tongue awaiting
          patent,
or do without.

We sing
in mutterings
to speak for ourselves.
     The turned field
black above us,
        the moon
high in her dominion.

Wedding-Ring

My wedding-ring lies in a basket
as if at the bottom of a well.
Nothing will come to fish it back up
and onto my finger again.
                    It lies
among keys to abandoned houses,
nails waiting to be needed and hammered
into some wall,
telephone numbers with no names attached,
idle paperclips.
                    It can't be given away
for fear of bringing ill-luck.
                    It can't be sold
for the marriage was good in its own
time, though that time is gone.
                    Could some artificer
beat into it bright stones, transform it
into a dazzling circlet no one could take
for solemn betrothal or to make promises
living will not let them keep? Change it
into a simple gift I could give in friendship?

A Son

A flamey monster—plumage and blossoms
        fountaining forth
                        from her round head,
        her feet
                squeezing mud between their toes,
        a tail of sorts
                        wagging hopefully
and a heart of cinders and dreamstuff,
                flecked with forever molten gold,
        drumrolling in her breast—
bore a son.

        His father? A man
not at ease with himself,

half-monster too,
half earnest earth,

fearful of monsterhood;
kindly, perplexed, a fire
smouldering.

The son
took, from both monsters, feathers
of pure flame,

and from his mother,

alchemical gold,
and from his father,

the salt of earth:

a triple goodness.

If to be artist
is to be monster,
he too was monster. But from his self
uprose a new fountain,
of wisdom, of in-seeing, of wingéd justice
flying unswerving
into the heart.

He and compassion
were not master and servant,
servant and master,
but comrades in pilgrimage.

What My House Would Be Like If It Were A Person

This person would be an animal.
This animal would be large, at least as large
as a workhorse. It would chew cud, like cows,
having several stomachs.
No one could follow it
into the dense brush to witness
its mating habits. Hidden by fur,
its sex would be hard to determine.

Definitely it would discourage
investigation. But it would be, if not teased,
a kind, amiable animal,
confiding as a chickadee. Its intelligence
would be of a high order,
neither human nor animal, elvish.
And it would purr, though of course,
it being a house, you would sit in *its* lap,
not it in yours.

Artist to Intellectual (Poet to Explainer)

i

'The lovely *obvious!* The feet
supporting the body's tree and its crown
of leafy flames, of fiery
knowledge roaming
into the eyes,
that are lakes, wells, open
skies! The lovely
evident, revealing
everything, more mysterious
than any
clueless inscription scraped in stone.
The ever-present, constantly vanishing,
carnal enigma!'

ii

'Do I prophesy? It is
for now, for no future.
Do I envision? I envision
that every seed
knows, what shadow
speaks unheard
and will not repeat.
My energy
has not direction,
tames no chaos,

creates, consumes, creates
unceasing its own
wildfires that none
shall measure.'

iii

'Don't want to measure, want to be
the worm slithering wholebodied
over the mud and grit of what
may be a mile,
may be forever—pausing
under the weeds to taste
eternity, burrowing
down not along,
rolling myself
up at a touch, outstretching
to undulate in abandon to exquisite rain,
returning, if so I desire, without
reaching that goal the measurers
think we must head for. Where is
my head? Am I not
worm all over? My own
orient!'

The Poet Li Po Admiring a Waterfall

Improvisation on a Xmas card for the composer
David del Tredici, at Yaddo,
Xmas, 1975

And listening to its
Japanese blues, the bass
of its steady plunging
tones of dark,
and within their roaring:
strands of thin
foamwhite, airbright
light inwoven!—all
falling
so far

so deep,
his two
acorn-hatted infant
acolytes fear
he will long to
fly like spray
and fall too, off
the sloping, pale
edge of the world,
entranced!

Postcard

The sunshine is wild here!
It laps our feet!
Wavelets of sunshine!
Spiky wavelets!
The sunshine snaps at our toes!
Thick handfuls of sunshine freeze
our fingers like ice,
like burning ice cream!
Farewell!
The towers of the city across
the gulf of sunshine are wavering!

Hidden Monsters at the Mount Auburn Cemetery.
A Found Poem.

I looked after the carving while it was executing at the prison,
and found it necessary to make only one slight deviation from the
model.
You may recollect that in most of the Egyptian cornices
there is on each side of the globe, a fabulous sort of animal,
with an inflated body, and a head like a serpent or crocodile . . .
As it was suggested that an uncouth Egyptian idol
might give offense to some persons,
I sought for some way of modifying it,
which might cover this difficulty

without departing from the main design.
I accordingly instructed the workmen to introduce
an Egyptian Lotus on each side,
the flower of which falls so as to conceal
the head of the monster,

leaving the spectator to imagine what he pleases behind it.

Dr. Jacob Bigelow to H.A.S. Dearborn,
Boston, January 13th, 1833

Blake's Baptismal Font

Behind the Tree the hands
of Eve and Adam almost
                              meet.
Only a single thick
rope of serpent
divides them.

Adam holds
his other hand on his heart
                              in fear
as Eve stretches out *her* other hand
across the front of the Tree.
          to offer him knowledge.
The apple the serpent holds in its mouth
and the twin apples of her breasts are all
exact replicas of the apple she holds.

Four prehensile, elegant, practical feet
stand among roots.
Above the heads
                    of man and woman and serpent,
dense leaves and a crown of apples hide
the font and its bas-relief stories—
              the sky's dome
upturned, an unknown cosmos.

For X . . .

I've never written poems for you, have I.
You rarely read poems,
your mind thrives
on other fruits and grains:

but just this once
a poem; to say:

As unthought gestures, turns of
common phrase, reveal
the living of life—
pathos, courage, comedy;

as in your work you witness
and show others
people's ordinary and always strange
histories;

so you give me from myself
an open secret,

a language other than my language, poetry,
in which to rest myself with you,

in which to laugh with you;

a cheerful privacy
like talking Flemish on a bus in Devon.

Love Poem

>   *'We are good for each other.'*
>   X

What you give me is

the extraordinary sun
splashing its light

              into astonished trees.

A branch
of berries, swaying

under the feet of a bird.

I know
other joys—they taste
bitter, distilled as they are
from roots, yet I thirst for them.

But you—
you give me

the flash of golden daylight
in the body's
midnight,
warmth of the fall noonday
between the sheets in the dark.

Chant: Sunset, Somerville, Late Fall '75

Cloudy luminous rose-mallow sundown,
                                    suffusing the whole
roof-and-branch-interrupted lofty
air, blue fishscale slates,
wires, poles, trolleycars, flash
of window,
rectangular Catholic tall campanile abstracted
above North Cambridge, people heads down
leaving the store with groceries, bathed—
all!—utterly
                in this deepening, poised,
                fading-to-ivory oxbowed river of
light,
one drop
of crimson lake to a brimming
floodwater chalice
and we at the lees of it—ah,
no need to float, to long
to float upward, into it, sky itself

is floating us into the dusk, we are motes
of gold brushed from the fur
of mothwings, night is
breathing
close to us,
dark, soft.

LIFE IN THE FOREST

For Jon:

·

Brother in dream

·

Sometime lover

·

Friend

·

Imaginer

Movement

Towards not being
anyone else's center
of gravity.
         A wanting
to love: not
to lean over towards
an other, and fall,
but feel within one
a flexible steel
upright, parallel
to the spine but
longer, from which to stretch;
one's own
grave springboard; the outflying spirit's
vertical trampoline.

Slowly

Spirit has been alone
of late. Built a house
of fallen leaves
among exposed tree-roots.
Plans dreamily
to fetch water

from a stone well.
Sleeps
hungrily.
         Waking,
is mute,
listening. Spirit
doesn't know
what the sound will be,
song or cry.
Perhaps

one word. Holds
at heart a
red thread, winding

back to the world,

to one who holds
the far end,
far off.
      Spirit
throws off the quilts
when darkness
is very heavy,

shuffles among
the leaves
upstairs and down
waiting.
      Wants
the thread to vibrate

again. Again! Crimson!

Meanwhile refuses
visitors, asks
those who come
no questions,
answers none. Digs in
for winter,
        slowly.

Life in the Forest

The woman whose hut was mumbled by termites
—it would have to go,
  be gone,
  not soon, but some day:
  she knew it and shrugged—
had friends among the feathers,
quick hearts.

And among crickets too,
brown and faithful,
creviced at hearthside winters.

But her desire
fixed on a chrysalis.

        How Eternity's
silver blade filed itself fine
on the whetstone of her life!
        How the deep velours
of the wings, the mystery of the feelers,
        drew amazed cries from her
when the butterfly came forth
and looked at her, looked at her, brilliantly gazing.
        It was a man, her own size,
and touched her everywhere.

And how, when Time, later,
once the Eternal had left to go wandering,
knocked and knocked on her door, she smiled,
        and would not open!

The trees
began to come in of themselves, evenings.
The termites labored.
The hut's green moss of shadows
gave harbor
to those who sheltered her.

She was marked
by the smile within her. Its teeth
bit and bit at her sense of loss.

Letter

You in your house among your roommate's plants
that seem at times, you tell me, an overgrown thicket of assertive
                                                        leaves,
obtrusive—

are lonely. Deeply,
with a plumb-line
stillness.
        I feel it,
two miles away.

You work, your typewriter clatters cheerfully,
scenes evolve; while Dylan sings on,
                                and the record-changer
proceeds with its duties.
But underneath all is that stillness.
You hear your own heartbeats.

                        And I in my house
of smaller plants, many books, colored rugs,
my typewriter silent,
                have been searching out for you,
though I forget how we came to speak of it, the name
of the three beings who shared
just the one fateful eye between them,
spitefully taking turns. I found them:
they were the Graiae, the Grey ones, who guarded

their sisters the Gorgons. Perseus outwitted them,
the hero who rescued Andromeda; he stole
that sinister vigilant marble, using the craftiness
that is given to heroes in time of need.

Also I found (looking for something else)
in the long, grown-up, valedictory poem
close to the end of *A Child's Garden of Verses*—
yes, in that elegy,
not in the black shadows of a drawing memory collaged
from the illustrations to earlier pages—
                                    I found
Babylon, and candles,
                        and the long night.

I too today,
the wind and the rain transforming
my house to an island, a bare rock in the sea,
am alone
and know I'm alone,
                        silent within the gusting weather.
The plumb-line
doesn't swing, it
comes to rest

a cold small weight
hung from its faithful cord
level with heart's core.

A Wanderer

i

The iris hazel, pupils
large in their round blackness,
his eyes
do see me,
he hugs me
tightly, but

he turns away,
he takes his grief
home with him,
my half of it
hides behind me as I
wave, he waves,
and it and I
close my door for the night.

ii

He has taken his sorrow
away to strangers.
They form a circle around it,
listening, touching,
drawing it forth.

It weeps among them,
begins to shed
cloaks and shawls, its old
gray and threadbare twisted bandages,
and show
pale skin, dark wounds.

My arms are empty,
my warm bed's empty,
I say no
to the lovers who want to warm themselves
in me.
     I want

to lie alone, dreaming awhile
about that ring dance,
that round
I don't know how to sing,
that language
strangers talk to him in,
speaking runes to his sorrow.

A Pilgrim Dreaming

By the fire light
of Imagination, brand
held high in the pilgrim's
upraised hand, he sees,
not knowing what boundaries it may have,

a well, a pool or river—
water's darkly shining
mirror, offering
his sought-for Self.

O, he silently
cries out, reaching gladly.
But *O*, again: he sees
dimly, beside the knowledge
he has sought, another:

now he hesitates—
she whose face attentively
looks from the water up to him,
tutelary spirit of this place,
of the water-mirror,

who is she. It is
not a question.
It is a question
and troubles him. The flames

flutter and fail, Imagination
falters. His image
vanishes, he is left
in a vague darkness.

Then it is
he fears the glimmering presence,
her image
vanished like his own,
yet not utterly. Only

when with his breath

he reawakens fire, the light
of vision, will he once more

know the steady look, the face
of his own life. Only in presence
of his Self
can he look gladly
at that other face,

the mirror's gazing spirit,
mute, eloquent, weak, a power,
powerless,
yet giving
what he desires, if he gives light.

Metamorphic Journal

Part I—December

A child, no-one to stare, I'd run full tilt to a tree,
hug it, hold fast, loving the stolid way it
stood there, girth
arms couldn't round,
                        the way
only the wind made it speak, gave it
an autumn ocean of thoughts
creaking on big wings into the clouds, or rolling
in steady uncountable sevens in
to the wild cliffs when I shut my eyes.

. . . .

If I came to a brook, off came my shoes,
looking could not be enough—
or my hands at least must be boats or fish for a minute,
to know the purling water at palm and wrist.
My mind would sink like a stone
and shine underwater,
dry dull brown
                        turned to an amber glow.

. . . .

My friend . . . My friend, I would like
to talk to myself about you: beginning
with your bright, hazel, attentive eyes,
the curving lines of your mouth.
I would like to ponder the way
I have grown so slowly aware those lines
are beautiful, generous. Energy lights your
whole face, matching
the way you walk. A gradual seeing,
not in a phantom flash of storm . . .
But I'm not ready
to speak about you,
Not yet.
Perhaps I will never be ready,
nor you to be spoken of.

. . . .

Whether or not I find
words for you, to tell myself who you are,

I shan't mistake you
for a tree to cling to. Let me speak of you
as of a river:
quick-gleaming, conjuring
little pyramids of light that pass
in laughter from bonded ripple to ripple;
but pausing, dark
in pools where boughs
lean over;
but never
at a standstill—

. . . .

            I don't know how deep,
how cold I want
to touch it, drink of it, open mouth
bent to it.

Sometimes as a child
I'd slip on the rocks and fall in.
Never mind.
I wanted to know
the river's riveriness with my self,

be stone or leaf, sink or be
swept downstream
to spin and vanish, spin
and hover, spin
and sweep on beyond sight.

Part II—February

'And what if the stream
is shallow?'

Then I will wade in it.

'—the current only a ripple
that will not bear you?'

I'll make my way,
not leaf nor stone, a human,
step by step, walking,
slipping, scrambling,
seeking the depth

where the waters will summon themselves
to lift me
off my feet.

I am looking always
for the sea.

. . . .

Let me say
it is I who am a river.
Someone
is walking along
the shore of me.

He is looking
sometimes at my surface,
the lights and the passing
wingshadows,

sometimes
through me, and down
towards rocks and sand,

sometimes across me
into another country.

Does he see me?

. . . .

I met a friend
as I walked by the river that runs
through my mind.

Or he himself
was the river,

for this river
rises in metamorphosis
when some confluence
of wills occurs far-off,
            where the gods are,

and could appear
as a man,
as my friend—

who would be unaware
then, of his river-nature,

his own eyes (not
hazel, as I thought,
but topaz, are they?)
fixed rather upon flames,

592

for it may be
fire, not a river flowing,
flickers and glows in his mind,

while to me, drawn
to water by the pull
of searching roots,

he would seem
a river, or a man
gazing searchingly
into the river,
a fellow-wanderer . . .

Part III—April

But what are
              the trees to which—
              (to whom, were they not beings,
              impassive but sentient? 'Dreamy, gloomy,
              friendly . . .')
                        —I ran long ago, and still
when I'm alone, embrace sometimes, shyly,
not impulsively: pensively;
      what within me or in those I love, or who draw me
towards themselves (as water
is pulled by roots out of the soil, to rise up
up, and up
              into the tower of the tree)
—what is the counterpart, then,
in these or myself,
to imagined, retrieved, pines and oaks of the past
uttering ocean on inland gusts of autumnal wind?
(Eyes closed, eyes closed,
                        swaying as they swayed,
              listening with the heart to envisioned breakers,
the senses confounded, my breathing
breathing with boughs' tossing
until delight
broke in me into a dance,
unwitnessed, secret, whirling,

as if I became
a heap of firstfallen leaves
                        to eddy and fly
joyfully over the field
and scatter—)
What within us is tree?
                        What
cannot be budged, the stock
'not moved' that stands and yet
draws us
            into ourselves, centers us,
                never rebuffs us, utters
our wildest dreams for us, dreams
of oceanic blessing,
our hymns of pure being?

. . . .

Neither mighty tree,
                    sounding
                            of ocean
nor river flooding toward
                        sea-depths;

my self is a grey-barked sapling
of a race that needs
                    a hundred years' growth
close to water.
                Its dryad soul
dreams of plunging, of
swallow-diving off the pliant
twigs of its crown
into fathomless caverns, sliding
through yielding glass.
Its roots
        inch their toes
toward hidden streamlets
planning to pull them
                        drop by drop
up through clay, gravel, thick
topsoil, to slake
            sip by sip

tree-thirst, flesh of wood that harbors
that dreamer.

. . . .

Are you flame among the branches,
unaware? You move flickering, swift, restless
in your own life,
but I see no path behind you
of blackened leaves.
     Yourself, is it,
you burn?

. . . .

Friend,
  more than friend,
     less than friend,
in dream I came to the home of your family
to deliver a message.
Messenger of the gods, I knew
nothing of what I was to tell. Only those
who received it would comprehend
what it was.
   You had a sister,
who resembled you—
   tall, curly-haired, with an aquiline, questing nose,
a sharp-edged presence, restless, charged
with some half-concealed wistful desire—
but resembled me too,
as if she and I were sisters: I knew this
though I know little of my own
presence, what it is.
    She was kind to me,
welcomed me warmly into the house
which was stirring with eager people, cousins,
  grandparents,
aunts and uncles, all talking quickly,
      moving through the rooms.
Everywhere green plants hung from baskets,
swaying in fish-swift ripples of light
as the family passed to and fro

595

smiling, vehement, pursuing
shining ribbons of concept that crisscrossed in mid-air
like strong fibers of gossamer.
I could not see you
though you were surely there
somewhere in that place where it was clear you belonged;
but your sister drew me kindly into the midst
and brought me the cup that is brought
to messengers from distant places, before they must

                                             speak.

. . . .

I see for sure now
        beginning to speak of you, ready,
        for a moment's grace, to speak at last
        of what I don't know but see in the dark:
the flame is Imagination's flame
that burns your spirit.
                 When you
are present, but
not present,
            when you
scarcely sink into sleep
but merely rest in the deadman's float
among waves that never for a moment
let up their jostling,
            where you are
            is with the envisioning fire
inside the cave of the mind
where Images ride to the hunt on the creviced walls
as the flame struggles out of the smoke.
All about you is watery, within you lies the dark
cave, and the fire.

. . . .

When you love me well
        it is when
          Imagination has flicked
                  its fire-tongue over you,
                  you are freed
        by that act of the mind
               to act.

You have
those moments of absolute sureness,
exploding, golden, in the shifting, smoky, uncertain
                                                    dimensions of the cave,
when the hunter's
                    quarry is under his hand,
                    breathing, trembling, its heart
racing, and he puts his mark on it,
letting it go until it returns of its own
accord;
        those instants
when the Creative Spirit, sisterly,
takes a Wanderer's cold and burning hand
in hers
and they enter the dance.

Magic
for Jon

The brass or bronze cup, stroked at the rim,
round and around, begins
to hum,
        the hum slowly
buzzes more loudly, and rapidly now
becomes
            the clang of the bell of the
            deep world, unshaken, sounding
            crescendo out of its wide mouth
                                one note,
            continuous,
                        gong
            of the universe, neither beginning nor ending,
but heard
only those times we take
the cup and stroke
the rim,
diminuendo,
only seeming
to cease when we cease
to listen . . .

CANDLES IN BABYLON

Candles in Babylon

Through the midnight streets of Babylon
between the steel towers of their arsenals,
between the torture castles with no windows,
we race by barefoot, holding tight
our candles, trying to shield
the shivering flames, crying
'Sleepers Awake!'
                    hoping
the rhyme's promise was true,
that we may return
from this place of terror
home to a calm dawn and
the work we had just begun.

I   WANDERER'S DAYSONG

Dwellers at the Hermitage

Grief sinks and sinks
into the old mineshaft
under their house,
how deep, who knows.
When they have need
for it, it's there.

Their joys
refused to share themselves,
fed from the hand
of one alone, browsed
for days in dappled
pathless woods
untamed.

Sorrow
is what one shares,
they say;
and happiness, the wistful gold

of our solitudes, is what
our dearest lovers,
our wingéd friends,
leave with us, in trust.

The Soothsayer

My daughters, the old woman says, the weaver
              of fictions, tapestries
              from which she pulls
              only a single thread each day, pursuing
              the theme at night—
my daughters? Delicate bloom
of polished stone. Their hair
ripples and shines like water, and mine
is dry and crisp as moss in fall.

Trunk, limbs, bark; roots under all of it:
the tree I am, she says, blossoms year after year,
random, euphoric;
the bees are young, who nuzzle their fur
into my many fragile hearts.
My daughters
have yet to bear
their fruit,
they have not imagined
the weight of it.

The Chill

Mother and Father have fulfilled their promise:
              the overture, the rise of the curtain, the imagined pomp
              of magic and artifice, all
              glows, as if music
              were made of candle flames, all
              flows, as if dancers
              were golden oil of music,
              the theater's marvelous smell is also
              the prickle of crimson velvet on bare skin—but

at the marrow of all this joy, the child
is swept by a sudden
chill of patience: notices wearily
the abyss that Time
opens before it.
                    Careful, careful—
no one must share
this knowledge.
The child tenderly, tense with protective love,
guards their innocent happiness,
                    kind Father,
                    kind Mother.
                              Quickly! Back to the long-desired,
the even-better-than-hoped-for treat.
                              Has one not run
                              more than once
            back from a strip of woods to open sunlight,
            hastily laughing, uttering
            not a word about
                                  white
                                        bones
            strewn in ivy,
                    and old feathers, raggéd?

Poet and Person

I send my messages ahead of me.
You read them, they speak to you
in siren tongues, ears of flame
spring from your heads to take them.

When I arrive, you love me,
for I sing those messages you've
learned by heart, and bring,
as housegifts, new ones. You hear

yourselves in them,
self after self. Your solitudes
utter their runes, your own
voices begin to rise in your throats.

But soon you love me less.
I brought with me
too much, too many laden coffers,
the panoply of residence,

improper to a visit.
Silks and furs, my enormous wings,
my crutches, and my spare crutches,
my desire to please, and worse—

my desire to judge what is right.

I take up
so much space.
You are living on what you can find,
you don't want charity, and you can't
support lingering guests.

When I leave, I leave
alone, as I came.

The Passing Bell

One by one
they fall away—

all whom they really
wanted to keep. People.
Things that were more than things.

The dog, the cat,
the doll with a silk dress,
the red penknife:
those were the first to go.

Then father, mother,
sister, brother,
wife and husband.
Now the child.

The child is grown,
the child is gone,
the child has said,
Don't touch me, don't call me,

your lights have gone out,
I don't love you.
No more.

The distant child
casts a tall shadow:
that's the dark.
And they are small.

The world is brittle,
seamed with cracks,
ready to shatter. Now

the old man steps
into a boat,
rows down the rainy street.
Old woman, she climbs up

into the steeple's eye.
Transmogrified, she's
the clapper of the bell.

The tolling begins.

Talking to Oneself

Try to remember, every April, not this one only
you feel you are walking underwater
in a lake stained by your blood.

When the east wind rips the sunlight
your neck feels thin and weak, your clothes
don't warm you.

You feel you are lurching away from
deft shears, rough hands, your fleece
lies at the shepherd's feet.

And in the first warm days each step
pushes you against a weight,
and you don't want

to resist that weight,
you want to stop, to return
to darkness
                —but treaties made
over your head force you to
waver forward.

Yes, this year you feel
at a loss, there is no Demeter
to whom to return

if for a moment you saw
yourself as Persephone.
It is she, Demeter, has gone
                down to the dark.

Or if it is Orpheus drawing you forth,
Eurydice,
he is inexorable, and does not look back
to let you go.

You are appalled to consider you may be destined
to live to a hundred.
But it is April,

there is nothing unique in your losses,
your pain is commonplace
and your road ordained:

your steps will hurt you,
you will arrive
as usual

at some condition you name *summer*:

an ample landscape,
voluptuous, calm,
of large, very still trees,
water meadows, dreamy
savannah distances,

where you will gather strength,
pulling ripe fruit from the boughs,
for winter and spring,
forgotten seasons.

Try to remember it is always this way.
You live
this April's pain
now,

you will come
to other Aprils,
each will astonish you.

Wanderer's Daysong

People like me can't feel
the full rush of air around us as we
plunge into swansdown billows of
dustgold fathomless happenstance—

                we leap but
we've known the leaden no-light
that's not darkness, that is
eclipse. When green
loses its green spirit. When vertigo
takes the wheeling swifts and drops them like separate
pebbles of rain. When rain
begins and stops, appalled at the discourse of bones it makes
on cracked clay. That no-light blunted us.

Yes, and we've known, we know
every day, our tall mothers and fathers
are gone, no one

has known us always,
we are ancient orphans,
parchment skins stretched upon crutches,
inscribed with epitaphs.

When mirrors tell us white beards
have not yet appeared from within us

nor pendulous breasts
hung themselves on our torsos like bundles
of parched herbs,

when the sun
gnaws its way out of its cage again,

when the skylark
tears itself out of our throats,

we do leap, we do
plunge into skylake's
haze of promise. But we feel

along with the air rushing, our own breath
rushing
out of us.
               See
for an instant the arc of
our vanishing.

The Dragonfly-Mother

I was setting out from my house
to keep my promise

but the Dragonfly-Mother stopped me.

I was to speak to a multitude
for a good cause, but at home

the Dragonfly-Mother was listening
not to a speech but to the creak of

                    stretching tissue,
tense hum of leaves unfurling.

Who is the Dragonfly-Mother?
What does she do?

She is the one who hovers
on stairways of air,
                    sometimes almost
grazing your cheekbone,
she is the one who darts unforeseeably
into unsuspected dimensions,

who sees in water
her own blue fire zigzag, and lifts
her self in laughter
into the tearful pale sky

that sails blurred clouds in the stream.

                    •

She sat at my round table,
we told one another dreams,
I stayed home breaking my promise.

When she left I slept
three hours, and arose

and wrote. I remember the cold
Waterwoman, in dragonfly dresses

and blue shoes, long ago.
She is the same,

whose children were thin,
left at home when she went out dancing.
She is the Dragonfly-Mother,

that cold
is only the rush of air

swiftness brings.

There is a summer
over the water, over

the river mirrors
where she hovers, a summer
fertile, abundant, where dreams
grow into acts and journeys.

Her children
are swimmers, nymphs and newts, metamorphic.
                        When she tells
her stories she listens; when she listens
she tells you the story you utter.

                    •

When I broke my promise,
and slept, and later
cooked and ate the food she had bought
and left in my kitchen,

I kept a tryst with myself,
a long promise that can be fulfilled
only poem by poem,
broken over and over.

                    I too,
a creature, grow among reeds,
        in mud, in air,
in sunbright cold, in fever
of blue-gold zenith, winds
of passage.

            Dragonfly-Mother's
a messenger,
if I don't trust her
I can't keep faith.

                There is a summer
in the sleep
of broken promises, fertile dreams,
acts of passage, hovering
journeys over the fathomless waters.

Improbable Truth

There are times
          no one seems to notice
                    when I move weightlessly
not flying exactly
          but stepping as if in
                    7 league boots—
yet not
     leagues at a time,
                    merely a modest matter of
feet or at most yards.
I don't
     know how it is that
                    no one sees it, or
could it be they do, and don't
               mention it
                    from embarrassment?
Certainly
     it is strange, I know,
                    and yet
there's no need for anyone to
               feel afraid. I prefer
not to suppose
          envy could cause their silence.
                         No,
more likely it's only
          so improbable,
                    they don't believe
their eyes.
For myself, I confess,
          it is a
                    great delight—
the springiness,
          the soft
               swing of it.
Especially I like
          to traverse
               a landscape this way
when there is no one
          looking.
There is
     a low hill rising from marshland I've been to lately
                    at twilight, an hour

of mist and mauve loomings of
               vast and benevolent
                              ancient trees—
I returned
         only when sensing myself
                         too close to the deepening water.

On the Way

On the way to the
valley of transformation
one arrives sometimes at
those evenings, late, the mirror gives one,
          (softlit, and folds or falls
          of silk or wool
          conspiring like the eyes of
          loyal friends)
when one's own image greets one with pleasure.
Pleasure! How one smiles back, still hearing
goodnights and laughter,
              how one turns up the radio's midnight blues
and dances,
and checks the mirror and sees,
yes, one is dancing there, looking
just the way dancers do when one watches
                         wistfully from the outskirts of music.
On the way down there are
these way stations
                where goodbyes
are festive lanterns by the edge of a lake
and the face in the glass has shed its agelines as if
they were the mirage.

The Art of the Octopus: Variations on a Found Theme

The octopus is a solitary creature, and for it,
          any shelter it can find is home.
Connoisseur of continents,
it embraces gratefully the flatlands where shadows

dance the largesse of sky and transpose
the gestures of clouds whose wagon trains
roll across domed springtime,

while simultaneously
another caressive tentacle
strokes the steel girders of the mountains'
refusal to budge, admiring their steadfast ranks,
their doctrine of patience.

When it gave up its protective shell it developed
many skills and virtues.

It can, for example, curl itself small
to live in attics where daybreak
is an alertness of red rooftiles that a moment ago
were a vague brown at the western window,
or it can untwine, stretching out starbeams into voluptuous
unexplored chains of high-vaulted thronerooms
beyond the scan of hurried, bone-aching throngs
below in the long streets.
                                        These are skills.
Virtues? Transparently
it ingests contrast, regarding it humbly
as joy. Nourished,
it gives forth peculiar light, a smoky radiance.
Some see this aura. Some think it poisonous,
others desire it. Of those who enter
that bright cloud, some vanish. Others begin
to grow long, wavering, extra arms, godlike,
so that at last they touch
many things at once, and reach
towards everything; they too begin
the solitary dance.

The May Mornings

May mornings wear
light cashmere shawls of quietness,
brush back waterfalls of

burnished silk from
clear and round brows.
When we see them approaching
over lawns, trailing
dewdark shadows and footprints,
we remember, ah,
yes, the May mornings,
how could we have forgotten,
what solace it would have been
to think of them,
what solace
it would be in the bitter violence
of fire then ice again we
apprehend—but
it seems the May mornings
are a presence known
only as they pass
lightstepped, seriously smiling, bearing
each a leaflined basket
of wakening flowers.

Rain Spirit Passing

Have you ever heard the rain at night
streaming its flaxen hair against
the walls of your house?

Have you ever heard the rain at night
drifting its black, shiny, seaweed hair
through multistoreyed arcades of leaves?

And have you risen then
from bed and felt your way
to the window, and raised the blind, and seen

       stillness, unmisted moonlight, the air
       dry? Street and garden
       empty and silent?

You had been lying awake; the rain
was no dream. Yet where is it?

When did that rain descend and descend,
filling your chalices
until their petals loosened

and wafted
down to rest
on grass and the wet ground,

and your roots in their burrows
stretched and sighed?

II   PIG DREAMS

Her Destiny

The beginning: piglet among piglets,
the soft mud caking
our mother's teats.
Sweetsqueal, grunt:
her stiff white lashes, the sleepy
glint of her precious
tiny eyes.

                    •

But I am Sylvia. Chosen.
I was established
pet. To be
the pig of dreams, the pig
any of us could be,
            taken out of the sty,
            away from the ravaged soil of pig-yards,
            freed from boredom and ugliness.
I was chosen to live without dread of slaughter.

                    •

For three days, after they took me,
I hungered. Nowhere a teat to suck from,
no piglet siblings to jostle and nudge.

At last
     in the full moon's sacred light
     in the human room where I'd run
     in circles till my tapping trotters
     almost gave way,
the He-human
        naked and white as my
        lost mother,
bent on all-fours over my untouched bowl,
his beard a veil before me,
and with musical loud sounds of guzzling
showed me *eating*. Gave me
the joy of survival.

              •

Quicklearner, soon
I could hold my shit.
I was rocked in warm
human arms.
I liked laps, the thighs
of humans.
Cuddling.
     Every pig
could be cuddled if there were justice.
     Every human
could have its intelligent pig,
     every pig
its dextrous human. Our lives
would be rich as creamy corn,
tasty as acorns.

Dogbrothers

Pigalone. Sylvia.
Sylvia Orphan Onlypig.
Even my She-human's lap
could not console.
But then I found
my Dogbrothers.

Bark and growl,
dog-laugh, waving
tails and the joy
of chasing, of whirling,
squealing, my dainty trotters
trilling beneath me
sharp and sure!
Of huddling to doze
in warm quickbreathing
muddle of dogs,
almost believing
I, Sylvia,
am dog not pig.

The Catpig

John the cat
is most my brother,
almost pig

even though he
leaps among branches,
climbs to high shelves,
is silky.

Black and white Catpig,
I outgrew you,
but once we matched.

She-human gave us
our milk from
our pitcher.

Quiet we sat
under the sumacs of Vermont
and watched

the birds leave,
the first snow
pepper each other's
somber faces.

Winterpig

At the quick of winter
moonbrightest
snowdeepest

we would set out.
I'd run up my ramp
into the pickup,

we'd rattle and shake
two midnight miles
to the right hill.

Then on foot,
slither and struggle
up it—

they'd
ready their sled
and toboggan down

and I'd
put down my nose and
spread my ears and

tear down beside them,
fountains of snow
spurting around me:

I and my Humans
shouting, grunting,
the three of us

wild with joy,
just missing
the huge maples.

Yes, over and over
up to the top of the
diamond hill—

the leanest, the fastest,
most snow-and-moon-and-midnight-bewitched
pig in the world!

The Bride

They sent me away to be bred.
I was afraid, going down the ramp
from the truck to the strange barn,
I tried to run for the farmyard—strangers
shouted, they drove me inside.

In the barn a beautiful, imperious boar
dwelt in majesty. They brought me to him.
In the hot smell of him, I who was delicate,
     Sylvia the pet,
          who smelled of
     acorns and the windscoured pasture,
     I, Sylvia the Dreamer,
was brought low,
was brought
into the depths
of desire.
     I steeped my soul
          in the sweet dirt,
          the stench of
    My Lord Boar

     •

Terrible, after the sensuous dark,
     the week of passion and feasting,
—terrible my return.
I screamed when they dragged me
outdoors to the truck. Harsh light
jumped at my eyes. My body's weight
sagged on my slender legs.

In the house of My Lord Boar
I had eaten rich swill.

Back home, I headed for my
private house, the house of Sylvia—
and my swill-swollen body
          would not enter,
          could not fit.

In shame I lay
many nights
on the ground outside my Humans' window
and passed my days silent and humble
in the bare pasture, until I was lean again,
               until I could enter
               my maiden chamber once more.

But now I carried in me
the fruit of my mating.

Her Task

My piglets cling to me,
perfect, quickbreathing, plump—
kernels of pearly sweetcorn,
milky with my milk.

These shall I housetrain, I swear it,
these shall dwell like their mother
among dextrous humans, to teach them
pig-wisdom. O Isis, bless
thy pig's piglets.

Her Secret

In the humans' house
fine things abound:
furniture, rugs by the hearth,
bowls and pitchers, freezer and fridge,
closets of food, baskets of apples,
the Musical Saw on which

my He-human plays
                    the songs I dream . . .

In my neat A-frame
they think there is nothing,
only the clean straw of my bed.
But under the floor I gather
beautiful tins, nutshells, ribbons,
shining buttons, the thousand baubles
a pig desires.

They are well hidden.
Piglets shall find one day
an inheritance of shapes,
textures, mysterious substances—

Rubber! Velvet! Aluminum! Paper!

Yes, I am founding,
     stick by stick,
     wrapper by wrapper,
     trinkets, toys—
Civilization!

Her Nightmare

The dream is blood: I swim,
which is forbidden to pigs,
and the doom comes: my sharp
flailing feet cut
into my thick throat
and the river water
is stained, and fills, and
thickens with bright blood
and darkens, and I'm
choking, drained,
too weak to heave
out of the sticky
crimson mud, and
I sink and sink in it

screaming, and then
voiceless, and
when I wake it's
the dark of the moon.

Yet, when I was young,
not knowing the prohibition,
I did swim. The corn
was tall, and my skin
was dry as old
parchment of husks,
the creviced earth
scorched, and no rain
had fallen
for long and long:
when my She-human plunged
into the lovely
cool and wet river,
I too
plunged, and swam.
It was easy to me
as if the water
were air, and I
a young bird in flight.
My pig-wings
flailed, but my throat
was not slit, and we crossed
the river, and rested
under splashed leaves
on the far shore,
and I thought I would always
be Sylvia Waterpig.
O it was sweet
to be upborne
on the fresh-running current,
a challenge to push
across it and gain
the moss and shade.
I escaped
the doom
then.
        But I grew

heavier, thick in the throat,
properly pigshaped,
and learned the Law.
And now,
this dream, on some
black nights, fills up
my bowl of sleep
with terror,
with blood.

Her Lament

When they caressed
and held in loving arms
the small pig that I was,
I was so glad, I blessed
my singular fate.
How could I know
my Humans would not grow
to fit me, as I became
Sylvia the Sow?
He-and-She-Human stayed the same, and now
even look smaller.
Perhaps I should not have learned
to adore
pleasures that could not last?
I grew so fast.
My destiny
kept me lean, and yet
my weight increased.
Great Sylvia, I must stay
under the table at the humans' feast.
And once, scratching my back on it,
I made the table fall
dishes and all!
How could a cherished piglet
have grown so tall?

Her Sadness

When days are short,
mountains already
white-headed, the west
red in its branchy
leafless nest, I know

more than a simple
sow should know.

I know
the days of a pig—
and the days of dogbrothers, catpigs,
cud-chewing cowfriends—
are numbered,

even the days of
Sylvia the Pet,

even the days
of humans are numbered.
Already

laps are denied me,
I cannot be cuddled,
they scratch my ears
as if I were anypig, fattening for bacon.

I shall grow heavier still,
even though I walk
for miles with my Humans,
through field and forest.

Mortality
weighs on my shoulders,
I know
too much about Time for a pig.

Her Sister

Kaya, my gentle
        Jersey cowfriend,
                you are no pig,
you are slow to think,
             your moods
                are like rounded clouds
drifting over the pasture,
            casting
               pleasant shadows.
You lift your head
          slowly
             up from the grass
to greet me.
         Occupied
           with your cud, you are
all cow,
      yet we are friends,
             or even sisters.
We worship
        the same goddess,
              we look
to the same humans
         with love,
            for love.
When I tread
        the mud in pigpatterns
              after a shower,
my footprints shine
        and reflect the sky:
              in this
they resemble your huge
         kindly eyes.
            My own
are small,
     as befits a pig,
          but I behold your steep
graygold side,
      a bulwark
        beside me.

Her Delight

I, Sylvia, tell you, my piglets:
it has been given me
to spend a whole day up to my snout
in the velvet wetness that is mud:

and to walk undriven, at dusk,
back to the human-house
and be welcomed there:

welcomed by humans and cats and dogs,
not reproached for my mantle
of graying mud:

welcomed, and given to eat
a food of human magic, resembling mud
and tasting
of bliss: and its holy name
is *chocolate*.

I, Sylvia, your mother,
have known
the grace of pig-joy.

Her Judgement

I love my own Humans and their friends,
but let it be said,
that my litters may heed it well,
their race is dangerous.

They mock the race of Swine, and call
'swinish' men they condemn.
Have they not appetites? Do *we*
plan for slaughter to fill our troughs?

Their fat ones, despised, waddle large-footed,
their thin ones hoard

inedible discs and scraps
called 'money.' Us they fatten,
us they exchange for this;

and they breed us not that our life
may be whole, pig-life
thriving alongside dog-life, bird-life,
grass-life, all
the lives of earth-creatures,

but that we may be devoured. Yet,
it's not being killed for food
destroys us. Other animals
hunt one another. But only Humans,

I think, first corrupt their prey
as we are corrupted, stuffed with temptation
until we can't move,

crowded until we turn on each other,
our name and nature abused.

It is their greed
overfattens us.
Dirt we lie in
is never unclean as their minds,
who take our deformed lives
without thought, without
respect for the Spirit Pig.

Pig-song

Walnut, hickory, beechmast,
apples and apples, a meadow
of applegrass dapple.
Walnut, hickory, beechmast.
And over the sunfall slope,
cool of the dark mudwallow.

Her Vision

My human love, my She-human,
speaks to me in Piggish. She knows
my thoughts, she sees my emotions
flower and fade, fade and flower
as my destiny unrolls
its carpet, its ice and apples.

Not even she
knows all my dreams.
Under the russet sky
at dusk
I have seen
the Great Boar pass

invisible save to me.

His tusks are
flecked with skyfoam.
His eyes
red stars.

Her Prayer

O Isis my goddess,
my goddess Isis,
forget not thy pig.

Isis Speaks

Sylvia, my faithful
Petpig, teacher
of humans, fount
of pig-wisdom:
you shall yet know
the grief of parting:
your humans, bowed with regret,

shall leave you.
But hear me,
this is no dream:
the time shall come
when you shall dwell,
revered,
in a house of your own
even finer than that you have.
And though you no longer
enter the houses of humans,
in springtimes to come
your black hide shall be strewn
with constellations of blossom.
Yes, in the deep summers,
apples shall bounce on your roof,
the ripe and round
fruit of your own appletree.
There you shall live long, and at peace,
redreaming the lore of your destiny.

III   PEOPLE, PLACES, VISIONS

An Arrival (North Wales, 1897)

The orphan arrived in outlandish hat,
proud pain of new button boots.
Her moss-agate eyes
photographed views of the noonday sleepy town
no one had noticed. Nostrils flaring,
she sniffed odors of hay and stone,
                    absence of Glamorgan coaldust,
and pasted her observations quickly
into the huge album of her mind.
Cousins, ready to back off like heifers
were staring:
                    amazed, they received
the gold funeral sovereigns she dispensed
along with talk strange to them as a sailor's parrot.

Auntie confiscated the gold;
the mourning finery, agleam with jet,
was put by to be altered. It had been chosen
by the child herself and was thought
unsuitable. She was to be
the minister's niece, now,
not her father's daughter.
                              Alone,
she would cut her way, through a new world's
graystone chapels, the steep and sideways
rockface cottages climbing
mountain streets,

enquiring, turning things over
in her heart,
                    weeping only in rage or when
the choirs in their great and dark and
golden glory broke forth and the hills
skipped like lambs.

Visitant

i

From under wide wings of blackest velvet
—a hat such as the Duse might have worn—
peered out at me my mother,
tiny and silver-white, her ancient skin delicately
pink, her eyes their familiar very dark
pebble-green, flecked with amber. 'Mother,'
I cried or mumbled, urgent but even now
embarrassed, 'can you forgive me? Did you,
as I've feared and feared, feel betrayed
when I failed to be there
at the worst time, and returned
too late? Am I forgiven?' But she looked vague
under the velvet, the ostrich-down, her face small;
if she said mildly, 'There is nothing to forgive,'
it seemed likely she wasn't listening,
she was preoccupied with some concerns

of that other life, and when she faded
I was left unabsolved still, the raven drama
of her hat more vivid to me
than she in her polite inattention.
                         This, I told myself,
is fitting: if the dead live
for a while in partial semblances
of their past selves, they have no time
to bear grudges or to bless us;
their own present
holds them intent. Yet perhaps
sometimes they dream us.

ii

Another time she arrived
through the French window at home
(the house that has no place now
to *be* in, except in me)
with gypsy bundles, laughing, excited,
old but not ancient yet, strong,
a lone traveller.
                         It was clear
she had come only to visit,
not to remain—
'It was a long trip,' she said,
'from Heaven to here!'
and we hugged and laughed and were comfortable.
I saw each thread
in the tapestry seat of a forgotten chair,
cloudy figures in the marble mantelpiece,
each detail of that vanished room.
A joyful meeting, and she
incandescent with joy.
Yet next day my perplexed grief
did not lift away but still,
like a mallard with clipped wings
circles me summer and winter, settled
for life in my life's reedy lake.

Marta (Brazil, 1928)

A Saxon peasant girl
darning a sock, is telling
household tales to her sleepy daughters.
'So the roasting pan
said to the little brown hen—'
Looking up, she sees
their eyes have closed. No need
to tell what it said.
She trims the lamp,
sits in the small circle of gold;
dark of the room's corners
is in league with the dark outside.
The forest
is not the familiar forest of proper trees
whose names she knew,
woodland of midsummer Sunday walks,
Grandmother's märchen,
understandable dangers.
This is the jungle. Here
enormous dazzling butterflies lure her children
into the underbrush among the snakes.
Birds whose violent beauty
makes her long for the humble brown
of a thrush, scream through vines
that everywhere
hide those unknowable trees, trunks
masked in green and blossom, boughs
a ceiling of dense foliage and flashes
of hot sky. At times
a band of monkeys will leap
to the ridge of her roof, which Hans
has built like a homeland roof,
sound and well-joined, from outlandish wood.
The creatures chatter:
their speech is strange, but no stranger
than what the people spoke whom they met
on the voyage and long journey to come here.
The clearing is still too small;
the jungle's too near, and grows
too fast, in endless rain and
steaming sunlight.

Oh,
where can he be? Three days already
have gone since he should have returned.
Oil for the lamp's
getting low . . . but what if right now
with a flashlight, he's making his way
back home? If there's no light,
it will seem like no welcome.

> *And Hans never comes. Has drowned*
> *a mile from home, falling*
> *face forward into a rainswollen stream,*
> *feet entangled in ropes of vine,*
> *pack of supplies holding him down,*
> *Months will pass*
> *before his bones are discovered.*

Marta rethreads her needle with bluegrey wool.
Her ears ache with listening:
silent slumber of Trudi,
just-audible breathing of Emmi,
unceasing hum and buzz and creaking and rustle
of Amazon forest,
                    thump of her heart.
Posture of waiting,
gesture of darning,
golden halo of lamplight—patient, unknowing,
Maria remains forever
a story without an ending,
broken off in the telling.

Winter Afternoons in the V. & A., pre-W.W. II

Rain unslanting, unceasing,
darkening afternoon streets.

Within lofty and vast halls,
no one but I, except for

the ancient guards, survivors
of long-ago battles, dozing

under a spell, perched
on the brittle chairs of their sinecure.

My shoes made no sound. I found
everything for myself,

everything in profusion.
Lace of wrought iron,

wrought jewels, Cellini's dreams,
disappearing fore-edge paintings,
chain mail, crinolines, Hokusai, Cotman.
Here was history

as I desired it: magical, specific,
jumbled, unstinting,

a world for the mind to sift
in its hourglass—now, while I was twelve,
or forever.

Heights, Depths, Silence, Unceasing Sound of the Surf

Are they birds or butterflies?
They are sailing, two, not a flock,
more silver-white than the high
clouds, blissful
solitary lovers in infinite azure.

Below them, within the reef,
green shallows, transparent.
                              Beyond,
bounded by angry lace that
flails the coral,
                the vast,
ironic dark Pacific.

Tonga, 1979

Tropic Ritual

Full moon's sharp
command transforms
the leafspine of each
palmfrond to curved
steel: in absolute
allegiance, uncountable scimitars
hail the unwitnessed hour. The humans
have withdrawn
curtained,
shuttered.
Stars fall, kamikaze
of ecstasy. The tide
submits and submits.
The moon exacts
penitent joy from lizards,
blood from dreaming women.
Dogs huddle
scared under the frangipani
which lets fall
silently one flower
into the sand.

Tonga, 1979

For Nikolai, Many Thousand Miles Away

The procession that has been crossing
the mountains of your mind since you were six
     and went to Mexico and Grandma showed you
     the trees or clouds moving
               along the horizon
traverses (clouds for now) this evening the Pacific,
up towards the Equator—horses, men,
centaurs, pilgrims, women with bundles, children;
refugees—or the wild heroes
of a mythology bearing its heavy altars
into the next of its worlds.
          In my hand,

a spiral shell I'd thought
an empty cornucopia
stirs—something looks out of it
and searches my palm with delicate
probing claws, annoyed.
Among the last stains of sundown
the stars return. I look about
for the Southern Cross, and am given—whist!
a shooting star.
                    The great world and its wars
are a long way off, news wavers over
the radio and goes out, you and your life
are half a world distant, and in daylight.
                                        Here
the surf the reef holds back
speaks without ceasing,
drawing breath
only to utter the next words of its rune.
Crickets begin—deaf to that great insistence—
to praise the night.
Above the dark ocean, over coral, over continents
the riders move, their power
felt but not understood, their will
remote.

For a Child

'In the field, a
        dark thing.'
'It was, oh, a
        bush or something'

'No no, a
        dark thing,
something that could
        look at me.'

'Was it like a bear?
        Was it like a moose?'
'No, it was a dark thing
        keeping still to look at me.'

'Was it fierce? Was it foul?
        Was it going to leap upon you?'
'No, it was a shy thing,
        keeping still to look at me.'

Continent
        for Dennis Lee

In Canada, a sense
of weight, of burden,
of under the belly of the live
animal land, a clod, or maybe
another beast that clutches
and hangs there. Florida
is its tail, muscular, succulent.

And in the U.S. sometimes
a draft, a current
of air, chills and heightens
the senses, an idea
of mind, of space, of less
dense flesh, something
not ethereal but poignant, a head
crowned with carved ice.

From the Train, Eastward

Furry blond wheatfield in
predawn light—I
thought it was a frozen pond.

                        •

Small town, early morning.
No cars. Sunlit
children wait for the green light.

                        •

A deer! It leapt the fence,
scared of the train!
Did anyone else see it?

And twenty miles later
again a deer,
the exact same arc of gold!

.

After the trumpets, the
kettledrums, the
bold crescendo of mountains—

prairie subtleties, verbs
declined in gray,
green tones sustained, vast plainsong.

Old People Dozing

Their thoughts are night gulls
following the ferry, gliding
in and out of the window light
and through the reflected wall there, the door
that holds at its center
an arabesque of foam
always at vanishing point,
                              night gulls
that drift on airstream, reverse, swoop
out of sight, return, memory
moving again through the closed door,
white and effortless, hungry.

Eyes And No-Eyes

Sewing together the bits of data
abandoned by the retina.

Well, here was a hand.
We never did see
the lines of its palm.
But fate had inscribed the knuckles,
anyway. Remember?

Oh—that shine,
that reflection on the dark
T.V. screen.
What I was looking at

was a violet,
a shy symbol in purple. No,
a whole jarful of violets.

Their stems are long, they seek
light, perhaps maligned
by imputations of modesty:
nothing cares to be praised by mistake.

                        That shine
of noon on dark glass
distracted me. Plus what I knew.
How briefly
I focussed on pointed petals and
the white sanctum,
the gold herm within,
the magic eyelash-fine stripes of
darker purple
that led to it like strips of prayer rug.

Two Artists

i

Rosalie Gascoigne.
Old nails, their large flat heads
a gray almost silver, bunched
in a blue-glazed stoneware pot—
flowers of the playful mind.
She has fenced one side

of an open invisible square with pickets of feathers—
and here's a bowlful of turret shells,
fingernail size, you can dip your hands in
as into millet, and hear
the music of jostled brittleness.
The room's a temple, the kind that's
thronged with casual, un-awestruck worshippers,
and crowded with small shrines, each
a surprise, and dedicated
each in its turn, to the principle
that nothing is boring, everything's
worth a second look. Presiding,
there's an escutcheon, its emblems
shapes unnamed by geometrists:
slabs of old wood, weathered, residual,
formed by the absence of what was cut
for forgotten purpose, out of their past:
they meet now, austere, graceful,
transfigured by being placed,
being seen.

ii

Memphis Wood.

A studio looped with huge
hanks of wool, of scarlet,
jute and velvet and blue,
rough, braid, swathe, yardage—
textures and colors so profuse, who
can tell noun from adjective,
the process continuous, table, wall,
the woven stitched tied construct
triumphant but never
disowning its origins, scissors
opening roads in landscapes of cloth,
pilgrim needles zigzagging
through gloss and viridian, crimson,
cotton, a motet of fabric, a lace forest
grown by two hands, one vision.

Williams: An Essay

His theme
over and over:

the twang of plucked
catgut
from which struggles
music,

the tufted swampgrass
quicksilvering
dank meadows,

a baby's resolute fury—metaphysic
of appetite and tension.

Not
the bald image, but always—
undulant, elusive, beyond reach
of any dull
staring eye—lodged

among the words, beneath
the skin of image: nerves,

muscles, rivers
of urgent blood, a mind

secret, disciplined, generous and
unfathomable.
                    Over

and over,
his theme
                    hid itself and
smilingly reappeared.
                            He loved
persistence—but it must
be linked to invention: landing
backwards, 'facing
into the wind's teeth,'
                    to please him.

He loved
the lotus cup, fragrant
upon the swaying water, loved

the wily mud
pressing swart riches into its roots,

and the long stem of connection.

IV   THE ACOLYTE

Holiday
   for K.

i   Postcard

It's not that I can't
get by without you
it's just that
I wasn't lonesome
before I met you.
It's something to do with
salt losing its savor
when that half of the world
one wants to share
stays in one's pocket, half
a crispy delicious bacon sandwich
saved, but for—oh, like Shelley's
posy of dewy flowers, remember,
how he turns to give it—
ah, to whom?

ii   Meeting Again

At Nepenthe, screaming
Steller jays adorn
the gulfs of air. We bask
in sea-sunwarmth. Trees

are blackly green, a phoenix
rages at its prey. I ask
for more coffee and more
of your story. You are telling
of suffering, I suffer
hearing it, but rejoice with you
in the jays' blue, their black
heads, the sheen
of feathers and of the sea.
Let's be
best friends: I'll love you
always if you'll love me.

iii   To Eros

Eros, O Eros, hail
thy palate, god who knows
good pasta,
good bread,
good Brie.
        The beauty
of freckled squid, flowers of the sea
fresh off the boat, graces
thy altar, Eros, which is in
our eyes. And on our lips
the blood of berries
before we kiss, before we
stumble to bed.
        Our bed
must be, in thy service, earth—
as the strawberry bed
is earth, a ground
for miracles.
        The flesh
is delicate, we must nourish it:
desire hungers
for wine, for clear plain water,
good strong coffee,
as well as for hard cock and
throbbing clitoris and the
glide and thrust of
sentence and paragraph in and up to the

last sweet sigh of a
chapter's ending.

iv   **Love Letter**

Fragrant with sandalwood, with lightest
oil of almond,

our hearts still flying around and around
            like silver wheels that
            can't stop spinning
                all in a moment,

we lay at rest, holding
tight to each other,
                not ready yet
to relax and
each move off into separateness.

Then in words
you gave me
to myself:

you made me know I'd
given you what I
wanted to give,
that I hadn't
been travelling alone . . .
                You wonder
who you are, if you exist, what
you can do with your energy, has it
a center?
        I tell you,
if you can love a woman
the way you love
blackberries,
strawberries in the sun,
the small red onions you plant,
or a hawk riding
the sway of wind over ocean,
if you can make her know it
even for a moment,

you are as real
as earth itself.
                    No one confirms
an other unless
he himself rays forth
from a center. This
is the human inscape, this
is the design our fragile
shifting molecules strive to utter
upon the airy spaces where it's
so hard to find foothold.

v   **Postcard**

There's a thistle here
smells of meadowsweet—
so sweet,
so meadow-fragrant
among its prickles.
Yarrow is plentiful,
                    that China and old England
                    both knew had occult
                    power—but I can divine
no messages.
                    The roses
have no scent. The sea
here is a landlocked Sound.
It says *I miss you*, breaking
quiet upon the dark sand.

She and the Muse

Away he goes, the hour's delightful hero,
arrivederci: and his horse clatters
out of the courtyard, raising
a flurry of straw and scattering hens.

He turns in the saddle waving a plumed hat,
his saddlebags are filled with talismans,
mirrors, parchment histories, gifts and stones,
indecipherable clues to destiny.

He rides off in the dustcloud of his own
story and when he has vanished she
who had stood firm to wave and watch
from the top step, goes in to the cool

flagstoned kitchen, clears honey and milk and bread
off the table, sweeps from the hearth
ashes of last night's fire, and climbs the stairs
to strip tumbled sheets from her wide bed.

          Now the long-desired
visit is over. The heroine
is a scribe. Returned to solitude,
eagerly she re-enters the third room,

the room hung with tapestries, scenes that change
whenever she looks away. Here is her lectern,
here her writing desk. She picks a quill,
dips it, begins to write. But not of him.

Volupté

Mmm, yes, narcissus, mmm.
Licking my scented fingers.
The squat bulb
complacent under its stars.

The Acolyte

The large kitchen is almost dark.
Across the plain of even, diffused light,
copper pans on the wall and the window geranium
tend separate campfires.
Herbs dangle their Spanish moss from rafters.

At the table, floury hands
kneading dough, feet planted
steady on flagstones,

a woman ponders the loaves-to-be.
Yeast and flour, water and salt,
have met in the huge bowl.

It's not
the baked and cooled and cut
bread she's thinking of,
but the way
the dough rises and has a life of its own,

not the oven she's thinking of
but the way
the sour smell changes
to fragrance.

She wants to put
a silver rose or a bell of diamonds
into each loaf;
she wants

to bake a curse into one loaf,
into another, the words that break
evil spells and release
transformed heroes into their selves;
she wants to make
bread that is more than bread.

V   AGE OF TERROR

The Split Mind

A Governor
is signing papers, arranging deals.
His adored grandchild
sits at his feet; he gives her
the architect's model of the nuclear plant to play with.
'A little house' she says,
'with funny fat chimneys.'
'Goddamn commies,' he mutters, crushing

the report on nuclear hazards into a ball and
tossing it across the room, ignoring
the wastebasket and plutonium and the idea
that he could be wrong, one gesture
sufficing for all.
                    He strokes
her shining hair. Her death
is in his hands; in hers
the simulacrum of his will to power,
a funerary playhouse. If he lives
to see her change
in the sick radiance later,
after the plant is built,
what will he tell himself?
How deep, how deep
does the split go, the fault line
under the planned facility,
into his mind?

Engraved

A man and woman
sit by the riverbank.
He fishes,
she reads.
The fish are not biting.
She has not turned the page
for an hour.
The light around them
holds itself taut,
no shadow moves,
but the sky and the woods,
look, are dark.
Night has advanced upon them.

The Vron Woods (North Wales)

In the night's dream of day
the woods were fragrant.

Carapaced, slender, vertical,
            red in the slant
            fragmented light, uprose
Scotch firs,
boughs a vague smoke of
green.
            Underfoot
                  the slipping
of tawny needles.

I was wholly there,
aware of each step
in the hum of quietness,
each breath.
                  Sunlight
a net
      of discs and lozenges, holding
odor of rosin.

These were the Vron Woods,
                  felled
      seven years before I was born,

      levelled,
                  to feed a war.

Sound of the Axe

Once a woman went into the woods.
The birds were silent. Why? she said.
Thunder, they told her,
thunder's coming.
She walked on, and the trees were dark
and rustled their leaves. Why? she said.
The great storm, they told her,
the great storm is coming.
She came to the river, it rushed by
without reply, she crossed the bridge,
she began to climb
up to the ridge where grey rocks

bleach themselves, waiting
for crack of doom,
and the hermit
had his hut, the wise man
who had lived since time began.
When she came to the hut
there was no one.
But she heard his axe.
She heard
the listening forest.
She dared not follow the sound
of the axe. Was it
the world-tree he was felling?
Was this the day?

Desolate Light

We turn to history looking
for vicious certainties through which
voices edged into song,

engorged fringes of anemone swaying
dreamily through deluge,

gray Lazarus bearing
the exquisite itch and ache of blood returning.

Reason has brought us
more dread than ignorance did.
Into the open
well of centuries

we gaze, and see gleaming,
deep in the black broth at the bottom,
chains of hope by which our forebears
hoisted themselves
hand over hand towards light.

But we
stand at the edge looking back in and knowing

too much to reasonably hope. Their desired light
burns us.

> *O dread,*
drought that dries
the ground of joy till it cracks and
caves in,

O dread,
wind that sweeps up the offal of lies,
sweep my knowledge, too, into oblivion,

drop me back in the well.

No avail.

Concurrence

Each day's terror, almost
a form of boredom—madmen
at the wheel and
stepping on the gas and
the brakes no good—
and each day one,
sometimes two, morning-glories,
faultless, blue, blue sometimes
flecked with magenta, each
lit from within with
the first sunlight.

An English Field in the Nuclear Age

To render it!—*this* moment,
                              haze and halos of
                sunbless'd particulars, knowing
no one,
        not lost and dearest nor
        the unfound,
could,

                    though summoned,
                    though present,
      partake nor proffer vision unless
                              (named, spun, tempered, stain of it
                              sunk into steel of utterance) it
                    be wrought:
                    (centuries furrowed in oakbole, *this* oak,
                    these dogrose pallors, that very company
                              of rooks plodding
                                    from stile to stile of the sky) :
      to render that isolate knowledge, certain
                    (shadow of oakleaves, larks
                    urging the green wheat into spires)
      there is no sharing save in the furnace,
      the transubstantiate, acts
                              of passion:
                                          (the way

            air, *this* minute, searches
            warm bare shoulders, blind, a lover,

            and how among
            thistles, nettles, subtle silver
            of long-dried cowpads,

            gold mirrors of buttercup satin
            assert eternity as they reflect
            nothing, everything, absolute instant,
            and dread

            holds its breath, for
            this minute at least was
            not the last).

Grey August

The dog's thigh, the absurd heaven,

the dog's thigh extended, thigh of an Odalisque,
the absurdly pale, shrinking, panic of the sky,
an arched heaven of terror,

like an Etruscan outstretched
to partake of wine the dark
relaxed dog, the heavens intimidated
by smog and preparations for thunder, the sensual patient
placing of himself on the cool linoleum
indoors, outdoors the white sky and humid
thick of air, a veiled twilight, his paws
not twitching, his head at rest,

at last something stirs the
ashleaves to sibilance, an ear
flicks up but disregards
this, the dog has not
seen the sky, he will know
thunder when it comes, if it comes
the heavens will retrieve
their pride, the dog's thigh
quivers, it will be,
for this day,
thunder, not war.

Beginners

Dedicated to the memory of Karen Silkwood and Eliot Gralla

'*From too much love of living,*
     Hope and desire set free,
Even the weariest river
     Winds somewhere to the sea—'

But we have only begun
to love the earth.

We have only begun
to imagine the fulness of life.

How could we tire of hope?
—so much is in bud.

How can desire fail?
—we have only begun

to imagine justice and mercy,
only begun to envision

how it might be
to live as siblings with beast and flower,
not as oppressors.

Surely our river
cannot already be hastening
into the sea of nonbeing?

Surely it cannot
drag, in the silt,
all that is innocent?

Not yet, not yet—
there is too much broken
that must be mended,

too much hurt we have done to each other
that cannot yet be forgiven.

We have only begun to know
the power that is in us if we would join
our solitudes in the communion of struggle.

So much is unfolding that must
complete its gesture,

so much is in bud.

Psalm: People Power at the Die-in

Over our scattered tents by night
lightning and thunder called to us.

Fierce rain blessed us,
catholic, all-encompassing.

We walked through blazing morning
into the city of law,

of corrupt order, of invested power.

By day and by night
we sat in the dust,

on the cement pavement we sat down and sang.

In the noon of a long day, sharing the work of the play,
we died together, enacting

the death by which all
shall perish unless we act.

.

Solitaries drew close, releasing
each solitude into its blossoming.

We gave to each other the roses
of our communion—

A culture of gardens, horticulture not agribusiness,
arbors among the lettuce, small terrains.

.

When we tasted the small, ephemeral
harvest of our striving,

great power flowed from us,
luminous, a promise. Yes! . . .

great energy flowed from solitude,
and great power from communion.

About Political Action in Which Each Individual Acts from the Heart

When solitaries draw close, releasing
each solitude into its blossoming,

when we give to each other the roses
of our communion—

a culture of gardens, horticulture not agribusiness,
arbors among the lettuce, small terrains—

when we taste in small victories sometimes
the small, ephemeral yet joyful
harvest of our striving,

great power flows from us,
luminous, a promise. Yes! . . . Then

great energy flows from solitude,
and great power from communion.

What It Could Be

Uranium, with which we know
only how to destroy,

lies always under
the most sacred lands—

Australia, Africa, America,
wherever it's found is found an oppressed
ancient people who knew
long before white men found and named it
that there under their feet

under rock, under mountain, deeper
than deepest watersprings, under
the vast deserts familiar
inch by inch to their children

lay a great power.
                    And they knew the folly
of wresting, wrestling, ravaging from the earth
that which it kept
                    so guarded.

Now, now, now at this instant,
men are gouging lumps of that power, that presence,
out of the tortured planet the ancients
say is our mother.
                            Breaking the doors
of her sanctum, tearing the secret
out of her flesh.

But left to lie, its metaphysical weight
might in a million years have proved
benign, its true force being to be
a clue to righteousness—
showing forth
the human power
not to kill, to choose
not to kill: to transcend
the dull force of our weight and will;

that known profound presence, *un*touched,
the sign
providing witness,
            occasion,
            ritual
for the continuing act of
*non*violence, of passionate
reverence, active love.

In Memory of Muriel Rukeyser

The last event
of Black Emphasis Week.
In the big auditorium, 2 or 3 Whites, 4 or 5 Blacks,
watch the lynching.

In technicolor,
fictive, not
documentary black and white—

the truth, nonetheless,
white and black.

And the burning.
Familiar—
torching of
brittle timber,
or straw.

      Asia or Alabama,
      the screen gives forth
      an odor. Fat. Hair.
      There will be bones
      in the hot rubble. Black
      bones, or yellow,
      ash white.

The film continues,
reel after reel. Ends. And now
the few who were here—
                  scattered, like dim lights
of prairie farms seen from a plane,
                 isolate,
                     lost—
have gone out when you turn to leave.

Out, now, into night.
The world is dark, the movie's over,
it's showing again in your head but
your sobs are silent,
you shake

with despair in the
night which holds

trees, soft air,
music pulsing from a dorm,

and a thousand students who chose
not to attend

the truth of fiction,
history, their own. 'No one

to witness and adjust,'

drifting.
     You think: *Perhaps*

we deserve
no more, we humans,
cruel and dull.
No more time.
          We've made
our cathedrals,
had our chance,

blown it.

     You will never
feel more alone than this. Or will you?
Yes. There are 'cliffs of fall'
steeper, deeper.

And you remember
the passion for life, the vision
of love and work

your great intelligent friend had,
who died last week.
Is this despair

a link of those chains she called
the sense of shame?

At Scottsboro she
saw plain,
in black and white,

terror
and hatred;

didn't despair,
grieved, worked,
moved beyond shame,

fought forty years more.

You cross
the darkness

still shaking, enter
the house you've been given,

turn up the desk light,
sit down to plan

the next day. How else
to show your respect?

'No one
to drive the car.' *Well,
let's walk then*, she says,
when you imagine her.

Now. Stop shaking. Imagine her.

She was a cathedral.

A Speech: For Antidraft Rally, D.C., March 22, 1980

As our planet swings and sways
into its new decade
under the raped moon's weary glance,

I've heard the voices
of high-school kids on the bus home to the projects,
of college students (some of them female, this time)
in the swimmingpool locker room, saying,

'If there's a war—' 'If there's a war—'
'I don't want to get drafted but
if there's a war I'll go'—'If there's a war
I'd like to fight' 'If there's a war
I'll get pregnant'
'Bomb Tehran'—'Bomb Moscow' I heard them say.

Ach! They're the same ones, male and female, who ask,
'Which came first, Vietnam or Korea?'

'What was My Lai?' The same kids who think
Ayatollah Khomeini's a, quote, 'Commie.' Who think
World War Two was fought against, quote, 'Reds,' namely
Hitler and some Japs.

No violence they've seen
on the flickering living-room screen familiar since infancy
or the movies of adolescent dates, the dark
so much fuller of themselves, of each other's presence than of
history (and the history anyway
twisted—not that they have a way to know that)—
  the dark
  vibrant with themselves, with warm breath,
  half suppressed mirth, the wonder
  of being alive, terrified, entranced
  by sexual fragrance each gives off
  among popcorn, clumsy
  gestures, the weird
  response of laughter when on that screen
  death's happening, Wow, *unreal*, and people
  suffer, or dream aloud . . . None of that spoon-fed violence
prepares them. The disgusting routine horror of war
eludes them. They think
they would die for something they call America,
vague, as true dreams are not; something they call
freedom, the *Free World*, without ever knowing
what *freedom* means, what *torture* means, what *relative* means.
They are free to spray walls with crude
assertions—numbers, pathetic names; free
to disco, to disagree—if they're in school—
with the professor. Great. They don't know
that's not enough, they don't know
ass from elbow, blood from ketchup, that knowledge
is kept from them, they've been taught to assume
if there's a war there's
also a future, they know
not only nothing,
in their criminally neglected imaginations, about
the way war always meant
not only dying but killing,
not only killing but seeing
not only your buddy dying but
your buddy in the act of killing, not nice,

not only
your buddy killing but the dying
of those you
killed yourself, not always
quick, and
not always soldiers.

Yes, not only do draft-age people mostly
not know how that kind of war's become almost a pastoral
compared to *new* war, the kind
in which they may find themselves (while the usual
pinkfaced men, smoothshaved, overfed, placed in power
by the parents of those expendable young, continue
to make the decisions they are programmed for) but also

they know nothing at all about radiation
nothing at all about lasers
nothing at all about how the bombs
the Pentagon sits on like some grotesque
chicken caged in its nest and fed
cancerous hormones, exceed and exceed and exceed
Hiroshima, over and over and over, in weight
                              in power
                              in horror
                              of genocide.
                    When they say
'If there's a war,
I'll go,' they don't know
they would be going to kill
                    themselves,
                         their mamas and papas,
                         brothers and sisters
                              lovers.
When they say, 'If there's a war, I'll get pregnant,'
          they don't seem to know
                              that war would destroy that baby.
When they say, 'I'd like to fight,'
                         for quote, 'freedom,'
                         for quote, the 'Free World,'
                         for quote, 'America,'—
for whatever they think they'd be fighting for,
               those children,
                    those children with braces on their teeth,

                    fears in their notebooks,
                 acne on their cheeks,
                 dreams in their
                         inarticulate hearts
            whom the powerful men at their desks
            designate as the age group suitable for registration,
they don't know they'd be fighting
very briefly, very
successfully,
quite conclusively,
for the destruction of this small
lurching planet, this confused
lump of
rock and soil, ocean and air,
on which our songs, cathedrals, gestures
of faith and splendor
have grown like delicate moss, and now
may or may not survive
the heavy footsteps of our inexcusable ignorance,
the chemical sprays of our rapacious idiocy,
our minds that are big enough
to imagine love, imagine peace, imagine
community—but may not
be big enough to learn in time
how to say no.
                    My dear
fellow-humans, friends, strangers, who would be friends
if there were time—
let us *make* time, let us unite to say
NO to the drift to war, the drift
to take care of little disasters by making a
big disaster and then
the last disaster,
                    from which
no witness will rise,
no seeds.
Let us unite to tell
all we have learned about old-fashioned war's
vomit and shit, about new fashioned war's
abrupt end to all hope—
unite to tell what we know to the wholebodied young,
unwitting victims lined up ready already
like calves at the pen for slaughter;

share what we know, until no more
young voices talk of 'If there's a war,' but all say
No, and again no to the draft, and no to war,
and no to the sacrifice
of anyone's blood to the corporate beast that dreams
it can always somehow
save its own skin.
                         Let our different dream,
and more than dream, our acts
of constructive refusal generate
struggle. And love. We must dare to win
not wars, but a future
in which to live.

For the New Year, 1981

I have a small grain of hope—
one small crystal that gleams
clear colors out of transparency.

I need more.

I break off a fragment
to send you.

Please take
this grain of a grain of hope
so that mine won't shrink.

Please share your fragment
so that yours will grow.

Only so, by division,
will hope increase,

like a clump of irises, which will cease to flower
unless you distribute
the clustered roots, unlikely source—
clumsy and earth-covered—
of grace.

Age of Terror

Between the fear
of the horror of Afterwards
and the despair
in the thought of no Afterwards,
we move abraded,
each gesture scraping us
on the millstones.

In dream
there was an Afterwards:
        the unknown device—
                a silver computer as big as a
                block of offices at least,
                                floating
                like Magritte's castle on its rock, aloft
                in blue sky—
        did explode,
                        there was
                a long moment of cataclysm,
                                        light
of a subdued rose-red suffused
all the air before
a rumbling confused darkness ensued,
but
I came to,
            face down,
                        and found
my young sister alive near me,
and knew my still younger brother
and our mother and father
                        were close by too,
and, passionately relieved, I
comforted my shocked sister,
                        still not daring
to raise my head,
only stroking and kissing her arm,
afraid to find devastation around us
though we, all five of us,
seemed to have survived—and I readied myself
to take rollcall: 'Paul Levertoff? Beatrice Levertoff?'

And then in dream—not knowing
if this device, this explosion, were radioactive or not,
but sure that where it had centered
there must be wreck, terror,
fire and dust—
the millstones
commenced their grinding again,

and as in daylight
again we were held between them, cramped,
scraped raw by questions:

perhaps, indeed, we were safe; perhaps
no worse was to follow?—but . . .
what of our gladness, when there,
          where the core of the strange
          roselight had flared up
          out of the detonation of brilliant
          angular silver,
there must be others, others in agony,
and as in waking daylight,
the broken dead?

Talk in the Dark

We live in history, says one.
We're flies on the hide of Leviathan, says another.

Either way, says one,
fears and losses.

And among losses, says another,
the special places our own roads were to lead to.

Our deaths, says one.
That's right, says another,
now it's to be a mass death.

Mass graves, says one, are nothing new.
No, says another, but this time there'll be no graves,
all the dead will lie where they fall.

Except, says one, those that burn to ash.
And are blown in the fiery wind, says another.

How can we live in this fear? says one.
From day to day, says another.

I still want to see, says one,
where my own road's going.

I want to live, says another, but where can I live
if the world is gone?

Writing in the Dark

It's not difficult.
Anyway, it's necessary.

Wait till morning, and you'll forget.
And who knows if morning will come.

Fumble for the light, and you'll be
stark awake, but the vision
will be fading, slipping
out of reach.

You must have paper at hand,
a felt-tip pen—ballpoints don't always flow,
pencil points tend to break. There's nothing
shameful in that much prudence: those are your tools.

Never mind about crossing your t's, dotting your i's—
but take care not to cover
one word with the next. Practice will reveal
how one hand instinctively comes to the aid of the other
to keep each line
clear of the next.

Keep writing in the dark:
a record of the night, or
words that pulled you from depths of unknowing,

words that flew through your mind, strange birds
crying their urgency with human voices,

or opened
as flowers of a tree that blooms
only once in a lifetime:

words that may have the power
to make the sun rise again.

Re-Rooting

We were trying to put the roots back,
wild and erratic straying root-limbs,
trying to fit them into the hole that was
cleancut in clay, deep but not
wide enough; or wide but too square—trying
to get the roots back into earth
before they dried out and died.
Ineptly we pulled and pushed
striving to encompass so many rivers
of wood and fiber in one confinement without
snapping the arteries of sap, the force
of life springing in them that made them
spring away from our hands—
we knew our own life was
tied to that strength, that strength we knew would
ebb away if we could not find within us
the blessed guile to tempt
its energy back into earth,
into the quiet depths from which we had
rashly torn it, and now clumsily
struggled to thrust it back not into sinuous corridors
fit for its subtleties, but obstinately
into an excavation dug by machine,
                    And I wake,
as if from dream, but discover
even this digging, better than nothing,
has not yet begun.

Unresolved

'*See the blood in the streets*'
Neruda

i

Fossil shells, far inland; a god; bones;
they lie exposed by the backhoe.

Little stars continue to confide their silken hopes
among rough leaves.

In blood, his own, a man writes on a wall,
Revolution or Death. Not then. Now.

Now in a dry crevice, the corn, His Grace
the God of Maíz,
wraps his parchment about the green nub
destined to be gold.

ii

When one has begun to believe
the grip of doubt tightens.

A child is born. Earthquake kills
20,000. That's the commonplace.

A dialectic always half perceived. We know
no synthesis.

iii

What we fear begins and begins. Fools and criminals
rule the world. Life is a handful of stones
loosely held in their fists.

iv

Merciful earthquake! Majestic lava pouring
unstinted from mountain's fire! Ceremonious flood!
You ravage but are not hideous. Compare:

chopped-off heads stare in El Salvador
at their steaming torsos, flat circles
                            that were their necks revealing
closepacked flesh and bone and the sectioned tubes
                                through which
food and drink used to pass, and breath. See it on film.

Run the scene over again. And over again.
For verisimilitude, many hundred times
will not be enough.
                        Just out of range—
of the camera, not of the bullets—
babies, tossed high for the Junta's
target practice, plummet
past their parents' upturned screaming faces and hit
the reddening river with small splashes.
Hear it. It sounds like someone idly pitching rocks;
as if a terrified dog were being stoned
while it swam in circles; while it drowned.

v

We know so much of daily bread,
of every thread of lovingly knit compassion;

garments of love clothe us, we rest
our heads upon darkness; when we wake

sapphire transparency calls forth our song.
And this is the very world, the same, the world
of vicious power, of massacre.
Our song is a bird that wants
to sing as it flies, to be
the wings of praise, but doubt

binds tight its wire to hold down
flightbones, choke back breath.
We know no synthesis.

The Great Wave

With my brother I ran
willingly into the sea:

our mother, our sister too,
all of us free and naked.

We knew nothing of risk,
only the sacred pleasure

of sun and sand and the
beckoning ocean:

in, into the leaping
green of the lilt of it.

But at once a vast wave
unfurled itself to seize me, furled

about me, bore me as a bubble
back and tilted aslant from

all shore; all sight, sound, thought of others swept
instantly into

remote distance—
                   Now is wholly
this lucent rampart up which

I can't climb but where
I cling, powerless, unable

to distinguish terror from delight, calm
only in the one wanhope, to keep

a breath alive above the enormous
roar of the sunlaughing utter

force of the great wave, ride
on in its dangerous cradle of swift
transparent silks that curve
in steel over and round me, bearing

westward, outward, beyond
all shores, the great

wave still mounting, moving,
poised and poised in its

flood of emerald, dark unshatterable
crystal of its

unfathomed purpose—

Mass for the Day of St. Thomas Didymus

> i **Kyrie**
> ii **Gloria**
> iii **Credo**
> iv **Sanctus**
> v **Benedictus**
> vi **Agnus Dei**

i   **Kyrie**

O deep unknown, guttering candle,
beloved nugget lodged
in the obscure heart's
last recess,
have mercy upon us.

We choose from the past, tearing morsels to feed
pride or grievance.
We live in terror
of what we know:

death, death, and the world's
death we imagine
        and cannot imagine,
we who may be
the first and the last witness.

We live in terror
of what we do not know,
in terror of not knowing,
of the limitless, through which freefalling
forever, our dread
sinks and sinks,

         or

    of the violent closure of all.

Yet our hope lies
in the unknown,
in our unknowing.

O deep, remote unknown,
O deep unknown,
Have mercy upon us.

ii   **Gloria**

Praise the wet snow
    falling early.
Praise the shadow
    my neighbor's chimney casts on the tile roof
even this gray October day that should, they say,
have been golden.
           Praise
the invisible sun burning beyond
   the white cold sky, giving us
light and the chimney's shadow.
Praise
god or the gods, the unknown,
that which imagined us, which stays
our hand,
our murderous hand,
             and gives us
still,
in the shadow of death,
     our daily life,
     and the dream still
of goodwill, of peace on earth.
Praise
flow and change, night and
the pulse of day.

iii   Credo

I believe the earth
exists, and
in each minim mote
of its dust the holy
glow of thy candle.
Thou
unknown I know,
thou spirit,
giver,
lover of making, of the
wrought letter,
wrought flower,
iron, deed, dream.
Dust of the earth,
help thou my
unbelief. Drift,
gray become gold, in the beam of
vision. I believe and
interrupt my belief with
doubt. I doubt and
interrupt my doubt with belief. Be,
belovéd, threatened world.
          Each minim
mote.
     Not the poisonous
luminescence forced
out of its privacy,
the sacred lock of its cell
broken. No,
the ordinary glow
of common dust in ancient sunlight.
Be, that I may believe. Amen.

iv   Sanctus

Powers and principalities—all the gods,
angels and demigods, eloquent animals, oracles,
storms of blessing and wrath—

all that Imagination
has wrought, has rendered,
striving, in throes of epiphany—

naming, forming—to give
to the Vast Loneliness
a hearth, a locus—

send forth their song towards
the harboring silence, uttering
the ecstasy of their names, the multiform
name of the Other, the known
Unknown, unknowable:

sanctus, hosanna, sanctus.

v   **Benedictus**

Blesséd is that which comes in the name of the spirit,
that which bears
the spirit within it.

The name of the spirit is written
in woodgrain, windripple, crystal,

in crystals of snow, in petal, leaf,
moss and moon, fossil and feather,

blood, bone, song, silence,
very word of
very word,
flesh and
vision.

      (But what of the deft infliction
      upon the earth, upon the innocent,
      of hell by human hands?

      Is the word
      audible under or over the gross
      cacophony of malevolence?
      Yet to be felt

on the palm, in the breast,
by deafmute dreamers,
a vibration
known in the fibers of
the tree of nerves, or witnessed
by the third eye to which
sight and sound are one?

What of the emptiness,
the destructive vortex that whirls
no word with it?)

In the lion's indolence,
    there spirit is,
in the tiger's fierceness
    that does not provide in advance
but springs
        only as hunger prompts,
        and the hunger
        of its young.

Blesséd is that which utters
its being,
the stone of stone,
the straw of straw,
            for there
spirit is.
            But can the name
utter itself
            in the downspin of time?
Can it enter
        the void?
                        Blesséd
be the dust. From dust the world
utters itself. We have no other
hope, no knowledge.
                The word
chose to become
flesh. In the blur of flesh
we bow, baffled.

vi   Agnus Dei

Given that lambs
are infant sheep, that sheep
are afraid and foolish, and lack
the means of self-protection, having
neither rage nor claws,
venom nor cunning,
what then
is this 'Lamb of God'?

This pretty creature, vigorous
to nuzzle at milky dugs,
woolbearer, bleater,
leaper in air for delight of being, who finds in astonishment
four legs to land on, the grass
all it knows of the world?
          With whom we would like to play,
whom we'd lead with ribbons, but may not bring
into our houses because
it would soil the floor with its droppings?

What terror lies concealed
in strangest words, *O lamb*
of God that taketh away
the Sins of the World: an innocence
                    smelling of ignorance,
                    born in bloody snowdrifts,
                    licked by forebearing
dogs more intelligent than its entire flock put together?

                    God then,
              encompassing all things, is
              defenseless? Omnipotence
              has been tossed away, reduced
              to a wisp of damp wool?

                    And we,
              frightened, bored, wanting
only to sleep till catastrophe
has raged, clashed, seethed and gone by without us,
                    wanting then
to awaken in quietude without remembrance of agony,

we who in shamefaced private hope
had looked to be plucked from fire and given
a bliss we deserved for having imagined it,

is it implied that *we*
must protect this perversely weak
animal, whose muzzle's nudgings
suppose there is milk to be found in us?
Must hold to our icy hearts
a shivering God?

.

So be it.
Come, rag of pungent
quiverings,
dim star.
Let's try
if something human still
can shield you,
spark
of remote light.

The Many Mansions

What I must not forget
is the world of the white herons

complete to the last hair of pondweed,
a world the size of an apple,

perfect and undefiled, with its own sky, its air,
flora and fauna, distance, mysteries.

What I must not forget
is the knowledge that vision gave me

that it was not a fragile, only, other world,
there were, there are (I learned) a host,

each unique, yet each having
the grace of recapitulating

a single radiance, multiform.

This is what, remembering,
I must try, telling myself again,

to tell you. For that the vision
was given me: to know and share,

     passing from hand to hand, although
     its clarity dwindles in our confusion,

the amulet of mercy.

OBLIQUE PRAYERS

I   DECIPHERINGS

Decipherings
for Guillevic

i

When I lose my center
of gravity
I can't fly:

levitation's
a stone
cast straight as a lark

to fall plumb
and rebound.

ii

Half a wheel's
a rising sun:
without spokes,
an arch:

half a loaf
reveals
the inner wheat:
leavened
transubstantiation.

iii

A child
grows in one's body,
pushes out and
breaks off :
       nerves

denying their
non-existence
twist and pinch
long after:
after that otherness
floats
far,
thistledown engine,

up and
over
horizon's ramparts.

iv

Felt life
grows in one's mind:
each semblance

forms and
reforms cloudy
links with
the next

and the next:
chimes and
gamelan gongs

resound:

pondering,
picking the tesserae,
blue or
perhaps vermilion,

what one aches for
is the mosaic music
makes in one's ears

transformed.

Broken Ghazals

Each life spins
              into its own orbit—rain
of meteor showers, sparkle of—
                     some brittle desire, is it?
                     the stab of deep pain?

Not without tearing
              a few fibers,
                    the magnet forces
pull apart. I. He. Being
              is not referential.

I wake: instant recollection—a shadow
                    threatens my son's life.
Others slide their elongations toward his spirit.

My being, unconformable
              to his perception,
moves on. Awake, I keep waking.

He survives
            and leaves, moving
through the apparition he sees and
                    away from it.

Again waking, I stretch a hand out
to stop the warning clock.
                 Time is another country.

Squinting toward light:
              a tree has filled it
with green diamonds. Or there's the air, bemused:
                    newfallen snow.
Shock waves of a music
              I don't hear
as you
      don't hear mine.
                 How they beat on the sea-wall!

The Gaze Salutes Lyonel Feininger While Crossing the New Jersey Wastelands

A certain delicacy in the desolation:
olive-green the polluted
stretches of grass and weeds, the small
meres and sloughs dark with the darkness
of smoked glass,
gray air at intervals slashed with
rust-red uprights,
cranes or derricks;
and at the horizon line,
otherwise indeterminate,
a spidery definition of viaducts and
arched bridges,
pale but clear in silverpoint.

Mappemonde

Nonchalant clouds below me
dangle shadows
into the curved river at Saskatoon.

Atlas of frontiers long-redrawn,
gazeteer of obsolete cities—
a jet-vapor garland
                    stretches and stretches to link
your incantations,
and breaks.
Still audible, stiffly revolving,
the globe of the world
creaks out enticements.
Decades pile up like thunderheads,
O Geography!
              On your thick syrops
I float and float,
I glide through your brew
of bitter herbs.

Múmbulla Mountain,
low and round,
hums in green and hums
in tune, down in the Dreamtime.
World, you grow vaster. Our
time cannot
encompass you.

Blue Africa

for Angela Jackson

As they roam over grassland
the elephants cast
a blue river of shadows.
Their ears flap as they listen.

One evening, caught
in icy wind,
the traffic snarling,
I saw for one moment
their fluent stride, and heard
a quiet in Africa,
hum without menace.
They listened to sunlight,
and flowed
onward, unhurried.
          Remember,
they are there
       now.
Each in turn
enters the river of blue.

Seers

They make mistakes:
they busy themselves,
anxious to see more, straining their necks to look
beyond blue trees at dusk,

forgetting it is
the dust at their feet reveals
the strangest, most needful truth.

They think they want
a cherishing love to protect them
from the anguish they must distribute, the way
        wives of cruel kings handed
          loaves of bread to the poor—
a love that delights in them: but when

ironic Time gives them such love
they discover—and only then—its weight, which,
if they received and kept it, would crush down
the power entrusted to them.
The tender lover,
aghast at what he sees them seeing, or blind
and gently denying it, would set
a wall of lead about them,
hold down their feathered
Hermes-feet,
close the eyes that brim
not with tears but with visions,
silence the savage music
such golden mouths
                are sworn to utter.

Lovers (I)

With one I learned
how roots turn
to grip loam,
learned
the pulse of stone,
mineral arteries,
skyless auroras.

Was it so indeed?
I remember now
only telling myself
it was so.

Another led me
under the wing of
the waterfall. Light
was fine mist.
My skin was myself.

I remember now
only the words,
what they tell is gone.

And others I loved—
what were their kingdoms?
What songs did I sing of them,
and gazed from what high windows
toward their borders?

I journeyed
onward, my road always
drawing me further.

Lovers (II) : Reminder

'But that other:
he danced like a gypsy's bear at the winter crossroads,
the days of your youth and his are a bit of blue glass
bevelled by oceans and kept in his pocket,
wherever he is is always
now.
Touch, mass, weight, warmth:
a language you found you knew.
He brought you
the bread of sunlight on great platters of laughter.'

Seeing for a Moment

I thought I was growing wings—
it was a cocoon.

I thought, now is the time to step
into the fire—
it was deep water.

Eschatology is a word I learned
as a child: the study of Last Things;

facing my mirror—no longer young,
     the news—always of death,
     the dogs—rising from sleep and clamoring
          and howling, howling,

nevertheless
I see for a moment
that's not it: it is
the First Things.

Word after word
floats through the glass.
Toward me.

Man Wearing Bird

*. . . one afternoon, I saw a patient standing in the middle of the drive-
way . . . Something was moving on his head. . . . Suddenly, two large
wings flapped over his head in the light breeze . . . He had rolled his
pants up to his knobby knees and wore an opened leather jacket over a
T-shirt with a large number 17 . . . the mesmerized motorists slowed to
a crawl for a longer look . . . The patient later told his therapist he had
. . . realized that people were startled by his appearance. In fact, he had
relished it . . .*
                    —Boston Globe, *December 1983*

I could be stone,
a live bird on my civic head.
They would not look twice.

This is my pigeon
and I its prophet.
No one but I

found it. It died
for me to find,
to lift like the Host

and place aloft, a soft
weight on my naked scalp,
where one more time

flailing wings can
contest with the wind.
I am a column, a pillar of

righteousness, upholding
mystery, a dead pigeon that spoke
and continues to speak, that told

no one but me what to do,
told me to hold still under its
cold flutterings, told me

to relish the foolish grins, the awestruck
staring of passing, passing,
tenuous motorists, stand

barelegged in the winter day, display—
with the same wind beating
upon it—the number life and its warders

assign me, inscribed on my thin shirt
over my heart:

I the prophet,
chosen from all, ennobled, singular,
by this unique
unfathomable death.

The Mourner

Instead of arms to hold you
I want longer limbs, vines,
to wrap you twofold, threefold.

I wrap you, I pick you up, I carry you,
your knees drawn up, your head bent,
your arms crossed on your breast.

You are heavy.
I walk, I walk.
You say nothing.

Onward. Hill and dale. Indoors.
Out again. You say nothing.
You grow smaller, I wrap you fourfold.

I show you all the wonders you showed me,
infinitesimal and immense.
You grow smaller, smaller,
and always heavier. Why will you not speak?

Sundown Sentences

Fogbillows crest over ocean, soundless, unbreaking,
infinitely patient.

Tier after tier, mountains rehearse
the passage from green to evening's amethyst.

Redwings repeat with unslaked thirst
their one sweet song.

The rain's cleared off and the cats are dreamily
watching the lucid world, perched on the fence-rail,
striving for nothing; their shadows grow long.

Delicately,
two hilltop deer
nibble the sky.

Counting Sheep

Mexico City—smog and light but no color.
Los Angeles—light and smog but no color.
San Francisco—arid pastels.
Brownstone and grime-gray and black glass—New York.
Boston—trees and clouds but no color.
Tawny Rome!
                    The pearl-gray sheen of Paris.
The dear soot-darkened Portland stone of London.
Soot-darkened stone of London.
Stone of London.
Dear. Soot-darkened. Stone.
Of London . . .

Of Necessity

Running before the storm, the older child
was beautiful, her gold hair flew about her,
her small plump legs twinkled amusingly.
It was the other needed help—
wailing, toiling along, a wisp
of misery. Sticky with jam,
her skin damp, her hands
spiders in my hair.
But carrying her, strangely I began
to cherish that discomfort.
The wind blew, the first large raindrops
were falling, the forest we were leaving
leaned darkly after us, waving
in threat or longing.
Quieted, my burden
held fast to me,
patiently trustful. Of necessity.

Grey Sweaters
for James Laughlin

You want your old grey sweater,
lost or given away, you
need it for life and death, your lines
are cast to pull it
back around you.
Last night I dreamed one—
a sweater, I mean, found in the woods,
knit by an oriole.
Once I had—have you seen one ever?
—an oriole's nest,
woven of silvery milkweed silk
and weathered light as a
spindrift timber
tempered ten saltwater seasons . . .
I wore it, a perfect
châtelaine at my waist,
till it slipped off and was lost again
in orchard leaves.
The sweater I dreamed
was like that.
        I meant,
waking, to offer it
as a replacement. It would stretch
to fit you. But then I recalled
that indeed you had conjured yours already
into a poem,
it and your need for it are
the knit and purl of the poem's rows
re–raveled.

Presence

Sunlight in Ohio, touching
frostbitten stubblefields
and the cabbagy yards, strewn
        with rusting downhill racers and
        abandoned rabbit-hutches,
of small frame houses near the railroad . . .

The spirit
of Jim Wright is strong here,

so strong it comes through into the train,
through the thick pane.

                         The sun's light hands
touch the land
blindly, careful to memorize
planes and expressive
inclinations. It fingers
the scrapyard, the silo'd farm, the schoolbus,
the windowless plant and the men
going in for the dayshift.

                        Jim
can't speak anymore, he's dead,
but I swear
he's here
            making me look, he's here
angry and loving and full
of *Sehnsucht*, he's in
this landscape
where industry straggles uncertainly
out into farmland, and farmland
shrinks and looks grey—

he's the kid
skilfully spinning a beat-up bike-wheel
along and along,

down a road that leads straight,
straight, straight to the edge of the world.

Another Revenant

One long-dead
  returned for a night
    to speak to us

to me and
   a shadowy other beside me—
      we who had known him in time past—

and to a third,
   our friend, genius of listening,
      fully attentive, smiling.

While the revenant
   spoke, we looked
      back and forth to each other
         across the table,

            wicks taking flame
            one from the next, beacons
            lit on ridges of dark—

            confirming the wonder:

he was telling
   all we had not even
      thought to ask, long ago,

unsuspected luminous eloquence
   of pages long-yellowed,
      interventions

of unrecorded, brick-upon-brick
   structures of early thought
      re-collected,

rooms, towers, arches
   rising from rubble, gateways
      open, inviting entrance:

            dimensions unguessed that change
               a story the way
                  our comprehension of some unaccountable flora

            would change
               if we knew a river's course had been altered
                  before there were maps—

altered with effort so strenuous, no-one,
      long after,
            had wanted or tried to remember it.

All we'd thought gone
   into ashes,
      clay,
         deep night—

memories to account for the
   gray unresonant
      gaps and rifts:

his memories,
      which in his life before death had seemed
         obliterate, buried beyond retrieval,

emerging: his gift
   to us, and
      yes, to himself—

visible threads
   woven amongst us, gleaming,
      a fabric
         one with our listening.

II   PRISONERS

"Silent Spring"

O, the great sky!

Green and steep
the solid waves of the land,
breasts, shoulders, haunches,
serene.

The waveless ocean
arches its vertical silver,
molten, translucent.

Fine rain
browses the valley, moves
inland.
And flocks
of sunlight fly
from hill to hill.
The land
smiles in its sleep.

But listen . . .

no crisp susurration of crickets.
One lone frog. One lone
faraway whippoorwill. Absence.
No hum, no whirr.
And look:

the tigerish thistles, bold
yesterday,
curl in sick yellowing.

Drop the wild lettuce!
Try not to breathe!
Laboriously
the spraytruck
has ground its way
this way.
Hear your own steps
in violent silence.

Vocation

I have been listening, years now,
to last breaths—martyrs dying
passionately
            in open blood,
            in closed cells:

to screams and surprised silence
of children torn from green grass
into the foul bite
                  of the great mower.

From a long way off
I listen, I look
with the eyes and ears concealed within me.
Ears and eyes of my body
know as I know:
I have no vocation to join the nameless great,

only to say to others, Watch! Hear them!
Through them alone
we keep our title, *human,*

word like an archway, a bridge, an altar.
(Sworn enemies
answering phrase to phrase,
used to sing in the same key, imagine!—
used to pick up the furious song and
sing it through
to the tonic resting place, the chord,
however harsh,
of resolution.)

Nowadays
I begin to hear a new sound:
a leaf seems as it slowly
twirls down
earthward
to hum,

a candle, silently
melting beneath its flame,
seems to implore
attention, that it not burn its life
unseen.

Thinking about El Salvador

Because every day they chop heads off
I'm silent.
In each person's head they chopped off
was a tongue,
for each tongue they silence
a word in my mouth
unsays itself.

From each person's head two eyes
looked at the world;
for each gaze they cut
a line of seeing unwords itself.

Because every day they chop heads off
no force
flows into language,
thoughts
think themselves worthless.

No blade of *machete*
threatens my neck,
but its muscles
cringe and tighten,
my voice
hides in its throat-cave
ashamed to sound
            into that silence,
the silence

of raped women,
of priests and peasants,
teachers and children,
of all whose heads every day
float down the river
and rot
and sink,
not Orpheus heads
still singing, bound for the sea,
but mute.

Perhaps No Poem But All I Can Say And I Cannot Be Silent

As a devout Christian, my father
took delight and pride in being
(like Christ and the Apostles)
a Jew.
  It was
  Hasidic lore, his heritage,
  he drew on to know
  the Holy Spirit as Shekinah.

My Gentile mother, Welsh through and through,
and like my father sustained
by deep faith, cherished
all her long life the words
of Israel Zangwill, who told her,
'You have a Jewish soul.'

I their daughter ('flesh of their flesh,
     bone of their bone')
writing, in this Age of Terror, a libretto
about El Salvador, the suffering,
    the martyrs,

look from my page to watch
the apportioned news—those foul
dollops of History
each day thrusts at us, pushing them
into our gullets—
    and see that,
    in Lebanon
  so-called Jews have permitted
  so-called Christians
  to wreak pogrom ('thunder of devastation')
  on helpless folk (of a tribe
  anciently kin to their own, and now
  concentrated
    in Camps . . .)

My father—my mother—
I have longed for you.

Now I see
        it is well you are dead,
dead and
gone from Time,
gone from this time whose weight
of shame your bones, weary already
from your own days and years of
tragic History,
could surely not have borne.

Deathly Diversions

In dark slick as
                plastic garbage bags,
spotlights play, color of
                canned grapefruit juice . . .
Half-heroes totter
                into the glare:
America,
        stalking its meat,
                        pounces.

Each time
        the same meal, monotony
of lead-tasting blood.
Catharsis blocked, America
chokes on its own
                clotted tears.
It is millions,
        each a loner.
                        Meanwhile,
bellies keep swelling,
        limbs dwindle
to bone, famine
        drags its feet over continents.

                        And meanwhile,
screened from half-heroes' ritual mourners
        by smoke of their little fires,
        their beguiled attention fixed

on dead phantasmal presidents,
innocuous dead singers,
and unheard while they wail, 'give peace a chance,'

vaster catastrophes
are planned.

Rocky Flats

As if they had tamed the wholesome undomesticated puffball,
men self-deceived are busily cultivating,
in nuclear mushroom sheds, amanita buttons,
embryonic gills undisclosed—rank buds of death.
Men shield their minds from horror, shield their hands
with rubber, work behind glass partitions,
yet breathe in, breathe out, that dust,
spreading throughout themselves, throughout the world,
spores of the Destroying Angel.

Watching *Dark Circle*

'Why, this is hell, nor am I out of it'
Marlowe, Dr. Faustus

Men are willing to observe
the writhing, the bubbling flesh and
swift but protracted charring of bone
while the subject pigs, placed in cages designed for this,
don't pass out but continue to scream as they turn to cinder.
The Pentagon wants to know
something a child could tell it:
it hurts to burn, and even a match
can make you scream, pigs or people,
even the smallest common flame can kill you.
This plutonic calefaction is redundant.

Men are willing
to call the roasting of live pigs
a simulation of certain conditions. It is

not a simulation. The pigs (with their high-rated intelligence,
their uncanny precognition of disaster) are real,
their agony real agony, the smell
is not archetypal breakfast nor ancient feasting
but a foul miasma irremovable from the nostrils,
and the simulation of hell these men
have carefully set up
is hell itself,

        and they in it, dead in their lives,
and what can redeem them? What can redeem them?

Gathered at the River

For Beatrice Hawley and John Jagel

As if the trees were not indifferent . . .

A breeze flutters the candles but the trees give off
a sense of listening, of hush.

The dust of August on their leaves.
But it grows dark. Their dark green
is something known about, not seen.

But summer twilight takes away
only color, not form. The tree-forms,
massive trunks and the great domed heads,
leaning in towards us, are visible,

a half-circle of attention.

They listen because the war
we speak of, the human war with ourselves,

the war against earth,
against nature,
is a war against them.

The words are spoken
of those who survived a while,
living shadowgraphs, eyes fixed forever

on witnessed horror,
who survived to give
testimony, that no-one
may plead ignorance.
Contra naturam. The trees,
the trees are not indifferent.

We intone together, *Never again,*

we stand in a circle,
singing, speaking, making vows,

remembering the dead
of Hiroshima,
of Nagasaki.

We are holding candles: we kneel to set them
afloat on the dark river
as they do
there in Hiroshima. We are invoking

saints and prophets,
heroes and heroines of justice and peace,
to be with us, to help us
stop the torment of our evil dreams . . .

Windthreatened flames bob on the current . . .

They don't get far from shore. But none capsizes
even in the swell of a boat's wake.

The waxy paper cups sheltering them
catch fire. But still the candles
sail their gold downstream.

And still the trees ponder our strange doings, as if
well aware that if we fail,
we fail also for them:
if our resolves and prayers are weak and fail

there will be nothing left of their slow and innocent wisdom,
no roots,
no bole nor branch,

no memory
of shade,
of leaf,

no pollen.

Prisoners

Though the road turn at last
to death's ordinary door,
and we knock there, ready
to enter and it opens
easily for us,
                    yet
all the long journey
we shall have gone in chains,
fed on knowledge-apples
acrid and riddled with grubs.

We taste other food that life,
like a charitable farm-girl,
holds out to us as we pass—
but our mouths are puckered,
a taint of ash on the tongue.

It's not joy that we've lost—
wildfire, it flares
in dark or shine as it will.
What's gone
is common happiness,
plain bread we could eat
with the old apple of knowledge.

That old one—it griped us sometimes,
but it was firm, tart,
sometimes delectable . . .

The ashen apple of these days
grew from poisoned soil. We are prisoners
and must eat
our ration. All the long road
in chains, even if, after all,
we come to
death's ordinary door, with time
smiling its ordinary
long-ago smile.

The Cry
Dedicated to Jonathan Schell

No pulsations
        of passionate rhetoric
                suffice
in this time
        in this time
                this time
we stammer in
        stammering dread
                or
parched, utter
        silence
                from
mouths gaping to
        'Aayy!'—
                this time when
in dense fog
        groping
                groping or simply standing
by mere luck balanced
        still
                on the
swaying
        aerial catwalk of
                survival
we've approached
        the last
                the last choice:

shall we
    we and our kindred
        we and
the sibling lives,
    animal,
        vegetable,
we've lorded it over,
    the powers we've
        taken in thrall,
waters,
    earths,
        airs,
shall they
    shall we
        by our own hand
undo our
    being,
        their being,
erase
    is
    and *was*
along with
    will be?
        Nothing
for eloquence
    no rhetoric
        fits
that *unrendering,*
    voiding,
        dis-
assemblement—If
    by luck
        chance
grace perhaps
    able
        even now
to turn
    to turn away from
        that dis-
solution—
    only, O
        maybe

some wholly
            holy
                    holy
unmerited call:
              bellbird
                        in branch of
snowrose
          blossoming
                      newborn cry
demanding
          with cherubim
                          and seraphim
eternity:
          being:
                  milk:

III FOURTEEN POEMS BY JEAN JOUBERT

Écriture du vent

à Serge Brindeau

Le poème ici né du matin, de la clarté
liquide où nage encore un songe,
tu le crois grand, tu flaires l'immortel
et te réjouis de ce parfum.
Rose céleste, mauve profond, musique,
tu le vois sûr au centre de la roue
dont tourne et geint dans les brouillards
le fer boueux. Le jour pourtant s'avance,
le poids du sang. Les mots sont vulnérables :
la pluie, le feu, la main qui erre,
l'égarement peuvent les assaillir.
C'est le signe de nos frontières,
il nous défend de l'excessif orgueil.
Il n'y a plus alors que des éclats de langue,
des lettres chues, des loques grises,
comme des voix au loin dans la vallée
que les échos déchirent. Et parfois rien:
le sable, le silence, l'écriture du vent.

Cette autre encore

Cette autre encore,
terrible femme qui criait sur les collines, pleurant
    la mort d'un roi.
On l'entendait avec effroi du côté des rivières, là
    où s'élèvent les demeures,
où sur le sommeil des jardins tirés à la corde, à la
    houe, le soir penche sa voile rose.
L'eau droite y court entre les simples, la terre est
    un berceau de feuilles, tout y prospère dans
    l'oubli des dieux.

Wind Script

To Serge Brindeau

The poem newborn of morning,
of the liquid clarity where a dream still swims:
you think it great, you catch the scent of immortality
and luxuriate in that perfume.
Celestial rose, profound mauve, music—
you see it securely at the center
of the turning wheel whose muddy iron
creaks through the fog. But the day proceeds,
the weight of blood. Words are vulnerable:
rain, fire, the errant hand,
confusion—all can assail them.
This marks our limits, guards us
from an excess of pride.
Then there are left only splinters of language,
fallen letters, gray tatters
like voices far across the valley,
which echoes fracture. And sometimes nothing:
sand, silence, calligraphy of the wind.

Again That Other

Again that other, the terrible one,
the woman who wailed on the hilltops
lamenting the deaths of kings . . .
With dread her voice has been heard
    by the riverbanks, down among dwellings, where
    over sleepy gardens laid out in rows well tilled,
    the evening reefs-in its rose-colored sail.
    There the water
    runs a straight course between herbs,
    the earth is a leafy cradle,
    all prospers there,
    forgotten by the gods.

Alors pourquoi suivre cette démente, guetter sa langue
son drapeau?
Certains complotent son massacre, d'autres un rire ou
un crachat.
Bouche étroite, basse saison! Nos enfants choisiront
dans la douleur et le mépris.

L'été se clôt

Le
temps
qui nous prendra

nous le
prenons parfois
par la
queue

comme un beau lézard
bleu qui se
brise

Pour un instant
scintille entre nos doigts
la frénétique lueur

Haut lieu de songe de
merveille

(Ainsi de toi Amour et du poème)

Why then follow this raving woman,
why pay heed to that flag of warning, her tongue?
Some people plot to kill her,
others just laugh and spit.
Narrow mouths,
mean and debased times!
It's our children
who'll have to make choices,
in pain and contempt.

from L'été se clôt

Time
which will
take us

we take
sometimes
by the tail

like a handsome blue
lizard which deftly
breaks itself off

For one wild moment
it gleams
between our fingers

high crest
of dream
of marvel

(Thus it is
with you, Love,
and with the poem).

Eau de lune

L'œil aiguisé
par ton
visage

j'ai vu au soir
la mer
violette

l'appel des
feux

puis l'eau
de
lune

Venise décembre

Renversée sous la mer, une forêt soutient
    la ville pourrissante,
qui fut lieu de péage, d'épice, de navire,
d'or sombre décharné d'un haut visage :
lieu de génie, de guerre, de sauvages prisons.

Les arbres froids vêtus de sel et dans le noir
    portent l'immonde, la merveille.

La ville glisse vers sa mort. Sur ses places
    les oiseaux gris cherchent l'ancien
    feuillage.

Les quatre réveils

La sourde est morte par une nuit de vent.
Le village sifflait. Des feuilles, des rafales.
Elle tourne dans son silence. L'ampoule nue
faiblit. Aux murs, des ombres louches.

Moonwater

With eyes made keen
by watching your face

I've seen at dusk
the sea
       violet

the beckoning
    points of light

then:
      moonwater.

December Venice

Up-ended under the sea, a forest supports
    the decaying city
which once was a place of levies, of spices, of a great fleet,
of a lean and haughty countenance cast in somber gold:
place of genius, of war, of savage prisons.

The chill trees robed in salt and blackness
    uphold the squalor, the marvel.

The city is sliding toward its death. In its piazzas
    gray birds look for the long-ago leaves.

The Four Alarm Clocks

The deaf woman died on a windy night.
The village wailed and whistled. Leaves, gusts and squalls.
She turns within her silence. The naked bulb
has grown dim. On the walls, enigmatic shadows.

"Je suis en plan," dit-elle, gémit dans le désert
et capitule. À l'aube, elle était froide.
Longtemps vigie à sa fenêtre,
pleureuse noire, rusée sorcière,
son livre d'heures s'est fermé.
Demeurent sur la table
quatre marrons dans une porcelaine,
une serviette grise parmi les miettes
et sur la maie, semblables, côte à côte,
quatre réveils qui continuent de battre.

La sentence

"Vous êtes tous condamnés à mort, dit-il.
La sentence sera exécutée pour chacun d'entre vous
quand et comme il conviendra.
Il n'y a pas d'appel. Rentrez dans vos prisons,
nous saurons vous trouver.
Nous avons le bras long, l'œil aigu, des registres.
En attendant, voici du tabac, de l'alcool.
Jouez, rêvez! Il n'est pas interdit d'imaginer parfois
le goût du dernier verre, de la dernière cigarette."

Chat vieux

Chat vieux comme le
village où je suis
et les racines,

chaque matin tes yeux
(l'un voilé)
sont plus grands.

Que vois-tu dans la brume
entre roche et cyprès? Tu veilles
maintenant couché sur ma poitrine.

'I'm through,' she said, trembling in the wilderness
and capitulated. By dawn she was cold.
She who for so long kept watch on everyone from her window,
black funeral-wailer, wily sorceress—
her book of hours is shut.
On the table remain
four chestnuts in a china bowl,
a gray cloth among crumbs,
and on the dresser, side by side, exactly alike,
four alarm clocks, still ticking away.

The Sentence

'All of you are condemned to death,' he said.
'The sentence will be carried out for each of you
when and in whatever way it is convenient.
There is no appeal. Return to your prisons,
we shall know how to find you.
We have long arms, sharp eyes, registers.
Meanwhile, here's tobacco and booze.
Go ahead, play, dream! It's not forbidden
to imagine the taste of the last glass sometimes,
or the last cigarette.'

Ancient Cat

Cat
old as this village
old as roots

each morning your eyes
(one of them veiled)
are larger.

What do you see in the haze
between rock and
cypress?
          These days you lie
stretched on my chest
to maintain your vigil.

Tu te plais à mon sang,
tes griffes me
devinent.

Sur ton échine maigre
je pose cette main
qui sait et ne veut pas savoir.

Dans la cuisine

Le feu craque dans la cuisine, et de grandes vapeurs échevelées collent aux vitres leurs visages.

Sur la table, l'enfant écrit. Penché, le père guide la main qui tremble. "Applique-toi!" dit-il "C'est mieux, c'est bien" puis "Il est tard."

L'enfant écrit *enfant*, et de ce mot s'étonne sur la page, comme d'une bête douce que tantôt, l'encre étant sèche, il pourra du doigt caresser.

De sa plus belle main, le père écrit *miroir* avec des pleins et des déliés, élégamment bouclés entre les lignes (Commis aux écritures à la fabrique).

Miroir copie l'enfant, puis soupire: "J'ai bien sommeil!" "Il neige" dit le père.

L'enfant écrit *Il neige* et, dans son tablier noir bordé de rouge, paisiblement s'endort.

My blood
pleases you, your claws
read me.

On your scrawny spine I place
this hand
        which knows and
wants not to know.

In the Kitchen

The fire crackles in the kitchen range, and big disheveled clouds of steam stick their faces up against the window-panes.

At the table, the child is writing. Leaning over him, the father guides his wobbling hand. 'Try!' he says. 'That's better—that's good.' Then, 'It's late.'

The child writes, *Child*, and is amazed at this word there on the page, like a friendly animal that soon, when the ink has dried, he'll be able to stroke with his finger.

In his best copperplate hand, the father writes *mirror*, the curves and uprights elegantly curlicued between the lines (he's a copying-clerk at the factory).

Mirror, the child copies; then sighs, 'I'm so sleepy.' 'It's snowing,' the father says.

The child writes, 'It's snowing,' and, in his black red-bordered pinafore, falls peacefully asleep.

Portrait d'homme
(Holbein)

Moi,
Marcus Silésius,
poète,
je me suis arraché du monde.
Dans la forêt, au plus noir, j'ai bâti
ma tanière de branches.
Là-bas, dans leurs palais, longtemps j'ai répété
que je voyais grandir le feu et la famine,
j'ai dénoncé l'orage et l'imminence du charnier.
Qui m'écoutait? Quelques fous, quelques enfants,
une femme qui apprêtait ses linges et ses larmes.
Les autres m'ont haï ou méprisé.
On se détourne ainsi des diseurs de lumière!
Dorénavant j'habite le silence,
je me lève à l'heure du sanglier,
j'attends le cerf au seuil de son royaume.
Je vieillis dans l'orgueil, mes oracles m'étouffent.
Parfois, du haut de la falaise,
je regarde très loin fumer les villes:
braises, cendres, déjà poussière.

Troisième hypothèse sur la mort d'Empédocle

Un peu avant la nuit, une voix s'éleva
dans le verger, l'appelant par son nom.
Il avait soupé seul sous la lampe, serré
le pain, le vin, caressé le silence.
Son chat dormait auprès du feu couvert.
C'est alors que la voix monta parmi les branches,
ne disant que son nom, mais si limpide, si
pressante qu'il ouvrit la porte et s'avança
sous les figuiers, à travers le jardin.

Portrait of a Man
(after Holbein)

I,
Marcus Silesius,
poet,
I tore myself out of the world.
In the darkest forest
I wove my lair out of branches.
Back there in their palaces
how long I had told them, over and over,
what I could see: famine and fire
growing and growing;
I warned them of tempests to come,
of carnage impending.
Who listened? Madmen, a few,
children, a few, a woman
making ready her tears and her bands of linen.
The rest either hated me or misunderstood.
That's how they turn away from those who utter the light!
Since then I inhabit silence,
I rise when the wild boar rises,
I await the stag at the threshold of his kingdom.
I have grown old in my pride,
my oracles choke me.
Sometimes, from high on the cliff,
I watch, far off, the smoke of cities:
embers, cinders, ashes—already dust.

Third Hypothesis on the Death of Empedocles

A little before nightfall, a voice was raised
in the orchard, calling him by his name.
He had supped alone under the lamp, cleared away
the bread and the wine, caressed the silence.
His cat was asleep by the banked fire.
It was then the voice rose up among the branches
uttering only his name, but with such clarity,
so insistently, that he opened his door and
went forward under the figtrees, across the garden.

Rien n'y avait changé, si ce n'est que la terre
poreuse s'imbibait de l'unique clarté.
Sur le rivage, des bêtes calmes l'attendaient.
Il entra souriant dans l'ombre de la lune.
Nul jamais plus ne le revit.

Est-ce le vent qui nous gouverne?

Est-ce le vent qui nous gouverne?
Celui-ci, passeur d'étangs,
chargé de songes et de crimes?
Ou celui-là, hautain,
ami des neiges où l'esprit
glisse et nage sur les cimes?
Ou bien encore tel autre :
bouffée de rage, haleine de ténèbre,
métamorphose, au petit jour, de la forêt
où tremble une eau de feuilles?
Dans la naissance du verger, chaque matin je m'interroge.
Je sens vibrer les liens qui me marient
à tant d'étoiles invisibles, à la lune
engloutie, au soleil dont le rire
empourpre la colline. Et la sève partout,
d'arbre en arbre, de fleur en fleur,
et dans les veines du jardin, coule
jusqu'à mes paumes qu'elle irrigue.
Un chien marche dans mes yeux. Le
chat bâille près d'une rose, tandis
qu'au loin des pies froissent les branches.
Et la jeune lumière avive la beauté
d'une toile où veille l'archange. Ensemble
nous prions. En silence nous recevons,
nous acceptons ce souffle immense qui nous lave.

Nothing had changed there, unless it was
that the porous earth drank-in that singular clearness.
By the waterside calm beasts awaited him.
Smiling, he entered the moon shadow.
No one saw him ever again.

Are We Ruled by the Wind?

Are we ruled by the wind?—that wind
which ferries over the ponds
a freight of dreams and crimes?
Or the haughty wind, familiar
of snowy peaks where the mind
glides and floats?
Or perhaps some other:
bluster of fury, breath of darkness,
the forest transformed, by daybreak,
to a trembling rain of leaves?
In the newborn orchard each morning
I ponder. And sense the vibration
of bonds that wed me
to the great host of invisible stars,
to the sunken moon,
to the sun whose laughter
flushes the hill with crimson.
And everywhere sap is rising
in tree after tree, and flows
in the very veins of the garden towards me, and bathes
the palms of my hands.
A passing dog
walks through my eyes. The cat
yawns by the roses,
magpies jostle the distant branches.
Early light
burnishes a web's perfection
where the archangel keeps vigil. Together
we pray, in silence
receive, accept
the immense breathing which laves us.

Éclat du ciel

Jamais entre les branches le ciel
n'a brillé d'un tel éclat, comme s'il
tendait vers moi toute sa lumière,
comme s'il essayait de me parler,
de me dire quoi, quel pressant mystère
sur cette bouche transparente?
Ni feuille ni rumeur! C'est dans l'hiver,
dans la vacance froide et le silence
que l'air ainsi soudain se creuse
et resplendit. Ce soir, ailleurs,
un ami est entré dans sa mort,
il sait, il marche seul parmi les arbres,
peut-être pour la dernière fois. Tant
d'amour, tant de combats s'effritent,
s'amenuisent, mais lorsqu'il a levé les yeux,
le ciel soudain s'est revêtu
de la même vertigineuse clarté.

L'arrière-saison du poète

Chaque matin en préparant le thé
je songe à l'ami mort.
Le soleil bas transperce les roseaux,
le chat rôde sur le seuil.

Printemps été automne hiver:
chaque saison apporte ses oiseaux
différents, que je nourris de miettes.

Voici novembre,
le rouge-gorge est au logis de branches.
Je suis seul, je n'écris plus, je remercie
les dieux de ce grand vide de lumière.

Parfois, au-dessus des collines,
un *jet* tire un trait blanc
qu'un vent hautain lentement ébouriffe.

Brilliant Sky

Never between the branches has the sky
burned with such brilliance, as if
it were offering all of its light to me,
as if it were trying to speak to me,
to say—what? what urgent mystery
strains at that transparent mouth?
No leaf, no rustle . . . It's in winter,
in cold emptiness and silence, that the air
suddenly arches itself like this into infinity,
and glitters.
        This evening, far from here,
a friend is entering his death,
he knows it, he walks
under bare trees alone,
perhaps for the last time. So much love,
so much struggle, spent and worn thin.
But when he looks up, suddenly the sky
is arrayed in this same vertiginous clarity.

The Poet's Late Autumn

Each morning, making tea,
I think of my dead friend.
The low sun slants through the reeds,
the cat prowls at the doorsill.

Spring, summer, autumn, winter:
each season brings
its particular birds, whom I feed with crumbs.

Now it's November, the redbreast
haunts its usual tree.
I am alone, I write nothing,
        I thank
the gods for this great breadth
        of empty light.

At times, over the hills a jet
leaves a white trail
a lofty wind
        slowly unravels.

IV   OF GOD AND OF THE GODS

Of Rivers

Rivers remember
        in the pulse of their springs,
        in curl and slide and onrush
        lakeward and seaward,
a touch
shuddering them forth,
a voice
intoning them into
their ebbing and flood:
        fingertip, breath
        of god or goddess in whom
their fealty rests
rendered by being unceasingly
the pilgrim conversation of waterflesh.

                That remembrance
                gives them their way
to know, in unknowing flowing,
the God of the gods, whom the gods
themselves have not imagined.

Of Gods

God gave the earth-gods
adamantine ignorance.

They think themselves
the spontaneous shimmering of fact—
brilliant wings with no history
of cramped egg or stifling cocoon.

Therein lies their power.

Poplar in Spring

The tall poplar
so late to leaf I thought, the first year,
it had died, but before I left
          it was rippling a close-wrapped cloak, sewn
          with teardrops of green, each held
          by a single stitch,

reaches now, in its time of advent,
for each day's primal shining.
Above the crouched garden, darkly asleep,
                              swing
seraphs, veiled in their own splendor,
          high in the bare pinnacle.

Last Night's Dream

I sing *tree*, making green
school after school of leaf-fish
flicker between the shade and sunlight
in nets of branch,
urging the students to see, to see—

and one says: *I* like
the *brown* tree. So I look:
she has conjured
one of those scrawny northern cedars,
arbor vitae, dead or alive, one can't tell,
earth-brown, sprouting
bits of dry fern-frond from random twigs,
disregarded;

and this tree, behold,
glows from within;
haloed in visible
invisible gold.

To the Morton Bay Figtree, Australia, a Tree-God

Soul-brother of the majestic beechtree,
thy sculpted buttresses only more sharp-angled,
leaves darker, like the leaves of ilex—

vast tree, named by fools who noticed only
thy small hard fruit, the figlike shape of it,
                nothing else—
not thy great girth and pallid sturdy bark,
thy alert and faithful retinue of roots,
the benign shade under the rule of thy crown:

Arbor-Emperor, to perceive thy solemn lustre
and not withhold due reverence—
may it not be for this, one might discover,
a lifetime led, after all?—not for
those guilts and expiations the mind's clock ticks over,
but to have sunk before thee in deep obeisance,
spirits rising in weightless joy?

The Avowal

    For Carolyn Kizer and John Woodbridge,
    Recalling Our Celebration
    of the 300th Birthday of George Herbert, 1983

As swimmers dare
to lie face to the sky
and water bears them,
as hawks rest upon air
and air sustains them,
so would I learn to attain
freefall, and float
into Creator Spirit's deep embrace,
knowing no effort earns
that all-surrounding grace.

The God of Flowers

Mouth, horn, cilia, sun—
multiform, multitude, galaxy, cosmos:
blossom on blossom, fragrance on fragrance, tint upon tint:
and no disdain, no clash
of opposites . . .
          But the god of flowers
sits not among petals but inside the minuscule
bulb of all bulbs, a Buddha, a hen on her eggs,
furled in the cell among cells that insists on growth,
sifted in soil, in bins, in leathery hands of gardeners,
sits and sits in the mustard seed.
And the unknown God of the gods
watches and smiles.

The Task

As if God were an old man
always upstairs, sitting about
in sleeveless undershirt, asleep,
arms folded, stomach rumbling,
his breath from open mouth
strident, presaging death . . .

No, God's in the wilderness next door
—that huge tundra room, no walls and a sky roof—
busy at the loom. Among the berry bushes,
rain or shine, that loud clacking and whirring,
irregular but continuous;
God is absorbed in work, and hears
the spacious hum of bees, not the din,
and hears far-off
our screams. Perhaps
listens for prayers in that wild solitude.
And hurries on with the weaving:
till it's done, the great garment woven,
our voices, clear under the familiar
      blocked-out clamor of the task,
can't stop their

terrible beseeching. God
imagines it sifting through, at last, to music
in the astounded quietness, the loom idle,
the weaver at rest.

St. Peter and the Angel

Delivered out of raw continual pain,
smell of darkness, groans of those others
to whom he was chained—

unchained, and led
past the sleepers,
door after door silently opening—
out!
     And along a long street's
majestic emptiness under the moon:

one hand on the angel's shoulder, one
feeling the air before him,
eyes open but fixed . . .

And not till he saw the angel had left him,
alone and free to resume
the ecstatic, dangerous, wearisome roads of
what he had still to do,
not till then did he recognize
this was no dream. More frightening
than arrest, than being chained to his warders:
he could hear his own footsteps suddenly.
Had the angel's feet
made any sound? He could not recall.
No one had missed him, no one was in pursuit.
He himself must be
the key, now, to the next door,
the next terrors of freedom and joy.

This Day

i

Dry wafer,
sour wine.

This day I see

God's in the dust,
not sifted

out from confusion.

ii

Perhaps, I thought,
passing the duckpond,
perhaps—seeing the brilliantly somber water
deranged by lost feathers and bits of
drowning bread—perhaps
these imperfections (the ducklings
practised their diving,
stylized feet vigorously cycling among débris)
are part of perfection,
a pristine nuance? our eyes,
our lives, too close to the canvas,
enmeshed within
the turning dance,
to see it?

iii

In so many Dutch 17th-century paintings
one perceives
a visible quietness, to which the concord
of lute and harpsichord contribute,
in which a smiling conversation
reposes:
'calme, luxe,' and—in auburn or mercurial sheen

of vessels, autumnal wealth
of fur-soft table-carpets,
blue snow-gleam of Delft—
'volupté'; but also the clutter
of fruit and herbs, pots, pans, poultry,
strewn on the floor: and isn't
the quiet upon them too, in them and of them,
aren't they wholly at one with the wonder?

iv

Dry wafer,
sour wine:

this day I see

the world, a word
intricately incarnate, offers—
          ravelled, honeycombed, veined, stained—
what hunger craves,

a sorrel grass,
a crust,
water,
salt.

Oblique Prayer

Not the profound *dark*
night of the soul

and not the austere desert
to scorch the heart at noon,
grip the mind
in teeth of ice at evening

but gray,
a place
without clear outlines,

the air
heavy and thick

the soft ground clogging
my feet if I walk,
sucking them downwards
if I stand.

Have you been here?
Is it

a part of human-ness

to enter
no man's land?

I can remember
                    (is it asking you
                        that
                        makes me remember?)
even here
the blesséd light that caressed the world
before I stumbled into
this place of mere
not-darkness.

The Antiphon

> 'L'Esprit souffle dans le silence
> là où les mots n'ont plus de voix'
> Anon

And then once more
all is eloquent—rain,
raindrops on branches, pavement brick
humbly uneven, twigs of a storm-stripped hedge revealed
shining deep scarlet,
speckled whistler shabby and
unconcerned, anything—all
utters itself, blessedness
soaks the ground and its wintering seeds.

'. . . That Passeth All Understanding'

An awe so quiet
I don't know when it began.

A gratitude
had begun
to sing in me.

Was there
some moment
dividing
song from no song?

When does dewfall begin?

When does night
fold its arms over our hearts
to cherish them?

When is daybreak?

Of Being

I know this happiness
is provisional:

       the looming presences—
       great suffering, great fear—

       withdraw only
       into peripheral vision:

but ineluctable this shimmering
of wind in the blue leaves:

this flood of stillness
widening the lake of sky:

this need to dance,
this need to kneel:
       this mystery:

Passage

The spirit that walked upon the face of the waters
walks the meadow of long grass;
green shines to silver where the spirit passes.

Wind from the compass points, sun at meridian,
these are forms the spirit enters,
breath, *ruach*, light that is witness and by which we witness.

The grasses numberless, bowing and rising, silently
cry hosanna as the spirit
moves them and moves burnishing

over and again upon mountain pastures
a day of spring, a needle's eye
space and time are passing through like a swathe of silk.

BREATHING THE WATER

"Was it so strange, the way things
are flung out at us, like the apples
of Atalanta perhaps, once we have
begun a certain onrush?"

Eudora Welty,
"Music from Spain,"
The Golden Apples

I

Variation on a Theme by Rilke
(The Book of Hours, Book I, Poem 1, Stanza 1)

A certain day became a presence to me;
there it was, confronting me—a sky, air, light:
a being. And before it started to descend
from the height of noon, it leaned over
and struck my shoulder as if with
the flat of a sword, granting me
honor and a task. The day's blow
rang out, metallic—or it was I, a bell awakened,
and what I heard was my whole self
saying and singing what it knew: *I can.*

Hunting the Phoenix

Leaf through discolored manuscripts,
make sure no words
lie thirsting, bleeding,
waiting for rescue. No:
old loves half-
articulated, moments forced
out of the stream of perception
to play 'statue',
and never released—
they had no blood to shed.
You must seek
the ashy nest itself
if you hope to find
charred feathers, smouldering flightbones,
and a twist of singing flame
rekindling.

August Daybreak

Slowly the crows patrol the parapet.
A leopard-slug, sated with leaf-juice, vanishes for the day.
Brown, untwirling, laburnum seedpods recapitulate
the golden rain of June.
                                 Indoors, the timid millipedes
venture a tango across the cellar floor.
I hear the books in all the rooms
breathing calmly, and remember a dream I had years ago:
my father—all that complexity, cabalistic lore,
childish vanity, heroic wisdom, goodness, weakness,
defeat and faith—had become, after traveling
through death's gated tunnel, a rose,
                        an old-fashioned dark-pink garden rose.

There is no breeze. A milky sky. Traces
of blue shadow
                    melting like ice.
The day will be hot.
Not shadow—wisps of night. I feel them
under my eyes; and after a deep breath
at the open window, draw down the blind.
It meant, I say to myself, he let knowledge
                        fall from his hands,
no longer needed: now he could be his essence,
            it was there all along, many-petaled, fragrant,
'a blissful foolish rose' in the sun.
                        I return to sleep
as if to the slippery fragrance
of pinewoods, the needles' shelving
in soft darkness, the last of night
retrieved.

A Blessing

For Joanna Macy

'Your river is in full flood,' she said,
'Work on—use these weeks well!'
She was leaving, with springy step, a woman

herself renewed, her life risen
up from the root of despair she'd
bent low to touch,
risen empowered. Her work now
could embrace more: she imagined anew
the man's totem tree and its taproot,
the woman's chosen lichen, patiently
composting rock, another's
needful swamp, the tribal migrations—
swaying skeins rotating their leaders,
pace unflagging—and the need
of each threatened thing
to be. She had met
with the *council*
of all beings.

                             'You give me
my life,' she said to the just-written poems,
long-legged foals surprised to be standing.

The poet waving farewell
is not so sure of the river.
Is it indeed
strong-flowing, generous? Was there largesse
for alluvial, black, seed-hungry fields?
Or had a flash-flood
swept down these tokens
to be plucked ashore, rescued
only to watch the waters recede
from stones of an arid valley?
But the traveler's words
are leaven. They work in the poet.
The river swiftly
goes on braiding its heavy tresses,
brown and flashing,
as far as the eye can see.

The Spirits Appeased

A wanderer comes at last
to the forest hut where it was promised

someone wise would receive him.
And there's no one there; birds and small animals
flutter and vanish, then return to observe.
No human eyes meet his.
But in the hut there's food,
set to keep warm beside glowing logs,
and fragrant garments to fit him, replacing
the rags of his journey,
and a bed of heather from the hills.
He stays there waiting. Each day the fire
is replenished, the pot refilled while he sleeps.
He draws up water from the well,
writes of his travels, listens for footsteps.
Little by little he finds
the absent sage is speaking to him,
is present.
                        This is the way
you have spoken to me, the way—startled—
I find I have heard you. When I need it,
a book or a slip of paper
appears in my hand, inscribed by yours: messages
waiting on cellar shelves, in forgotten boxes
until I would listen.
                        Your spirits relax;
now she is looking, you say to each other,
now she begins to see.

II   SPINOFFS, ONE

A Doorkey for Cordova

    . . . And light made of itself an amber
transparency one sundown, restoring
Moorish atavistic imprints almost
to memory, patterns tight-closed
eyes used to make in childhood when
the greenish thickwoven cotton tablecover,
frayed and become an ironing sheet, linked itself somehow
to a Septembery casbah imagined
before any casbah became knowledge . . .

Athanor

Tempered wood. Wrought light. Carved
rags. Curdled gold, the thin
sheets of it. The leaves of it.
The wet essence of it infused.
Effluvia of gold suffused throughout. The saturation.
The drying. The flaking. The absorption.
It is a paper sack, a paper sack for dogfood, dry,
the dry wafers of a sacrament, a sacred sack,
its brownish pallor illumined, inscribed with red,
upheld by a many-layered substance
plush as moss, chocolate-dark, dense, which is shadow,
and backed by a tentative, a tremulous
evanescence which is wood
or which is the tardy sungleam from under cloudbank
just before evening settles,
that percolates through cobwebs and thick glass.
Which is the fleeting conjugation
of wood and light, embrace that leaves wood
dizzy and insubstantial, and leaves light
awestruck again at its own destiny.

Window-Blind

Much happens when we're not there.
Many trees, not only that famous one, over and over,
fall in the forest. We don't see, but something sees,
or someone, a different kind of someone,
a different molecular model, or entities
not made of molecules anyway; or nothing, no one:
but something has taken place, taken space, been present, absent,
returned. Much moves in and out of open windows
when our attention is somewhere else,
just as our souls move in and out of our bodies sometimes.
Everyone used to know this,
but for a hundred years or more
we've been losing our memories, moulting, shedding,
like animals or plants that are not well.
Things happen anyway,

whether we are aware or whether
the garage door comes down by remote control over our
recognitions, shuts off, cuts off—.
We are animals and plants that are not well.
We are not well but while we look away,
on the other side of that guillotine or through
the crack of day disdainfully left open below the blind
a very strong luminous arm reaches in,
or from an unsuspected place, in the room with us,
where it was calmly waiting, reaches outward.
And though it may have nothing at all to do with us,
and though we can't fathom its designs,
nevertheless our condition thereby changes:
cells shift, a rustling barely audible as of tarlatan
flickers through closed books, one or two leaves
fall, and when we read them we can perceive,
if we are truthful, that we were not dreaming,
not dreaming but once more witnessing.

The Spy

Everything was very delicately striped.
You could see the wood-pulse exquisitely throb
under paint's thin tissue, beside
the mirror limpid in its film
of silver,
most justly beveled,
most faintly steam-blurred,
most faintly warped as if with just sufficient
bruise to tinge
with tenderness its icy patience.
A few sheets of paper were still on the roll;
the austere and efficient holder cast, in the shadows,
a sprightly fantasy of itself in stronger shadow, crossing
the beveled molding. This the glass
never could reflect,
never unless the entire closet door, wrenched from its hinges,
were placed across the room and
forced to look back,
or a second mirror

brought in to face it: neither of them
with a word to say.
There was blue, there was brown paler than ivory, a half-curtain,
there were other blues and an aspiration to whiteness,
there were preludes to green, pink, gold and aluminum,
mostly there was the sense that though
the light would fade
and return next day and slowly move
from right to left and again
fade and return, yet
the stillness here, so delicate,
pulse unquickened, could outwait
every move.

Embrasure

The wind behind the window moves the leaves.

James with his cockleshell or Genevieve
a fraction westward move each day
in ruby beads,

a rosary let fall (*with lily, germander, and sops-in-wine*)
decade by decade through the year
across the wall, along the floor.

The figures ripple and the colors quicken.
In cloud or dark invisible
yet moving always, and in light

turning—the circle
east by west or west by east
day after day

constant in pilgrimage. The wind
behind the window moves
the leaves, the bare

branches stir or hold
their breath, their buds,
up to remotest stars.

And dustmote congregations file
endlessly through the slanted amethyst.

III

Zeroing In

'I am a landscape,' he said,
'a landscape and a person walking in that landscape.
There are daunting cliffs there,
and plains glad in their way
of brown monotony. But especially
there are sinkholes, places
of sudden terror, of small circumference
and malevolent depths.'
'I know,' she said. 'When I set forth
to walk in myself, as it might be
on a fine afternoon, forgetting,
sooner or later I come to where sedge
and clumps of white flowers, rue perhaps,
mark the bogland, and I know
there are quagmires there that can pull you
down, and sink you in bubbling mud.'
'We had an old dog,' he told her, 'when I was a boy,
a good dog, friendly. But there was an injured spot
on his head, if you happened
just to touch it he'd jump up yelping
and bite you. He bit a young child,
they had to take him down to the vet's and destroy him.'
'No one knows where it is,' she said,
'and even by accident no one touches it.
It's inside my landscape, and only I, making my way
preoccupied through my life, crossing my hills,
sleeping on green moss of my own woods,
I myself without warning touch it,
and leap up at myself—'

'—or flinch back
just in time.'
                    'Yes, we learn that.
It's not terror, it's pain we're talking about:
those places in us, like your dog's bruised head,
that are bruised forever, that time
never assuages, never.'

The Absentee

Uninterpreted, the days
are falling.

The spring wind
is shaking and shaking the trees.

A nest of eggs,
a nest of deaths.

Falling
abandoned.

The palms rattle, the eucalyptus
shed bark and blossom. Uninterpreted.

Captive Flower

This morning's morning-glory
trying to thrust
through the wire mesh towards the sun
is trapped
                half-open.
I ease it back
to see better its unfurling,

but only slowly it resigns
the dream. Its petals
are scarred.

I had not thought myself
a jailor.

The Mockingbird of Mockingbirds

A greyish bird
the size perhaps of two plump sparrows,
fallen in some field,
soon flattened, a dry
mess of feathers—
and no one knows
this was a prince among his kind,
virtuoso of virtuosos,
lord of a thousand songs,
debonair, elaborate in invention, fantasist,
rival of nightingales.

In Memory: After a Friend's Sudden Death
(A.N., 1943–1985)

Others will speak of her spirit's tendrils reaching
almost palpably into the world;

but I will remember her body's unexpected beauty
seen in the fragrant redwood sauna,

young, vestal, though she was nearing fifty
and had borne daughters and a son—

a 15th century widehipped grace,
small waist and curving belly,

breasts with that look
of inexhaustible gentleness,
shoulders narrow but strong.

And I will speak
not of her work, her words, her search
for a new pathway, her need

to heedfully walk and sing through dailiness
noticing stones and flowers,

but of the great encompassing *Aah!* she would utter,
entering slowly, completely, into the welcoming whirlpool.

Missing Beatrice
(For B.H., 1944–1985)

Goodness was
a fever in you. Anyone

might glow in the heat of it,
go home comforted—

for them a shawl, for you
fire at the bone.

•

You knew
more than was good for you.
Your innocence
was peat-bog water, subtle and dark,
that cold it was,
that pure.

•

Kindness—didn't we act as though
we could cut an endless supply from you
like turf from a bog?

•

Smoke of that empty hearth
fragrant still.
Your words
cupped in our hands to drink.
But you—

you're gone and we never
really saw you.

To Olga

When the last sunlight had all seeped
down behind the woods and taken
colors and shadows with it, leaving us
not in darkness but in
the presence of an absence, with everything
still visible but
empty of soul—

when we trudged on knowing our home was
miles and hours away and the real dark
overtaking us, and mother and father waiting
anxious by now and soon
growing angry because again
we'd traveled too far out and away, leaving
almost as if
not to return—

what did you, almost grown up, feel
as we spoke less and less, too tired
for fantasy? I was afraid for them,
for their fear and of
its show of anger, but not of the night.
I felt the veil
of sadness descend

but I was never afraid for us,
we were benighted but not lost, and I trusted
utterly that at last,
however late, we'd get home.
No owl, no lights, the dun ridges
of ploughland fading. No matter.
I trusted you.

But you? Irritably you'd ask me
why I was silent. Was it because

you felt untrusted, or had no trust
in yourself? Could it,
could it have been that
you, you were afraid,
my brave, my lost
sister?

*

Ceremonies

The ash tree drops the few dry leaves it bore in May,
stands naked by mid-July.
When each day's evil news drains into the next,
a monotonous overflow,
has a tree's dying lost the right to be mourned?
No—life's indivisible. And this tree,
rooted beyond my fence, has been,
branch and curved twig, in leaf or bare, the net
that held the sky in my window.
Trunk in deep shade, its lofting crown
offers to each long day's
pale glow after the sun
is almost down, an answering gold—
the last light
held and caressed.

Every Day

Three men spoke to me today.

One, bereaved, told me his grief, saying
Had God abandoned him, or was there
no God to abandon him?

One, condemned, told me his epitaph,
'Groomed to die.' On Death Row he remembers
the underside of his gradeschool desk, air-raid drill.
He never expected to live
even this long.

He sticks his head back down between his knees,
'not even sad.'

One, a young father, told me
how he had needed his child, even
before she was conceived.
How he had planted a garden too big to hoe.
He told me about the small leaves near his window,
how he had seen in them their desire to be,
to be the world.

With this one I sat laughing,
eating, drinking wine. 'The same word,'
he said, 'she has the same word for me and the dog!
She loves us!'

Every day, every day I hear
enough to fill
a year of nights with wondering.

To One Steeped in Bitterness

Nail the rose
                to your mind's door
like a rat, a thwarted chickenhawk.
Yes, it has had its day.

And the water
                poured for you
which you disdain to drink,
yes, throw it away.

Yet the fierce rose
                stole nothing
from your cooped heart,
nor plucked your timid eye;

and from inviolate rock
                the liquid light
was drawn, that's dusty now
and your lips dry.

IV

The Stricken Children

The Wishing Well was a spring
bubbling clear and soundless into a shallow pool
less than three feet across, a hood of rocks
protecting it, smallest of grottoes, from falling leaves,
the pebbles of past wishes peacefully under-water, old desires
forgotten or fulfilled. No one threw money in, one had to search
for the right small stone.

This was the place from which
year after year in childhood I demanded my departure,
my journeying forth into the world of magical
cities, mountains, otherness—the place which gave
what I asked, and more; to which
still wandering, I returned this year, as if
to gaze once more at the face
of an ancient grandmother.
And I found the well
filled to the shallow brim
with debris of a culture's sickness—
with bottles, tins, paper, plastic—
the soiled bandages
of its aching unconsciousness.

Does the clogged spring still moisten
the underlayer of waste?
Was it children threw in the rubbish?
Children who don't dream, or dismiss
their own desires and
toss them down, discarded packaging?
I move away, walking fast, the impetus
of so many journeys pushes me on,
but where are the stricken children of this time, this place,
to travel to, in Time if not in Place,
the grandmother wellspring choked, and themselves not aware
of all they are doing-without?

During a Son's Dangerous Illness

You could die before me—
I've known it
always, the
dreaded worst, 'unnatural' but
possible
in the play
of matter, matter and
growth and
fate.

                   ·

My sister Philippa died
twelve years before I was born—
the perfect, laughing firstborn,
a gift to be cherished as my orphaned mother
had not been cherished. Suddenly:
death, a baby

cold and still.

                   ·

Parent, child—death ignores
protocol, a sweep of its cape brushes
this one or that one at random
into the dust, it was
not even looking.
                  What becomes
of the past if the future
snaps off, brittle,
the present left as a jagged edge
opening on nothing?

                   ·

Grief for the menaced world—lost rivers,
poisoned lakes–all creatures, perhaps,
to be fireblasted
                 off the

whirling cinder we
loved, but not enough . . .
The grief I'd know if I
lived into
your unthinkable death
is a splinter
of that selfsame grief,
infinitely smaller but
the same in kind:
one
stretching the mind's fibers to touch
eternal nothingness,
the other
tasting, in fear, the
desolation of
survival.

Carapace

I am growing mine
though I have regretted yours.

>   She says, Sure I saw him: he wanted
>   to run, the Guardia Civil
>   shot him before he reached the patio wall.
>   Do I understand 'subversive'? Yes,
>   the word means
>   people who know their rights,
>   if they work but don't get enough to eat
>   they protest. He was
>   a lay preacher, my father,
>   he preached the Gospel,
>   he was subversive.

>   She is 12.

My shell is growing
nicely, not very hard, just
a thin protection but it's
better than just skin. Have you

completed yours? It seems
there will be chinks in it though,
the cartilaginous
plates don't quite meet, do yours?

    A 9 year old boy whose father has 'disappeared' three weeks now,
    asked how he feels, says
    with the shrug of a man of sixty,
    'sad,' He nods. 'Yes; sad . . .'

That burning, blistering glare
off the world's desert
still pushes in; oh, filter it, grow faster,
hide me in shadow,
    my carapace!

Urgent Whisper

It could be the râle of Earth's tight chest,
her lungs scarred from old fevers, and she asleep—

but there's no news from the seismographs,
the crystal pendant
hangs plumb from its hook;

and yet at times (and I whisper because
it's a fearful thing I tell you)
a subtle shudder has passed
from outside me into my bones,

up from the ground beneath me,
beneath this house, beneath
the road and the trees:

a silent delicate trembling no one has spoken of,
as if a beaten child or a captive animal
lay waiting the next blow.

It comes from the Earth herself, I tell you,

Earth herself. I whisper
because I'm ashamed. Isn't the Earth our mother?
Isn't it we who've brought
this terror upon her?

From the Image-Flow—South Africa 1986

Africa, gigantic slave-ship, not anchored yet not moving,
all hatches battened down, living tormented cargo
visible through dark but transparent sides. The sea
writhing too, but slowly, serpentine. In the vast hold,
vinelike hands reach out from crowded souls, strike sparks
                                              from chains,
light fires in what space they make between their bodies:
not the ship only begins to burn,
                        the viscous depths it rides on
already smoulder.

Making Peace

A voice from the dark called out,
        'The poets must give us
imagination of peace, to oust the intense, familiar
imagination of disaster. Peace, not only
the absence of war.'
                        But peace, like a poem,
is not there ahead of itself,
can't be imagined before it is made,
can't be known except
in the words of its making,
grammar of justice,
syntax of mutual aid.
                        A feeling towards it,
dimly sensing a rhythm, is all we have
until we begin to utter its metaphors,
learning them as we speak.
                        A line of peace might appear
if we restructured the sentence our lives are making,

revoked its reaffirmation of profit and power,
questioned our needs, allowed
long pauses . . .
                    A cadence of peace might balance its weight
on that different fulcrum; peace, a presence,
an energy field more intense than war,
might pulse then,
stanza by stanza into the world,
each act of living
one of its words, each word
a vibration of light—facets
of the forming crystal.

From the Image-Flow—Summer of 1986

'Only Hope remained there within the rim of the great jar'
(after Pandora had let loose disaster and affliction).

These days—these years—
when powers and principalities of death
weigh down the world, deeper, deeper
than we ever thought it could fall and still
                        keep slowly spinning,
Hope, caught under the jar's rim, crawls
like a golden fly
round and around, a sentinel:
it can't get out, it can't fly free
among our heavy hearts—
but does not die, keeps up its pace,
pausing only as if to meditate
a saving strategy . . .

V   SPINOFFS, TWO

'She wept, and the women consoled her.'

The flow of tears ebbed,
her blouse began to dry.
But the sobs that
took her by the shoulders and
shook her came back
for unknown reasons
and shook her again, like soldiers
coming back when everyone had gone.
History's traffic had speeded up and
smashed into gridlock all around her;
the women consoled her but she couldn't get out.
Bent forward as she was,
she found herself looking at her legs.
They were old, the skin
shiny over swollen ankles,
and blotched. They meant nothing to her
but they were all she could see.
Her fallen tears had left their traces
like snail-tracks on them.

'The day longs for the evening.'

The zenith longs for the banâl horizon.
The north wind longs for the south,
and the trudging clouds are
searching, searching for that land
of glowing fruit, of polished marble;
but the wind that drives them
is bitter, they bring winter with them,
What is that promised evening?
The day, the day knows
in spite of everything,
that evening will not fail,
the ancient evening,
the luminous evening.

'The last heavy fairytale, in which one lays one's heart bare before the knife.'

The room is small, the table plain,
white pine well-scrubbed.
The house is deep in the forest.
Each comes alone, but watched,
carefully holding in two hands
that heart which till now
was drumming and drumming away
in its own interior anteroom—
comes to center it, bare and still beating,
on the plain table
in the small room
where the knife will appear, new-sharpened, held
invisibly.

'The sea's repeated gesture.'

Stroking its blue shore
throughout the night, patient, patient,
determined rhetoric that never
persuades, the rocks unwilling
to be pebbles, nights and days and
centuries passing before the pebbles
dwindle to join the sand, the sand itself
at last barring the sea's way
into the land, an island
forming from the silt. Yet still
all this night and all
the nights of our life the sea
stroking its blue shore,
patient, patient—

'The myriad past, it enters us and disappears. Except that within it somewhere, like diamonds, exist the fragments that refuse to be consumed.'

Until sometimes an ancient
mind or body—it's not clear any more
which it may be—
those indurate insistences
having crowded out all else,
becomes all diamond:
hard transparence cut
to a thousand facets gleaming
with lights of the unseen,
a primal iridescence,
rainbow of death.

'The Holy One, blessed be he, wanders again,' said Jacob, 'He is wandering and looks for a place where he can rest.'

Between the pages
a wren's feather
to mark what passage?
Blood, not dry,
beaded scarlet on dusty stones.
A look of wonder
barely perceived on a turning face—
what, who had they seen?
Traces.
Here's the cold inn,
the wanderer passed it by
searching once more
for a stable's warmth,
a birthplace.

'I learned that her name was Proverb.'

And the secret names
of all we meet who lead us deeper
into our labyrinth
of valleys and mountains, twisting valleys
and steeper mountains—
their hidden names are always,
like Proverb, promises:
Rune, Omen, Fable, Parable,
those we meet for only
one crucial moment, gaze to gaze,
or for years know and don't recognize

but of whom later a word
sings back to us
as if from high among leaves,
still near but beyond sight

drawing us from tree to tree
towards the time and the unknown place
where we shall know
what it is to arrive.

VI

In Praise of Allium

No one celebrates the allium.
The way each purposeful stem
ends in a globe, a domed umbel,
makes people think,
'Drumsticks', and that's that.
Besides, it's related to the onion.
Is that any reason
for disregard? The flowers—look—
are bouquets of miniature florets,
each with six elfin pointed petals
and some narrower ones my eyes

aren't sharp enough to count,
and three stamens about the size
of a long eyelash.
Every root
sends up a sheaf of sturdy
ridged stems, bounty
to fill your embrace. The bees
care for the allium, if you don't—
hear them now, doing their research,
humming the arias
of a honey opera, *Allium* it's called,
gold fur voluptuously
brushing that dreamy mauve.

Poet Power

Riding by taxi, Brooklyn to Queens,
a grey spring day. The Hispanic driver,
when I ask, 'Es Usted Mexicano?' tells me
No, he's an exile from Uruguay. And I say,
'The only other Uruguayan I've met
was a writer—maybe
you know his name?—
                    Mario Benedetti?'
   And he takes both hands
off the wheel and swings round,
glittering with joy: '*Benedetti!*
Mario Benedetti!!'
                  There are
hallelujas in his voice—
we execute a perfect
figure 8 on the shining highway,
and rise aloft, high above traffic, flying
all the rest of the way in the blue sky, azul, azul!

The Well

At sixteen I believed the moonlight
could change me if it would.
            I moved my head
on the pillow, even moved my bed
as the moon slowly
crossed the open lattice.

I wanted beauty, a dangerous
gleam of steel, my body thinner,
my pale face paler.
            I moonbathed
diligently, as others sunbathe.
But the moon's unsmiling stare
kept me awake. Mornings,
I was flushed and cross.

It was on dark nights of deep sleep
that I dreamed the most, sunk in the well,
and woke rested, and if not beautiful,
filled with some other power.

Girls

1 The Cherry Orchard

Not innocence; it was ignorance
lifted our chattering hoyden voices.
The orchard path, a shortcut to the village
where, when we got there, what was there to do?
—nothing to buy
but a handful of sticky sweets
our taste had outgrown.
Without mercy, without malice,
we tore off polished rubies, doubles and triples
of garnet baubles from the bent branches
to adorn our ears, wreathe in our Alice headbands,
devour. We spat the pale stones

from stained mouths, or from thumb and finger
flipped them to the treetops,
outscreaming the jays. We were indignant
when the farmer appeared
and raised his stick and shouted.
Our thieving troupe was beyond his reach.

2 Vineyards

Later, and older. Now we had suffered—a little.
When the way south became
a white road between fields of
fabled abundance, ranged in such weedless
elegance of order, we had no impulse, the two of us,
to trespass far into the serried vine;
but fruit nearest the verge we still thought
ours by right, to break our fast
as the dew vanished, the sun climbed. We slept
on bare ground, under stars, the nights of those days.

Not one by one but in passionate clusters
we pressed the grapes to our lips.
Their bloom was bloom,
the dust plain dust,
a time of happiness.
We had suffered
only a little, still,—our ignorance grown
only a little more shallow. There was something now
of innocence in us perhaps—we would not ask ourselves that
until we were almost old.

From the Image-Flow—Death of Chausson, 1899

Green in his mind the bows flicker, flicker and stream,
the piano's violet dapples the riverbed in arpeggios,
green, green the leaves.

Filled with summer his mind rises, his mind floats
a voice under branches, whisper of light, flying—
the leaves, the leaves:

and the road's long slope hums down to the shaded hollow,
a rushing scale, his wheels are spinning, his hat takes wing,
faster, faster, the brakes are asleep or deaf,
he is flying through green and violet
to the unseen wall, the silence.

Wavering

Flickering curtain, scintillations, junebugs,
rain of fireflies low in the rippling fog,
motes abundant, random, pinpoints of intelligence
floating like bright snow . . .
A world, the world, where *live shell*
can explode on impact or, curled elaborate bone,
be an architecture, domicile
of wincing leisurely flesh.
                    The attention
sets out toward a cell, its hermit,
                the rapt years all one day,
                telling and telling beads and vision—
            toward a river forever
            sweeping worn stones without impatience,
            holding its gesture, palm upraised—
but at once wavers: the shimmering curtain, wet strands
of hair, sound of the thick reeds jostled by what they hide,
life on the move, a caravan of event. Water an intermittent gleaming,
pools, marshes, a different river.

VII

Caedmon

All others talked as if
talk were a dance.
Clodhopper I, with clumsy feet
would break the gliding ring.
Early I learned to

hunch myself
close by the door:
then when the talk began
I'd wipe my
mouth and wend
unnoticed back to the barn
to be with the warm beasts,
dumb among body sounds
of the simple ones.
I'd see by a twist
of lit rush the motes
of gold moving
from shadow to shadow
slow in the wake
of deep untroubled sighs.
The cows
munched or stirred or were still. I
was at home and lonely,
both in good measure. Until
the sudden angel affrighted me—light effacing
my feeble beam,
a forest of torches, feathers of flame, sparks upflying:
but the cows as before
were calm, and nothing was burning,
          nothing but I, as that hand of fire
touched my lips and scorched my tongue
and pulled my voice
               into the ring of the dance.

The Servant-Girl at Emmaus (A Painting by Velázquez)

She listens, listens, holding
her breath. Surely that voice
is his—the one
who had looked at her, once, across the crowd,
as no one ever had looked?
Had seen her? Had spoken as if to her?

Surely those hands were his,
taking the platter of bread from hers just now?
Hands he'd laid on the dying and made them well?

Surely that face—?

The man they'd crucified for sedition and blasphemy.
The man whose body disappeared from its tomb.
The man it was rumored now some women had seen this morning, alive?

Those who had brought this stranger home to their table
don't recognize yet with whom they sit.
But she in the kitchen, absently touching the winejug she's to take in,
a young Black servant intently listening,

swings round and sees
the light around him
and is sure.

Standoff

Assail God's hearing with gull-screech knifeblades.

Cozen the saints to plead our cause, claiming
grace abounding.

God crucified on the resolve not to displume
our unused wings

hears: nailed palms
cannot beat off the flames of insistent sound,

strident or plaintive,
nor reach to annul freedom—

nor would God renege.

Our shoulders ache. The abyss
gapes at us.

When shall we
dare to fly?

On a Theme from Julian's Chapter XX

Six hours outstretched in the sun, yes,
hot wood, the nails, blood trickling
into the eyes, yes—
but the thieves on their neighbor crosses
survived till after the soldiers
had come to fracture their legs, or longer.
Why single out this agony? What's
a mere six hours?
Torture then, torture now,
the same, the pain's the same,
immemorial branding iron,
electric prod.
Hasn't a child
dazed in the hospital ward they reserve
for the most abused, known worse?
This air we're breathing,
these very clouds, ephemeral billows
languid upon the sky's
moody ocean, we share
with women and men who've held out
days and weeks on the rack—
and in the ancient dust of the world
what particles
of the long tormented,
what ashes.

But Julian's lucid spirit leapt
to the difference:
perceived why no awe could measure
that brief day's endless length,
why among all the tortured
One only is 'King of Grief'.
The oneing, she saw, *the oneing*
with the Godhead opened Him utterly
to the pain of all minds, all bodies
—sands of the sea, of the desert—
from first beginning
to last day. The great wonder is
that the human cells of His flesh and bone
didn't explode

when utmost Imagination rose
in that flood of knowledge. Unique
in agony, Infinite strength, Incarnate,
empowered Him to endure
inside of history,
through those hours when He took to Himself
the sum total of anguish and drank
even the lees of that cup:

within the mesh of the web, Himself
woven within it, yet seeing it,
seeing it whole. *Every sorrow and desolation*
He saw, and sorrowed in kinship.

Candlemas

With certitude
Simeon opened
ancient arms
to infant light.
Decades
before the cross, the tomb
and the new life,
he knew
new life.
What depth
of faith he drew on,
turning illumined
towards deep night.

Variation on a Theme by Rilke
(The Book of Hours, Book I, Poem 4*)*

All these images (said the old monk,
closing the book) these inspired depictions,
are true. Yes—not one—Giotto's,
Van Eyck's, Rembrandt's, Rouault's,
how many others'—

not one is a fancy, a willed fiction,
each of them shows us exactly
the manifold countenance
of the Holy One, Blessed be He.
The seraph buttress flying
to support a cathedral's external walls,
the shadowy ribs of the vaulted sanctuary:
aren't both—and equally—
the form of a holy place?—whose windows' ruby
and celestial sapphire can be seen
only from inside, but then
only when light enters from without?
From the divine twilight, neither dark nor day,
blossoms the morning. Each, at work in his art,
perceived his neighbor. Thus the Infinite
plays, and in grace
gives us clues to His mystery.

La Cordelle

Be here:
surrounded
by stone,

by hewn stone, tints
of ochre, carnelian,

fieldstone graying
to dim white—

stones placed
one by one, a labor
arduous and exact.

Be here:
in presence
of stones, of silence,

of silence holding a pale
memory of shame,

of the cross
defiled (brandished
in war as a weapon)

of the poor
later, encamped
among charred
stones, time
of abandonment,
the altar fallen.

Be here:
where columns, arches
colors
of hay, of chaff,
of hedge-rose dust,
recall

the time of
stored grain, time
of sheep wintering,
drifted snow
heaped at
the broken door.

Be here, surrounded
by stone, by time,
by sunlight entering
like a bee at the
arched portal.

Here, where so long
no altar stood,
there stands, hewn
but not carved,
a block
of plain
stone unadorned,

and on the floor
before it, a gray
stoneware jar holds

(held, itself,
in the careful
space which
within the peace
of these ancient
stones
sustains us)

fading goldenrod,
fresh marguerites and
ardently pink
dahlias, dahlias
of bright
scarlet, dahlias
of garnet crimson,
almost black,
both reds
bloodred,

the entire bouquet
singing its colors
the livelong
empty day, the stones
resanctified.

The Showings: Lady Julian of Norwich, 1342–1416

1

Julian, there are vast gaps we call black holes,
unable to picture what's both dense and vacant;

and there's the dizzying multiplication of all
language can name or fail to name, unutterable
swarming of molecules. All Pascal
imagined he could not stretch his mind to imagine
is known to exceed his dread.

And there's the earth of our daily history,
its memories, its present filled with the grain

of one particular scrap of carpentered wood we happen
to be next to, its waking light on one especial leaf,
this word or that, a tune in this key not another,
beat of our hearts *now*, good or bad,
dying or being born, eroded, vanishing—

And you ask us to turn our gaze
inside out, and see
a little thing, the size of a hazelnut, and believe
it is our world? Ask us to see it lying
in God's pierced palm? That it encompasses
every awareness our minds contain? All Time?
All limitless space given form in this
medieval enigma?
                              Yes, this is indeed
what you ask, sharing
the mystery you were shown: *all that is made:*
a little thing, the size of a hazelnut, held safe
in God's pierced palm.

2

What she petitioned for was never
instead of something else.
Thirty was older than it is now. She had not married
but was no starveling; if she had loved,
she had been loved. Death or some other destiny
bore him away, death or some other bride
changed him. Whatever that story,
long since she had travelled
through and beyond it. Somehow,
reading or read to, she'd spiralled
up within tall towers
of learning, steeples of discourse.
Bells in her spirit
rang new changes.
                              Swept beyond event, one longing
outstripped all others: that reality,
supreme reality,
be witnessed. To desire wounds—
three, no less, no more—
is audacity, not, five centuries early, neurosis;

it's the desire to enact metaphor, for flesh to make known
to intellect (as uttered song
                    makes known to voice,
                    as image to eye)
make known in bone and breath
(and not die) God's agony.

3

'To understand her, you must imagine . . .'
A childhood, then;
the dairy's bowls of clabber, of rich cream,
ghost-white in shade, and outside
the midsummer gold, humming of dandelions.
To run back and forth, into the chill again,
the sweat of slate, a cake of butter
set on a green leaf—out once more
over slab of stone into hot light, hot
wood, the swinging gate!
A spire we think ancient split the blue
between two trees, a half-century old—
she thought it ancient.
Her father's hall, her mother's bower,
nothing was dull. The cuckoo
was changing its tune. In the church
there was glass in the windows, glass
colored like the world. You could see
Christ and his mother and his cross,
you could see his blood, and the throne of God.
In the fields
calves were lowing, the shepherd was taking the sheep
to new pasture.
                    Julian perhaps
not yet her name, this child's
that vivid woman.

4

God's wounded hand
reached out to place in hers
the entire world, 'round as a ball,
small as a hazelnut'. Just so one day

of infant light remembered
her mother might have given
into her two cupped palms
a newlaid egg, warm from the hen;
just so her brother
risked to her solemn joy
his delicate treasure,
a sparrow's egg from the hedgerow.
What can this be? *the eye of her understanding* marveled.

God for a moment in our history
placed in that five-fingered
human nest
the macrocosmic egg, sublime paradox,
brown hazelnut of All that Is—
made, and belov'd, and preserved.
As still, waking each day within
our microcosm, we find it, and ourselves.

5   *Chapter Thirteen*

Why did she laugh?
In scorn of malice.

What did they think?
They thought she was dying.

They caught her laugh?
Even the priest—

the dark small room
quivered with merriment,

all unaccountably
lightened.

If they had known
what she was seeing—

     the very
     spirit of evil,

the Fiend they dreaded,
seen to be oafish, ridiculous, vanquished—

what amazement! Stupid,
stupid his mar-plot malevolence!

Silly as his horns and
imaginary tail!

Why did her laughter
stop? Her mind moved on:

the cost, the cost,
the passion it took to undo
the deeds of malice.
The deathly

wounds and the anguished
heart.
And they?

They were abashed,
stranded in hilarity.

But when she recovered,
they told one another:

'Remember how we laughed
without knowing why?
That was the turning-point!'

6

Julian laughing aloud, glad
with *a most high inward happiness*,

Julian open calmly to dismissive judgements
flung backward down the centuries—
'delirium', 'hallucination';

Julian walking under-water
on the green hills of moss, the detailed sand and seaweed,
pilgrim of the depths, unfearing;

twenty years later carefully retelling
each unfading vision, each
pondered understanding;

Julian of whom we know
she had two serving-maids, Alice and Sara,
and kept a cat, and looked God in the face
and lived—

Julian nevertheless
said that *deeds are done so evil, injuries inflicted*
so great, it seems to us
impossible any good
can come of them—

any redemption, then, transform them . . .

She lived in dark times, as we do:
war, and the Black Death, hunger, strife,
torture, massacre. She knew
all of this, she felt it
sorrowfully, mournfully,
shaken as men shake
a cloth in the wind.

            But Julian, Julian—
I turn to you:
          you clung to joy though tears and sweat
rolled down your face like the blood
you watched pour down *in beads uncountable*
as rain from the eaves:
clung like an acrobat, by your teeth, fiercely,
to a cobweb-thin high-wire, your certainty
of infinite mercy, witnessed
with your own eyes, with outward sight
in your small room, with inward sight
in your untrammeled spirit—
knowledge we long to share:
Love was his meaning.

Variation and Reflection on a Theme by Rilke

(The Book of Hours, Book I, Poem 7*)*

1

If just for once the swing of cause and effect, cause and effect,
would come to rest; if casual events would halt,
and the machine that supplies meaningless laughter
ran down, and my bustling senses, taking a deep breath
fell silent
and left my attention free at last . . .

then my thought, single and multifold,
could think you into itself
until it filled with you to the very brim,
bounding the whole flood of your boundlessness:

and at that timeless moment of possession,
fleeting as a smile, surrender you
and let you flow back into all creation.

2

There will never be that stillness.
Within the pulse of flesh,
in the dust of being, where we trudge,
        turning our hungry gaze this way and that,
the wings of the morning
brush through our blood
as cloud-shadows brush the land.
What we desire travels with us.
We must breathe time as fishes breathe water.
God's flight circles us.

A DOOR IN THE HIVE

I

To Rilke

Once, in dream,
             the boat
pushed off from the shore.
You at the prow were the man—
all voice, though silent—who bound
rowers and voyagers to the needful journey,
the veiled distance, imperative mystery.

All the crouched effort,
         creak of oarlocks, odor of sweat,
         sound of waters
         running against us
was transcended: your gaze
held as we crossed. Its dragonfly blue
restored to us
             a shimmering destination.

I had not read yet of your Nile journey,
the enabling voice
drawing that boat upstream in your parable.
Strange that I knew
your silence was just such a song.

To R.D., March 4th 1988

You were my mentor. Without knowing it,
I outgrew the need for a mentor.
Without knowing it, you resented that,
and attacked me. I bitterly resented
the attack, and without knowing it
freed myself to move forward
without a mentor. Love and long friendship
corroded, shrank, and vanished from sight
into some underlayer of being.
The years rose and fell, rose and fell,
and the news of your death after years of illness

was a fact without resonance for me,
I had lost you long before, and mourned you,
and put you away like a folded cloth
put away in a drawer. But today I woke
while it was dark, from a dream
that brought you live into my life:
I was in a church, near the Lady Chapel
at the head of the west aisle. Hearing a step
I turned: you were about to enter
the row behind me, but our eyes met
and you smiled at me, your unfocussed eyes
focussing in that smile to renew
all the reality our foolish pride extinguished.
You moved past me then, and as you sat down
beside me, I put a welcoming hand
over yours, and your hand was warm.
I had no need
for a mentor, nor you to be one;
but I was once more
your chosen sister, and you
my chosen brother.
We heard strong harmonies rise and begin to fill
the arching stone,
sounds that had risen here through centuries.

Intimation

I am impatient with these branches, this light.
The sky, however blue, intrudes.
Because I've begun to see
there is something else I must do,
I can't quite catch the rhythm
of days I moved well to in other winters.
The steeple tree
was cut down, the one that daybreak
used to gild—that fervor of birds and cherubim
subdued. Drought has dulled
many a green blade.
                    Because
I know a different need has begun

to cast its lines out from me into
a place unknown, I reach
for a silence almost present,
elusive among my heartbeats.

A Traveler

If it's chariots or sandals,
I'll take sandals.
I like the high prow of the chariot,
the daredevil speed, the wind
a quick tune you can't
quite catch
        but I want to go
a long way
and I want to follow
paths where wheels deadlock.
               And I don't want always
to be among gear and horses,
     blood, foam, dust. I'd like
to wean myself from their strange allure.
I'll chance
the pilgrim sandals.

Entering Another Chapter

The nights pass, sleep and dreams, the ship rolling and creaking;
and days, clouds rolling soundlessly, creak of seabirds' wings
veering, battling headwinds. Nights, days, out on the main,
passage of years, decades, no landfall fragrance, peppery breeze.
Then a morning comes, this one, of light different
                            as light in childhood
          when we opened our eyes to an altered ceiling,
          customary shadows absent,
          tenor of morning changed—afraid for a moment,
          then we knew, and jumped out of bed to look,
             and yes, the mystery
         was indeed the mystery of snowfall.

Today, awakening shows a color of ocean
unrecognized. And there are islands. Birds of new species
                              follow the wake.
The sky too is a sky not witnessed before, its hue
not imagined. Coastal villages, mountain contours almost
                              remembered—yet this
is not any place from which we left, some cognate rather. Travelers
not noticed before stand at the rail beside us. No sense of arrival;
a sense of approach. Some meet our eyes, we begin to speak, to hear
how their story—the long land journey, the port, delays, embarkation,
    storms, doldrums, then the seductive furrowing through time,
                              anything else
    receding, paling, fuzzy and then forgotten,
    only the sea present and real, and the ship nosing its way
    under moon and sun—
                              was our own story.

For Instance

Often, it's nowhere special: maybe
a train rattling not fast or slow
from Melbourne to Sydney, and the light's fading,
we've passed that wide river remembered
from a tale about boyhood and fatal love, written
in vodka prose, clear and burning—
the light's fading and then
beside the tracks this particular
straggle of eucalyptus, an inconsequential
bit of a wood, a coppice, looks your way,
not at you, through you, through the train,
over it—gazes with branches and rags of bark
to something beyond your passing. It's not,
this shred of seeing, more beautiful
than a million others, less so than many;
you have no past here, no memories,
and you'll never set foot among these shadowy
tentative presences. Perhaps when you've left this continent
you'll never return; but it stays with you:
years later, whenever
its blurry image flicks on in your head,

786

it wrenches from you the old cry:
O Earth, belovéd Earth!
                         —like many another faint
constellation of landscape does, or fragment
of lichened stone, or some old shed
where you took refuge once from pelting rain
in Essex, leaning on wheel or shafts
of a dusty cart, and came out when you heard
a blackbird return to song though the rain
was not quite over; and, as you thought there'd be,
there was, in the dark quarter where frowning clouds
were still clustered, a hesitant trace
of rainbow; and across from that the expected
gleam of East Anglian afternoon light, and leaves
dripping and shining. Puddles, and the roadside weeds
washed of their dust. Earth,
that inward cry again—
Erde, du liebe . . .

The Blind Man's House at the Edge of the Cliff

At the jutting rim of the land he lives,
but not from ignorance,
not from despair.
He knows one extra step from his seaward
wide-open door would be
a step into salt air,
and he has no longing to shatter himself
far below, where the breakers
grind granite to sand.
No, he has chosen a life
pitched at the brink, a nest on the swaying
tip of a branch, for good reason:

dazzling within his darkness
is the elusive deep horizon. Here
nothing intrudes, palpable shade,
between his eager
inward gaze
and the vast enigma.

If he could fly he would drift forever
into that veil, soft and receding.

He knows that if he could see
he would be no wiser.
High on the windy cliff he breathes
face to face with desire.

II

Distanced

> "If one's fate is to survive only
> sorrow, one has no right to the name survivor."

Shepherds in summer pastures
watched the invaders, a rectangular wave,
advance on the city far below. Smoke,
and towers falling. A straggling river
pouring from breached walls.
This high, no noises reached them.

They marvelled, they sorrowed.
Each had wished some day
to see for himself the city's
alien glories; all felt pity and dread.
They knew the river
was people fleeing.

But they could see no faces,
and no blood.

Land of Death-Squads

The vultures thrive,
clustered in lofty blue above
refuse-dumps where humans too
search for food, dreading

what else may be found.
Noble their wingspread,
hideous their descent
to those who know
what they may feast on:
sons, daughters.
And meanwhile,
the quetzal, bird of life, gleaming
green, glittering red, is driven
always further, higher,
into remote
ever-dwindling forests.

El Salvador: Requiem and Invocation
(A Libretto)

Not long after the murders of Archbishop Oscar Romero and of the three American nuns and a lay sister in El Salvador, I was asked by the composer Newell Hendricks to provide a text for him to work with in composing an oratorio. I suggested El Salvador as a theme, and these martyrdoms as a focus; and he was receptive to the idea. Drawing on my knowledge of Mexico and some research into Salvadoran history, I also obtained copies of letters written home by the four assassinated women as well as excerpts from Archbishop Romero's homilies. What I then attempted to write was not conceived as a poem so much as a working text for the composer—that is to say, I wanted to avoid certain nuances of rhythm and pitch in my words in order to produce something deliberately incomplete, something broadly sketched which would call precisely for that development the still-unwritten music would give it. Please see the note on pages 1034–35 for further details of the piece's sources and development.   —D.L.

Chorus (Words of Terror and Violence)

Blood Rape Kill Mutilate Death-squad Massacre
Torture Acid Order National Guard Thirst Pain
Crying Screaming Bloated Naked Helicopter
Slaughter Shoot Machine-gunned Beaten Vomit
Slash Burning Slit Bullhorns Sprayed Blinded
Bullets Machete Wounds Smash

(Phrases of Terror and Violence)
They cut off their heads They cut off their hands
They cut off their balls They cut off their breasts
Chopped up his face Hacking dead meat
The crops are burning 'Mama they're burning
my dress!' 'The empire of hell' 'Hit them—hit them
again' 'We've hit them already—they'll
just die—leave them'
'I had a terrible thirst' 'The water was full of blood'
'Blood of my children' 'I kept drinking, drinking
the water. It was full of blood.'
'Kill the survivors' 'Tie their thumbs behind their
backs.' 'Acid is thrown in their faces.'
'We have seen too much, too many dead.'*
The air is black with smoke. No one is safe.

Voice of Questioner

O Mayan land! El Salvador!
What brought you to this time
of horror? Long ago
           it was not so—
Chorus

Long ago
it was not so,
the land was generous,
the people lived at peace.
The land and people
were one, and lived
at peace:

Narrator

Long ago, in the far millenia,
already the Mayan folk were tending
pumpkins & chili,
corn and beans:
the earth was bountiful,
it gave freely:

*Actual quotations from eyewitness accounts

Chorus

avocado, guava, papaya,
blackberry, elderberry,
tomato and calabash,
sapote, nopale–

Narrator

The people lived
with reverence, knowing
the daily mystery:
earth, sky, plants, men & women,
inseparable,
a single mystery:

The hoe, the digging stick,
were tools of a sacrament.
Prayers rose night & day
from the deep valleys,
from the lowlands,
from the mountainslopes
in the shimmering dust of months that are hot & dry,
in the great rains of summer
when thunder cracks its whip.
They knew the cycle, the rituals:
earth & sky,
fruits, animals,
humans:

Prayer (Chorus)

'O God,
Lord of the hills & valleys,
I am beneath thy feet,
beneath thy hands—
O God, my grandfather,
O God, my grandmother,
        God of the hills,
        God of the valleys,
my holy God:
            I make to you my offering
            with all my soul.
Be patient with me in what I am doing.

It is needful that you give me
all I am going to sow here,
here where I have my work,
my cornfield;
watch it for me,
guard my field for me, my *milpa*,
let it be safe,
from the time of sowing
to the time of harvest.'*

Narrator

And once a year
for five days there was silence—

Chorus

Once a year
hide
in darkness
under roofs,
indoors—
do nothing,
don't eat
don't make love
don't speak,
hide
in darkness

the gods
are not here
not there
we know
nothing
we must
be still
be patient
in limbo,
holding our breath,
for then,
after silence
life will

* Kakehi Indian prayer

792

continue,
earth & sky,
fruit and folk . . .

Narrator

And life continued, slow, long ago, the rhythms
of that slow dance, grandmother earth,
grandfather sky, their children & children's children.

Voice of Questioner

And then, and then?
  How did the horror begin?
Was it a thunderclap? Did men
blaspheme?

Narrator

Not with a thunderclap,
but yes,
with blasphemy:
but not the Maya blasphemed:
men from a far place,
a few, & a few, then more,
more—yet still
only a few, but powerful
with alien power—
came seeking gold,
        seeking wealth,
        denying
        the mystery of the land,
        the sacred harmony,
        breaking the rhythm
        taking the earth unto themselves
        to use it—

Chorus

To use it for money,
to send its fruits far away for money,
for others to use,
for people who had not seen the land
to eat and drink of its fruits,

to spend the money bought of its fruits:
the sacred fields given over
> to indigo
> to sugar
> to making rum out of sugar
> to cotton
> to coffee . . .

The land was raped,
forced to bear crops that
could not feed us.

Narrator

With pomp and circumstance
they came,
and new names for God:

they came speaking of goodness,
of good and evil;

they brought evil.
Our people were brought
under their domination, powerless.

Voices from Chorus

The lands of God our Golden Corn,
who nourishes us
were taken away from us,
taken away from Him:

Voices from Chorus

The lands of God our Dark Mother
the Cocoa Plant, *Madre Cacao*,
who gives us a sacred potion to drink,
were taken away from us,
taken away from Her.

Voices from Chorus

They made us use
cocoa-beans for small change.
Corn and cocoa and all plants

by which our bodies were sustained
                    or warmed
                    or clothed
and our spirits
                    lightened or instructed—
all these were taken from us
and from our gods,
          the gods that dwelt in root and blossom,
                              in leaf and fruit—
taken, and put to strange uses.

Narrator

And time passed.
The conqueror's cattle
foraged and trampled the *milpas*.
Like hungry ghosts,
forced off the land,
the disinherited wandered to work
now here, now there,
or were rounded up,
their huts set on fire.
They were taken away into slavery.

Chorus

And time passed.
For one of the centuries
it was cane we served,
that turned into rum,
which whenever we could we drank
to make us forget
hunger and loss
and loss of the gods they said
the new god had conquered.

And time passed.
For one of the centuries
our slavery was to indigo.
Stench
of rotten indigo buzzing with flies
lay heavy over our compounds.
Brown hands

turned blue.
Fevers killed many.
Many escaped at night
to eat poison roots
or to hang themselves in the forest.

Narrator

And time passed.
As cane for rum
had supplanted the corn,
and then indigo
made more of a profit than rum,
now the dye gave place
to coffee.

Chorus

We worked, we worked, the cycle
of sun and rain continued but we
were hungry,
hungry, hungry,
our children were few,
they died,
our numbers dwindled,
yet there was no longer food enough in the land
for the land's own people.

Narrator

Thus the crops changed
as demand changed,
but the people,
the people were still enslaved.

Chorus

We were hungry, hungry, hungry, hungry,
hungry and enslaved.

Narrator (Staccato; like a huckster)

And the century
was the fifth since the conquest,

the 20th century,
the market for coffee
was big.
                    For this was the century
that got where the others were going,
and made
                    the whole world into a marketplace!

Chorus

And at last we could bear
no more: and the people,
we the poor
we the hungry,
we the enslaved,
tried to throw off our chains—

tried when a peasant, our own brother,
Farabundo Martí
rose up to lead us,
tried
        to rise with him:

tried and failed,
crushed by the power of their guns,
money and guns,
their machine guns bought with the money
our labor provided, coffee
exchanged for money, money
given back in exchange for guns,
machine guns to murder the people to show
the people they cannot rebel, to keep
the people enslaved, working to grow
the coffee to sell for money the people
don't ever see, the money to buy
the machine guns . . . coffee money blood murder
machine guns buy sell enslaved . . .

[Cacophonous babble ensues, followed by orchestral interlude]

Narrator

But now among those
who long ago had come with the conquerors

bearing aloft the image of a God they said was good,
in whose name they and
the conquerors, soldiers of fortune,
took power,
    took power and gave to the people
not God's good but evil;
who crushed the people as they
crushed the old gods,
who came as priests of conquest—
now among these were heard
 new voices
 voices of mercy
 voices of pity
 voices of love for the poor;

Chorus

and now
the nuns, priests, bishops,
not only spoke but listened,

and listening gave
the great gift of attention,
and fed the hungry
not with scraps and crumbs of
 uncharitable charity
but with respect,
calling for justice.

Narrator

And strongest among them, a voice leading the chorus,
Oscar Romero, the Arch-
bishop, 'prince of the church,' whose riches
were faith, hope, and love,
who, day by day,
 week by week,
gathered testimony of terror,
of 'the insulted and injured'—

Romero

'the clamor of the people, the aching
of so much crime, the ignominy
of so much violence'*

Narrator

—and broadcast it, Sunday by Sunday

Chorus

—that no general
        no member of the Junta
        no National Guardsman
        no business tycoon
could claim innocence, ignorance;
no side of the great multifaceted
crime of oppression
would go undenounced.

Narrator

And each week he read
the roll of names of the newly dead—
of the men, women, and children
abducted, tortured, killed, disappeared
that week.
        He was Archbishop:
the junta's anger
smouldered.

Romero

ANTONIO FLORES
SANDRA MARITZA GALICIA
EVE CATALINA HERNANDEZ
DENIS ORLANDO GALLARDO
BORIS NAPOLEAN MARTINEZ
JAIME ANDRES LOPEZ CASTELLON
SONIA ELIZABETH MEJIA
JUAN RAMON PEREZ SANDOVAL
BLANCA ESTELA CONTRERAS

---

* This and all subsequent speech by Romero when set within quotation marks are
taken from his public statements.

RAMIRO ENRIQUEZ
RAUL OMAR ROSALES CAMPOS
RICARDO ERNESTO ORELLANA
EDWIN CHAVEZ
ADILSON MELENDEZ SOMOZA
DEMESIO ZETINO RODRIQUEZ
LORI ROBERTO ORELLANA SANCHES
JOSE ROBERTO PONCE VELASQUEZ
JOSE GUIERMO CARPIO
MARCO ANTONIO CARCAMO DONA
ANTONIO DUBON SANCHEZ
ARISTIDES WILFREDO CASTILLO
EFRIAN MENJIVAR
YURI ELMER ARIA NOVOA
CLAUDIA INES CUELLAR COTO
JUAN MANUEL RODRIQUEZ
ADOLFO BERNAL MEJIA
MARIA CRISTINA JUAREZ
MARIA ALICIA PEREZ
ROSA MARGARITA JOAQUIN
LUIS ALBERTO DIAZ SERRANO
LUZ VASQUEZ MEJIA RIVERA
IVAN CUELLAS GIRON
CARLOS ARMANDO SERRANO
NAPOLEAN DE MONGE RIVERA
MARIA TERESA MANJIVAR
CARLOS ARMANDO MEDINA
HAYDEE YANIRA RIVERA
JORGE ANDRES CHACON SEQURA
ROXANA QUITANILLA
RENE SANTOS
EDUARDO SANTOS
ELMA MOJICA
SERGIO MOJICA SANTOS
WALTER SANTOS
DELMA SANTOS
MORENA SANTOS
BEATRIZ SANTOS
SONIA MOJICA
TOMMASA SANTOS
HERMINA SANTOS
ERASMO VLADIMIRO SANTOS

VENECIA AND VICTORIA SANTOS
ROSA SANTOS
TERESA SANTOS
ELBA SANTOS
ROSA MOJICA
MARCOS MOJICA SANTOS
HUGO MOJICA SANTOS . . .

[Voice continues diminuendo *behind chorus]*

Chorus

The pain, the murders,
the hunger, the tortures,
all continued,
and continue still,
and increase—

yet the voices that tell us
our broken bodies are not after all
worthless rubbish, but hold
sparks of the God—
                      these voices
begin to give us our freedom:

Half Chorus

Though we have lost
knowledge of old harmonies,
old ways we spoke to the earth,
            sang to the sky—
though we have lost
the knowledge we had
      of grandfather, grandmother
      god in the ear of corn,
      god in the cocoa-bean,
      god the rain and
      god the sun—

Chorus

Yet now
our dignity grows in us
once more,

we believe
there is life in our land
to be lived,
that our anguish
moves us onward, forward towards
a time of justice . . .

Narrator

And time was passing,
quickly, quickly,
here in the small land of El Salvador
as in the rest of the troubled globe,
where wars and hunger and fear
convulse and contort
like vast and poisonous clouds
battling in nightmare skies
as the century's last quarter
hurtles toward the unknown—
and into this chaos
    where daily among the people
    priests and nuns risked with the rest
    torture, 'disappearance,' mutilation.

Chorus

FATHER MARCIEL SERRANO
FATHER ERNESTO ABREGO
FATHER RUTILIO GRANDE
SISTER SYLVIA MARIBEL ARRIOLA . . .

[Chorus continues with additional names]

Narrator

and into this chaos arrived four women
out of the north—

Chorus

—out of that land
whose money and power and weapons
support our oppressors, and teach
the junta's killers

new ways of killing:
four Yanqui nuns—

Narrator

—arrived to join
their sisters and serve the people:
Ita, Maura, Jean, Dorothy.

Dorothy

'We have come to a land that
is writhing in pain . . .
Yet a land that's waiting, hoping,
yearning for peace.'*

Maura

'We came in answer
to a call. The need
is overwhelming.'

Ita

'We came to live with the poor.
To be
evangelized by the poor.'

Jean

'I was a lay missioner.
I came to give
two years of myself.
I was not planning to stay.'

All Four

'We have come to a land that
is writhing in pain.
Yet a land that's waiting, hoping,
yearning for peace.'

---

*This and all subsequent lines spoken by the four sisters when set within quotation
marks are taken from their letters.

Narrator

And Romero spoke to the soldiers,
the National Guard, the police,
                    saying,

Romero

'Brothers, you belong
to our own people! You kill
your brother peasants!
Stop the killing—for no one
has to comply with immoral orders,
immoral laws.'

Narrator

And Romero spoke to the government,
saying,

Romero

'Reforms mean nothing
when they are bathed
in so much blood.'

Chorus

We are refugees
in our own country,
herded and huddled
now here, now there—

Sisters (Singly)

'We came to bring food and shelter'
'To search for the missing'
'To help in the struggle to break
out of the bonds
          of oppression
          and hunger
          and violence'—

Sisters (Together)

'in a land that is writhing in pain,
yearning for peace—'

Chorus (Overlap echo effect)

So much blood
          So much blood

So many deaths
          So many deaths

So much courage
          So much courage

So much endurance
          So much endurance

So much faith
          So much faith

Chorus

We learned
how the old gods, our grandparents, long betrayed,
unite with the god our martyred friends
brought in their hearts to us: the crucified—
          who refused to be bought,
          who suffered like us,
          who returned from the dead.

Sisters (Together)

'In a land that is writhing in pain,
yearning for peace,'

to suffer the powerlessness of the poor
and to go beyond it,

to discover,
to discover and to reveal

the power of that powerlessness.

Chorus (With irony)

Powerless, feathers in a whirlpool,
they were killed,
of course. (**Echo**: Of course, of course, of course . . .)

Voice of Questioner

O Mayan land! El Salvador!
what brought you to this time
of horror?

Narrator

Archbishop Romero gunned down
in the hospice for incurables,
named for Divine Providence:
his killers
chose their moment.
He fell
at the altar, saying
a requiem mass, saying
'Let us unite'—

Romero

'Let us unite in faith and hope
as we pray
for the dead
and for ourselves.'

Narrator

A magnum slug,
his heart torn open,
a single shot,
a hired killer,
a distance of 20 meters.

Half Chorus

His killers
were ironic;
*but in martyrdom
is a seed of power!*

Narrator

The sisters, travelling
on their road of mercy,
were ambushed,
raped,
killed,
flung in a pit.

Half Chorus (Bitterly ironic)

Raped, killed, flung in a pit—
the usual way.
The soldiers
had practice.
But in martyrdom
is a seed of power.

Voice of Questioner

What do they ask,
the martyrs,
of those who hear them,
who know
the story, the cry,
who know what brought
our land to this grief?
What do their deaths demand?

Romero and Four Sisters

We ask that our story be known
not as the story of Salvador only;
everywhere, greed
exploits the people,
everywhere, greed
gives birth to violence,
everywhere, violence
at last is answered with violence:
   the desperate turn,
convulsed with pain,
to desperate means.

Half Chorus

Those who were martyred
bequeathed, a gift to the living,
their vision:
they saw, they told in their lives that violence
is not justice, that merciless justice
is not justice, that mercy
does not bind up
festering wounds,
but scrapes out the poison.

That 'no one has to comply
with immoral laws,'

that power abused is powerless to crush
the spirit.

Half Chorus

Now we still writhe in agony,
violent against
the unceasing violence of greed,
the greed for profit, the greed for power,
the greed of faraway strangers
to hold the world's power in their hands.
Desperation
drives us: we take no joy
in bloodshed: our longing,
our longing, our longing,
is for Peace and the works of Peace:

even now in the hidden villages,
in the mountain camps,
schools for the people spring up
like corn in the ancient *milpas*—
play and knowledge for children,
dignity for women, hope for men,
poems and songs of the people:
all of this
is for Peace. For this
our martyrs died.
Their deaths

enjoin upon us, the living,
not to give up the vision
of lives freed from the lead weight
of centuries, clear of the stain
                of indigo, stench
                of fermenting sugar,
                whistle of whiplash,
                cramps of hunger,
                ache of lost dignity, loss
                of the ancient rhythms—
vision of simple peace,
sharing our minds, our labor, our soup,
teaching hope to our children,
putting behind us
the terror of centuries.

Chorus

Those who were martyred—
Romero,
        Maura,
            Ita,
                Dorothy,
                    Jean—
and those whose names
are lost along with their bodies—
all the Marias and Juans, the Josés and Pedros,
Elenas and Glorias—they tell us,
                we in El Salvador, you
our sisters and brothers who know
the story,
all of us, all—
they tell us that horror
won't cease on the earth
till the hungry are fed,

that the fruits of the earth
don't grow that a few may profit,

that injustice here
is one with injustice anywhere,
all of us *are*
our brother's keepers,

members one of another,
responsible, culpable, and—

able to change.
This is the knowledge
that grows in power
out of the seeds of their martyrdom.

Romero and Four Sisters

Let us unite
in faith and hope
as we pray
for the dead
and for ourselves.

All

Let us unite
in faith and hope
as we pray:
as we pray for the dead
in faith and hope:
in faith and hope
as we pray:

as we pray for ourselves
for faith
as we pray
for hope.

The Book Without Words
    (From a painting by Anselm Kiefer)

The gray waves gnash
their teeth of foam.

Behind this verge,
the barren plain,
seamed, fissured.

Ahead, limitless ocean.
The sky's low ceiling
bears down upon it,
dark and darkening.

Here at the end of land
(not earth but cinders)

was to have been given
the ultimate direction.
The sea-voyage was to begin.

And indeed the book
is here, a huge volume,
open and upright—
it levitates, close to the hiss of spume,

immutable, desolate, cast
in lead. Wordless.
If with great force its pages
were made to turn,
they would knock, unresonant,

one on another,
void upon void.
You have come to the shore.
There are no instructions.

Variation on a Theme by Rilke
(The Book of Hours, Poem 8)

Soon, the end of a century. Is the great scroll
being shaken, the scroll
inscribed by God and daubed with our lives' graffiti,

to raise this wind that churns
the sleep of listeners?
What holds aloft
that banner, that undeciphered legend?

Familiar powers extend towards it
their fingers of bone—
it lifts
        beyond reach,
an elusive kite.

And the wind
rises and rises, the powers
exchange dark looks, the sleepers
watch and listen.

                        Is there more parchment
wound, still, on the heavy spindle?
If, when the scroll unfurls, it reveals
a pallid, empty field,
                    what shall be written there?
Where, if we discover the runes continue,
shall we seek out
                    their hierophant?

In California: Morning, Evening, Late January

Pale, then enkindled,
light
advancing,
emblazoning
summits of palm and pine,

the dew
lingering,
scripture of
scintillas.

Soon the roar
of mowers
cropping the already short
grass of lawns,

men with long-nozzled
cylinders of pesticide

poking at weeds,
at moss in cracks of cement,

and louder roar
of helicopters off to spray
vineyards where *braceros* try
to hold their breath,

and in the distance, bulldozers, excavators,
babel of destructive construction.

Banded by deep
oakshadow, airy
shadow of eucalyptus,

miner's lettuce,
tender, untasted,
and other grass, unmown
luxuriant,
no green more brilliant.

Fragile paradise.

    . . . .

At day's end the whole sky,
vast, unstinting, flooded with transparent
mauve,
tint of wisteria,
cloudless
over the malls, the industrial parks,
the homes with the lights going on,
the homeless arranging their bundles.

    . . . .

Who can utter
the poignance of all that is constantly
threatened, invaded, expended

and constantly
nevertheless
persists in beauty,

tranquil as this young moon
just risen and slowly
drinking light
from the vanished sun.

Who can utter
the praise of such generosity
or the shame?

Those Who Want Out

In their homes, much glass and steel. Their cars
are fast—walking's for children, except in rooms.
When they take longer trips, they think with contempt
of the jet's archaic slowness. Monastic
in dedication to work, they apply honed skills,
impatient of less than perfection. They sleep by day
when the bustle of lives might disturb their research,
and labor beneath fluorescent light in controlled environments
fitting their needs, as the dialects
in which they converse, with each other or with
the machines (which are not called machines)
are controlled and fitting. The air they breathe
is conditioned. Coffee and coke keep them alert.
But no one can say they don't dream,
that they have no vision. Their vision
consumes them, they think all the time
of the city in space, they long for the permanent colony,
not just a lab up there, the whole works,
malls, raquet courts, hot tubs, state-of-the-art
ski machines, entertainment . . . Imagine it, they think,
way out there, outside of 'nature,' unhampered,
a place contrived by man, supreme
triumph of reason. They know it will happen.
They do not love the earth.

Two Threnodies and a Psalm

I

It is not approaching.
It has arrived.
We are not circumventing it.

It is happening.
It is happening now.
We are not preventing it.
We are within it.

    •

The sound of its happening
is splitting other ears.
The sight of its happening
is searing other eyes.
The grip of its happening
is strangling other throats.

    •

Without intermission it spins,
without cessation we circle its edge
as leaf or crumb will float circling
a long time at the outer rim
before centripetal force
tugs it down.

II

The body being savaged
is alive.
It is our own.

While the eagle-vulture
tears the earth's liver,
while the heart-worm burrows
into earth's heart,

we are distant from what devours us
only as far as our extremities are from our minds,
which is no great distance.

.

Extremities, we are in
unacknowledged *extremis*.
We feel only
a chill as the pulse of life
recedes.

We don't beat off the devouring beak,
the talons. We don't dig out what burrows
into our core. *It is not*
our heart, we think (but do not say).
It is the world's, poor world, but I
am other.

III

Our clear water
one with the infested water
      women walk miles to
        each day they live.
One with the rivers tainted with detritus
                  of our ambitions,
and with the dishonored ocean.
Our unbroken skin
one with the ripped skin of the tortured,
      the shot-down, bombed, napalmed,
      the burned alive.
One with the sore and filthy skin of the destitute.

.

We utter the words
we are one
but their truth
is not real to us.

Spirit, waken
our understanding.
Out of the stasis
in which we perish,
the sullen immobility
to which the lead weight of our disbelief
condemns us,
only our rushing wind
can lift us.

       .

Our flesh and theirs
one with the flesh of fruit and tree.

Our blood
one with the blood of whale and sparrow.

Our bones
ash and cinder of star-fire.

Our being
tinder for primal light.

       .

Lift us, Spirit, impel
our rising
into that knowledge.

Make truth real to us,
flame on our lips.

Lift us to seize the present,
wrench it
out of its downspin.

Kin and Kin

For William Everson

Perhaps Jeffers was right, our species
best unborn, and once born
better soon gone, a criminal kind,
the planet's nightmare. Our going
would leave no hauntings at all, unless
to the last of those we've tamed or caged;
after those, a world
fierce in the hunt but free from malice
and free from remembrance.

Yet there have been the wise, the earthen elders
humble before the grass.
When from the torturers, picking their teeth
after a full meal, relaxed
after a full day of their routine job, we turn
to regard such others, remote as they are, yet kin—
as wheat and weed are kin, each
having root, stem, seed—or when
we hear some note of kindness
innocent of its own courage amid
the clamor of lies, it seems after all

there might be open to us, even now,
a chance to evolve, a swerve we could take,
a destiny still held out (if we would look)
in the Spirit's palm.

On the Mystery of the Incarnation

It's when we face for a moment
the worst our kind can do, and shudder to know
the taint in our own selves, that awe
cracks the mind's shell and enters the heart:
not to a flower, not to a dolphin,
to no innocent form
but to this creature vainly sure
it and no other is god-like, God
(out of compassion for our ugly

failure to evolve) entrusts,
as guest, as brother,
the Word.

III

Where Is the Angel?

Where is the angel for me to wrestle?
No driving snow in the glass bubble,
but mild September.

Outside, the stark shadows
menace, and fling their huge arms about
unheard. I breathe

a tepid air, the blur
of asters, of brown fern and gold-dust
seems to murmur,

and that's what I hear, only that.
Such clear walls of curved glass:
I see the violent gesticulations

and feel—no, not nothing. But in this
gentle haze, nothing commensurate.
It is pleasant in here. History

mouths, volume turned off. A band of iron,
like they put round a split tree,
circles my heart. In here

it is pleasant, but when I open
my mouth to speak, I too
am soundless. Where is the angel

to wrestle with me and wound
not my thigh but my throat,
so curses and blessings flow storming out

and the glass shatters, and the iron sunders?

Soutine (Two Paintings)

As if the forks themselves
were avid for the fish,
dead scrawny fish
on dead-white plate.
As if the red steps
were clutching the hill,
famished,
crawling toward the summit.
O desperate things,
living lives unheeded,
disbelieved
by those who made them!
O grey void, usurping
the abandoned cup's
parched hollow!

And houses lean, wavering,
to watch if the steps will ever
arrive, and what could there be,
up there,
to fulfil desire?

The Love of Morning

It is hard sometimes to drag ourselves
back to the love of morning
after we've lain in the dark crying out
O God, save us from the horror. . . .

God has saved the world one more day
even with its leaden burden of human evil;
we wake to birdsong.
And if sunlight's gossamer lifts in its net
the weight of all that is solid,
our hearts, too, are lifted,
swung like laughing infants;

but on gray mornings,
all incident—our own hunger,

the dear tasks of continuance,
the footsteps before us in the earth's
belovéd dust, leading the way—all,
is hard to love again
for we resent a summons
that disregards our sloth, and this
calls us, calls us.

The Winter Stars

Last night the stars had a brilliance more insistent
than I'd seen for months. The sword of Orion poised
ready to strike—one of the few constellations I know.
        Once for a short while
I lived by a lake. Each day a gentle man
who knew much about poetry, much about William Blake,
but spoke with a painful stutter, brought to my door
food, messages, friendship;
sometimes his two young sons came with him,
one of them just recovered from dangerous illness.
It snowed while I was there
and I took a photo that caught
the large loose flakes descending
among awestruck tall and straight young trees.
But mostly that winter it was so warm
by noon you could sit outdoors
and the Canada geese had halted
on their way south, encamped, like me, on the shore.
Heading out each day in captained hundreds
to forage, they returned at dusk,
troop by troop, and barked the day's luck to each other,
a multifold, intimate tribal lay . . .
In the cottage, where all was old, delicate, friendly,
I wrote a poem to the antique clock that for years
had peacefully kept its own time.
Before sleep I would stop outdoors:
the lake silent, no wind in the trees,
the throng of geese at rest, but always
a few of them stirring;
and the winter stars.

Later the man and one of his sons
(I never found out which one, whether the boy
death had already fingered and left,
or the one more robust)
were killed by a drunken driver.
The wife and the lonely brother
moved away. 'Eating the bread of bitterness' was the phrase
that came to my mind. There had been
much love and kindness among those four.
　　There are clusters, constellations,
one can perceive as grouped
but which suggest no figure of myth,
no meaning. The stars which give
a clue to the pattern
are too many light-years away, perhaps,
for our eyes, or our telescopes,
or even our inner vision.
Those we perceive can seem
to threaten us or implore, so insistently
their remote beauty glitters upon us,
and with such silence.

Two Mountains

> "To perceive the aura of an object, we look at means to invest it
> with the ability to look at us in return."
> *Walter Benjamin*

For a month (a minute)
I lived in sight of two mountains.
One was a sheer bastion
of pale rock. 'A rockface,' one says,
without thought of features, expression—
it's an abstract term.
　　But one says, too,
'a stony-faced man,' or 'she maintained
a stony silence.' This mountain,
had it had eyes, would have looked always
past one or through one; its mouth,
if it had one, would purse thin lips,
implacable, ceding nothing, nothing at all.

The other mountain gave forth
a quite different silence.
Even (beyond my range of hearing)
it may have been singing.
Ravines, forests, bare rock that peaked, off-center
in a sharp and elegant cone or horn, had an air
of pleasure, pleasure in being.
At this one I looked and looked
but could devise
no ruse to coax it to meet my gaze.
I had to accept its complete indifference,
my own complete insignificance.
my self
         unknowable to the mountain
as a single needle of spruce or fir
on its distant slopes, to me.

In Tonga

the sacred bats
hang in their chosen grove,
         sinister old dustbags,
         charcoal gray,
doze upside down,
         alien, innocent.
Restless, like seals on a rock,
they nudge one another,
they slip off into air to circle
                  the trees and
return, squeaking their utterance,
a fluttering language, and others, disturbed,
squeak in reproof.
                  All day in the heat
they wait
for dusk and the high
invisible orchards.

If they could think
it would not be of us.

A Sound

1

An unexplained sound, today,
in the early sunlight
and no wind stirring the leaves,
of something breathing

                      surrounds the house,
quiet, regular, as of someone
peacefully dreaming; something close,
yet not located: one can't say,
'it comes from beneath the southwest window,'
for, go to the north window,
it breathes there too.

2

                      They say that once,
and in living memory, orchards of apricot,
nectarine, peach, filled this valley.
In spring it drifted in ruffles
of lacy white, of lacy pink.
And before that time, for centuries
months would go by each year when no human gaze
witnessed the changes here. Forest or grassland,
green to tawny and slowly
back to green as the seasons
paced in their circle-dance. The oaks
were thick on the hills.

3

Whatever was breathing nearby,
early today, I can't hear
now that the sun is high.
It woke, perhaps, and softly
removed itself. Or maybe
it turned in its sleep,
lowered itself to new depths of dream,
soundless. I think I shall hear it
breathing some day again. Or if I'm gone,
no matter—I think the sound
will recur. It need not be heard.

Envy

The bare trees
have made up their seed bundles.
They are ready now.
The warm brown light
pauses briefly, shrugs and moves on.
They are ready now
to play dead for a while.
I, human, have not as yet devised
how to obtain
such privilege.
Their Spring will find them rested.
I and my kind
battle a wakeful way
to ours.

Complicity

On the young tree's highest twig,
a dark leaf, dry, solitary, left over
from winter, among the small new buds.
But it turns its head!
                              It's a hummingbird,
tranquil, at rest, taking time off
from the hummingbird world of swift intensities—
yet no less attentive. Taking
a long and secret look at the day,
like a child whose hiding-place
has not been discovered, who hasn't even
been missed. No hue and cry.
                                        I saw
a leaf: I shall not betray you.

Flickering Mind

Lord, not you,
it is I who am absent.

At first
belief was a joy I kept in secret,
stealing alone
into sacred places:
a quick glance, and away—and back,
circling.
I have long since uttered your name
but now
I elude your presence.
I stop
to think about you, and my mind
at once
like a minnow darts away,
darts
into the shadows, into gleams that fret
unceasing over
the river's purling and passing.
Not for one second
will my self hold still, but wanders
anywhere,
everywhere it can turn. Not you,
it is I am absent.
You are the stream, the fish, the light,
the pulsing shadow,
you the unchanging presence, in whom all
moves and changes.
How can I focus my flickering, perceive
at the fountain's heart
the sapphire I know is there?

IV

A Woodcut

(Jean Duvet, 1480–1561)

St. John, as Duvet's angel leads him
(roused from his arbor beyond
the river's moored boats and conversing swans)
through clouds, above the earthly orchards,
writes as he walks. But when he reaches

burnished Jerusalem, thronged with the blessèd,
most of them upward-gazing in adoration, some
leaning their arms on a balustrade
to dreamily scan implicit horizons
level with their celestial vantage-point,

he kneels wordless, gazing too—upward, outward,
back at the angel (now behind him), downward, inward—
his ink-bottle, slung at his hip
as before, but his notebook
vanished, perhaps discarded.

A Stone from Iona

Men who planned to be hermits, hoped to be saints, arrived
in a round boat of wicker and skin at a pebbled cove.
Behind them, dangerous leagues of mist and wave
and behind those, a land belov'd and renounced. Before them,
beyond the slope of stones and the massed green
spears of iris, waited the island, habitation of birds
and of spirits unknown, dwellers in mounds and hummocks.

Under Columba's saltwashed toes, then jostled beneath
sacks of provisions, and briefly hidden under the coracle
brothers lifted to safety above the tideline, lay
this stone, almost a seabird's egg in form, in color
a white that, placed upon white, is revealed as pearl grey.
Now worn down by fourteen more centuries, its lustre
perhaps has increased, as if moonlight, patiently
blanching and stroking, had aided weather and water
in its perfecting.
                                    Hold the stone in your palm:
it fills it, warm when your need is for warmth,
cool when you seek the touch of shadow. Its weight
gives pleasure. One stone is not like another.

The Sculptor (Homage to Chillida)

A man who lives with his shadow
on equal terms,

who learns from his shadow the arcane power
of right-angles:
                            ascension and lever,
                            taproot and flower.

A man who transmutes
mass into fire: from red, gold; from gold, white—
                            iron accepting rapture, moving,
                            returning satisfied to its purpled
                            black density, secretly curved.

Who permits stone
to acknowledge the inward void it compresses.

And to the impatient sea, the sea who knows everything,
gives immutable combs for its rushing tresses,

new gestures lifted
to the wind, new spouts
for the water curled by the wind
to pour itself into and leap from, shouting.

Early

From behind the hill,
flowing through somber
palm, eucalyptus, web
of oakboughs, rises
light so pale a gold
it bathes in silver
the cool and still
air a single bird
stirs with tentative song.

The Braiding

The way the willow-bark
braids its furrows
is answered by the willow-branches
swaying their green leaf-weavings
over the river shallows,
assenting, affirming.

At One

The mountain's spine, the cow's ridge,
the saddle dip,
          high flanks,
spur of ranged
spruce, tail
to brush at flies, valley air
between them, and
          nothing else.

Web

      Intricate and untraceable
      weaving and interweaving,
      dark strand with light:

      designed, beyond
      all spiderly contrivance,
      to link, not to entrap:

elation, grief, joy, contrition, entwined;
shaking, changing,
        forever
          forming,
            transforming:

all praise,
    all praise to the
        great web.

The Sorcerer

Blue-eyed Oberon prances
for joy in winter dusk,
the stars
are sparks from his deep, cold fur.
Motifs of Samoyed song
float forth from black lips.
                              For my part
I want the indoors, hot tea,
cherry jam. Yet I linger:
everything
instant by instant
intensifies,
dusk darker, stars wilder.
                              And Oberon,
strange-eyed Oberon,
meets my gaze in stillness
and holds it
                    before
he dances homeward,
dog and shaman.

Flying High

So much is happening above the overcast!
Cloud poets, metaphysicians, essayists,
fabulists of the troposphere,
all at work, the material
their own metamorphic substance:
here a frank exposition, suds you could wash your clothes in,
there an abstract brocade that loops and swivels
in rivers of air. We glide low
across a forest, league on league
of trees in abundant leaf,
but white, silver-white, smudged with blue, tinged
with pink, like peonies—an entire summer
conjured in milky vapor, smoke of alabaster, slivers
of pearl. League on league
to a horizon more remote

than earth's horizons. Fading now,
curling, unfolding, imperceptibly flowing,
the blush paling. Dense thickets migrate
slowly across the fertile cloud-savannah, browsing.
And far aloft, in the sky's own sky, reclined,
the shepherd moon, propped on one elbow, watches
the flocks of drowsy cloud-lambs nibble their way out of being:
for darkness, even here, is gathering; the lunar gaze
dilates and begins to gleam,
while our enormous air-bus, throbbing west and south,
seems to tarry, fleck of metallic dust,
in this firmament where dreamy energies
sculpt themselves and winnow
epic epiphanies.

Praise of a Palmtree

Tufts of brassy henna in the palm's
shaggy topknot—O Palm,
I like it, I like it!
                    And the dingy underlayer,
bedraggled skirt, tattered collar
around your furrowed neck, or is it your body,
that stout column?
                    You stay awake
all night every night
and tonight will be full moon. It's March,
and the ground beneath you
crunches under bicycle tires
where you littered it with your fruit,
those shiny brown things—I must take
a nutcracker to one some day, are they edible?
You let them fall
like a kid in the movies dropping a trail of popcorn.
                    Are you asleep up there,
your tousled green uncombed,
sunning yourself? Your way of paying
no attention, feline, and yet
strutting your crazy finery fit to kill,
I like it, I like it.

August Houseplant

Is there someone,
                an intruder,
in my back yard? That slight
scraping sound again—only a cat
maybe?
                —I look from the screendoor:
Ah! It's you, dear leaves,
only you, big, wildly branching leaves
of the philodendron,
summering on the deck,
                touching the floor of it, feeling
                the chair,
                                exploring.
As if you knew
                fall is coming, you seem to desire
        everything that surrounds you,
                        all of air,
                                all of light,
                                all of shade.
How am I going to carry you in,
when it gets cold?
                        It's not
that I can't manage the weight
of your pot of earth, though it's heavy.
It's those long, ever-longer, reaching arms
that don't fit through the door.
                        And when you're manoeuvered in,
how small the room will become;
        how can I set you
                where your green questions
won't lean over human shoulders, obscuring
books and notepads, interrupting
trains of thought
                        to enquire,
                        mutely patient,
                        about the walls?

Rearrangement

Old chimney bricks, dull red,
sometimes charred in a manner resembling
the way some painters shade
tone into deeper tone:
I'm using them to mark
a new-dug bed where yesterday,
weak and uncertain-looking,
small annuals were planted. Things
get moved around, purposes
redefined.
The bricks aren't beautiful—but time
may change them, after their years
of heat and smoke. Time in the rain.

A Surrogate

The nearest leaves, outside the glass,
let through no light

but those beyond them
are so filled with ecstatic green
it brims over, cloud of brilliance,
                hovering ocean, glowing
        behind the dark others

that sway, ornate, specific, lobed, opaque,
each with its destiny,

defined upon that dazzling screen
which seems the very source,
for this hour,
of illumination.

V

On the Parables of the Mustard Seed
(Matthew 17.20, Mark 4.30–32,
Luke 13.18–19)

Who ever saw the mustard-plant,
wayside weed or tended crop,
grow tall as a shrub, let alone a tree, a treeful
of shade and nests and songs?
Acres of yellow,
not a bird of the air in sight.

No, He who knew
the west wind brings
the rain, the south wind
thunder, who walked the field-paths
running His hand along wheatstems to glean
those intimate milky kernels, good
to break on the tongue,

was talking of miracle, the seed
within us, so small
we take it for worthless, a mustard-seed, dust,
nothing.
        Glib generations mistake
the metaphor, not looking at fields and trees,
not noticing paradox. Mountains
remain unmoved.

Faith is rare, He must have been saying,
prodigious, unique—
one infinitesimal grain divided
like loaves and fishes,

as if from a mustard-seed
a great shade-tree grew. That rare,
that strange: the kingdom
        a tree. The soul
a bird. A great concourse of birds
at home there, wings among yellow flowers.

The waiting
kingdom of faith, the seed
waiting to be sown.

The Life of Art

The borderland—that's where, if one knew how,
one would establish residence. That watershed,
that spine, that looking-glass . . . I mean the edge
between impasto surface, burnt sienna, thick,
      striate, gleaming—swathes and windrows
      of carnal paint—
      or, canvas barely stained,
      where warp and weft peer through,

and fictive truth: a room, a vase, an open door
giving upon the clouds.

A step back, and you have
the likeness, its own world. Step to the wall again,
and you're so near the paint you could lick it,
you breathe its ghostly turpentine.
                         But there's an interface,
immeasurable, elusive—an equilibrium
just attainable, sometimes, when the attention's rightly poised,
where you are opulently received
by the bravura gestures hand and brush
proffer (as if a courtier twirled
a feathered velvet hat to bow you in)
and yet, without losing sight of one stroke,
                one scrape of the knife,
you are drawn through *into* that room, into
its air and temperature.

Couldn't one learn to maintain
that exquisite balance more than a second?
                         (One sees even
the pencilled understrokes, and shivers
in pleasure—*and* one's fingertips
touch the carpet's nubs of wool, the cold fruit in a bowl:

one almost sees
what lies beyond the window, past the frame, beyond . . .

Annunciation

> *'Hail, space for the uncontained God'*
> *From the Agathistos Hymn,*
> *Greece, VIc*

We know the scene: the room, variously furnished,
almost always a lectern, a book; always
the tall lily.
            Arrived on solemn grandeur of great wings,
the angelic ambassador, standing or hovering,
whom she acknowledges, a guest.

But we are told of meek obedience. No one mentions
courage.
           The engendering Spirit
did not enter her without consent.
                    God waited.

She was free
to accept or to refuse, choice
integral to humanness.

Aren't there annunciations
of one sort or another
in most lives?
           Some unwillingly
undertake great destinies,
enact them in sullen pride,
uncomprehending.
         More often
those moments
    when roads of light and storm
    open from darkness in a man or woman,
are turned away from

in dread, in a wave of weakness, in despair
and with relief.
Ordinary lives continue.
                         God does not smite them.
But the gates close, the pathway vanishes.

———————————————

She had been a child who played, ate, slept
like any other child—but unlike others,
wept only for pity, laughed
in joy not triumph.
Compassion and intelligence
fused in her, indivisible.

Called to a destiny more momentous
than any in all of Time,
she did not quail,
                    only asked
a simple, 'How can this be?'
and gravely, courteously,
took to heart the angel's reply,
perceiving instantly
the astounding ministry she was offered:

to bear in her womb
Infinite weight and lightness; to carry
in hidden, finite inwardness,
nine months of Eternity; to contain
in slender vase of being,
the sum of power—
in narrow flesh,
the sum of light.
                    Then bring to birth,
push out into air, a Man-child
needing, like any other,
milk and love—

but who was God.

This was the minute no one speaks of,
when she could still refuse.

A breath unbreathed,
                    Spirit,
                              suspended,
                                        waiting.

———————————————

She did not cry, 'I cannot, I am not worthy,'
nor, 'I have not the strength.'
She did not submit with gritted teeth,
                              raging, coerced.
Bravest of all humans,
                    consent illumined her.
The room filled with its light,
the lily glowed in it,
                    and the iridescent wings.
Consent,
          courage unparalleled,
opened her utterly.

Wings in the Pedlar's Pack

The certainty of wings: a child's bold heart,
not, good little *Schul*-boy, Torah or Talmud
gave it to you, a practical vision:
wings were needed, why should people
plod forever on foot, not glide like herons
through the blue and white
promise unfolding
over their heads, over
the river's thawing?
Therefore the pedlar. (But why did they not
avail themselves of his wares?)

Later, *ochetz moy*, when you discovered
wings for your soul, the same bold heart
empowered you. From Prussia east and southward
verst after *verst* you willed the train to go faster,
skimming the rails home to the Dnieper valley.
You bore such news, so longed-for,
fulfilling a hope so ancient

My father, as a
child, sees the
magic pedlar
Marc Chagall
was also to see
a few years
later. The one
intuited that he
carried wings,
the other
painted him,
wingless but
floating high
over Vitepsk.

My father, as a
student, discov-
ers the Messiah,

it had almost become dry parchment, not hope any more.
At the station you hailed a *droshky*,
greeted the driver like a brother. At last
there was the street, there was the house:

and hurries
home with the
good news,

but when you arrived
they would not listen.
They laughed at you. And then they wept.
But would not listen.

but is not believed.

Inheritance

Even in her nineties she recalled
the smooth hands of the village woman
who sometimes came from down the street
and gently, with the softest
of soft old flannel,
soaped and rinsed and dried
her grubby face, while upstairs
the stepmother lay abed bitterly sleeping,
the uncorked opiate bottle
wafting out sticky sweetness
into a noontime dusk.
Those hands, that slow refreshment,
were so kind, I too,
another lifetime beyond them,
shall carry towards my death
their memory,
grateful, and longing
once again to feel them soothe me.

Nativity: An Altarpiece

The wise men are still on the road, searching,
crowns and gifts packed in their saddlebags.

The shepherds are still asleep on the hill, their woolen
caps pulled over their ears, their campfire low.

It's the wondering animals, ox and ass, unused
to human company after dark, who witness,

alone with Mary and Joseph, the birth; who hear
the cry, the first cry

of earthly breath drawn through the newborn lungs
of God.
           And the cord is cut, and the shepherds
that selfsame moment have sprung to their feet

in a golden shower of angels, terrified, then
rejoicing. They lope downhill to the barn

to see their Redeemer. A cloud of
celestial music surrounds them.

                         The wise men
are still far off, alone on the road with a star.

But the ox and the ass
are kneeling already, the Family's oldest friends,

in the glow of light that illumines the byre, the straw,
their eyes and the human eyes—a glow

shed from no source but the living Child Himself.

The Open Sentence

To look out over roofs
of a different city—

steaming tiles, chimney pots, mansards,
the gleam on distant spires
if after a downpour—

To look out
(and the air freshens)
and say to oneself,
Today . . .

The Past

Somewhere, married and in love,
we walked through streets planted with linden trees.
There were ramparts, buttresses, ancient fragments
bonded with newer masonry that was old too.
The warmth of the day just ending
stretched itself on the stones, a golden dog.
People were strolling, there were no cars to speak of,
and we, we were only passing through.
What chance imperative held us on course
toward what train? Nothing I can remember,
no better city.
                  Quiet avenues. Lamps coming on.
The sky still full of light.
I can't remember arriving nor leaving,
and even while we were there it seems
we were somewhere else, inattentive. But the lindens
were blossoming, their perfume, mysterious, pianissimo,
filled the whole town: every few years that remembrance
briefly returns, as if
a fragment of dream; but I know
it was history, a bit of my life,
a bit of the life of Europe. The past.
We failed to linger—as if the lindens
only spoke over this gulf of time.

A Calvary Path

Where the stone steps
falter and come to an end
but the hillside rises
yet more steeply,
obtruded roots of the pines
have braided themselves
across the path to continue
the zigzag staircase.
In times past the non-human—
plants, animals—
often, with such gestures,

intervened in our lives,
or so our forebears
believed when all lives were seen
as travellings-forth of souls.
One can perceive
few come here now—
it's nothing special,
not even very old,
a naive piety,
artless, narrow. And yet
this ladder of roots
draws one onward, coaxing
feet to become
pilgrim feet, that climb
(silenced by layers
of fallen needles,
but step by step
held from sliding)
up to the last
cross of the calvary.

The Past (II)

> 'The witnesses are old things, undimmed, dense
> With the life of human hands'
>
> *Czeslaw Milosz*

My hand on chiseled stone, fitting
into the invisible
                        print of the mason's own
                        where it lay
a moment of that year the nave
was still half-risen, roofless . . .

There's a past that won't suffice:
years in billions,
walls of strata. My need roams
history, centuries not aeons.
And replica is useless.

The new dust
floated past, his mate
from the scaffolding reached down
for the water-jug.

               This stone
or another: no inch of all
untouched. Cold, yes,

but that human trace
will burn my palm.
This is a hunger.

Reflections

The mountain trembles in the dark lake,
its golden cliffs dipping
from almost-sunset light
deep into almost-evening waters.
Round them the forest
floats, brushstrokes
                    blurred just a little.

Death and the past
move closer, move
away again and once more
come closer, swaying, unhurried,
like the sound
of cowbells wandering
down the steep pastures.

Midnight Gladness

> *'Peace be upon each thing my eye takes in,*
> *Upon each thing my mouth takes in.'*
> *Carmina Gadelica*

The pleated lampshade, slightly askew,
dust a silverish muting of the lamp's fake brass.

My sock-monkey on the pillow, tail and limbs asprawl,
weary after a day of watching sunlight
                prowl the house like a wolf.
Gleams of water in my bedside glass.
Miraculous water, so peacefully
waiting to be consumed.

The day's crowding arrived
at this abundant stillness. Each thing
given to the eye before sleep, and water
at my lips before darkness. Gift after gift.

VI

St. Thomas Didymus

In the hot street at noon I saw him
                                a small man
        gray but vivid, standing forth
                                beyond the crowd's buzzing
holding in desperate grip his shaking
                                teethgnashing son,

and thought him my brother.

I heard him cry out, weeping, and speak
                                those words,
Lord, I believe, help thou
                mine unbelief,

and knew him
        my twin:

a man whose entire being
                had knotted itself
into the one tightdrawn question,
                                Why,
why has this child lost his childhood in suffering,
                why is this child who will soon be a man

tormented, torn, twisted?
                              Why is he cruelly punished
who has done nothing except be born?

The twin of my birth
                         was not so close
as that man I heard
                         say what my heart
sighed with each beat, my breath silently
                                          cried in and out,
in and out.

After the healing,
                    he, with his wondering
newly peaceful boy, receded;
                              no one
dwells on the gratitude, the astonished joy,
                                             the swift
acceptance and forgetting.
                           I did not follow
to see their changed lives.
                            What I retained
was the flash of kinship.
                          Despite
all that I witnessed,
                      his question remained
my question, throbbed like a stealthy cancer,
                                             known
only to doctor and patient. To others
                                      I seemed well enough.

So it was
          that after Golgotha
                              my spirit in secret
lurched in the same convulsed writhings
                                        that tore that child
before he was healed.
                      And after the empty tomb
when they told me He lived, had spoken to Magdalen,
                                                   told me
that though He had passed through the door like a ghost

                                    He had breathed on them
the breath of a living man—
                              even then
when hope tried with a flutter of wings
                                  to lift me—
still, alone with myself,
                        my heavy cry was the same: *Lord,*
I believe,
            help thou mine unbelief.

I needed
            blood to tell me the truth,
the touch
            of blood. Even
my sight of the dark crust of it
                              round the nailholes
didn't thrust its meaning all the way through
                                    to that manifold knot in me
that willed to possess all knowledge,
                                  refusing to loosen
unless that insistence won
                          the battle I fought with life.

But when my hand
                    led by His hand's firm clasp
entered the unhealed wound,
                          my fingers encountering
rib-bone and pulsing heat,
                        what I felt was not
scalding pain, shame for my
                          obstinate need,
but light, light streaming
                          into me, over me, filling the room
as if I had lived till then
                          in a cold cave, and now
coming forth for the first time,
                            the knot that bound me unravelling,
I witnessed
            all things quicken to color, to form,
my question

846

not answered but given
                              its part
in a vast unfolding design lit
                        by a risen sun.

Dream 'Cello

When he improvised, from what
unpremeditated congeries of wisdoms
did the sounds appear, woven
like laser tracings on the screen of air?
Music out of 'nowhere,' that granary,
that palace of Arabian serpents,
of sleek rats plush as
young seals. What do words, too,
do there, the real ones,
while we dally with their pale
understudies, or swim
through choppy floods, too busy
with breathing to summon them?
Could we live there? Is it dark?
Could the grain shoals
not light us with their gold sheen?
Invisible hive, has it no small door
we could find if we stood
quite still and listened?

Ikon: The Harrowing of Hell

Down through the tomb's inward arch
He has shouldered out into Limbo
to gather them, dazed, from dreamless slumber:
the merciful dead, the prophets,
the innocents just His own age and those
unnumbered others waiting here
unaware, in an endless void He is ending
now, stooping to tug at their hands,
to pull them from their sarcophagi,

dazzled, almost unwilling. Didmas,
neighbor in death, Golgotha dust
still streaked on the dried sweat of his body
no one had washed and anointed, is here,
for sequence is not known in Limbo;
the promise, given from cross to cross
at noon, arches beyond sunset and dawn.
All these He will swiftly lead
to the Paradise road: they are safe.
That done, there must take place that struggle
no human presumes to picture:
living, dying, descending to rescue the just
from shadow, were lesser travails
than this: to break
through earth and stone of the faithless world
hack to the cold sepulchre, tearstained
stifling shroud; to break from *them*
back into breath and heartbeat, and walk
the world again, closed into days and weeks again,
wounds of His anguish open, and Spirit
streaming through every cell of flesh
so that if mortal sight could bear
to perceive it, it would be seen
His mortal flesh was lit from within, now,
and aching for home. He must return,
first, in Divine patience, and know
hunger again, and give
to humble friends the joy
of giving Him food—fish and a honeycomb.

Lent 1988

Variation on a Theme by Rilke
(*The Book of Hours*, Book I, #15)

With chips and shards, rubble of being,
we construct
            not You but our hope of You.
We say—we dustmotes in the cosmos—
'You dome, arching above us!':

as if You were the sanctuary
by which we seek to define You.

Our cities pulverize, proud technologies
spawn catastrophe. The jaws of our inventions
snap down and lock.
                              Their purpose will be forgotten;
Time is aeons
and we live in minutes,
flies on a windowpane.

Who can conceive the span of You,
great vault, ribbed cauldron slung beneath the abyss,
cage of eternity?

Metaphors shatter, mirrors of poverty.

But something in us, while the millennia
monotonously pass
                              and pass,
hungers to offer up
our specks of life as fragile tesserae
towards the vast mosaic—temple, eidolon;

to be, ourselves, imbedded in its fabric,
as if, once, it was from that we were broken off.

EVENING TRAIN

I   Lake Mountain Moon

Settling

I was welcomed here—clear gold
of late summer, of opening autumn,
the dawn eagle sunning himself on the highest tree,
the mountain revealing herself unclouded, her snow
tinted apricot as she looked west,
tolerant, in her steadfastness, of the restless sun
forever rising and setting.
                      Now I am given
a taste of the grey foretold by all and sundry,
a grey both heavy and chill. I've boasted I would not care,
I'm London-born. And I won't. I'll dig in,
into my days, having come here to live, not to visit.
Grey is the price
of neighboring with eagles, of knowing
a mountain's vast presence, seen or unseen.

Elusive

The mountain comes and goes
on the horizon,

            a rhythm elusive as that of a sea-wave
            higher than all the rest, riding to shore
            flying its silver banners—

you count to seven, but no,
its measure
          slips by you with each recurrence.

Morning Mist

The mountain absent,
a remote folk-memory.

The peninsula
vanished, hill, trees—
gone, shoreline
a rumour.

And we equate
God with these absences—
Deus absconditus.
But God

is imaged
as well or better
in the white stillness

resting everywhere,

giving to all things
an hour of Sabbath,

no leaf stirring,
the hidden places

tranquil in solitude.

Presence

Though the mountain's the same warm-tinted ivory
as the clouds (as if red ground had been laid beneath
not quite translucent white) and though the clouds
disguise its shoulders, and rise tall to left and right,
and soften the pale summit with mist,
                                        yet one perceives
the massive presence, obdurate, unconcerned
among those filmy guardians.

Effacement

Today the mountain
is cloud,
pale cone of shadow
veiled by a paler scrim—

majestic presence become
one cloud among others,
humble vapor,
barely discernible,

like the archangel walking
with Tobias on dusty roads.

Heron I

St. Simon Heron,
standing, standing, standing
upon his offshore pillar,

suddenly, subtly,
dips his head to drink,
three, then a fourth,
and more times, that legato
arabesque of the neck,
the small head almost a serpent's,
smoothly one with its flexible stem.
Body and tall legs
move not an inch.
                        Hunger,
thirst, fulfillment
are ripples that lap his surface;
his patience absorbs them.
Time does not pass, for him;
it is the lake, and full, and still,
and he has all of it, and wades to strike
when he will upon his fish.

Heron II

Elegantly gray, the blue heron
rises from perfect stillness on wide wings,
          flies a few beats
   sideways,
            trails his feet in the lake,
   and rises again to circle
from marker to marker (the posts
that show where the bottom shelves downward)
choosing:
and lands on the floating dock where the gulls cluster—

a tall prince come down from the castle to walk,
proud and awkward, in the market square,
while squat villagers
break off their deals
and look askance.

Taking Charge

Here comes the moon,
bright rim
slicing importantly
through windrows of
grey thistledown cloud just losing
their sundown flush.

Abruptly

The last warm day, I caught,
almost unnoticing,
      that high shrilling like thin
wires of spun silver, glint
of wheeling flight—some small tribe
leaving.
            That night
the moon was full; by morning
autumn had come.

October Moonrise

1

Moon, wisp of opal fire, then slowly
revealed as orb arising,
still half-hidden; the dark
bulk of the wooded ridge defined
by serrations of pine and fir against
this glow
　　　　　that begins to change
from lambent red to a golden
pervasive mist of light as the whole
fullness of moon
floats clear of the hill.

2

Risen, the gold moon
will shrink and blanch
but for now, still
low in the sky,

her pallor is veiled
as if by a net of
gilded gossamer

and the path she has laid down
over the ripples of
dark lake water

is gold unalloyed.

Daily Bread

A gull far-off
rises and falls, arc of a breath,
two sparrows pause on the telephone wire,
chirp a brief interchange, fly back to the ground,
the bus picks up one passenger and zooms on up the hill,

across the water the four poplars
conceal their tremor, feet together, arms pressed to their sides,
behind them the banked conifers dark and steep;
my peartree drops a brown pear from its inaccessible height
into the bramble and ivy tangle, grey sky
whitens a little, now one can see vague forms of cloud
pencilled lightly across it.
This is the day that the Lord hath made,
let us rejoice and be glad in it.

Open Secret

Perhaps one day I shall let myself
approach the mountain—
hear the streams which must flow down it,
lie in a flowering meadow, even
touch my hand to the snow.
Perhaps not. I have no longing to do so.
I have visited other mountain heights.
This one is not, I think, to be known
by close scrutiny, by touch of foot or hand
or entire outstretched body; not by any
familiarity of behavior, any acquaintance
with its geology or the scarring roads
humans have carved in its flanks.
This mountain's power
lies in the open secret of its remote
apparition, silvery low-relief
coming and going moonlike at the horizon,
always loftier, lonelier, than I ever remember.

II   The Two Magnets

The Two Magnets

Where broken gods, faded saints, (powerful in antique presence
as old dancers with straight backs, loftily confident,

or old men in threadbare wellcut coats) preside casually
over the venerable conversations of cypress and olive,
there intrudes, like a child interrupting, tugging at my mind,
incongruous, persistent,
the image of young salmon in round ponds at the hatchery
across an ocean and a continent, circling
with muscular swiftness—tints of green, pink, blue,
glowing mysteriously through slate gray, under trees
unknown here, whose names I forget because
they were unknown to me too when I was young.

And there on the western edge of America—home to me now,
and calling me with this image of something I love,
yet still unknown—I dream of cathedrals,
of the worn stone of human centuries.
Guarded by lions with blunted muzzles
or griffins verdant with moss, gateposts open in me
to effaced avenues.
Part of me lives under nettle-grown foundations.
Part of me wanders west and west, and has reached
the edge of the mist where salmon wait the day
when something shall lift them and give them to deeper waters.

Steadfast

Tattooed in black and gold, lichened nymphs,
sentinels faithful to their garden wall,
face the impertinent back of a new villa,
their view of the lake usurped.

Stele

   (I–II c. B.C.)

They part at the edge of substance.
Henceforth, he will be shadow
in a land of shadow.
And she—she too will be going
slowly down a road of cloud,

weightless, untouched, untouching.
This is the last crossroad.
Her right hand and his left
are clasped, but already,
muffled in his acceptance of fate,
his attention recedes from her.
Her left hand rises, fingertips trace
the curve of his warm face
as it cools and fades.
He has looked down his road,
he is ready to go, not willingly
yet without useless resistance.
She too accepts the truth, there is no way back,
but she has not looked, yet, at the path
accorded to her. She has not given herself,
not yet, to her shadowhood.

The Faithful Lover

Play with a few decades, shift them:
try to imagine Ruskin in the New World,
walking with John Muir in the wilderness.

He, whose enraptured first sight of the Alps
transformed him, that meek Protestant Sunday
when he and Mama and Papa and dull cousin Mary
were patiently waiting the secular week's beginning
before attempting the sights,

                    but all unawares
came face to face
with the sublime—unmistakeably not clouds,
surpassing all that engravings had promised,
floating west of Schaffhausen, sharp, *tinged with rose—
far into blue—suddenly—beyond!*

—changed him from docile prig (poor child: he was 14 and knew
so much and so little) to a man of passion,
whatever his failings.

Imagine him in Yosemite. Would loyalties already divided
—Rock Simple or Rock Wrought,
strata of mountains, strata of human craft,
tools of Geology or tools of Art—have split him?
Would wilderness, legends unknown, or if known offering
no toe-hold for his mind's expectant footing,
have swept him wholly into its torrents of non-human grandeur?

Or wouldn't Art have pulled him back in the end
to layered history felt in the bones,
(even Geology a fraction of that insistence, loved
for its poetry of form, color, textures,
not as a scientist loves it)?
Back to where human hands created

rich tessellations or the *shadowy Rialto*
threw its colossal curve slowly
forth . . . that strange curve, so delicate,
so adamantine, strong as a mountain cavern,
graceful as a bow just bent—?

Back to where Nature—even the Alps, still so remote,
unsung through so many centuries—

lay in the net or nest of perception,
seen then re-seen, recognized, wrought in myth.

A Little Visit to Doves and Chickens
For Page Smith

Demure and peaceful, quiet above
the crooning chickens (who peck and strut,
equally peaceful in winter sun, a level below them,
as if on the ground-floor of a two-storey house),
the doves
are softly pale: gray warmed by brown;
and each one wears a collar, narrow and black
as the velvet ribbon girls and dowagers
used to clasp at the throat with a diamond.
Unlike their cousins the city pigeons,

they don't seem obsessed by sex or food,
don't chase one another in circles,
don't keep talking. They are as calm
in motion as in repose.
                    The chickens meanwhile
remind me of wealthy peasants
in an ancient culture—their rustic finery, gold,
scarlet, opulent umber, brighter and just as beautiful
as the doves' patrician sobriety, and their manners
good but less formal. Their comforts
are earned by their labors. One wonders
if from the doves also their keeper extracts a tithe,
or retains them merely to be
their dreamy selves.

No, there's no moral nor irony
lurking among these words, no message—
unless the sense
                    that it's pleasant to visit a while
                    a modest, indeed a minute, poultry yard
                    where such content may be witnessed
                    and even a pair of guineafowl don't seem nervous
is itself a message simply because
it's wistful, the leisure of mind
to lean on the fence and simply look, and not feel
the need to press for a subtext, being so rare.

The Composition

> (*Woman at the Harpsichord,*
> *Emmanuel de Witte, 1617–1692*
> *Musée des Beaux Arts, Montreal*)

> *For Jean Joubert and for Howard Fussiner*

Two rooms away, seen through the open door,
the servant-maid raises her head to listen,
times the strokes of her broom to the music's crisp
golden wavelets. Autumn sun
and shadows well-defined overlay the floortiles,
antiphonal transverse strips over squares

of white and black. Filtered through little panes
in long and lofty windows, the light
hints at green in its morning pallor. But red,
red is the lord of color here: the draperies,
bedside carpet, ceiling-beams, elaborate
hanging lamp, a chair, all these and more
are a glowing Indian red; and red above all,
with its canopy, valance, ample curtains,
the big four-poster. Up and dressed, the young wife,
(white cap and dimly auburn skirts, red jacket
basqued with ermine-tips) is playing
the harpsichord, beginning the day with delight,
while snug, still, in the bed's half-dark reclines
the young husband, leaning his head on one hand,
intently, blissfully, watching and listening.
A human scene: apex of civilized joy, attained
in Holland, the autumn of 1660, never surpassed, probably
never to be matched.
                    But if
the same scene had been painted differently—
not only with other colors but from another
distance, perspectives differently disposed, more curves,
less play of severe rectangles; if it had been
a composition that lacked this austere
counterpoint of forms which evoke,
in brave resplendent red, the very
twang and trill and wiry
ground bass of the notes ringing forth
under her fingers: if it had been
reduced to anecdote—we'd never have known
that once, in eternity,
this peaceful joy had blessed an autumnal morning.

III   Ancient Airs

Broken Pact

A face ages quicker than a mind.

And thighs, arms, breasts,
take on an air of indifference.
Heart's desire has wearied them, they chose to forget
whatever they once promised.

But mind and heart continue
their eager conversation,
they argue, they share epiphanies,
sometimes all night they raise
antiphonal laments.

Face and body have betrayed them,

they are alone together,
unsure how to proceed.

Diptych

1 Mysterious Movement

Though no wind is blowing, the lake,
        as if to reënact the remote day
        when, as a journeying river, it first flowed
        into the long hollow of its bed
        and met the embracing shores
        and could go no further,
is pressing strongly, darkly,
southward in fading light, this waning hour
near the close of the year—

although it can go no further.

2 Midwinter

A sky stained
even at midmorning
with the water and blood of daybreak . . .

And the mountain,
strangely approachable
this winter day,
has moved forward into the middle distance,
humbly letting valleys and dark
seams of rock be perceived,
like a woman not trying to hide
her loss of youth from the light.
Her snows are gray.

Ancient Airs and Dances

I

I knew too well
what had befallen me
when, one night, I put my lips to his wineglass
after he left—an impulse I thought was locked away with a smile
into memory's museum.

When he took me to visit friends and the sea, he lay
asleep in the next room's dark where the fire
rustled all night; and I, from a warm bed, sleepless,
watched through the open door
that glowing hearth, and heard,
humming the roof, the rain's
insistent heartbeat.

Greyhaired, I have not grown wiser,
unless to perceive absurdity
is wisdom. A powerless wisdom.

II

Shameless heart! Did you not vow to learn
        stillness from the heron,
        quiet from the mists of fall,
        and from the mountain—what was it?
        Pride? Remoteness?
You have forgotten already!
And now you clamor again
like an obstinate child demanding attention,
interrupting study and contemplation.
You try my patience. Bound as we are
together for life, must you now,
so late in the day, go hounding sideways,
trying to drag me with you?

Time for Rivets

Reinforced though it was
with stoic strapping,
my heart was breaking again. Damn!
Just when I had so much to do,
a list as long as your arm.
The world news slithered
toward the probable worst
of a lifetime's bad news,
and as for me (as if in that shadow it mattered—
but it did) in two days' time
I'd be saying goodbye to someone I thought of
'day and night,' as I'd not been planning to think
of anyone ever again.

I'd believed it would hold, yes,
I'd considered my serviceable heart
long-since well-mended,
and equal to what demands
might still confront it.
And hadn't I written, still longer ago,
that these metaphorical hearts, although
they 'break for nothing,' do so

in surface fissures only, a web
of hairline fractures, the way
old pieplates do, rimmed with a blue design
as if someone had pressed them all round
with tines of a fork well-dipped in indigo?
All true enough, but surely by now
mine, though made like such plates
for use, not show, must need
those clamps of metal with which
cracked vessels of finer porcelain are held.
For the moment I'd have to do
with tape and crossed fingers.

Arrived

Away from home,
the reality of home
evades me. Chairs,
sofa, table, a cup—
I can enumerate objects
one by one, but they're inventory,
not Gestalt. This house
I've stayed in often before,
the open suitcase,
my friends who live here,
that's what's real.
And that face
so vivid to me these past three months
evades me too: the shape
of his head, or
color of his eyes appear
at moments, but I can't
assemble feature with feature.
I seem to have landed
upon this *now*
as if on a mid-ocean island,
past and future two continents, both
lost in immense distance,
the mist and seasons
of months at sea—the voyage
from yesterday to today.

IV   Flowers of Sophia

Range

Peak upon peak, brown, dustily gold, crowded,
sharp juttings, razorbacks, angular undulations,
so many we seem not to move above them, confusion
of multitudinous upthrust forms, pushing
against one another, surging.
                                        Valley forests
look from the air like dark green water,
but if there are lakes
they are hidden. A dry country
unless when the snows melt.

But at last
when a true lake shows itself
it is blue, blue, blue,
a cupful of sky.

The Plains

Tiepolo clouds—
tinge of beige in diaphanous shadow
over cornfields and western bluffs
where no one has seen
how they hang also above
ascensions, veils,
ecstatic saints and the heads
of cherubim . . .

Down Under

Bloodred, viridian, poison aqua:
round mineral pools or pits in the Nullarbor.
My photo, taken through scratched glass from the air,
was to have been a gift for an artist son,

but came out blurred and pale
and was never given.
                    Years later,
flying above a different desert,
I see with mind's eye the painting I imagined
he might have made from the pattern's
aboriginal mystery.

Milky Way

Sky-wave breaks
in surf, and leaves
the lace of it to border
an obscure, etherial,
sinuous coastline—

phosphorescent for that lingering
instant which is to us
time immemorial.

Eye Mask

In this dark I rest,
unready for the light which dawns
day after day,
eager to be shared.
Black silk, shelter me.
I need
more of the night before I open
eyes and heart
to illumination. I must still
grow in the dark like a root
not ready, not ready at all.

Entre Loup et Chien

Night's broken wing
and its wide untorn one
hobble across the paling sky
dropping black feathers down on black trees.
Day is still forming itself.
This is the gap,
the time between the sagacious, taciturn wolf
and the plain dog who will yap into place
when dawn has flared and faded.

On the Eve
For Melanie

The moon was white
in the stillness. Daylight
changed without moving,
a hint of sundown
stained the sky. We walked
the short grass,
the dry ground of the hill,
beholding
the tinted west. We talked
of change in our lives. The moon
tuned its whiteness a tone higher.

River

Dreaming the sea that
                    lies beyond me
I have enough depth
                    to know I am shallow.

I have my pools, my bowls
                    of rock I flow
into and fill, but I must
                    brim my own banks, persist,

vanish at last in greater flood

yet still within it

follow my task,

dreaming towards

the calling sea.

Brother Ivy

Between road and sidewalk, the broadleafed ivy,
unloved, dusty, littered, sanctuary of rats,
gets on with its life. New leaves shine gaily
among dogged older ones
that have lost their polish.
It does not require appreciation. The foliage
conceals a brown tangle of stems
thick as a mangrove swamp; the roots
are spread tenaciously. Unwatered
throughout the long droughts, it simply
grips the dry ground by the scruff of the neck.

I am not its steward.
If we are siblings, and I
my brother's keeper therefore,
the relation is reciprocal. The ivy
meets its obligation by pure
undoubtable being.

Idyll

The neighbor's Black Labrador, his owners
out at work, unconscious anyone
is watching him, rises again and again
on hind legs to bend with his paws
the figtree's curving branches
and reach the sweet figs with his black lips.

Arctic Spring

The polar she-bear, dirty ivory
against the blue-white steep
slope of ice
rolls and slides like a cub,
happy to stretch cramped limbs after four
months in the stuffy den;
but quickly lopes
upward with toed-in undulant grace
back to the bleating summons
of three new bears, their first time out,
hind feet still in the tunnel,
black astonished eyes regarding
their mother at play, black noses
twitching, smelling
strange wonders of air and light.

Flowers of Sophia

Flax, chicory, scabious—
flowers with ugly names,
they grow in waste ground, sidewalk edges,
fumes, grime, trash.
Each kind has a delicate form, distinctive;
it would be pleasant to draw them.
All are a dreamy blue,
a gentle mysterious blue,
wise beyond comprehension.

V   Evening Train

In Love

Over gin and tonic (an unusual treat) the ancient poet
haltingly—not because mind and memory
                falter, but because language, now,

weary from so many years
of intense partnership,
comes stiffly to her summons,
with unsure footing—
recounts, for the first time in my hearing, each step
of that graceful sarabande, her husband's
last days, last minutes, fifteen years ago.

She files her belongings freestyle, jumbled
in plastic bags—poems, old letters, ribbons,
old socks, an empty pictureframe;
but keeps her fifty years of marriage wrapped, flawless,
in something we sense and almost see—
diaphanous as those saris one can pass through a wedding ring.

Venerable Optimist

He saw the dark as a ragged garment
spread out to air.
Through its rents and moth-holes
the silver light came pouring.

Letter to a Friend

As if we were sitting as we have done so often,
over a cup of tea, and I knew how
to read the leaves, let me look closely into
this card you have sent, this image you say
holds for you something you feel is yourself.
A woman sits outdoors by a white-cloth'd table
(blue in shadow); but it's not a café;
there are columns, masonry, perhaps a ruin behind her,
and also a stretch of open lawn or pasture,
and trees beyond. She has opened—a parasol?
or an umbrella? There's enough light to suggest
a parasol, but the coat she wears
is not for summer: passionate red is muted
almost to russet, and high collar, sleeves

that narrow from elbow to wrist, imply weight,
warm cloth. Yet the silken shelter's pale cerulean,
shot with gold, seems too light for rain.
Perhaps it is rainbow weather, flying showers
on a gleaming day in spring.
Not a young girl any more, this woman's
fresh color and shining hair are not yet
beginning to fade; but in her eyes one sees
knowledge, though in their clear, steady,
almost challenging gaze there's a certain innocence;
and her lips are firmly closed. Bareheaded,
(despite her coat) she is quietly seated,
not poised to leave; one arm rests on the chair's
green embracing arm.
                    Most notable in this portrait:
her solitude. She may or may not be waiting for someone;
whether or not, she looks out from the picture-plane
not at the painter but straight through time
at me looking back at her. She's not sad,
not angry, not joyful: but open, open
to what shall befall.
                  The image is only
a detail, fragment of a larger whole.
The context might change my reading. Companions
perhaps are nearby, unseen by us; perhaps she too
doesn't see them. The place she is in
might be defined if one saw the rest of the painting.
One might deduce from it why she is there,
where she will go. But the more I look, the more
I perceive what her eyes express: it's courage.
That's what told me this woman is innocent but not ignorant.
Courage knows the price of living. Courage itself
is a form of innocence, of trust or faith.
Your sense of being portrayed no doubt refers
to less than this; to her solitude, it may be.
It's against the rules to tell your own fortune,
and I, after all, am able only to descry
the images in the leaves, not to construe their meaning.
Some day one of us may discover the painting's whereabouts,
see the whole of it. Then we'll divine
what fortune her gaze betokens.

Becca

Becca. Each washday,
steamy scullery, yellow soap-smell, whites
boiled in the copper. Becca brandishing
a stick, huge spoon to stir the bubbling
soup of linens.
A child had best keep out of the way.
And skreak of the mangle turning
hurt to hear.
Outdoors, though,
clotheslines made streets across the lawn,
walled with sheets, a billowing village.
Becca, bandy-legged, sturdy
under the weight, brought forth
the round wicker basket,
stretched wet
huge arms to the line to peg,
with gypsy pegs that stuffed
her apron pockets, more and more
clean clothes, mangle-wrung,
and the washday wind
slapped them, slapped
me as I dodged from door to invisible door, Becca
shouting, but not at me,
she was deaf I think, I think we never
exchanged a word, she just
appeared and then it was washday, but not
after I was six, perhaps five, perhaps four, yes,
early—for me she existed
at our washtub only, and in our garden,
with no in-between, no home, no story,
toothlessly smiling (not at me).
Lodged in my head
forever, primordial. Becca.
Known. Unknown.

For Bet

You danced ahead of me, I took
none of those last steps with you
when your *enchainement* led you
uphill to the hospital and a death sentence
or before that when language
twirled round and tripped your voice.
Dancers must learn to walk
slowly across a stage, unfaltering;
we practiced that, long ago.
You faltered, but only in the wings,
that week when *timor mortis*
lunged at you. And you shook off
that devouring terror, held up
your head, straightened
your back, and moved in grace
(they tell me—I was not at your side
but far away,
intent on a different music)
into the light of that last stage,
a hospice garden, where you could say,
breathing the ripened fragrance of August mornings,
'yes, and evenings too are beautiful.'

Link

Half memory of what my mother
at over ninety could still see
clear in mind's eye, transferring,
like earrings or brooches,
her lapidary trove
into my vision; half imprint
of that charcoal-burner with his boy,
gazing at thickets towering up
around the sleeping palace
in my childhood treasure of treasures,
Dulac's Perrault,
                    I carry
into this alien epoch, year by year,

the presence of that venerable great-
or great-great uncle to whom,
precociously observant five-year-old,
she was taken one summer day
and told to remember always
that *he* could remember Waterloo,
when he was a drummer-boy, a lad
of twelve perhaps, and how Napoleon—
Boney, the bogeyman disobedient children
were threatened with—rode off on his mountainous
black horse.

The ancient's dark nets were spread
before his cottage; drowsing waves
lapped the Welsh strand and his beached coracle,
reflections wavering on the brilliant whitewash.
White hair grew to his shoulders, kneebritches left
his brown legs bare, his feet were bare.
Indoors, the earth floor, hard as flagstones,
had for ornament patterns he drew
with the staining juice of a certain plant.
                    I perceive, seeing him there,
his life, glimpsed that day and held
in the amber pendant I inherit, belongs
to any of several centuries, though now
it has no place except in me, as if memory travelled
fingertip to outstretched fingertip
across the longest lives, an electric gesture
learned of Adam, dwindling
to meanings we no longer know,
but only know our sense of history
has only such barely-touchings, uninterpreted
not-forgettings, to suffice
for its continuance.

The Opportunity

My father once, after his death,
appeared to me as a rose,
passed beyond intellect.

This time, he resumes
human form to become
a boy of six.
I kneel to hug him,
kiss the child's bare shoulder;
near us the ocean
sighs and murmurs,
firm sand reflects
the turn of the wave.

This is my chance to tell him,
'Much has happened, over the years,
many travels.
In the world,
in myself.
Along the way,
I have come to believe
the truth of what you believe.'

The child, with good grace,
permits
my brief embrace; he smiles:
the words
are lazy waves above and around him,
he absorbs their tone,
knows he is loved.
Knows only that.

This was my chance
to speak. I've taken it,
we are both content.

Dream Instruction

In the language-root place (a wooden
hall, homestead; warm, Homeric, Beowulfian shelter)
candles are glowing, shadows in rhythm
rise and fall. Into this haven have swept,
blown by gusting winds, figures whose drama
makes a stage, for a while, of place and time,

enthralling attention, prompting action,
so that my mind meshes itself in their story
until with promises, tears, laughter, they sweep
out once more into night. Ruefully,
'Life!' I stammer, as the wake of their passage
ebbs and vanishes, 'It rushes and rushes toward me
like Niagara—I don't have time
to write it, to write it down, to hold it, it never
pauses!'   And she whom I address,
the old mother sitting in bed, cheerful, spritely,
cushions behind her, saucer in one hand,
porcelain cup in the other, sipping her fragrant tea,
smiles in wisdom and tells me
that need will pass; she herself
has come to live in what happens, not in the telling.
She quotes to me what a woman
born in slavery said, when she was free and ancient:
I sits here, in my rocker, evenin's,
and just

       purely
          be's.

The vision
of mighty falls bearing down on me still
thundering in my mind, I see
a crimson candle guttering, flaring, and another, too,
whose wax is an amber yellow almost
the gold of its flame. Colors
of passionate life. I recall
Out, out, brief candle. 'Shall I snuff them?' 'Leave them—
they'll still themselves
as the air hushes.'
               I think of the travellers
gone into dark, 'They were only
passing through,' I say, surprised,
to her, to myself,
relieved and in awe, learning to know
those oncoming waters rushed through the aeons
before me, and rush on beyond me,
and I have now, as the task before me, to *be*,
to arrive at being,
as she the Old Mother has done
in the root place, the hewn

wooden cave, home
of shadow and flame, of
language, gradual stillness,
blessing.

Evening Train

An old man sleeping in the evening train,
face upturned, mouth discreetly closed,
hands clasped, with fingers interlaced.
Those large hands
lie on the fur lining of his wife's coat
he's holding for her, and the fur
looks like a limp dog, docile and affectionate.
The man himself is a peasant
in city clothes, moderately prosperous—
rich by the standards of his youth;
one can read that in his hands,
his sleeping features.
How tired he is, how tired.
I called him old, but then I remember
my own age, and acknowledge he's likely
no older than I. But in the dimension
that moves with us but itself keeps still
like the bubble in a carpenter's level,
I'm fourteen, watching the faces I saw each day
on the train going in to London,
and never spoke to; or guessing
from a row of shoes what sort of faces
I'd see if I raised my eyes.
Everyone has an unchanging age (or sometimes two)
carried within them, beyond expression.
This man perhaps
is ten, putting in a few hours most days
in a crowded schoolroom, and a lot more
at work in the fields; a boy who's always
making plans to go fishing his first free day.
The train moves through the dark quite swiftly
(the Italian dark, as it happens)
with its load of people, each

with a conscious destination, each
with a known age and that other,
the hidden one—except for those
still young, or not young but slower to focus,
who haven't reached yet that state of being
which will become
not a point of arrest but a core
around which the mind develops, reflections circle,
events accrue—a center.
                              A girl with braids
sits in this corner seat, invisible,
pleased with her solitude. And across from her
an invisible boy, dreaming. She knows
she cannot imagine his dreams. Quite swiftly
we move through our lives; swiftly, steadily the train
rocks and bounces onward through sleeping fields,
our unknown stillness
holding level as water sealed in glass.

VI   Witnessing from Afar

The Reminder

Composed by nature, time, human art,
an earthy paradise. A haze that is not smog
gentles the light. Mountains delicately frosted,
timbered autumnal hillsides copper and bronze.
Black-green of pine, gray-green of olive.
Nothing is missing. Ferries' long wakes pattern the water,
send to still shores a minor music of waves.
Dark perpendiculars
of cypress, grouped or single, cross immemorial
horizontals of terraced slopes, the outstretched wings,
creamy yellow, of villas more elegant
in slight disrepair than anything spick and span
ever could be. And all perceived
not through our own crude gaze alone but by the accretion
of others' vision—language, paint, memory transmitted.
Here, just now, the malady
we know the earth endures seems in remission—

or *we* are, from that knowledge that gnaws at us.
But only seems. Down by the lake the sign:
"Swim at your own risk. The lake is polluted."
Not badly, someone says, blithely irrelevant.
We can avoid looking that way,
if we choose. That's at our own risk.
Deep underneath remission's fragile peace,
the misshaped cells remain.

Lago di Como, 1989

Mysterious Disappearance of May's Past Perfect

Even as the beaches blacken again with oil,
reporters tell us, 'If the ship had had
a double hull, the spill
may not have occurred.' And now a poet
writing of one who died some years ago
too young, recounts that had she been and done
otherwise than she was and did, it's thought she
'*may* have survived.' The poet does not agree—
but this impoverished grammar, nonetheless,
places in doubt an undeniable death.

      Is it collective fear suppresses
might have, fear that causes do
produce effects? Does *may* still trail with it,
misused, a comforting openness, illusion
that what has already happened, after all
can be revoked, reversed?

                  Or, in these years
when from our mother-tongue some words
were carelessly tossed away, while others hastily
were being invented—chief among them, *overkill*—
has the other meaning, swollen as never before,
of *might* thrust out of memory its minor
homonym, so apt for the precise
nuance of elegy, for the hint of judgement,
reproachful clarities of tense and sense?

Tragic Error

The earth is the Lord's, we gabbled,
and the fullness thereof—
while we looted and pillaged, claiming indemnity:
the fullness thereof
given over to us, to our use—
while we preened ourselves, sure of our power,
wilful or ignorant, through the centuries.

Miswritten, misread, that charge:
subdue was the false, the misplaced word in the story.
Surely we were to have been
earth's mind, mirror, reflective source.
Surely our task
was to have been
to love the earth,
to *dress and keep it* like Eden's garden.

That would have been our *dominion*:
to be those cells of earth's body that could
perceive and imagine, could bring the planet
into the haven it is to be known
(as the eye blesses the hand, perceiving
its form and the work it can do).

Mid-American Tragedy

They want to be their own old vision
of Mom and Dad. They want their dying son
to be eight years old again, not a gay man,
not ill, not dying. They have accepted him,
they would say if asked, unlike some who shut
errant sons out of house and heart,
and this makes them preen a little, secretly;
but enough of that, some voice within them
whispers, even more secretly, *he's our kid*,
Mom and Dad are going to give him
what all kids long for, a trip to Disney World,
what fun, the best Xmas ever.

And he, his wheelchair strung with bottles and tubes,
glass and metal glittering in winter sun,
shivers and sweats and tries to breathe as *Jingle Bells*
pervades the air and his mother, his father,
chatter and still won't talk, won't listen,
will never listen, never give him
the healing silence
in which they could have heard
his questions, his answers,
his life at last.

The Batterers

A man sits by the bed
of a woman he has beaten,
dresses her wounds,
gingerly dabs at bruises.
Her blood pools about her,
darkens.

Astonished, he finds he's begun
to cherish her. He is terrified.
Why had he never
seen, before, what she was?
What if she stops breathing?

Earth, can we not love you
unless we believe the end is near?
Believe in your life
unless we think you are dying?

Airshow Practice

Sinister wreathing mist in midsummer sky
slowly disperses
as it descends
over the wooded hill, the lake, the bathing children:

streaks of exhaust left by Blue Angels as they
scream back and forth, virtuosos of costly power,
swifter than hurricane—

to whom a multitude
gazes upward, craving
a violent awe, numb to all else.

Watching TV

So many men—and not the worst of them,
the brutally corrupt, no, others,

liberal, intelligent if not
notably imaginative,

men with likeable eyes—

have mouths that are weak, cruel, twisted,
alien to desire:

mouths that don't match their eyes.

And our wretched history
utters through those mouths

the perfidies their hurt eyes evade.

Protesters

Living on the rim
of the raging cauldron, disasters

witnessed but
not suffered in the flesh.

The choice: to speak
or not to speak.
We spoke.

Those of whom we spoke
had not that choice.

At every epicenter, beneath
roar and tumult,

enforced:
their silence.

Hoping

All my life hoping the nightmare
I dreamed as a child (and could make recur
if perverse fascination willed it)
was not prophetic:
                    all the animals
seated in peaceful council by candleglow
in a shadowy, fragrant barn,
timeless, unmenaced—then without warning,
without any flash or noise,
the crumbling to black ash, ash
corrugated, writhing, as filmy shreds
of paper used to when sheets of it,
placed round the firescreen to coax the draft
upward and liven the coals, would themselves
catch fire and float, newsprint curdling,
dreadfully out from the hearth towards me.
All my life hoping; having to hope
because decades brought no reassurance.

The Certainty

They have refined the means of destruction,
abstract science almost visibly shining,
it is so highly polished. Immaterial weapons
no one could ever hold in their hands
streak across darkness, across great distances,
threading through mazes to arrive
at targets that are concepts—

But one ancient certainty
remains: war
means blood spilling from living bodies,
means severed limbs, blindness, terror,
means grief, agony, orphans, starvation,
prolonged misery, prolonged resentment and hatred and guilt,
means all of these multiplied, multiplied,
means death, death, death and death.

The Youth Program

The children have been practicing,
    diligent before their screens, playing
        a million missions a week.
A few teddybears, cuddly tigers, unicorns,
    still lie prone
        on youthbed pillows.
In antique-shops
    you may find sometimes
        a few small bows and arrows,
    Arthurian picturebooks,
        even cardboard theaters with cut-out
fairytale characters—
    Aladdin, Rose Red, Rose White—
        saved by chance from the garbage;
but the children
    don't even know such things
        gave pleasure once, and are gone.
They're busy with the new
    play-learning: they may not know
        the words *millennium*, *apocalypse*,
but the expensive games are already
    putting them ahead:
        pilots today, a spokesman says,
have attained
    new speeds of reflex,
        though trained on earlier models.
These children
    are preparing,
        being prepared.

But before their war
     begins,
          others, in which
their brothers, their young fathers
     will be deployed,
may have *taken out*
     the world.
          Perhaps someone
should tell the children, interrupt
     their wasted time?
          Persuade them to run
outdoors for a while, and take
     a look at the unfamiliar
          while it is there—
sky, tree, bird? Or even
     risk their annoyance and
          turn off the power?

Misnomer

They speak of the art of war,
but the arts
draw their light from the soul's well,
and warfare
dries up the soul and draws its power
from a dark and burning wasteland.
When Leonardo
set his genius to devising
machines of destruction he was not
acting in the service of art,
he was suspending
the life of art
over an abyss,
as if one were to hold
a living child out of an airplane window
at thirty thousand feet.

Witnessing from Afar the New Escalation of Savage Power

She was getting old, had seen a lot,
knew a lot.
But something innocent
enlivened her,
upheld her spirits.
She tended a small altar,
kept a candle shielded there,
or tried to. There was a crash and throb
of harsh sound audible
always, but distant.
She believed
she had it in her
to fend for herself and hold
despair at bay.
Now when she came to the ridge and saw
the world's raw gash
reopened, the whole world
a valley of steaming blood,
her small wisdom
guttered in the uprush;
rubbledust, meatpulse—
darkness and the blast
levelled her. (Not her own death,
that was not yet.) The deafening
downrush. Shock, shame
no memory, no knowledge
nor dark imagination
had prepared her for.

January–March 1991

News Report, September 1991
U.S. BURIED IRAQI SOLDIERS ALIVE IN GULF WAR

> *"What you saw was a
> bunch of trenches with
> arms sticking out."*
> "Plows mounted on

tanks. Combat
earthmovers."
"Defiant."
"Buried."
"Carefully planned and
rehearsed."
*"When we
went through there wasn't
anybody left."*
"Awarded
Silver Star."
"Reporters
banned."
"Not a single
American killed."
"Bodycount
impossible."
*"For all I know,
thousands,* said
Colonel Moreno."
*"What you
saw was a bunch of
buried trenches
with people's
arms and things
sticking out."*
"Secretary Cheney
made no mention."
"Every single American
was inside
the juggernaut
impervious
to small-arms
fire." *"I know
burying people
like that sounds
pretty nasty,* said
Colonel Maggart,
But . . . ."
"His force buried
about six hundred
and fifty

in a thinner line
of trenches."
*"People's arms
sticking out."*
"Every American
inside."
"The juggernaut."
*"I'm not
going to sacrifice
the lives
of my soldiers,*
Moreno said, *it's not
cost-effective."*
*"The tactic was designed
to terrorize,*
Lieutenant Colonel Hawkins
said, who helped
devise it."
"Schwartzkopf's staff
privately
estimated fifty to seventy
thousand killed
in the trenches."
"Private Joe Queen was
awarded
a Bronze Star for burying
trenches with his
earthmover."
"Inside
the juggernaut."
"Impervious."
*"A lot of the guys
were scared,* he said,
*but I
enjoyed it."*
*"A bunch of
trenches. People's
arms and things
sticking out."*
"Cost-effective."

In California During the Gulf War

Among the blight-killed eucalyptus, among
trees and bushes rusted by Christmas frosts,
the yards and hillsides exhausted by five years of drought,

certain airy white blossoms punctually
reappeared, and dense clusters of pale pink, dark pink—
a delicate abundance. They seemed

like guests arriving joyfully on the accustomed
festival day, unaware of the year's events, not perceiving
the sackcloth others were wearing.

To some of us, the dejected landscape consorted well
with our shame and bitterness. Skies ever-blue,
daily sunshine, disgusted us like smile-buttons.

Yet the blossoms, clinging to thin branches
more lightly than birds alert for flight,
lifted the sunken heart

even against its will.
                              But not
as symbols of hope: they were flimsy
as our resistance to the crimes committed

—again, again—in our name; and yes, they return,
year after year, and yes, they briefly shone with serene joy
over against the dark glare

of evil days. They *are*, and their presence
is quietness ineffable—and the bombings *are*, were,
no doubt will be; that quiet, that huge cacophony

simultaneous. No promise was being accorded, the blossoms
were not doves, there was no rainbow. And when it was claimed
the war had ended, it had not ended.

In the Land of Shinar

Each day the shadow swings
round from west to east till night overtakes it, hiding
half the slow circle. Each year
the tower grows taller, spiralling
out of its monstrous root-circumference, ramps and colonnades
mounting tier by lessening tier the way a searching
bird of prey wheels and mounts the sky, driven
by hungers unsated by blood and bones.
And the shadow lengthens, our homes nearby are dark
half the day, and the bricklayers, stonecutters, carpenters bivouac
high in the scaffolded arcades, further and further above the ground,
weary from longer and longer comings and goings. At times
a worksong twirls down the autumn leaf of a phrase, but mostly
                                  we catch
only the harsher sounds of their labor itself, and that seems only
an echo now of the bustle and clamor there was long ago
when the fields were cleared, the hole was dug, the foundations laid
with boasting and fanfares, the work begun.
The tower, great circular honeycomb, rises and rises and still
                                the heavens
arch above and evade it, while the great shadow engulfs
more and more of the land, our lives
dark with the fear a day will blaze, or a full-moon night defining
with icy brilliance the dense shade, when all the immense
weight of this wood and brick and stone and metal and massive
weight of dream and weight of will
will collapse, crumble, thunder and fall,
fall upon us, the dwellers in shadow.

VII   The Almost-Island

One December Night . . .

This I had not expected:
the moon coming right into my kitchen,
the full moon, gently bumping
angles of furniture,

seeming to like the round table
but not resenting corners.

Somehow the moon
filled all the space and yet
left room for whatever
was there already, including me,
and for movement. Like a balloon,
the moon stirred at a breath
and unlike a balloon did not
rise to the ceiling, but wandered
as if sleep-walking,
no more than a foot from the floor.

Music accompanied this lunar visitation—
you would imagine harp or lute, but no,
I'd say it was steel drums,
played with an airy whispering touch.
(Those scooped concavities
might serve as moon-mirrors.)
The greenish tint of white spider-chrysanthemums
resembled the moon's color,
but that was lighter, lighter.

I have been given much, but why this also?
I was abashed. What grand gesture of welcome
was I to make? I bowed, curtsied, but the modest moon
appeared unaware of homage.
I breathed, I gazed; and slowly, mildly,
the moon hovered, touring stove and cupboards,
bookshelves and sink, glimmering
over a bowl of tangerines. And gently
withdrew, just as I thought to summon courage
to offer honey-mead or slivovitz.

Myopic Birdwatcher

One day the solitary heron,
so tall, so immobile on his usual post,
seemed to have shrunk and grown darker.

Had I imagined
his distinction? Now,
when I wanted my friend to see
what I had seen, it was gone.
And the changed heron had two companions,
somber and hunkered down on neighboring posts.

On succeeding days I saw him again
with and without his doubles,
but even alone he looked shabby, fidgetty,
almost sinister, diminished.
I thought it perhaps a matter
of winter plumage,
seasonal behavior.
Till another friend
came with me to the shore.
'Cormorants,' he said.

It lightened my spirits. My heron's place was usurped,
he disdains to return till they leave—
and they may not leave;
but at least I know
it's not he who,
shrugging his wings to dry them
(a vulgar gesture,
though required, it seems,
by cormorant feathers) displays
the high-shouldered baleful silhouette
of Teutonic eagles on old postage-stamps,
black on a sallow ground
of winter lake-light.
At least I know
I didn't deceive myself:
my absent heron's air of austere dignity
was real, whatever hunger
sustains his watchfulness.

Mirage

Ethereal mountain,
snowwhite foam hovering
far above blue, cloudy ridges—
can one believe you are not a mirage?

Against Intrusion

When my friend drove up the mountain
it changed itself into a big
lump of land with lots of snow on it
and slopes of arid scree.
Another friend climbed it the hard way:
exciting to stay the course, get to the top—
but no sense of height there, nothing to see but
generic mist and snow.
As for me,
when my photos come back developed,
there's just the lake, the south shore of the lake,
the middle distance. No mountain.
                How clearly it speaks! *Respect, perspective,*
privacy, it teaches. *Indulgence*
of curiosity increases
ignorance of the essential.
What does it serve to insist
on knowing more than that a mountain,
forbearing—so far—from volcanic rage,
blesses the city it is poised above, angelic guardian
at rest on sustaining air; and that its vanishings
are needful, as silence is to music?

Looking Through

White as cloud above
a less-white band of cloud
the mountain
stands clear on a sky of

palest blue,
no other clouds in all
the sunny arch
of summer's last holiday.
And the mountain's
deep clefts and hollows,
the shadowy crevasses,
are that same
palest blue, as if
snow and rock,
the whole great mass of mountain,
were transparent
and one could look
through at more sky
southward.
Luminous mountain,
real, unreal sky.

Whisper

Today the white mist that is weather
is mixed with the sallow tint
of the mist that is smog.
And from it, through it, breathes
a vast whisper:
the mountain.

Witness

Sometimes the mountain
is hidden from me in veils
of cloud, sometimes
I am hidden from the mountain
in veils of inattention, apathy, fatigue,
when I forget or refuse to go
down to the shore or a few yards
up the road, on a clear day,
to reconfirm
that witnessing presence.

A Reward

Tired and hungry, late in the day, impelled
to leave the house and search for what
might lift me back to what I had fallen away from,
I stood by the shore waiting.
I had walked in the silent woods:
the trees withdrew into their secrets.
Dusk was smoothing breadths of silk
over the lake, watery amethyst fading to gray.
Ducks were clustered in sleeping companies
afloat on their element as I was not
on mine. I turned homeward, unsatisfied.
But after a few steps, I paused, impelled again
to linger, to look North before nightfall—the expanse
of calm, of calming water, last wafts
of rose in the few high clouds.
And was rewarded:
the heron, unseen for weeks, came flying
widewinged toward me, settled
just offshore on his post,
took up his vigil.
                    If you ask
why this cleared a fog from my spirit,
I have no answer.

Indian Summer

Zones of flickering
                    water-diamonds
converse with almost-still
        glint of leaves along the poplar-row.

A dispersed array of water-birds relaxes
        afloat in autumn light,
one or another sometimes
                    diving casually.

                    And far across
        near the other shore,

      the lake is wearing a narrow, trembling
    band of silver,
a silver barely tinged with gold,
delicate tarnish.

      Someone's tapedeck booms and yells
      crescendo . . .
      pulses by and zooms
      out of the park.

      And quiet resumes,
      holding off as best it can
      peripheral sounds of human action—
      planes, subliminal traffic,
      (only one motorboat yet,
      it's a workday morning)—

      but admits
    the long and distant old-time wail of a train:
this quiet, this autumn sun,
      cool air and pale
      diaphanous light,
are generous.

Contrasting Gestures

Coots, heads bobbing, forever urging themselves
fussily onward . . . How strong their neck-muscles
must be! One is put in mind of human philistines
toiling and spinning through their lives
anxiously complacent in pursuit of trivia.
But coots without warning effortlessly
dive, leaving barely a crease on the black polished-satin
surface—vanishing
into the primal element—!
                   That gesture
of absolute abandon, absolute
release into clear or cloudy
inner flow of the lake: it's what
artists and mystics want to attain, abjuring

acquisition, drunk on occasional
intuitions, on the sense that
depth, height, breadth don't express the dimension
which invites them, which evades them . . .
(Though mystics desire submersion
to transform them, as it does not transform
the coots, who resume
their pushing and nodding forward
after each plunge. And artists
want not themselves transformed
but their work. The plunge itself
their desire, a way to be
subsumed, consumed utterly
into their work.)

The Almost-Island

The woods which give me their silence,
their ancient Douglas firs and red cedars, their ferns,
are not the wilderness. They're contained
in the two-mile circumference of an almost-island,
a park in city limits. Pleasure-boats crowd at weekends
into the small bay. The veils hiding the mountain
are not always natural cloud. Eagle and heron
speak of solitude, but when you emerge from forest shade
the downtown skyline rears up, phantasmagoric but near,
across the water. Yet the woods, the lake,
the great-winged birds, the vast mountain at the horizon,
are Nature: metonymy of the spirit's understanding
knows them to be a concentrate
of all Thoreau or Wordsworth knew by that word,
Nature: 'a never-failing principle
of joy and purest passion.' Thoreau's own pond
was bounded by the railroad, punctuated
by the 'telegraph trees' and their Aeolian wires.
All of my dread and all of my longing hope that Earth
may outwit the huge stupidity of its humans,
can find their signs and portents here, their recapitulations
of joy and awe. This fine, incised two inches
of goldsmith-work just drifted down, can speak

as well for *tree* as a thousand forest acres,
and tree means depth of roots, uprisen height, outreaching branches.
This musical speech of wavelets jounced against reeds
as a boat's wake tardily reaches the shore,
is *voice of the waters*, voice of all the blue
encircling the terrestrial globe
which as a child I loved to spin
slowly upon its creaking axis—blue globe
we have seen now, round, small as an apple,
afloat in the wilderness we name
so casually, as if we knew it
or ever could know it, 'Space.'

VIII   The Tide

After *Mindwalk*

Once we've laboriously
disconnected our old conjunctions—
'physical,' 'solid,' 'real,' 'material'—freed them
from antique measure to admit what,
even through eyes not naked but robed
in optic devices, is not perceptible (oh,
precisely is not perceptible!): admitted
that 'large' and 'small' are bereft
of meaning, since not matter but process only, process only,
gathers itself to appear
knowable: *world, universe*—

then what we feel
in moments of bleak arrest,
panic's black cloth falling
over our faces, over our breath,

is a new twist of Pascal's dread,
a shift of scrutiny,
                                its object now
inside our flesh, the *infinite spaces* discovered

within our own atoms, inside the least
particle of what we supposed
our mortal selves (and *in* and *out*side,
what are they?)—its object now

bits of the Void left over from before
the Fiat Lux, immeasurably
incorporate in our discarnate, fictive,
(yes, but sentient) notion of substance,
inaccurate as our language,
flux which the soul alone
pervades, elusive but persistent.

Namings

Three hours wholly absorbed: trying to identify one rainsoaked
wormridden mushroom. And the ducks—bufflehead or goldeneye?

The markings once clearly recognized, a glow or grace clarifies
other matters of doubt. They dive, resurface, I know their name.

'What's the most useful thing I can do for you?' I asked the old poet,
lost and distraite in a new apartment. 'Identify things!' she answered.

'What are these?' An empty frame. A box of buttons.
An ivory paper knife. For the moment nothing makes sense.

The need to know *maenad* from *dryad*, to know when you see the
     green drift
of watergrass combed by current, the word you desire is *naiad*.

Sorting. Sifting. The ancient tasks, the hero trials, ways to survive,
ways to grow wise. Taxonomies, need to arrange, need to instruct.

We don't trust the stars. *O bright star*—! No, look,
it's moving. Afraid to feel delight.

Tonight two. One was a plane, plodding slowly towards the airport.
One was a star, very silvery. It's still there.

Embracing the Multipede

(I) Embracing the Multipede

On the dream sidewalk
moving towards you
a caterpillar, shiny, hairless, not cute.
Move it
out of harm's way!
It's ringed like an earthworm,
repulsively fecal in color,
with snail-eyes searching about.
Rescue it!
Footsteps will crush it!
It's not so much
like nothing you've seen before
as it is a mixture
of millipede and scorpion.
It's moving towards you,
not cute.
Offer it
your help! It looks
hostile, it may sting you,
but it's small,
each of the multiple feet
the size of an eyelash.
wavering eyes like pinheads.
It's hairless, shiny, repulsive,
scoop it carefully
into your hands,
take it to safety! Not cute, not cute,
it shrinks as you move to meet it,
don't let it vanish before you have time
to give it your heart, a work of mercy.

(II) Questioning the Creature

Where are you going, you
disgusting creature?

It's rumoured
there's a barn, lady,

outside of town,
where anyone may scuttle.

And what would you do there,
vile one?

I'd meet
fellow vile ones, sir,
we'd scuttle, we'd scuttle,
in safety.

And what else, loathsome worm?

God knows.
God would hide in our midst
and we'd seek him.

(III) Pondering the Creature

Return to my dreams,
little leper of my heart:

I want to know—
who are you?

What is the pitiful, wormish,
dangerously creeping thing

I must protect?
Is this a trick to lure me

under the stones,
under the punkwood crevices,

insect shanties that harbor
you and your boneless kin?

Why did the servile answer
you made to insults

twist in its glistening
exuded track to claim

God as your intimate,
ready to join

your lowly games,
to seek and be found?

(IV) The Creature Absent: An Underpass

'Cherish the mystery.'
(a voice responds)
'the mystery of this metamorphic
apparition.
       Does it insidiously
claim your pity? Give it some,
You can spare it.
         Is it treacherous, malevolent?
Give it the benefit
of your ample doubt. You have
no positive evidence
it bites or stings.
Perhaps it has for you
some message,
a talisman brought from whatever distance
it travelled to arrive
at you, you in particular,
you only.'

      Who was speaking?
The creature
was absent, not one shadow
changed shape to mark its trail. Echo
of words remained, as if halloo, halloo,
were sounding in a tunnel.

What the Figtree Said

Literal minds! Embarrassed humans! His friends
were blushing for Him
in secret; wouldn't admit they were shocked.
They thought Him

petulant to curse me!—yet how could the Lord
be unfair?—so they looked away,
then and now.
But I, I knew that
helplessly barren though I was,
my day had come. I served
Christ the Poet,
who spoke in images: I was at hand,
a metaphor for their failure to bring forth
what is within them (as figs
were *not* within me). They, who had walked
in His sunlight presence,
they could have ripened,
could have perceived His thirst and hunger,
His innocent appetite;
they could have offered
human fruits—compassion, comprehension—
without being asked,
without being told of need.
My absent fruit
stood for their barren hearts. He cursed
not me, not them, but
(ears that hear not, eyes that see not)
their dullness, that witholds
gifts *unimagined*.

Contraband

The tree of knowledge was the tree of reason.
That's why the taste of it
drove us from Eden. That fruit
was meant to be dried and milled to a fine powder
for use a pinch at a time, a condiment.
God had probably planned to tell us later
about this new pleasure.
                              We stuffed our mouths full of it,
gorged on *but* and *if* and *how* and again
but, knowing no better.
It's toxic in large quantities; fumes
swirled in our heads and around us

to form a dense cloud that hardened to steel,
a wall between us and God, Who was Paradise.
Not that God is unreasonable—but reason
in such excess was tyranny
and locked us into its own limits, a polished cell
reflecting our own faces. God lives
on the other side of that mirror,
but through the slit where the barrier doesn't
quite touch ground, manages still
to squeeze in—as filtered light,
splinters of fire, a strain of music heard
then lost, then heard again.

On a Theme by Thomas Merton

'Adam, where are you?'
                              God's hands
palpate darkness, the void
that is Adam's inattention,
his confused attention to everything,
impassioned by multiplicity, his despair.

Multiplicity, his despair;
                              God's hands
enacting blindness. Like a child
at a barbaric fairgrounds—
noise, lights, the violent odors—
Adam fragments himself. The whirling rides!

Fragmented Adam stares.
                              God's hands
unseen, the whirling rides
dazzle, the lights blind him. Fragmented,
he is not present to himself. God
suffers the void that is his absence.

Salvator Mundi: Via Crucis

Maybe He looked indeed
much as Rembrandt envisioned Him
in those small heads that seem in fact
portraits of more than a model.
A dark, still young, very intelligent face,
a soul-mirror gaze of deep understanding, unjudging.
That face, in extremis, would have clenched its teeth
in a grimace not shown in even the great crucifixions.
The burden of humanness (I begin to see) exacted from Him
that He taste also the humiliation of dread,
cold sweat of wanting to let the whole thing go,
like any mortal hero out of his depth,
like anyone who has taken a step too far
and wants herself back.
The painters, even the greatest, don't show how,
in the midnight Garden,
or staggering uphill under the weight of the Cross,
he went through with even the human longing
to simply cease, to not be.
Not torture of body,
not the hideous betrayals humans commit
nor the faithless weakness of friends, and surely
not the anticipation of death (not then, in agony's grip)
was Incarnation's heaviest weight,
but this sickened desire to renege,
to step back from what He, Who was God,
had promised Himself, and had entered
time and flesh to enact.
Sublime acceptance, to be absolute, had to have welled
up from those depths where purpose
drifted for mortal moments.

Ascension

Stretching Himself as if again,
        through downpress of dust
                upward, soil giving way

to thread of white, that reaches
        for daylight, to open as green
                leaf that it is . . .
Can Ascension
        not have been
                arduous, almost,
as the return
        from Sheol, and
                back through the tomb
into breath?
        Matter reanimate
                now must relinquish
itself, its
        human cells,
                molecules, five
senses, linear
        vision endured
                as Man—
the sole
        all-encompassing gaze
                resumed now,
Eye of Eternity.
        Relinquished, earth's
                broken Eden.
Expulsion,
        liberation,
                last
self-enjoined task
        of Incarnation.
                He again
Fathering Himself.
        Seed-case
                splitting,
He again
        Mothering His birth:
                torture and bliss.

The Tide

Where is the Giver to whom my gratitude
rose? In this emptiness
there seems no Presence.

.

How confidently the desires
of God are spoken of!
Perhaps God wants
something quite different.
Or nothing, nothing at all.

.

Blue smoke from small
peaceable hearths ascending
without resistance in luminous
evening air.
Or eager mornings—waking
as if to a song's call.
Easily I can conjure
a myriad images
of faith.
Remote. They pass
as I turn a page.

.

Outlying houses, and the train's rhythm
slows, there's a signal box.
People are taking their luggage
down from the racks.
Then you wake and discover
you have not left
to begin the journey.

.

Faith's a tide, it seems, ebbs and flows responsive
to action and inaction.

Remain in stasis, blown sand
stings your face, anemones
shrivel in rock pools no wave renews.
Clean the littered beach, clear
the lines of a forming poem,
the waters flood inward.
Dull stones again fulfill
their glowing destinies, and emptiness
is a cup, and holds
the ocean.

Suspended

1 had grasped God's garment in the void
but my hand slipped
on the rich silk of it.
The 'everlasting arms' my sister loved to remember
must have upheld my leaden weight
from falling, even so,
for though I claw at empty air and feel
nothing, no embrace,
I have not plummetted.

SANDS OF THE WELL

I   Crow Spring

What Harbinger?

Glitter of grey
oarstrokes over
the waveless, dark,
secretive water.
A boat is moving
toward me
slowly, but who
is rowing and what
it brings I can't
yet see.

Uncertain Oneiromancy

I spent the entire night leading a blind man
through an immense museum
so that (by internal bridges, or tunnels?
somehow!) he could avoid the streets,
the most dangerous avenues, all the swift
chaotic traffic . . .   I persuaded him
to allow my guidance, through to the other
distant doors, though once inside, labyrinthine corridors,
steps, jutting chests and chairs and stone arches
bewildered him as I named them at each swerve,
and were hard for me to manoeuver him
around and between. As he could perceive nothing,
I too saw only the obstacles, the objects
with sharp corners; not one painting, not one carved
credenza or limestone martyr.   We did at last
emerge, however, into that part of the city
he had been headed for when I took over;
he raised his hat in farewell, and went on, uphill,
tapping his stick. I stood looking after him,
watching as the street enfolded him, wondering
if he would make it, and after I woke, wondering still
what in me he was, and who

the *I* was that took that long short-cut with him
through room after room of beauty his blindness
hid from me as if it had never been.

Threat

You can live for years next door
to a big pinetree, honored to have
so venerable a neighbor, even
when it sheds needles all over your flowers
or wakes you, dropping big cones
onto your deck at still of night.
Only when, before dawn one year
at the vernal equinox, the wind
rises and rises, raising images
of cockleshell boats tossed among huge
advancing walls of waves,
do you become aware that always,
under respect, under your faith
in the pinetree's beauty, there lies
the fear it will crash some day
down on your house, on you in your bed,
on the fragility of the safe
dailiness you have almost
grown used to.

In Question

A sunset of such aqueous hints, subdued
opaline gleamings, so much grey among its
wan folds, fading
tangerine roses;
            and in a rosetree—not a rosetree,
            a young tree of some other species
            which has become the noble
            support, patient, perhaps eager,
            of a capricious Gloire de Dijon—

           in this green
symbiosis of elder and wildening
rose, the evening wind is pulsing,
and the sound nearby
of a saxophone, slowly wistful
without being strictly sad.

For the first time, the certainty of return
to this imprinted scene, unchanging but for the height
of green thicket, rising year by year
beyond the cobwebbed windowpanes,
can not be assumed.

The Wound

My tree
had a secret wound.
Not lethal. And it was young.
But one withered branch
hung down.

Wall

When distant ocean's big V of silver
reaches straight up, rearing
between the hills that hold it,
don't you feel you could go and go
swift as hurricane till you
flung yourself at its wall, its
blue wall of spider silver,
and passed like Alice
into the blind mirror?

Wondering

> *"The very act of lighting*
> *the candle is prayer."*
> Bro. David Steindl-Rast

Just to light the candle,
just to draw the breath
of a sigh towards the match,
is an act?
   A prayer?

Can it bridge the gulf
between our sense of being—
node, synapse, locus of hidden counsels
—and the multitudinous force of
world?

The Danger Moments

Some days, some moments
shiver in extreme fragility.
A trembling brittleness
of oak and iron. Splinterings, glassy shatterings,
threaten.
Evaporations of granite.
These are the danger moments:

different from fear of what we do, have done,
may do. Different from apprehension
of mortality, the closing cadence
of lived phrases, a continuum.

These are outside the pattern.

You've heard the way infant and ancient sleepers
stop sometimes between
one breath and the next?
You know the terror
of watching them.
It's like that.

As if the world were a thought
God was thinking and then
not thinking. Divine attention
turned away. Will breath and thought
resume?
            They do, for now.

Empty Hands

In the night foundations crumble.
God's image was contrived
of beaten alloy. A thin clatter
as it tumbles from its niche.

Parts of your body ache,
each separate, ominous,
linked only by emplacement within
a worn skin. Convictions

wheel and scatter,
white birds affrighted.

In time you sleep. But wake
to the same sensation: adrift
mid-ocean, frayed mooring ropes
trailing behind you, swirling.

Yet when you open
unwilling eyes, you see the day
is sunlit. You walk
down to the real shore.

Over the city,
a scum of brown. But it is quiet
among the trees, grass
strewn with first-fallen leaves,
a sheen of dew. The past night

remains with you, but your attention
is drawn away from it
to taste the autumn light, falling
into your empty hands.

What Goes Unsaid

In each mind, even the most candid,
there are forests, where needled haze overshadows
the slippery duff and patches of snow long-frozen,
or else where mangroves, proliferant, vine-entwisted,
loom over warm mud that slowly bubbles.
In these forests there live certain events, shards
of memory, scraps of once-heard lore, intimations
once familiar—some painful, shameful, some
drably or laughably inconsequent, others
thoughts that the thinker
could never hold fast and begin to tell.
And some—a few—that are noble, tender,
and so complete in themselves, they had
no need of saying.
                            There they dwell,
no sky above them, resting
like dragonflies on the dense air, or nested
on inaccessible twigs.
It is right that there are these secrets
(even the weightless ones have perhaps
some part to play in the unperceiveable whole)
and these forests; privacies
and the deep terrain to receive them.
Right that they rise at times into our ken,
and are acknowledged.

Fair Warning

Rain and the dark. The owl,
terror of those he must hunt,
flies back and forth, hungry.

Darkly, solemnly, softly, over and over,
he makes known his presence,
his call a falling of mournful notes,
his tone much like the dove's.

The Glittering Noise

To tell the truth,
I believe I could be happy
doing nothing but reading old diaries
morning to night. Silk and muslin
brush my hands like moths
passing by, the dancers
go up and down the room, no one
has learned the Valse as yet,
fiddle and flute and fortepiano
return to the older rhythms.
Birth and death, the fortunes of war,
fear and relief from fear
compel attention, yet
they're veiled in the mild Septembery
haze of time—blessedly present, blessedly
long gone by. Aware of the shame
I ought to feel—defecting
so willingly from my own century—
I stroll calmly through candlelit rooms
and down to the quay, to board
a waiting vessel that sails with the tide
into *the finest clear night*
possible, the Comet more beautiful
than anything I ever saw,
and the noise of the herrings,
which passed us
in immense shoals, glittering
in the Sea, like fire . . .

As the Moon Was Waning

Small intimations of destiny wove
a hammock about me out of fine
wiry fibers, a steel gossamer swaying
calmly in chaos. What I needed
was to examine it inch by inch,
discover it true or false, shelter or prison.
Instead, I lay low, evasive,
imagining mortal weariness that it's not yet time for.
Only the neighbor's new, very delicate, distant,
mercurial windbells promised,
if not tonight, then some night soon, to recall me
to that scrutiny, that obligation deferred—
as if their music,
sparse, random, uninsistent, nevertheless
would prove, in time,
a summons I'd not resist.

Advising Myself

When the world comes to you muffled *as through a glass
darkly*—jubilance, anguish, declined into
faded postcards—remember how, seventeen, you said
you no longer felt or saw with the old
intensity, and knew that the flamelight
would not rekindle; and how Bet scoffed
and refused to believe you. And how many thousand times,
burning with joy or despair, you've known she was right.

Concordance

Brown bird, irresolute as a dry
leaf, swerved in flight
just as my thought
changed course, as if I heard
a new motif enter a music I'd not
till then attended to.

A Gift

Just when you seem to yourself
nothing but a flimsy web
of questions, you are given
the questions of others to hold
in the emptiness of your hands,
songbird eggs that can still hatch
if you keep them warm,
butterflies opening and closing themselves
in your cupped palms, trusting you not to injure
their scintillant fur, their dust.
You are given the questions of others
as if they were answers
to all you ask. Yes, perhaps
this gift is your answer.

Crow Spring

The crows are tossing themselves
recklessly in the random winds
of spring.
            One friend has died, one disappeared
        (for now, at least) leaving no address;
        I've lost the whereabouts
        of a wandering third. That seems to be,
        this year, the nature of this season.
        Is it a message about relinquishment?
Across the water, rain's veil, gray silk,
flattens the woods to two dimensions.
While close at hand
the crows' black fountain
jets and falls, jets and blows
this way and that.
How they scoop themselves
up from airy nadirs!

II Sojourns in the Parallel World

Salvation

They are going to
                    daylight a river here—
that's what they call it, noun to verb.
A stream turned out
                    years ago from its channel
to run in cement tunnels, dank and airless
                    till it joined a sewer,
will be released—to sun, rain, pebbles, mud,
                    yellow iris, the sky above it
and trees leaning over to be reflected!

At night, stars or at least streetlamps
                    will gleam in it,
fish and waterbugs swim again in its ripples;
                    and though its course,
more or less the old one it followed before its
                    years of humiliation,
will pass near shops and the parking lot's
                    glittering metallic desert, yet
this unhoped-for pardon will once more permit
                    the stream to offer itself at last
to the lake, the lake will accept it, take it
                    into itself,
the stream restored will become pure lake.

Secret Diversion

Where a fold of fog
briefly lifts by the headland,
it reveals a shoal of
wave-glitterings
imitating fish as the ocean
plays unobserved.

Singled Out

Expanse of gray, of silver.
Only this one rockstrewn
shallow bay singled out
to be luminous jade.
                            Its breakers
sing hard, sing loud, the sound
heard clear on the hilltop. Perhaps
the red-tailed hawk, swaying its flight
so much higher, hears it as well.

Rage and Relenting

Hail, ricocheting off stone and cement, angrily
sprinkling its rock-salt among fallen
blossoms on earth's
half-awakened darkness,
                            enters
        the folds of sturdy camellias
        as if to seek
        refuge in those phyllo-layers of immaculate soft red,
        a place in which
                    to come to rest,
                            to melt.

The 6:30 Bus, Late May

The mountain
a moonflower in late
blue afternoon.

The bus
grinds and growls.
At each stop

someone gets off,
the workday over,
heads for home.

Trees in their first
abundance of green
hold their breath,

the sky is
so quiet, cloudless.
The mountain

mutely
by arcane power
summons the moon.

Midsummer Eve

All day the mountain boldly
displayed its white splendor,
disavowing all ambiguity,

but now, the long June day
just closing, the pale sky
still blue, the risen moon
well aloft, the mountain
retreats from so much pomp,
such flagrant and superficial pride,

and drifts above the horizon,
ghostly, irresolute, more akin
to a frail white moth

than to the massive tension
of rock, its own bones, beneath
its flesh of snow.

The Mountain Assailed

Animal mountain,
some of your snows are melting,
dark streaks reveal

your clefts, your secret creases.
The light quivers,
is it blue, is it gold?
I feel your breath
over the distance,
you are panting, the sun
gives you no respite.

Pentimento

To be discerned
             only by those
                      alert to likelihood—

the mountain's form
               beneath the milky radiance
                            which revokes it.

It lingers—
        a draft
            the artist may return to.

3 Short Solos

1

Softest of shadows
brave the mist, diluted gold
films the puddles.
Gingerly the sun
lowers itself
behind the hill of houses,
calling for evening:
it is only March, this day
has lasted long enough.

2

The red madrone's
undone by some unknown
disease. A robin
witlessly repeats among its branches
the old news, *spring,*
spring is begun.

3

Wickering from the lake, a bird
barely rising seems to ride
its own wake into air—only
to splash down nearby on the waveless water.

A Song of Degrees

Pearblossom bright white
against green young leaves that frame
each tuft, black
pinewoods, graybrown buildings—

but rich
cream against strewn
feathers of cloud that float
slowly through new
blue of an April morning.

Rainbow Weather

The rain-curtains are blowing
north past the woods

and now the sun
looks out of its blue window

and they blow
right into a rainbow

arched above the lake
to see its own reflection

crinkled among the somber
festivities of fish!

Alchemy

Deep night, deep woods,
valley far below the steep
thigh of the hill, the sky too
a hazy darkness—yet the moon,
small and high, discovers
a wide stretch of river
to be its mirror, steel
brighter than its own
fogmuffled radiance.

Double Vision

Artery of ice,
winding sinuous down between
scarred hillsides, remnant
forests, clearcut raw
scraggy declivities. Above,
pale capillaries mark where,
when it thaws, this
frozen stream will take
the thin soil down with it.
Meanwhile it lies
white on gradations
of nuanced grey,
flowing to black, elegant design
to be acknowledged,
detached arabesque, a beauty
not to be denied.

Webs

What the spider weaves
is targets, dart-boards
of delicate design.
Flimsy prey, too insubstantial
to have a common name,
come blundering into them,
arrows each breeze
deflects from vague intentions.
Autumn raindrops adorn
the dead, the living,
the beauty of the web.
The entire arrangement
shakes and steadies, shakes
and steadies, complacent,
exquisite, efficient.

Bearing the Light

Rain-diamonds, this winter morning,
embellish the tangle of unpruned
pear-tree twigs; each solitaire,
placed, it appears, with considered
judgement, bears the light
beneath the rifted clouds—the indivisible
shared out in endless abundance.

In Summer

When the light, late in the afternoon, pauses among
the highest branches of the highest trees,
they stir a little, as if in pleasure. Light and a passing breeze
become one and the same, a caress. Then the lower branches,
leaves or needles in shadow, take up the lilt
of that response, their green with its hint of blue forming
what, if it were sound, could be called
a chord with the almost yellow of those
the sunlight tarries with.

Flowers Before Dark

Stillness of flowers. Colors
a slow intense fire, faces
cool to the touch, burning.
Massed flowers in dusk, crimson,
magenta, orange,
unflickering furnace, gaze
unswerving, innocent scarlet,
ardent white, afloat
on late light, serene passion
stiller than silence.

Firmament

Fish in the sky of water—silvery
as travelling moon through cloud-hills—
down current whisks, or deeper
fins into depths, to rise or sagely
wait in the milky mist of
disturbed sediment, wheeling briskly
at least whim, at one
with the aqueous everything it shines in.

Agon

The sea barely crinkled, breathing
calmly. Islands and shore
pure darkness, uncompromised,
outline and mass without
perplexity of component forms,
the salt grasses at water's edge
a frieze, immobile. All of this
a visible gravity,
not sad but serious.
                     And above,
the light to which this somber peace
has not yet awoken, the sun

struggling to rise as one fights sometimes
to break out of fearful dreams
unable to shout or move—and clouds
in delicate brilliance sweeping
long aquiline curves, wild arabesques
across the east, drinking the rising
light, light, as it streams
out from that mortal struggle from which
the sun is already gasping free.

Warning

Island or dark
hollow of advancing wave?
Beyond
surf and spray a somber
horizontal. As if the sea
raised up
a sudden bulwark.
A menacing land, if land—
frowning escarpment, ephemeral
yet enduring, uncharted,
rumored. If wave,
a thundered prophetic word
in ocean's tongue, a bar of blackest
iron brandished aloft
in two fists of a water-god,
a warning not meant kindly.

Swan in Falling Snow

Upon the darkish, thin, half-broken ice
there seemed to lie a barrel-sized, heart-shaped snowball,
frozen hard, its white
identical with the untrodden white
of the lake shore. Closer, its somber face—
mask and beak—came clear, the neck's
long cylinder, and the splayed feet, balanced,

weary, immobile. Black water traced, behind it,
an abandoned gesture. Soft
in still air, snowflakes
fell and fell. Silence
deepened, deepened. The short day
suspended itself, endless.

Creature to Creature

Almost too late to walk in the woods, but I did,
anyway. And stepping aside for a moment
from the shadowy path to enter
darker shadow, a favorite circle of fir trees,
received a gift from the dusk:

a small owl, not affrighted, merely
moving deliberately
to a branch a few feet
further from me, looked
full at me—a long regard,
steady, acknowledging, unbiased.

A Wren

Quiet among the leaves, a wren,
fearless as if I were invisible
or moved with a silence like its own.

From bush to bush
it flies without hesitation,
no flutter or whirring of wings.
I feel myself lifted,
lightened, dispersed:

it has turned me to air,
it can fly right through me.

Like Noah's Rainbow

And again—after an absence
of months, first his, then mine—
when I return greyhearted
to the sunny shore, and find
St. Simon Heron has returned too:
that startled, glad
intake of breath, that sense
of blessing! Surely these sightings,
familiar but always
strange with unearned joy,
are a sign of covenant it's
grossly churlish to disregard. Heavily,
I begin to lift my wings.

Meeting the Ferret

One of my best encounters with animals
was meeting the ferret.
                    Stoats, weasels, ferrets
have evil reputations, and are indeed
without mercy (but has any creature but ourselves
even the potential for mercy
unless within its own species?
Rarely though we use it, amongst us or beyond,
we do have it, it's a human
distinguishing mark, like some colored
underwing feather or prehensile digit;
an offshoot of Imagination).
                    This ferret,
svelte, alert, but not long woken
from a daytime nap, showed, when it yawned,
those sharp little teeth that can draw from rabbits
the unforgettable scream they give with a last breath,
a scream filling the woods, echoing
down a listener's decades. But named, petted,
consenting to walk on a leash,
this ferret, out for a stroll
in the public park of a small town

somewhere in America,
came to my hands as if smiling, clambered
onto my shoulder, twined cosily
round my neck, rubbed noses with me.
I've never felt fur cloud-softer. I envied
the boy it lived with—I can't say 'owner,'
or 'tamer'—it seemed neither owned nor tamed
but a creature willing to try out
the Peaceable Kingdom: to just
begin it, without waiting.
                                    I knew
it was restless, nocturnal, demanding,
and wouldn't fit into my life. But I longed,
nevertheless, to have my own ferret.

Sojourns in the Parallel World

We live our lives of human passions,
cruelties, dreams, concepts,
crimes and the exercise of virtue
in and beside a world devoid
of our preoccupations, free
from apprehension—though affected,
certainly, by our actions. A world
parallel to our own though overlapping.
We call it 'Nature;' only reluctantly
admitting ourselves to be 'Nature' too.
Whenever we lose track of our own obsessions,
our self-concerns, because we drift for a minute,
an hour even, of pure (almost pure)
response to that insouciant life:
cloud, bird, fox, the flow of light, the dancing
pilgrimage of water, vast stillness
of spellbound ephemerae on a lit windowpane,
animal voices, mineral hum, wind
conversing with rain, ocean with rock, stuttering
of fire to coal—then something tethered
in us, hobbled like a donkey on its patch
of gnawed grass and thistles, breaks free.
No one discovers

just where we've been, when we're caught up again
into our own sphere (where we must
return, indeed, to evolve our destinies)
—but we have changed, a little.

III   It Should Be Visible

Protesting at the Nuclear Test Site

A year before, this desert
had raised its claws to me,
importunate and indifferent, half-naked beggar
displaying sores at the city gates.
Now again, in the raw glare
of Lent. Spikes, thorns, spines.
Where was the beauty others perceived?
I could not.
             But when the Shoshone elder spoke,
last year and now once more,
slowly I began to see what I saw as ugly were marks
of torture. When he was young this was desert, too,
but of different aspect, austere but joyful.
A people's reverence illumined stony ground.
Now, as my mind knew but imagination strained to acknowledge,
deep, deep and narrow the holes were bored
into the land's innards, and there, in savage routine,
Hiroshima blasts exploded, exploded, rape
repeated month after month for years.
What repelled me here was no common aridity
unappealing to lovers of lakes and trees,
but anguish, lineaments drab with anguish. This terrain
turned to the human world a gaze
of scorn, victim to tormentor.
                  Slowly,
revulsion unstiffened itself, I learned
almost to love
the dry and hostile earth, its dusty growth
of low harsh plants, sparse in unceasing wind;
could almost have bent
to kiss that leper face.

The News and a Green Moon. July 1994.

The green moon, almost full.
Huge telescopes are trained on catastrophe:
comet fragments crash into Jupiter, gouging
craters gleeful astronomers say are bigger than Earth
(or profound displacements, others claim—tunnels, if you will—
                        in that planet's gaseous insubstantiality).

Visualize that. Visualize the News. The radio
has an hour to deliver so much. Cooperate.
Two thirds of what's left of Rwanda's people after the massacres
milling about in foodless, waterless camps.
Or not milling about, because they're dying

or dead. The green moon, or maybe
when it rises tomorrow in Rwanda or Zaire it will look
white, yellow, serenely silver. Here in the steamy gray
of heatwave dusk it's green as lime. Twenty five years ago
absurd figures, Michelin tire logos, bounced on the moon, whitely.

An audio report from Haiti: Voodoo believers
scrub themselves frantically under a waterfall,
wailing and shouting—you can hear the water behind them.
A purification ritual. Not a response to astronomical events
but to misery. Names change, the Tonton Macoute not mentioned

of late, but misery's tentacles don't relax. Babies now
(as the mike moves on), more wailing, no shouting, a hospital,
mothers and nuns sing hymns, there's not much food to give out.
Young men's bodies, hands tied behind them, litter the streets
of Port au Prince. (As rivers and lakes

in Africa have been littered recently, and not long ago in Salvador—
a familiar item of News.) The crowded boats (again) set out,
sink or are turned back. There could be, a scientist says
(the program returns to Jupiter) an untracked comet any time
heading for Earth. No way to stop it. Meanwhile

an aging astronaut says he regrets we're not sending men to Mars,
that would be progress, he thinks, a mild-mannered man, he thinks
too much has been spent on Welfare, all his devotion given to leaving

uncherished Earth behind, none to some one particular field or tree
and whatever knows it as home, none to the human past either,

certainly none to sacred mountains and wells or nontechnological
orders of knowledge. And meanwhile I'm reading Leonardo Sciascia's
furious refinements of ironic analysis, mirrored pathways
of the world's corruption in Sicily's microcosm. I feel the weight
of moral torpor; the old buoyant will for change that found me actions

to reflect itself (as the moon finds mirrors in seas and puddles)
butts its head on surfaces that give back no image. Slowly, one speck
to a square meter, cometary dust, continually as if from an
    inexhaustible
talcum shaker, falls unseen, adding century by century its increment
to Earth's burden. Covered in that unseen dust I'm peering up to see

the haze of green radiance the moon gives off this night, this one quick
breath of time. No lunamancy tells me its significance, if it has one.
It is beautiful, a beryl, a disk of soft jade melting
into its own light. So silent.
And earth's cries of anguish almost audible.

It Should Be Visible

If from Space not only sapphire continents,
swirling oceans, were visible, but the wars—
like bonfires, wildfires, forest conflagrations,
flame and smoky smoulder—the Earth would seem
a bitter pomander ball bristling with poison cloves.
And each war fuelled with weapons: it should be visible
that great sums of money have been exchanged,
great profits made, workers gainfully employed
to construct destruction, national economies distorted
so that these fires, these wars, may burn
and consume the joy of this one planet
which, seen from outside its transparent tender shell,
is so serene, so fortunate, with its water, air
and myriad forms of 'life that wants to live.'
It should be visible that this bluegreen globe
suffers a canker which is devouring it.

In the Woods

Everything is threatened, but meanwhile
everything presents itself:
the trees, that day and night
steadily stand there, amassing
lifetimes and moss, the bushes
eager with buds sharp as green
pencil-points. Bark of cedar,
brown braids, bark of fir, deep-creviced,
winter sunlight favoring
here a sapling, there an ancient snag,
ferns, lichen. And the lake
always ready to change its skin
to match the sky's least inflection.
Everything answers the rollcall,
and even, as is the custom,
speaks for those that are gone.
—Clearly, beyond sound:
that revolutionary *'Presente!'*

IV   Anamnesis

The Sea Inland

Heather, bracken, the tall Scotch Firs.
There on the mountain, as the wind
came and went in the trees, she could hear
the sea. Closing her eyes she watched it
leaping upon the strand and slowly
returning into itself, tumbling the shingle with it,
to leap again, the over and over
rush, leap forward, and slow withdrawal.
And watched seaweed sway in the pools,
and stretches of wet sand reflect
a gleam of jade as the waves
poised before plunging.
All this she heard and saw on the mountain,
days when there was no school—

long before I was born—as I do now
under Douglas Firs in a western land
long after her death, my now, her then
intermingled as vision and sound
mingle, and what is fleeting and what remains
outside of time.

The Change

For years the dead
were the terrible weight of their absence,
the weight of what one had not put in their hands.
Rarely a visitation—dream or vision—
lifted that load for a moment, like someone
standing behind one and briefly taking
the heft of a frameless pack.
But the straps remained, and the ache—
though you can learn not to feel it
except when malicious memory
pulls downward with sudden force.
Slowly there comes a sense
that for some time the burden
has been what you need anyway.
How flimsy to be without it, ungrounded, blown
hither and thither, colliding with stern solids.
And then they begin to return, the dead:
but not as visions. They're not
separate now, not to be seen, no,
it's they who see: they displace,
for seconds, for minutes, maybe longer,
the mourner's gaze with their own. Just now,
that shift of light, arpeggio
on ocean's harp—
not the accustomed bearer
of heavy absence saw it, it was perceived
by the long-dead, long absent, looking
out from within one's wideopen eyes.

Something More

Sometimes I'd make of Valentines, long ago,
a wilder place than it was—
the sluice where a man-made lake spilled into Cranbrook
perceived as a cascade huge in mesmeric power:
I'd lean my arms on the 'rustic' fence
and gaze myself into almost-trance.
And now, leaving my sixth decade, I attribute sometimes
the freedom and shy charm of mountain rills in Wales
to the tiny stream that playfully
runs past the ponds at the hatchery, forming
miniature falls before, through stonework channels
built in the Thirties, it passes
under the road and joins the lake.
Viciously sentimental, this habit would be,
of vesting the commonplace in robes of glory
if I deceived myself a fraction more.
But even in childhood I knew
the difference, saw with a double vision.
And I've found the custom gives, in time,
new spirit to fact—or restores it. Places
reveal, as it were, their longings. Inherent dreams.
With the will to see
more than is there, one comes, at moments,
to perceive the more that there is:
from behind gray curtains of low expectation
it is drawn forth, resplendent.

The Past III

You try to keep the present
        uppermost in your mind, counting its blessings
                (which today are many) because
although you are not without hope for the world, crazy
        as that seems to your gloomier friends and often
                to yourself, yet your own hopes
have shrunk, options are less abundant. Ages ago
        you enjoyed thinking of names
                for a daughter; later you still entertained,

at least as hypothesis, the notion
          of a not impossible love, requited passion;
                    or resolved modestly to learn
some craft, various languages.
          And all those sparks of future
                    winked out behind you, forgettable. So—
the present. Its blessings
          many today:
                    the fresh, ornate
blossoms of the simplest trees a sudden
          irregular pattern everywhere, audacious white,
                    flamingo pink in a haze of early warmth.
But perversely it's not
          what you crave. You want
                    the past. Oh, not your own,
no reliving of anything—no, what you hanker after
          is a compost,
                    a forest floor, thick, saturate,
fathoms deep, palimpsestuous, its surface a mosaic
          of infinitely fragile, lacy, tenacious
                    skeleton leaves. When you put your ear
to that odorous ground you can catch the unmusical, undefeated
          belling note, as of a wounded stag escaped triumphant,
                    of lives long gone.

Sheep in the Weeds

Simmer and drowse of August. And the sheep
single file
threading a wavering path, because
the mood takes them, or took
the bellwether, to go
this way, not that,
the length of the long field.
Coarse grass,
a powdery green. Hum
of bees, heat of noon
among seeding thistles. Silver,
purple.

Almost bodily
something returns,
a heavy
note or two of sensual music.
A moment
of milkweed sweetness
long past,

a river
unseen beyond
the field's vague edge.

Without nostalgia,
a neutral
timelessness. Its shadow,
still tight as skin around it,
rehearses in silence
the message
it will deliver later,
about time.

The London Plane

> *"Xerxes' strange* Lydian *love,*
> *the* Platane *tree."*
> John Donne, 'The Autumnal'

Primrose dapple on grey. Majestic
trunk and limbs, and then
the toy-like bobbles among the tangle
of small branches, random twigs.
Strange Lydian love, you evoke, anywhere,
the old streets of my city, forever filled
with promise and history.

Anamnesis at the Faultline

For Barbara Thomas, after experiencing her installation, "What is Found, What Is Lost, What Is Remembered," 1992

I

In each house, imprinted,
a journey.   Partings, tearings
                              apart: storm, loss, hands
                              upraised for rescue,
                              onrush of wave,
                              exile.
Long-hidden, the time
of arrival, plumb-line,
first foundation.

How does memory
serve, serve the earth?
                              Columns
                              of turned wood placed
                              among broken stones,
                              perches for companion
                              ravens. A way
                              of witness.

II

House, hill-field, open
shell of stillness:
                              passage
                              through
                              from doorless
                              doorway
                              to doorway
                              to sky.
The wind
        where it listeth.

III

In each bird,
storm-voyage.

In each tilted
cross, human
dreams,
clouds,
the shifting
seasons.

And in each grave.

> In each stasis,
> impetus. Dark
> edifice, backlit, bigger
> than house or grave. White
> gold of its aura.

Complaint and Rejoinder

There's a kind of despair, when your friends
are scattered across the world; you see
how therefore never is there a way
each can envision truly
the others of whom you speak.
     Oceans divide your life,
you want to place all of it—
people, places, their tones, atmospheres,
everything shared uniquely with each—
into a single bowl, like petals, like sand
in a pail. No one can ever hear or tell
the whole story.

(And do you really think
this would not be so if you lived
all of your life on an island,
in a village too small to contain
a single stranger?)

The Trace

My friendships with one or two, yes, three
men for whom once I felt
the wildest, most painful longing,
still retain, in their enduring transformation,
some fragrance of those times,
like a box where once
the leaves of an exotic herb were kept,
an herb of varied properties, useful and dangerous,
long since consumed.

The Great Black Heron

Since I stroll in the woods more often
than on this frequented path, it's usually
trees I observe; but among fellow humans
what I like best is to see an old woman
fishing alone at the end of a jetty,
hours on end, plainly content.
The Russians mushroom-hunting after a rain
trail after themselves a world of red sarafans,
nightingales, samovars, stoves to sleep on
(though without doubt those are not
what they can remember). Vietnamese families
fishing or simply sitting as close as they can
to the water, make me recall that lake in Hanoi
in the amber light, our first, jet-lagged evening,
peace in the war we had come to witness.
This woman engaged in her pleasure evokes
an entire culture, tenacious field-flower
growing itself among rows of cotton
in red-earth country, under the feet
of mules and masters. I see her
a barefoot child by a muddy river
learning her skill with the pole. What battles
has she survived, what labors?
She's gathered up all the time in the world
—nothing else—and waits for scanty trophies,
complete in herself as a heron.

The Cult of Relics

My father's serviette ring,
silver incised with a design
of Scotch thistles, the central medallion
uninitialled, a blank oval.
                              The two massive
German kitchen knives, pre-1914, not-stainless steel,
which my mother carefully scoured with Vim
after each use.
                    My daily use
of these and other such things
links me to hands long gone.

Medieval con-men disgust and amuse us,
we think we'd never have fallen
for such crude deceptions—unholy
animal bones, nails from any old barn,
splinters enough from the Cross to fill
a whole lumber-yard.
                          But can we
with decency mock the gullible
for desiring these things?
                              Who doesn't want
to hold what hands belov'd or venerated
were accustomed to hold?—You? I?
                              who wouldn't want
to put their lips to the true chalice?

For Steve

The morning after your midnight death
I wake to Lieder—
Schumann, Schubert, the Goethe settings.
Why did I not make sure that you
(and your partner also before his death,
whose cabaret songs would perhaps
have pleased Franz Schubert) came to know
this music?
              This is the way

mourning always begins to take root
and add itself to one's life. A new
pearl-grey thread entering the weave:
this longing to show, to share,
which runs full tilt into absence.

Le Motif

Southwest the moon
full and clear,

eastward, the sky
reddening, cloudless
over fir trees, the dark hill.

I remember, decades ago,
'day coming and the moon not gone,'
the low ridge of the Luberon
beyond the well

and Ste. Victoire
shifting its planes and angles
yet again.

V   Representations

Representations

Daybreak

A winding uphill road. The valley still
deep in shadow. Sunlight
scales the mountain, reaches in
to towers, pinnacles—a city
transformed by daybreak and distance.
Larger than life, a human figure
backlit by the dazzle. Black and white,

but we see it as gold, we see it
as gold and silver.

Pilgrims

Pilgrims among the dune-grass, returning
to their small beached boat. Hurry,
or else the tide will lift it
to drift out to sea! They stumble
in soft sand tufted
with starry flowers.

Seeing the Unseen

Snow, large flakes,
whirling in midnight air,
unseen, coming to rest
on a fast-asleep, very small village
set among rocky fields; not one
lit square of wakeful window.

In Private

He silent and angry,
she silent and afraid, each looking
out the cab windows,
he to the left, she to the right,
both dressed for winter, driving
somewhere neither wants to go.

Moongaze

Full moon's unequivocal
curious stare: the palm-trees
range their lanky shadows defiantly
on the sand for inspection,
motionless as resting spiders.

Alleluia

Angels carved from oak surround
the empty tomb, holding
the hammer and nails, the dice,

949

the crown of rose-thorns. Mute air
of bitter praises in their singing mouths.
What sharp-ridged wings, what shine
of oaken feathers!

Station of Solitude

Alone in his tiny station, the platform latticed with shadows
that tell us a simple fencelike gate is behind him,
shut at the level crossing, the stationmaster watches
the train slowly grow larger. The signal is ready.
Puffing and clanging, *forte, fortissimo*:
a second to go, and it's here—
the first event of the day.
                              There's a single track.
At dusk, when the whitish sky consents
to be briefly brilliant, he'll watch the same train dwindle
back up the line, curve into distance; and silence,
complacently, like a cat dislodged yet again
from its place by the hearth, will reoccupy all the air.
He'll furl the redundant flag. The second event
will be over. That's all. No express
with its scream of triumph, its flash
of glittering windows, of rosy-shaded dining-car lamps
ever passed this way, ever will.

Male Voice Choir

They move from left to right on the road below,
a column of Russian soldiers marching or being marched
to the onion-domed church for Sunday liturgy, sergeant
bringing up the rear, officer on horseback leading,
none of them welcome here
in Poland, 1910.
                 From a grassy bank
the bride from a distant country, resting
in summer sun, watches, and later sees them return,
shriven and springy, swinging their arms, singing.
Hearing the basses, mineshaft deep,
the altos climbing like larks,
the folksong's yearning, the merry sudden
accelerations, a dance of voices, she remembers

the colliers practicing for an Eisteddfod, twilights of summer,
her childhood village.
                              A free afternoon is stretching
before the Tzar's mouzhik conscripts, prospect
of vodka and sleep. They are far from home.
                                          She holds

her husband's hand, warm, smooth, and safe.
But there are tears on her cheeks, the live coals
of such harmonies brand her heart.

                                          Time Retrieved

It is late in a mild English autumn. All of the leaves
have fallen, and now (the now of the eighteen eighties,
eternal) lie in the long trafficless road that leads
away into fields, past the lit windows of one last
large building, a school or seminary. One figure
servant or seamstress, quietly recedes from us, scarcely
rustling the pavement leaves, carrying a basket; she's gazing
over a garden wall to the source of the lemony glow tinting
a sky cloudless yet faintly bonfire-smoky: the sun
is just now dipping below the woods she can see
though we can only deduce their branchy darkness
from these roadside trees, so black, so confident
in their stripped beauty, intricate logic of twigs. A wall
across the street encloses the grounds
of an unseen house; wiry strands of a bare vine
interlace themselves with pale twig-shadow——the fading gold
still almost red on the bricks. From the russet carpet
up through the muffled tawny low horizon
to the transparent muted yellow above,
which is almost already
tinged with the wistful green it may hold
for a minute or two before dark, that glow
suffuses all, it touches the girl's cheek
just seen as she moves homeward, and the edge of her cap,
and the closed door to the hidden garden.

VI   Raga

The Visual Element

Feet moving only to shift weight, the conductor
dances, an old bamboo leaning
a flexible torso into the gusting music,
precisely waving, uttering choreographically
the song the orchestra
makes audible.

String players barely glance his way,
long since linked to him
by unseen strands of spider-silk;
bows move in unison,
like wheat stirred in the wind's
rhythmic passing.
And wind-players glance
left and right, secretly watchful
like small animals. Twitch of an eyebrow:
silent appoggiatura.

Unaccompanied

Violinist, alone as on a martyr's cross,
you have forgotten us.
It's not always this way,
I've seen plenty of others playing
the audience along with the music;
but you, exposed, tortured, ecstatic—
should we not close our eyes?
Have we the right to perceive
the blindness of you, your white face,
badly tailored suit, awkward stance
and deeply erotic abandon, as well as to accept
this intricate energy, this weight, this outpouring
of light which Bach
permits you to suffer, permits you to offer?

Bruckner

Angel with heavy wings
weathering the stormwracked air,
listing heavenward.

The Mystery of Deep Candor

Intervals
so frank,
open and major as you like,
rhythms
a child could keep—

only Haydn dared
make magic from such
morning suns,
roadside gold, each dandelion
dipped in his elixir,
the secret depths of candor.

A Trio by Henze

The golden brushwood! But that
says nothing to you. Think perhaps
of strokes calligraphic yet delineatory,
sepia, the ground grayish,
a subtle wrist guiding
the rather dry brush—it turns,
lifts.
        And then
recollection of bells, one moment only.
And moving on. Moving
along the brief path, charged
with still unlit brands that will gild the dark.

Raga

The fluteplayer
can't be seen to draw breath,
doesn't even
part his lips. But music
flows from the
wooden flute, a river
of honey over-
flowing the honeycomb.

VII   A South Wind

Looking, Walking, Being

"The world is not something to look at, it is something to be in."
Mark Rudman

I look and look.
Looking's a way of being: one becomes,
sometimes, a pair of eyes walking.
Walking wherever looking takes one.

The eyes
dig and burrow into the world.
They touch
fanfare, howl, madrigal, clamor.
World and the past of it,
not only
visible present, solid and shadow
that looks at one looking.

And language? Rhythms
of echo and interruption?
That's
a way of breathing,

breathing to sustain
looking,

walking and looking,
through the world,
in it.

A South Wind

Short grass, electric green, the ground
soggy from winter rain, Chaucerian
eyes of day, minute petals rose-tinted,
nourished by droppings of ducks and geese.
Hold fast what seem ephemera—
plain details that rise clear
beyond the fog of half-thoughts,
that rustling static, empty of metaphor.
Nothing much, or everything; all depends
on how you regard it.
                    On *if* you regard it.
                                    Note the chalk—
yellow of hazel catkins, how in the wet
mild wind they swing toward spring.

The Lyre-Tree

There was a dead tree in the woods
whose two remaining limbs sprang upward
in semblance of a lyre.
                    And now
one has snapped off. What remains
cannot signify.
            O Orpheus,
lend me power to sing
the unheard music of that vanished lyre.

Witness: Incommunicado

They speak of bonding. Of the infant, the primitive
without sense of boundary, everything as much
or as little itself as itself.
                          Yet what loneliness,
the solitude
of thought before language. A kind of darkness
stirring the mind, blurring
the glare and glitter of vision,
steam on the white mirror.

Primal Speech

If there's an Ur-language still among us,
hiding out like a pygmy pterodactyl
in the woods, sighted at daybreak sometimes,
perched on a telephone wire, or like
prehistoric fish discovered in ocean's
deepest grottoes, then it's the exclamation,
universal whatever the sound, the triumphant,
wondering, infant utterance, 'This! This!',
showing and proffering the thing, anything,
the affirmation even before the naming.

For Those Whom the Gods Love Less

When you discover
your new work travels the ground you had traversed
decades ago, you wonder, panicked,
'Have I outlived my vocation? Said already
all that was mine to say?'
                        There's a remedy—
only one—for the paralysis seizing your throat to mute you,
numbing your hands: Remember the great ones, remember Cézanne
doggedly *sur le motif*, his mountain
a tireless noonday angel he grappled like Jacob,
demanding reluctant blessing. Remember James rehearsing

over and over his theme, the loss
of innocence and the attainment
(note by separate note sounding its tone
until by accretion a chord resounds) of somber
understanding. Each life in art
goes forth to meet dragons that rise from their bloody scales
in cyclic rhythm: Know and forget, know and forget.
It's not only
the passion for *getting it right* (though it's that, too)
it's the way
radiant epiphanies recur, recur,
consuming, pristine, unrecognized—
until remembrance dismays you. And then, look,
some inflection of light, some wing of shadow
is other, unvoiced. You can, you must
proceed.

The Hymn

Had I died, or was I
very old and blind, or
was the dream—
this hymn, this ecstatic paean,
this woven music
of color and form, of the sense
of airy space—
was the dream
showing forth the power
of Memory, now, today or at any
moment of need? Or the power
of the inner eye, distinct
from Memory, Imagination's power,
greater than we remember,
in abeyance, the well in which
we forget to dip our cups?

At all events,
that broad hillside of trees
all in leaf, trees of all kinds,
all hues of green, gold-greens, blue-greens,

black-greens, pure and essential
green-greens, and warm and deep
maroons, too, and the almost purple
of smoketrees—all perceived
in their mass of rounded, composed forms
across a half mile of breezy air,
yet with each leaf
rippling, gleaming,
visible almost to vein and serration:

at all events, that sight
brought with it, in dream
such gladness, I wept
tears of gratitude
(such as I've never wept, only read
that such tears sometimes
are shed) amazed to know
this power was mine, a thing given,
to see so well, though asleep,
though blind,
though gone from the earth.

Writer and Reader

When a poem has come to me,
almost complete as it makes its way
into daylight, out through arm, hand, pen,
onto page; or needing
draft after draft, the increments
of change toward itself, what's missing
brought to it, grafted
into it, trammels of excess
peeled away till it can breathe
and leave me—

then I feel awe at being
chosen for the task
again; and delight, and the strange and familiar
sense of destiny.

But when I read or hear
a perfect poem, brought into being
by someone else, someone perhaps
I've never heard of before—a poem
bringing me pristine visions, music
beyond what I thought I could hear,
a stirring, a leaping
of new anguish, of new hope, a poem
trembling with its own
vital power—

then I'm caught up beyond
that isolate awe, that narrow delight,
into what singers must feel in a great choir,
each with humility and zest partaking
of harmonies they combine to make,
waves and ripples of music's ocean,
who hush to listen when the aria
arches above them in halcyon stillness.

Your Heron

for Ben Saenz

From stillness
the Great Blue Heron
rose without warning,

winged in robust decision
up and across
the sky-filled water.

You shared
the unfailing joy of it,
we laughed in pleasure.

Later the heron
turned white in your mind,
conflated with egrets.

Memory and dream, joined in Imagination's
'esemplastic power,' gave you the great
winged symbol, rising

or plummeting, as the creative
work required, experience feeding
the mind's vision, that moves

with beating wings
into and over
the page, the parable.

Hymns to Darkness

Beauty growls from the fertile dark.
Don't disturb
the glow. Shadows
are not contrivances devised
for your confusion. They grow
in subtle simplicity from the root,
silence.

      And words put forth
before there's time to hesitate about
their strangeness, are swaying bridges
(quick! You're across) to further
dark illumination,
lovely tarnish of old silver,
bronze long-buried.

    ·

Alders crowd to the pool's edge.
From roots and bark seeps down
their dark spirit,
a gift to the water that assuages
their thirst. It dyes
the pool to a blacker depth,
a clarity
deeper and less apparent.

•

Imagine the down of black swans.
Hidden beneath the smooth layers
of black breast-feathers, preened by red beaks.
That's the tender dark of certain nights
in summer, when the moon's away,
stars invisible over the moist
low roof of fog.
How good it would be to spend such a night
wholly attentive to its obscurity,
without thought of history, of words like
Dark Ages, Enlightment, or especially
Contemporary, the shameful news each day.
Wholly present to the beneficent
swansdown grace of a single night,
unlit by even a candle.

VIII   Close to a Lake

'In Whom We Live and Move and Have Our Being'

Birds afloat in air's current,
sacred breath? No, not breath of God,
it seems, but God
the air enveloping the whole
globe of being.
It's we who breathe, in, out, in, the sacred,
leaves astir, our wings
rising, ruffled—but only the saints
take flight. We cower
in cliff-crevice or edge out gingerly
on branches close to the nest. The wind
marks the passage of holy ones riding
that ocean of air. Slowly their wake
reaches us, rocks us.
But storm or still,
numb or poised in attention,

we inhale, exhale, inhale,
encompassed, encompassed.

What One Receives from Living Close to a Lake

That it is wide,
and still—yet subtly
stirring; wide and
level, reflecting the intangible sky's
vaster breadth in its own
fresh, cold, serene
surface we can
touch, enter, taste.
That it is wide
and uninterrupted save by
here a sail, there
a constellation of waterfowl—
a meadow of water
you could say,
a clearing amid the entangled
forest of forms and voices,
anxious intentions, urgent
memories: a deep, clear
breath to fill
the soul, an internal
gesture, arms
flung wide to echo
that mute
generous outstretching
we call *lake*.

The Beginning of Wisdom
Proverbs 9:10

You have brought me so far.

.

I know so much. Names, verbs, images. My mind
overflows, a drawer that can't close.

> •

Unscathed among the tortured. Ignorant parchment
uninscribed, light strokes only, where a scribe
tried out a pen.

> •

I am so small, a speck of dust
moving across the huge world. The world
a speck of dust in the universe.

> •

Are you holding
the universe? You hold
onto my smallness. How do you grasp it,
how does it not
slip away?

> •

I know so little.

> •

You have brought me so far.

Poetics of Faith

'Straight to the point'
           can ricochet,
                      unconvincing.
Circumlocution, analogy,
              parable's ambiguities, provide
                      context, stepping-stones.

Most of the time. And then

the lightning power
              amidst these indirections,
                      of plain

unheralded miracle!
        For example,
                as if forgetting
to prepare them, He simply
        walks on water
                toward them, casually—
and impetuous Peter, empowered,
        jumps from the boat and rushes
                on wave-tip to meet Him—
a few steps, anyway—
        (till it occurs to him,
                'I can't, this is preposterous'
and Jesus has to grab him,
        tumble his weight
                back over the gunwale).
Sustaining those light and swift
        steps was more than Peter
                could manage. Still,
years later,
        his toes and insteps, just before sleep,
                would remember their passage.

Conversion of Brother Lawrence

'Let us enter into
ourselves, Time
presses.'
Brother Lawrence
1611–1691

1

What leafless tree plunging
into what pent sky was it
convinced you Spring, bound to return
in all its unlikelihood, was a word
of God, a Divine message?
Custom, natural reason, are everyone's assurance;
we take the daylight for granted, the moon,
the measured tides. A particular tree, though,

one day in your eighteenth winter,
said more, an oracle. Clumsy footman,
apt to drop the ornate objects handed to you,
cursed and cuffed by butlers and grooms,
your inner life unsuspected,
you heard, that day, a more-than-green
voice from the stripped branches.
Wooden lace, a celestial geometry, uttered
more than familiar rhythms of growth.
It said *By the Grace of God.*
Midsummer rustled around you that wintry moment.
Was it elm, ash, poplar, a fruit-tree, your rooted
twig-winged angel of annunciation?

      2

Out from the chateau park it sent you
(by some back lane, no doubt,
not through the wide gates of curled iron),
by ways untold, by soldier's marches, to the obscure
clatter and heat of a monastery kitchen,
a broom's rhythmic whisper for music,
your torment the drudgery of household ledgers. Destiny
without visible glory. 'Time pressed.' Among pots and pans,
heart-still through the bustle of chores,
your labors, hard as the pain in your lame leg,
grew slowly easier over the years, the years
when, though your soul felt darkened, heavy, worthless,
yet God, you discovered, never abandoned you but walked
at your side keeping pace as comrades had
on the long hard roads of war. You entered then
the unending 'silent secret conversation',
the life of steadfast attention.
Not work transformed you; work, even drudgery,
was transformed: that discourse
pierced through its monotones, infused them
with streams of sparkling color.
What needed doing, you did; journeyed if need be
on rocking boats, lame though you were,
to the vineyard country to purchase the year's wine
for a hundred Brothers, laughably rolling yourself
over the deck-stacked barrels when you couldn't

keep your footing; and managed deals with the vintners
to your own surprise, though business was nothing to you.
Your secret was not the craftsman's delight in process,
which doesn't distinguish work from pleasure—
your way was not to exalt nor avoid
the Adamic legacy, you simply made it irrelevant:
everything faded, thinned to nothing, beside
the light which bathed and warmed, the Presence
your being had opened to. Where it shone,
there life was, and abundantly; it touched
your dullest task, and the task was easy.
                    Joyful, absorbed,
you 'practiced the presence of God' as a musician
practices hour after hour his art:
'A stone before the carver,'
you 'entered into yourself.'

Dom Helder Camara at the Nuclear Test Site

Dom Helder, octagenarian wisp
of human substance arrived from Brazil,
raises his arms and gazes toward
a sky pallid with heat, to implore
'Peace!'
          —then waves a 'goodbye for now'
to God, as to a *compadre*.
'The Mass is over, go in peace
to love and serve the Lord': he walks
down with the rest of us to cross
the cattle-grid, entering forbidden ground
where marshals wait with their handcuffs.

After hours of waiting,
penned into two wire-fenced enclosures, sun
climbing to cloudless zenith, till everyone
has been processed, booked, released to trudge
one by one up the slope to the boundary line
back to a freedom that's not so free,
we are all reassembled. We form
two circles, one contained in the other, to dance

clockwise and counterclockwise
like children in Duncan's vision.
But not to the song of ashes, of falling:
we dance in the unity that brought us here,
instinct pulls us into the ancient
rotation, symbol of continuance.
Light and persistent as tumbleweed,
but not adrift, Dom Helder, too,
faithful pilgrim, dances,
dances at the turning core.

On Belief in the Physical Resurrection of Jesus

It is for all
    'literalists of the imagination,'
        poets or not,
that miracle
      is possible,
           possible and essential.
Are some intricate minds
        nourished
           on concept,
as epiphytes flourish
      high in the canopy?
           Can they
subsist on the light,
      on the half
        of metaphor that's not
grounded in dust, grit,
      heavy
        carnal clay?
Do signs contain and utter,
        for them
           all the reality
that they need? Resurrection, for them,
      an internal power, but not
        a matter of flesh?
For the others,
      of whom I am one,
        miracles (ultimate need, bread

of life) are miracles just because
people so tuned
to the humdrum laws:
gravity, mortality—
can't open
to symbol's power
unless convinced of its ground,
its roots
in bone and blood.
We must feel
the pulse in the wound
to believe
that 'with God
all things
are possible,'
taste
bread at Emmaus
that warm hands
broke and blessed.

Psalm Fragments (Schnittke String Trio)

This clinging to a God
for whom one does
nothing.
A loyalty
without deeds.

•

Tyrant God.
Cruel God.
Heartless God.

God who permits
the endless outrage we call
History.

Deaf God.
Blind God.
Idiot God.

(Scapegoat god. Finally
running out of accusations
we deny Your existence.)

·

I don't forget
that downhill street
of spilled garbage and beat-up cars,
the gray faces
looking up, all color
gone with the sun—
disconsolate, prosaic twilight
at midday.   And the fear
of blindness.

It's harder to recall
the relief when plain
daylight returned

subtly, softly,
without the fuss
of trumpets.
                    Yet
our faces had been upturned
like those of gazers
into a sky of angels
at Birth or Ascension.

·

Lord, I curl in Thy grey
gossamer hammock

that swings by one
elastic thread to thin
twigs that could, that should
break but don't.

·

I do nothing, I give You
nothing. Yet You hold me

minute by minute
from falling.

Lord, You provide.

The Prayer Plant (*Maranta Leuconeura*)

The prayer plant must long
for darkness, that it may fold and raise
its many pairs of green hands
to speak at last, in that gesture;

the way a shy believer,
at last in solitude, at last,
with what relief
kneels down to praise You.

What Time Is Made From

The hand that inscribed Genesis left out
the creation of Time. Dividing
darkness from light, God paused to reach
into the substance of Eternity,
teased out a strand of it,
and wound its arabesques throughout
the workshop of creation, looping it through
the arches of newmade days and nights,
pulling and stretching each of them into aeons.
Our own lifetimes and centuries
were formed from leftover
bits and pieces, frayed
ends of God's ribbon, rags
from the Eternal scrapbag.

A Heresy

When God makes dust of our cooling magma,
musingly crumbling the last
galls and studs of our being,

the only place we can go if we're not
destined for hell, or there already,
is purgatory——for certainly heaven's
no place for a film of dust to settle;

and I see no reason why purgatory
may not be reincarnation, the soul
passing from human to another
earth-form more innocent—even to try

the human again, ablaze
with outsetting infant wonder—from which
to learn, as expiation progressed,
neglected tasks.
                 Then

the sifting again, between thoughtful fingers,
the rubbing to finer substance.
                             Then perhaps
time for the floating
                into light,
                       to rest suspended
                       mote by silvery mote
                in that bright veil to await
the common resurrection.

A Blessing

Hovering light embraces
the yellowing poplars, four spires
evenly spaced, a dozen clustered
apart, all of them backed by foresty dark,
a curtain of conifers.

Waking and sleeping, there was grace, reassurance,
during the hours of darkness:
a change in perception, such as we read of
in 19th-century stories, when someone in fever
visibly passed from danger into a calm lagoon
of slumber, promising health.

The light on the trees a nimbus now
of downy yellow, embrace without pressure of weight,
compassionate light.

A Yellow Tulip

The yellow tulip in the room's warmth
            opens.
Can I say it, and not seem to taunt
all who live in torment? Believe it, yet
remain aware of the world's anguish?
But it's so: a caravan arrives constantly
out of desert dust, laden
with gift beyond gift, beyond reason.
        Item: a yellow tulip
        opens; at its center
        a star of greenish indigo,
        a subtle wash of ink
        at the base of each of
        six large petals.
        The black stamens
        are dotted with white.
        At the core, the ovary,
        applegreen fullness
        tapering to proffer—sheltered
        in the wide cup of primary
        yellow—its triune stigma, clove
        of green and gold.
That's one, at nightfall of a day which brought
a dozen treasures, exotic surprises, landscapes,
music, words, acts of friendship, all of them wrapped
in mysterious silk, each unique.
How is it possible?

The yellow tulip
              in the room's warmth
                              opens.

Sands of the Well

The golden particles
descend, descend,
traverse the water's
depth and come to rest
on the level bed
of the well until,
the full descent
accomplished, water's
absolute transparence
is complete, unclouded
by constellations
of bright sand.
Is this
the place where you
are brought in meditation?
Transparency
seen for itself—
as if its quality
were not, after all,
to enable
perception *not* of itself?
With a wand
of willow I again
trouble the envisioned pool,
the cloudy nebulae
form and disperse,
the separate
grains again
slowly, slowly
perform their descent,
and again,
stillness ensues,
and the mystery
of that sheer
clarity, is it water indeed,
or air, or light?

Altars

1

Again before your altar, silent Lord.
And here the sound of rushing waters,
a dove's crooning.

Not every temple serves
as your resting-place.
Here, though, today,
over the river's continuo,
under the dove's soliloquy,
your hospitable silence.

2

Again before thy altar, silent Lord.

Thy presence is made known
by untraced interventions
like those legendary baskets filled
with bread and wine, discovered
at the door by someone at wit's end
returning home empty-handed
after a day of looking for work.

To Live in the Mercy of God

To lie back under the tallest
oldest trees. How far the stems
rise, rise
            before ribs of shelter
                        open!

To live in the mercy of God. The complete
sentence too adequate, has no give.
Awe, not comfort. Stone, elbows of
stony wood beneath lenient
moss bed.

And awe suddenly
passing beyond itself. Becomes
a form of comfort.
                    Becomes the steady
        air you glide on, arms
stretched like the wings of flying foxes.
To hear the multiple silence
of trees, the rainy
forest depths of their listening.

To float, upheld,
        as salt water
        would hold you,
                    once you dared.

        •

To live in the mercy of God.

To feel vibrate the enraptured
waterfall flinging itself
unabating down and down
                    to clenched fists of rock.
Swiftness of plunge,
hour after year after century,
                    O or Ah
uninterrupted, voice
many-stranded.
                    To breathe
spray. The smoke of it.
                    Arcs
of steelwhite foam, glissades
of fugitive jade barely perceptible. Such passion—
rage or joy?
                    Thus, not mild, not temperate,
God's love for the world. Vast
flood of mercy
            flung on resistance.

Primary Wonder

Days pass when I forget the mystery.
Problems insoluble and problems offering
their own ignored solutions
jostle for my attention, they crowd its antechamber
along with a host of diversions, my courtiers, wearing
their colored clothes; cap and bells.
                              And then
once more the quiet mystery
is present to me, the throng's clamor
recedes: the mystery
that there is anything, anything at all,
let alone cosmos, joy, memory, everything,
rather than void: and that, O Lord,
Creator, Hallowed One, You still,
hour by hour sustain it.

THIS GREAT UNKNOWING

From Below

I move among the ankles
of forest Elders, tread
their moist rugs of moss,
duff of their soft brown carpets.
Far above, their arms are held
open wide to each other, or waving—

what they know, what
perplexities and wisdoms they exchange,
unknown to me as were the thoughts
of grownups when in infancy I wandered
into a roofed clearing amidst
human feet and legs and the massive
carved legs of the table,

the minds of people, the minds of trees
equally remote, my attention then
filled with sensations, my attention now
caught by leaf and bark at eye level
and by thoughts of my own, but sometimes
drawn to upgazing—up and up: to wonder
about what rises
so far above me into the light.

For the Asking

'You would not seek Me if you did not already possess Me.'
—Pascal

Augustine said his soul
was a house so cramped
God could barely squeeze in.
Knock down the mean partitions,
he prayed, so You may enter!
Raise the oppressive ceilings!
                    Augustine's soul
didn't become a mansion large enough
to welcome, along with God, the women he'd loved,
except for his mother (though one, perhaps,
his son's mother, did remain to inhabit

a small dark room). God, therefore,
would never have felt
fully at home as his guest.
                            Nevertheless,
it's clear desire
fulfilled itself in the asking, revealing prayer's
dynamic action, that scoops out channels
like water on stone, or builds like layers
of grainy sediment steadily
forming sandstone. The walls, with each thought,
each feeling, each word he set down,
expanded, unnoticed; the roof
rose, and a skylight opened.

Celebration

Brilliant, this day—a young virtuoso of a day.
Morning shadows cut by sharpest scissors,
deft hands. And every prodigy of green—
whether it's ferns or lichen or needles
or impatient points of bud on spindly bushes—
greener than ever before.
                            And the way the conifers
hold new cones to the light for blessing,
a festive rite, and sing the oceanic chant the wind
transcribes for them!
A day that shines in the cold
like a first-prize brass band swinging along the street
of a coal-dusty village, wholly at odds
with the claims of reasonable gloom.

Patience

What patience a landscape has, like an old horse,
head down in its field.
                            Grey days,
air and fine rain cling, become one, hovering till at last,
languidly, rain relinquishes that embrace, consents

to fall. What patience a hill, a plain,
a band of woodland holding still, have, and the slow falling
of grey rain . . . Is it blind faith? Is it
merely a way to deeply rest? Is the horse
only resigned, or has it
some desirable knowledge, an enclosed meadow
quite other than its sodden field,
which patience is the key to? Has it already,
within itself, entered that sunwarmed shelter?

Ancient Stairway

Footsteps like water hollow
the broad curves of stone
ascending, descending
century by century.
Who can say if the last
to climb these stairs
will be journeying
downward or upward?

First Love

It was a flower.

There had been,
before I could even speak,
another infant, girl or boy unknown,
who drew me—I had
an obscure desire to become
connected in some way to this other,
even to *be* what I faltered after, falling
to hands and knees, crawling
a foot or two, clambering
up to follow further until
arms swooped down to bear me away.
But that one left no face, had exchanged
no gaze with me.

This flower:
            suddenly
there was *Before I saw it*, the vague
past, and *Now*. Forever. Nearby
was the sandy sweep of the Roman Road,
and where we sat the grass
was thin. From a bare patch
of that poor soil, solitary,
sprang the flower, face upturned,
looking completely, openly
into my eyes.
            I was barely
old enough to ask and repeat its name.
'Convolvulus,' said my mother.
Pale shell-pink, a chalice
no wider across than a silver sixpence.

It looked at me, I looked
back, delight
filled me as if
I, not the flower,
were a flower and were brimful of rain.
And there was endlessness.
Perhaps through a lifetime what I've desired
has always been to return
to that endless giving and receiving, the wholeness
of that attention,
that once-in-a-lifetime
secret communion.

Beyond the Field

Light, flake by flake touching down on surface tension
of ocean, strolling there before diving forever under.

Tectonic plates inaudibly grinding, shifting—
monumental fidgets.

The mind's far edges twitch, sensing
kinships beyond reach.

Too much unseen, unknown, unknowable,
assumed missing therefore:

shadings, clues, transitions linking
rivers of event, imaged, not imaged, a flood

that rushes towards us, through us, away
beyond us before we wheel to face what seems

a trace of passage, ripple already stilling itself
in tall grass near the fence of the mind's field.

The Métier of Blossoming

Fully occupied with growing—that's
the amaryllis. Growing especially
at night: it would take
only a bit more patience than I've got
to sit keeping watch with it till daylight;
the naked eye could register every hour's
increase in height. Like a child against a barn door,
proudly topping each year's achievement,
steadily up
goes each green stem, smooth, matte,
traces of reddish purple at the base, and almost
imperceptible vertical ridges
running the length of them:
Two robust stems from each bulb,
sometimes with sturdy leaves for company,
elegant sweeps of blade with rounded points.
Aloft, the gravid buds, shiny with fullness.

One morning—and so soon!—the first flower
has opened when you wake. Or you catch it poised
in a single, brief
moment of hesitation.
Next day, another,
shy at first like a foal,
even a third, a fourth,
carried triumphantly at the summit

of those strong columns, and each
a Juno, calm in brilliance,
a maiden giantess in modest splendor.
If humans could be
that intensely whole, undistracted, unhurried,
swift from sheer
unswerving impetus! If we could blossom
out of ourselves, giving
nothing imperfect, withholding nothing!

A Hundred a Day

'A million species of plants and animals will be extinct by the
turn of the century, an average of a hundred a day.'
—*Dr. Mustafa Tolba, Director-General of the*
U.N. Environment Program

Dear 19th century! Give me refuge
in your unconscious sanctuary for a while,
let me lose myself behind sententious bombazine,
rest in the threadbare brown merino of dowerless girls.
Yes, you had your own horrors, your dirt, disease,
profound injustices; yet the illusion of endless time
to reform, if not themselves, then the world,
gave solace even to gloomy minds. Nature, for you,
was to be marvelled at, praised and conquered,
a handsome heiress; any debate concerned
the origin and subsequent behaviour of species,
not their demise. Virtue, in your heyday
(blessed century, fictive but so real!) was confident
of its own powers. Laxly guarded, your Hesperides
was an ordinary orchard, its fruit
apples of simple hope and happiness.
And though the *ignorant armies*, then as always,
clashed by night, there was
a beckoning future to look to, that bright
Victorian cloud in the eastern sky. The dodo
was pathetic, grotesque in its singular extinction,
its own stupidity surely to blame. It stood alone
on some low hillock of the mind
and was not seen as shocking, nor as omen.

That Day

Across a lake in Switzerland, fifty years ago,
light was jousting with long lances, fencing with broadswords
back and forth among cloudy peaks and foothills.
We watched from a small pavilion, my mother and I,
enthralled.
                And then, behold, a shaft, a column,
a defined body, not of light but of silver rain,
formed and set out from the distant shore, leaving behind
the silent feints and thrusts, and advanced
unswervingly, at a steady pace,
toward us.
                I knew this! I'd seen it! Not the sensation
of déjà vu: it was Blake's inkwash vision,
'The Spirit of God Moving Upon the Face of the Waters'!
The column steadily came on
across the lake toward us; on each side of it,
there was no rain. We rose to our feet, breathless—
and then it reached us, took us
into its veil of silver, wrapped us
in finest weave of wet,
and we laughed for joy, astonished.

Elephant Ears

I've given up wearing earrings.
Like my mother's my ears are large—
and mine are lopsided. Now, with age,
the lobes show a crease, and seem to droop
like a Buddha's. But Buddhist tradition
links such big ears to wisdom—
should that console me? My big-eared mother,
although not foolish, was not so much wise
as ardent, responsive, eager to learn.
At the age I am now, she still wore her various pairs
of beautiful earrings with confidence,
and they became her. Perhaps that éclat
was her wisdom—for now, and maybe forever,
a wisdom beyond my reach.

Should I call upon Buddha, on Ganesh,
upon that part of my mother
which lives in me, for enlightenment?
For the *chutzpa* to dangle jewels
from long and uneven lobes?

Animal Spirits

When I was five and
undifferentiated energy, animal spirits,
pent-up desire for the unknown built in me
a head of steam I had
no other way to let off, I ran
at top speed back and forth
end to end of the drawingroom,
bay to French window, shouting—
roaring, really—slamming
deliberately into the rosewood
desk at one end, the shaken
window-frames at the other, till the fit
wore out or some grownup stopped me.

But when I was six I found better means:
on its merry gallows
of dark-green wood my swing, new-built,
awaited my pleasure, I rushed
out to it, pulled the seat
all the way back to get a good start, and
vigorously pumped it up to the highest arc:
my legs were oars, I was rowing a boat in air—
and then, then from the furthest
forward swing of the ropes
                        I let go and flew!
At large in the unsustaining air,
flew clear over the lawn across
the breadth of the garden
and fell, Icarian, dazed,
among hollyhocks, snapdragons, love-in-a-mist,
and stood up uninjured, ready
to swing and fly over and over.

The need passed as I grew;
the mind took over, devising
paths for that force in me, and the body curled up,
sedentary, glad to be quiet and read and read,
save once in a while, when it demanded
to leap about or to whirl—or later still
to walk swiftly in wind and rain
long and far and into the dusk,
wanting some absolute, some exhaustion.

The Poodle Palace

I never pass the Poodle Palace
with its barber pole in the shape
of a striped beribboned bone and the sign:
Specializing in Large and Matted Dogs,
without remembering the bitter wonder
of the taxi-driver from somewhere in India
who asked me,
'What is that, Poodle Palace?
What does it mean?'—and when I told him,
laughed, and for blocks,
laughed intermittently, a laughter
dry as fissured earth,
angry and sharp as the ineradicable
knowledge of chronic famine,
of human lives given to destitution
from birth to death. A laugh
in which the stench of ordure
simmered, round which a fog of flies
hovered, a laugh laughed to himself,
whether in despair or hatred, and not
as a form of address: he was indifferent
to whether I heard it or not.

Swift Month

The spirit of each day passes, head down
under the wind, arms folded.
Ambiguous brothers of those envisioned
'daughters of Time,' proffering neither
gifts nor scorn, their hands
grip elbows, hidden in wide sleeves
of shadow-colored caftans. Day after day
and none lagging, the pace of their stride
not hurried, yet swift, too swift.

A New Flower

Most of the sunflower's bright petals
had fallen, so I stripped the few
poised to go, and found myself
with a new flower: the center,
that round cushion of dark-roast
coffee brown, tipped with uncountable
minute florets of gold, more noticeable
now that the clear, shiny yellow was gone,
and around it a ring of green, the petals
from behind the petals, there all the time,
each having the form of sacred flame
or bo-tree leaf, a playful, jubilant form
(taken for granted in Paisley patterns)
and the light coming through them, so that
where, in double or triple rank, like a bevy
of Renaissance angels, they overlapped,
there was shadow, a darker shade
of the same spring green—a new flower
on this fall day, revealed within
the autumn of its own brief bloom.

A Cryptic Sign

August. The woods are silent.
No sway of treetops, no skitter of squirrels,
no startled bird. Sky fragments
in rifts of canopy,
palest silken blue.
                    In the crook
of an old and tattered snag
something gleams amid the stillness,
drawing the gaze: some bit of heartwood
so long exposed, weather and time
have polished it, as centuries
of awed lips, touching
a hand of stone, rub it
to somber gleaming.

Feet

I

In the forties, wartime London, I read
an ode by Neruda I've never found again,
about celery—celery the peasant, trudging
stony Andean ridges to market on poor
frayed feet.
                I could search out the *Obras Completas*
I know . . . But even if I never find it again,
those green fibrous feet, upholding
the tall stooped form with its flimsy cockscomb
of yellowing leaves, plodded
through me as if through the thin
mountain air, maintaining
their steady, painful, necessitous trudge, and left
their prints in my dust.

II

Travestied by Disney, the Mermaid's real story
has gone underground for now, as books do

if they're abused. As Andersen told it, the tale
was not for young children, not even called
'The Little'—just, 'The Mermaid.' It's about love and grief,
a myth of longing and sacrifice, far closer, say,
to Goethe's *Parable* than to any jovial folktale,
much less to today's manufactured juvenile distractions.

The Mer-folk live for three hundred years, then dissolve
in a foam of the wave, and forever vanish
into non-being; humans, the mermaid learns, rarely live
for even one hundred years, often far fewer, but they possess
immortal souls, and rise to continue living
in starlit regions merfolk can never see.
                        In her resolve to love and be loved
by the human prince she had rescued once
from storm and shipwreck, and gain for herself
such a soul, the mermaid goes to the terrible
ocean witch, and obtains a potion to turn her golden-scaled
fish-tail into legs and feet—
and gives up her voice in payment. She does this
knowing each gliding, graceful step she will take
will bring her the pain of walking on knives.
She does this for love, and the dream
of human joys and a deathless soul.
                        There's more,
much more to the story—even a kind of
happy ending, after the final sacrifice, a concession
Andersen made to his time and place. But what endures
along with the evocation of the undersea gardens,
of moonlight, of icebergs and coral, and of that same yearning
we find in the Silkie tales and in *The Forsaken Merman*,
are the knifeblades under her feet, unguessed-at
by any who see her glide and dance; and the torment
of having no tongue to speak her love, to speak
her longing to earn a soul.
                        Something in this
made my mother shed tears when she read it aloud,
her voice for a moment baffled—
and this when her closet was full of elegant shoes
with the pointed toes of fashion. Did she foresee (and forget
till the next reading) the misery
old age and poor circulation and years of those narrow shoes

would bring her? Certainly she had no doubt
of her own soul; no, what hurt her
was the mermaid's feet. Her agony without complaint,
her great love, courage, unfathomed sorrow,
would not have equally moved my mother
without that focussed sense of each step the mermaid took
being unbearable, yet borne, the firm support
we count on torn away, invisibly shredded.

III

I watched a man whose feet were neatly wrapped in green plastic enter
the restaurant that advertised a $2.00 special. Sloppy Joes. And I saw
him immediately come out again. It was cold and wet, and I was shel-
tering under the canvas awning till my bus was due. He stood there,
too and I could sense that he was fuming. 'What happened?' I ven-
tured. He looked at me. Good eyes, I thought. 'No shoes,' he said.

I know the rule, 'no shoes, no service' is supposed to be in the interests
of hygiene, but I've never understood how. Whatever dirt and germs
bare feet bring in, shoes bring too. Why anyone would want to walk
barefoot on filthy sidewalks is another mystery—but that's a matter of
personal choice. In this instance the man was, in any case, not bare-
foot: several layers of heavy-duty green garbage-bag plastic hid his
feet and were tied firmly at the ankles. The arrangement made me
think of Russian serfs, birchbark shoes . . .

'I've got the money,' he said, and showed it me in his hand—two
bucks, and a few pennies for tax. How *unfair*! He fumed, I fumed, the
rain poured off the awning, a steady curtain. He looked quite young,
under 40. Did I say he was Black? He hadn't the look of a drunk or a
druggy; looked a bit young for a Vietnam Vet. When I offered to go
in and protest to the manager he didn't like the idea, and I saw he
would feel it a humiliation. I shouldn't have suggested that.

'What happened to your shoes—did they fall apart?' I asked shyly. 'A
guy stole them in the night.' I acknowledged, silently, the naiveté of
my own shock at this robbery of one destitute man by another. He
could get some second-hand shoes at Goodwill or the Salvation Army,
he told me, but he was hungry, had wanted to eat before the long walk
to the missions. I guessed he had spent the night under the freeway.
This street where we stood, near the college, was mostly upscale—

this 'luncheon special' at a place which referred to itself as an 'Eatery,' was the only thing of its kind. I thought with disgust of Sloppy Joes, trying to imagine being hungry enough to want one.

I offered him the price of a pair of the cheapest shoes you could buy; I'd noticed them in the window of an Outlet store. He accepted with dignity. When I found myself wondering if in fact he would spend the money on shoes, I realized he might do better with good hand-me-downs than cheap new ones. By then the rain let up and we went our ways.

If affluent Whites took it into their heads to wrap their feet in plastic, a new fashion, how long would the 'eateries' exclude them?

IV

Still in her 80s when she first lived there,
       she loved
              to tramp over the *cerro* above the town;
it reminded her
       of Wales and the freedom
            of long girlhood walks in all weathers.
Here as there, the hills and mountains,
       layer beyond layer,
            ranged themselves like advancing breakers,
though they broke on no shore;
       cloud-shadows stroked them, brightness
            flowed in again as the shadows
moved on. But in time
       her strength failed her.
            She walked only down to the town's
mercado to buy the fruit she craved,
       and exchange a word or two
            with the market women,
the vendors of juice or trinkets, and give her letters,
       into the hands of sour-faced
            post-office clerks. In the *Zócalo*
she could watch with pleasure the playing children
       or with amusement
            the foolish antics of tourists. Everywhere
the familiar faces of strangers.
       Then, climbing back up the hilly streets,
            ill-paved, high-kerbed, often,

by her mid-80s, she needed to pause,
        to stop and rest in a cool dark church.
                Once, and more than once, perhaps,
her feet pained her so much that weakness
        overcame her,
                she sat there crying,
desolate in the need to rise and walk on,
        four or five blocks to her room,
                her bed, her books, her patio—
accidental pilgrim
        in a strange land.
                When, my next visit,
I'd found her slippers padded and soft
        yet sturdy enough for the *calle*
                you'd think I'd brought her the moon and stars . . .

We begin our lives with such small,
        such plump and perfect
                infant feet, slivers of pink pearl for toenails,
it's laughable to think of their ever sustaining
        the whole weight of a body.
                And end them sometimes
with gnarled and twisted objects
        in which are inscribed
                whole histories—wars, and uprootings,
and long
        patient or impatient sufferings,
                layer beyond layer,
successions of light and shadow, whole ranges.
        But no recollection
                of what our feet were like
before we put them to work.

V

Certain phrases recur—not main motifs but occasional
mini-cadenzas on flute, curling
brief as foam above stir and onrush of waves.
'Beautiful are the feet of the swallow
folded unseen past the mountain'—
or, 'Blessèd are the feet
of him who brings good tidings.'

Beautiful, too one's own feet if they've stayed
more or less straight and strong through decades,
and one walks for miles by the sea or through fields and woods
or spends a joyful day in a great museum, arriving
at opening time, staying till closing, grateful to be so upheld.

Yet what prevails is harsh. The mermaid's knives.
My mother's tears. Or the shame
an aging poet felt when, bulky in body, diabetic,
she had to call upon someone to cut her toenails, and not just anyone,
someone (small and deft) in whose country we were guests,
a country our own was bombing, defoliating, attempting,
with all its mechanical power,
                                    to obliterate.
With exacting care the Vietnamese nurse performed the procedure,
a doctor checked to see all was as close to well as possible,
and Muriel obediently stretched out her long thin legs, submitting,
grateful but deeply embarrassed: these ministrations
were given by those accustomed to dress the wounds
of footless or armless children,
of peasants whose hands were gone. Her feet
felt better, her soul was mortified.

And still those brief cadenzas
recur—'Blessèd are the feet
of him who brings good tidings,'—'Beautiful
are the feet of the swallow
folded unseen past the mountain.'

VI

Maundy Thursday. As prearranged, twelve chairs
are placed in a row before the altar, and twelve parishioners
seat themselves, and take off their shoes and clean socks.
As the old priest and the young one bend to their task,
one stiff, one supple, and carry the shining bowls of fresh warm water
to each presented pair of prewashed feet,
and wash them again and dry them on white, white towels,
the humble ritual, so ancient, so much an act of the body,
a sanctification of flesh (even though, at times,
proud prelates and small bigotted men have been the enactors)
stirs the heart, as true theater must, even in an age
with so loose or lost a connection to symbolic power.

But this is a good time to reflect on how dusty,
scarred by worn sandals, dirty between the toes, grime
on the calloused soles, the apostles' feet would have been.
And mind moves on to worse: old winos stumbling along,
unwashed, their long nails thick as horn, shoes wrong-sized, broken.
And not just winos—anyone homeless, who has to keep moving all day
with no place to go, even if shelter at night
gives them a chance to bathe their blisters, must know
week by week an accretion of weariness, once-good shoes
grown thin; must know a mounting sense of frayed and helpless
fiber at the ends of swollen legs, although they have never imagined
the endless foot-after-foot journey of peasant celery.

Fugitives

The Red Cross vans, laden with tanks of
drinking water, can go no further:
the road has become a river.
The dry, dusty, potholed road
that was waiting the rainy season
is flowing with men and women
(especially women) and children.
Silent in stumbling haste,
almost all of them. Only the wailing
of young babies, hungry and terrified,
wafts over the lava-flow
that brims and hurries, dividing briefly
to pass the impediment that each van
is to them, impervious to their purpose
(the first one caught in the flood,
the remaining small convoy already attempting
to back, inch by inch, to where, miles behind them,
they might turn).
                        From a plane,
the road—the river—would look
like one of those horrible nature films
about insects moving as one in some
instinctive ritual; horrible because
though one by one each creature might have
some appealing feature, *en masse* they are

inexorable, a repulsive teeming collective . . .
But these are people, and the Red Cross driver,
one of the last to remain in what seems
an unhelpable land of terror, knows it,
sees it, feels it. He has not the distant
impersonal gaze of a pilot high overhead watching
an insect swarm. He deeply perceives
war has deprived these humans, his fellows,
of choice of action. Diminished them. And they advance,
dazed, haggard, unstoppable, driven
less by what shreds of hope may cling to their bodies
than by a despair that might well have left them
paralyzed in the dust, inert before imminent slaughter,
but which some reflex, some ancient trigger in brain-tissue,
propels into grim motion thousand upon thousand,
westward to zones Relief has already fled from.

Dark Looks

Strange: today the mountain
—circled by curly cherub clouds
beyond the glittering lake
and vague middle-distance—

looks dark, not snowy,
at odds with the benign
October light, a frowning
humorless old prophet,

sullen among the *putti*.

'Memory demands so much'

Memory demands so much,
it wants every fiber
told and retold.
                It gives and gives
but for a price, making you

risk drudgery, lapse
into document, treacheries
of glaring noon and a slow march.
Leaf never before
seen or envisioned, flying spider
of rose-red autumn, playing
a lone current of undecided wind,
lift me with you, take me
off this ground of memory that clings
to my feet like thick clay,
exacting gratitude for gifts and gifts.
Take me flying before
you vanish, leaf, before
I have time to remember you,
intent instead on being
in the midst of that flight,
of those unforeseeable words.

Roast Potatoes

Before the Wholesale Produce Market
moved to the Bronx, what wild
Arabian scenes there'd be each night
across from our 5th floor window—
the trucks arriving from all over
as if at a caravanserai under the weird
orange-bright streetlights
(or was it the canvas awnings that were orange,
sheltering the carrots, the actual oranges . . .)
Great mounds of fruit, mountain ranges
of vegetables spread in the stalls, and now
more unloading, and the retail trucks
rolling up to bargain and buy till dawn . . .
Unemployed men, casual labor, hung around,
waiting for clean-up jobs; some were glad
to get some bruised produce if no work.
And the Catholic Worker pickup
 came by at the last
for anything unsold, unsaleable (but not
uncookable). In the '60s

there was the Bowery, yes, and ordinary
urban winos, but not
throngs of homeless men
and hardly ever a homeless woman except
for those you'd see down at Maryhouse or sometimes
(conspicuous, embarrassing), in the waiting room at Grand Central.
There were men, though, among those frequenting the market,
who clearly had no fixed abode; we though of them
as old fashioned hobos.
Some time in the night, or weekends
when the big parking lot, the whole
commercial neighborhood (vanished now), was deserted,
they'd build fires in old metal barrels
and sit round them on upturned crates
roasting fallen potatoes they'd salvaged,
(a regular feast once when a truck
lost its load) and talking, telling stories,
passing a bottle if they had one.
The war was (remotely) gearing up,
Vietnam a still unfamiliar name,
the men were down on their luck,
some White, some Black, not noticeably hostile,
most of them probably drunks:
you couldn't call it
a Golden Age; and yet
around those fires, those roasting potatoes,
you could see, even from our top-storey windows,
not even down there catching the smoky
potato-skin smell or hearing
fragments of talk and laughter—*something*
—you name it, if you know, I can't . . .
something you might call blessèd? Is that hyperbole? Something kind?
Something not to be found in the '90s, anyway.
Something it seems we'll have to enter the next millennium
lacking, and for the young,
                              unknown to memory.

Visitation. Overflow.

1

The slender evidence . . .

The *you must take*
my word for it.

The intake of a word.
Its taste, cloud in the mouth.

The presence, invisible,
impalpable, air to
outstretched arms,

but voiced, tracked easily
in room's geography,
among the maps, the gazing-window,
door, fire, all in place, internal
space immutable.

The slenderness
of evidence, narrow backed
tapir undulating
away on
rainforest paths, each tapir bearing
a human soul.

2

Amazon basin,
filling, overflowing,
spirits in every
plant, in bark, in every
animal, in
juice of bark. Words taken

by lips, tongue, teeth, throat,
down into body's
caverns, to enter

blood, bone, breath, as here:

as here the presence
next to that window, appearance

known not to sight,
                to touch,
but to hearing, yes, and yet
appearing, apprehended

in form, in color, by
some sense unnamed,

3

moving slenderly
doorwards, assured, re-
assuring, leaving

a trace, of certainty, promise
broader than slender
tapir's disappearing
sturdy back, the
you can only
take my
word for it, a life,
a phase,
beyond the
known geography, beyond familiar

inward, outward,
outward, inward. A

'time and place' (other terms
                unavailing)
of learning, of casting
off of dross, as when

hunters steam off fur, skin,
feathers in cauldrons, leaving

the flesh to share
with all, the humble
feast, slender

evidence, take it
or leave it, I give you
my word.

'The mountain's daily speech is silence'

The mountain's daily speech is silence.
Profound as the Great Silence
between the last Office and the first.
Uninterrupted as the silence God maintains
throughout the layered centuries.
All the mountain's moods,
frank or evasive,
its whiteness, its blueness,
are shown to sight alone.
Yet it is known
that fire seethes in its depths
and will surely rise one day, breaking open
the mute imperturbable summit. Will the roar of eruption be
the mountain's own repressed voice,
or that of the fire? Does the mountain
harbor a demon distinct from itself?

'Scraps of moon'

Scraps of moon
bobbing discarded on broken water

but sky-moon
complete, transcending

all violation.

Mass of the Moon Eclipse

Not more slowly than frayed
human attention can bear, but slow
enough to be stately, deliberate, a ritual
we can't be sure will indeed move
from death into resurrection.
As the bright silver inch by inch
is diminished, options vanish,
life's allurements. The last sliver
lies face down, back hunched, a husk.

But then, obscured, the whole sphere can be seen
to glow from behind its barrier shadow: bronze,
unquenchable, blood-light. And slowly,
more slowly than desolation overcame, overtook
the light, the light
is restored, outspread in a cloudless pasture of
spring darkness where firefly planes
fuss to and fro, and humans
turn off their brief attention
in secret relief. No matter: the rite
contains its power, whether or not
our witness rises toward it;
grandeur plays out the implacable drama
without even flicking aside our trivial
absence, the impatience with which we
fail to respond.
               And yet

we are spoken to, and sometimes
we do stop, do, do give ourselves leave
to listen, to watch. The moon,
the moon we do after all
love, is dying, are we to live
on in a world without moon? We swallow
a sour terror. Then
that coppery sphere, no-moon become once more
full-moon, visible in absence.
And still without haste, silver
increment by silver
increment, the familiar, desired,

disregarded brilliance
is given again, given and given.

Once Only

All which, because it was
flame and song and granted us
joy, we thought we'd do, be, revisit,
turns out to have been what it was
that *once*, only; every initiation
did not begin
a series, a build-up: the marvelous
       did happen in our lives, our stories
       are not drab with its absence: but don't
expect now to return for more. Whatever more
there will be will be
unique as those were unique. Try
to acknowledge the next
song in its body-halo of flames as utterly
present, as now or never.

Mid-December

Westering a sun a mist of gold
between solemnities of crowded vertical
poplar twigs. The mountain's
western slope is touched
weightlessly with what will be, soon,
the afterglow.

Translucence

Once I understood (till I forget, at least)
the immediacy of new life, Vita Nuova,
redemption not stuck in linear delays,
I perceived also (for now) the source

of unconscious light in faces
I believe are holy, not quite transparent,
more like the half-opaque whiteness
of Japanese screens or lampshades,
grass or petals imbedded in that paper-thin
substance which is not paper as this is paper,
and which permits the passage of what is luminous
though forms remain unseen behind its protection.
I perceived that in such faces, through
the translucence we see, the light we intuit
is of the already resurrected, each
a Lazarus, but a Lazarus (man or woman)
without the memory of tomb or of any
swaddling bands except perhaps
the comforting ones of their first
infant hours, the warm receiving-blanket . . .
They know of themselves nothing different
from anyone else. This great unknowing
is part of their holiness. They are always trying
to share out joy as if it were cake or water,
something ordinary, not rare at all.

Drawn in Air

The arc of branch is not perfect.
Before it reaches
conclusion (and the gratuitous
upcurve of terminal twig,
a playful coda), it falters, losing
for a moment the impetus
that arched its outsetting.
This brief hesitation into
straightness; that post-arrival
flourish; and the way,
being a branch, it tapers, even
the arc's upmost passage
more slender than when it left
the main stem: these,
taken together, are what
gives this unremarkable branch

of an aging, tallish, unpruned peartree
its peculiar charm,
the charm of a master's line—
Degas, Holbein, chalk or pencil,
gathering strength and emphasis,
letting it wane, suggesting
contour but offering to the eyes
a pleasure in simply
line as line.

Noblesse Oblige

With great clarity, great precision, today
the mountain presents not only
all of its height but a keener sense
of breadth. It seems
nearer than usual;
yet it maintains
the lonely grandeur nothing can challenge:
this open approach,
this way of proclaiming that spring
at last is come, this ceremonious
baring of snowy breast as if
its arms were thrown wide, is not
an attempt at intimacy.
                    (Meanwhile,
          the April sun, cold though it is,
          has opened the small daisies,
          so many and so humble they get underfoot—
          and don't care. Each one
          a form of laughter.)
The mountain graciously continues
its measured self-disclosure.

Masquerade

Today the mountain,
playful and not omniscient, thinks itself

concealed among
attendant clouds.
                        Their white and blue
            are a perfect match for yours,
            O mountain! But you are no more hidden
            by complacent cumulus
            than Venus by a mask
            of black Venetian velvet.
            Like a *cavaliere*
            astounded, in the piazza's twilight throng,
            to discern her goddess-flesh,
            I recognize
            amidst imponderable white
            wafting billows, your naive force,
            mountain,
                dense, unmoving.

Enduring Love

It was the way
as they climbed the steps
they appeared bit by bit
yet swiftly—
the tops of their hats
then their faces
looking in as they reached
the top step by the door, then
as I flung the door open
their dear corporeal selves,
first him, then her. It was
the simultaneously
swift and gradual advent
of such mercy after
I had been wounded.
It was the little familiar
net attached to her hat,
it was especially
the thick soft cloth of his black
clerical overcoat,
and their short stature

and their complete
comforting embrace,
the long-dead
visiting time from eternity.

Immersion

There is anger abroad in the world, a numb thunder,
because of God's silence. But how naive,
to keep wanting words we could speak ourselves,
English, Urdu, Tagalog, the French of Tours,
the French of Haiti . . .
                              Yes, that was one way omnipotence chose
to address us—Hebrew, Aramaic, or whatever the patriarchs
chose in their turn to call what they heard. Moses
demanded the word, spoken and written. But perfect freedom
assured other ways of speech. God is surely
patiently trying to immerse us in a different language,
events of grace, horrifying scrolls of history
and the unearned retrieval of blessings lost for ever,
the poor grass returning after drought, timid, persistent.
God's abstention is only from human dialects. The holy vice
utters its woe and glory in myriad musics, in signs and portents.
Our own words are for us to speak, a way to ask and to answer.

A Clearing

What lies at the end of enticing
country driveways, curving
off among trees? Often only
a car graveyard, a house-trailer,
a trashy bungalow. But this one,
for once, brings you
through the shade of its green tunnel
to a paradise of cedars,
of lawns mown but not too closely,
of iris, moss, fern, rivers of stone rounded
by sea or stream,

of a wooden unassertive large-windowed house.
The big trees enclose
an expanse of sky, trees and sky
together protect the clearing.
One is sheltered here
from the assaultive world
as if escaped from it, and yet
once arrived, is given (oneself
and others being a part of that world)
a generous welcome.
                              It's paradise
as a paradigm for how
to live on earth,
how to be private and open
quiet and richly eloquent.
Everything man-made here
was truly made by the hands
of those who live here, of those
who live with what they have made.
It took time, and is growing still
because it's alive.
It is paradise, and paradise
is a kind of poem; it has
a poem's characteristics:
inspiration; starting with the given;
unexpected harmonies; revelations.
It's rare among
the worlds one finds
at the end of enticing driveways.

Southern Cross

(After a sculpture by Philip McCracken)

A darkness rivered, swirled, meandered
by fathomless fiery currents.
Dense abyss of planes and angles,
pinned by unblinking constellations,
celestial stigmata.
And at the core,
bright blood of the wounded wood

(not cut, riven
by secret canker
now revealed)
tardily down the rough cleft
descends and beads.

Descending Sequence

'It was a fearful thing
to come into a man's heart . . . '
—*William Carlos Williams, "Winter Sunset"*

What I thought to be a river
turned out to be sky.
What I thought were shore, island,
rocks, river-mist,
turned out to be cloud, shadow,
shot-holes in sky's canvas.
Even the deepest shade
down near the horizon
turned out not to be earth,
the real horizon was lower still.
At the oblong world's
very base,
further darkness, a round-topped tree,
a telephone pole, the sharp
ridge of a roof, chimney, gable end:
silhouettes on a sky
differently white, not the illusory
river's whiteness—and all
very small under the huge
vista above. Small,
as if in fear.

Alienation in Silicon Valley

I'd like to invoke a different world,
a history more past than future, yes,
but present in fragments, hinting itself onward

in here a word or there a grace that's
taken for granted—evoke and hold it.
Ancestral, painful, but mine by right.
But soberly I have to admit
it's only by virtue of being outside those worlds
I can perceive them.
                        What can I make, then,
of this one, inside it
but not at home? 'Here,' de Toqueville said,
(not this far west, but at what was then the edge)
'they live from hand to mouth,
like an army on the march—'
severed from history.
I am told of orchards, clouds of blossom,
crimson peaches, fragrant apricots,
forty years back, fifty at most, where now
a vacuous clutter of buildings fills up
square mile after mile; and I can cast
on my mind's screen an orchard,
acres of orchards—but I never
touched their earth. Nostalgia
comes if it must, but is not for borrowing.
I see, I know, the desecration, I taste
the degrading sickly bile of that knowledge—
but I did not witness flower or fruit,
a specific locus, ancestral ground.
What I hold are the links the mind
forges between a vanished field of imagined trees
and their peers remembered, the shine
of stolen cherries, far off
in time and in place; and also by now perhaps
vanished, that field built over.

Moments of Joy

A scholar takes a room on the next street,
the better to concentrate on his unending work, his word,
his world. His grown children
feel bereft. He comes and goes while they sleep.
But at times it happens a son or daughter

wakes in the dark and finds him sitting
at the foot of the bed
in the old rocker; sleepless
in his old coat, gazing
into invisible distance, but clearly there to protect
as he had always done.
                        The child springs up and flings
arms about him, presses
a cheek to his temple, taking him by surprise,
and exclaims, 'Abba!'—the old, intimate name
from the days of infancy.
And the old scholar, the father,
is deeply glad to be found.
That's how it is, Lord, sometimes:
You seek, and I find.

Thinking about Paul Celan

Saint Celan,
stretched on the cross
of survival,

pray for us. You
at last could endure
no more. But we

live and live,
blithe in a world
where children kill children.

We shake off
the weight of
our own exemption,

we flourish,
we exceed
our allotted days.

Saint Celan,
pray for us
that we receive

at least a bruise,
blue, blue, unfading,
we who accept survival.

Aware

When I opened the door
I found the vine leaves
speaking among themselves in abundant
whispers.
        My presence made them
hush their green breath,
embarrassed, the way
humans stand up, buttoning their jackets,
acting as if they were leaving anyway, as if
the conversation had ended
just before you arrived.
                I liked
the glimpse I had, though,
of their obscure
gestures. I liked the sound
of such private voices. Next time
I'll move like cautious sunlight, open
the door by fractions, eavesdrop
peacefully.

AFTERWORD

by PAUL A. LACEY
and
ANNE DEWEY

Collected here are all the books of poetry Denise Levertov published or intended to publish, starting from her earliest poems in World War II and her first book, *The Double Image* (1946), which she never reprinted in full except in a late fine-press limited edition (Brooding Heron Press, 1991), through eighteen more books, concluding with her posthumous *This Great Unknowing* (1999). Two mutually reinforcing ways to understand Levertov's body of work are to trace her life's trajectory in it and to name some of her dominant themes. She said she always wrote from what was happening in her life, and her poetry gives eloquent voice to what she has seen, heard and experienced of family life, of war and injustice, and as a powerful witness for social, political and economic justice as the foundation of peace. In "The Phone Call" (1974) she calls politics "the word I use to mean striving for peace and for mercy . . . " As a child, she met intellectual leaders and artists, refugees sheltered in her family's home and she demonstrated publicly with her parents and sister against fascism. She sold copies of *The Daily Worker* and wanted to join the British communist party but was too young.

She always writes out of her life as daughter and sister, wife and mother, lover, lifelong pilgrim and seeker for spiritual meaning, from belief in the power of the artist's transformative vision. Her career emerges with the full flowering of literary modernism, the aftermath of World War One and the Great Depression; and her poetry's changes and innovations strive to continue the experimentation driven by a modernist sense of the poet's vocation as a seer and craftsperson to meet the challenges of the modern world: its worldwide political and social revolutions (the rise of communism, fascism and Nazism, the Spanish Civil War, World War Two, the Cold War and prolonged conflicts in Nicaragua and El Salvador, Vietnam and the Persian Gulf), struggles for race and gender equality, a global, political and ecological consciousness and multiplicity of cultural and religious traditions. In her later years she wrote intense, touchstone poems on religious experience, which this essay examines below.

From her youth, Levertov had a facility with language and delighted in the auditory, visual and musical dimensions of the natural world, which she described and celebrated in her poetry. Primarily home-schooled until the age of twelve, she wrote her first poem at age five, studied ballet, drew, and played the piano, pursuing ballet seriously until she decided to enter nurse's training at age nineteen. Her strong sense of a literary vocation led her as a teenager to seek advice from T. S. Eliot and Herbert Read, and her first published poems reflect the lush neoromanticism pervasive in British writing of the 1940s.

In 1948, Levertov and her husband Mitchell Goodman moved to New York. Their son Nikolai was born a year later. Her creative process developed around several generative friendships from which emerged the new poetics of presence evident in her next two books, *Here and Now* (1956) and *Overland to the Islands* (1958), and formalized in her 1965 "Some Notes on Organic Form." A significant articulation of the poetics of a new generation of innovative poets, the essay calls for fidelity to "organic" form as not merely an extension but "a revelation of content," of the thing or interplay among things as perceived in the poet's "inscape" and reflected in poetic "instress," words she adopted from Gerard Manly Hopkins.

Levertov followed a lifelong practice of keeping extensive journals and notebooks in which she recorded quotations from her reading, ideas for and drafts of poems, notations of her daily experience, and reflections on the working of her conscious mind. She always kept track of her dream-life and what the unconscious taught her. Her poetry also emerged in rich dialogue with others. During the next decade, she became immersed in the post-war avant garde, forming close friendships with older poets such as William Carlos Williams and H.D.; and those of her generation such as Robert Creeley and Robert Duncan, who, among others, were assimilating Pound's craft and Williams's concrete sensuality and American idiom. Together they forged the poetics of presence and orality central to post-war experimentation. These were heady times for poets who had been working in isolation, now thrilling at the discovery of kindred spirits and entering into intense exchanges about poetry and poetics. Envelopes thick with letters and typescripts crossed continents and oceans, were received with excitement, marked up, commented on, and returned to the author to spark the next breakthrough. Finally, translation proved a third significant place for Levertov's experimentation and creative development, leading sometimes to publication but often not, simply enabling exploration of her own language and style through continual conversation with friends. These extensive records, archived with her papers in the Green Library at Stanford University, undergird her finished poetry and prose.

The small, isolated poetry communities of the 1950s (New York, San Francisco, Black Mountain) grew, gained consciousness of their role as leaders in the New American Poetry and became increasingly politicized, involved in the growing youth movements and political protests against the Vietnam War, for liberal reform in the U.S., and for racial and gender equality. Like many, Levertov was moved to adapt her poetics of presence to record and lend her vision to the war resistance movement and write protest poetry. With this growth, her circle of interlocutors and debate widens to include questions of how to write political poetry, exchanges on feminism with Adrienne Rich, on feminism and resistance to racism with Audre Lorde and Lucille Clifton. In the 1950s, she and Mitch had refused to take shelter during mock air raids, along with pacifist organizations and members of the Catholic Worker Movement. This was the first of many demonstrations in which she was arrested. By 1968 they were central figures in draft resistance. Perhaps some student of her public life will be able to document how often she got arrested and how many nights she spent in jail. Her documentary long poem "To Stay Alive" (1972) remains significant testimony to the intense pressures on poets who tried to address politics in relation to the crisis of poetic authority and democratic voice. That crisis produced both a great deal of conflicted political poetry in the 1960s and also powerful creative response to the tension. The crisis of overextended life and poetry recorded in "To Stay Alive" leads Levertov to question her earlier poetics; she experiments with new formal devices, such as making something like an abecedary catalogue, to find her way back to language she can trust to tell the truth again. She seeks the stability of her childhood European and literary roots to sustain and refresh the earlier transformative power of her poetic vision and craft. She struggles to anchor poetic vision as responsive and responsible to a community, itself difficult to forge in the socially fragmented, politically disillusioned post-1960s world. Present and past, both literary and political, fuse in her later poetry, which Paul Giles has described as "a magical transposition of past and present," a "double vision" or "transatlantic circuit linked by the disjunctive juxtapositions of surrealism."

Levertov's intensified religious spirituality and her ecological consciousness grow in tandem as forces of unity and empathy in which to ground community and poetic vision. Both Catholic spirituality and literary touchstones, from Julian of Norwich to Rilke, become the ground that sustains and inspires her new poetic vision.

Levertov breaks significant new ground in establishing women as professionals in a poetry establishment changing rapidly with second-wave feminism. She chose emphatically not to call herself a feminist ("I don't believe I have ever made an aesthetic decision based on my gender"). "If a writer has [an intense awareness of artistic ethics], his or her art will transcend gender." Yet both her professional activity and her poetry help to transform gender hierarchies.

She resists being cast in the role of protégée to mentor, attempting instead to open more egalitarian relationships with Duncan, Rexroth, Zukofsky and others. As reviewer and poetry editor for Norton Publishers and poetry editor for *The New Republic* and at least interim editor in other journals, she shapes critical taste and the terms on which her generation's poetry is received. If her work as editor establishes an authoritative woman's voice shaping poetry as institution during her generation, her poetry also helps free women from traditional roles in its courage in rewriting traditional feminine and sexual roles, its imagination of feminine muses and goddesses as a source of poetic vision.

Space permits only a brief noting of her favorite touchstone-words, among them "dreams" and its associated forms—"wanderer" and "pilgrim." These recur and sketch in many of the contours of her life. Levertov did not accept Freud's analysis of the dream-life as evidence of neurosis, turning instead to Carl Jung's emphasis on the health-giving character of the deep-welled collective unconscious. Whenever she sought the help of therapy, she turned to Jungian analysts. In her foreword to Robert Bosnak's book, *A Little Course in Dreams* (Shambala, 1986) she says Bosnak "leads the reader to perceive the importance to society, the political value, of increasing our attention to those powerful aspects of our being that go uncomprehended in the ignored dreamlife of billions."

Albert Gelpi calls her way of perceiving the world "incarnational." Others praise her "sacramental vision." That is to say, it exemplifies the catechism's definition: discerning in the outward world visible signs of an inward and spiritual grace. Though for many of her adult years, she described herself as an agnostic, her writing always grew out of reverence. In "Some Notes on Organic Form" (1965) she calls finding the organic form a method of apperception, based on practicing observation as contemplation, i.e. the activity that occurs in the temple, "in the presence of a god."

In her later poetry, even as she continues to struggle with belief, "god" becomes "God," addressed as "Thou" in the "Credo" of her

"Mass for the Day of St. Thomas Didymus." She believes and interrupts her belief with doubt; doubts and interrupts it with belief. This reminds us that an agnostic is one who cannot be sure of what she can know. Two powerful poems in *Candles in Babylon* (1982), "Talk in the Dark" and "Writing in the Dark," tell what it means to keep faith with whatever little we know. The epigraph to *Life in the Forest* (1978) is Henry James's poignant "We work in the dark. We do what we can. We give what we have. Our doubt is our passion. Our passion is our task. The rest is the madness of art."

"Writing in the Dark" precisely describes how to record with paper and pencil, words and images brought to us in sleep. In both poems, darkness is a benign matrix allowing true speech and poetry to emerge. In her earliest poems, the rhythms are regular, and rhyme—which she later called "anachronistic" in contemporary poetry—appears infrequently but deliberately. In the two quatrains of "Listening to Distant Guns" (1940) she rhymes "eye," "dry" and "fly," "screams" and "dreams." "A Dream of Cornwall" (1946) uses rhyme to close the first and fourth lines of its three quatrains. In some of her late, avowedly Christian, poetry we recognize deliberate but light use of rhyme, notably in some sections of "Mass for the Day of St. Thomas Didymus" (*Candles in Babylon*) and "The Avowal" in homage to George Herbert (*Oblique Prayers*). She seems to want these poems to capture the stateliness of traditional Christian liturgy and music.

"Poem" (1946) introduces another of her lifelong preoccupations, the life of the wanderer: "Some are too much at home in the role of wanderer, / / watcher, listener . . ." Though she loves and cherishes her family roles, a settled life seems temporary for her. There is always the lure of the pilgrim's or wanderer's hard, dry life, trudging—another of her favorite words, here from "The Olga Poems" (*The Sorrow Dance*, 1967)—over dusty roads, always the seeker.

If it is the pilgrim's calling to live in a spiritual quest, Levertov also knows that the obverse of the pilgrim would be the restless outcast. In "Poet and Person" (*Candles in Babylon*) she writes of hosts who are happy to see her arrive but soon glad to see her go. "I brought with me / too much . . . my desire to please and worse— / my desire to judge." So she says she leaves as she came, alone. In a late essay about place, she calls herself an "airplant," growing in midair, without place or need to put down roots.

For her, art grants a provisional, vital resting place for the driven seeker, the outcast pilgrim. Art thrives in the borderland, provides "an interface / immeasurable, elusive—an equilibrium. . . ." From birth

"A goy among Jews, a Jew among Christians," she imagines "The borderland—that's where if one knew how, one would establish residence. . . ." There "fictive truth" emerges from "impasto surface" "thick striate . . . swathes of carnal paint." She gives the same intense, reverent attention to details in works of art as she does the natural world.

She draws on the deep streams of childhood recollection, especially the pleasures of Valentines Park and its wishing well. When she reads Martin Buber's *Tales of the Hasidim*, she locates herself at the intersection of her parents' bloodlines. "Illustrious Ancestors" (*Overland to the Islands*) affirms her Jewish line of descent from "the Rav of Northern White Russia" equally with her descent from "Angel Jones of Mold," the Welsh mystic and tailor who sews his meditations into the garments he makes. "Believing some line still taut" between herself and those ancestors, she embraces the qualities of their two vocations to write poems direct, hard, sound, mysterious and silent.

In her writing, as in her daily life, maintaining connection matters deeply. Her first, tentative experiments in the William Carlos Williams mode, "An Innocent (I and II)" date from the mid-1950s. In "Williams: an Essay" (*Candles in Babylon*) she says:

> He loved
> persistence—but it must
> be linked to invention: landing
> backwards 'facing
> into the wind's teeth,'
>   to please him.
>
> He loved
> the lotus cup . . .
>
> and the long stem of connection.

With *Relearning the Alphabet* (1970) the prolongation of the Vietnam War so darkens her vision that she distrusts the ease with which she previously wrote out of what she now thinks her unearned, incarnational, sacramental vision. "A Cloak" begins with an epigram from W. B. Yeats's poem of the same title: "there's more enterprise in walking naked." Hobbled by doubt, in "The Cold Spring" she asks "what if my poem is deathsongs?" In "Advent, 1966" she says the napalm burning of children in Vietnam has filmed over her poet's "clear caressive sight."

The poem "Relearning the Alphabet" marks a new beginning through a return to the elementary building-blocks of written language. Before the poem comes the alphabet, the child's abecedary book and the little song that has helped us learn the letters and their essential, exact order. This perfect mnemonic teaching-song organizes the letters into a rhyming poem:

> abcd efg
> hijk lmnop
> qrs tuv
> wx y(&)z.

Alphabetizing is a brilliant intellectual invention which gives us a tool to organize and categorize the overwhelming accumulation of information and facts in our libraries. It is a tool available to anyone who memorizes that little mnemonic.

Only *Candles in Babylon*, which recalls the childhood rhyme, "How Many Miles to Babylon?" suggests a comparable return to first things and the comfort of a promise "that we may return / from this place of terror / home to a calm dawn and / the work we had just begun."

Though she never completely stopped grieving for the lost vision, she persisted in writing from her life's passionate concerns. She found herself turning away from her agnosticism to Christian praxis, initially back to the High Church Anglicanism of her upbringing and ultimately to communion in the Roman Catholic Church. About her "Mass for the Day of St. Thomas Didymus"—doubting Thomas, her patron saint—she has said that she was an agnostic when she began writing it and had become once more a Christian when the Mass was completed. Exploring the Mass, the liturgical form she had known from childhood, she had imagined and written and prayed her way back to faith. Her openness to Christian mystics, especially *The Showings of Dame Julian of Norwich* and Brother Lawrence's *The Practice of the Presence of God* inspired her several Julian poems and "The Conversion of Brother Lawrence." "Caedmon" elaborates the Venerable Bede's story of another outcast, the lonely, tongue-tied brother who goes to keep company with the barn animals, where divine inspiration unlocks his tongue and gives him poems. Velázquez's painting "The Servant-Girl at Emmaus" appears in the same section of *Breathing the Water* (1987) with "Caedmon" and some of the Julian poems.

The term "religious poetry" is commonly used but needs examination. Samuel Johnson argues in *The Life of Waller* that since poetry must be inventive and create delight by producing unexpected surprises, there can be no religious poetry, since the "topics of devotion" are few, already known to all believers and therefore unable to produce surprise. That argument might have made sense in a time when belief was widely shared in a culture, but Johnson's was not such an age, a fact he dealt with by denying doubts and abusing doubters. He ignored George Herbert's *Sacred Poems*, which he loved. Of course, he never got to read (and perhaps would have deplored) Matthew Arnold's "Dover Beach," whose sea of faith has receded in a "melancholy, long, withdrawing roar" nor Thomas Hardy's "The Oxen," where the poet recalls the fantasy that the oxen kneel in the stable on Christmas Eve. "So fair a fancy few would weave / In these years," though he wishes "it might be so." Johnson could not have imagined the devout Jesuit Gerard Manly Hopkins's "I'll not, carrion comfort, Despair, / not feed on thee." Nor could he have read Wallace Stevens' "Sunday Morning," whose speaker, though living "unsponsored, free" in elegant quiet comfort in a skeptical age, says, "But in contentment I still feel / The need of some imperishable bliss." He could not know the profound influence of T. S. Eliot's "Ash Wednesday," "Because I do not hope to turn again. / Because I do not hope," inevitably pointing to the turmoil and doubt of Good Friday, and the *Four Quartets'* "Dry Salvages," "People change and smile, but the agony abides." Johnson would not have imagined W. H. Auden's Christmas Oratorio "For the Time Being" (1944), nor his "Friday's Child" in memory of Dietrich Bonhoeffer: "Now, did He really break the seal / And rise again? We dare not say; / But conscious unbelievers feel / Quite sure of Judgment Day."

Those are all poems from the world of anxious doubt and tentative faith which Levertov and we have inherited. They show it is possible to recast sacred stories, to meditate on the paintings of Velázquez and the writings of Julian of Norwich, to make midrash and poetry of such content. Johnson easily speaks of "topics of devotion," but Levertov does not entertain "topics;" she testifies to faith's birth-throes and fragile survival out of disbelief. "Devotion" means practicing Levertov's "oblique prayers," intense focusing of the mind and spirit on Eliot's "hints followed by guesses." Devotion animates the pilgrim's search, and the doubter's affirmation, "you can, you must proceed."

Can we imagine modern poetry without that kind of devotional poetry?

In *Breathing the Water* she tells in "The Spirits Appeased" of finding books she needs, waiting for her on her parents' bookshelves, inscribed by their hands, and imagines them saying "Now she is paying attention, now she sees . . ."

Sands of the Well returns to variations and reflections on themes in Rilke's poetry. "Primal Speech" and "For Those Whom the Gods Love Less" each take us to another borderland, this one connecting the living and the beloved dead. In "For Those Whom the Gods Love Less" she takes us into another time of despair, solaced by the example of the great artists. Cézanne, who tests every new stage in his work by returning again and again "sur le motif" to paint Mont Saint-Victoire, is an inspiration to persist. "You can, you must proceed."

Levertov's prose and poetry give strength to each other. Fittingly, she names her first book of essays *The Poet in the World* (1973). Two subsequent collections follow: *Light Up The Cave* (1981) and *New and Selected Essays* (1992). Her essays explore all the themes and preoccupations of her poetic life: the craft of poetry; close reading; and celebration of her other illustrious ancestors and living companions, poets she admires, among them Rilke and Chekhov, Robert Duncan, Robert Creeley, H.D., Hayden Carruth, Anne Sexton, Hilda Morley. Above all, she is a close reader of William Carlos Williams and writes extended and precise examinations of form and measure in his poetry. How Williams employs the triadic line and line breaks are cornerstones of Levertov's criticism. Many of her essays begin as spoken lectures and speeches at public rallies. Her essays dwell at length on connections between poetry and politics and her own political convictions. Her essays are close companions to the poetry and enlarge our understanding of form, dominant themes and subjects in her thought.

She was a lifelong inveterate letter-writer, in a way we will probably never see again. Her business letters were typed by a secretary, but everything else was hand-written, often along the vertical side of ordinary blank tablet paper, on both sides with afterthoughts squeezed into the margins. We have the published interchange of letters between Levertov and William Carlos Williams (edited by Christopher MacGowan) as well as the monumental collection of letters between her and Robert Duncan (edited by Robert J. Bertholf and Albert Gelpi). There is no way of estimating how many letters she wrote in her lifetime, nor the number of correspondents with whom she kept up, but many of her letters are in the Green Library at Stanford and perhaps in other libraries in the archives of such friends as James Laughlin. In *Tesserae: Memories and Suppositions* (1993), she composes autobiographical mosaics, tiny pieces assembled to make patterns. Here again the materials of the prose and the poetry throw light back and forth on the whole of her life. Sometimes she puts some prose pieces in among her poems, finding no other place to publish them. *Tesserae: Memories and Suppositions* contained short lightly fictionalized autobiography, a prose recollection of a dream, and her later work includes a speech at an antiwar rally and one work she entitled "Perhaps No Poem, But All I Can Say and I Cannot Be Silent."

Her life's poetry shows us an arc from sacramental vision, the wonderful innocent celebration of the world, through political engagement with war and injustice, deaths of parents and loved ones, family estrangements, back to a hard-won, profound spirituality and openness. She does indeed write out of her own life, witnessing to mystical vision without mystification. She might once have been "arrogant in innocence" but now every grace, every eloquence is hard-won. Robert Creeley, her friend from her earliest days in the United States, offers this summing up: "The exceptional grace—a dancer's I liked to think—of her work, the movement so particular to a complex of thought and feeling accomplished a rare unity. That quality is present in all she does. . . . "

NOTES

Though Denise Levertov published most of her books with New Directions, she sometimes arranged for the printing of special editions of books or parts, such as "Conversation in Moscow." Some of these were fine press limited editions and some were printed on behalf of causes she supported. Where there are variants (very few), the *Collected Poems* adopts the New Directions version. Over time, New Directions gathered the early books chronologically into multi-volume collections, thus keeping all her work in print. There are a few variants to the single volumes in these compilations, but none substantial. With the exception of correcting errors, we have honored the authority of the single volumes, since there we have the strongest evidence that Levertov scrutinized, edited, and meticulously corrected the proofs of her poems to her satisfaction.

Levertov sometimes changed typography. We have chosen to largely simplify the format for dedications, epigraphs, dates, and other elements for consistency in the *Collected Poems*. We have also placed almost all of her notes, which initially appeared at the ends of sections or volumes, together at the very end of this book. Anne Dewey consulted multiple print editions and typed and holograph versions of the poems in the Levertov Papers at Stanford University to aid in choosing variations in text, particularly to distinguish indented from wraparound lines that had to be broken in the published New Directions volumes. Where the documents were clear and space permitted, we have restored the wraparounds. In all this, we have tried to keep faith with the physician's promise first to do no harm.

Levertov sometimes included previously published poems in new volumes of poetry when she believed that they belonged in the new context of the later volume. The *Collected Poems* prints each poem only once. Our decisions on where to print the repeated poems, as well as their placement in the volumes from which the *Collected* omits them, are explained in the Notes.

1 *Early and Uncollected Poems* Levertov's Author's Note to the 1979 *Collected Earlier Poems 1940-1960*:

"I began writing at five years old, but have lost the poems that precede my first *published* poem, 'Listening to Distant Guns,' written during or just before Dunkirk. In Buckinghamshire, where I was 'evacuated,' one could hear the big guns across the Channel even though Bucks is an inland county. I have also lost many of the poems written between that one and those included in my first book, *The Double Image*, which was published in 1946 by The Cresset Press. The earliest poems in *The Double Image* were written when I was eighteen or nineteen, and the latest in 1945 (a full year having passed between acceptance and publication).

"Of the poems included in the 'Early and Uncollected' section of this present collection, some, as will be seen, were composed in England and Europe before I arrived in the United States at the end of 1948, while a few belong to my life in New York City in the 1950's. This whole group is not arranged in strict chronological order, though I have noted the year of composition and, when recalled, the place. Only the last in the group postdates my first U.S. books, *Here and Now* and *Overland to the Islands*.

"I would like to mention here my curious publishing history and some kindnesses that helped me along my way long ago: When I was twelve I had the temerity to send some poems to T. S. Eliot, even though I had not shown most of them even to my sister, and certainly to no one else. Months later, when I had forgotten all about this impulsive act, a two- or even three-page typewritten letter from him arrived, full of excellent advice. (Alas, the letter, treasured for many years, vanished in some move from one apartment to another in the 1950's; I've never ceased to hope it may one day resurface . . .) When I was sixteen I became acquainted with Herbert (later Sir Herbert) Read, as I have elsewhere recounted. From him also I received the most kindly encouragement. When I was nineteen I met Charles Wrey Gardiner, and he began to publish me in his magazine, *Poetry Quarterly* (the same that had printed 'Listening to Distant Guns,' though he had not then been the editor). This led to publication in other little magazines, such as *Outposts* and *Voices*. The editor of one of these—either Denys Val Baker or Howard Sergeant, I'm afraid I can no longer remember which it was—suggested that I take a book-length manuscript to a friend of his at Sylvan Press. Excited, I did so; but Sylvan Press was about to go out of business. The day I picked up my manuscript from them, as requested (I was too naïve to have sent a stamped addressed envelope with it!) I had just succeeded in landing a nursing job I wanted, at St. Luke's Hospital, Fitzroy Square; and so, carried on the wave of my satisfaction about that, I walked into the offices of The Cresset Press, which I caught sight of at the corner of the square upon completing my successful interview with the matron of St. Luke's. Accidentally, I entered by way of the stockroom, and a packer there let me ascend to Irene Calverley's office. She was courteously but firmly instructing me that this was not the way to approach a publisher when something—my youthful appearance (I was twenty-one but looked seventeen) or crestfallen expression—made her decide to look into my ill-typed manuscript anyway. She then told me to leave the package and my address and phone number with her. A few days later she called to say John Hayward had read the poems and accepted them for publication. I remember going into a church somewhere in Soho to kneel in awe because my destiny, which I had always known as a certain but vague form on the far horizon, was beginning to *happen*.

"*The Double Image* came out in 1946, and as previously noted I came to the United States in 1948. I took no steps towards publication of another book, but Kenneth Rexroth included my poems in his anthology *New British Poets* (1949) and friendship with Robert Creeley led to publication in *Origin* and in the *Black Mountain Review*. In the mid-50's (when I was living in New York City) I received a letter from Weldon Kees, who was only a name to me, saying that he'd read and liked my work and wanted to publish a book of it in a small press series he and a printer friend were planning. I was delighted, and sent him a manuscript, with which he was pleased. But before the book went into production came news of his death, or at least of his presumed death by a leap from the Golden Gate Bridge. I never met him. Perhaps a year later, one 'Larry Ferling,' as Lawrence Ferlinghetti then called himself, wrote to say that my poems had come into his hands after Weldon Kees' death and that he would like to publish them; he was just starting the City Lights Series then.

"Not much later Jonathan Williams wrote to say he would like to do a book. Because the Kees/Ferlinghetti offer had come first, I offered Ferlinghetti first choice of all the poems I had by then accumulated (a somewhat larger group than the original Kees project) and gave Jonathan the 'rejects' plus what still newer work I had done in the intervening months. Thus, poems that should really have been in a single book together because of their interrelationships were arbitrarily divided between *Here and Now* and *Overland to the Islands*. Robert Duncan, who had read them all in typescript, pointed out to me that I should not have let either book be so loosely, thoughtlessly thrown together; and for the first time I realized that a book of separate poems can in itself be a composition, and that to *compose* a book is preferable to randomly gathering one.

"Of all these kindnesses none exceeds, in effect or duration, that of Kenneth Rexroth. He 'discovered' me before I came to the United States, and continued to 'promote' me after I came here. Probably it was he who showed my poems to Kees and then to Ferlinghetti. Most certainly it was he who persistently brought me to James Laughlin's attention, and so—once James Laughlin felt I had a voice of my own—to the happiness and honor of becoming in 1959 a New Directions author. I have actually met Kenneth only a few times in all the years, and after 1948 rarely exchanged letters with him; yet his unswerving concern for my work has undoubtedly benefitted my life and fortune. Publication of this book seems a fitting time to say thanks to him, and to the others I've mentioned."

17 *The Double Image* was first published in 1946 by Cresset Press, under original name spelling, Levertoff. Levertov's prefatory note reads: "I would like to thank Mr. John Hayward, Mr. Herbert Read and Mr. Charles Wrey Gardiner, for their invaluable criticism and encouragement. I hope one day to justify their interest by a better book. Acknowledgements are due to the Editors of 'Poetry Quarterly,' 'Voices,' and 'Gangrel' to reprint poems which have appeared in their periodicals; also to the B.B.C. for the use of a poem that was broadcast."

Editors' note: The table of contents of *The Double Image* divides the volume into two parts, "Fears" (through "Meditation and Voices") and "Promises" (from "Ballad" to end).

21 Editors' note: "Durgan": Dedication "For J.M." included in *Collected Earlier Poems* but not in *The Double Image*.

23 Editors' note: "Casselden Road, N.W. 10": Dedication "For M." appears in *The Double Image* version only.

41 Editors' note: *Here and Now* was first published in 1957 by City Lights Pocket Poets Series (no. 6). We print the poems in *Collected Earlier Poems*, which follow the named Contents of the City Lights edition.

47 The quoted words were spoken by Blake in my dream. This was London, 1945.

54 "Mrs. Cobweb": a lady who used to send me her poems in the mid '50s; mad poems in which here and there a marvelous image gleamed.

63 *Overland to the Islands* was first published in 1958 by Jonathan Williams, Jargon Press.

67 "A Story, a Play": *A Dream of Love* by WCW and *Jardou* by RC. Editors' note: William Carlos Williams and Robert Creeley.

89 *With Eyes at the Back of Our Heads.* Editors' note: the single volume dedication reads "for Mitchell and Nikolai Goodman."

106 "Notes of a Scale": See 'The True Wonder' anecdote of Rabbi Elimélekh of Lijensk in Buber's *Tales of the Hasidim: The Early Masters.*

127 In a footnote to "Art," Levertov identified the three speakers: Cézanne for "the thrill of continuance with the appearance of all its changes"; Jean Hélion for "art becomes a realization with which the urge to live collaborates as a mason"; and Ruskin for "the mind's tongue, that works and tastes into the very rock heart."

131 *The Jacob's Ladder.* Editors' note: We omit from this section poems which originally appeared in the Jargon Society's edition of *Overland to the Islands* and then were reprinted in a final section (titled "Poems from *Overland to the Islands* (1958)") of New Directions' edition of *The Jacob's Ladder*: "Overland to the Islands," "Scenes from the Life of the Peppertrees," "The Whirlwind," "One A.M.," "The Absence," "Lonely Man," "Merritt Parkway," "Turning," "The Springtime," "A Stir in the Air," "Sunday Afternoon," "The Recognition," "Illustrious Ancestors."

176 In "The Peachtree, ii" of "During the Eichmann Trial," Levertov's note stated that "this poem is based on the earliest mention, during the trial, of this incident. In a later statement it was said the fruit was cherries, that the boy was already in the garden, doing forced labor, when he was accused of taking the fruit, and that Eichmann killed him in a tool shed, not beneath the tree. The poem therefore is not to be taken as a report of what happened but of what I envisioned."

233 Editors' note: *The Sorrow Dance*: The single volume contains a dedication: "Dedicated to / Harry Green / in memory of Olga / and to / Betty Kray." To avoid repetition, we omit here poems that Levertov decided had to be reprinted in *To Stay Alive*: "Olga Poems" (after "A Lamentation"), "Life at War," and "What Were They Like?" (after "The Pulse"); "Enquiry" as part i of "Two Variations"; "A Note to Olga (1966)" (after "The Altars in the Street" as "A Note to Olga, 1966").

273 *Relearning the Alphabet:* Editors' note: To avoid repeating poems which Levertov decided belonged in her subsequent collection *To Stay Alive*, we omit poems reprinted in *To Stay Alive*: "Advent 1966" (after "The Broken Sandal"), "Tenebrae" (after "Despair"), "An Interim" (after "For Paul and Sally Goodman," retitled "Prologue: An Interim" in *To Stay Alive*), "From a Notebook: October '68—May '69" (after "Dialogue," retitled "Part I (*October '68—May '69*)" in *To Stay Alive*).

331 *To Stay Alive*: Editors' note: *To Stay Alive* includes poems reprinted from *The Sorrow Dance* and *Relearning the Alphabet*. For the original placement of these poems, see notes on each volume.

Levertov's original "Author's Preface 1971" to the volume states:

"As one goes on living and working, themes recur, transposed into another key perhaps. Single poems that seemed isolated perceptions when one wrote them prove to have struck the first note of a scale or a melody. I have heard professors of literature snicker with embarrassment because a poet quoted himself: they thought it immodest, narcissistic. Their attitude, a common one, reveals a failure to understand that though *the artist as craftsman* is engaged in making discrete and autonomous works—each of which, like a chair or a table, will have, as Ezra Pound said, the requisite number of legs and not wobble—yet at the same time, more unconsciously, as these attempts accumulate over the years, *the artist as explorer in language of the experiences of his or her life* is, willy-nilly, weaving a fabric, building a whole in which each discrete work is a part that functions in some way in relation to all the others. It happens at times that the poet becomes aware of the relationships that exist between poem and poem; is conscious, after the act, of one poem, one line or stanza, having been the precursor of another. It may be years later; and then, to get the design clear—'for himself and thereby for others,' Ibsen put it—he must in honesty pick up that thread, bring the cross reference into its rightful place in the inscape, the Gestalt of his life (his work)/his work (his life).

"In *Relearning the Alphabet* I published some sections of a poem then called, as a working title, 'From a Notebook,' which I was aware was 'unfinished,' openended. In pursuing it further I came to realize that the long poem 'An Interim,' published in a different section of the same volume, was really a prelude or introduction to the Notebook poem. And Mitch Goodman and Hayden Carruth, on reading new parts of the Notebook, showed me that other, earlier poems—such as those I had written about my sister Olga after her death in 1964, and included in *The Sorrow Dance*—had a relation to it that seemed to demand their reissue in juxtaposition. It was Hayden who, years ago, pointed out to me how, in writing about my childhood in England, my diction became English—and this fact becomes itself one of the themes of the Notebook poem; for the sense my individual history gives me of being straddled between *places* extends to the more universal sense any writer my age—rooted in a cultural past barely shared by younger readers, yet committed to a solidarity of hope and struggle with the revolutionary young—must have of being almost unbearably, painfully, straddled across *time*.

"In the pendant to 'Olga Poems'—A Note to Olga (1966) two years after her death—occurs the first mention in my work of one of those public occasions, demonstrations, that have become for many of us such familiar parts of our lives. Later, not as a deliberate repetition but because the events were of importance to me, other such occasions were spoken of in other poems. The sense of community, of fellowship, experienced in the People's Park in Berkeley in 1969, deepened and intensified under the vicious police attack that, for middle-class whites especially, was so instructive. The personal response that moves from the identification of my lost sister, as a worker for human rights, with the pacifists 'going limp' as they are dragged to the paddywagon in Times Square in 1966, to the understanding by 1970 that 'there comes a time when only anger/is love,' is one shared by many of us who have come bit by bit to the knowledge that opposition to war, whose foul air we have breathed so long that by now we are almost choked forever by it, cannot be separated from opposition to the whole system of insane greed, of racism and imperialism, of which war is only the inevitable expression. In 'Prologue: An Interim' some of my heroes—that is, those who stand for integrity, honesty, love of life—are draft resisters who go to jail in testimony of their refusal to take part in carnage. In the same poem I invoked the self-immolators—Vietnamese and American—not as models but as flares to keep us moving in the dark. I spoke with love—a love I still feel—of those who 'disdain to kill.' But later I found that Gandhi himself had said it was better to 'cultivate the art of killing and being killed rather than in a cowardly manner to flee from danger.' In the later sections of the Notebook the sense of who the guardians of life, of integrity, are, is extended to include not only those who 'disdain to kill' but all who struggle, violently if need be, to pull down this obscene system before it destroys all life on earth.

"The justification, then, of including in a new volume of poems which are available in other collections, is esthetic—it assembles separated parts of a whole. And I am given courage to do so by the hope of that whole being seen as having some value not as mere 'confessional' autobiography, but as a document of some historical value, a record of one person's inner/outer experience in America during the '60's and the beginning of the '70's, an experience which is shared by so many and transcends the peculiar details of each life, though it can only be expressed in and through such details."

Levertov included an additional note regarding *To Stay Alive*: "Some people mentioned in these poems, Dennis Riordon, Chuck Matthei, Bob Gilliam, David Worstell, de Courcy Squire and Jennie Orvino were young active war-resisters. 'Robert' referred to the poet Robert Duncan, 'Bromige' to the poet David Bromige. Mitch was my husband Mitch Goodman; the trial referred to in 'Prologue: An Interim' was the one in which he, Dr. Benjamin Spock and three others were defendants. Richard, Boat and Neil were young members of revolutionary collectives. Other personal names refer to various friends, living and dead."

338 The quoted lines—'a clearing/in the selva oscura . . . ' —are an adaptation of some lines in 'Selva Oscura' by the late Louis MacNeice, a poem much loved by my sister, Olga.

352 *Life that/wants to live.* Albert Schweitzer's phrase, in formulating the basis of his sense of 'reverence for life': 'I am life that wants to live, among other forms of life that want to live.'

(*Unlived life/of which one can die.*) Rilke's phrase from *The Notebooks of Malte Laurids Brigge.*

355 'Goldengrove/is unleaving all around me'—refers to Gerard Manley Hopkins's 'Spring and Fall: To a Young Child.'

364 *Thursday, May 15th*—the day in 1969 when James Rector was killed, Alan Blanchard, an artist, blinded, and many people wounded by police buckshot fire while protesting the destruction of the People's Park.

365 WHAT PEOPLE CAN DO—from an issue of *The Instant News*, a daily information sheet published in Berkeley during the weeks of demonstrations.

368 The lines from Brecht are a refrain of a song about slaves casting off their chains: 'No one or everyone, all or nothing!'

372 'Casa Felice'—the house of friends on Cape Cod.

374 'I Thirst'—Words of Jesus from the Cross, according to John 19:28. The demonstration of May 9, 1970, attempted to make clear the relationship between war abroad and racism and political oppression at home.

380 Powell—the British right-wing politician Enoch Powell.

381 'Imagination of disaster . . . life/ferocious and sinister'—Henry James, in a letter to Henry Adams.

383 José Yglesias—the quotation is from *In the Fist of the Revolution.*

391 'By the post house . . . *Wild Mulberry Branch.*' 'Now snowstorms . . . travel-ling-clothes.' From a translation by David Lattimore of Mao Chi'i-ling, 'To the Air: Southern Branch (At an inn west of the Huai I receive a letter from Ch'en Ching-chih. Sent with a reply.)'

394 Mayakovsky—the Russian poet Vladimir Mayakovsky (1893–1930). The quotation is from his *How Are Verses Made?* Though William Carlos Williams did not read Russian, he did *see* Mayakovsky's poems; and though his own structural inventions came out of rhythmic, sonic, expressive necessities of his own, I surmise the visual impression of Mayakovsky's lines may have remained with him as a hint. See his 'Russia,' first published in *The Clouds* (1948), and included in *The Collected Later Poems* [now *The Collected Poems of William Carlos Williams, Volume II*].
      'Stone/breaks stone . . . ' From an inscription on an ancient Chinese painting, 'Hamlet Between Cliffs,' by Tao Chi.

396 'Let us become men'—adapted from what Father Berrigan said in his last 'underground' speech, before his recapture in 1970, at a rally in support of the people who had destroyed draft files by immersing them in chemicals manufac-tured by the Du Pont Corporation. He said, in part: 'Let us therefore trust what we have done. Let us multiply the same and similar acts. Let us trust one another. Let us draw near across great differences, exorcise together our fear. Let us do that one thing . . . which by common and cowardly agreement is forbidden in America today—let us be men.'
      Etheridge Knight—the poet, editor and part author of *Black Voices from Prison*. The quotation is from 'To Dan Berrigan,' in the November, 1970, issue of *Motive*, of which Knight was poetry editor; the magazine also carried the text of Father Berrigan's speech, cited above.

397 Levertov noted about *Footprints:* "About two thirds of the poems in this vol-ume were written concurrently with the 'notebook' poem that gave its name to *To Stay Alive.* The rest were written—some in England during the summer of 1971—subsequently, except for a few which got 'lost' during the compilation of earlier volumes."

399 'Hut'—This poem is a pendant to the poem 'Relearning the Alphabet.'

404 '*L'homme est . . . /en lui-même*'—'Humans are strange creatures, whose center of gravity lies outside their own body.' These words are by the French poet Francis Ponge.

406 'Time to Breathe'—adapted from an untitled prose poem in *Ombres*, by Jean-Pierre Burgart.

407 'Hunza'—residents of a small mountain kingdom in northwest Kashmir, noted for their health and longevity.
      'M. C. 5'—the rock group associated with the White Panthers in Motor City. John Sinclair: poet, revolutionary, sometime political prisoner. The poem was writ-ten while listening to the record album *Kick Out the Jams* during the moon landings.

417 '*Richard* (ii)'—the quoted lines are adapted from *The Maurizius Case*, by Jakob Wasserman (1928).

429 'Antonio, Antonio,/the old wound's/bleeding.'—a quote from 'Cranach,' in Sir Herbert Read's *Collected Poems*.

432 The italicized lines are from Edmund Waller.

433 'Life Is Not a Walk across a Field'—Boris Pasternak, from a Russian proverb.

435 'Alice Transfixed'—see Chapter V of Lewis Carroll's *Alice in Wonderland*.
The italicized words are all quotes from John Keats's letters, as in the phrase 'the Vale of Soulmaking.' The 'Vale of Health' is a part of Hampstead Heath, London, near which the poet lived.

438 'Both Taine and the inland English child'—H. A. Taine was the French literary historian (1828–93), while the 'English child' is mentioned in an essay by G. K. Chesterton.

443 '*chercheuses de poux*'—a reference to the poem 'The Women Hunting Lice' by Arthur Rimbaud (1854–91). The prose translation by Anthony Hartley in *The Penguin Book of French Verse*, Volume III, begins: 'When the child's brow full of red torments begs for the white swarm of lazy dreams, tall charming sisters with delicate fingers and silvery nails come near his bed.'

509 Levertov's Introductory Note to *Life in the Forest*:
"In 1975 or '6 I found in Cesare Pavese's poems of the 1930's, *Lavorare Stanca*, read in the Penguin edition translated by Margaret Crosland, a kind of ratification for a direction I was already obscurely taking in my own work. Pavese's beautiful poems are about various persons other than himself; though he is a presence in them also, their focus is definitely not autobiographical and egocentric, and in his accompanying essays he speaks of his concept of suggesting a narrative through the depiction of a scene, a landscape, rather than through direct recounting of events as such. The poems I had been moving towards were impelled by two forces: first, a recurring need—dealt with earlier by resort to a diarylike form, a poem long enough to include prose passages and discrete lyrics—to vary a habitual lyric mode; not to abandon it, by any means, but from time to time to explore more expansive means; and second, the decision to try to avoid overuse of the autobiographical, the dominant first-person singular of so much of the American poetry—good and bad—of recent years.
"Those poems of my own which have, I feel, some humble affinity—however oblique—with what Pavese achieved in *Lavorare Stanca*, tend to rather long lines and a discursive structure. The content of the last five of them is, however, shared by certain other poems—the first three of *Continuum*—that do not belong, in tone and structure, to the *Homage to Pavese* section of this book. This is not wholly true of 'A Soul-Cake': formally it could belong with the *Homage to Pavese* poems; but its more emphatic use of the first person unfits it for that group. By placing it, together with 'A Visit' and 'Death Psalm,' at the beginning of *Continuum*, I hope to suggest to the reader alternative ways of reading all eight poems—i.e., they can be

considered as belonging to their respective sections, or they can be read as an internal grouping that spans the two sections.

"The poem in *Homage to Pavese* called 'Chekhov on the West Heath' grew out of being asked to contribute something to the Chekhov Festival organized by James McConkey at Cornell University early in 1977. Though originally I had considered presenting a prose piece I found myself stimulated into a poem. In this instance I felt that, despite the frankly autobiographical standpoint taken, the poem belonged in the 'Pavese' section by virtue of its focus on other persons and on place.

"The group called *Modulations for Solo Voice* appeared in a limited edition published by Five Trees Press in San Francisco as a benefit to provide funds for publication of a young, unknown, woman poet. These poems are definitely a sequence, and make the most sense read in the order in which they are arranged—which, however, differs from that of their original printing in one particular: the last two poems are reversed, what was originally called 'Litany' now becoming the coda or 'Epilogue.'

"Throughout the rest of the book the arrangement is less chronological than by kind and, within such kinship groups, by internal association from poem to poem."

516 The West Heath is a section of Hampstead Heath, the tract of never-cultivated land that overlooks London from the north and includes the point of highest elevation in the London area.

517 'The small, dark-green volumes. / The awkward, heroic versions' refers to the English collected edition of Constance Garnett's pioneer translations.
Für Elise is a short piano piece by Beethoven.

518 'The Black Monk' is a Chekhov story often, or perhaps I should say usually, interpreted quite differently—that is, as being a sad story about illusion. I did not then, and do not now, see it that way. All the *apparent* illusion in it is in fact what is strong and positive!
'The betrothed girl' is the heroine of the story variously translated as 'The Betrothed,' 'A Marriageable Girl,' 'The Bride,' etc.

520 'tender, delightful, ironic'—from Gorki's reminiscences of Chekhov. However, just about everyone who ever described Chekhov mentioned his smile in very similar terms.

549 shadowgraph—this is factual and may be viewed at Hiroshima.

556 Debs—Eugene V. Debs, who declared in a speech in court on September 11, 1918: ' . . . while there is a lower class, I am in it; while there is a criminal element, I am of it; while there is a soul in prison, I am not free.'

560 'Dream: Château de Galais' refers to Alain Fournier's *Le Grand Meaulnes* (*The Wanderer*).

567 *'the divine animal/who carries us through the world.'* Ralph Waldo Emerson, *The Poet*: '. . . beyond the energy of [the] possessed and conscious intellect [one] is capable of a new energy (as of an intellect doubled on itself,) by abandonment to the nature of things . . . . As a traveller who has lost his way throws his reins on his horse's neck and trusts to the instinct of the animal to find his road, so must we do with the divine animal who carries us through this world.'

579   The Font, in St. James's, Piccadilly, is one of Grinling Gibbons's few works in marble.

608   Readers of 'The Dragon-Fly Mother' may be interested to read 'The Earth-woman and the Waterwoman' (page 45), a poem written in 1957, to which this 1979 poem makes some allusions.

653   The opening stanza of 'Beginners' is Swinburne, slightly misquoted because I had remembered it this way for many years.

654–55   'Psalm: People Power . . . ' and 'About Political Action . . . ' The long version derives directly from events described in prose as 'With the Seabrook Natural Guard in Washington, 1978' (*Light Up the Cave*). The short version, detached from that particular occasion, is an alternative rather than a substitute.

660   'A Speech . . . ' Written for an antidraft rally (which was attended by 35,000) this piece really *is* a speech, and not properly classifiable as a poem. I decided to include it because it is not prose either, and because many people—draft counsellors and high-school teachers especially—have requested me to make it generally available.

681   *Oblique Prayers* was introduced with an Author's Note:
"The four sections of this book represent a thematic, not a chronological order. Similarly, the poems within each section are arranged in what has seemed to me the most appropriate sequence, whether or not it was that in which they were composed.
     "The section of translations from Jean Joubert requires a word of introduction. Joubert was born in 1928 in Châlette-sur-Loing (Loiret), France. He has lived in Languedoc for the last twenty-five years and teaches American literature at the Université Paul Valéry at Montpellier. He has published novels and children's stories as well as poetry, and his collection *Poèmes: 1955–1975* was awarded the prize of the Académie Mallarmé in 1978. Most of these poems are taken from a later volume, *Cinquante toiles pour un espace blanc.* I hope to present a book-length selection of translations from his work in the future; meanwhile, it is hoped that these poems will serve to introduce him to the American public."

700   Levertov noted in 1984 that "the title of 'Thinking About El Salvador' originally included the date 1982, but alas, the death squads and the army continue the slaughter, with U.S. help."

739   'Variations on Themes by Rilke.' Those who read German will be able to see what images and ideas are taken from the original and which are my own. The proportions vary from poem to poem. (Also see pages 770, 779, 811, and 848.)

740   The phrase 'a blissful foolish rose' is from 'A Ring of Changes' in *With Eyes at the Back of Our Heads* (New Directions, 1959).
     'A Blessing.' Joanna Macy is the author of *Despair and Personal Power in the*

Nuclear Age. 'The Council of All Beings' is a periodic gathering concerned with the concept of Deep Ecology.

742 'Spinoffs, One.' These 'span off' from photographs by Peter McAfee Brown when I was preparing to write an introduction to his work for a forthcoming publication. They should not be mistaken for descriptions.

753 'The Stricken Children.' Originally titled 'In Thatcher's England 1985.' That title was appropriate but—alas—too restrictive.

755 'Carapace.' This draws on a PBS *Frontline* program on El Salvador.

757 'The imagination of disaster' is Henry James's phrase. He said Americans had it—but do they still? Imagination is what makes reality real to the mind (which is why it's so hard to imagine peace, for it has not been experienced in the reality of our life in history except as the absence of war). Yet not only peace but the disastrous realities of our time go unimagined, even when 'known about,' when 'psychic numbing' veils them; and thus the energy to act constructively, which *imaginative* knowledge could generate, is repressed.

759 'Spinoffs, Two.' In the same way that the poems of 'Spinoffs, First Group,' 'span off' from photographs, these did so from sentences, taken out of context, in what I happened to be reading at the time—Ernst Wiechert, James Salter, others I have forgotten. The exact sources are not relevant to the poems except in one case, 'I learned that her name was Proverb,' which comes from the dream which Thomas Merton recounted in a letter to Boris Pasternak (quoted in a review by Father Basil Pennington of Michael Mott's biography of Thomas Merton (*National Catholic Reporter*, January 11, 1985)). The letter which is alluded to by Mott is in the Thomas Merton Studies center at Bellarmine, Kentucky. The poems are not a sequence, i.e., their order is arbitrary. A 'spinoff,' then, is a verbal construct which neither describes nor comments but moves off at a tangent to, or parallel with, its inspiration.

765 Ernest Chausson, composer, 1855–1899.

766 'Caedmon.' The story comes, of course, from The Venerable Bede's *History of the English Church and People*, but I first read it as a child in John Richard Green's *History of the English People*, 1855. The poem forms a companion piece to 'St. Peter and the Angel' in *Oblique Prayers*.

767 The painting 'The Servant-Girl at Emmaus' is in the collection at Russborough House, County Wicklow, Ireland. Before it was cleaned, the subject was not apparent: only when the figures at table in a room behind her were revealed was her previously ambiguous expression clearly legible as acutely attentive.

769 This is from the longer text of Julian of Norwich's *Showings* (or *Revelations*). The quoted lines follow the Grace Warrack transcription (1901). Warrack uses the word 'kinship' in her title-heading for the chapter, though in the text itself she says 'kindness,' thus—as in her Glossary—reminding one of the roots common to both words.

770 'Candlemas' draws on a sermon given by Father Benignus at Stanford, Candlemas 1985.

771 La Cordelle is a small chapel on the hillside below Vézelay.

773–78 The quotations are taken from the Pelican and the *Classics of Western Spirituality* editions.

783 The allusion is to Rilke's prose piece 'Concerning the Poet' (*Where Silence Reigns*, New Directions).
'To R.D., March 4th 1988.' Robert Duncan died on February 3, 1988.

787 The German quotation is from the ninth of Rilke's *Duino Elegies*.

788 My source was a quotation in a review of Jonathan Maslow's *Bird of Life, Bird of Death*. His focus in that book was on Guatemala, where he sought the quetzal in the dwindling forests; but of course the bodies of the 'disappeared' have been found in garbage dumps in other countries as well.

789 'El Salvador: Requiem and Invocation' was performed in May 1983 at Sanders Theatre, Harvard University, by the Back Bay Chorale, with soloists, and the Pro Arte Chamber Orchestra, conducted by the late Larry Hill—these two groups having commissioned the work. I had supplied the composer Newell Hendricks with the text in three installments, and he had worked on the music in that same sequence; the joint project took around a year for us to complete. Until a final rehearsal I did not hear the music, except for a brief orchestral rehearsal tape, as I was in California during the rehearsal period. I had, however, included in my text a few 'stage directions,' as it were; for in order to meet the challenge of my task at all I had to *imagine* the music in some degree. Thus, with the opening words and phrases I included the suggestion not only that they were for chorus but also that their sounds be loud, harsh, cacophonous; or elsewhere that voices overlap and die away into silence, or perhaps be followed by an orchestral interlude. Newell followed through on all my concepts most intuitively, and produced what I and the audience felt was a very strong and remarkable piece of music.

The basic models in my listening experience were the Bach Passions and various Handel and Haydn oratorios. The Narrator, then, plays a role equivalent to that of the Evangelist in the St. Matthew or St. John Passion music. The Chorus represents the people of El Salvador. Occasionally a solo voice emerges from the chorus as an unspecified Questioner. And then there are the solo voices of the Archbishop and the four women.

The narrative line—after the initial outburst of violent words and sounds representing the extremity of El Salvador's present condition—moves from pre-Columbian times through a condensed history of the intervening centuries (which could equally be that of other Central American countries) to very recent events. During the pre-Columbian passages I adapted some actual Mayan prayers; and when I came to contemporary times, I quoted directly from Archbishop Romero's sermons and from the letters by Sisters Dorothy, Maura, and Ita and lay worker Jean, supplied to me by the Maryknoll Sisters. At one point in the text, Romero intones the names of civilians known to have been killed during the previous week:

these are actual names, many of them, in this instance, belonging to members (mainly children) of a single family. It is an authentic, typical sampling of those weekly listings of murders done by right-wing death-squads which the Archbishop had the great courage to announce. Similarly, the list, at another point in the text, of priests and nuns murdered in the same manner consists of actual names. It should have been much longer, to be really representative.

The audience at the first performance of the oratorio in 1983 was provided with a program published by the Back Bay Chorale which included the text together with forewords by the composer, the conductor, myself, and the artist Michael Mazur who created a visual setting for the event, designed the program cover, and also sang as a member of the Chorale. A new edition was subsequently printed as a contribution to the organizations which are working to help Salvadoran and Guatemalan refugees, develop the ecumenical Covenant of Sanctuary movement, raise public awareness of the true situation, and give medical aid and moral support to the Salvadoran and other Central American people, as well as to protest United States military intervention. Copies were provided free to these organizations (and to a few individuals) for them to sell at whatever price they deemed appropriate.

814 'Those Who Want Out.' ' . . . that the earth is an inert lump of matter, that our relationship to it is merely utilitarian, even that we might find a paradise outside it in space colonies. Such monstrous aberrations of thought are symptoms of the enchantment which blinds us to reality.'—John Michell, *The Earth Spirit: Its Ways, Shrines, & Mysteries*.

853–58 The poems in Section I, 'Lake Mountain Moon,' were published as a limited edition chapbook by Tangram Press.

858–63 The poems in Section II, 'Two Magnets,' and several others including 'Evening Train,' were written at the Villa Serbelloni, Bellagio, where I spent five weeks in 1989 on a fellowship from the Rockefeller Foundation.

859 'Stele' was inspired by a stone relief in the Musée de Grenoble, France.

860–61 The quotations in 'The Faithful Lover' are all from Ruskin, mainly from *Praeterita*.

862 'The Composition': A duplicate of this painting is in the Boymans Museum in Rotterdam. Witold Rybczinski, in *Home: A Short History of an Idea*, gives a different interpretation of the scene, I discovered. I believe my own is equally valid.

870 'Entre Loup et Chien': the French expression 'entre chien et loup' ('between the dog and the wolf') refers to the evening twilight. Here the image is reversed for the predawn twilight.

889 'News Report,' a found poem, is collaged from *The Seattle Times* of September 12, 1991. To the best of my knowledge it was not followed up and seems to have gone virtually unnoticed in the national media—and the national consciousness.

901   *Mindwalk* is a film by Bernt Capra based on writings by Fritjof Capra.

903–5   The suite, 'Embracing the Multipede,' was published as a limited edition chapbook by Tangram Press.

907   The theme alluded to is in one of the tapes of informal lectures given at Gethsemani in the 1960s.

921   'The Glittering Noise.' The italicized lines are quoted from *The Wynne Diaries 1789–1820*, edited by Anne Fremantle.

929, 931, 932, 942   'Alchemy,' 'Double Vision,' 'Firmament,' 'Agon,' 'Warning,' 'Swan in Falling Snow,' and 'Sheep in the Weeds.' From photographs by Mary Randlett.

938   The allusion is to Schweitzer's phrase: 'I am life that wants to live, among other lives that want to live.'

960   'Esemplastic power': Coleridge's term.

964   The quotations are from Brother Lawrence's 'The Practice of the Presence of God' (available in many editions), and the biographical allusions are based on the original introduction.

977   *This Great Unknowing: Last Poems* was published posthumously. The editor of *This Great Unknowing* noted that had Levertov lived longer, it might have contained more poems and had a different title. It would probably have been organized into subsections, by thematic or other aesthetic principles, as she "composed" her books from *The Sorrow Dance* on, carefully ordering poems so that both individual works and groups of poems could throw light on one another and themes and counterthemes could weave larger patterns.

The editor of *This Great Unknowing* chose to print the poems as they appear in a loose-leaf book where, according to Levertov's last secretary, Marlene Muller, "in general the poems are numbered from the oldest to the most recent." Since Levertov kept her working notebook of finished poems separate from a second copy used for readings, we have some confidence that we are seeing how the poems emerged more or less chronologically. We can examine how subjects, images, and themes develop over time, imagining how they might make larger, more significant patterns or reading them as a rough chronicle of the poet's creative life in poetry in the last months of her life.

INDEX OF TITLES

INDEX OF FIRST LINES

The roses tremble, 3
The sacred bats, 823
The screendoor whines, clacks, 141
The sea barely crinkled, breathing, 931
The sea quiet, shadow-colored and, 60
These days—these years, 758
The shifting, the shaded, 72
The singing robes fly onto your body . . . , 498
The sink is full of dishes. Oh well, 68
The sleeping sensual head, 22
The slender evidence . . . , 999
'The solution,' they said to my friend, 546
The Soul's dark Cottage, batter'd any decay'd, 432
The spirit of each day passes, head down, 988
The spirit that walked upon the face of the waters, 735
The stairway is not, 158
The sunshine is wild here!, 578
The tall poplar, 727
The theater of war. Offstage, 405
The tree of knowledge was the tree of reason, 906
The trees' black hair electric, 425
The turnpike, without history, a function, 449
The vultures thrive, 788
The washing hanging from the lemon tree, 94
The way sorrow enters the bone, 570
The way the willow-bark, 829
The wayside bushes waiting, waiting, 441
'The will is given us that we may know, 47
The wind behind the window moves the leaves, 745
The wind would fan the life-green fires, 23
The wise men are still on the road, searching, 839
The Wishing Well was a spring, 753
The woman whose hut was mumbled by termites, 584
The wood-dove utters, 446

The woods which give me their silence, 900
The world alive with love, where leaves tremble, 19
The world comes back at me, 433
The world is round, 553
The world is, 213
The worm artist, 242
They are going to, 924
The yellow tulip in the room's warmth, 972
They enter the bare wood, drawn, 215
They have refined the means of destruction, 886
They make mistakes, 687
The young elm that must be cut, 248
They part at the edge of substance, 859
They sent me away to be bred, 619
They speak of bonding, 956
They speak of the art of war, 888
They want to be their own old vision, 883
The zenith longs for the banal horizon, 759
This carpentered, unpainted, aging house, 502
This clinging to a God, 968
This day has no centre, 36
This I had not expected, 893
This is the year the old ones, 186
This lagoon with its glass shadows, 95
This morning's morning-glory, 747
This person would be an animal, 575
This wild night, gathering the washing as if it were flowers, 165
Those groans men use, 252
Though no wind is blowing, the lake, 864
Though the mountain's the same warm-tinted ivory, 854
Though the road turn at last, 706
Three hours wholly absorbed, 902
Three men spoke to me today, 751
Through the high leafy branches, 545
Through the midnight streets of Babylon, 601

Wring the swan's neck seeking, 470

Xochipilli, god of spring, 124

'Yáchchiderálum, pútzele mútzele,
    271
Yes, he is here in this, 279
Yes, I'm nettled, 400
You can live for years next door, 916
You could die before me, 754
You danced ahead of me, I took, 876
You have brought me so far, 962
You have my, 58
You invaded my country by acci-
    dent, 456
You in your house among your
    roommate's plants, 585
Your beauty, which I lost sight of
    once, 184
'Your river is in full flood,' she said,
    740
You try to keep the present, 941
You want your old grey sweater, 694
You were my mentor, 783
You who are so beautiful, 426

Zaddik, you showed me, 162
Zones of flickering, 898

Audio files of Denise Levertov reading from her work are available
for download or listening on the New Directions website:
http://ndbooks.com/LevertovReading